Vauxhall Victor & VX 4/90 FE series Owners Workshop Manual

D1740940

by J H Haynes
Member of the Guild of Motoring Writers
and B L Chalmers-Hunt
TEng (CEI), AMIMI, AMIRTE, AMVBRA

Models covered

Victor series:
  Victor Saloon & Estate 1759cc
  Victor Saloon & Estate 2279cc
  VX 4/90 Saloon 2279cc

VX series:
  VX 1800 Saloon & Estate 1759cc
  VX 2300 Saloon & Estate 2279cc
  VX 4/90 Saloon 2279cc
  VX 2300 GLS Saloon & Estate 2279cc

ISBN 0 85696 541 3

ABCDE
FGHIJ
KLMNO
PQRS

Printed in England   (108 - 1E2)

HAYNES PUBLISHING GROUP
SPARKFORD YEOVIL SOMERSET ENGLAND
distributed in the USA by
HAYNES PUBLICATIONS INC
861 LAWRENCE DRIVE
NEWBURY PARK
CALIFORNIA 91320
USA

Acknowledgements

Thanks are due to Vauxhall Motors Limited for the supply of technical information and permission to reproduce certain illustrations; Castrol Limited who supplied details on lubrication, and the Champion Sparking Plug Company Ltd who supplied the illustrations showing the various sparking plug conditions. The bodywork repair photographs used in this manual were provided by Lloyds Industries Limited who supply 'Turtle Wax', 'Dupli-color Holts' and other Holts range products.

Lastly, thanks are due to all those people at Sparkford who helped in the production of this manual, particularly Stanley Randolph, Bruce Gilmour and John Rose.

About this manual

Its aim

The aim of this manual is to help you get the best value from your car. It can do so in several ways. It can help you decide what work must be done (even should you choose to get it done by a garage), provide information on routine maintenance and servicing, and give a logical course of action and diagnosis when random faults occur. However, it is hoped that you will make full use of the manual by tackling the work yourself. On simpler jobs it may even be quicker than booking the car into a garage, and having to go there twice, to leave and collect it. Perhaps most important, a lot of money can be saved by avoiding the costs the garage must charge to cover its labour and overheads.

The manual has drawings and descriptions to show the function of the various components so that their layout can be understood. Then the tasks are described and photographed in a step-by-step sequence so that even a novice can do the work.

Its arrangement

The manual is divided into thirteen Chapters, each covering a logical sub-division of the vehicle. The Chapters are each divided into consecutively numbered Sections and the Sections into paragraphs (or sub-sections) which are numbered following on from the Section they are in, eg 5.1, 5.2, 5.3 etc.

It is freely illustrated, especially in those parts where there is a detailed sequence of operations to be carried out. There are two forms of illustration: figures and photographs. The figures are numbered in sequence with decimal numbers, according to their position in the Chapter; eg, Fig.6.4 is the 4th drawing/illustration in Chapter 6. Photographs are numbered (either individually or in related groups) the same as the Section or sub-section of the text where the operation they show is described.

There is an alphabetical index at the back of the manual as well as a contents list at the front.

References to the 'left' or 'right' of the vehicle are in the sense of a person facing forwards in the driver's seat.

Whilst every care is taken to ensure that the information in this manual is correct no liability can be accepted by the authors or publishers for loss, damage or injury caused by any errors in, or omissions from, the information given.

Contents

Introduction

The 'Transcontinental' was introduced in February of 1972 as Vauxhall's new model to update their Victor range. The 'FD', the previous model had only been in production for some four years, when almost overnight , a new completely restyled Victor was announced using a very young 'European' marketing approach. Inwardly, however, little was changed although engine sizes were juggled so that the smaller model has an 1800 engine as opposed to the 1600, and the larger has a 2300 engine as opposed to the 2000 engine. The usual range options of automatic transmission, an estate car and the increased performance VX4/90 model are available. Altogether, the 'FE' model is larger, certainly more expensive but generally improved over the 'FD' and to most eyes better looking, particularly the estate car. Whilst it is not going to make anyone greatly enthuse about it, it does provide a worthy successor in the 'Victor' range and offers yet another choice in this highly competitive slice of the market.

Ordering spare parts

Buy genuine Vauxhall spares from a Vauxhall dealer direct or through a local garage. If you go to an authorised dealer, genuine parts can usually be supplied from stock.

Always have details of the car's serial number and engine number available when ordering parts. If you can also take along the part to be renewed it is helpful. Modifications are continually being made and many are not publicised. A storeman in a parts department is quite justified in saying that he cannot guarantee the correctness of a part unless the relevant numbers are available.

The vehicle identification plate is attached to the instrument panel, at the left hand side, and can be read through the windshield glass. This plate is stamped with the model and chassis number (Fig.1).

A service parts identification plate is attached to the right hand front inner wing panel adjacent to the battery. This plate bears the following information in the following sequence: Model, Destination, Job number, Paint code, Trim code, Option codes. (Fig.2).

The engine number is stamped on the rear right hand side of the cylinder block adjacent to the clutch bellhousing (Fig.3).

There is a code letter 'S' or 'EL' cast on the side of the cylinder block to differentiate between 1759cc and 2279cc engines respectively (Fig.4).

A further code letter 'H' or 'L' stamped on the cylinder block, adjacent to the distributor identifies between 'high' and 'low' compression engines (Fig.5).

The transmission unit has a special manufacture date code stamped on the extension housing (Fig.6).

Where an overdrive unit is fitted a serial number plate is attached to the right hand side of the main casing. The number must have a prefix of 28/115805/ (Fig.7).

The rear axle has a special manufacture date code stamped on the housing cover (Fig.8). The axle ratio is indicated by a letter stamped on the pinion housing (Fig.9). The code is as follows:

C	10/39
D	11/38
H	11/34
J	10/41
K	11/41

When obtaining new parts remember that many assemblies can be exchanged. This is very much cheaper than buying them outright and throwing the old part away. Before handing back an item in exchange always clean it to remove dirt and oil.

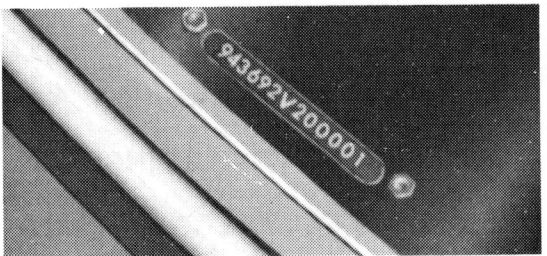

1. Vehicle identification plate

2. Service parts identification plate

3. Engine number

4. Cylinder block identification

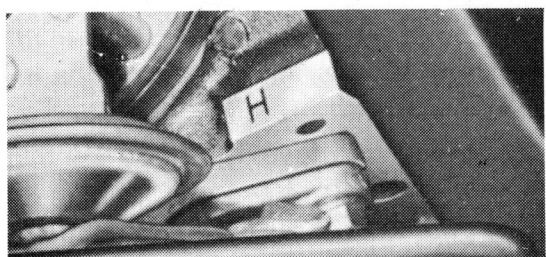

5. Engine compression ratio code

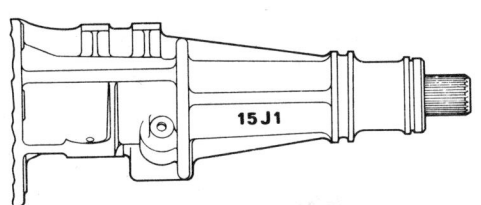

6. Transmission unit date code

7. Overdrive serial number plate

8. Rear axle date code

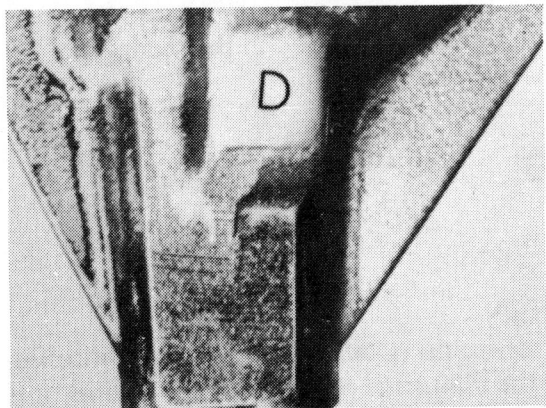

9. Rear axle ratio code letter

VICTOR FE '1800'

VICTOR FE ESTATE

VAUXHALL VX 2300 GLS

Routine maintenance

The manufacturers base their own servicing operations on a time factor rather than on mileage covered. They take 12,000 miles per annum as an average to base this service plan. This system is very satisfactory as it enables both the owner and garage to plan servicing in advance on a regular basis and confirms that deterioration of a vehicle's performance and safety is not necessarily connected with the number of miles covered. Where mileage is consistently and significantly in excess of the average, the time intervals between services may be reduced in proportion.

By implication, the servicing cycle recommended by the manufacturers gives a 6,000 mile interval between engine oil changes. Many owners prefer to change the oil more frequently particularly where much of the driving is in short runs or stop/start situations, where the engine does not get opportunity to warm up completely or operates consistently in heavy traffic. These conditions take far more out of an engine than steady runs in top gear.

The maintenance information given is not detailed in this section as information will be found in the appropriate chapters of this book.

Weekly
Coolant level in radiator.
    1 inch (25 mm) below bottom edge of filler neck.
Engine oil level - dipstick.
    Level must be above 'Add oil' mark. Quantity required from 'Add oil' to 'Full' is 2.85 pints (1.62 litres).
Battery electrolyte level.
    Should just cover the plate separators. Wipe away moisture or dirt from battery case exterior.
Tyre pressures.
    Examine also tread depth and for signs of other damage.

Safety check service S.
Brakes.
    Master cylinder fluid level.
    Hydraulic pipes and hoses inspection.
    Wheel cylinder inspection.
    Brake shoes - adjustment.
    Handbrake lever setting.
Steering.
    Tyre condition.
    Front wheel hub bearings adjustment
    Track rods and ball joints - damage and/or wear.
Suspension.
    Suspension arm upper and lower ball joints - wear
    Springs - level and unbroken
Automatic transmission
    Fluid level correct
General
    Lights in order
    Exhaust system intact
    Windscreen wiper blades serviceable
    Seat belts and anchorage points in order.

Service A
Brakes
    Examine linings and pads for wear. Renew if necessary and adjust.
Clutch and transmission
    Check and adjust clutch lever free play
    Gearbox oil level - check and top up
    Rear axle oil level - check and top up
Engine
    Renew oil and oil filter cartridge
    Carburettor damper dashpots(s) (Stromberg carburettors only) - check oil
    Fuel pump - clean filter
    Spark plugs - remove, clean and reset
    Distributor contact points - adjust gap. Clean or renew if necessary

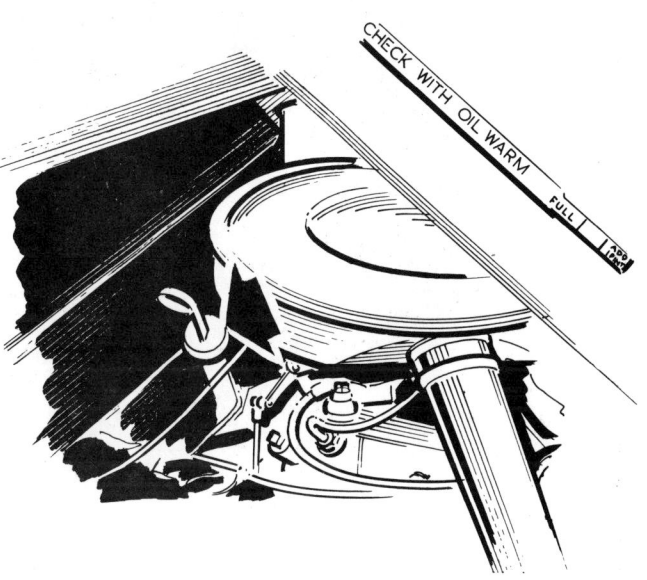

Oil level dipstick

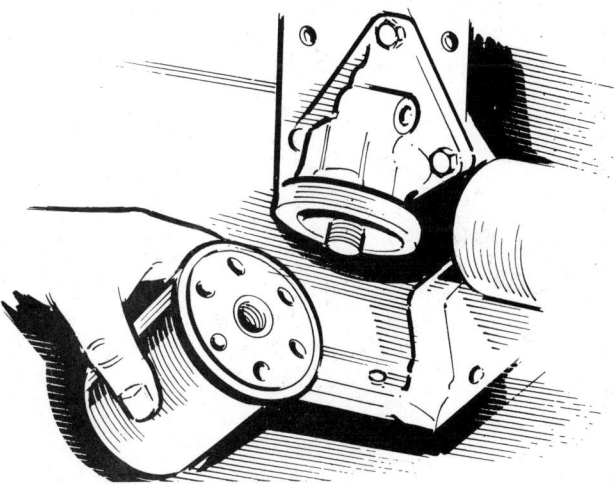

Oil filter cartridge renewal

Valve clearances - check and adjust
Fan belt - check and adjust tension
Engine idling speed - adjust carburettor if necessary.

Service B

Carry out service 'A' and add the following:

Brakes

Disc brake servo air filter - renew

Automatic transmission

Clean all ventilation holes and slots around the torque convertor cover. Scrape all dirt accumulations from surrounding areas

Engine

Spark plugs - renew
Carburettor air cleaner - renew paper element

Distributor - lubricate

Suspension

Grease upper and lower arm ball joints

Service C

Carry out Service B and add the following:

Steering

Remove front wheel bearings, clean and repack with grease

Brakes

Renew hydraulic fluid and cylinder seals

Automatic transmission

Renew fluid
Renew oil pump suction screen
Adjust low band servo.

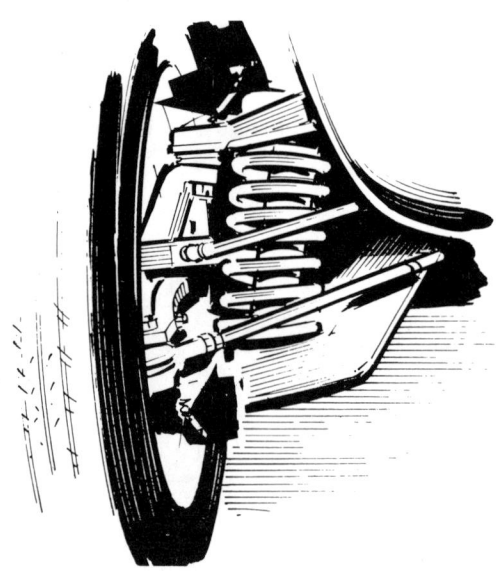

Front suspension arm ball joint grease nipples

Clutch pedal free play adjustment

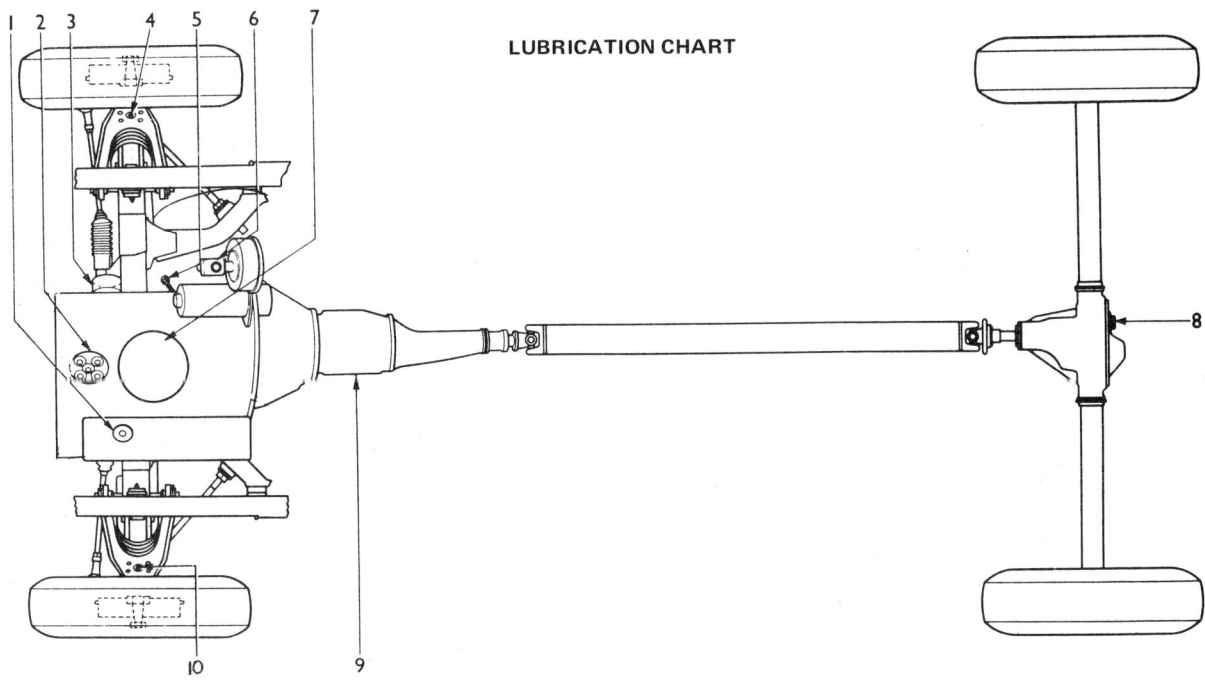

LUBRICATION CHART

Engine oil
Weekly
Check the oil level using the dipstick (5) and if necessary add sufficient Castrol GTX through the filler orifice (1) to bring the level up to the 'FULL' mark. 2.85 pints (1.62 litres) will raise the level from the 'ADD oil' to 'FULL' marks.

Service A
When warm, undo the sump drain plug and drain old oil. Renew the oil filter element (3). Replace the drain plug and refill with fresh Castrol GTX. Under abnormal conditions (city traffic, excess mileage, dusty or extreme temperature conditions), change the oil more frequently.
Capacity - dry: — 8.5 pints (4.83 litres
Refill including filter: — 8 pints (4.55 litres)

Gearbox oil

Service A
Remove the filler plug (9) and top up if necessary to the level of the plug orifice with Castrol Hypoy 90, examine for any signs of leaks.
Capacity - Less overdrive — 2.4 pints (1.36 litres)
Capacity - With overdrive — 3.0 pints (1.70 litres)

Automatic transmission
Check the fluid level on the dipstick whilst engine is running at normal working temperature. Top up as necessary with Castrol TQ 'Dexron' (R).
Service 'C' - Drain and refill
Capacity - refill — 4.5 pints (2.56 litres)

Rear axle oil
Service A
Remove filler plug (8) and top up if necessary to the level of plug orifice with Castrol Hypoy 90. Examine the casing for any signs of leakage.

Air filter

Service B
Renew paper element (7).

Hydraulic brake master cylinder reservoir

Service 'S'
Clean cap and surrounding area and after removing cap, top up if necessary to 0.25 inch (6 mm) below the lower edge of the filler neck. Use Castrol Girling Brake Fluid.

Distributor

Service B
Remove distributor cap and remove the two screws that secure the rotor. Put a few drops of Castrol GTX through the hole marked 'oil' and a drop on each end of the two advance weight pivots. A smear of petroleum jelly (vaseline) should be put on the cam surfaces. Do not over lubricate.

Front suspension arm ball joints
Service B
Grease two nipples each side, top and bottom (4 and 10) with Castrol MS3 Grease.

Recommended lubricants

COMPONENT	TYPE OF LUBRICANT OR FLUID	CORRECT CASTROL PRODUCTS
ENGINE	Multi-grade engine oil 20W/50	... Castrol GTX
GEARBOX/FINAL DRIVE	Gear oil SAE 90EP	... Castrol Hypoy
AUTOMATIC TRANSMISSION ...	... ...	... Castrol TQ Dexron R
FRONT WHEEL BEARINGS ...	Medium grade multi-purpose grease	... Castrol LM Grease
FRONT SUSPENSION BALL JOINTS ...	Medium grade Molybdenum Grease ...	... Castrol MS3 Grease
DISTRIBUTOR & GENERATOR BEAR-INGS	Engine or light oil	... Castrol GTX or 'Everyman'
CARBURETTOR DASHPOT(STROMBERG)	Engine or light oil	... Castrol GTX or 'Everyman'
UPPER CYLINDER LUBRICANT	Refined mineral oil	... Castrollo
BRAKE AND CLUTCH MASTER CYLINDERS	Hydraulic fluid	... Castrol/Girling Brake Fluid
ANTIFREEZE	GLYCOL ANTIFREEZE	... Castrol Antifreeze
CONTACT BREAKER CAM	Petroleum jelly (vaseline)	
BATTERY TERMINALS	Petroleum jelly (vaseline)	

Additionally Castrol GTX can be used to lubricate locks, hinges, cable linkages and latch mechanisms.

Chapter 1 Engine

Contents

Specifications

Type	4 cylinder in line 45° inclined, ohc

Capacity:

1800	1759 cc (107.4 cu in)
2300	2279 cc (139.0 cu in)

Bore:

1800	85.73 mm (3.375 in)
2300	97.54 mm (3.84 in)

Stroke	76.2 mm (3.0 in)

Firing order	1 3 4 2

Compression ratio:

HC (standard)..	8.5 : 1
LC	7.3 : 1

Compression pressure (HOT) - minimum:

HC	125 lb/sq in (8.76 kg/sq cm)
LC	110 lb/sq in (7.7 kg/sq cm)
max cylinder variation	20 lb/sq in (1.41 kg/sq cm)

Oil pressure (HOT)	45 - 55 lb/sq in (3.17 - 3.87 kg/sq cm) at 3000 rpm

Camshaft:

Journal diameter:

No 1 (front)	2.3735 - 2.3740 in	(60.28 - 60.30 mm)
No 2	2.3575 - 2.3580 in	(59.88 - 58.90 mm)
No 3	2.3425 - 2.3430 in	(59.50 - 59.52 mm)

No 4	2.3265 - 2.3270 in	(59.09 - 59.11 mm)
No 5	2.0605 - 2.0610 in	(52.33 - 52.35 mm)
Clearance in housing	0.0010 - 0.0025 in	(0.03 - 0.06 mm)
End float	0.001 - 0.007 in	(0.02 - 0.18 mm)
Thrust washer thickness	0.157 - 0.160 in	(3.99 - 4.06 mm)

Permissible dimension - cam peak to base:

1800

Inlet	1.877 in (47.93 mm) minimum	
Exhaust	1.868 in (47.45 mm) minimum	

2300

Inlet	1.902 in (48.31 mm) minimum	
Exhaust	1.893 in (48.08 mm) minimum	

Auxiliary shaft:

Front journal diameter	1.749 - 1.750 in	(44.42 - 44.44 mm)
Rear journal diameter	1.686 - 1.687 in	(42.82 - 42.84 mm)
Bearing clearance	0.001 - 0.003 in	(0.02 - 0.08 mm)
Thrust washer thickness	0.116 - 0.118 in	(2.95 - 3.00 mm)
End float	0.002 - 0.008 in	(0.05 - 0.20 mm)

Cylinder block:

Cylinder bore diameter - nominal standard

1800	3.375 in (85.73 mm)	
2300	3.84 in (97.54 mm)	

Top face distortion - max permissible

Longitudinally	0.005 in (0.13 mm)	
Transversely	0.003 in (0.08 mm)	

Permissible depth of block after refacing (Top face to centre of main bearing housing)	8.567 in (217.6 mm)	

Cylinder liners - 1800:

Cylinder bore diameter for liner fitment	3.553 - 3.554 in	(90.26 - 90.27 mm)

Piston rings:

Number per piston	3	

Ring gap in cylinder bore:

1800

Top ring	0.014 - 0.025 in	(0.36 - 0.63 mm)
Centre ring	0.007 - 0.024 in	(0.19 - 0.60 mm)

2300

Top ring	0.015 - 0.026 in	(0.37 - 0.65 mm)
Centre ring	0.009 - 0.026 in	(0.24 - 0.65 mm)

Thickness (top to bottom face)		
Top and centre rings	0.077 - 0.078 in	(1.95 - 1.98 mm)
Clearance in piston groove:		
Top ring	0.0015 - 0.0035 in	(0.04 - 0.09 mm)
Centre ring	0.001 - 0.003 in	(0.03 - 0.08 mm)

Pistons:

Type	Aluminium alloy solid skirt	
Clearance in cylinder bore	0.0015 - 0.0020 in	(0.04 - 0.05 mm)

Piston pins:

Clearance in piston bosses at 20° C	0.0003 - 0.0005 in (0.008 - 0.013 mm)	

Connecting rods:

Bearing housing bore	2.1460 - 2.1465 in	54.51 - 54.52 mm)
End float on crankpin	0.008 - 0.014 in	(0.20 - 0.36 mm)

Crankshaft and bearings:

Type	5 bearing, cast iron - copper/lead shells	
Crankpin diameter - standard	1.9975 - 1.9985 in	(50.75 - 50.76 mm)
Crankpin clearance in bearing	0.0010 - 0.0032 in	(0.03 - 0.08 mm)
Crankpin fillet radius	0.125 in (3.18 mm)	
Crank throw	1.497 - 1.502 in	(38.02 - 38.15 mm)
Main journal diameter - standard:		
No 1, 2, 3, 4 journals	2.4995 - 2.5005 in	(63.49 - 63.51 mm)
No 5 (rear) journal	2.5000 - 2.5005 in	(63.50 - 63.51 mm)

Main journal clearance in bearing:

No 1, 2, 3, 4 journals	0.0008 - 0.0028 in	(0.02 - 0.07 mm)
No 5 (rear) journal	0.0008 - 0.0025 in	(0.02 - 0.06 mm)
Main journal fillet radius	0.125 in	(3.18 mm)
Crankshaft end float	0.002 - 0.010 in	(0.05 - 0.25 mm)
Permissible crankshaft run-out	0.0015 in	(0.04 mm) max.
Main bearing housing bores	2.6655 - 2.6660 in	(67.70 - 67.72 mm)

Rear main journal - required length:

0.010 in undersize	1.346 - 1.350 in	(34.19 - 34.29 mm)
0.020 in undersize	1.351 - 1.355 in	(34.32 - 34.42 mm)
0.040 in undersize	1.356 - 1.360 in	(34.44 - 34.54 mm)

Rear main bearing width:

Standard	1.337 - 1.339 in	(33.96 - 34.01 mm)
0.010 in undersize	1.342 - 1.344 in	(34.09 - 34.14 mm)
0.020 in undersize	1.347 - 1.349 in	(34.21 - 34.26 mm)
0.040 in undersize	1.352 - 1.354 in	(34.34 - 34.39 mm)

Valves and valve seats:

Valve seat angle	45º	

Valve seat width:

Inlet	0.035 - 0.060 in	(0.89 - 1.52 mm)
Exhaust	0.055 - 0.085 in	(1.40 - 2.16 mm)

Stem diameter standard:

Inlet	0.3410 - 0.3417 in	(8.66 - 8.68 mm)
Exhaust	0.3403 - 0.3410 in	(8.64 - 8.66 mm)

Stem clearance in guide:

Inlet	0.0010 - 0.0027 in	(0.03 - 0.07 mm)
Exhaust	0.0017 - 0.0034 in	(0.04 - 0.09 mm)
Seat angle	44º	

Valve head thickness:

Inlet	0.025 in	(0.6 mm) minimum
Exhaust	0.035 in	(0.9 mm) minimum
Assembled length of valve in head	1.13 in	(28.5 mm) maximum

Valve springs:

Free length - nominal:

Inner	1.40 in	(35.5 mm)
Outer	1.64 in	(41.5 mm)

Spring force:

Inner at 0.83 in (21 mm)	72 lb (32.4 kg)
Outer at 1.00 in (25.5 mm)	139 lb (62.55 kg)

Valve tappets:

Diameter	1.4365 - 1.437 in	(36.49 - 36.57 mm)
Clearance in guide	0.0010 - 0.0015 in	(0.03 - 0.04 mm)

Valve clearance - hot:

Inlet	0.007 - 0.010 in	(0.18 - 0.25 mm)
Exhaust	0.015 - 0.018 in	(0.38 - 0.46 mm)

Valve timing:

Inlet valve maximum opening point	106º after TDC

Capacities:

Dry engine	8.5 pints (4.8 litres)
Refill with new oil filter	8.0 pints (4.6 litres)
Refill	7.5 pints (4.3 litres)

Torque wrench settings:

	lb ft	kg fm
Connecting rod cap bolts*	47	6.47
Main bearing cap bolts*	82	11.3
Flywheel and flex plate bolts	48	6.6
Cylinder head bolts	82	11.3
Camshaft housing bolts	25	3.5
Clutch to flywheel bolts	14	1.94
Torque converter to flex plate bolts	42	5.81

*Oiled threads

1 General description

The engine fitted to models covered by this manual is available in two capacities, 1759cc (1800) and 2279cc (2300). They are basically identical with the exception of the cylinder bore which has been increased on the larger capacity version.

It is of the four cylinder, water cooled, overhead camshaft design and is mounted with the clutch and gearbox within the engine compartment on flexible mountings.

The cylinder block and crankcase are cast together and have integral cylinder liners each one being surrounded by the water jacket. One unusual feature is that when fitted the cylinder axis is inclined to the left at an angle of 45°. The solid skirt pistons are made from aluminium alloy and have two compression rings and one steel rail type compression/oil control ring fitted, all above the gudgeon pin. The connecting rod is attached by this piston pin which is a running fit with piston bosses and shrunk into the little end.

The crankshaft is of cast iron and runs in five renewable copper/lead steel backed shells. End float control is at the rear main bearing (no. 5).

The I section steel forged connecting rods are fitted to the crankshaft by means of renewable copper lead steel backed shells at the big end. No bush is used in the connecting rod little end as the gudgeon pin is a shrink fit to the connecting rod.

The cast iron camshaft is positioned on the top of the cylinder head and is driven from the crankshaft by a special internally toothed reinforced rubber belt. The camshaft rotates in five bearings which are machined in the aluminium camshaft housing. End float is controlled by a thrust washer located between the rear face of the rear bearing and the retaining washer which is bolted to the end of the camshaft.

Also driven by the rubber toothed drive belt is the auxiliary shaft and this runs in two steel backed white metal bearings positioned in a housing within the cylinder block. The fuel pump operates from this shaft as does the distributor and oil pump. End float of the auxiliary shaft is taken by a thrust washer which is located in a groove at the front of its main journal.

The drive belt is tensioned by a smooth surface jockey pulley which runs on double row type ball bearings.

The cross flow type cast iron cylinder head is mounted on the cylinder block and carries the aluminium camshaft housing and valve assemblies. The overhead valves are retained in position with split type cotters which are located in the tapered bore of the valve spring retaining cap and double coil type valve springs. The valve guides are integral with the cylinder head. Because of the overhead mounted camshaft the valves are actuated directly by means of 'bracket-type' tappets which move in bores in the camshaft housing. Each tappet incorporates an angled wedge type adjusting screw.

The oil pump is driven via the distributor from the auxiliary shaft and may be of either the rotor or vane type. It has a special built in pressure relief valve which opens when the oil pressure exceeds normal operating pressure. The oil filter is of the disposable cartridge type and is mounted on the outside, right hand side of the cylinder block. Further details of the engine lubrication system will be found in Section 26. The majority of nuts, bolts and screws used on the engine are to Unified standard specifications so before any work is started make sure that a selection of suitable spanners and sockets is available.

2 Major operations with engine in place

The following major operations can be carried out to the engine with it in place in the car:
1 Removal and replacement of the camshaft and housing.
2 Removal and replacement of the camshaft drive belt.
3 Removal and replacement of the cylinder head.
4 Removal and replacement of the engine mountings.
5 Removal of sump (after removal of suspension crossmember assembly).

6 Removal of flywheel (not recommended without availability of raised ramps or a pit).
7 Removal of crankshaft front oil seal.
8 Removal of pistons and connecting rods. - not recommended.

3 Major operations with engine removed

The following major operations must be carried out with the engine out of the car and on a bench or floor.
1 Removal and replacement of the main bearings.
2 Removal and replacement of the crankshaft.

4 Methods of engine removal

There are two methods of engine removal: complete with clutch and gearbox or without the gearbox. Both methods are described.

It is easier if a hydraulic trolley jack is used in conjunction with two axle stands, so that the car can be raised sufficiently to allow easy access underneath the car. Overhead lifting tackle will be necessary in both cases.

NOTE Cars fitted with automatic transmission necessitating engine and transmission removal should have the transmission removed FIRST as described in Chapter 6. The transmission, even on its own, is very heavy.

5 Engine - removal with gearbox

1 The complete unit can be removed easily in about four hours. It is essential to have a good hoist, and two strong axle stands if an inspection pit is not available. Engine removal will be much easier if there is someone to assist especially during the later stages.
2 With few exceptions, it is simplest to lift out the engine with all ancillaries (alternator, distributor, carburettor, exhaust manifold) still attached.
3 Before beginning work it is worthwhile to get all the accumulated dirt cleaned off the engine unit at a garage which is equipped with steam or high pressure air and water cleaning equipment. It helps to make the job quicker, easier and of course much cleaner.
4 Detach the windscreen washer feed pipe from the bonnet jet connection (photo).
5 Using a pencil or scriber mark the outline of the bonnet hinge on either side to act as a datum for refitting. An assistant should now take the bonnet stay. Undo and remove the four bolts, spring and plain washers. Carefully lift the bonnet up and then over the front of the car. Store in a safe place where it will not be scratched, (photo). Push down hinges to stop any accidents.
6 Undo and remove the positive and then the negative battery terminal clamp bolts. Detach the terminal connectors (photo).
7 Undo and remove the wing nuts securing the battery clamp. Lift away the clamp and then the battery (photo).
8 Working under the car, place a container of 10 pints (6 litres) under the sump drain plug and remove the sump plug. When the oil has finished draining out refit the plug.
9 Using a scriber or file mark the propeller shaft at the rear flange and final drive coupling so that it may be refitted in its original position (photo)
10 Undo and remove the four nuts and bolts that secure the flange to the coupling. Detach the flange from the coupling, draw the propeller shaft rearwards and lower to the ground. Wrap the end of the gearbox extension housing in rag and then slide a polythene bag over the end and tie firmly with a piece of string or wire (photos)
11 Detach the speedometer drive cable from the right hand side of the extension housing by undoing the knurled sleeve nut. Draw the cable from the housing (photo).
12 Detach the gear change lever by releasing the spring clip on the end of the clevis pin. Push the clevis pin forwards. Note the

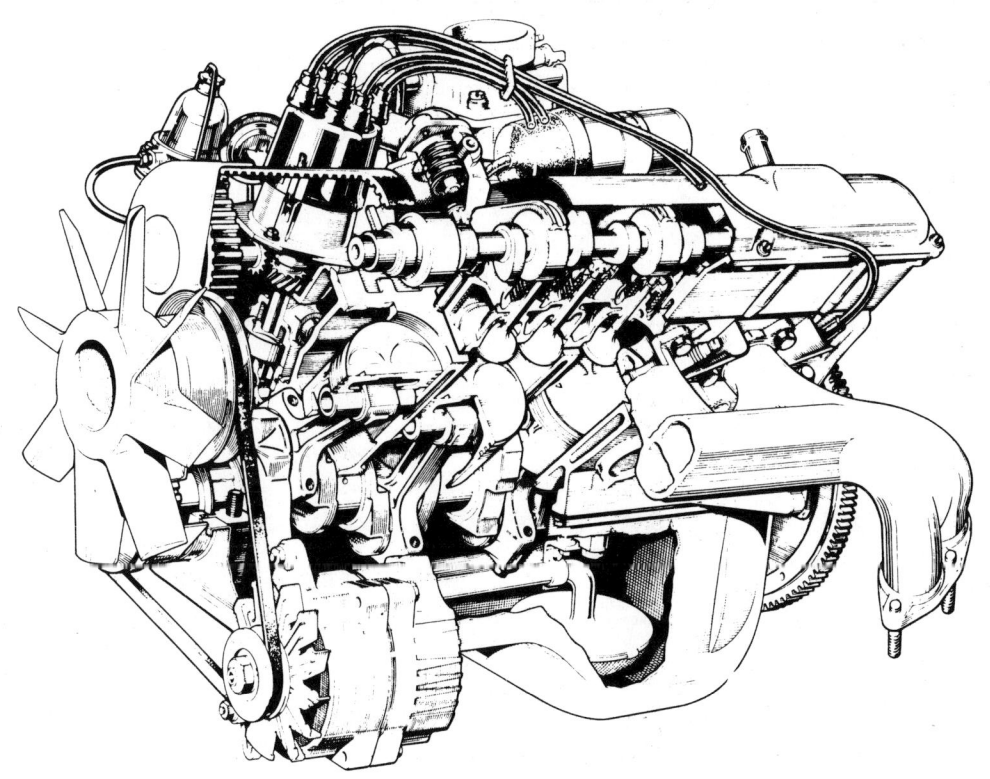

Fig. 1.1. Cutaway (top) and cross section (bottom) views of engine

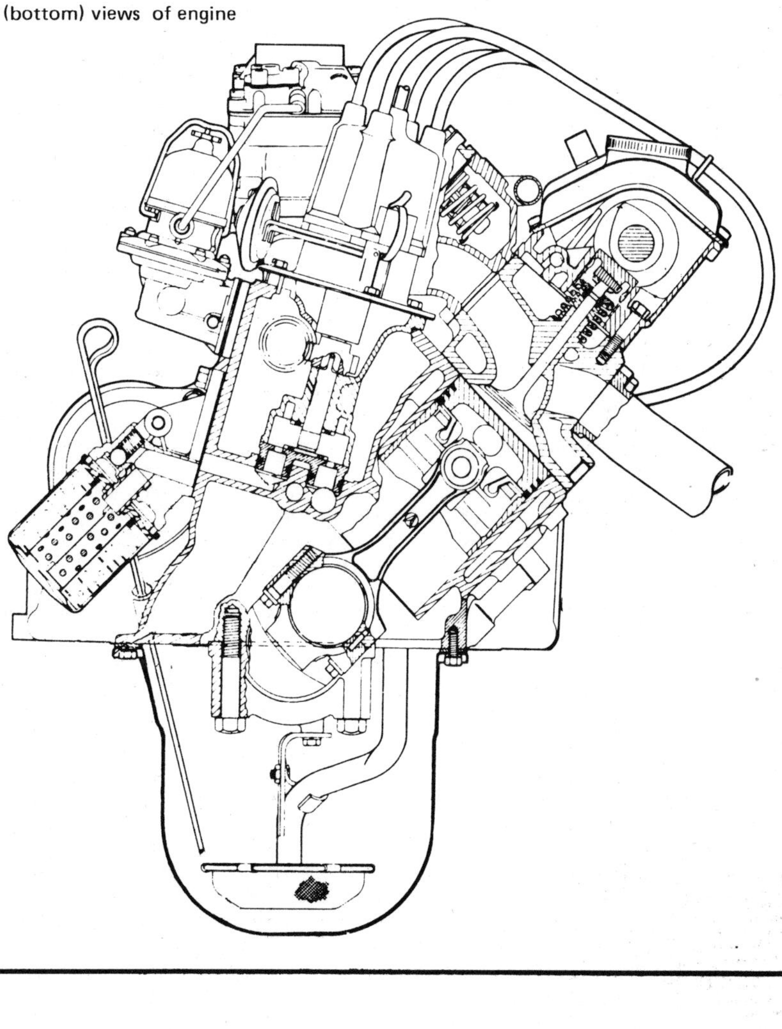

5.4 Releasing washer pipes

5.5 Removing bonnet securing bolts

5.6 Removing battery terminals

5.7 Battery clamp release

5.9 Alignment marks on propeller shaft flange

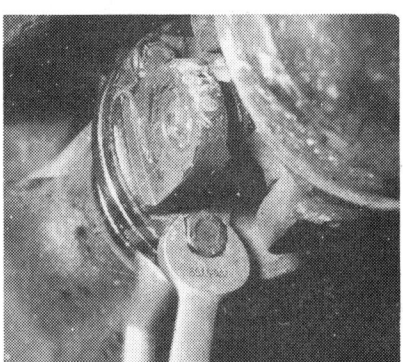

5.10a Undoing propeller shaft securing bolts

Belville washer at the clevis pin lead end (photos)

13 Detach the clutch cable return spring from the bracket on the side of the gearbox (photo).

14 Release the clutch cable adjustment nut lock nut, remove the locknut, adjustment nut, plain washer and nylon and rubber block. Slide off the rubber sleeve and then rubber connection boot. Draw back the cable and recover the plain 'C' washer.

15 Undo and remove 4 brass nuts and spring washers that secure the exhaust downpipe to manifold flange joint. Slide down the flange joint and recover the two asbestos rings. Tuck the exhaust downpipe under the wheel arch (photo).

16 Pull the two terminal blocks from the rear of the alternator. Unclip the wires from the front of the sump and also from the right hand side of the sump (photo).

17 Undo the battery earth strap retaining bolt which is located just underneath the oil filter canister.(photo).

18 Undo and remove the four self tapping screws that secure the cowl to the radiator. Push the cowl back over the blades (photo)

19 Place a wide container under the radiator bottom hose, slacken the hose clip at radiator end and draw off the hose (photo)

20 Slacken the top hose clip at the thermostat housing. Detach the top hose

21 Slacken the nuts that secure the radiator mountings to the front panel (photo).

22 Lift the radiator upwards and away from the engine compartment (photo).

23 Lift away the radiator cowling (photo).

24 Slacken the bottom hose connection at the water pump and detach the bottom hose (photo).

25 Slacken the hose clip at the rear of the air cleaner assembly and detach the hose (photo).

26 Undo and remove the three through bolts that hold the air cleaner assembly to the carburettor air intake. Lift away the air cleaner assembly (photo).

27 Slacken the clip that secures the servo unit hose to the inlet

28 Release the choke outer cable from the carburettor mounted bracket by springing off the clip with a screwdriver (photo).

29 Release the choke inner cable by undoing the bolt and withdrawing the cable (photo).

30 Using a screwdriver release the spring clip securing the throttle inner cable to the spindle. Withdraw the clevis pin.

31 Slacken the throttle cable locknut. Slacken the adjustment nut and slide from the side of the mounting bracket.

32 Note the cable connections to the starter solenoid. Undo and remove the nut and spring washer that secures the heavy duty cables. Also release the Lucar connectors (photo).

33 Pull off the temperature sender unit cable Lucar connector (photo).

34 Pull off the Lucar connector on the oil pressure switch located beneath the inlet manifold behind the starter motor (photo).

35 Pull the plastic cap from the top of the ignition coil. This will also release the HT cable.

36 Detach the cable from the switch side of the ignition coil (white with a yellow tracer) (photo).

37 Slacken the clip and detach the front heater pipe at the water pump connection (photo). Unclip this hose from the front of the top cover.

38 Slacken the clip and detach the heater hose from the small union pipe on the side of the thermostat housing (photo).

39 Because all the hoses are clipped together, release the top cover breather hose from the engine top cover (photo). Also detach heater hose from the tap on the bulkhead top panel and tuck hoses back beside the screen washer bottle (photo).

40 Undo and remove the bolt and plain washer that secures the rubber splash shield to the right hand inner wing. Unclip the shield from the anti-roll bar and push downwards (photo).

41 Using a pair of pliers open the fuel pipe joint clip and pull off the flexible hose. Plug the end with a pencil to stop dirt ingress (photo).

42 To stop accidental damage to the horn nearest the engine,

5.10b Withdrawing propeller shaft from gearbox

5.11 Removing speedometer drive cable

5.12a Gear lever to linkage attachment

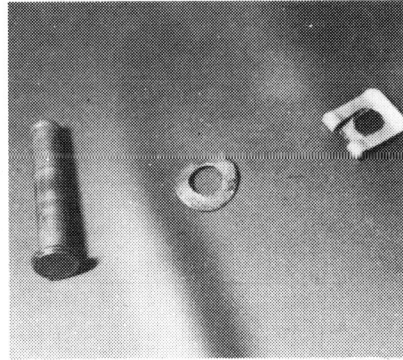

5.12b Clevis pin, spring clip and Belville washer

5.13 Clutch cable return spring detachment

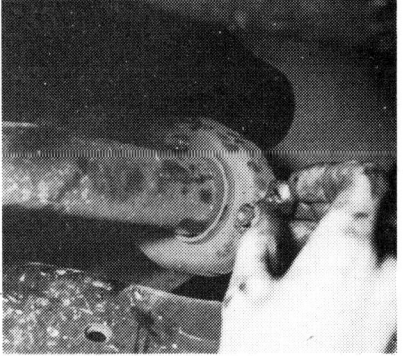

5.15 Exhaust manifold to downpipe attachment

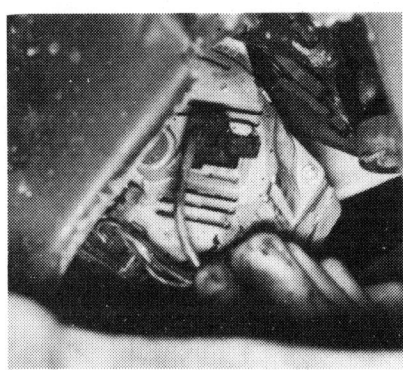

5.16 Rear of alternator showing terminal connectors

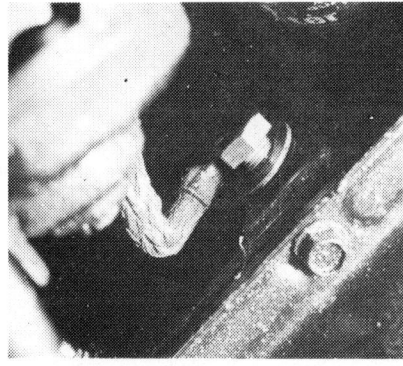

5.17 Earth strap attachment on engine

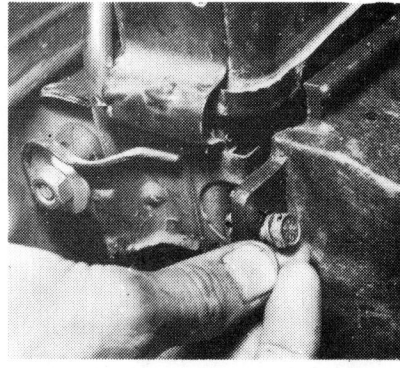

5.18 Cowl securing bolt removal

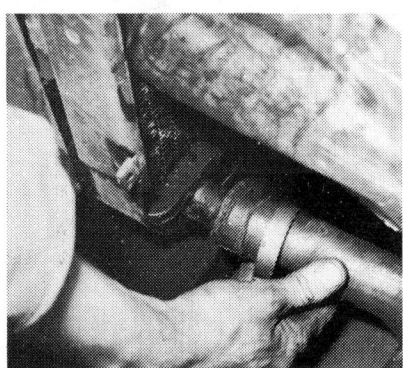

5.19 Bottom hose detachment

5.21 Radiator mounting bracket

5.22 Lifting away radiator

5.23 Lifting away cowl

5.24 Detaching bottom hose from pump

5.25 Hose attachment at rear of air cleaner assembly

5.26 Air cleaner attachment to carburettor air intake

5.27 Servo unit hose to inlet manifold adaptor attachment

5.28 Choke outer cable retaining clip removal

5.29 Choke inner cable removal

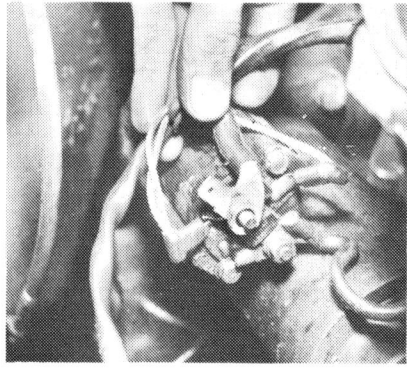

5.32 Cable connections at rear of starter motor

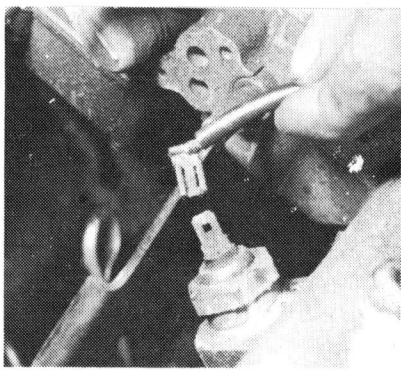

5.33 Temperature sender unit cable removal

5.34 Oil pressure switch cable removal

5.36 Detachment of cable from ignition coil

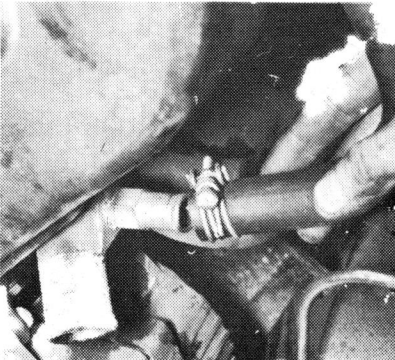

5.37 Front heater pipe removal at water pump connector

5.38 Heater pipe removal at thermostat housing

5.39a Hose removal from engine top cpver

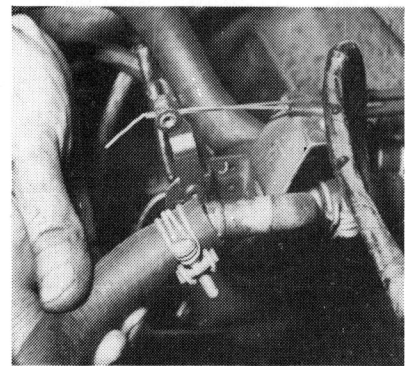
5.39b Heater pipe from bulkhead top panel

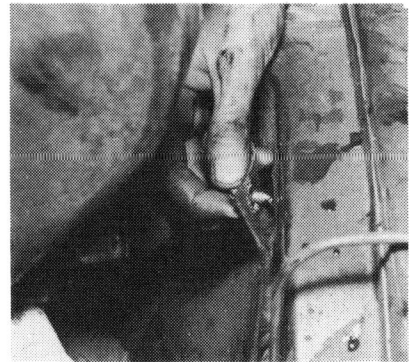
5.40 Splash shield detachment

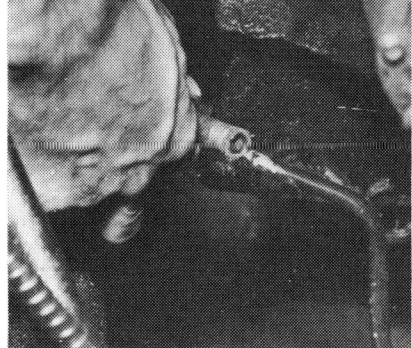
5.41 Fuel pipe joint clip removal

5.42 Removing the horns

5.43 Engine mounting detachment

5.45 Distributor cap removal

5.46 Removal of rotor arm

5.50 Removing gearbox mounting nut and washer

5.51 Supporting the gearbox

5.53a Commencing to lift engine

detach the cable and then undo and remove the one retaining bolt (photo).

43 Undo and remove the nut, shakeproof and plain washer that secures the right hand engine mounting to the front suspension cross member bracket (photo) (Fig.1.2).

44 Repeat the sequence in the last paragraph for the left hand engine mounting.

45 Release the distributor cap retaining clips and lift away the cap (photo).

46 Also remove the rotor arm by undoing and removing the rotor arm securing screws (photo).

47 Use a strong rope or chains to support the weight of the engine.

48 Place a small jack under the gearbox and support its weight. It will probably be necessary to place a block of wood on the jack saddle.

49 Undo and remove the bolt, spring washer and spacer from the right hand side gearbox mounting bracket. Slacken the left hand bolt but do not remove.

50 Undo and remove the nut and shakeproof washer that secures the gearbox extension housing mounting to the mounting bracket. Pivot the mounting bracket round to the left (photo).

51 Lower the jack under the gearbox and be prepared to commence lifting the complete power unit from the engine compartment. Make sure that all pipes, hoses, cables and controls have been detached and tucked well out of the way (photo)

52 To remove the power unit, it has to be lifted at an angle of 45° so make sure that the rope or chains will stand this position without slipping.

53 Raise the engine and draw forwards. Check that the exhaust flange clears the left hand mounting bracket, also the top cover clears the bulkhead. As lifting continues make sure the starter motor clears the heater tap (photos)

54 Continue to raise the engine until the rear of the sump is clear of the front cross member. The rear of the gearbox can now be lifted by hand over this cross member as the car is pushed rearwards or the hoist is drawn away from the engine compartment (photo). Lower the unit to the ground away from the car.

55 Check that the engine compartment and floor area around the car are clear of loose nuts and bolts as well as tools.

6 Engine - removal less gearbox

1 If it is necessary to remove only the engine, leaving the gearbox in position the engine can be detached from the gearbox and then lifted away.

2 Follow the instructions given in Section 5 paragraphs 2 - 8, 13 - 47.

3 Using a hydraulic jack support the weight of the gearbox.

4 Undo and remove the two bolts and spring washers that secure the starter motor to the clutch housing. Lift away the starter motor.

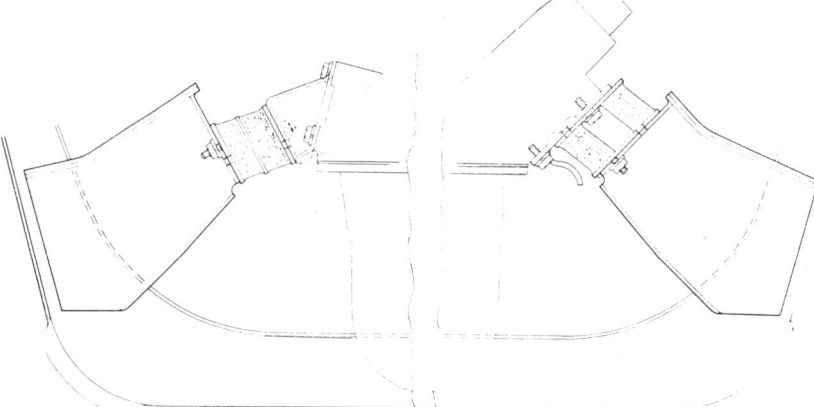

Fig. 1.2. Engine mountings

5.53b Note the angle at which the engine
      has to be tilted

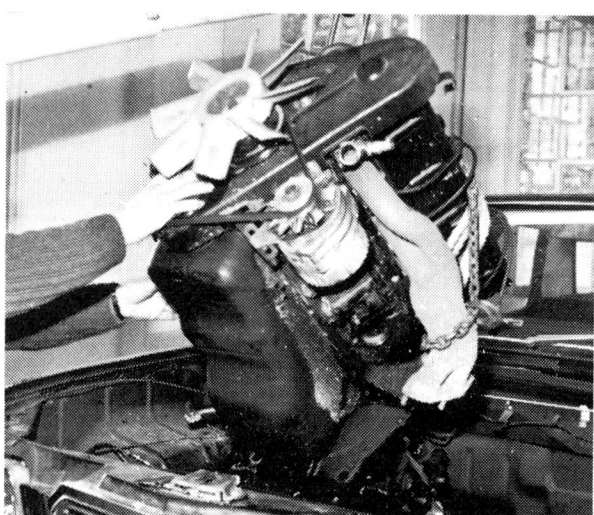

5.54 Engine removal - final stage

5 Place a rope sling or chains around the engine and support its weight using an overhead hoist.

6 Undo and remove the remaining nuts, bolts and spring washers that secure the engine to the gearbox bellhousing. Then release the engine mountings.

7 Check that no controls, cables or pipes have been left connected to the engine and that they are safely tucked to one side where they will not be caught as the unit is being removed.

8 Raise the engine slightly to enable the engine mountings to clear their mounting brackets and move it forwards until the clutch is clear of the input shaft. Continue lifting the unit taking care not to damage the front cross member. Then lower the engine to the floor.

9 To complete, clear out any loose nuts and bolts and tools from the engine compartment and the floor area.

7 Dismantling the engine - general

1 Keen d.i.y. mechanics who dismantle a lot of engines will probably have a stand on which to put them but most will make do with a work bench which should be large enough to spread the inevitable bits and pieces and tools around on, and strong enough to support the engine weight. If the floor is the only possible place try and ensure that the engine rests on a hardwood platform or similar rather than on concrete.

2 Spend some time on cleaning the unit. If you have been wise this will have been done before the engine was removed, at a service bay. Good solvents such as 'Gunk' will help to 'float' off caked dirt/grease under a water jet. Once the exterior is clean, dismantling may begin. As parts are removed clean them in petrol or paraffin (do not immerse parts with oilways in paraffin - clean them with a petrol soaked cloth and clear oilways with nylon pipe cleaners. If an air line is available so much the better for final cleaning off. Paraffin, which could possibly remain in oilways would dilute the oil for initial lubrication after reassembly).

3 Where components are fitted with seals and gaskets it is always best to fit new ones - but do NOT throw the old ones away until you have the new one to hand. A pattern is then available if they have to be made specially. Hang them on a convenient hook.

4 In general it is best to work from the top of the engine downwards. In any case support the engine firmly so that it does not topple over when you are undoing stubborn nuts and bolts.

5 Always place nuts and bolts back with their components or place of attachment if possible - it saves so much confusion later. Otherwise put them in small, separate pots or jars so that their groups are easily identified.

6 If you are lucky enough to have an area where parts can be laid out on sheets of paper do so - putting the nuts and bolts with them. If you are able to look at all the components in this way it helps to avoid missing something on reassembly because it is tucked away on a shelf or whatever.

7 Even though you may be dismantling the engine only partly - possibly with it still in the car - the principles still apply. It is appreciated that most people prefer to do engine repairs if possible with the engine in position. Consequently an indication will be given as to what is necessary to lead up to carrying out repairs on a particular component. Generally speaking the engine is easy enough to get at as far as repairs and renewals of the ancillaries are concerned. When it comes to repair of the major engine components, however, it is only fair to say that repairs with the engine in position are more difficult than with it out.

8 Engine ancillaries - removal

1 If you are stripping the engine completely or preparing to install a reconditioned unit, all the ancillaries must be removed first. If you are going to obtain a reconditioned 'short' motor (block, crankshaft, pistons and connecting rods) then obviously the cambox, cylinder head and associated parts will need retention for fitting to the new engine. It is advisable to check just what you will get with a reconditioned unit as changes are made from time to time.

2 The removal of all those items connected with fuel, ignition and charging systems are detailed in the respective chapters so for brevity they are merely listed here.

Distributor
Carburettor (can be removed together with inlet manifold).
Alternator
Fuel pump
Water pump
Starter motor
Thermostat

9 Engine mountings - removal and replacement

1 Jack up the engine with the saddle suitably padded with wood just sufficiently to take the weight.

2 Undo and remove the securing bolts and washers to the side of the crankcase and the lower mounting nut, shakeproof and plain washer.

3 Lift away the mounting. Fitting the new mounting is the reverse sequence to removal. These mountings are interchangeable side to side.

10 Oil filter and adaptor - removal and replacement

1 The oil filter is a throwaway cartridge which is changed regularly under service procedures. The adaptor into which it screws is held to the block by three bolts. A gasket is used.

2 The adaptor may be removed for cleaning and checking of the spring loaded bypass valve. The bypass valve opens to permit oil to flow in the event that the filter should get blocked.

3 Always fit a new gasket when refitting the adaptor (photo).

4 Smear the filter element sealing ring with lubricant before fitting to prevent binding and removal difficulty later (photos).

11 Bellhousing and cover plate - removal and replacement

1 The bellhousing can be removed with the engine in the car but first the gearbox has to be removed and the engine disengaged from its mountings in order to get at the top two securing bolts on the left side. Unless a hoist or pit is available this operation is very difficult and it is recommended the engine be taken from the car first.

2 Remove all the bolts holding the bellhousing to the block and the lower cover plate to the bellhousing including those of the starter motor if not removed already. The housing will have the clutch actuating arm attached to it. Pull the housing off the dowel pegs. The clutch actuating arm can be pulled off the pivot pin - it is held by a spring clip.

3 Replacement is a reversal of this procedure.

4 Note that the bellhousing is never removed or replaced together with the gearbox.

12 Flywheel - removal, inspection and renovation

1 The flywheel is held to the rear of the crankshaft by five bolts and located by two dowel pegs. It can be removed with the engine in the car but the bell housing has to come off first and this is not recommended for the reasons given in the last section.

2 If the engine is removed from the car take the flywheel off first after the bellhousing. Undo the bolts with a socket spanner and pull the flywheel off square. It is important not to damage the mating surfaces or the dowel pegs and holes.

3 The flywheel clutch friction surface should be shiny and unscored. Minor blemishes and scratches can be overlooked but

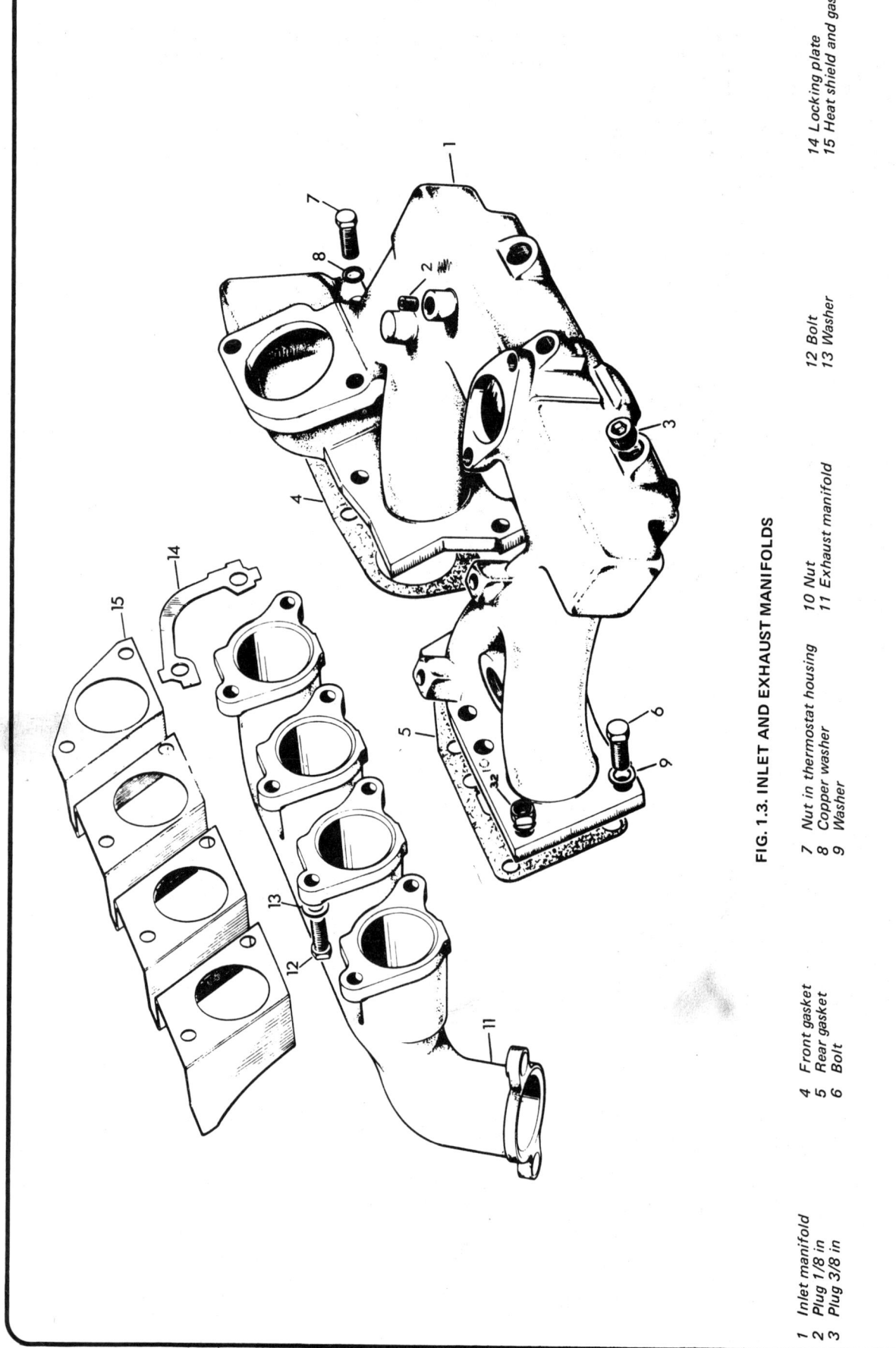

FIG. 1.3. INLET AND EXHAUST MANIFOLDS

1 Inlet manifold	4 Front gasket	7 Nut in thermostat housing	10 Nut	14 Locking plate
2 Plug 1/8 in	5 Rear gasket	8 Copper washer	11 Exhaust manifold	15 Heat shield and gasket
3 Plug 3/8 in	6 Bolt	9 Washer	12 Bolt	
			13 Washer	

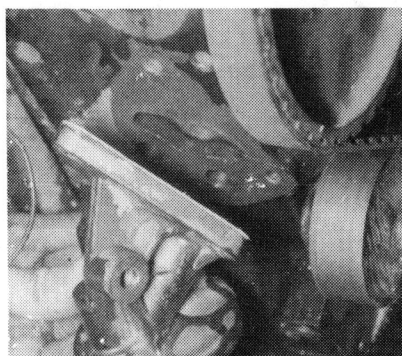

10.3 Replace oil filter adaptor bracket to block

10.4a Lubricating the oil filter cartridge sealing ring before replacement

10.4b Replacing the oil filter cartridge

13.2 Mark on timing belt to show direction of travel before removal

14.1 Levering off the crankshaft pulley

14.4a Fitting the crankshaft key

deep grooves will probably cause clutch problems in time. Renewal may be advisable.

If the starter ring gear teeth are badly worn the ring can be removed by first splitting it between two teeth with a chisel. Do not try and drive it off because it rests in a shallow groove. If you have never fitted a new ring gear yourself it is best to have it done for you. It needs heating to a temperature of 200°C evenly in order to shrink fit it on the flywheel. The chamfers on the ring gear must face in the direction the flywheel normally rotates. On later models the chamfer is on one side of the teeth only and this must be towards the clutch side of the flywheel.

13 Drive belt for camshaft and auxiliary shaft - removal

1 The drive belt may be removed with the engine installed but it will be necessary to remove the cover first and this, in turn, will involve removal of the fan and crankshaft V belt pulleys.

The crankshaft pulley is held by a central bolt which can be undone with a socket. The V section is separate from the toothed section but located on the common crankshaft woodruff key. It should pull off easily. The fan pulley is held to the water pump shaft by the four bolts which also carry the fan blades.

2 Before removing the belt certain precautions should be taken, depending on the reasons for removing it, so as to minimise the risk of making mistakes on replacement, and, of course, to save time. For all conditions mark the belt with a piece of chalk to indicate the direction of travel. This ensures that the wear pattern of the teeth stays the same and wear does not become excessive (photo).

3 In all situations other than complete engine dismantling, refer to the section on 'Valve timing and drive belt replacement' and set the pulleys in position before taking the belt off. In such situations do not move any pulleys (other than the one you may have to) until the belt is replaced.

If any of the pulleys are to be removed from their shafts later, first slacken the centre retaining bolt before removing the belt. Independent movement of the camshaft and crankshaft with the belt off will not only lose the valve timing position, but also cause valves to touch the crowns of pistons at TDC.

4 Slacken the bolts securing the belt jockey pulley mounting bracket. The belt may then be slid off the pulleys. Do not let it get kinked, damaged or contaminated. It is expensive. Normally it should last indefinitely and require no adjustment.

14 Crankshaft pulley, auxiliary shaft pulley and camshaft pulley - removal and replacement

1 All three pulleys are held onto their respective shafts in the same way - namely by a woodruff key in a parallel shaft. They should all pull off easily once the centre bolt is removed (photo).

2 The centre bolt should be slackened before the drive belt is removed - and then the drive belt should be taken off as described in the previous section.

3 The crankshaft pulley is slightly different in that it is in three parts - the outer V belt section, the timing belt section and the inner flange.

4 The two belt sections each engage half of the Woodruff key and the flange locates in a hand on the back of the timing belt pulley (photos).

5 It should be remembered that if any one of the three shafts is moved when the belt is off, the timing must be reset before replacing the belt.

15 Camshaft housing, camshaft and tappets - removal and inspection

1 The operation described can be carried out with the engine installed.

14.4b Fitting the crankshaft pulley (note how half the key engages each part of the pulley)

15.12 Camshaft housing, the punch is indicating the fine oil spray orifice

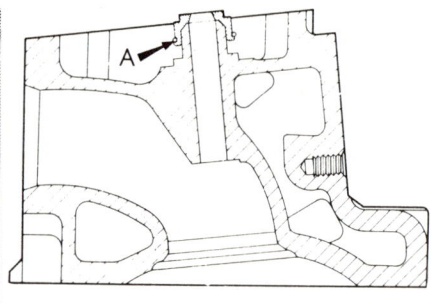

FIG.1.4. VALVE GUIDE OIL SEAL

Valve stem seal fitted round guide boss of head and secured by a circlip

2   The camshaft is removed together with the housing from the top of the cylinder head (ie you cannot move the camshaft with the housing fitted to the head).

3   Disconnect the leads from the spark plugs and then unclip them from the cambox cover.

4   Remove the timing belt as described in the previous section having first slackened the camshaft pulley bolt.

5   The camshaft housing is held to the head by ten bolts inside the housing. After removing the cover each bolt should be slackened a little at a time, evenly over the whole area until the valve springs held under tension are completely relaxed. Due to the narrow access to the bolt heads it will be found that a ½ inch drive socket set will be too big so unless you have a 3/8 inch or ¼ inch drive set buy a tubular spanner to fit. The bolts are not very tight.

6   Having loosened all bolts lift them out. Before lifting the cam housing you should be aware that the tappets can all fall out and this must be prevented. As soon as the tappets are clear of the valves, therefore, tip the housing so that they will stay in their locations. When they are removed from the housing place them in a suitable container which marks clearly which position they are from.

7   To remove the camshaft first take off the pulley which is keyed to the shaft. Under no circumstances grip the pulley in a vice. If you forget to slacken the bolt use the timing belt to grip the pulley when removing it. Alternatively, grip the camshaft on an unmachined portion with a pair of self grips to hold it.

8   Remove the housing end cover from the rear. The thrust washer retaining bolt underneath is then undone and for this it is all right to clamp the nose of the camshaft in a vice with the jaws suitably covered with soft material.

9   The oil seal at the front end should now be prised out of the housing. Make sure you have a new one available as the old one will be no longer of any use.

10   The camshaft can be drawn out of the front of the housing. Take care not to catch the bearings with the cam lobes.

11   The bearing surfaces of the cam lobes and tappets should be flat and unpitted. If otherwise you may expect rapid wear to occur in the future. Badly worn cam lobes affect the opening of the valves and consequently engine performance.

 If lack of lubrication has occurred the tappets may have become badly worn in the housing bores. In any of these circumstance it will be necessary to renew the affected parts.

12   The camshaft housing has an oil gallery lining its full length with fine jet holes opposite each tappet bore. It is essential that this is perfectly clean. To clean the gallery properly unscrew the blanking plugs at each end and blow out the five jets and gallery with an air line. Do not try to enlarge the jet holes - they are of a particular size in order to maintain oil pressure and an adequate spray to the tappets and cams (photo).

13   Each tappet contains a screw with a wedge shaped flat on it for the purposes of adjusting the valve tappet clearances. Should these be damaged or need renewal for other reasons (see 'Valve clearance adjustment') they may be screwed out of the tappets using an Allen key.

16 Inlet and exhaust manifolds - removal and replacement

 Details of how to remove the exhaust and inlet manifolds are given in the next section dealing with cylinder head removal. The only difference is that if you are not removing the cylinder head it is not necessary to remove the camshaft housing first. Replacement is covered in Section 34 dealing with cylinder head replacement.

17 Cylinder head , valves and springs - removal, inspection and renovation

1   The cylinder head can be removed with the engine in the car. Remove the camshaft housing as described in the previous section, and drain the cooling system of about four pints.

2   Undo the exhaust pipe from the manifold by removing the two nuts with a socket and extension from underneath.

3   To get at all the cylinder head bolts the exhaust manifold has to be removed first. The exhaust manifold is secured by eight bolts each pair having a double tab lockwasher. Bend back the tabs and remove the bolts with a socket or tubular spanner. Lift off the manifold and the heat shield gasket behind it.

4   The inlet manifold may be removed before or after the head is removed. Note that one of the securing bolt heads is inside the thermostat housing. The housing cover and thermostat should first be removed (see Chapter 2) and the bolt taken out. Note the copper sealing washer under the head of the bolt. Undo the water pipe union into the manifold from the water pump.

5   The cylinder head bolts are tight and if the engine is out of the car it must be securely supported whilst they are slackened. Use only a good quality socket spanner for this job. Bolts should be slackened from the ends towards the centre - preferably in the reverse sequence of tightening as shown in Fig.1.17 (page 40)

6   Undo the bolt which holds the inlet elbow for the water pump to the front of the head.

7   The head is located on two small dowels to the block and should lift straight off. Tapping the sides will not do much good if it sticks and no form of lever should be forced between the head and block. A lever can be arranged across the lower front corner, however, where it projects over the block.

8   Even if the valves are not being removed it is best to remove all carbon deposits from the combustion chamber with a wire brush in a power drill. If no power drill is available scrape the carbon off with an old screwdriver.

9   To remove the valves from the cylinder head requires a special 'G' clamp spring compressor. This is positioned with the screw head on the head of the valve and the claw end over the valve spring collar. The screw is turned until the two split collars round the valve stem are freed and can be renewed. If the spring collar tends to stick so that the compressor cannot be tightened, tap the top of the spring (while the clamp is on) to free it.

 Slacken off the compressor and the valve springs and collar will be released and can be lifted off. On later engines an oil seal

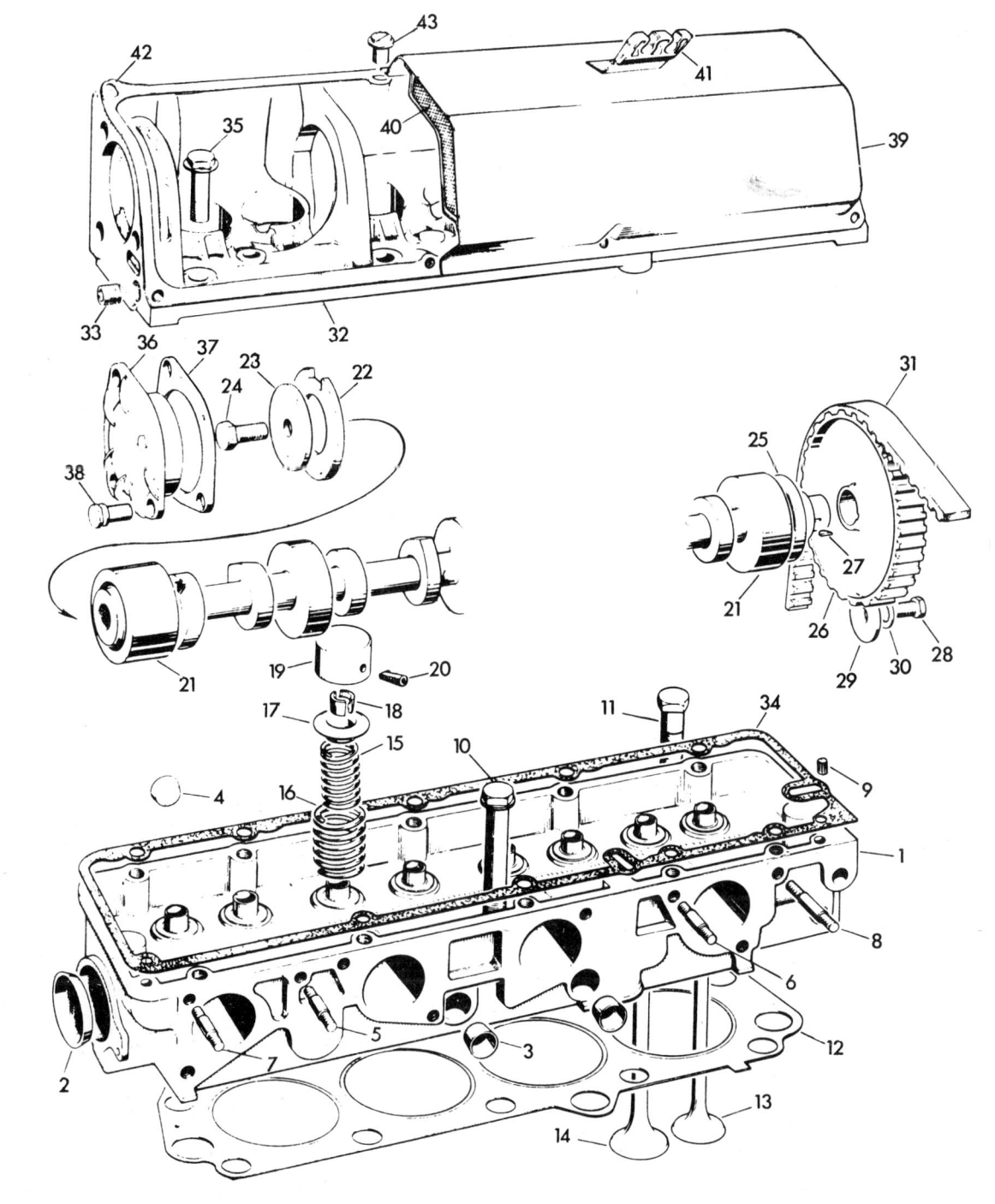

FIG. 1.5. CYLINDER HEAD, CAMSHAFT AND HOUSING

1	Cylinder head	12	Head gasket	23	Retaining washer	34	Gasket
2	Cup plug 1½ inch	13	Exhaust valve	24	Self locking bolt	35	Housing bolts
3	Cup plug ¾ inch	14	Inlet valve	25	Oil seal	36	Rear cover
4	Cup plug 5/8 inch	15	Inner valve spring	26	Camshaft pulley	37	Gasket
5	Stud-inlet manifold 5/16"	16	Outer valve spring	27	Woodruff key	38	Cover bolt
6	Stud-inlet manifold 7/16"	17	Valve spring cup	28	Pulley bolt	39	Housing cover
7	Stud-inlet manifold 5/8"	18	Valve collets	29	Washer	40	Breather element
8	Stud-inlet manifold 2.1/8"	19	Tappet	30	Lockwasher	41	Spark plug lead bracket
9	Knurled dowel peg	20	Adjuster screw	31	Drive belt	42	Cover gasket
10	Cylinder head bolt-long	21	Camshaft	32	Camshaft housing	43	Cover screw and washer
11	Cylinder head bolt-short	22	Camshaft thrust washer	33	Oil gallery plug		

cup is fitted round each valve guide shoulder and retained by a circlip. These should be renewed. Valves should be drawn out from the guides with care. Any tightness is probably caused by burring at the end of the stem so clean this up before drawing the valves through. The guides will not then be scored.

10 Valves, seats and guides should be examined in conjunction. Any valve which is cracked or burnt away at the edges must be discarded. Valves which are a slack fit in the guides should be discarded also if further rapid deterioration and poor seating are to be avoided. To decide whether a valve is a slack fit replace it in its bore and feel how much it rocks at the end. Then judge if this represents a gap of more than .003 inch between stem and bore.

11 If valves are obviously a very slack fit the remedy is to ream the guides out oversize to accept oversize valves. Valves are available in oversizes of 0.003, 0.006, 0.012 and 0.024 inch (0.0762, 0.1524, 0.3048, 0.6096 mm). Reaming should be done from the top of the head. Unless you have the proper reamers and experience of their use you are strongly advised to have this work done by a specialist. It will not be possible to decide what oversize valves will be required until the guide bore oversize is established by reaming out.

12 Where a valve has deteriorated badly at the seat the corresponding seat in the cylinder head must be examined. Light pitting or scoring may be removed by grinding the valve into the seat with carborundum paste. If worse, then the seat may need recutting with a special tool. Check again, if you do not have the correct tool it is best to have the work done by a specialist.

13 When grinding in valves to their seats all carbon must first of all be removed from the head and head end of the stem. This is effectively done by fitting the valve in a power drill chuck, clamping the drill in a vice and then scraping the carbon off the rotating valve with an old screwdriver. It is essential to protect the eyes with suitable goggles when doing this (photo).

New valves may also be ground into their seats but check first whether the ones you get have any special coating on them. The procedure for grinding in valves is as follows: Obtain a tin of carborundum paste which contains coarse and fine varieties and also a grinding tool consisting of a rubber suction cup on the end of a wooden handle. Smear a trace of coarse carborundum paste on the seat face and apply a suction grinder tool to the valve head. With a semi-rotary motion, grind the valve head to its seat, lifting the valve occasionally to redistribute the grinding paste. When a dull matt even surface finish is produced on both the valve seat and the valve, then wipe off the paste and repeat the process with fine carborundum paste, lifting and turning the valve to redistribute the paste as before. A light spring placed under the valve head will greatly ease this operation. When a smooth unbroken ring of light grey matt finish is produced, on both valve and valve seat faces, the grinding operation is complete.

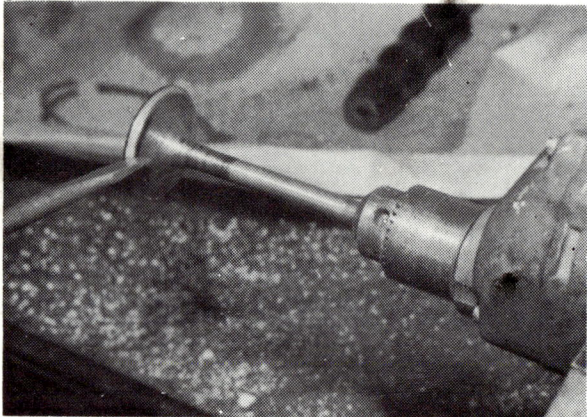

17.13 Cleaning carbon from a valve.
Power drill held in vice

14 After grinding, the thickness of the valve head (as indicated in Fig.1.6) should not be less than specified. Also the width of the seating should not be more than specified. If it is it means that the seating in the head may need recutting.

15 After the valve seats have been recut in the head the valve will naturally protrude further above the head. This protrusion should not exceed specification either (Fig.1.6). If you think of remedying this by grinding something off the end of the valve stem you could get into difficulties with valve clearances. It may be possible to fit valve seat inserts but the manufacturers do not recommend it. Being a relatively new engine, experience by specialist firms has not yet been built up on this feature.

16 When the grinding in process has finished all traces of carborundum paste must be removed. This is best done by flushing the head with paraffin and hosing out with water.

17 If the reason for removal of the head has been a blown gasket make sure that the surface is perfectly flat before it is refitted. This requires an accurate steel straight edge and a feeler gauge for checking. If there is any sign of warp over 0.003 inch (0.0762 mm) it is worthwhile getting it machined flat.

18 Each valve has an inner and outer spring and these should, of course, not have any broken coils. The overall length of each spring must be no less than the specified and if it is it must be discarded. The normal practice is to renew all springs when some are defective.

18 Oil pump - removal and inspection

1 The oil pump may be removed after the distributor has been taken off as described in Chapter 4, and the fuel pump removed as described in Chapter 3.

2 To lift the pump out insert a suitable lever into the fuel pump lever hole and prise the pump upwards so as to draw the bottom of the pump out of the two ports in the block. Do not try and prise it by the upper flange which may bend or break.

3 Once the pump is clear it should be turned 90° clockwise so that it can be lifted out.

4 Two types of pump are used - bi-rotor or vane type. To check the pump it is necessary to remove the bottom cover. Mark it first in relation to the main body and remove the four screws. Using a feeler gauge and straight edge the clearances between rotors and vanes, and the body housing them should be checked. On bi-rotor types the clearance between the tip of inner rotor and convex radius of outer rotor should not exceed 0.005 inch (0.1270 mm). The clearance between the outer rotor and the housing should not exceed 0.010 inch (0.254 mm). End float of rotors is 0.005 inch (0.1270 mm) maximum - measured with feeler blade and straight edge across the housing.

On vane type pumps the clearances between vanes and rotor, rotor and body (on the high point of the eccentric) and rotor end float should not exceed 0.005 inch (0.1270 mm). Tip clearance of the vanes opposite the high point of the rotor eccentric should not exceed 0.010 inch (0.254 mm).

If any or all of the clearances are excessive and the shaft is a slack fit in the body then it is best to obtain a new pump.

After checking the pump make sure that both the upper and lower rotor centre rings are properly located in relation to the vanes in the vane type pump and that the radiused edges of the vanes face outwards. On rotor type pumps the outer rotor is assembled with the chamfered edge inwards. In the side of the pump body below the gear opening there is a small hole which delivers oil to lubricate the auxiliary gears. Make sure it is quite clear.

19 Auxiliary shaft - removal, inspection and renovation

1 The auxiliary shaft may be removed after the drive belt, the shaft pulley, distributor and fuel pump. Refer to the appropriate chapter and sections for details of their removal.

2 The shaft is held in position by the oil seal. The oil seal cannot be removed without damage to it so make sure a new one is available beforehand.

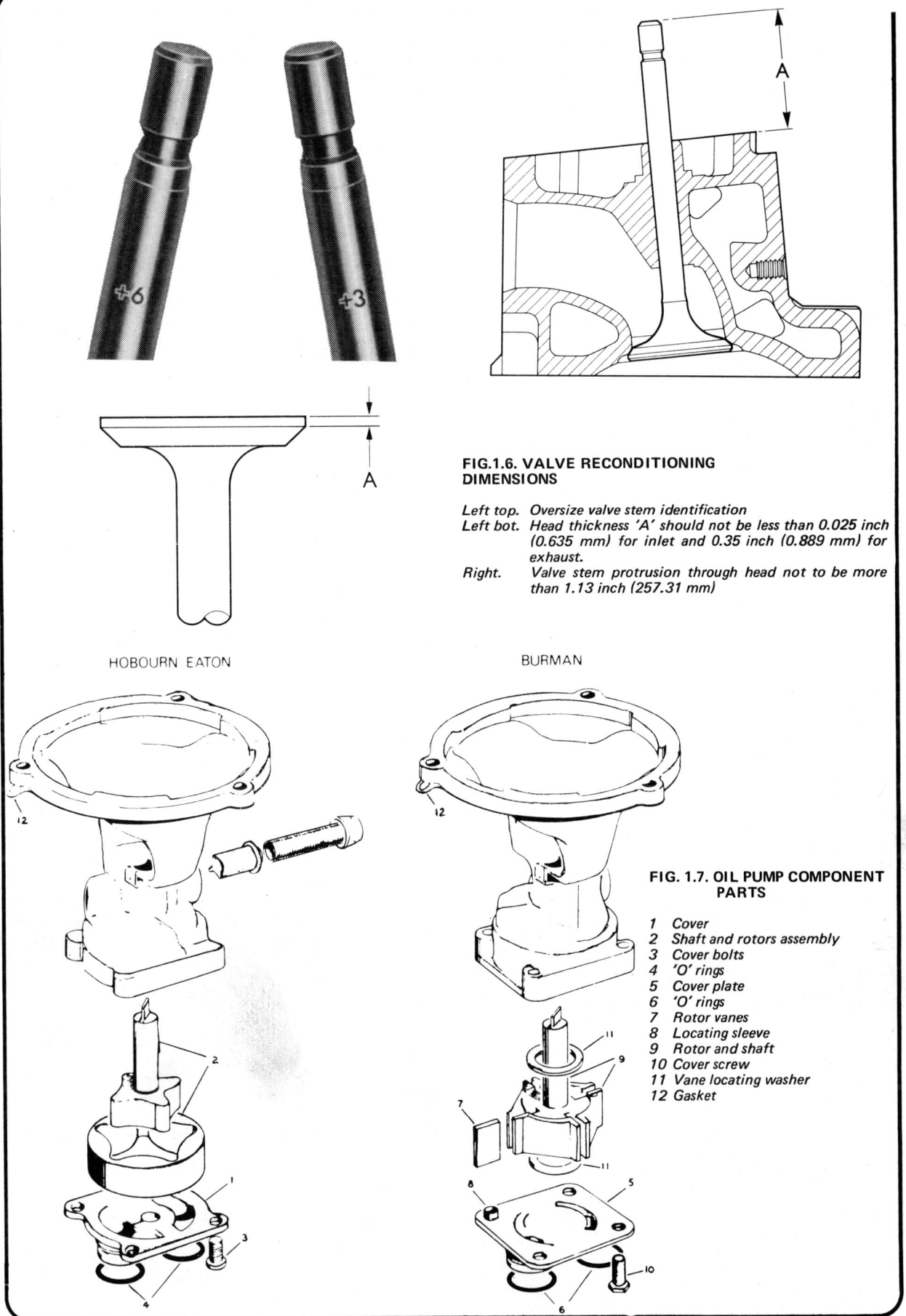

FIG.1.6. VALVE RECONDITIONING DIMENSIONS

Left top. Oversize valve stem identification
Left bot. Head thickness 'A' should not be less than 0.025 inch
           (0.635 mm) for inlet and 0.35 inch (0.889 mm) for
           exhaust.
Right.   Valve stem protrusion through head not to be more
           than 1.13 inch (257.31 mm)

HOBOURN EATON

BURMAN

FIG. 1.7. OIL PUMP COMPONENT PARTS

1 Cover
2 Shaft and rotors assembly
3 Cover bolts
4 'O' rings
5 Cover plate
6 'O' rings
7 Rotor vanes
8 Locating sleeve
9 Rotor and shaft
10 Cover screw
11 Vane locating washer
12 Gasket

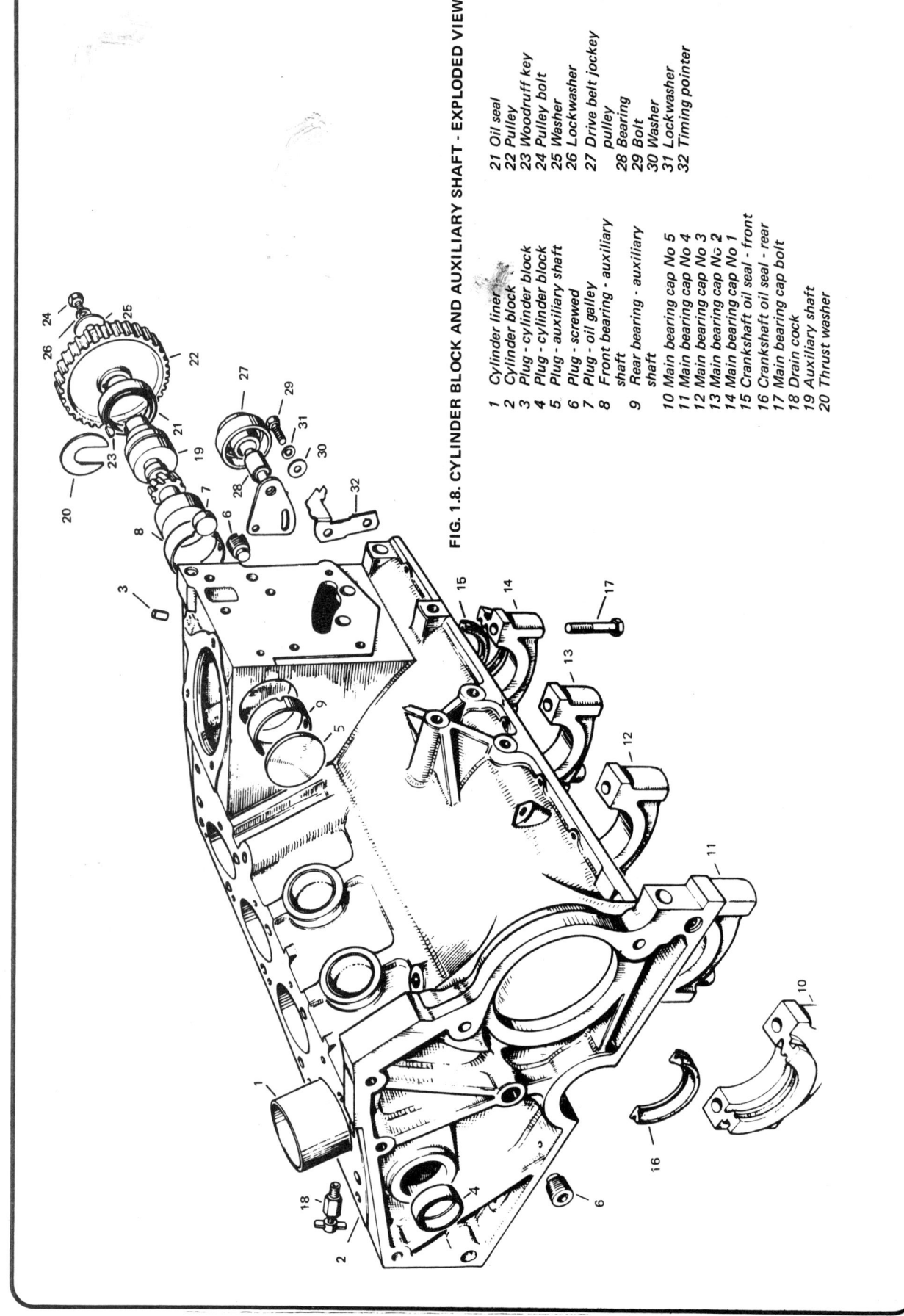

FIG. 1.8. CYLINDER BLOCK AND AUXILIARY SHAFT - EXPLODED VIEW

1 Cylinder liner
2 Cylinder block
3 Plug - cylinder block
4 Plug - cylinder block
5 Plug - auxiliary shaft
6 Plug - screwed
7 Plug - oil galley
8 Front bearing - auxiliary shaft
9 Rear bearing - auxiliary shaft
10 Main bearing cap No 5
11 Main bearing cap No 4
12 Main bearing cap No 3
13 Main bearing cap No 2
14 Main bearing cap No 1
15 Crankshaft oil seal - front
16 Crankshaft oil seal - rear
17 Main bearing cap bolt
18 Drain cock
19 Auxiliary shaft
20 Thrust washer
21 Oil seal
22 Pulley
23 Woodruff key
24 Pulley bolt
25 Washer
26 Lockwasher
27 Drive belt jockey pulley
28 Bearing
29 Bolt
30 Washer
31 Lockwasher
32 Timing pointer

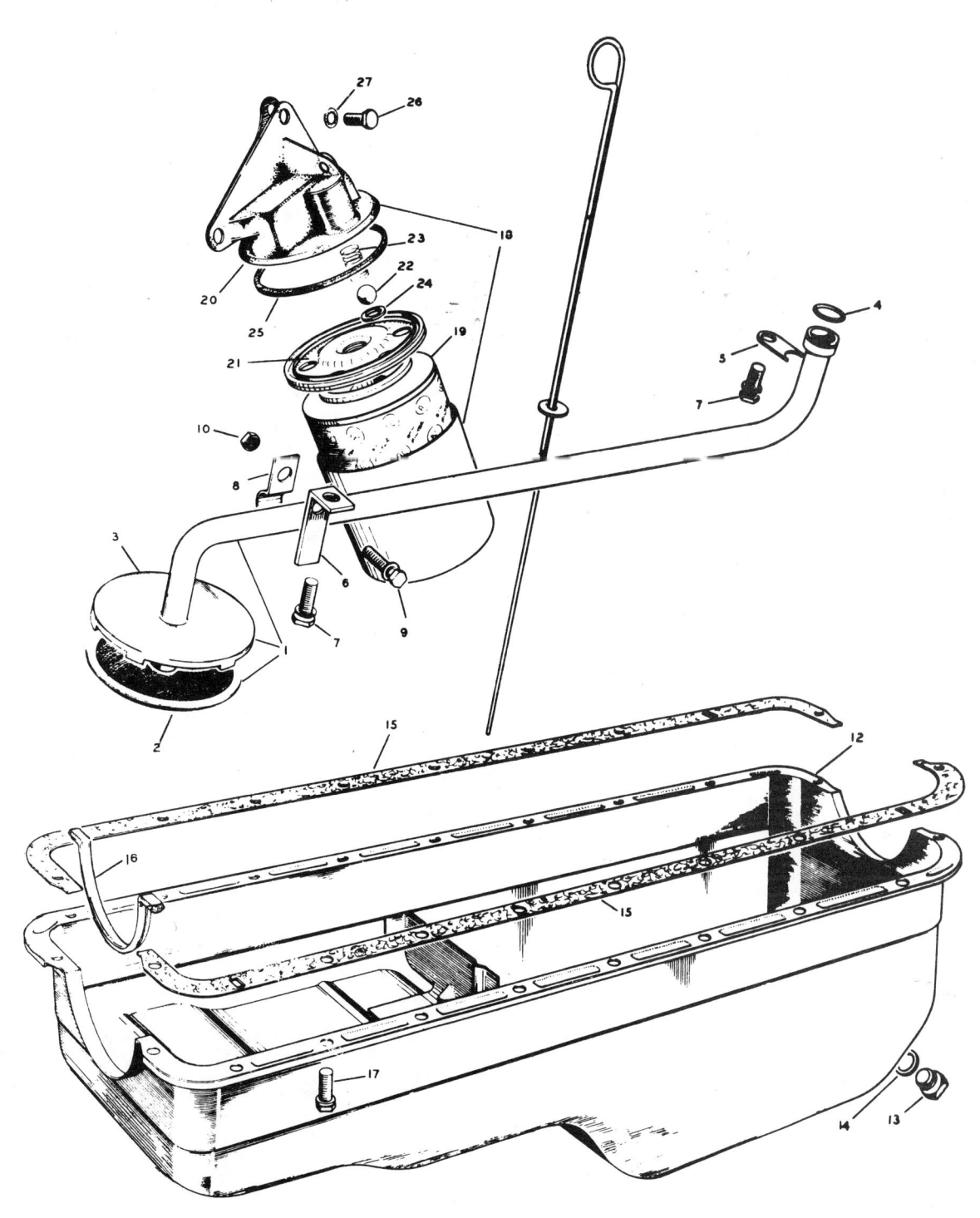

FIG. 1.9. SUMP, OIL SUCTION PIPE AND FILTER ASSEMBLIES

1 Screw and suction pipe assembly	7 Bolt	14 Washer	21 Valve seat
2 Screw	8 Clamp plate	15 Gasket	22 Steel ball
3 Cover	9 Clamp bolt	16 Seal	23 Spring
4 'O' ring	10 Nut	17 Screw and lockwasher	24 Sealing ring
5 Clamp plate	11 Gasket	18 Oil filter assembly	25 Gasket
6 Support bracket	12 Sump	19 Filter element	26 Bolt
	13 Drain plug	20 Adaptor lead	27 Lockwasher

3 Prise it out with a suitable tool and avoid scratching the shaft or the bore in the housing.

4 The shaft complete with thrust washer will then come out.

5 If the shaft gear is damaged or badly worn calling for renewal of the shaft then the distributor drive gear should also be renewed.

6 Wear on the thrust washer will be indicated by grooves and this also calls for renewal.

7 End float should be as specified and if there is any noticeable play between the shaft and bearings new bearing shells should be fitted.

8 The front and rear bearing shells can be drifted out although the rear one will come out with the block sealing plug.

9 When fitting new bearings see that the rear one has the offset hole and that the hole lines up with the passageway in the block.

10 The cut-out on the edge of the rear bearing should face the rear. Line up the hole for the front bearing with the cut-out facing the front.

11 Fit a new sealing plug at the rear using jointing compound to make it oil tight.

20 Sump - removal

1 To remove the sump means either lifting the engine out of the car or removing the front crossmember assembly.

2 If the engine is undergoing overhaul then, of course, it will be removed anyway.

3 If the problem is only leaking sump gaskets it is probably easiest to lower the front suspension. It is essential, however, to have proper stands to support the front of the car. Remove all the screws, marking the position of the one which holds the clutch cable clip. The sump can then be taken off.

21 Oil suction pipe and strainer - removal and replacement

1 The suction pipe and strainer can be removed when the sump is off.

2 It is held by a bolted clip to No 4 main bearing cap and a retaining plate held by a bolt at the elbow where the pipe goes into the block (photos).

3 With these removed the pipe can be pulled out.

4 Note the sealing ring round the pipe which is very important and should be renewed on replacement (photo).

5 Refitting is a straightforward reversal of these procedures.

22 Pistons, connecting rods and bearings - removal

1 To remove the pistons and connecting rods the engine should be removed from the car and the sump and cylinder head removed first as already described.

2 It is possible to make a preliminary examination of the state of the pistons relative to the bores with the engine in the car after removal of the cylinder head so bear this in mind where the inspection details are given in the next section.

3 Each connecting rod, bearing cap and piston is matched to each other and the cylinder, and must be replaced in the same position. Before removing anything mark each connecting rod near the cap with a light punch mark to indicate which cylinder it comes from. There is usually a makers number on the rod and cap so there should be no need to worry about mixing them up. If no numbers are apparent then mark the cap as well.

4 It is also important to ensure that the connecting rods and pistons go on the crankshaft the proper way round (the pistons are offset to the thrust side on the gudgeon pins). The best way to record this is by noting which side of the engine block the marks you have made or the existing numbers face. Provided the pistons are not being renewed then they can be arrowed with chalk on the crown pointing to the front but if they are separated from the connecting rods you still want to know which way

the rods go.

5 Having made quite sure that positions are clear undo the connecting rod cap bolts with a socket spanner. A normal 7/16 AF socket does not fit properly - a flank drive is needed - but an 11 mm metric socket is quite satisfactory.

6 Having removed the bearing caps the connecting rods and pistons may be pushed out through the top of the block.

7 The shell bearings may be slid round to remove them from the connecting rods and caps.

8 To separate the pistons from the connecting rods a great deal of pressure is needed to free the pins out of the small ends. This is not possible with anything other than a proper press and tools. Attempts with other methods will probably result in bent connecting rods or broken pistons. If new pistons are needed anyway it will need an experienced man to heat the connecting rods to fit the new gudgeon pins so the same man may as well take the old ones off.

23 Pistons, piston rings and cylinder bores - inspection and renovation

1 Examine the pistons for signs of damage on the crown and around the top edge. If any of the piston rings have broken there could be quite noticeable damage to the grooves, in which case the piston must be renewed. Deep scores in the piston walls also call for renewal. If the cylinders are being rebored new oversize pistons and rings will be needed anyway. If the cylinders do not need reboring and the pistons are in good condition only the rings need to be checked.

2 Unless new rings are to be fitted for certain, care has to be taken that rings are not broken on removal. Starting with the top ring first (all rings are to be removed from the top of the piston) ease one end out of its groove and place a thin piece of metal behind it.

Then move the metal strip carefully round behind the ring, at the same time nudging the ring upwards so that it rests on the surface of the piston above until the whole ring is clear and can be slid off. With the second and third rings which must also come off the top, arrange the strip of metal to carry them over the other grooves.

Note where each ring has come from (pierce a piece of paper with each ring showing 'top 1', 'middle 1' etc).

3 To check the existing rings, place them in the cylinder bore and press each down in turn to the bottom of the stroke. In this case a distance of 2½ inches from the top of the cylinder will be satisfactory. Use an inverted piston to press them down square. With a feeler gauge measure the gap for each ring which should be as given in the specifications at the beginning of this Chapter. If the gap is too large, the rings will need renewal.

4 Check also that each ring gives a clearance in the piston groove according to specifications. If the gap is too great, new pistons and rings will be required if Vauxhall spares are used. However, independent specialist producers of pistons and rings can normally provide the rings required separately. If new Vauxhall pistons and rings are being obtained it will be necessary to have the ridge ground away from the top of each cylinder bore. If specialist oil control rings are being obtained from an independent supplier the ridge removal will not be necessary as the top rings will be stepped to provide the necessary clearance. If the top ring of a new set is not stepped it will hit the ridge made by the former ring and break.

5 If new pistons are obtained the rings will be included, so it must be emphasised that the top ring be stepped if fitted to an un-reground bore (or un-deridged bore).

6 The new rings should be placed in the bores and the gap checked. If an un-reground bore check the gap above the line of the ridge (photo). Any gaps which are too small should be increased by filing one end of the ring with a fine file. Be careful not to break the ring as they are brittle (and expensive). On no account make the gap less than specification. If the gap should close when under normal operating temperatures the ring will break.

21.2a Oil pump suction pipe securing bracket

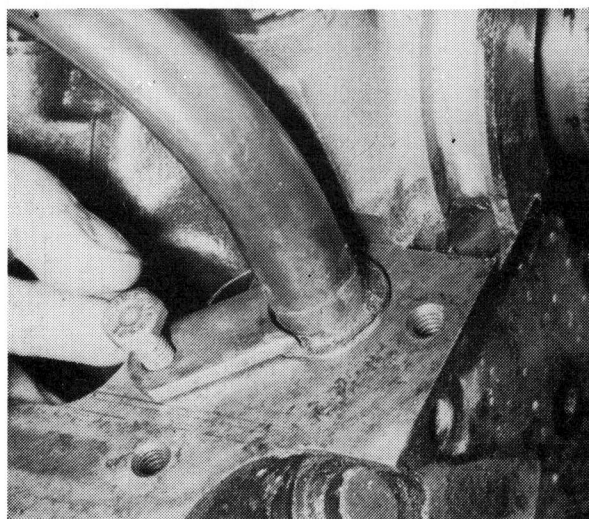

21.2b Oil pump suction pipe securing plate

21.4 Oil pump suction pipe 'O' ring seal

23.6 Checking a new ring gap above the ridge in an un rebored cylinder

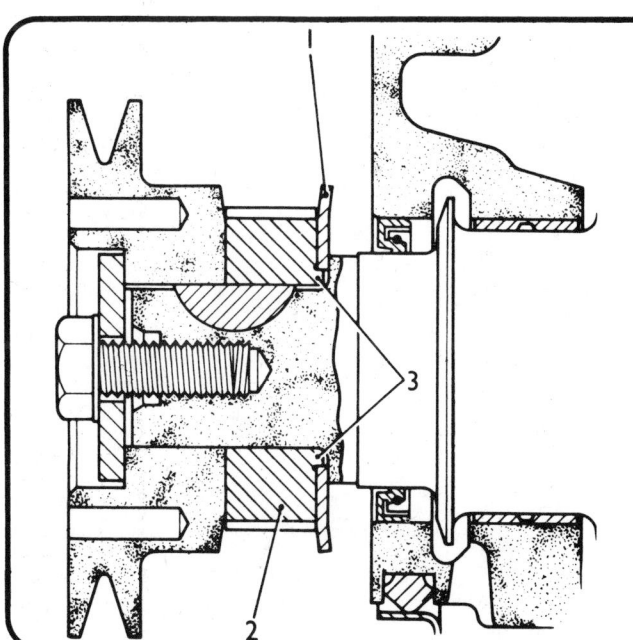

FIG. 1.10. CRANKSHAFT PULLEY WHEEL ASSEMBLY - CROSS SECTION

1 Flange
2 Toothed pulley
3 Register for flange

7 The groove clearance of new rings in old pistons should be within the specified tolerances. If it is not enough, the rings could stick in the piston grooves causing loss of compression. The piston grooves in this case will need machining out to accept the new rings.

8 Before putting new rings onto an old piston clean out the grooves with a piece of old broken ring (photo).

9 Refit the new rings with care, in the same order as the old ones were removed. Note that some special oil control rings are supplied in three separate pieces (photo). The cylinder bores must be checked for ovality, scoring, scratching and pitting. Starting from the top, look for a ridge where the top piston ring reaches the limit of its upward travel. The depth of this ridge will give a good indication of the degree of wear and can be checked with the engine in the car and the cylinder head removed.

10 Measure the bore diameter across the block and just below any ridge. This can be done with an internal micrometer or a Mercer gauge. Compare this with the diameter of the bottom of the bore, which is not subject to wear. If no micrometer measuring instruments are available, use a piston from which the rings have been removed and measure the gap between it and the cylinder wall with a feeler gauge.

11 If the difference in bore diameters at top and bottom is 0.010 inch (0.254 mm) or more, then the cylinders need reboring. If less than 0.010 inch (0.254 mm), then the fitting of new and special rings to the pistons can cure the trouble.

12 If the cylinders have already been bored out to their maximum it may be possible to have liners fitted. This situation will not often be encountered.

13 As mentioned in the previous section, new pistons should be fitted to the connecting rods by the firm which rebores the block.

24 Crankshaft - removal and inspection

1 With the engine removed from the car, remove the sump and oil suction pipe as described in Sections 20 and 21. If the cylinder head is also removed so much the better as the engine can be stood firmly in an inverted position.

2 Remove the connecting rod bearing caps. This will already have been done if the pistons are removed.

3 Using a good quality socket wrench remove the two cap bolts from each of the five main bearing caps.

4 Lift off each cap carefully. Each one is marked with the bearing number.

5 The bearing cap shells will probably come off with the caps, in which case they can be removed by pushing them round from

the end opposite the notch and lifting them out.

6 Grip the crankshaft firmly at each end and lift it out. Put it somewhere safe where it cannot fall. Remove the shell bearings from the inner housings noting that No 5 has a flange on each side. There is a two piece oil seal embedded in grooves of the crankcase and bearing cap of No 5 (rear) bearing. These should be levered out and the grooves properly cleaned. The circular oil seal on the front of the shaft should be pulled off.

7 Examine all the crankpins and main bearing journals for signs of scoring or scratches. If all surfaces are undamaged check next that all the bearing journals are round. This can be done with a micrometer or caliper gauge, taking readings across the diameter at 6 or 7 points for each journal. If you do not own or know how to use a micrometer, take the crankshaft to your local engineering works and ask them to 'mike it up' for you.

8 If the crankshaft is ridged or scored it must be reground. If the ovality exceeds 0.002 inch on measurement, but there are no signs of scoring or scratching on the surfaces, regrinding may still be necessary. It would be advisable to ask the advice of the engineering works to whom you entrust the work of regrinding in such instances.

25 Main and big end bearing shells - inspection and renewal

1 Big end bearing failure is normally indicated by a pronounced knocking from the crankcase and a slight drop in oil pressure. Main bearing failure is normally accompanied by vibration, which can be quite severe at high engine speeds, and a more significant drop in oil pressure.

2 The shell bearing surfaces should be matt grey in colour with no sign of pitting or scoring. If they are obviously in bad condition it is essential to examine the crankshaft before fitting new ones.

3 Replacement shell bearings are supplied in a series of thicknesses dependent on the degree of regrinding that the crankshaft requires, which is done in multiples of .010 inch. Thus depending on how much it is necessary to grind off, so bearing shells are supplied as '.010 inch undersize' and so on. The engineering works regrinding the crankshaft will normally supply the correct shells with the reground crank.

4 If an engine is removed for overhaul regularly it is worthwhile renewing big end bearings every 30,000 miles as a matter of course and main bearings every 50,000 miles. This will add many thousands of miles to the life of the engine before any regrinding of crankshafts is necessary. Make sure that bearing shells renewed are standard dimensions if the crankshaft has not been reground.

23.8 Cleaning out the ring groove in a
piston with a piece of broken ring

23.9 Fitting a 3 part oil control ring in
the bottom groove

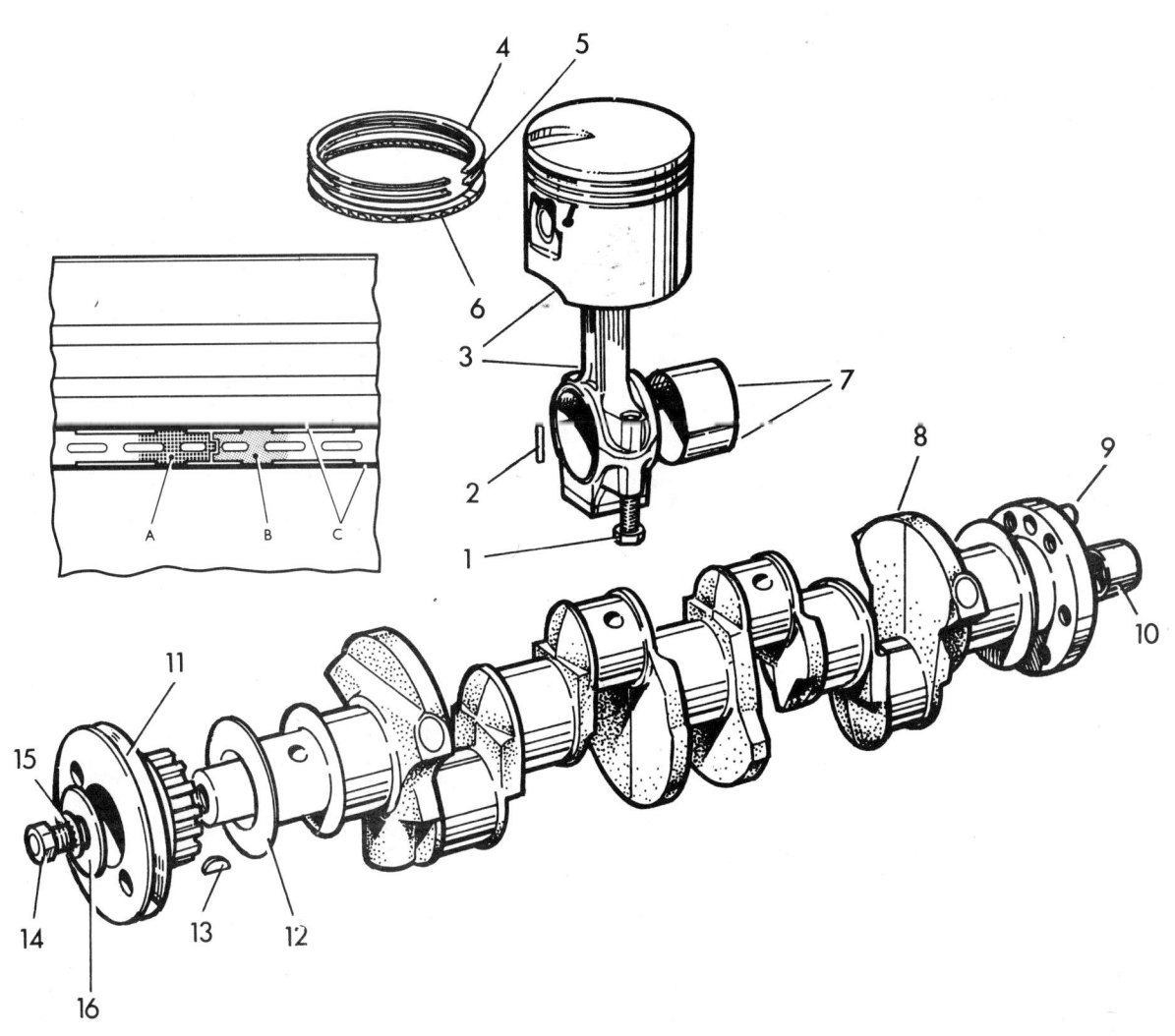

FIG. 1.11. CRANKSHAFT AND PISTONS

1 Big end bearing cap bolt	5 Lower compression ring	9 Dowel peg	13 Woodruff key
2 Dowel pin	6 Oil control ring	10 Input shaft pilot bush	14 Crankshaft pulley bolt
3 Piston and connecting rod	7 Big end shell bearings	11 Crankshaft pulley	15 Lockwasher
4 Top compression ring	8 Crankshaft	12 Pulley flange	16 Large plain washer

Inset.   Ends A and B must not overlap   C   Oil control ring rails

5 It is very important, if in doubt, to take the old bearing shells along if you want replacements of the same size. Some original crankshafts are .010 undersize on journals or crankpins and the appropriate bearings must be used.

26 Lubrication System - general description

The oil pump is driven via the distributor shaft from the auxiliary shaft and may be of either the vane or rotor type. Incorporated in the body is the pressure relief valve which opens when the oil pressure in the lubrication system is in excess of the normal operating pressure. The oil filter is of the disposable cartridge type and located on the right hand side of the cylinder block in front of the engine mounting. Incorporated in the filter is a little spring loaded by-pass valve which opens should the flow of oil through the filter drop due to severe contamination of the filter element.

The oil pump draws oil from the sump by a pick up pipe and wire gauge filter. It passes the oil through the oil filter element and into the main oil gallery.

The crankshaft main bearings are supplied under pressure from cross drillings from the main oil gallery whilst the connecting rod big end bearings are lubricated from the main bearings by oil forced through the crankshaft drillings. The camshaft bearings are fed from a drilling from the main oil gallery. The cams and tappets are individually lubricated by little jet holes.

The cylinder walls, pistons and piston pins are lubricated by oil splashed up by the crankshaft webs.

An oil pressure gauge is fitted to the instrument panel to give the driver an indication of the oil pressure in the main oil gallery.

Ventilation of the crankcase is by means of an outlet pipe connecting the camshaft housing to the filtered air side of the air cleaner.

27 Engine reassembly - general

1 To ensure maximum life with minimum trouble from a rebuilt engine, not only must everything be correctly assembled, but everything must be spotlessly clean, all the oilways must be clear, locking washers and spring washers must always be fitted where indicated and all bearing and other working surfaces must be thoroughly lubricated during assembly.

2 Before assembly begins renew any bolts or studs, the threads of which are in any way damaged, and whenever possible use new spring washers.

3 Apart from your normal tools, a supply of clean rag, an oil can filled with engine oil (an empty plastic detergent bottle thoroughly cleaned and washed out, will invariably do just as well), a new supply of assorted spring washers, a set of new gaskets, and a torque spanner should be collected together.

4 It is well worthwhile sitting down with a pencil and paper and listing all those items which you intend to renew and acquire all of them before reassembly. If you have   experience of

shopping around for parts you will appreciate that they cannot all be obtained quickly. Do not underestimate the cost either. Spare parts are relatively much more expensive now that they were a few years ago.

28 Pistons and connecting rods - replacement in cylinders

1 If the crankshaft has been removed, fit the pistons before replacing it. The pistons, complete with connecting rods and new shell bearings can be fitted to the cylinder bores in the following sequence:

2 With a wad of clean rag wipe the cylinder bores clean. If new rings are being fitted any surface oil 'glaze' on the walls should be removed by rubbing with a very fine abrasive. This can be a very fine (400 grade) 'wet and dry' paper as used for rubbing down paintwork. This enables new rings to bed into the cylinders properly which would otherwise be prevented or at least delayed for a long time. Make sure that all traces of abrasive are confined to the cylinder bores and are completely cleaned off before assembling the pistons into the cylinders. Then oil the pistons, rings, and cylinder bores generously with engine oil. Space the piston ring gaps equally around the piston (photo).

3 The pistons, complete with connecting rods, are fitted to their bores from above.

4 As each piston is inserted into its bore ensure that it is the correct piston/connecting rod assembly for that particular bore and that the connecting rod is the right way round, and that the front of the piston (which is marked) is towards the front of the engine.

5 The piston will only slide into the bore as far as the oil control ring. It is necessary to compress the piston rings into a clamp and to gently tap the piston into the cylinder bore with a wooden or plastic hammer. If a proper piston ring clamp is not available then a hose clip may be used (photo).

6 If new pistons and rings are being fitted to a rebored block the clearances are very small and care has to be taken to make sure that no part of a piston ring catches the edge of the bore before being pressed down. They are very brittle and easily broken. For this reason it is acceptable practice to chamfer the lip of the cylinder very slightly to provide a lead for the rings into the cylinder. The chamfer should be at an angle of 45° and should not be cut back more than .010 inch. If some form of hose clip is being used to compress the piston rings it may be found that the screw housing prevents the clip from lying exactly flush with the cylinder head. Here again watch carefully to ensure that no part of the ring slips from under the control of the clamp. Make sure also that the clamp is not gripping the piston tightly otherwise you will not be able to move it into the bore (photo).

7 When all four assemblies have been inserted position the connecting rods so that they will not interfere with the crankshaft when it is replaced. Check that the connecting rod bearing shells are properly positioned with the notches engaging in their respective positons.

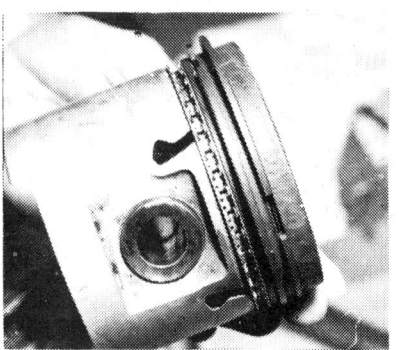
28.2 Ring gaps spaced equally round the piston

28.5 Clamping piston rings and putting the pistons and connecting rods into the cylinders

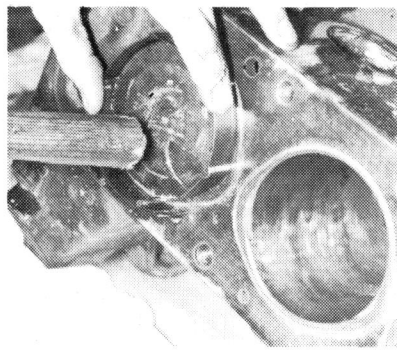
28.6 Tapping the piston into the bore

29 Crankshaft and seals - replacement

1 It is simpler to replace the pistons and connecting rods before the crankshaft. Ensure that the crankcase is thoroughly clean and that all oilways are clear. If possible blow the drillings out with compressed air.

2 It is best to take out the plug at each end of the main gallery in the cylinder block and so clean out the oilways to the crankshaft bearing housings. Replace the plugs using jointing compound to make an oil tight seal.

3 Treat the crankshaft in the same fashion and then inject engine oil into the crankshaft oilways.

4 Thoroughly clean the main bearing shell locations in the crankcase and carefully fit each half shell into the five locations.

5 The centre bearing shell has no oil groove and the No 5 bearing shell is flanged to control the crankshaft end float (photos).

6 New bearings may have over-thick flanges which will need reducing in order to permit the crankshaft to be replaced and fitted with the correct amount of end float, which is from 0.002 inch to 0.010 inch (0.0508 to 0.254 mm). End float, which is the amount a crankshaft can move endways, is measured between the centre bearing upper shell flange and the bearing surface on the web of the crankshaft, with the crankshaft moved to one extreme of its end float travel.

7 It will be necessary to reduce the shell bearing flange thickness by rubbing it down evenly on an engineers flat bed covered with fine emery cloth. This is done progressively until a feeler blade of 0.002 inch (0.0508 mm) thickness can be placed between the flange and the crankshaft web.

8 NOTE that at the back of each bearing is a tab which engages in locating grooves in either the crankcase or the main bearing cap housings.

9 If new bearings are being fitted, carefully clean away all traces of any protective grease or coating with which they may have been treated.

10 With the upper bearing shells securely in place, wipe the lower bearing cap housing and fit the five lower shell bearings to their caps ensuring that the right shell goes into the right cap.

Check that the rear oil seal groove in the crankcase is completely free of old jointing compound and that the bearing cap faces throughout are similarly clean. Remove all traces of oil. When quite clean and dry apply 'Hylomar' jointing compound sparingly into the crankcase seal groove. Then fit the half of the seal into the groove firmly and with the ends protruding above the face of the crankcase (photo). Early engines were fitted with rubber composition seals and later models with braided fabric versions. Both are provided in the gasket set and either may be used.

With the fabric seal make sure it is pressed fully into place - use a wooden hammer handle. The ends must be carefully trimmed to protrude no more than 0.020 inch (0.508 mm) and no frayed threads must be left to get trapped between the bearing cap and crankcase. Coat the seal with molybdenum paste or grease (Castrol MS3).

11 Thoroughly lubricate the main bearing shells with engine oil and lower the crankshaft carefully into position. Check the end float with a feeler gauge as described in paragraph 7.(photos)

12 Next fit the other half of the rear bearing oil seal into the groove in the cap, having first lightly smeared the groove with 'Hylomar' jointing compound. Take the same precaution as for the other half when using the braided fabric seal (photo).

13 Clean the bearing surface of the caps and position all the five shell bearings to them in the same way as was done for the others.

14 The front and rear main bearing caps need a trace of 'Hylomar' jointing compound across them to prevent oil leaks. It should be sparingly applied in the positions indicated in Fig.1.12 (photo).

15 Next lubricate all the journals with engine oil and fit the front and rear caps in position with the flat end faces flush with the ends of the crankcase (photo).

16 Place the other three caps in position the correct way round - as a guide the members should all be the same way (photos).

17 Replace the cap bolts in all bearings and nip them all up lightly. Turn the crankshaft to ensure it revolves freely and then start with No 1 and tighten the bolts of each cap to the correct torque of 82 lb ft (11.3 Kg m) (photo).

18 After tightening each cap turn the crankshaft by hand to ensure it is not binding. A reground crank may be a little stiff but it should be possible to turn it by hand without excess effort. If any bearing binds tight then something is wrong.

19 If the crank is a reground one check the journal diameters and bearing shell sizes. Do not hope that a very tight fit will ease up later after some running. It might - but 99 times out of 100 the bearing will bind and the surface 'pick up'. Then you will have to take everything apart once more.

20 The crankshaft front seal can be renewed if necessary without engine removal. All that is required is for the drive belt, fan belt and crankshaft pulley wheel to be removed.

21 Ideally the seal is removed by a special threaded tube puller which bites into the internal diameter. However, if care is taken it can be dug out with a sharp pointed tool. When this is done the shaft itself must not be scored - neither should the seal housing.

22 When fitting a new seal first ensure that the housing is quite clean. Smear the seal lip with molybdenum paste or grease and the outer periphery with Hylomar sealing compound (photo).

23 Carefully drive it in squarely with a flat nosed punch or drift until it is flush with crankcase and bearing cap face (photos)

Fig. 1.12. Crankshaft front and rear main bearing caps. Application of 'Hylomar' jointing compound (arrowed)

29.5a Main bearing showing plain centre shell No 3

29.5b Main bearing showing flanged rear shell No 5

29.10 Fit half the seal into the crankcase seal groove with the ends protruding above the face of the crankcase

29.11a Lubricate the bearing shells

29.11b Crankshaft ready to go into the bearings

29.11c Crankshaft in position

29.12 Fitting the other half of the rear bearing oil seal

29.14 Smearing jointing compound on the bearing caps

29.15 Lubricating the crankshaft journals

29.16a Replacing bearing caps

29.16b Note number on bearing cap

29.17 Tightening main bearing cap bolts with a torque wrench

29.22 Preparing the crankshaft front oil seal

29.23a Refitting the crankshaft oil seal

29.23b Drifting the oil seal home

30.3a Fitting big end cap

30.3b Check the numbers match

30.5 Tightening big end bearing bolts with a torque wrench

31.3 Fitting the sump end seals into the bearing cap grooves

31.4 Putting 'Bostik' 771 sealing compound onto the sump seal ends

31.5 Positioning the sump gasket

31.6a Fitting sump gasket and sump

31.6b Tightening down sump

32.1 Flywheel replacement

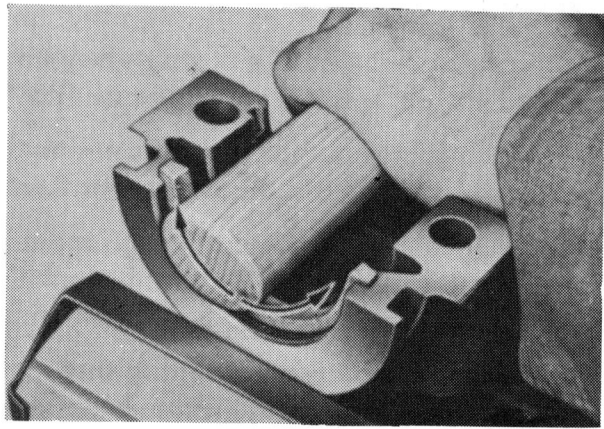

Fig. 1.13. Crankshaft rear main bearing fabric seal. Using hammer to press seal into groove

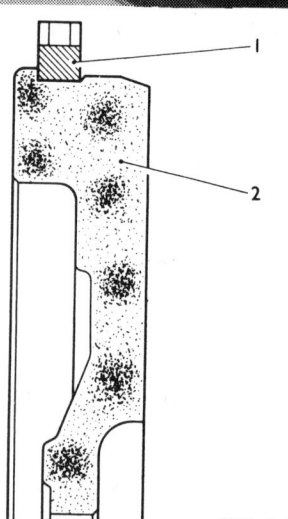

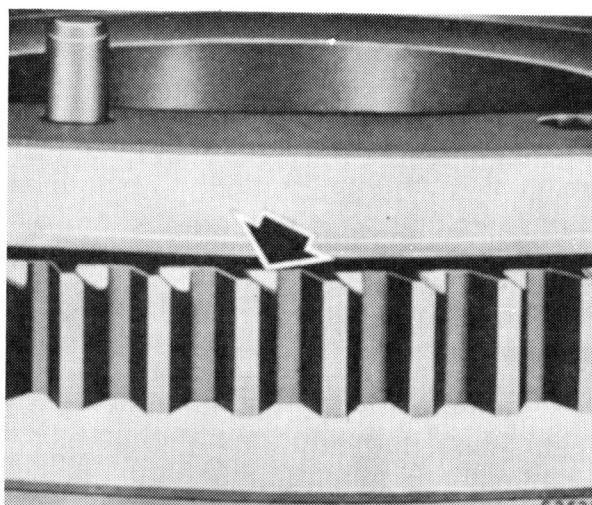

FIG. 1.14. FLYWHEEL CROSS SECTION TO SHOW STARTER RING GEAR

1 Ring gear

2 Flywheel

Arrow shows tooth chamfer towards transmission.

---

30 Connecting rods (big ends) - refitting to crankshaft

1 With the crankshaft replaced and all main bearing bolts tightened the pistons replaced in the cylinders and shell bearings fitted in their rods with the locating tongues in their grooves, position the crankshaft so that the two centre or two end crankpins are conveniently placed for drawing the connecting rods up to them.

2 If not already done wipe the connecting rod bearing cap and back of the shell bearing clean, and fit the shell bearing in position ensuring that the locating tongue at the back of the bearing engages with the locating groove in the connecting cap.

3 Make sure the cap fits the correct rod by checking the numbers matching marks already made and see that the spring dowel pins are intact (photos)

4 Generously lubricate the shell bearing and offer up the connecting rod bearing cap to the connecting rod.

5 Fit the connecting rod bolts with oiled threads and tighten them down with a torque spanner to 47 lb ft (6.47 Kg m) (photo).

6 Rotate the crankshaft (it will be fairly stiff because of the drag of the piston rings in the bores - if very stiff slacken the bearing caps to ensure it is not due to a binding bearing) so that the other two crankpins are in position for the connecting rods and replace them in the same way.

7 Oil the cylinder bores generously for initial lubrication.

31 Sump - replacement

1 Before fitting the sump check that the oil pump section pipe and strainer are correctly fitted (Section 21) and that all bearing cap bolts are tight.

2 The sump should have been thoroughly cleaned out and the flange mating surfaces of both the sump and crankcase perfectly cleaned free of all traces of old gasket. Check that the sump lies flat on the crankcase and that the flanges are not bent or damaged in any way.

3 Two specially shaped seals (included in the gasket set) are provided for the front and rear bearing caps. Ensure that the grooves and steps where the ends fit are perfectly clean and dry. Then apply a smear of 'Hylomar' jointing compound into the grooves and onto the step where the ends fit and place the seals into the grooves (photo).

4 Place a blob of Bostik 771 compound on top of the ends of the seal as well (photo).

5 Put the cork sump gaskets in position on the crankcase so that the ends bed with the compound and overlap the end seals. If the sump is being replaced with the engine in the car it is a good idea to stick the cork gasket to the crankcase with grease to hold it in place. It is not recommended that jointing compound be used (photo).

6 Refit the sump without disturbing the position of the gaskets and replace all the set screws (remembering the clutch cable clip on the one you marked) and tighten them evenly. Do not over-tighten (photos).

32 Flywheel - replacement

1   The flywheel is located on two dowel pegs and can only be fitted one way because the five bolt holes are not symmetrically arranged (photo).
2   Locate the flywheel on the dowels and tap it home square.
3   Replace the five bolts (there are no washers) and tighten them evenly to the correct torque of 48 lb ft (6.6 kg m) on clean dry threads. The flywheel may be held with a screwdriver in the teeth wedged against the bellhousing dowel peg whilst the bolts are being tightened (photos).

33 Valves and springs - reassembly to cylinder head

1   The valves and head should all be thoroughly clean before reassembly. If the same valves are being refitted they should return to the same place. It is good practice to smear the stems with a molybdenum or graphite paste before inserting them in the guides (photo).
2   Fit new valve stem seals and clips (these may be fitted on early engines which did not have them originally) over the shoulders of the valve guide extension on the top of the head.
3   Replace the inner and outer coil springs and the retaining collar over them (photos).
4   Compress the springs using the tool until it is possible to fit the two split collars around the valve stem so that they engage the groove (photo).
5   Release the spring compressor whilst watching to ensure that the two collets do not slip out of the groove. When released tap the valve stem end with a mallet to 'bounce' it and ensure that everything is properly seated.

34 Cylinder head - replacement

1   Before replacing the cylinder head check that the oil passageway is clear. Early engines have a port flush with the block surface but later engines have either a hollow spring pin protruding .12 inch from the block with an 'O' ring round it; or a combined dowel and restrictor fitted with an even larger 'O' ring. If you have an early head which you wish to fit to a new half engine fitted with a dowel and restrictor then the oil passage hole in the head should be drilled out to 5/16 inch to a depth of ½ inch. At the same time the two holes for the head locating pegs will also have to be drilled out with a 0.281 inch (7.144 mm) drill to a depth of 0.5 inch (12.7 mm). This is because with the restrictor, the locating pins fitted are larger so that they engage first when the head is replaced. Note that the camshaft housing may need modification also (see subsequent section). It is also possible to fit the hollow spring pin and 'O' ring to those early engines which may have had leakage difficulties from the oil transfer passage.
2   The surfaces of both cylinder block and head must be perfectly clean and dry.
3   Place the cylinder head gasket in position on the block making quite sure that it is the correct way up - it will be fairly obvious if it is not. The gaskets for 1759cc and 2279cc engines are different. The cylinder apertures for the larger engine are circular and there is an identifying tab (see Fig.1.16).
    Do not use any seal or grease on the head gasket.
4   Place the cylinder head squarely in position, taking care not to damage the protruding pegs before it fits over them (photo).
5   Replace the ten cylinder head bolts and nip them all down lightly.
6   Cylinder head bolts are very tight and must be tightened

32.3a Tightening flywheel bolts

32.3b Holding the flywheel while tightening the bolts

33.1 Fitting valve into guide

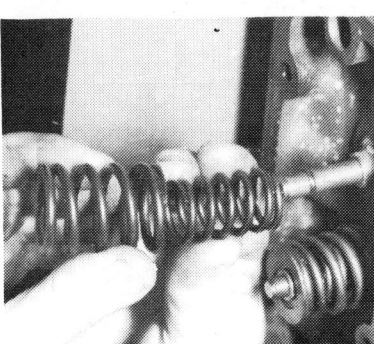
33.3a Replacing valve springs

33.3b Replacing valve upper collar

33.4 Compressing the valve springs and fitting the collets

down evenly and in the correct order as indicated in Fig.1.17. Tighten all bolts down first to a torque of 45 lb ft (6.22 Kg m) in the order shown and then go round again tightening to the final torque of 82 lb ft (11.3 Kg m) (photo).

7 The inlet and exhaust manifolds may be replaced next or after the camshaft housing if wished.

8 The exhaust manifold requires a combined heat shield and gasket. A used gasket may be re-used provided it is not damaged or burnt. Carefully clean off any carbon traces. The bolts are replaced with a lock tab to each pair and should be tightened up moderately. Do not overdo it, and break a bolt (photos).

9 Bend down a tab against a convenient flat on each bolt head.

10 The inlet manifold can be replaced with the carburettor fitted or otherwise. First of all make sure you fit the correct gaskets.(photos)

11 Check that the manifold studs in the head are tight and before placing the gaskets in position smear sealing compound round the water jacket holes on both sides.

12 Replace the bolts and the nuts - all of which have lock-washers and tighten them evenly. The bolt which fits inside the thermostat aperture should have a new copper washer under the head. Do not forget to reconnect the water pipe from the pump.

35 Camshaft, camshaft housing and tappets - reassembly

1 The camshaft must be fitted into the housing before fitting the housing to the head.

2 Smear all the bearing surfaces of the camshaft with an oil treated with graphite or molybdenum disulphide.

3 To check the end float, before fitting the shaft into the housing fit the thrust washer, retaining washer and original securing bolt to the rear end and check the gap between the two washers.

4 If you are fitting an early type camshaft housing to a later type cylinder head (see Section 34) with a dowel/restrictor fitted in the oil transfer port it will be necessary to bore out the corresponding port in the camshaft housing to 0.188 inch (4.763 mm). The depth of the hole should be no more than 0.74 inch (18.65 mm) below the housing bottom face (Fig.1.18).

5 Lubricate the bearings and then insert the camshaft into the housing from the front (photos).

6 Fit the thrust washer so that the cut-out faces upwards where it will engage with the lug in the cover (photo).

7 The retaining bolt is locked with a nylon insert and a new

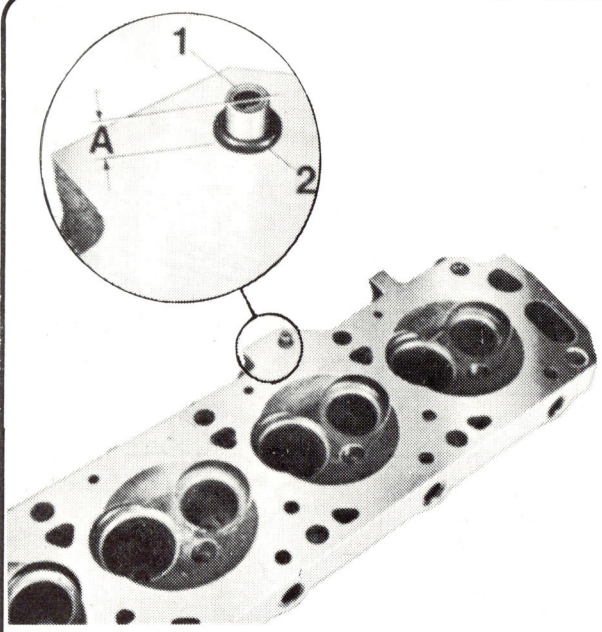

Fig. 1.15. Cylinder head - oil transfer passage from cylinder block fitted with spring pin (1) and 'O' ring. Dimension:

A = 0.12 inch   (3.008 mm)

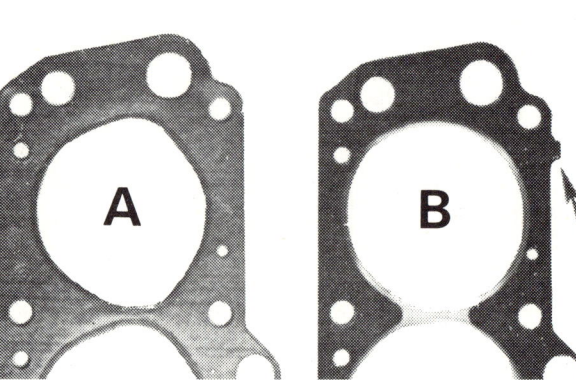

Fig. 1.16. Cylinder head gasket identification

A 1759 cc engine
B 2279 cc engine

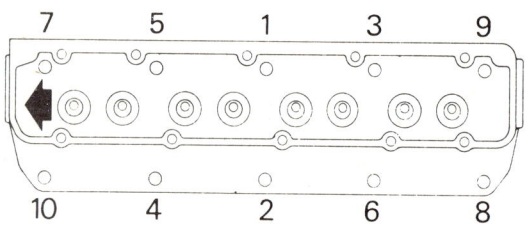

Fig. 1.17. Cylinder head bolt tightening sequence. Arrow points to front

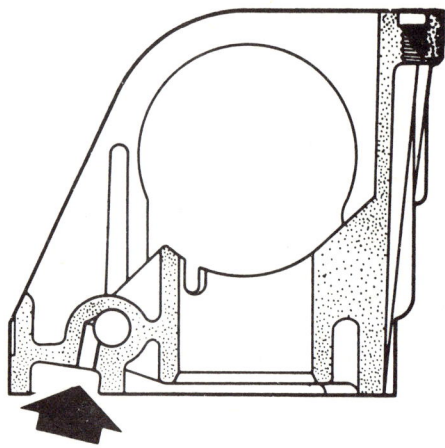

Fig. 1 18. Camshaft housing - cross section showing oil gallery transfer orifice (arrowed)

34.4 Replacing the cylinder head

34.6 Tightening cylinder head bolts

34.8a Replacing exhaust manifold

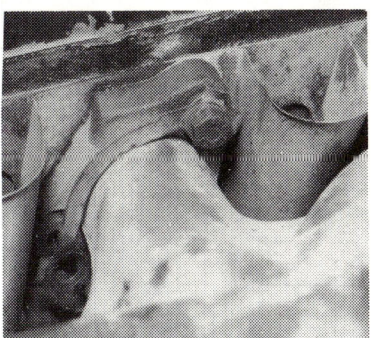

34.8b Lock tabs and bolts on exhaust manifold

34.10a Inlet manifold replacement showing two different gaskets

34.10b Tightening of the securing nut in the thermostat housing

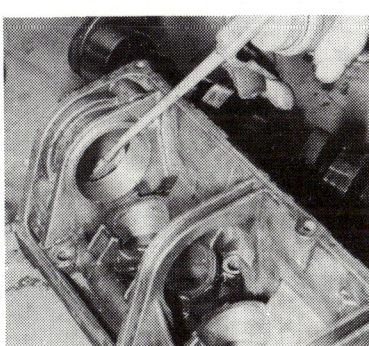

35.5a Lubricating camshaft bearings before reassembly

35.5b Inserting the camshaft into its bearings

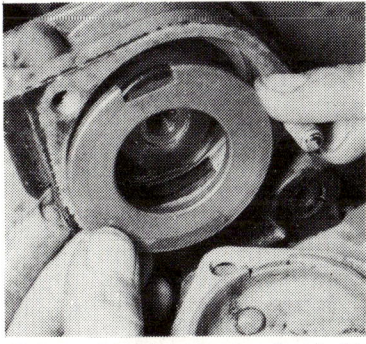

35.6 Camshaft thrust washer fitted with cut-out upwards

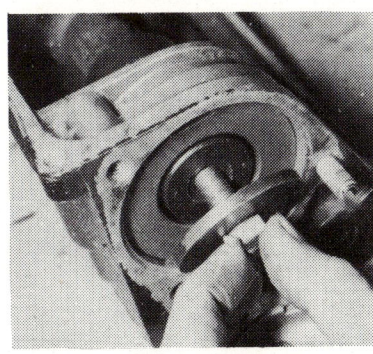

35.7 Replacing the camshaft washer and bolt

35.8 Tightening the camshaft bolt using a self grip wrench to hold the camshaft

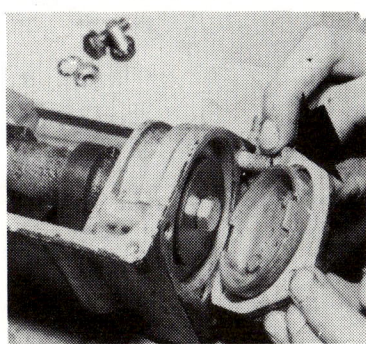

35.9 Fitting camshaft rear end cover. Note lug (arrowed) which engages in thrust washer cut-out

one should be used. If not, use a proprietary locking compound on the bolt threads (photo).

8 Grip the camshaft with self-grips whilst tightening the bolt (photo).

9 Using a new gasket refit the end cover so that the lug engages in the thrust washer cut-out and tighten the securing bolts (photo).

10 Fit a new oil seal in the front end of the housing. Smear the inner lip with molybdenum paste or grease and fit it facing inwards. Tap it home square (photos).

11 Lubricate the tappet bores in the housing and replace the tappets into the same locations from which they came. If you have removed the tappet adjusting screws for any reason they should be screwed in first so that the flat section faces the open end of the tappet and is approximately central across the tappet diameter. If any of the tappets look like dropping out easily under gravity use a smear of grease to hold them in position (photo).

36 Camshaft housing assembly - replacement

1 Make sure the cylinder head bolts are all correctly tightened down.

2 Place a new gasket in position on the cylinder head noting that the hole for the oil transfer passage should line up (photo).

3 Make sure that the crankshaft pulley timing mark is set approximately 90° BTDC to ensure valve to piston crown clearance (all pistons are halfway down the cylinders in this position).

4 Place the camshaft housing assembly in position without letting the tappets fall out of their locations in the process. Engage it over the dowels at each end of the head, and ensure the gasket position is not disturbed (photo).

5 The assembly will not seat right down yet because some valves will be opposite cams in the open position. Replace all the mounting bolts and using a pattern similar to that of tightening the cylinder head, tighten them all evenly a little at a time to the correct torque of 15 lb ft (2.07 Kg m) (photo).

6 Replace the pulley wheel over the key and fit the washer and bolt. The bolts may be tightened fully later after the belt has been replaced.(photo)

37 Auxiliary shaft - replacement

1 The drive belt and pulley, fuel pump and distributor must be removed before the shaft can be refitted.

2 Lubricate the bearings with oil (treated with graphite or molybdenum disulphide) and place the shaft with the 'U' shaped thrust washer located in the shaft groove into position in the block. The small notch in the thrust washer should engage the dowel peg in the housing (photo).

3 Lubricate the oil seal lip with molybdenum paste or grease and place it over the shaft open side first (photo).

4 Carefully tap the seal squarely into position until it stops up against the thrust washer.

5 Fit the pulley over the key and replace the washer and bolt. The bolt can be tightened after the belt is replaced (photo).

38 Oil pump - replacement

1 The oil pump may be refitted with the auxiliary shaft in position or not.

2 Fit new 'O' rings into the grooves around the ports in the bottom cover and oil the ports in the cylinder block where they will press in. It is important that the 'O' rings are not dragged out of position when the pump is pushed in position (photo).

3 Place a new gasket in position on the block (photo).

4 If the auxiliary shaft is installed hold the pump so that the opening in the body (for the gear of the auxiliary shaft) is 90° clockwise from the gear position. Put the pump into the housing and turn it anticlockwise 90° to line up the ports at the bottom

(photo).

5 Do not press the flange of the pump body to push it down into position. Use a tube or socket of some sort in the centre of the body in order to tap it down (photo).

6 The pump is finally secured by the same bolts that hold the distributor in position.

39 Drive belt replacement and valve timing

1 The drive belt controls the valve timing and it is imperative to get it fitted in exactly the correct tooth.

2 Before running the drive belt for any reason other than when an engine is undergoing a complete overhaul the crankshaft pulley timing mark must be set at 90° BTDC. In this position all the pistons are halfway down the cylinders and there is no chance of them fouling the valves when the camshaft pulley is independently turned.

3 When replacing the belt the crankshaft pulley should first be positioned, as for removal.

4 The auxiliary shaft and camshaft should then be turned so that their timing marks and the shaft centre lines are aligned; the timing marks being at the ends of that line.

5 The camshaft pulley mark is a round depression on the front face and the auxiliary pulley mark is a V notch on the front face. Ignore the circular mark on the rear of the auxiliary shaft pulley.

6 Use a straight edge to line up the marks and centres (photo).

7 Next turn the crankshaft clockwise (use a spanner on the pulley bolt) until the timing mark in the front face of the flange is lined up with the TDC pointer (the upper one). If a belt cover is fitted it will be necessary to replace this temporarily as the timing marks are moulded on its front face.

8 Without disturbing the position of the pulleys, fit the drive belt with the chalked arrow pointing in the direction of movement. There should be very little slack apparent between the auxiliary and camshaft pulleys and camshaft and crankshaft pulleys when the teeth are engaged. There will be more between the crankshaft and auxiliary shaft pulleys as this is where the jockey pulley goes (photo).

9 Position the lock and jockey pulley to give moderate tension (photo). Then rotate the crankshaft once more and stop at TDC again. This will automatically put the correct tension on the section of belt between the camshaft and crankshaft pulleys because the greatest valve spring drag will be applied to the camshaft in this position. (If you inadvertently overshoot the TDC position go round again. Do not reverse!).

10 The rest of the belt tension is adjusted by movement of the jockey pulley. A 10 lb (4.5 Kg) load applied midway between the auxiliary and camshaft pulleys should deflect the belt 0.30 inch (7.62 mm). It is important to remember that this tension must be checked only when the tension between camshaft and crankshaft pulleys has been set and left as described in the previous paragraph.

11 A belt set too tight will whine. A slack belt wears out quickly.

12 Tighten all pulley bolts.

40 Valve tappet clearances - adjustment

1 In order that the valves open the correct amount and to provide tolerance for thermal expansion the gap between the face of the cam and the tappet (which fits over the end of the valve stem) must be correctly set.

2 The clearances may be set with the engine in the car after removal of the camshaft housing cover.

3 Each tappet contains a screw running laterally across it with a tapered flat in the screw which bears on the end of the valve stem. The movement of the screw in or out alters the relative distance between the end of the valve stem and the tappet face.

4 Access to the end of the adjusting screw is through a hole in the side of the tappet. This hole must be aligned with the cut-out part of the housing by revolving the tappet. There are

35.10a Fitting a camshaft front oil seal

35.10b Tapping home the camshaft front oil seal

35.11 Replacing tappets in camshaft housing

36.2 Fitting camshaft housing gasket to cylinder head

36.4 Placing the camshaft housing assembly into position

36.5 Tightening the camshaft housing bolts to the cylinder head

36.6 Replacing the camshaft pulley and locking bolt

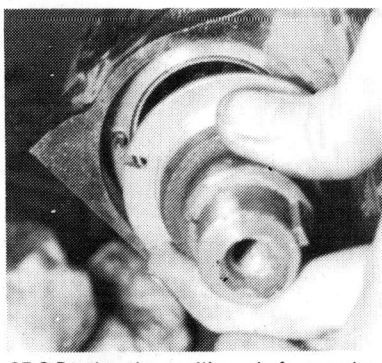

37.2 Putting the auxiliary shaft together with the thrust washer into the block. Note notch which engages the peg in the bearing housing

37.3 Placing the auxiliary shaft retainer oil seal in position

37.5 Replacing the auxiliary shaft pulley

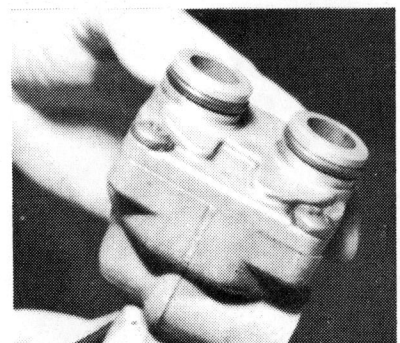

38.2 Oil pump showing oil port 'O' rings in position

38.3 Placing oil pump gasket **into** position

38.4 Putting the oil pump into position

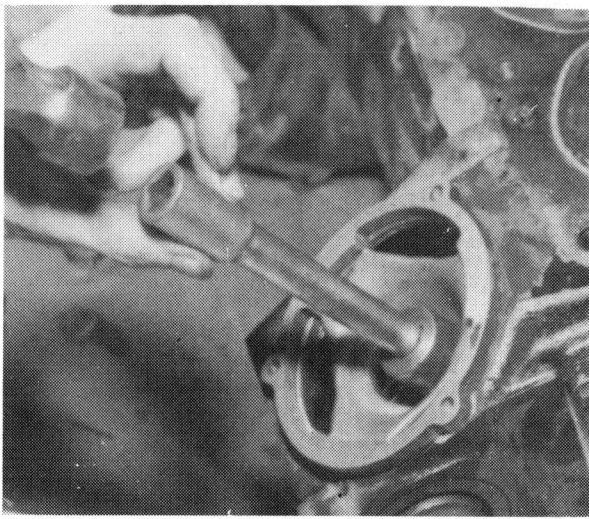
38.5 Tapping the oil pump down onto its seating using a socket and extension

39.6 Lining up the camshaft and auxiliary shaft timing marks with a straight edge

39.8 Fitting the timing belt (it is not yet round the crankshaft pulley)

39.9 Adjusting the drive belt jockey pulley

40.7 Turning the tappet with a screwdriver in the notch

Fig. 1.19. Drive belt replacement. Positioning crankshaft pulley timing mark (1) 90° before TDC pointer (2) to ensure valve/piston clearance

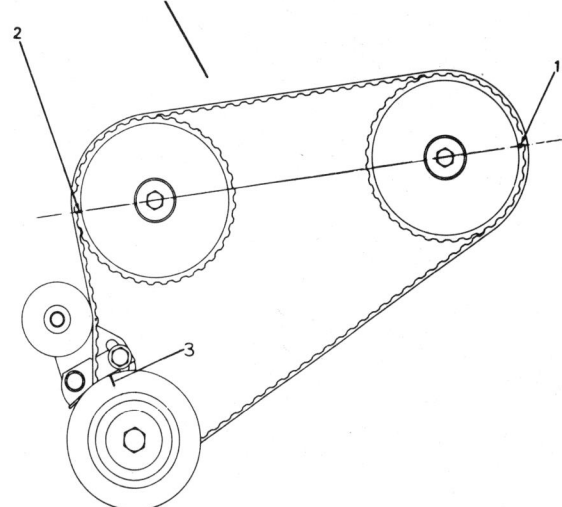

Fig. 1.20. Camshaft drive belt. Alignment of camshaft pulley timing mark '1' and auxiliary shaft pulley mark '2' with crankshaft pulley mark '3' at TDC

Fig. 1.21. Drive belt cover
Note securing points (arrowed) and ignition timing marks (1 and 2)

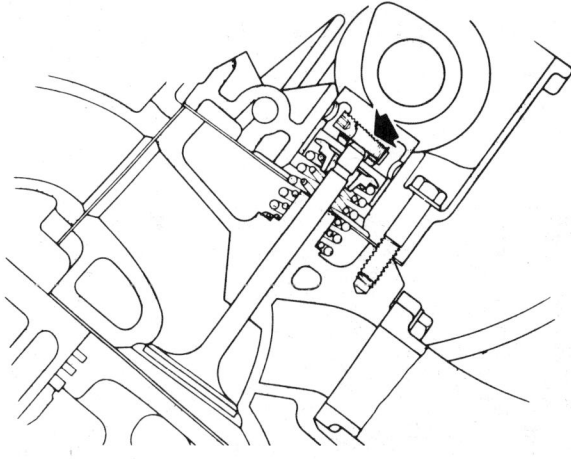

Fig. 1.22. Cylinder head/camshaft housing

Cross section to show position of valve clearance adjustment screw relative to tappet and valve stem

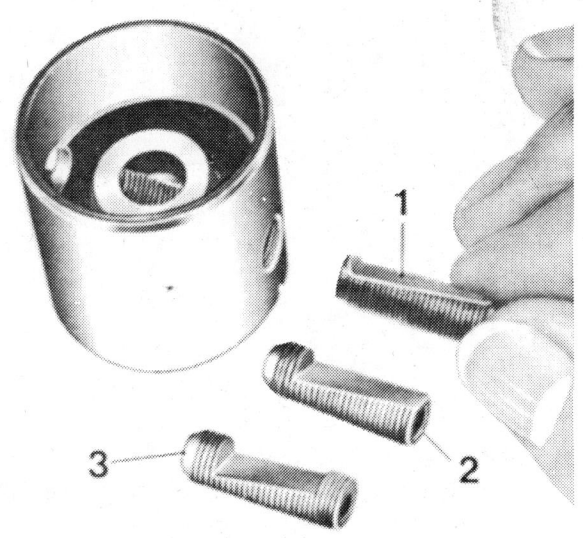

FIG. 1.23. VALVE CLEARANCE ADJUSTMENT

Three types of adjustment screw:
1 Standard
2 1st undersize (inadequate gap obtainable with standard screw)
3 2nd undersize (inadequate gap obtainable with 1st undersize screw)

holes in the tappet at both ends of the screw and the one which has the socket head is indicated by a small notch in the top edge of the tappet.

5 In order to identify the valve clearance requirement, early engines with the smaller clearances can be recognised by a groove in the front end of the camshaft behind the pulley.

6 Valve clearances are set when the valve is fully closed - that is when the tappet is bearing on the lowest point of the cam - this position is easy to see - the higest point of the cam is directly opposite.

7 Turn the tappet with a screwdriver in the notch in the top edge until the screw opening is visible (photo).

8 Measure the gap with a feeler blade. If the engine has not been run because of overhaul and is therefore cold the gap initially should be .003 inch less than specified (photo).

9 Having measured the gap accurately adjustment is necessary if it is not within the given range (which is inclusive).

10 The adjusting screw must be turned one complete revolution clockwise or anticlockwise to decrease or increase the gap respectively by 0.003 inch (0.0762 mm) (photo). A measured gap of 0.006 inch (0.1524 mm) will therefore be increased to 0.009 inch (0.2286 mm) if the adjusting screw is given one

complete anticlockwise turn.(photo) .

If a measured gap of 0.005 in (0.127 mm) occurred on a cold engine, one would decide whether 0.008 in/0.203 mm (ie 0.005 + 0.003 in/0.127 + 0.076 mm) fell within the specified range and adjust as necessary.

11 Once the cold clearances have been set they must be checked and adjusted again if necessary, when the engine is hot.

12 Refit the camshaft housing cover carefully - and preferably with a new gasket. As the gasket curves it is important to ensure that it is not dislodged during replacement (photos).

41 Engine - final reassembly after major overhaul

The ancillary components which were removed as listed in Section 6 (Engine anciliaries - removal) should be replaced as far as possible before putting the engine back in the car. Accessibility will be far better. One particular point to take care over is the fitting of the water pump inlet elbow short hose. Make sure the joining surfaces are clean and the hose is in good condition.

It may be worthwhile replacing the manufacturers wire type hose clips with the more positive worm screw drive type.

40.8 Measuring tappet clearance with a feeler gauge

40.10 Turning the tappet clearance adjusting screw with hexagonal section key

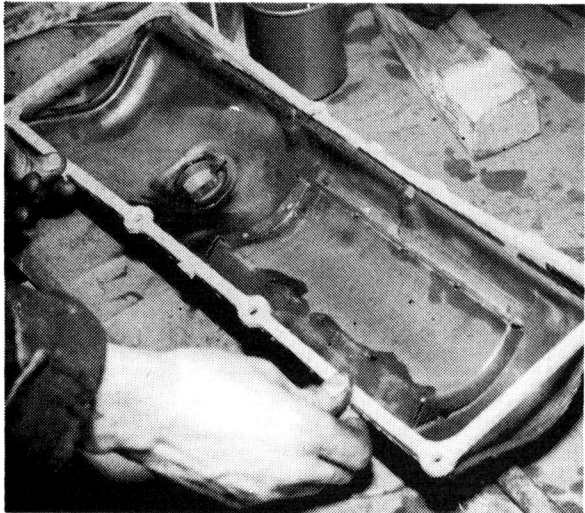

40.12a Fitting a new gasket to the camshaft housing cover

40.12b Fitting the camshaft housing

42 Engine - replacement in car

1 Replacement of the engine is a reversal of the removal procedure. A little trouble in getting the engine properly slung so that it takes up a suspended attitude similar to its final position will pay off when it comes to getting it set easily on the front engine mountings.

2 Refit the gearbox propeller shaft as described in the appropriate chapters. Do not forget to connect the exhaust pipe to the manifold.

3 It is likely that the engine will be initially stiff to turn if new bearings and rings have been fitted and it will save a lot of irritation if the battery is well charged. After a rebore the stiffness may be more than the battery can cope with so be prepared to link another up in parallel with jumper leads.

4 The following final check list should ensure that the engine starts safely and with the minimum of delay:

a) Fuel lines to pump and carburettor - connected and tightened.
b) Water hoses connected and clipped.
c) Radiator and engine drain taps closed.
d) Cooling system replenished.
e) Sump drain plug fitted and tight.
f) Oil in engine.
g) Oil in gearbox and level plug tight.
h) LT wires connected to distributor and coil.
j) Oil pressure and water temperature sender units screwed in tight and leads connected.
k) Spark plugs tight.
l) Tappet clearances set correctly.
m) HT leads connected securely to distributor, spark plugs and coil.
n) Rotor arm replaced in distributor.
o) Choke and throttle cables connected.
p) Braided earthing cable, engine to frame reconnected.
q) Starter motor lead connected.
r) Fan belt fitted and correctly tensioned.
s) Alternator leads connected.
t) Battery charged and leads connected to clean terminals.

43 Engine - initial start up after overhaul and major repair

Make sure that the battery is fully charged and that all lubricants, coolants and fuel are replenished.

If the fuel system has been dismantled, it will require several revolutions of the engine on the starter motor to pump petrol to the carburettor(s). An initial 'prime' of about 1/3 cupful of petrol down the air intake(s) or the carburettor(s) will help the engine to fire quickly, thus relieving the load on the battery. Do not overdo this however, as flooding may result.

As soon as the engine fires and runs, keep it going at a fast tickover only (no faster) and bring it up to normal working temperatures.

As the engine warms up, there will be odd smells and some smoke from parts getting hot and burning off oil deposits.

Look for water or oil which will be obvious if serious. Check also the clamp connection of the exhaust pipe to the manifold as these do not always 'find' their exact gas tight position until the warmth and vibration have acted on them, and it is almost certain that they will need tightening further. This should be done of course, with the engine stopped.

When the engine running temperature has been reached, adjust the idling speed as described in Chapter 3.

Stop the engine and wait a few minutes to see if any lubricant or coolant drips out.

Road test the car to check that the timing is correct and giving the necessary smoothness and power. Do not race the engine. If new bearings and/or pistons and rings have been fitted, it should be treated as a new engine and run in at reduced revolutions for 500 miles (800 km).

See page 48 for 'Fault Diagnosis'.

NOTE: When investigating starting and uneven running faults do not be tempted into a snap diagnosis. Start from the beginning of the check procedure and follow it through. It will take less time in the long run. Poor performance from an engine in terms of power and economy is not normally diagnosed quickly. In any event the ignition and fuel systems must be checked first before assuming any further investigation needs to be made.

Symptom	Reason/s	Remedy
Engine will not turn over when starter switch is operated	Flat battery Bad battery connections Bad connections at solenoid switch and/or starter motor	Check that battery is fully charged and that all connections are clean and tight.
	Starter motor jammed	Turn the square headed end of the starter motor shaft with a spanner to free it. Where a pre-engaged starter is fitted rock the car back and forth with a gear engaged. If this does not free pinion remove starter.
	Defective solenoid	Bridge the main terminals of the solenoid switch with a piece of heavy duty cable in order to operate the starter.
	Starter motor defective	Remove and overhaul starter motor.
Engine turns over normally but fails to fire and run	No spark at plugs	Check ignition system according to procedures given in Chapter 4.
	No fuel reaching engine	Check fuel system according to procedures given in Chapter 3.
	Too much fuel reaching the engine (flooding)	Check the fuel system as above.
Engine starts but runs unevenly and misfires	Ignition and/or fuel system faults	Check the ignition and fuel systems as though the engine had failed to start.
	Incorrect valve clearances	Check and reset clearances.
	Burnt out valves Blown cylinder head gasket	Remove cylinder head and examine and overhaul as necessary.
	Worn out piston rings Worn cylinder bores	Remove cylinder head and examine pistons and cylinder bores. Overhaul as necessary.
Lack of power	Ignition and/or fuel system faults	Check the ignition and fuel systems for correct ignition timing and carburettor settings.
	Incorrect valve clearances	Check and reset the clearances.
	Burnt out valves Blown cylinder head gasket	Remove cylinder head and examine and overhaul as necessary.
	Worn out piston rings Worn cylinder bores	Remove cylinder head and examine pistons and cylinder bores. Overhaul as necessary.
Excessive oil consumption	Oil leaks from crankshaft front and rear oil seals, camshaft oil seal, auxiliary shaft oil seal, cambox gasket, oil filter, sump gasket or drain plug	Identify source of leak and renew seal as appropriate.
	Worn piston rings or cylinder bores resulting in oil being burnt by engine, smoky exhaust is an indication	Fit new rings or rebore cylinders and fit new pistons, depending on degree of wear.
	Worn valve guides and/or defective valve stem seals	Remove cylinder heads and recondition valve stem bores and valves and seals as necessary.
Excessive mechanical noise from engine	Wrong valve clearances	Adjust valve clearances.
	Worn crankshaft bearings Worn cylinders (piston slap)	Inspect and overhaul where necessary.
Unusual vibration	Fan blade broken off	Break off another fan blade to balance fan until renewal is possible.
	Broken engine/gearbox mounting	Renew mounting.
	Misfiring on one or more cylinders	Check ignition system.

Chapter 2 Cooling system

Contents

Specifications

Type of system	Pressurised, pump assisted circulation with thermostat temperature control

Capacity:

1759 cc engine (manual transmission)

Without heater	13 pints (7.4 litres)
With heater	13.5 pints (7.7 litres)

1759 cc (automatic transmission) and 2279 cc engine

Without heater	14.0 pints (8.0 litres)
With heater	14.5 pints (8.2 litres)

Radiator:

Type	Tube and centre core soldered direct to top and bottom water tanks
Leak test pressure	20 lb/sq in (1.41 kg/sq cm)
Filler cap valve opening pressure	15 lb/sq in (1.05 kg/sq cm)

Fan belt:

Type	V pulley drive
Tension	Set to 0.24 in (6 mm) midway between pump and alternator pulleys 80 lb (36 kg) linear tension

Thermostat:

Type	AC Western Thompson
Opening temperature	82°C (179° 6' F) 88°C (190° 4' F)

NOTE: Models fitted with automatic transmission have an oil cooler incorporated in the bottom water tank

1 General description

The engine cooling water is circulated by a thermo syphon, water pump assisted system, and the coolant is pressurised. This is both to prevent the loss of water down the overflow pipe with the radiator cap in position and to prevent premature boiling in adverse conditions.

The radiator cap is, in effect, a safety valve designed to open at a pressure of 15 lb/sq.in (1.05 Kg/sq.cm) which means that the coolant can reach a temperature above 100°C (212°F) before it opens the valve. It then boils off, steam escaping down the overflow pipe. When the temperature, therefore the pressure, decreases, the valve reseats until the temperature builds up again. This means that the engine can operate at its most efficient temperature which is around the normal boiling point of water without the water boiling away.

In addition there is a vacuum in the cap which permits air to enter the system as it cools down thereby preventing collapse of the radiator or hoses.

It is therefore important to check that the radiator cap fitted is of the correct specification (the release pressure is stamped on the top) and in good condition, and that the spring behind the sealing washer has not weakened. Some garages have a device in which radiator caps can be tested. Check that the rubber sealing washer is in good condition, without signs of distortion or perishing.

The system functions in the following manner: Cold water in the bottom of the radiator circulates up the lower radiator hose to the water pump where it is pushed round the water passages in the cylinder block, helping to keep the cylinder bores and pistons cool.

The water then travels up the cylinder head and circulates round the combustion space and valve seats absorbing more heat, and then when the engine is at its correct operating temperature water flows around the inlet manifold water jacket, past the open thermostat into the upper radiator hose, and so into the radiator header tank.

The water travels down the radiator where it is cooled by the inrush of cold air through the radiator core, which is created by both the fan and motion of the car. The water, now much cooler, reaches the bottom of the radiator, whereupon the cycle is repeated.

When the engine is cold the thermostat (a valve which opens and closes according to the temperature of the water) maintains the circulation of the same water in the engine excluding that in the radiator.

The cooling system comprises the radiator, top and bottom water hoses, heater hoses (if heater/demister fitted) the impeller water pump (mounted on the front of the engine it carries the fan blades and is driven by the fan belt), the thermostat and two drain taps.

Only when the correct minimum operating temperature has been reached does the thermostat begin to open allowing water to return to the radiator.

2 Cooling system-draining

With the car on level ground drain the system as follows:
1 If the engine is cold, remove the filler cap from the radiator by turning the cap anti-clockwise. If the engine is hot, then turn the filler cap very slightly until the pressure in the system has had time to disperse. Use a rag over the cap to protect your hand from escaping steam. If, with the engine very hot the cap is released suddenly the drop in pressure can cause the water to boil. With the pressure released the cap can be removed.
2 If anti-freeze is in the radiator drain it into a clean bowl for re-use. A wide bowl will be necessary to catch all the coolant.
3 Slacken the hose clip at the radiator bottom hose and draw off the hose. No radiator drain tap or plug is fitted. Next remove the drain plug located at the left hand side manifold branch.
4 When the water has finished running probe the big orifice with a short piece of wire to dislodge any particles of rust or sediment which may be causing a blockage and preventing all the water draining out.
5 It is important to note that detaching the bottom radiator hose only, will not completely drain the cylinder block.

3 Cooling system - flushing

1 With time the cooling system will gradually lose its efficiency as the radiator becomes choked with rust scale, deposits from the water and other sediment. To clean the system out, remove the radiator cap and leave a hose running in the radiator cap orifice for ten to fifteen minutes.
2 In very bad cases the radiator should be reverse flushed. This can be done with the radiator in position. A hose must be arranged to feed water into the lower radiator outlet pipe. Water, under pressure, is then forced up through the radiator and out of the header tank filler orifice.
3 The hose is removed and placed in the filler orifice and the radiator washed out in the usual manner.

4 Cooling system - filling

1 Reconnect the bottom hose and tighten the clip. Clean the threads of the cylinder block drain plug and coat with a little Hylomar SQ32/M or similar non setting sealant. Refit the drain plug and tighten.
2 Move the heater control to the hot position and slowly fill the system to ensure that air locks are minimised.
3 Do not fill the system higher than within 0.5 inch (12.7 mm) of the filler cap orifice. Overfilling will merely result in wastage, which is especially to be avoided when anti-freeze is in use.
4 Only use anti-freeze mixture with an ethylene glycol base. See section 9 for further information.
5 Always add 3 fl oz (85 ml) of Vauxhall Corrosion Preventative when refilling the cooling system with plain water. Replace

the radiator cap.
6 Run the engine at a fast idle speed for approximately half a minute and remove the radiator filler cap slowly. Top up as necessary and finally replace the filler cap turning it clockwise firmly to lock it in position.

5 Radiator - removal, inspection, cleaning and replacement

1 Refer to Section 2 and drain the cooling system.
2 Slacken the clip which holds the top water hose to the thermostat elbow and carefully pull off the hose.
3 Where a heater is fitted slacken the clip which holds the heater hose to the hose connector attached to the bottom hose. Detach the heater hose.
4 Models fitted with 1759cc engine and manual transmission.
a) Unscrew the four self tapping screws that secure the top and bottom panels to the radiator support panels. Lift away the top and bottom panels.
b) Slacken the radiator side mounting bracket securing nuts. Then lift the radiator upwards and away from the front of the car.
5 Models fitted with 2279cc engine and automatic transmission.
a) Unscrew the four self tapping screws that secure the shaped cowl to the radiator. Draw the shaped cowl rearwards as far as possible.
b) Models fitted with automatic transmission have an oil cooler housed in the bottom of the radiator. Detach the pipes at the oil cooler and plug the ends to stop syphoning off the oil and dirt ingress.
c) Slacken the radiator side mounting bracket securing nuts. Then lift the radiator upwards and away from the front of the car.
6 Clean out the inside of the radiator by flushing as described in Section 3. When the radiator is out of the car it is well worthwhile to invert it for reverse flushing. Clean the exterior of the radiator by hosing down the matrix with a strong water jet to clear away embedded dirt and insects which will impede the air flow.
7 If it is thought that the radiator is partially blocked, a good proprietary chemical product such as 'Radflush' should be used to clean it.
8 With the radiator away from the car any leaks can be soldered or repaired with a suitable substance such as 'Cataloy'. Full information and instructions for use will be found on the pack.
9 Inspect the radiator hoses for cracks, internal or external perishing and damage caused by the securing clips. Replace the hoses as necessary. Examine the radiator hose securing clips and renew them if they are rusted or distorted.
10 Refitting the radiator is the reverse sequence to removal. If automatic transmission is fitted check and top up its fluid level as described in Chapter 6.

6 Thermostat - removal, testing and replacement

1 To remove the thermostat, partially drain the cooling system as described in Section 2. 4 pints (2.27 litres) is usually enough.
2 Slacken the radiator top hose at the thermostat housing elbow and carefully draw it off the elbow.
3 Unscrew the two set bolts and spring washers securing the thermostat housing elbow 'and lift the housing and gasket away. If it has stuck because a sealing compound has been previously used, tap with a soft faced hammer to break the seal.
4 Lift out the thermostat and observe if it is stuck open. If this is the case discard it.
5 Suspend it by a piece of string together with a thermometer in a saucepan of cold water. Neither the thermostat or the thermometer should touch the sides or bottom of the saucepan otherwise a false reading could be obtained.
6 Heat the water, stirring it gently with the thermometer to

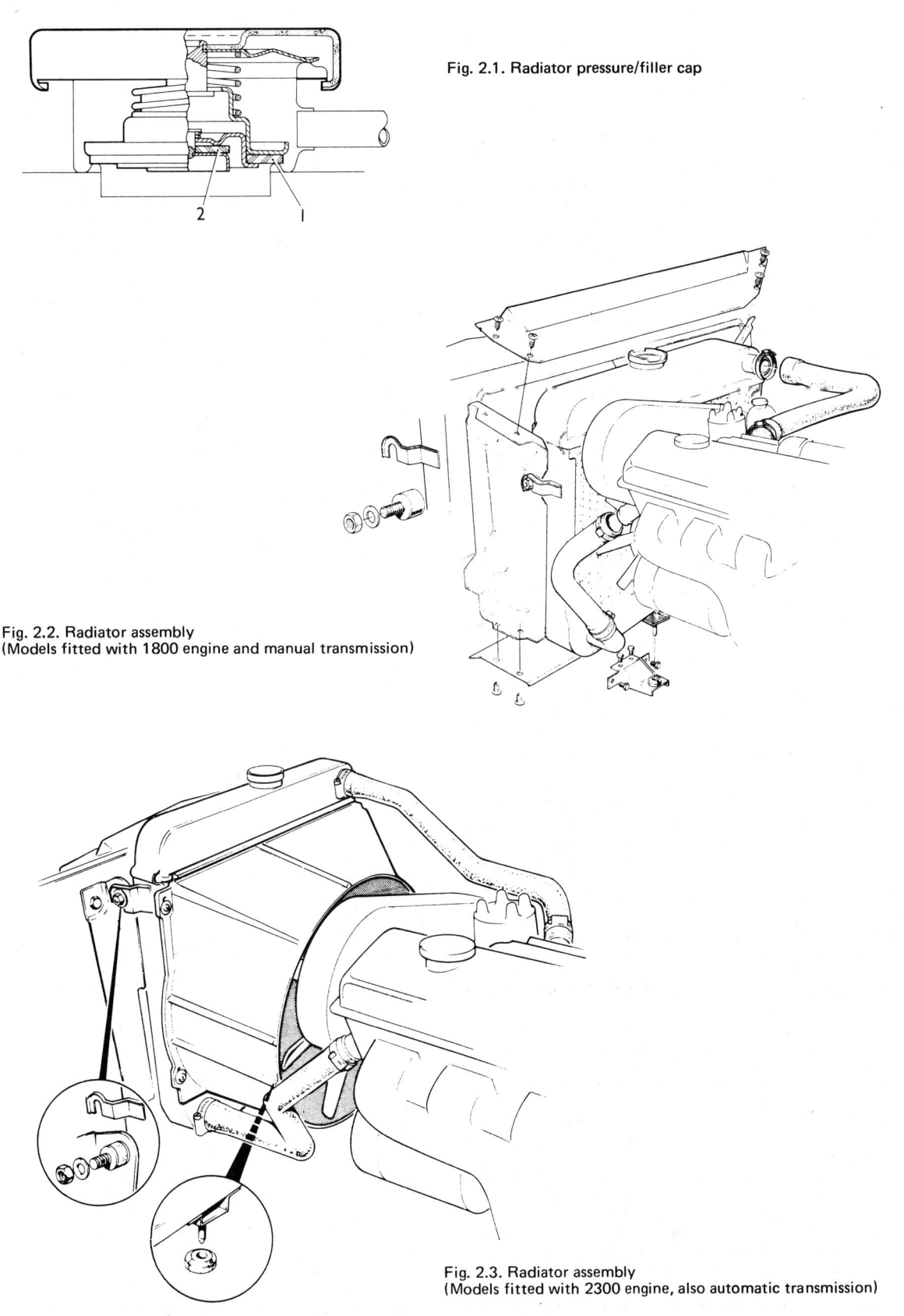

Fig. 2.1. Radiator pressure/filler cap

Fig. 2.2. Radiator assembly
(Models fitted with 1800 engine and manual transmission)

Fig. 2.3. Radiator assembly
(Models fitted with 2300 engine, also automatic transmission)

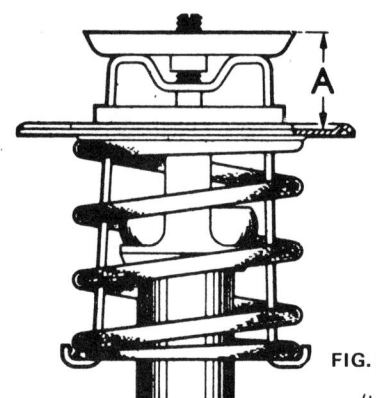
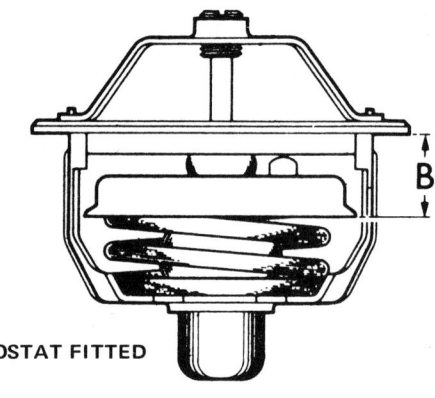

FIG. 2.4. TWO TYPES OF THERMOSTAT FITTED

(left)   Western Thompson
(right) A C

Fully open position dimensions:
A   0.51 inch   (12.95 mm)
B   0.48 inch   (12.19 mm)

ensure temperature uniformity, and note when the thermostat begins to open. Note the temperature and this should be comparable with the figure given in the specifications at the beginning of this chapter.

7   Continue heating the water until the thermostat is fully open. Now let it cool down naturally and check that it closes fully. If the thermostat does not fully open or close then it must be discarded and a new one obtained.

8   Replace the thermostat in a reverse of the removal procedure. Always clean the mating faces and use a new paper gasket.

7   Water pump - removal and replacement

1   To gain access to the water pump, the radiator, fan, fan belt, crankshaft pulley and engine front cover must be removed. Full information on removal will be found in Section 5 of this chapter and then in Chapter 1.

2   Slacken the bottom hose clip and carefully detach the hose from the water pump if this has not been done already.

3   Detach the heater pipe union from the water pump body adjacent to the bottom hose location.

4   Undo and remove the four bolts and spring washers that secure the water pump body to the cylinder block. Lift away the water pump and recover the old gasket.

5   Refitting the water pump is the reverse sequence to removal but the following additional points should be noted.

a)   Make sure the mating faces of the pump body and cylinder block are clean. Always use a new gasket.

b)   Refer to Section 9 and adjust the fan belt tension. If the belt is too tight undue strain will be placed on the water pump and alternator bearings. If the belt is too loose, it will slip and wear rapidly as well as giving rise to possible engine overheating and low alternator output.

8   Water pump - dismantling and reassembly

1   Before dismantling the water pump check the economics of overhaul compared with cost of a guaranteed new unit. Then make quite sure all the spare parts required are to hand.

2   To renew the bearing shaft assembly or the seal and thrust washer it is first necessary to draw off the rotor. To do this hold the pump body firmly in a vice and using a universal three leg puller, ease the rotor from the shaft as shown in Fig.2.6.

3   Squeeze the sides and lift out the shaft and bearing locking clip from the nose of the water pump body (Fig.2.7).

4   Withdraw the seal assembly from the water pump body.

5   Using a soft metal drift carefully drive the old shaft and

bearing assembly forwards through the pump body.

6   The pulley flange may now be drawn from the shaft with the universal three leg puller.

7   To reassemble first drift the new shaft and bearing assembly into the pump body so that the locking ring groove in the bearing coincides with the groove in the body. The front of the shaft is easily identified by its larger diameter.

8   Carefully insert the shaft and bearing locking clip.

9   Assemble the seal assembly so that the grooves in the sleeve engage with the pipe in the casing. Next smear a little Castrol Girling Red Rubber Grease onto the outer rim of the seal and install into the water pump body.

10   The pulley flange and rotor may now be pressed onto the shaft using a large bench vice or suitable diameter tubes and hammer. Refer to Fig. 2.8 and ensure that dimensions A and B are achieved.

11   The water pump assembly is now ready for refitting.

9   Anti-freeze coolant solution

1   Where temperatures are likely to drop below freezing point (0°C, 32°F) the cooling system must be adequately protected by the addition of anti-freeze. It is still possible for water to freeze in the radiator with the engine running in very cold conditions - particularly if the engine cooling is being adequately dealt with by the heater radiator. The thermostat will remain closed and the coolant in the radiator will not circulate.

2   Before refilling the cooling system with an anti-freeze solution it is best to drain and flush the system as described in Sections 2 and 3 of this chapter.

3   Because anti-freeze has a greater searching effect than water make sure that all hoses and joints are in good condition.

4   The table below gives the details of the anti-freeze percentage to be used:

%	Complete protection	
25	−11°C	12.2°F
30	−14°C	6.8°F
35	−19°C	−2.2°F
40	−23°C	−9.4°F
45	−29°C	−20.2°F
50	−35°C	−31.0°F

5   Mix the required quantity of anti-freeze with four pints (2.27 litres) of water and pour into the cooling system. Top up with water and check the level as described in Section 4, paragraph 6.

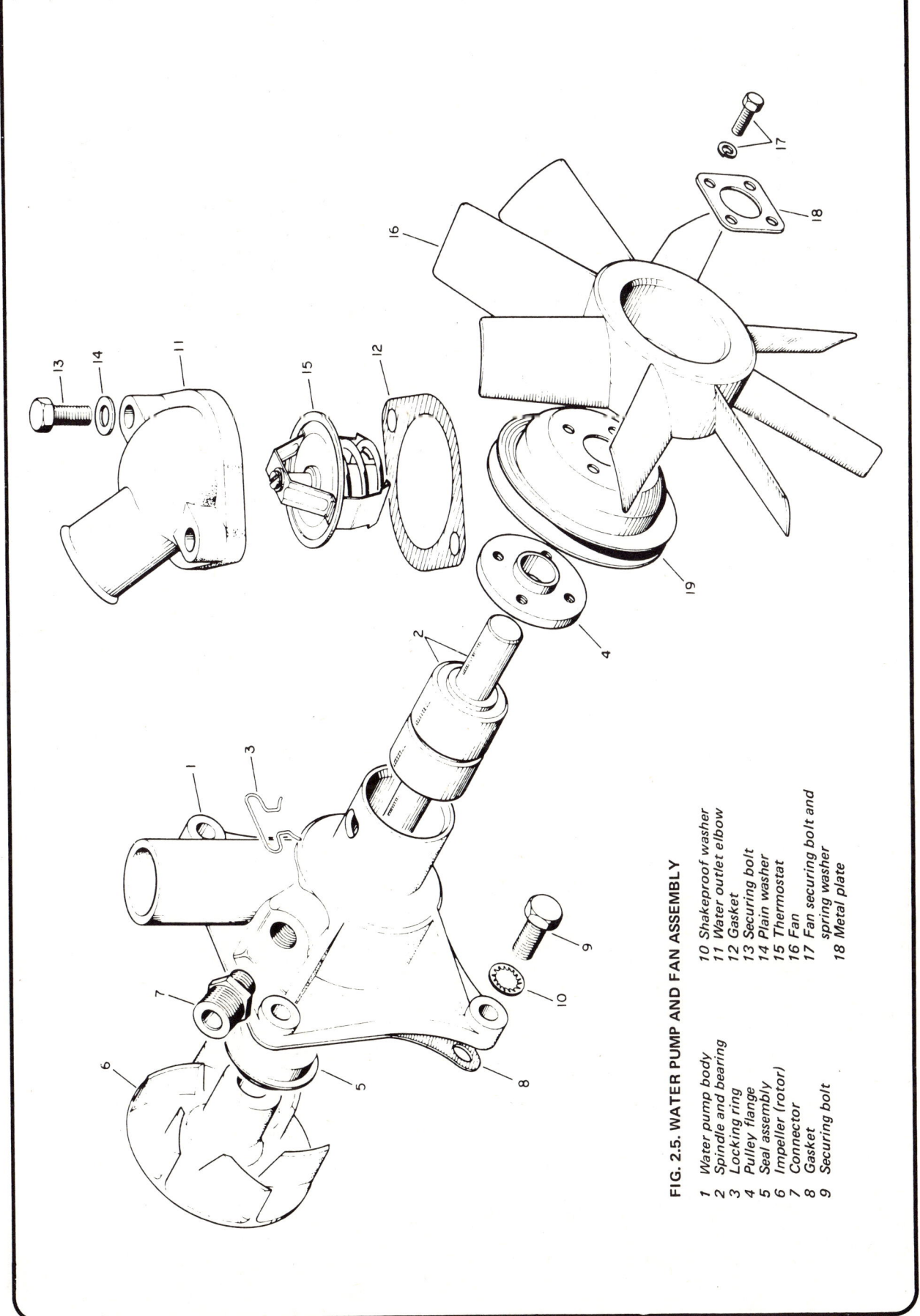

FIG. 2.5. WATER PUMP AND FAN ASSEMBLY

1	Water pump body	10	Shakeproof washer
2	Spindle and bearing	11	Water outlet elbow
3	Locking ring	12	Gasket
4	Pulley flange	13	Securing bolt
5	Seal assembly	14	Plain washer
6	Impeller (rotor)	15	Thermostat
7	Connector	16	Fan
8	Gasket	17	Fan securing bolt and
9	Securing bolt		spring washer
		18	Metal plate

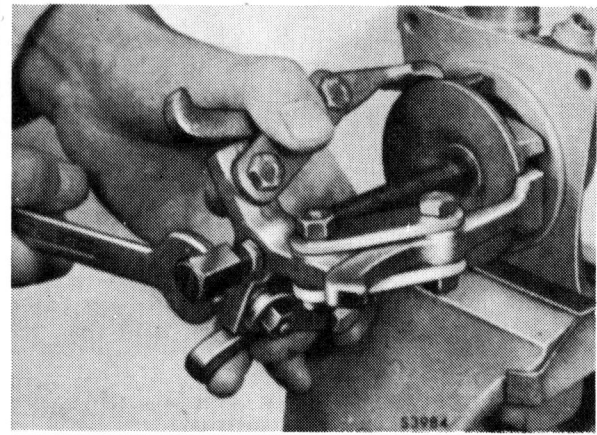

Fig. 2.6. Removal of rotor with universal puller

Fig. 2.7. Withdrawal of locking ring

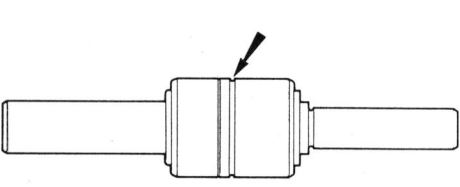

Fig. 2.8. Groove in bearing assembly into which locking ring engages

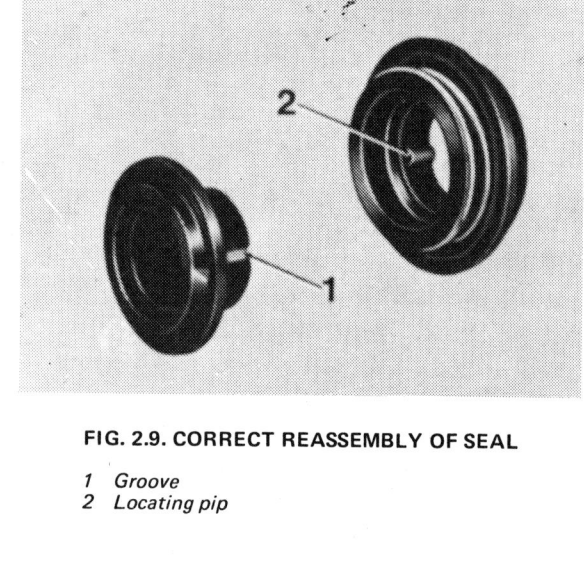

FIG. 2.9. CORRECT REASSEMBLY OF SEAL

1   Groove
2   Locating pip

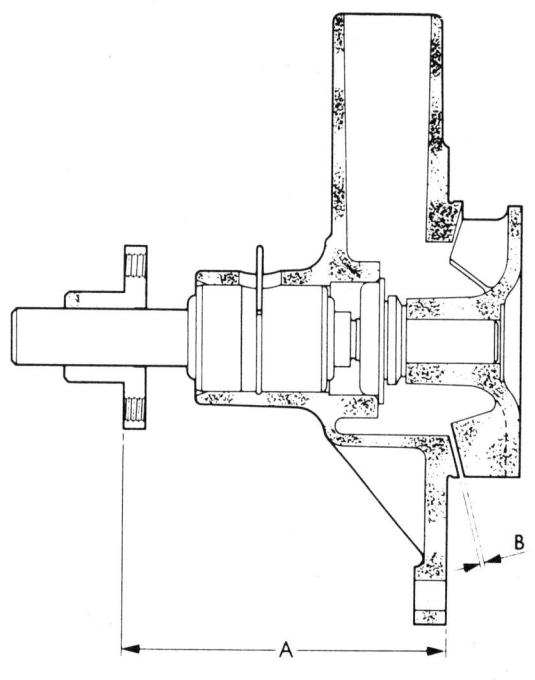

FIG. 2.10. WATER PUMP CROSS SECTION

A	3.78 inch	(96 mm)
B	0.03 - 0.05 inch	(0.75 - 1.30 mm)

10 Fan belt - removal, replacement and adjustment

1 If the fan belt is worn or has stretched unduly it should be replaced. The most usual reason for replacement is breakage in use. Always carry a spare.

2 Even though the belt may have broken and fallen off, go through the removal routine. First of all loosen the two alternator pivot bolts and the nut on the adjustment link. Push the alternator towards the engine and lift off the old belt.

3 Position the new belt over the pulleys.

4 The alternator must now be used as a tensioner in effect by pulling it away from the engine and locking it in the required position. This can call for some sustained effort unless the pivot bolts are slackened only a little so that the alternator is quite stiff to move. A lever between the alternator and cylinder block will help. However, avoid applying pressure to the rear end cover or it may break. Always tighten the front end cover securing bolts first.

5 The tension of the belt, mid-way between the water pump and alternator pulleys should be set to 0.25 in (6 mm), (under an 80 lb (36 kg) pressure). If in doubt it is better to be a little too slack than too tight. Only slipping will occur if it is too slack. If too tight, damage can be caused by excessive strain on the pulley bearings.

6 When the adjustment is correct tighten the alternator mountings fully.

7 With a new belt check the tension 250 miles (400 km) after fitting.

8 Periodic checking of the belt tension is necessary and there is no hard and fast rule as to the most suitable interval, because a fan belt does not necessarily stretch or wear at a pre-determined rate. Assuming most owners check their own oil and water levels regularly it is suggested as a good habit to check the fan belt tension every time the bonnet is opened.

11 Water temperature warning indicator

1 The water temperature gauge is operated by a heat sensitive switch which is screwed into the water jacket of the inlet manifold.

2 Normally the gauge needle should stay out of the red sector when normal engine temperature is being maintained and the ignition switched on.

3 The instrument may be tested by detaching the lead from the temperature sender unit and placing it on a good earth point.

4 If the gauge needle moves into the red position when the ignition is switched on, the sender unit is faulty and must be renewed.

5 If there is still no reaction from the indicator then there is an electrical fault (fuse, wiring gauge etc), and further investigation is necessary.

12   Fault diagnosis

Cause	Reason/s	Remedy
SYMPTOM: OVERHEATING		
Heat generated in cylinder not being successfully disposed of by radiator	Insufficient water in cooling system	Top up radiator
	Fan belt slipping (Accompanied by a shrieking noise on rapid engine acceleration)	Tighten fan belt to recommended tension or replace if worn.
	Radiator core blocked or radiator grill restricted	Reverse flush radiator, remove obstructions
	Bottom water hose collapsed, impeding flow	Remove and fit new hose.
	Thermostat not opening properly	Remove and fit new thermostat.
	Ignition advance and retard incorrectly set (Accompanied by loss of power and perhaps misfiring)	Check and reset ignition timing.
	Carburettor incorrectly adjusted (mixture too weak)	Tune carburettor.
	Exhaust system partially blocked	Check exhaust pipe for constrictive dents and blockages.
	Oil level in sump too low	Top up sump to full mark on dipstick.
	Blown cylinder head gasket (Water/steam being forced down the radiator overflow pipe under pressure)	Remove cylinder head, fit new gasket.
	Engine not yet run-in	Run-in slowly and carefully.
	Brakes binding	Check and adjust brakes if necessary.
SYMPTOM: UNDERHEATING		
Too much heat being dispersed by radiator	Thermostat jammed open	Remove and renew thermostat.
	Incorrect grade of thermostat fitted allowing premature opening of valve	Remove and replace with new thermostat which opens at a higher temperature.
	Thermostat missing	Check and fit correct thermostat.
SYMPTOM: LOSS OF COOLING WATER		
Leaks in system	Loose clips on water hoses	Check and tighten clips if necessary.
	Top, bottom, or by-pass water hoses perished and leaking	Check and replace any faulty hoses.
	Radiator core leaking	Remove radiator and repair.
	Thermostat gasket leaking	Inspect and renew gasket.
	Radiator pressure cap spring worn or seal ineffective	Renew radiator pressure cap.
	Blown cylinder head gasket (Pressure in system forcing water/steam down overflow pipe).	Remove cylinder head and fit new gasket.
	Cylinder wall or head cracked	Dismantle engine, dispatch to engineering works for repair.

Chapter 3 Fuel system and carburation

Contents

Specifications

Fuel pump:

Standard	AC Two port	
Recirculating	AC Three port	
Delivery pressure:		
Standard	2.5 - 3.5 lb sq in	(0.185 - 0.245 kg sq cm)
Recirculating	2.75 - 4.25 lb sq in	(0.193 - 0.299 kg sq cm)
Diaphragm spring force when compressed to 0.64 in (16.5 mm):		
Standard	8 - 8.5 lb	(3.6 - 3.825 kg)
Recirculating	9.25 - 10 lb	(4.16 - 4.5 kg)

Fuel tank:

Location	Between body side rails beneath luggage compartment floor
Capacity	14.25 gallons (65 litres)
Petrol grade:	
Low compression engine	90 octane (minimum)
High compression engine	95 octane (minimum)

Air cleaner:

Type	Renewable dry paper element
Optional	Oil bath

Carburettor — 1759 cc, Zenith manufacture:

Identification number:	Manual transmission (standard)	361V (3415)	
	Automatic transmission (standard)	361VT (3416)	
	European exhaust emission control models (EEEC)	361 VE (3518)	

	Standard	EEEC
Choke tube	29 mm	25 mm
Main jet	105	85
Compensation jet	120	120
Idling jet	50	45
Pump jet	55	55
Needle valve	1.75 mm	1.75 mm
Needle valve washer thickness	2 mm	2 mm

Float position with carburettor cover inverted and needle roller seating highest point of floats should be ... ...   30.5 - 31.5 mm above face of cover gasket

	Standard	EEEC
Engine idle speed:		
Manual transmission	725 - 775 rpm	725 - 775 rpm
Automatic transmission	See text	See text
Permissible exhaust CO at idling speed	See text	See text
High altitude jet settings:		
Main jet		
5,000 - 7,000 ft (1,500 - 2,000m)	102	82
7,000 - 10,000 ft (2,000 - 3,000m)	100	80
10,000 - 15,000 ft (3,000 - 4,500m)	95	77
Compensation jet		
7,000 - 10,000 ft (2,000 - 3,000m)	117	117
10,000 - 15,000 ft (3,000 - 4,500m)	115	115

Carburettor — 2279 cc, Zenith/Stromberg manufacture:

Identification number:	
Manual transmission (standard)	175CD - 2S (3411)
Automatic transmission (standard)	175CD - 2ST (3412)
European exhaust emission control models (EEEC)	175CD - 2S (3411B)
VX 4/90 - twin installation of identical carburettors	

	All models	VX 4/90 (two)
Metering needle	BIBM	BI BU
Jet orifice	2.54 mm	2.54 mm
Air valve spring identification colour	Red	Red
Fast idle cam:		
Manual transmission	W	D
Automatic transmission	C4	A6
Cold start needle	M1	K
Needle valve	1.75 mm	1.75 mm
Needle valve washer thickness	1.6 mm	1.6 mm
Float position with carburettor inverted and needle valve on seating, highest point of floats should be	15.5 - 16.5 mm above face of main body - gasket removed	
Engine idle speed:		
Manual transmission	725 - 775 rpm	725 - 775 rpm
Automatic transmission	See text	See text
Permissible exhaust CO at idling speed	See text	See text

1 General description

The fuel system comprises a fuel tank at the rear of the car, a mechanical fuel pump located on the front right hand side of the cylinder block and a single Zenith Carburettor (Victor models) or twin Zenith/Stromberg Carburettors (VX 4/90 models). A renewable paper element air cleaner is fitted as standard with an option of an oil bath type.

The fuel pump draws petrol from the fuel tank and delivers it to the carburettor installation. The level of petrol in the carburettor is controlled by a float operated needle valve. Petrol flows past the needle until the float rises sufficiently to close the valve. The pump will then free wheel under slight back pressure until the petrol level drops. The needle valve will then open and petrol continue to flow until the level rises again.

The petrol/air charge is drawn into the cylinders via the water heated inlet manifold on each induction stroke of the pistons, the air being first filtered to remove harmful dust.

2 Air cleaners - removal and replacement

Paper element - 1759cc engine

1 The air cleaner assembly is secured to the carburettor by a Jubilee type clip which must be first released to remove the complete assembly. Before lifting away note the relative position of the air cleaner intake.
2 To gain access to the element undo and remove the seven self tapping screws securing the top cover to the main body. Lift away the top cover followed by the paper element and two sealing rings.
3 Refitting or reassembly is the reverse sequence to removal.

Paper element - 2279cc engine (Victor)

1 The air cleaner assembly is secured to the carburettor air intake flange by three bolts which pass through the body of the assembly. Removal is simply a matter of unscrewing these three bolts and lifting away the air cleaner assembly.
2 To gain access to the element undo and remove the five self tapping screws securing the cover to the main body. Lift away the top cover followed by the paper element and two sealing rings.
3 Refitting or reassembly is the reverse sequence to removal.

Paper element - 2279cc engine (VX 4/90)

1 The twin element air cleaner assembly is mounted on adaptors which are bolted to the carburettor air intake flanges. The assembly must be dismantled as described in paragraph 2, prior to removal.
2 To gain access to the elements undo and remove the two nuts, one bolt, plain washers and sealing washers that secure the body to the adaptors. Lift away body followed by the two elements.
3 Should it be necessary to remove the adaptors undo and remove the three retaining nuts, bolts and spring washers. Note that the adaptors are marked 'Front' and 'Rear' and must not be interchanged.
4 Reassembly is the reverse sequence to removal but the following additional points must be noted:
a) Make sure that the rubber sealing gaskets on the circumference of the adaptors are correctly in position.
b) Ensure the sleeve and seal washer are fitted to the bolt and sealing washers and plain washers to the studs.
c) Before refitting the retaining bolt apply a little Loctite Grade B to the bolt thread.

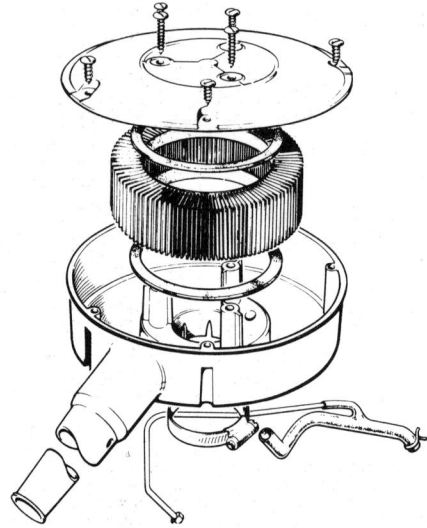

Fig. 3.1. Paper element air cleaner (1800 engines)

Fig. 3.2. Air cleaner assembly (2300 engines)

Fig. 3.3. Air cleaner assembly (VX4/90)

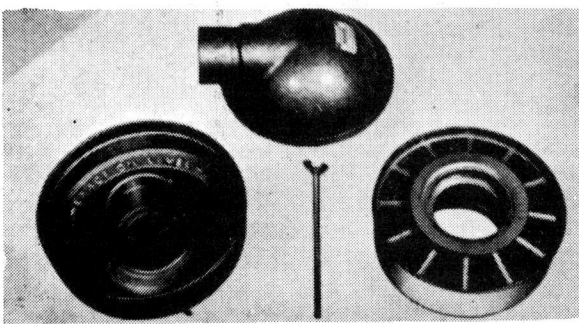

Fig. 3.4. Oil bath type air cleaner

Oil bath type - optional

1 On some cars an oil bath type air cleaner is fitted. It is mounted on a bracket secured to the left hand side of the engine compartment.
2 To gain access to the wire mesh element undo and remove the one wing top bolt and lift away the top cover.
3 Lift out the element, noting which way round it is fitted and wash out in paraffin. Allow to drain or blow dry using compressed air.
4 Wash out the oil bath and wipe clean with an absorbant cloth. Refill the oil bath with SAE 50 grade oil up to the level indicated. Reassembly is now the reverse sequence to removal.

3 Fuel pump - description

The mechanically operated AC fuel pump is actuated through a spring loaded rocker arm. One arm of the rocker is coupled by a rod and link to an eccentric on the auxiliary shaft and the other arm operates a diaphragm pull rod.

As the auxiliary shaft rotates the pivoted rocker arm moves outwards and this in turn pulls the diaphragm pull rod and diaphragm down against the pressure of the diaphragm spring.

This creates sufficient vacuum in the pump chamber to draw in fuel from the tank through the sediment chamber, fuel filter gauze and non-return inlet valve.

The rocker arm is held in constant contact with the eccentric of an anti-rattle spring and as the auxiliary shaft continues to rotate the eccentric allows the rocker arm to move inwards. The diaphragm spring is thus free to push the diaphragm upwards thereby pushing the fuel in the pump chamber out to the carburettor through the non return outlet valve.

When the float chamber in the carburettor installation is full the float chamber needle valve will close so preventing further flow from the fuel pump.

The pressure in the delivery line will hold the diaphragm downwards against the pressure of the diaphragm spring, and it will remain in this position until the needle valve in the float chamber opens to admit more petrol.

On models fitted with a recirculatory fuel system, the fuel pump has an additional port with a restricted hole on the outlet side of the pump. This port is connected to a fuel return pipe to an extra tube in the fuel gauge tank sender unit.

4 Fuel pump - removal and replacement

1 Disconnect the fuel pipes by unscrewing their unions on the fuel pump body. Plug the inlet fuel line from the tank to prevent dirt ingress.
2 Undo and remove the two bolts and spring washers which secure the fuel pump to the cylinder block. Lift away the pump noting carefully the number of gaskets used between the pump and cylinder block mating faces.
3 Replacement is a straightforward reversal of removal. If possible always use new gaskets.

5 Fuel pump - dismantling, inspection and reassembly

1 Before dismantling, clean the exterior of the pump and then make a mark across the centre and base casting mating flanges so that they may be refitted in their original positions ((Fig.3.7).
2 Undo the knurled screw on the stirrup that holds the glass bowl in position, swing the stirrup to one side and lift off the bowl.
3 Lift the filter screen from the top of the centre casting.
4 Undo and remove the six screws and spring washers that secure the centre to the base casting and carefully lift off the centre casting. It is possible for the diaphragm to stick to the mating flanges so if this is the case ease free with a sharp knife.
5 To release the diaphragm, depress the centre and turn through 90°. This will release the diaphragm pull rod from the

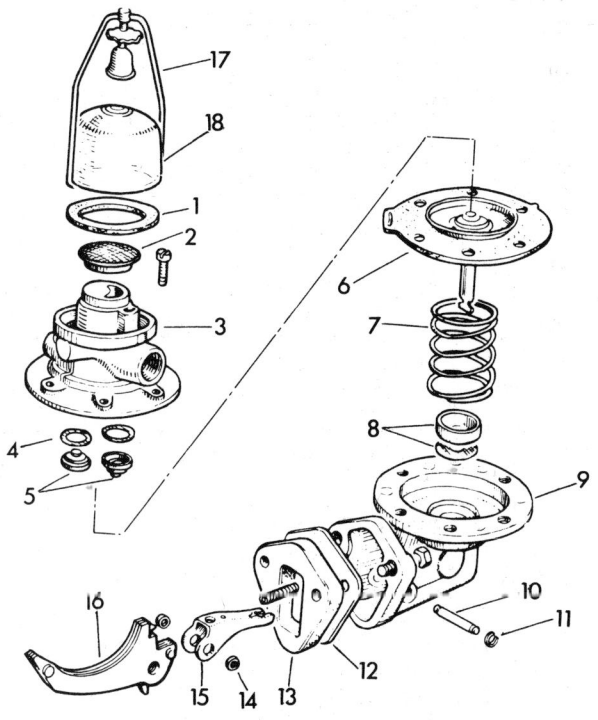

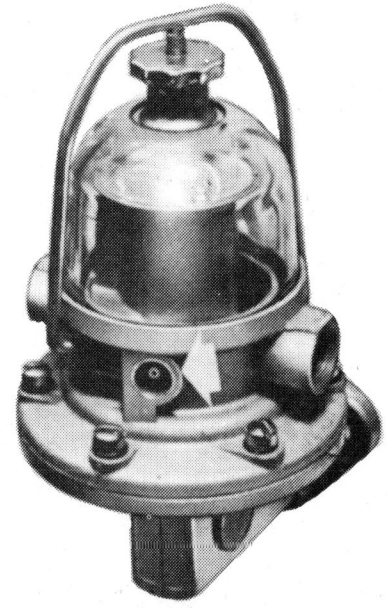

Fig. 3.6. Second outlet port - recirculating system

FIG. 3.5. FUEL PUMP COMPONENTS

1	Seal	10	Rockar arm pin
2	Filler	11	Pin clip
3	Upper pump body	12	Gasket
4	Seal	13	Insulator
5	Valves	14	Spacer
6	Diaphragm	15	Link
7	Spring	16	Rocker
8	Seal and retainer	17	Clamp
9	Lower pump body	18	Bowl

Fig. 3.9. Correct location of diaphragm

Fig. 3.7. Upper and lower body marked flanges

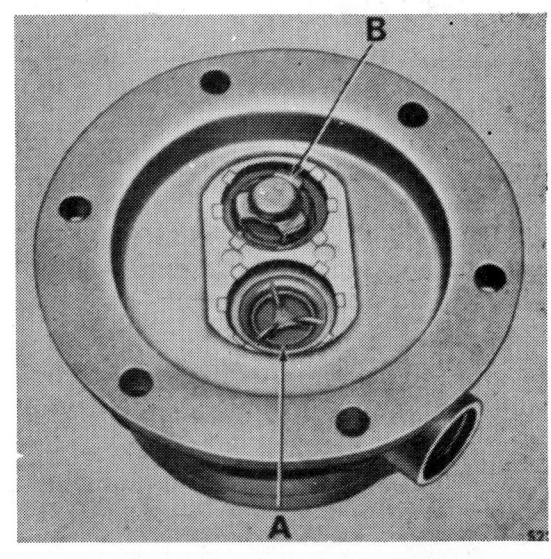

FIG. 3.8. VALVE IDENTIFICATION

A Outlet valve   B Inlet valve

stirrup in the operating link. Lift out the seal and seal retainer.

6 Do not remove the rocker arm and pivot pin from the base casting unless there are obvious signs of excessive wear - in which case it would probably be more economical to obtain an exchange pump.

7 To remove the valve assemblies from the body centre, undo and remove the two retaining plate securing screws and lift out each valve and the gasket behind. Note which way round the valves are fitted. It may be found that on later produced pumps these two valves are staked in position so if this is the case removal should not be attempted unless absolutely necessary. The staking may be removed with a small sharp chisel (Fig.3.8).

8 Carefully examine the diaphragm for signs of splitting or cracking and renew it if in any doubt.

9 If the valves are suspected of malfunctioning, replace them.

10 The filter screen should be intact with no signs of elongated holes or broken strands. If blocked use an old toothbrush and wash in petrol.

11 Obtain a new oil seal ready for reassembly.

12 Clean up the recesses where the valves are located and insert a new gasket into the valve location. Carefully position the valves so that the inlet valve has its spring facing the bottom of the pump. The outlet valve is positioned the other way up.

13 Secure the valves by either restaking using a pointed centre punch or refitting the retaining plate and securing screws.

14 To refit the diaphragm first put a new oil seal followed by the retainer into the body base. Put the diaphragm pull rod through the seal and the slot in the rocker arm link. Then turn the diaphragm anticlockwise 90° so that it lines up with the screw holes and the lug on the body aligns with the tab on the diaphragm (Fig.3.9).

15 Move the rocker arm until the diaphragm is level with the body flanges and hold the arm in this position. Reassemble the two halves of the pump ensuring that the previously made marks on the flanges are adjacent to each other.

16 Refit the six screws and spring washers and tighten them down finger tight.

17 Move the rocker arm up and down several times to centralise the diaphragm, and then with the arm held down, tighten the screws securely in a diagonal and progressive manner.

18 Replace the gauze filter. Fit the sealing ring followed by the glass bowl and secure with the stirrup. Tighten the knurled screw finger tight.

---

6   Fuel pump - testing

If operation of the fuel pump is suspect, or it has been overhauled, it may be quickly dry tested by holding a finger over the inlet nozzle and operating the rocker lever through three complete strokes. When the finger is released a suction noise should be heard. Next hold a finger over the outlet nozzle and press the rocker arm fully. The pressure generated should hold for a minimum of fifteen seconds. **NOTE:** *For fuel pumps which have a second outlet port (see Fig. 3.6), this port must be plugged while testing the pump.*

---

7   Zenith 361 V series carburettors - description

Models covered by this manual fitted with the 1759cc engine use the 361 V series fixed choke downdraught carburettor. It is fitted with an accelerator pump and incorporates an economy unit to correct fuel mixture at certain intermediate engine speeds. The principle of operation is as follows:

At full throttle opening with the choke flap open, the depression (low pressure) in the choke tube draws a fuel/air mixture from the main discharge beak.

The fuel/air mixture has been emulsified in the emulsion tube below the discharge beak. The fuel reaches the emulsion tube via the reserve well, from the main jet located in the float chamber.

When the engine is cold and the choke flap closed ready for engine starting the throttle flap is automatically opened slightly

FIG 3.10. ZENITH 361V SERIES CARBURETTOR (MANUAL TRANSMISSION)

1 Economiser cover screw	34 Pump link
2 Spring washer	35 Interconnection link
3 Economiser valve cover	36 Emulsion block screw
4 Spring	37 Spring washer
5 Gasket	38 Emulsion block seal
6 Diaphragm	39 Emulsion block
7 Cover screw (short)	40 Pump jet
8 Cover screw (long)	41 Plug
9 Float chamber cover	42 Pump discharge valve
10 Gasket	43 Valve ball circlip
11 Pump lever nut	44 Valve ball
12 Washer	45 Slow running jet
13 Pump lever	46 Pump piston
14 Retaining ring	47 Bracket
15 Float pivot	48 Screw
16 Float assembly	49 Clip
17 Main jet	50 Clevis pin
18 Compensating jet	51 Plain washer
19 Needle seating washer	52 Lever
20 Needle and seating	53 Pump spindle
21 Volume control screw	54 Choke spindle
22 Spring	55 Spring
23 Throttle flap	56 Circlip
24 Screw	57 Screw
25 Throttle spindle	58 Choke control lever
26 Throttle lever	59 Lever spring
27 Washer	60 Spindle washer
28 Throttle stop	61 Choke flap
29 Locating lever	62 Screw
30 Nut	63 Insulator
31 Shakeproof washer	64 Gasket
32 Throttle stop screw	65 Stud
33 Spring	66 Nut

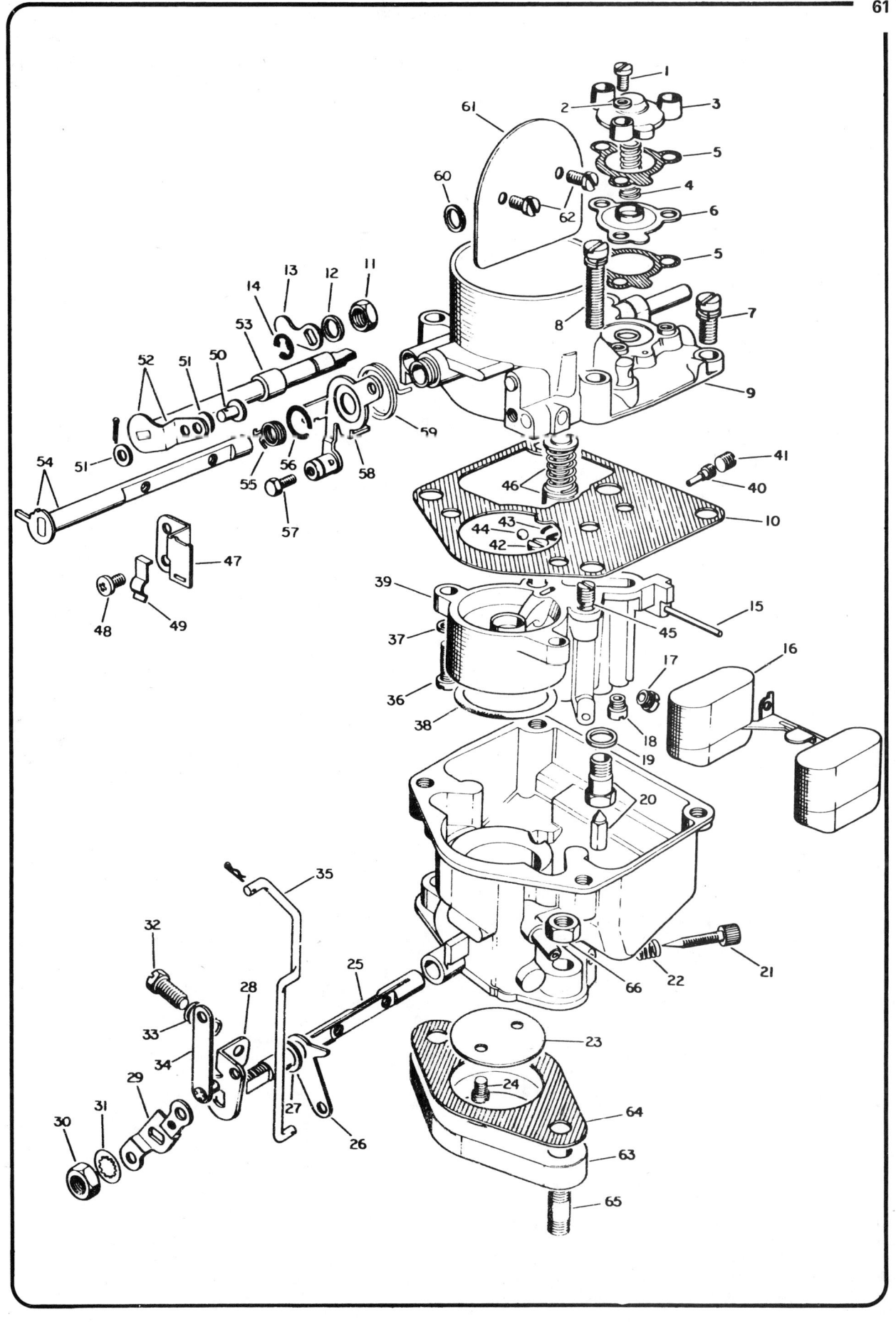

to allow the charge to pass into the inlet manifold. The choke tube depression draws principally on the discharge beak and therefore a very rich mixture reaches the engine, as air from the main air inlet has been closed off.

At engine idle speed with the throttle flap shut, there is no depression at the main discharge beak. It is now concentrated at the idling discharge orifice on the engine side of the throttle flap. Fuel from the main reserve well is drawn via the pilot jet to this orifice, taking the requisite amount of air for the mixture through the pilot air bleed by-pass orifice. The volume of the mixture supplied is controlled by the idling mixture control screw.

As soon as the throttle is opened further, the by-pass orifice is then also subject to depression, so instead of feeding air in one direction to the idling discharge orifice, it now delivers fuel/air mixture in the other direction until the throttle is open sufficiently for the main discharge beak to take over.

The economy unit augments the fuel flow from the main jet automatically through the economy jet when the choke tube depression is low. At cruising speeds, when the depression is high, a diaphragm operated valve shuts off the economy jet.

There is also an accelerator pump which delivers a metered jet of neat fuel into the choke tube whenever the accelerator pedal is depressed quickly. This gives the richer mixture necessary for rapid acceleration. The fuel is drawn from the float chamber into the pump chamber via a non return valve at the bottom of the float chamber. When the pump is operated quickly (i.e. sudden accelerator pedal operation) the pump release valve is forced shut under pressure and the fuel passes through the injector. If the pump is operated slowly, the pressure is insufficient to close the release valve, so fuel passes through it back to the float chamber rather than out of the injector.

The 361 VT carburettor is fitted to 1759cc engines on cars with automatic transmission and is basically similar to the 361 V type with the exception that it has a water heated automatic choke unit contained in a housing which is attached to the main carburettor body.

The automatic choke piston is connected to an offset spindle via a rod and bell crank as shown in Fig.3.11. The choke flap is attached to the spindle. Located in the base of the cylinder is a drilling which connects with further drillings in the carburettor body and finishes at a port positioned below the throttle flap. A pin attached to one arm of the bell crank engages the outer end of the thermostat coil which is anchored at one end to a large solid metal disc.

When starting a cold engine the accelerator pedal must be depressed once and then released. This will set the choke flap and fast idle cam in a position which is dependant on under-bonnet temperature. The choke flap is held in the closed position by the thermostat and the choke piston will be in the raised position when engine temperature is below 21ºC (69.8ºF)

As soon as the engine starts, inlet manifold depression is applied to the choke piston and moves it down in the cylinder. This action is transmitted through the bell crank and flap spindle so opening the choke flap by a small amount against the torque reaction of the thermostat coil. This will provide a weaker mixture whilst retaining a fast idle.

When the accelerator pedal is depressed, the depression under the piston will increase and the choke flap will move to the closed position therefore enrichening the mixture. This occurs because the thermostat coil is now not under the influence of the choke piston.

As the engine temperature rises the coolant temperature also rises and heats up the temperature of the large solid metal disc. This will reduce the thermostat coil torque action and the choke flap will move to the open position.

The 361 VE carburettor is used on 1759cc engines destined to be operated in areas under European Exhaust Emission Control. It is similar to the 361 V type with the exception of difference in specifications including the accelerator pump stroke setting and the use of a sealed calibration screw.

8 Zenith 361 V carburettor - removal and replacement

1 Refer to Section 2 and remove the air cleaner assembly.
2 Slacken the choke inner cable clamp screw and detach the outer cable clip from its support bracket. Withdraw the cable.
3 Detach the throttle return spring and then using a screwdriver ease the spring clip from the end of the clevis pin attaching the inner cable yoke to the throttle lever. Withdraw the clevis pin.
4 Unscrew the outer cable adjustment nut and locknut and detach from the support bracket.
5 Detach the fuel feed pipe from the top cover and the distributor vacuum advance/retard pipe from the carburettor body.
6 Undo and remove the two nuts and washers that secure the carburettor to the inlet manifold and lift the carburettor from the studs.
7 Recover the gaskets, insulator, correction bar and throttle cable support bracket carefully noting the correct order for reassembly.
8 Refitting the carburettor is the reverse sequence to removal but the following additional points should be noted:
a) A new gasket must be used between each mating face of the carburettor, heat insulator and bracket.
b) Make sure that the corrector bar is fitted so that the ends locate in the insulator cut outs (Fig.3.12).
c) Adjust the throttle control linkage as described in Section 25.

9 Zenith 361 V carburettor - dismantling and reassembly

1 As most of the important parts of the carburettor are located in the top cover it is usually not necessary to remove the carburettor from the engine for cleaning purposes.
2 Withdraw the spring pins and detach the pump linkage and choke control rod (Fig.3.13).
3 Undo and remove the four screws and spring washers that secure the top cover to the main body. Note the location of these screws as they are of different lengths.
4 Carefully lift the cover from the main body so as not to tear the gasket, bend or damage the delicate float assembly which are all attached to the cover.
5 To gain access to the jets and accelerator pump the emulsion block must be removed from the underside of the cover (Fig.3.14).
6 Withdraw the float arm pivot pin and lift away the float assembly. Lift out the small needle valve.
7 Using a suitable size box spanner unscrew the needle valve seat and lift it away together with the special washer.
8 Unscrew the two screws that secure the emulsion block to the cover. Lift the emulsion block upwards and take care to prevent the accelerator pump and spring dropping out. Recover the sealing ring.
9 The economy device is held on the top cover by three screws and spring washers which should next be removed. Lift away the cover, diaphragm and spring.
10 Unscrew the jets in the top cover and put in a safe place. The pump jet may be removed from the emulsion block after removing the plug located on the side.
11 Wash the top cover in petrol and probe the drillings with a piece of wire. Inspect the economy device diaphragm for signs of damage and, if evident, obtain a new one ready for reassembly.
12 Reassembly starts with the refitting of the emulsion block to the cover. Refer to Fig.3.15 and make sure that the accelerator pump inlet ball and circlip are installed in the bottom of the cylinder. Refit the jets to the top cover.
13 Fit the new gasket to the top cover and ensure that the accelerator pump lever is correctly positioned as shown in Fig.3.16.
14 Examine the needle valve for any signs of ridging on the bevelled face and renew both the needle and seat if in doubt.
15 Position the emulsion block on the top cover and secure with the two screws.

FIG. 3.11. ZENITH 361 VT CARBURETTOR AUTOMATIC CHOKE

1 Water jacket   4 Bell crank
2 Heat mass   5 Choke piston
3 Thermostat coil   6 Offset spindle

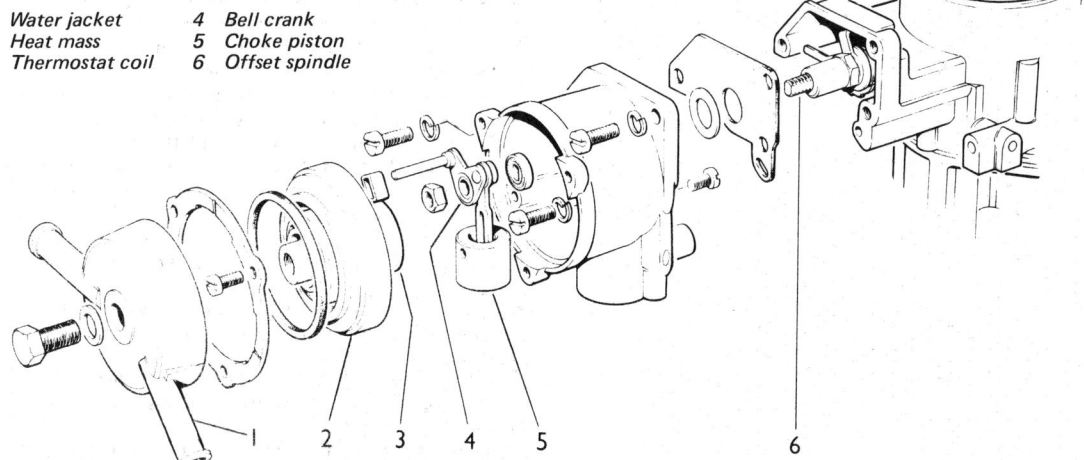

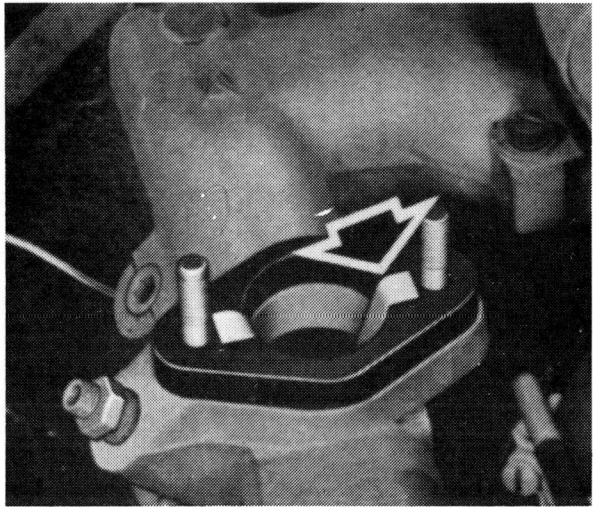

Fig. 3.12. Correct location of corrector bar

FIG. 3.13. PUMP LEVER LINKAGE

1 Pump lever link attachment
2 Choke control rod

Fig. 3.14. Emulsion block attachment points

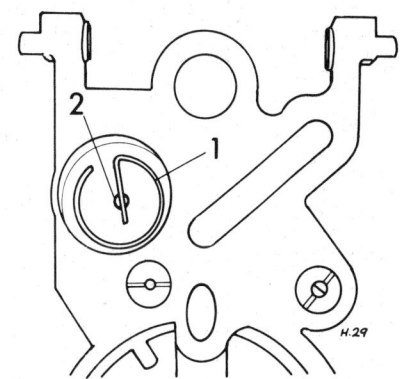

FIG. 3.15. LOCATION OF ACCELERATOR PUMP INLET BALL AND LOCATING CLIP IN THE EMULSION BLOCK

1 Locating clip   2 Ball

Fig.3.16. Location of accelerator pump lever

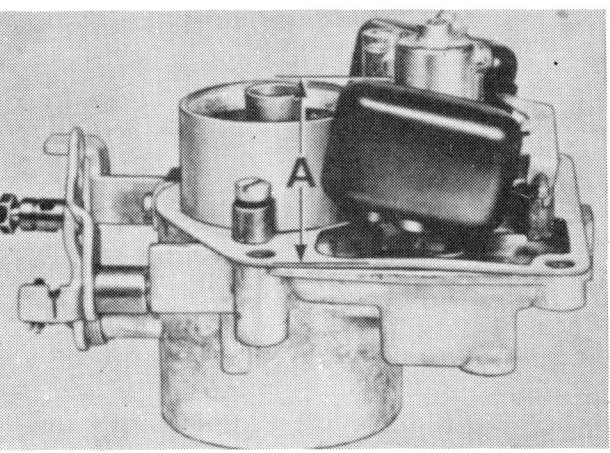

FIG.3.17. FLOAT LEVEL SETTING

A = 30.5 - 31.5 mm

Fig.3.18. Location of sealing ring

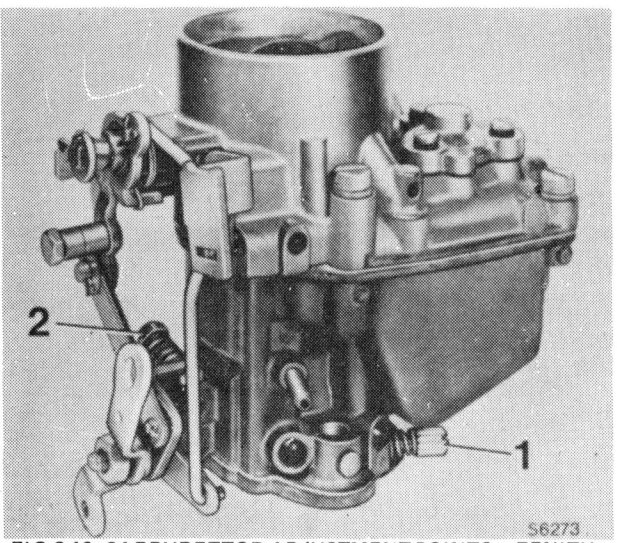

FIG.3.19. CARBURETTOR ADJUSTMENT POINTS – ZENITH 36IV SERIES

1   Volume control screen   2   Throttle stop screw

16 Refit the needle valve seating and special washer. Insert the needle.

17 Refit the float assembly and retain in position with the spindle. Hold the cover upside down and measure the distance from the bottom of the floats to the face of the cover gaskets. It should be 30.5 - 31.5 mm. Make any adjustments necessary by carefully bending the float arm centre tag which contacts the needle. This setting is important (Fig.3.17).

18 Before replacing the cover onto the body check that the sealing ring located as shown in Fig.3.18 is in good order. A bad seal will result in fuel leaking from the float chamber. Secure the cover with the four screws and spring washers. Take care because these are of different lengths.

19 Reconnect the accelerator pump linkage noting that the pin should always be fitted to the upper hole in the pump spindle lever.

20 The choke control rod is not provided with any obvious adjustment. With the choke flap held shut there should be a 0.040 inch (1 mm) gap down the side of the throttle flap. For this a number 61 drill is useful. Bend the control rod if necessary to obtain this setting.

21 The choke flap spindle return spring must engage the first notch on the lever.

10 Zenith 361 V carburettor - adjustment

1 If it is known that the reason for adjustment is something more than just slow running, then check the setting as described in the previous section.

2 Slow running is carried out by the throttle stop screw and volume control screw together. These are shown in Fig.3.19.

3 First run the engine until it has reached its normal operating temperature and then set the volume control screw 1½ turns out from full closed. Next set the throttle stop screw so that the engine runs fast enough not to stall. Adjust the volume control screw one way or the other so that the engine speed increases and then reduce speed using the throttle stop screw. Keep doing this in stages until the idle speed of 725 - 775 rpm with even running.

11 Zenith 361 VT carburettor - removal and replacement

1 Refer to Chapter 2 Section 2 and partially drain the cooling system.

2 Refer to Section 2 and remove the air cleaner assembly.

3 Slacken the two hose clips at the automatic choke unit and carefully detach the hoses.

4 Refer to Section 8 and follow the instructions given in paragraph 3 onwards.

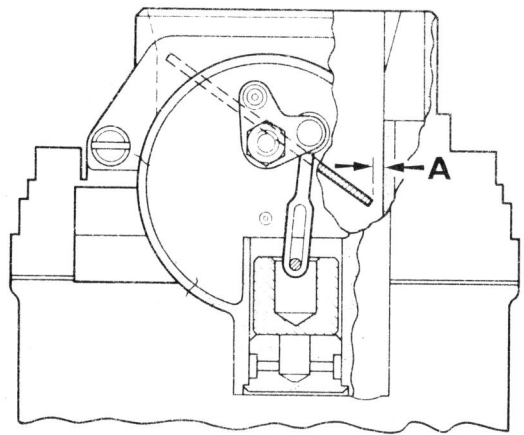

FIG.3.20. CHOKE FLAT SETTING

A = 2.8 mm

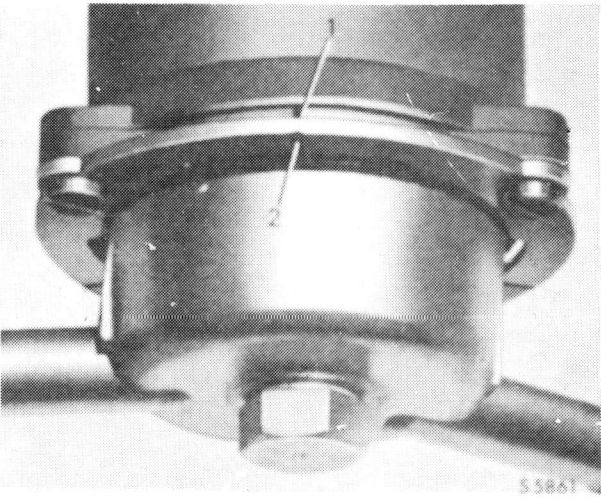

Fig. 3.21 Thermostat alignment marks

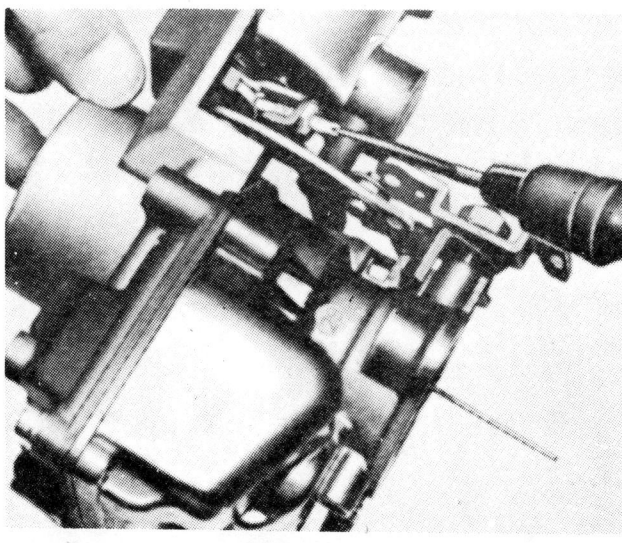

Fig.3.22. Adjustment of fast idle screw - Zenith 361 VT carburettor

12 Zenith 361 VT carburettor - dismantling and reassembly

1   The procedure for dismantling the main carburettor is basically identical to that as described for the 361 V type in section 9. However, disregard reference to the choke assembly.
2   Undo the two screws that retain the choke flap to the spindle and remove the choke flap.
3   Refer to Fig.3.11 and remove the three retaining screws and clamp that secure the thermostatic spring and water housing unit to the carburettor automatic choke housing. Lift away the housing from the choke housing.
4   Locate the three screws and spring washers that retain the automatic choke housing and spindle to the carburettor body. One screw is positioned on each side of the barrel and the other on the inside of the housing on the right of the piston bore. Undo and remove the screws and spring washers and remove the automatic choke housing and spindle.
5   Undo the choke spindle retaining nut and lift away the nut, plain washer and spindle.
6   Lift away the gasket, cam and choke lever.
7   Withdraw the piston from the bore.
8   Should it be necessary to separate the cover from the large solid metal disc undo and remove the centre bolt and washer.
9   Reassembly is the reverse sequence to dismantling but the following additional points should be noted:
a)   Check that all drillings relevant to the operation of the automatic choke are free from blockage.
b)   Before the thermostat housing is refitted assemble a new gasket, sealing washer and locating washer (serrated side facing outwards) onto the choke flap spindle.
c)   When the choke piston crank is assembled to the choke flap spindle with the piston at the bottom of the cylinder there must be a gap 'A' (Fig.3.20), between the choke flap and body of 2.8 mm. This is easily determined using a number 35 drill.
d)   When refitting the thermostat assembly make sure that the hook of the thermostat engages with the crankpin.
e)   When fully assembled the thermostat must be set so that the scribed line on the rim of the large solid metal disc is aligned with the mark on the clamping plate. This is shown in Fig.3.21.

13 Zenith 361 VT carburettor - adjustment

The adjustment sequence is identical to that as described in Section 10 with the exception that the fast idle screw must not be disturbed as it is set during initial assembly and should normally not require adjustment.

If this setting has been disturbed then it may be reset with the carburettor away from the engine. Fully close the choke flap and adjust the fast idle screw against the top step of the cam so as to give a gap at the edge of the throttle flap of 1.1 mm. Use a number 57 drill to ensure accuracy.

On cars fitted with automatic transmission the idling adjustment must be made with a drive range selected.

14 Zenith 361 VE carburettor - adjustment

Adjustment of this carburettor is basically identical to that of the 361 V type with the exception of the sealed calibration screw (see also Section 7).

It is important that the percentage of carbon monoxide (CO) in the exhaust gases at engine idle speed must be within the limits of 2.5 - 3.5% at normal engine operating temperature. For this exhaust gas analysis equipment is necessary.

On cars with automatic transmission, once the exhaust gas CO content has been checked at engine idle speed with one of the drive range selected, it must be rechecked in the 'Park' or 'Neutral' positions.

Should a smooth engine idle be difficult to obtain within the previously given limits, the spark plugs, contact breaker points, ignition timing and valve clearances must be checked and reset.

15 Zenith/Stromberg 175CD - 2S series carburettors - description

This type of carburettor has a single horizontal variable choke and is quite different in principle of operation to the fixed choke Zenith 361 VE series. The air intake is variably restricted by a cylindrical air valve which moves vertically.

A tapered needle is fitted to the base of the air valve and runs in and out of a fixed jet orifice through which fuel is drawn from the float chamber located beneath the main body. Suction from the engine inlet manifold passes through a hole in the base of the air valve to the suction chamber. This suction acts on the diaphragm, to which the air valve and metering needle are attached and raises them. This increases the air flow through the choke tube and the fuel flow through the jet as the tapered needle withdraws. As the air valve rises the degree of suction through the air valve hole is reduced and the valve reaches a point of equilibrium, balanced against the throttle opening and air valve height.

Sudden acceleration demands would apparently cause the air valve to rise sharply, thus tending to weaken the mixture. In fact the rise of the air valve is dampened by an oil controlled piston. Thus when the throttle is opened suddenly the initial suction is concentrated at the fuel jet and the quantity of air let through to reduce the mixture richness to normal occurs slightly later as the piston rises. The taper of the metering needle is obviously the main controlling feature of the carburettor's performance and this controls the fuel/air mixture at all heights of the valve. At the same time the height of the air valve is nicely balanced, according th throttle opening, in conjunction with the metering needle. The jet itself is adjustable by raising or lowering, thus altering the position of the jet orifice in relation to the taper of the needle.

For cold starts there is a special device mounted on the side and comprises a rotating disc with a number of holes drilled in it. When the disc is moved by the control lever a passage way is opened up. Depending on the number of holes uncovered so the fuel flow is restricted. The fuel from the float chamber can then be drawn direct into the choke tube supplementing that from the main jet.

The 175 CD - ST is fitted to cars with 2279 cc engines and automatic transmission and is basically similar to the 175 CD - 2S type with the exception that it has a water heated automatic cold start device instead of the normal manually operated disc type.

The cold start device supplies fuel to the mixing chamber to facilitate starting when the engine is cold and will continue to supply fuel in a gradually reducing amount as the engine warms up.

The tapered needle (see Fig.3.24) allows fuel into the carburettor mixing chamber and is operated by a thermostat lever which is moved under certain conditions by the vacuum kick rod and piston. The vacuum kick rod is cut away so as to allow partial independent movement of the thermostat lever. The thermostat lever and the fast idle cam are mounted on a common shaft and are interconnected by a spring which controls movement of the fast idle cam relative to the thermostat lever.

The location of the thermostat lever is controlled by a bi-metal spring thermostat which is heated by engine coolant water passing through the water jacket.

When starting the engine from cold the accelerator pedal must be depressed once and then released so as to allow the thermostat lever and fast idle cam to take up a rich position which will depend on the under bonnet temperature. Under these conditions the needle is lifted off its seating so as to allow fuel to pass through into the carburettor mixing chamber.

Once the engine is running inlet manifold vacuum is passed behind the piston which will then cause it to move against its spring. The movement is then transferred through the vacuum kick rod to the thermostat lever which will allow the needle to ride in a lower position thereby providing a weaker mixture whilst retaining a fast idle.

FIG.3.23. STROMBERG 175 CD - 2S SERIES CARBURETTOR COMPONENTS

1 Suction chamber cover screw	29 Screw
2 Damper assembly	30 Return spring
3 Retaining ring	31 Fast idle lever
4 Piston	32 Throttle lever
5 'E' clip	33 Lockwasher
6 Washer	34 Nut
7 Diaphragm	35 Throttle stop screw
8 Diaphragm retaining plate	36 Spring
9 Screw	37 Fast idle screw
10 Retaining ring	38 Locknut
11 Air valve spring	39 Cold start device
12 Jet	40 Screw
13 Jet spring	41 Lockwasher
14 'O' ring	42 Control cable bracket
15 Jet bush	43 Clip
16 Washer	44 Screw
17 Jet retainer	48 Float chamber
18 'O' ring	49 Gasket
19 Jet adjuster 'O' ring	50 Cover screw
20 Jet adjuster	51 Cover screw
21 'O' ring	52 Float
22 Air valve lifting pin	53 Float pivot pin
23 Pin spring	54 Needle valve
24 Clip	55 Washer
25 Needle	57 Insulator
26 Retaining screw	58 Gasket
27 Throttle spindle	59 Mounting stud
28 Throttle flap	60 Mounting nut
	61 Gasket - air filter

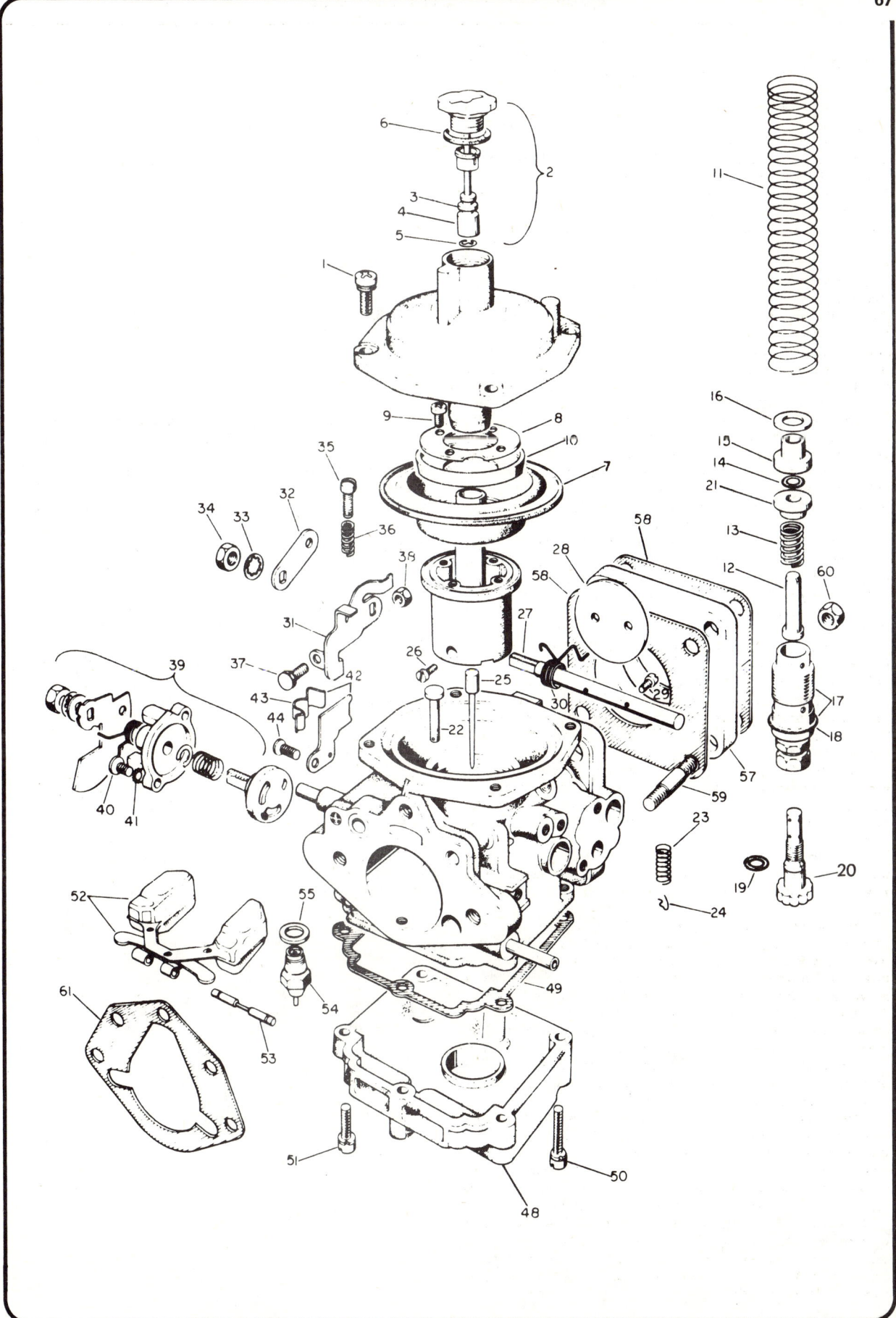

Should the accelerator pedal be depressed before the engine has reached its normal operating temperature the vacuum at the rear of the piston will drop allowing spring pressure to move the piston outwards. This movement is transferred to the needle which will ride a high position resulting in a richer mixture under open throttle conditions.

When the engine has reached its normal operating temperature the thermostat will allow the lever to completely seat the needle thereby stopping any fuel from entering the mixing chamber. The fast idle cam will then take up the normal running position.

Twin Zenith/Stromberg 175CD - 2S carburettors are used on the VX 4/90 models with manual transmission and they are basically identical to the single 175CD - 2S with the exception that a disc type cold start is fitted to the front carburettor only. A small pipe connects the front and rear carburettors together. The throttle control spindles are interconnected by a rod and two spring clamp couplings.

VX 4/90 models fitted with automatic transmission use two Zenith/Stromberg 175CD - 2ST carburettors and these are basically identical to the single 175CD - 2ST with the exception that the vacuum kick rod piston in the cold start device has no vacuum leak drilling.

16 Zenith/Stromberg 175CD - 2S - removal and replacement

1 Refer to Section 2 and remove the air cleaner.
2 Using a screwdriver ease the clip from the end of the clevis pin attaching the throttle inner cable yoke to the throttle yoke. Withdraw the clevis pin.
3 Unscrew the outer cable adjustment nut and locknut and detach from the support bracket.
4 Slacken the choke inner cable clamp screw and detach the outer cable clip from its support bracket. Withdraw the cable.
5 Detach the fuel feed pip from the carburettor and the distributor vacuum advance/retard pipe from the carburettor body.
6 Undo and remove the four nuts and washers that secure the carburettor to the inlet manifold. Also undo and remove the one bolt, spring and plain washer that secures the support bracket at the engine mounting upper end. Lift the carburettor from the studs.
7 Recover the gaskets and insulator from the inlet manifold.
8 Refitting the carburettor is the reverse sequence to removal but the following additional points should be noted:
a) A new gasket must be used between each mating face of the carburettor and insulator.
b) Top up the hydraulic damper with Castrol GTX so that the level is 0.030 in (8 mm) below the top of the air valve guide.

17 Zenith/Stromberg 175CD - 2S - dismantling and reassembly

1 With the carburettor on the bench, undo and remove the damper cap and plunger. Mark the relative positions of the suction chamber cover and main body and then undo and remove the four screws and spring washers which hold the suction chamber cover in place. Lift away the cover.
2 The air valve complete with needle and diaphragm may now be lifted away. Handle the assembly with the greatest of care as it is very easy to damage the needle accidently.
3 The bottom of the float chamber may next be removed. Undo and remove the six retaining screws and spring washers noting that they are of different lengths. Lift away the float chamber and gasket.
4 Withdraw the pin that acts as a pivot/retainer from the float assembly. Lift away the float assembly.
5 If desired, the needle may be removed from the air valve by slackening the small grub screw in the side of the piston (Fig.3.25).
6 To remove the diaphragm from the piston, simply undo the

four screws and washers which hold the diaphragm retaining ring in place.
7 Undo and remove the jet locking nut and carefully lift away the associated parts. Note the order of assembly.
8 Undo and remove the two screws and spring washers that secure the cold start device to the side of the main body.
9 On some versions of this carburettor a temperature compensator is fitted. It alters the amount of air which can by pass the main air valve and is controlled by a tapered plug operated by a bi-metal strip. Heat transferred to the carburettor body acts on the strip and makes fine adjustments to the air bleed. Do not tamper with it.
10 On reassembly there are several points which should be noted particularly. The first is that if fitting a new needle to the piston ensure it has the same markings stamped on it as the old one (Fig.3.26). Fit it so that the needle shoulder is perfectly flush with the base of the piston. This can be done by placing a metal rule across the base of the valve and pulling the needle out until it abuts the rule. The needle must lean away from the depression holes (Fig.3.27).
11 Thoroughly clean the piston and its cylinder in paraffin.
12 Refit the jet and associated parts, then the piston and finally the jet assembly.
13 Turn the mixture adjusting nut clockwise until the tip of the jet just stands proud into the choke tube. Now loosen the jet bush retainer about one turn so as to free the bush.
14 Allow the piston to fall. As it drops the needle will enter the orifice and automatically centralise it. With the needle still in the orifice tighten the jet assembly slowly frequently raising and dropping the piston 0.25 in (6.35 mm) to ensure the orifice bush has not moved. Finally check that the piston drops freely without hesitation and hits the bridge with a soft click.
15 Make sure that the holes in the diaphragm line up with the screw holes in the piston and retaining ring, and that the diaphragm is correctly positioned with the upper and lower tongues engaged in the slots in piston and body. Reassembly is otherwise a straightforward reversal of the dismantling sequence.
16 The cold start device can be set to operate in two positions. The two position stop can be set to control the maximum amount to which the unit may rotate. With the cross pin in the slot the device may rotate to its full extent but this is not usually needed unless the temperature drops below - 18°C (- 0.4°F). The fast idle cam operates against the throttle lever via an adjusting screw which may be set to ensure a suitably fast idling speed under cold start conditions (Fig.3.28).
17 To adjust the fast idle, the cold start cam must be set correctly in relation to the throttle flap. To do this put the cold start setting pin in the normal (vertical) position and press the cam against the end of the pin. Then move the adjusting screw on the throttle control lever against the cam until there is a gap between the throttle flap and carburettor body of 0.035 in (0.9 mm). Use a number 64 drill to assist in obtaining accuracy (Fig.3.29).

18 Zenith/Stromberg 175CD - 2S - float chamber fuel level setting

1 Refer to Section 2 and remove the air cleaner assembly.
2 Slacken the jet bush retainer and undo the six screws and spring washers which hold the float chamber to the base of the carburettor. Note that these bolts are of different lengths. Lift away the float chamber.
3 Turn the carburettor body upside down and accurately measure the highest point of the floats. This should be 15.5 - 16.5 mm above the flange which mates with the float chamber. During this operation make sure that the needle is against its seating. (Fig.3.30).
4 Should it be necessary to reset the level carefully bend the tag which bears against the end of the needle.
5 Recentre the jet after replacing the float chamber as described in Section 17, paragraph 13 and 14.

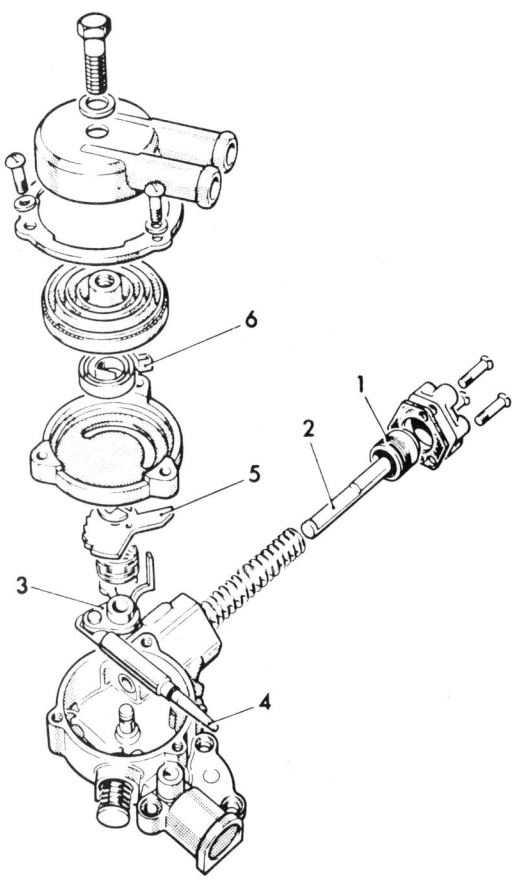

FIG.3.24. AUTOMATIC START DEVICE -
STROMBERG 175 CD–ST

1 Piston
2 Vacuum link rod
3 Thermostat - lever
4 Tapered needle
5 Fast idle cam
6 Thermostat bi-metal spring

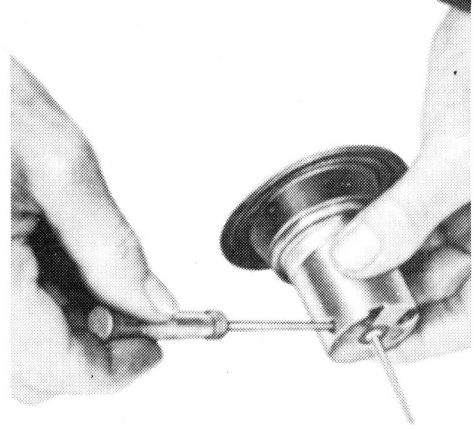

Fig.3.25. Removal of needle from piston

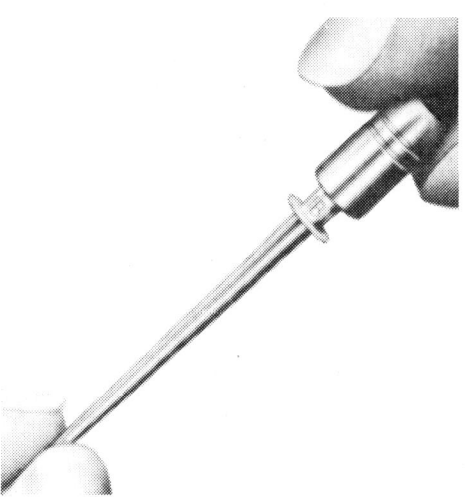

Fig.3.26. Needle identification

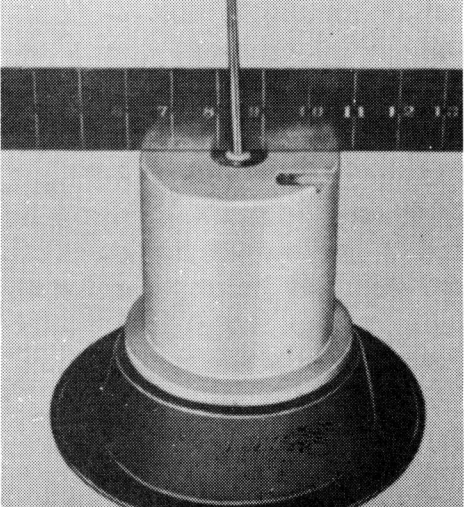

Fig.3.27. The needle shoulder must be flush with base of piston

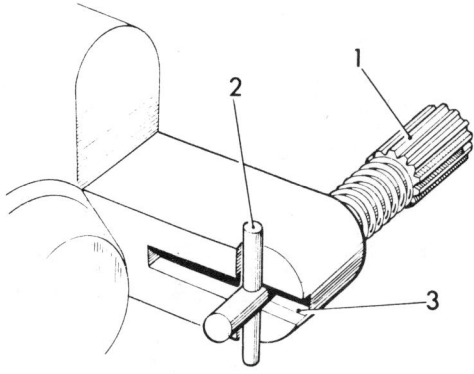

FIG.3.28. COLD START DEVICE SETTING

1 Spring loaded stop
2 Pin
3 Groove

19 Zenith/Stromberg 175CD - 2S - adjustment

1 As there is no separate idling jet, the petrol/air mixture for all conditions is supplied by the main jet and variable choke. Thus the strength of the mixture throughout the range depends on the height of the jet in the carburettor body and when the idling mixture is correct, the mixture will be correct throughout the range unless of course if the needle or jet are are worn.

2 A knurled screw at the base of the carburettor increases or decreases the strength of the mixture. Turning the screw clockwise raises the jet and weakens the mixture. Turning the screw anti-clockwise enriches the mixture. The engine idle speed is controlled by the throttle stop screw.

3 To adjust a Stromberg carburettor from scratch it is assumed that the fast idle cam has already been correctly set as described in Section 17, paragraphs 16 and 17. Start the engine and allow to run until it reaches its normal operating temperature. Refer to Section 2 and remove the air cleaner assembly.

4 Insert a 0.002 in (0.05 mm) feeler gauge between the air valve and carburettor body and screw in the jet adjusting screw until it touches the air valve (Fig.3.31). The feeler gauge should now be withdrawn and the adjuster unscrewed two complete revolutions. This will give an approximate setting. Start the engine and adjust the throttle stop screw so that the engine runs fairly slowly and smoothly (about 750 rpm) without oscillating on its mountings. To let the engine run smoothly at this speed it may be necessary to turn the jet adjuster nut a small amount in either direction.

5 To test if the correct setting has been found, lift the air valve piston 00.04 in (1 mm) with a small electrician's screwdriver. This is a very small amount and care must be taken to lift the piston only by this amount.

6 If the engine speed increases and stays at the new speed then the mixture is too rich. If it hesitates and is unstable it is too weak. Re-adjust the jet adjusting nut - see paragraph 2 - and recheck. All is correct when the engine speed rises momentarily and then drops when the air valve piston is lifted the specified 0.04 in (1 mm).

7 Make sure that the air valve damper is correctly filled with engine oil. With the air cleaner assembly removed and the plunger withdrawn the level should be 0.25 in (6.35 mm) below the top of the air valve guide. Lift the air valve up with a finger placed through the air intake during the topping up operation. Use Castrol GTX. Refit the air cleaner.

20 Zenith/Stromberg 175CD - 2ST - removal and replacement

1 Refer to Chapter 2, Section 2 and partially drain the cooling system.

2 Refer to Section 2, and remove the air cleaner assembly.

3 Slacken the two hose clips at the automatic choke unit and carefully detach the hose.

4 Refer to Section 16, and follow the instructions given in paragraphs 2, 3 and 5 onwards.

21 Zenith/Stromberg 175CD - 2ST - dismantling and reassembly

1 The procedure for dismantling the main carburettor is basically identical to that as described for the 175CD - 2S type in Section 17.

2 It is not recommended that this item is tampered with but in the event of the owner deciding to investigate because of a malfunction the following instructions should be followed.

3 Upon reference to Fig.3.24 it will be seen that the water jacket, heat mass and heat insulator are held in position by a plate which is retained in position with three screws. These should first be removed and the assembly withdrawn.

4 Carefully remove the 'E' clip on the end of the pivot pin and

withdraw the fast idle cam and thermostat lever.

5 Undo and remove the three screws and spring washers that secure the end cover. Lift away the end cover and gasket. Carefully withdraw the vacuum kick assembly.

6 The needle may now be withdrawn through the hole in the top of the housing once the threaded plug has been removed.

7 The fast idle plunger is assembled with an internal 'C' clip and cannot be withdrawn from the housing. The thermostat and heat mass are produced as a calibrated assembly and must not be separated.

8 Probe all drillings with a piece of wire to ensure that they are not blocked. Make sure that the needle and piston move freely in their respective bores and also that the 'O' ring on the needle is not damaged. The pivot pin nut located at the rear of the housing must be tight.

9 When reassembling the fast idle cam and thermostat lever make sure that the lever peg engages in the taper needle slot and the spade in the flat in the vacuum kick rod (Fig.3.32).

10 The interconnecting spring must be fitted so that the inner end goes over the long arm of the thermostat lever and the other end hooks into the hole in the fast idle cam afterwards.

11 The clearance between the fast idle screw and cam (on the base circle) should be 0.020 in (0.5 mm) when the thermostat lever is rotated fully anticlockwise. The fast idle screw can be adjusted as required and resecured using Loctite grade AA.

12 When refitting the water jacket and cover make sure that the square loop on the thermostat spring engages with the peg on the thermostat lever.

13 Correct positioning of the thermostat after assembly is indicated by line up marks on the housing and rims. No variations may be made (Fig.3.33)

22 Zenith/Stromberg 175CD - 2ST - adjustment

The adjustment sequence is identical to that as described in Section 19. The engine idle speed screw is controlled by the screw 1 (Fig.3.34), whereas the fast idle screw 2 is set and sealed on assembly and adjustment should normally not be attempted in service.

If the fast idle cam should stick in the open position for some reason it can be moved back manually. Remove the screwed plug in the housing and insert a piece of 0.1875 in (4.7625 mm) diameter rod and push the thermostat lever and fast idle cam fully anticlockwise.

For this the rod must have a flat end. Before refitting the plug coat the threads with Loctite Grade AA.

On cars fitted with automatic transmission the idling adjustment must be carried out with a drive range selected.

23 Zenith/Stromberg 175CD - 2S (European Exhaust Emission Control) - adjustment

Adjustment of this carburettor is basically identical to that of the standard 175CD - 2S type with the exceptions that the exhaust emission must be within defined limits.

It is important that the percentage of carbon monoxide (CO) in the exhaust gases at engine idle speed must be within the limits of 2.5 - 3.5% at normal engine operating temperature. For this obviously exhaust gas analysis equipment is necessary.

On cars with automatic transmission, once the exhaust gas CO content has been checked at engine idle speed with one of the drive range selected, it must be rechecked in the 'Park' or 'Neutral' positions.

Should a smooth engine idle be difficult to obtain within the previously given limits the spark plugs, contact breaker points, ignition timing and valve clearances must be checked and reset as necessary.

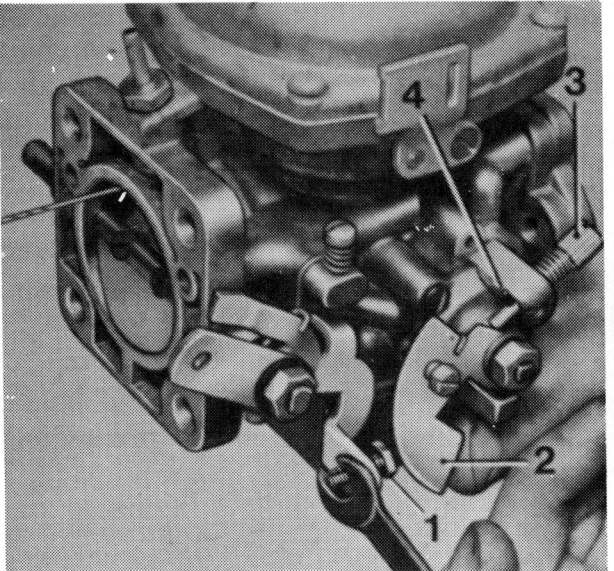

FIG.3.29. SETTING FAST IDLE

1 Stop screw   3 Stop
2 Fast idle cam   4 Stop pin

FIG.3.32. REFITTING POSITIONS OF FAST IDLE CAM AND THERMOSTAT LEVER

1 lever peg
2 Lever spade
3 Vacuum kick rod

FIG.3.30. FLOAT LEVEL SETTING

A = 15.5 – 16.5 mm

Fig.3.33. Alignment marks on housing and rims

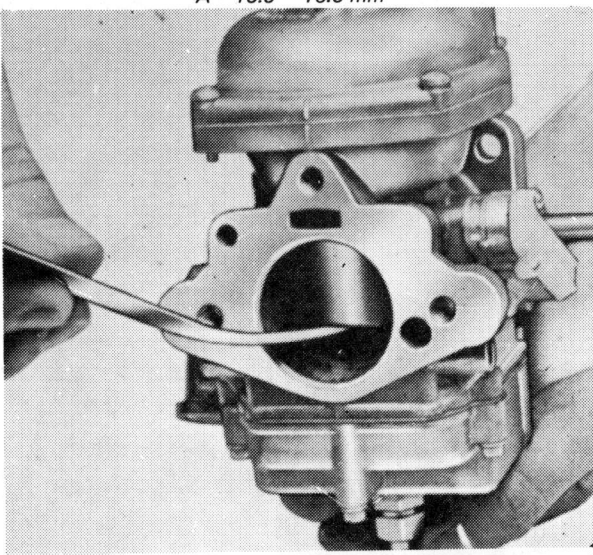

Fig.3.31. Insertion of feeler gauge between carburettor bore and pad on underside of air valve piston

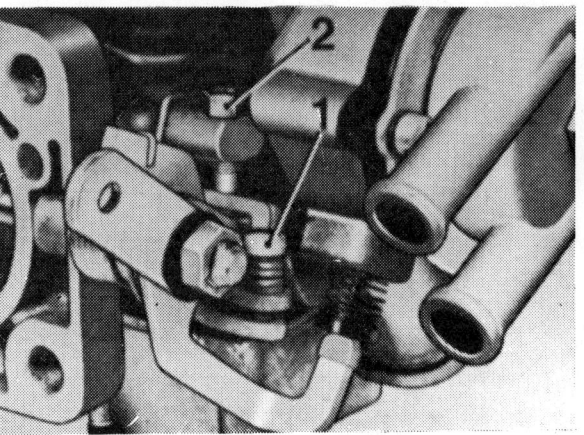

FIG.3.34. IDLE ADJUSTMENT – STROMBERG 175 CD–2ST

1 Screw - engine idle speed   2 Fast idle screw

FIG.3.35. CARBURETTOR LINKAGE - VX4/90 MODELS

1   Throttle coupling rear clamp bolt   2   Stop screw

24 Twin Zenith/Stromberg 175CD - 2S carburettors (VX 4/90) general

1   For a general description of the installation refer to Section 15.

2   Removal of the carburettors is basically identical to that described in Section 16 with the exception that the interconnecting rod also has to be disconnected. When reconnecting, with the throttle coupling rear clamp bolt slack make sure that the throttle spindle of the rear carburettor rotates freely in the coupling. Also make sure that the throttle cable is not holding the throttle abutment lever away from the stop screw. The coupling clamps must be positioned at 90° to one another.

3   To adjust the carburettors slacken one clamp bolt and then allow the engine to run until it reaches normal operating temperature. Adjust the throttle stop screw on each carburettor until an idle speed of 725 - 775 rpm is attained. Use of a piece of tubing to listen to the air hiss at the air intake will assist in this setting.

Retighten the clamp bolt: the final mixture setting may now be made to obtain smooth idling by turning each jet adjuster by an equal amount. Should the engine idle speed now be outside the limits the two throttle stop screws must be reset.

For cars being operated in areas under European Exhaust Emission Control it is important that the percentage of carbon monoxide (CO) in the exhaust gases at engine idle speed must be within the limits of 2.5 - 3.5% at normal engine operating temperature. For this exhaust gas analysis equipment is necessary.

On cars with automatic transmission, once the exhaust gas CO content has been checked at engine idle speed with one of the drive range selected it must be rechecked in the 'Park' or 'Neutral' positions.

Should a smooth engine idle be difficult to obtain and within the previously given limits the spark plugs, contact breaker points, ignition timing and valve clearance must be checked and reset as necessary.

25 Throttle control linkage

1   All models covered by this manual have a cable operated throttle control. Upon reference to Fig.3.36, it will be seen that the inner cable ball end locates in a bracket welded to the throttle pedal shaft lever.

2   The pedal and shaft position is governed by an adjustable pedal stop on the shaft lever and should be set to give a pedal angle of 20° from the vertical plane.

3   Any adjustment of the cable may be made at the threaded

sleeve and two nuts on the carburettor end of the outer cable. The nuts should be set to provide a small degree of slackness in the inner cable when the pedal stop is in contact with the bulkhead panel and the carburettor throttle lever is in the closed position.

4   A second cable, called a detent valve operating cable, is connected to a second bracket on the pedal shaft lever for models fitted with automatic transmission. The outer cover of the throttle cable at the pedal end is connected to a spring loaded over ride plunger in the casing, the latter being a push fit into a rubber sleeve contained in the cable housing.

The detent valve operating cable also has a spring loaded over ride plunger but this casing is screwed into the cable housing.

5   When adjusting the throttle cable on models fitted with an automatic choke it is important to ensure that the fast idle cam is not in operation before making any adjustment. This can be done by removing the air cleaner assembly (Section 2). On Zenith 361 V series carburettors hold the choke flap open and operate the throttle linkages so as to allow the fast idle cam to return to the normal running position. With Zenith/Stromberg 175CD - 2S series carburettors the fast idle cam may be returned manually to the normal running position by unscrewing the brass plug and inserting a piece of 0.1875 in (4.7625 mm) diameter rod and pushing the thermostat lever and fast idle cam fully anticlockwise. For this the rod must have a flat end. Before refitting the plug coat the threads with Loctite grade AA.

6   The detent cable is made up in two parts incorporating an adjuster. Should it be necessary to adjust this cable, unscrew the adjuster locknut and screw adjuster on the front cable casing until the threaded portion of casing protrudes through the adjuster. Make sure that the two cables are connected. Hold the accelerator pedal fully down and tension the inner cable by pulling the outer casings apart until the detent valve is felt to bottom against the stop. Hold this tension and rotate the adjuster until the flange on the rear casing is in contact with the adjuster. Turn back the adjuster half a turn and lock with the nut.

26 Fuel tank - removal and replacement

1   For safety reasons disconnect the battery. Make sure that there are no open flames in the vicinity. DO NOT smoke during this operation.

2   The tank outlet pipe is on the front of the tank and should be disconnected by pulling off the flexible pipe connection. If a recirculating fuel system is fitted a return tube is situated below the outlet tube and this should also be detached.

3   Detach the electric cable connection from the sender unit.

4   If the fuel tank is to be drained this should be done now by attaching a longer piece of pipe to the outlet and syphoning the contents out.

5   Slacken the clip securing the filler pipe to the tank neck (Fig.3.37).

6   Support the weight of the tank and undo and remove the five retaining bolts and spring washers. Lift away the fuel tank taking care not to spill any petrol left in the tank (Fig.3.38)

7   With time it is likely that sediment will collect in the bottom of the fuel tank. Condensation, resulting in rust and other impurities, is sometimes found in the fuel tank.

8   When the tank is removed, it should be rigorously flushed out and turned upside down and, if facilities are available, steam cleaned.

9   Repairs to the fuel tank to stop leaks are best carried out using resin adhesive and hardeners as supplied by most accessory shops. In cases of repairs being done to large areas, glass fibre mats or perforated Zinc sheet may be required to give the area support. If any soldering welding or brazing is contemplated, the tank must be steamed out to remove any traces of petroleum vapour. It is dangerous to use naked flames on a fuel tank without this, even though it may have been lying empty for a considerable period.

10   Refitting the fuel tank is the reverse sequence to removal.

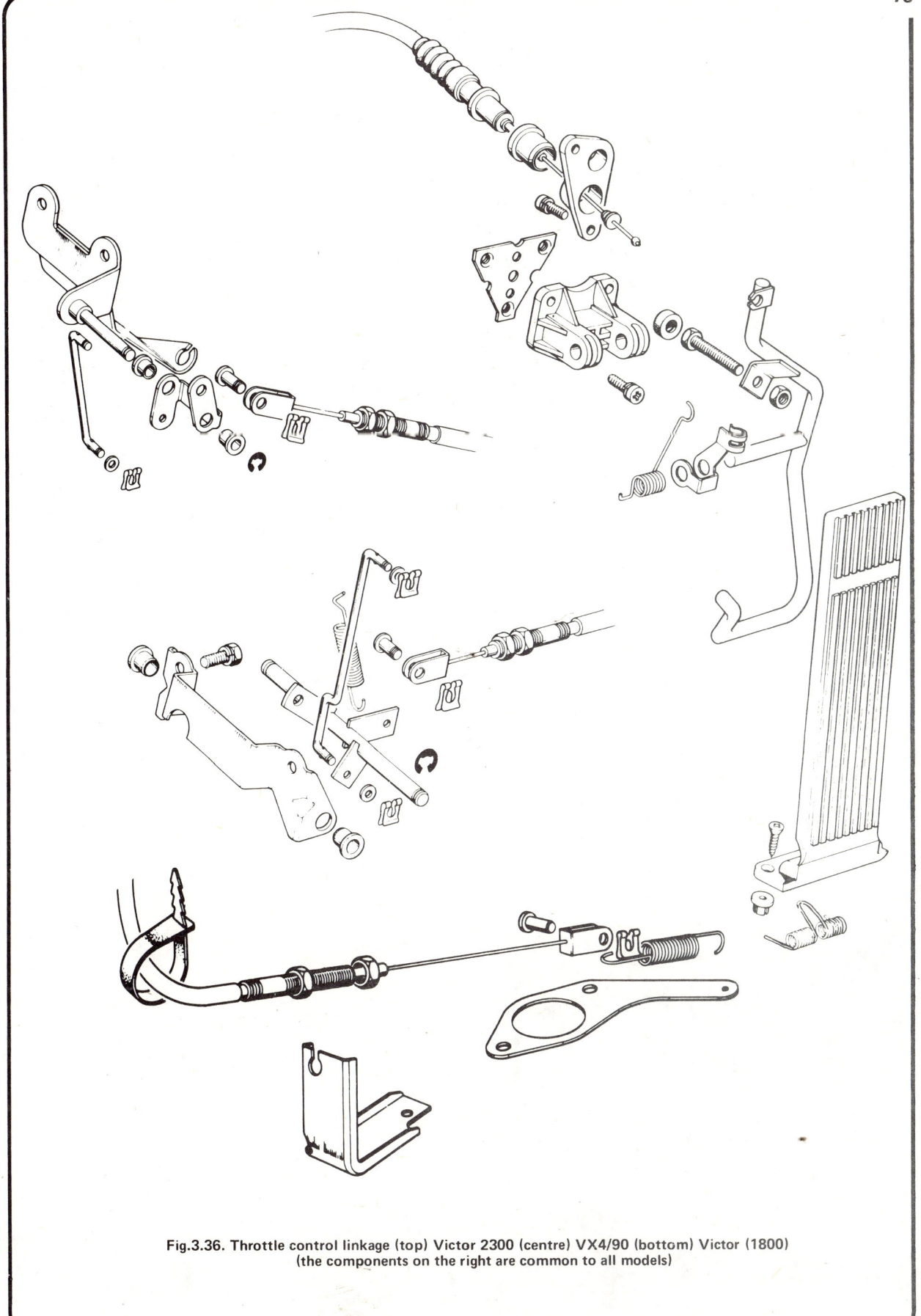

**Fig.3.36. Throttle control linkage (top) Victor 2300 (centre) VX4/90 (bottom) Victor (1800)
(the components on the right are common to all models)**

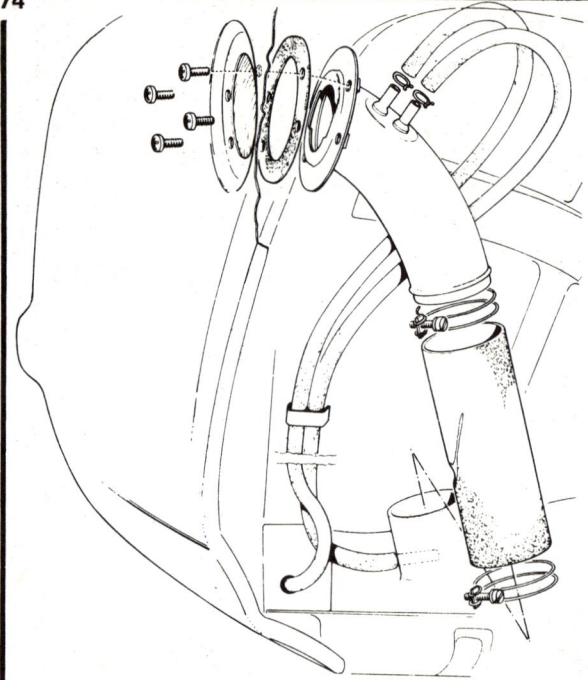

Fig.3.37. Fuel tank filler pipe and breather assembly

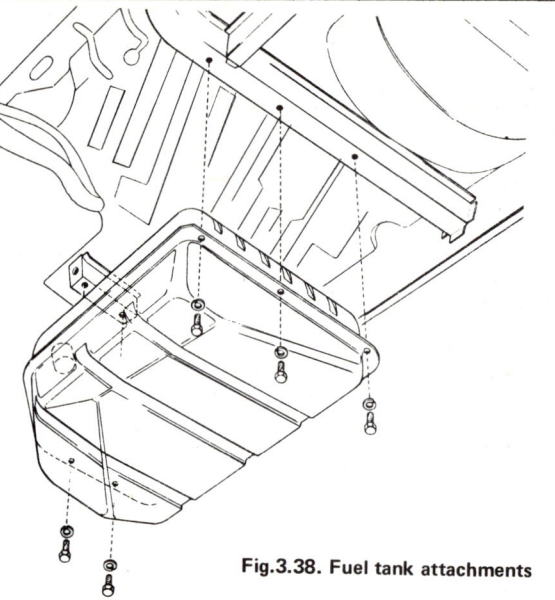

Fig.3.38. Fuel tank attachments

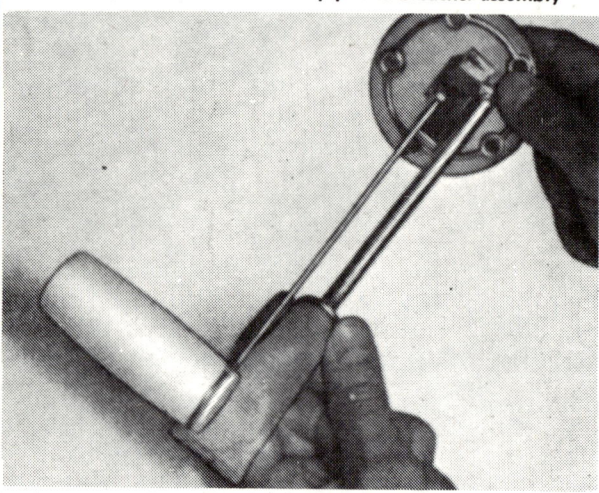

Fig.3.39. Fitting new filter to pick-up pipe

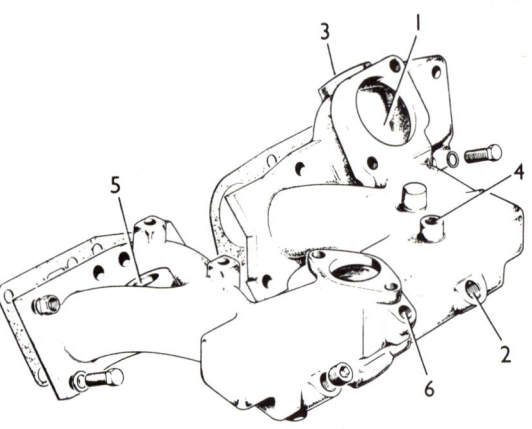

FIG.3.40. INLET MANIFOLD (1800 cc SHOWN)

1 Thermostat aperture
2 Water temperature gauge
   sender unit
3 Heater water hose
   connection

4 Brake servo vacuum pipe
5 Water pipe to pump
   connection
6 Breather pipe

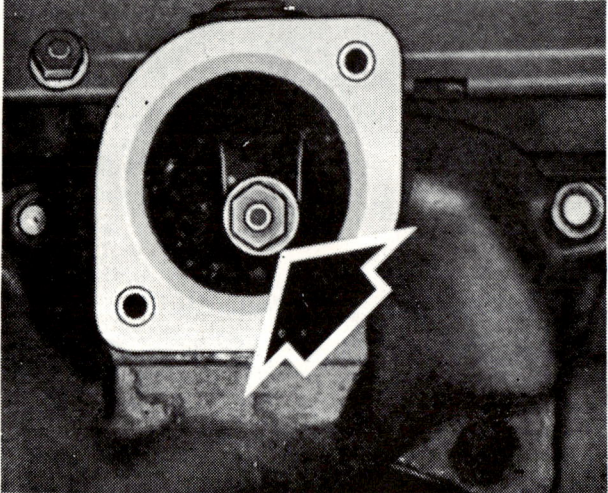

Fig.3.41. Location of inlet manifold nut and copper washer

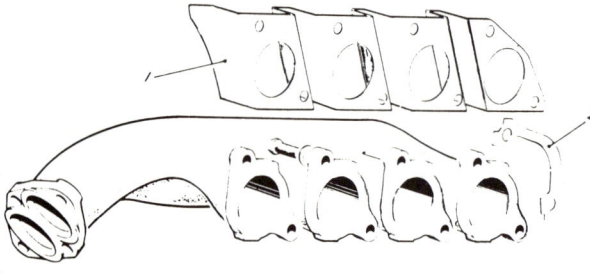

FIG.3.42. EXHAUST MANIFOLD AND HEAT SHIELD

1 Spark plug heat shield   2 Lock plate

27 Fuel gauge sender unit - fault finding

1   The sender unit is mounted on right hand front of the fuel tank and incorporates the outlet pipe. On models with the recirculation type fuel system the return pipe is also attached to the sender unit.

2   If the fuel gauge does not work correctly then the fault is either in the sender unit, the gauge in the instrument panel, the wiring or the voltage stabilizer.

3   The first test for operation is to switch on the ignition and observe if the fuel and temperature gauges operate. If only one operates it can be assumed the voltage stabilizer is satisfactory. However, if neither operates then check the stabilizer as described in Chapter 10.

4   To check the sender unit first disconnect the wire from the unit at the connector. Switch on the ignition and the gauge should read 'Empty'. Now connect the lead to earth and the gauge should read 'Full'. Allow 30 seconds for each reading.

5   If both of these situations are correct then the fault lies in the sender unit.

6   If the gauge does not read 'Empty' with the wire disconnected from the sender unit, the wire should then also be disconnected from the gauge to the sender unit.

7   If not, the gauge is faulty and should be replaced. (For details see Chapter 10).

8   With the wire disconnected from the sender unit and earthed, if the gauge reads anything other than 'FULL' check the rest of the circuit (see Chapter 10 for the wiring diagram).

9   To remove the unit, first make sure that the level of fuel in the tank is below the lower edge of the unit mounting flange.

10 Disconnect the battery and then the sender unit wire. Also detach the fuel line/s. Undo and remove the six mounting screws and spring washers. Carefully withdraw the sender unit so that the wire or float are not damaged or bent. Similarly the fuel pick up pipe must not be bent otherwise its position relative to the bottom of the tank will be upset. Recover the flange gasket.

11 If it is necessary to fit a new pick up pipe filter, first smear Loctite Grade AVV around the pipe at approximately 1.6 in (40 mm) from the end. Hold the filter end cap, push onto the pipe taper and rotate the cap to wedge the filter right on the pipe.

Align the filter and parallel with the float (Fig.3.39)

12 Refitting the fuel tank sender unit is the reverse sequence to removal. If possible always use a new gasket. The flange must be positioned so that the electrical blade terminal is directly to the right of the outlet tube.

28 Inlet manifold, exhaust manifold and system - general

The cylinder head has individual valve ports with the inlet manifold fitted on the right hand side and the exhaust manifold on the left hand side. The inlet manifold incorporates a hot water jacket to assist fuel vaporization. The cooling system thermostat is located in the water jacket aperture. Other connections are available for water temperature gauge unit, heater water hose connector, brake servo vacuum pipe, water pipe to water pump connection and breather pipe.

Before removing the inlet manifold, the cooling system must be partially drained (see Chapter 2, Section 2) and then the thermostat removed. This will give access to one nut and copper washer located inside the manifold.

Prior to refitting smear a little sealing compound to either side of the gaskets around the holes corresponding with the water passage between the cylinder head and manifold. Always smear the stud, new copper washer and nut with a sealing compound before refitting inside the manifold.

The exhaust manifold is secured with nuts or bolts and spring washers. Additionally the bolts are retained with lock plates. Removal is straightforward, access to the lower bolts being gained from under the car. Always ensure that the spark plug heat shield is refitted between the manifold and cylinder head. When refitting to the downpipe tighten the centre nuts of the exhaust pipe flange evenly and then the other two nuts. Recheck tightness of the first two nuts.

The exhaust system consists of a twin branch downpipe, a front intermediate pipe and silencer and a rear pipe resonator having a single tail pipe. Support for the silencer and tail pipes is by rubber rings which are hooked to under body panel mounted brackets. It is important that there is a gap of at least 1 inch (25 mm) between any part of the exhaust system and the under body panels.

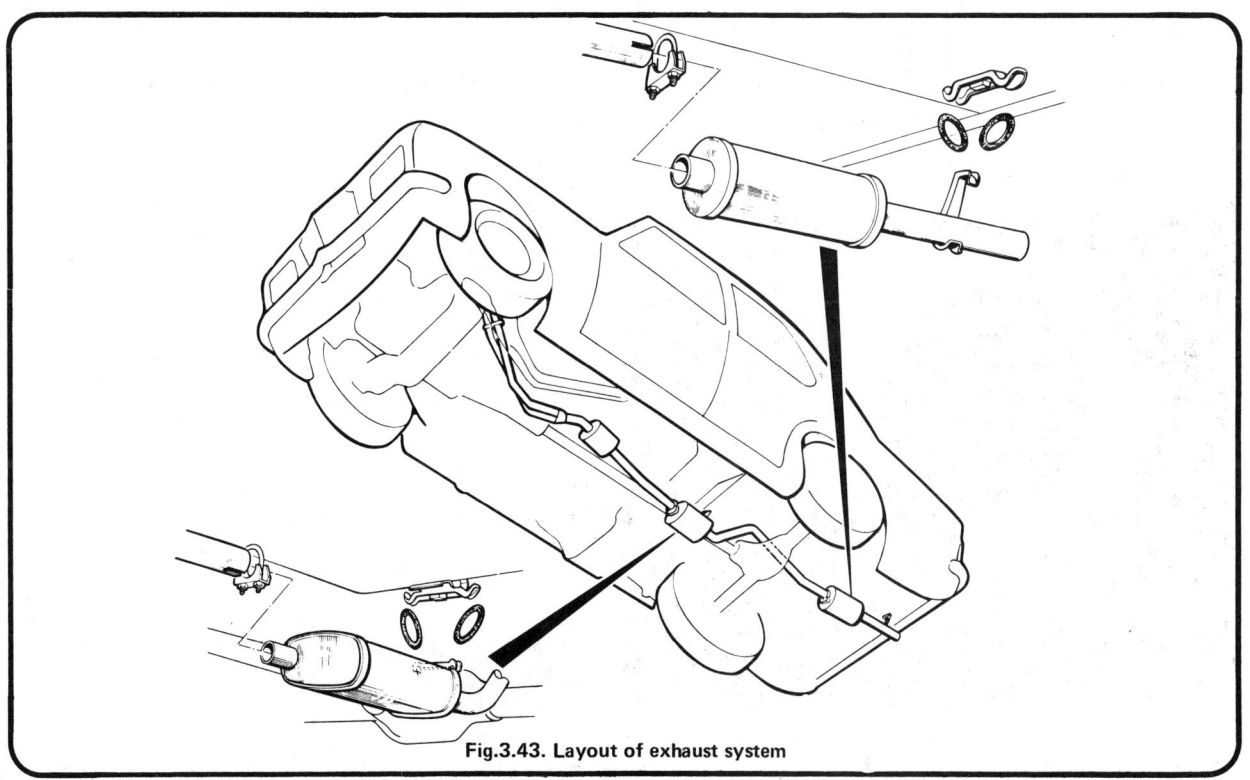

Fig.3.43. Layout of exhaust system

Fault diagnosis

Unsatisfactory engine performance and excessive fuel consumption are not necessarily the fault of the fuel system or carburettor. In fact they more commonly occur as a result of ignition faults. Before acting on the fuel system it is necessary to check the ignition system first. Even though a fault may lie in the fuel system it will be difficult to trace unless the ignition is correct.

The table below therefore, assumes that the ignition system is in order.

Symptom	Reason/s	Remedy
Smell of petrol when engine is stopped	Leaking fuel lines or unions Leaking fuel tank	Repair or renew as necessary. Fill fuel tank to capacity and examine carefully at seams, unions and filler pipe connections. Repair as necessary.
Smell of petrol when engine is idling	Leaking fuel line unions between pump and carburettor Overflow of fuel from float chamber due to wrong level setting or ineffective needle valve or punctured float	Check line and unions and tighten or repair. Check fuel level setting and condition of float and needle valve and renew if necessary.
Excessive fuel consumption for reasons not covered by leaks or float chamber faults	Worn needle Sticking needle	Renew needles. Check correct movement of needle body.
Difficult starting, uneven running, lack of power, cutting out	One or more blockages Float chamber fuel level too low or needle sticking Fuel pump not delivering sufficient fuel Intake manifold gaskets leaking, or manifold fractured	Dismantle and clean out float chamber and body. Dismantle and check fuel level and needle. Check pump delivery and clean or repair as required. Check tightness of mounting nuts and inspect manifold.

Chapter 4 Ignition system

Contents

Specifications

Spark plugs:

1759 cc engine	AC R41TS
2279 cc engine	AC R42TS
Electrode gap - normal running	0.030 in (0.75 mm)
running in	0.026 in (0.65 mm)

Coil: ... ... Delco-Remy

Type ... ... Oil filled, LT resistor in circuit bypassed for additional starting voltage

Coil feed resistance ... ... 2 ohms

Distributor: ... ... Delco-Remy D300

Rotation	Anti-clockwise
Firing order	1 3 4 2
Contact breaker points gap - new	0.022 in (0.55 mm)
used	0.020 in (0.5 mm)
Contact arm spring tension	22 - 26 ounces
Cam dwell angle	35 - 37°
Mainshaft clearances in bushes	0.0001 - 0.0011 in (0.003 - 0.028 mm)
Mainshaft end float	0.085 - 0.175 in (2.12 - 4.44 mm)

Ignition timing: ... ... 9° BTDC

Vacuum advance:

Vacuum (in.Hg.)	Distributor degrees
4	0
6	0 - 2½
7 and over	1½ - 3½

Centrifugal advance:

1759 cc engine

Cut in speed ... ... 350 - 550 rpm

Distributor rpm	Distributor degrees
350	0
550	0 - 4½
750	4½ - 8
1000	7 - 9
1500	9 - 11½
2000	11½ - 13½
2500 and over	12½ - 14½

2279 cc engine

Cut in speed ... ... 375 - 525 rpm

Distributor rpm	Distributor degrees
375	0
525	0 - 2
600	1 - 3
900	4½ - 7
1250	6½ - 9
2000	9 - 11
2500	10½ - 12½

Distributor rpm	Distributor degrees
2750 and over	11 - 13½

Torque wrench settings:

Spark plugs	15 lb ft	2.07 kg m

1 General description

In order that the engine can run it is necessary for an electrical spark to ignite the fuel/air mixture in the combustion chamber at exactly the right moment in relation to the engine speed and load.

The ignition system is based on feeding low tension voltage from the battery to the ignition coil where it is converted to high tension voltage. The high tension voltage is powerful enough to jump the spark plug gap in the cylinders many times a second under high compression pressures, providing that the system is in good condition and that all adjustments are correct.

The ignition system is divided into two circuits. The low tension circuit and the high tension circuit.

The low tension (sometimes known as the primary) circuit consists of the battery, lead to the control box, lead to the ignition switch, lead from the ignition switch to the low tension or primary coil windings (terminal SW), and the lead from the low tension coil windings (terminal CB) to the contact breaker points and condenser in the distributor.

The high tension circuit consists of the high tension or secondary coil windings, the heavy duty ignition lead from the centre of the coil to the centre of the distributor cap, the rotor arm, and the spark plug leads and spark plugs.

The system functions in the following manner: High tension voltage is generated in the coil by the interruption of the low tension circuit. The interruption is effected by the opening of the contact breaker points in the low tension circuit.

High tension voltage is fed via the carbon brush in the centre of the distributor cap to the rotor arm of the distributor.

The rotor arm revolves anti clockwise at half engine speed inside the distributor cap, and each time it comes in line with one of the four metal segments in the cap, which are in turn connected to the spark plug leads, the opening and closing of the contact breaker points causes the high tension voltage to build up, jump the gap from the rotor arm to the appropriate metal segment and so via the spark plug lead to the spark plug, where it finally jumps the spark plug gap before going to earth.

The ignition is advanced and retarded automatically, to ensure the spark occurs at just the right instant for the particular load at the prevailing engine speed.

The ignition advance is controlled both mechanically and by a vacuum operated system. The mechanised governor mechanism comprises two weights, which move out from the distributor shaft as the engine speed rises, due to centrifugal force. As they move outwards they rotate the cam relative to the distributor shaft, and so advance the spark. The weights are held in position by two springs and it is the tension of these springs which is largely responsible for correct spark advancement.

The vacuum control comprises a diaphragm, one side of which is connected via a small bore tube to the carburettor, which varies with engine speed and throttle opening, causing the diaphragm to move, so moving the contact breaker plate, and advancing or retarding the spark. A fine degree of control is achieved by a spring in the vacuum assembly.

2 Distributor rotor - removal and replacement

1 Having removed the distributor cap by first releasing the two spring clips, undo and remove the two securing screws and spring washers that secure the rotor to the main shaft and cam assembly.
2 Carefully lift the rotor upwards and away from the distributor.

3 It will be observed that on the underside of the rotor there are two locating pegs. One is round and the other square. These must fit into the corresponding holes in the mainshaft and cam assembly when the rotor is refitted (Fig.4.2).
4 The contact spring on the rotor must not be bent or damaged in any way. The height of the spring should be set to 1.38 - 1.44 in (35 - 37 mm) above the base of the rotor as shown in Fig.4.3 .
5 Refitting the rotor is the reverse sequence to removal. The two retaining screws and spring washers must be tightened firmly but not overtight otherwise the rotor could fracture.

3 Contact breaker points - adjustment

1 To adjust the contact breaker points first release the two clips that secure the distributor cap to the distributor body. Lift away the cap.
2 Clean the cap inside and out with a dry cloth. It is unlikely that the four segments will be badly burned or scored, but if they are, the cap will have to be renewed.
3 Check the carbon brush insert located in the top of the cap to make sure that it is not broken or missing.
4 To give better access to the contract breaker points the rotor should be removed as described in Section 2.
5 Gently prise the contact breaker points open to examine the condition of their faces. If they are rough, pitted or dirty, it will be necessary to remove them for resurfacing or for replacement points to be fitted.
6 Presuming the points are satisfactory, or that they have been cleaned and refitted, measure the gap between the points by turning the engine over until the contact breaker arm is on the peak of one of the four cam lobes.
7 A 0.020 in (0.5 mm) feeler gauge should now just fit between the points (0.002 in (0.55 cm) for new points).
8 If the gap varies from this amount, slacken the two securing screws (Fig.4.4) .
9 Adjust the contact gap by inserting a screwdriver in the slot in the fixed plate and levering it. It is best to do this with the securing screws holding the plate sufficiently to prevent uncontrolled movement.
10 Always check the gap again after tightening the screws. Sometimes during the final tightening the points are moved slightly from their original setting.

4 Contact breaker points - removal and replacement

1 Release the two spring clips and remove the distributor cap. Undo and remove the two securing screws and spring washers that secure the rotor to the mainshaft and cam assembly.
2 Carefully lift the rotor upwards and away from the distributor. Refer to Section 2, paragraph 3 for information on the correct location of the rotor arm.
3 Unscrew and remove the two screws that secure the contact breaker points to the mounting plate.
4 Carefully ease the end of the moving contact spring out of the insulator.
5 Lift the complete contact set assembly from the pivot pin of the mounting plate.
6 If the condition of the points is not too bad they can be reconditioned by rubbing the contacts clean with fine emery cloth or a fine carborundum stone. It is important that the faces are rubbed flat and parallel to each other so that there will be complete face to face contact when the points are closed. One of the points will be pitted and the other will have a deposit on it.

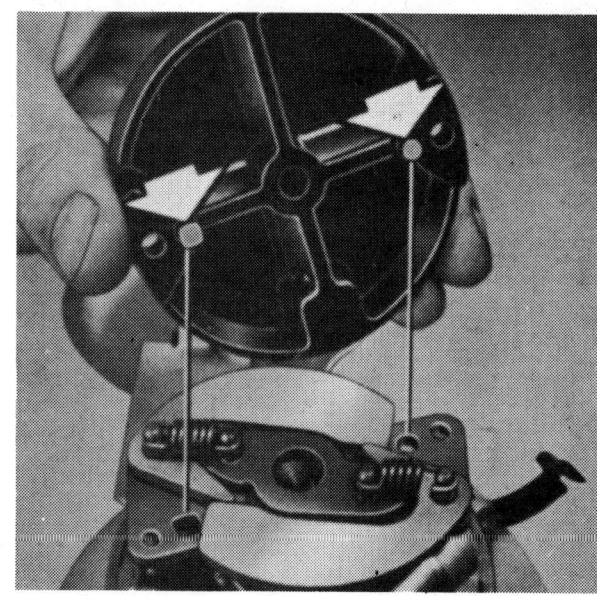

Fig.4.2. Lifting away rotor

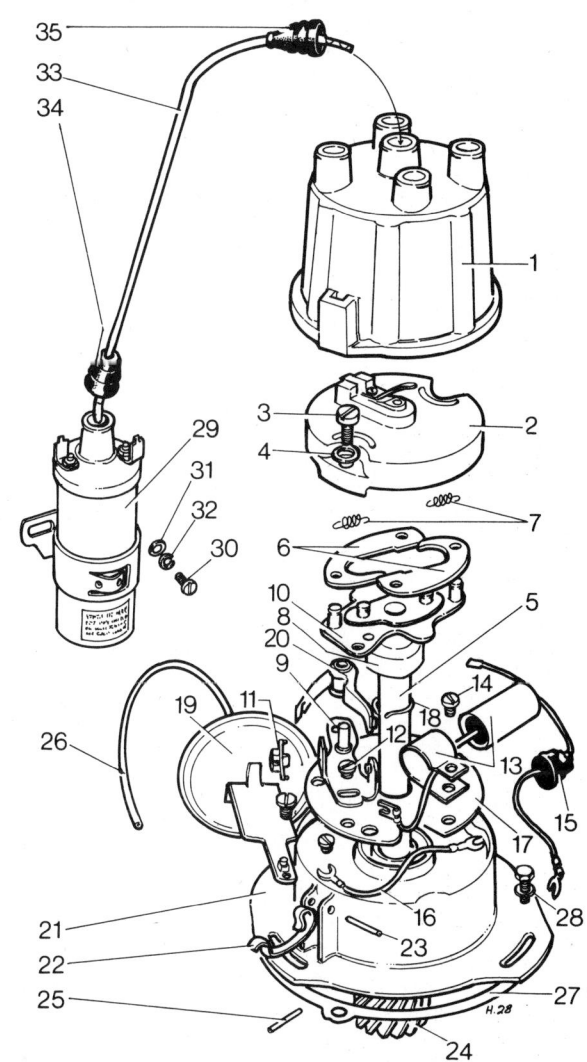

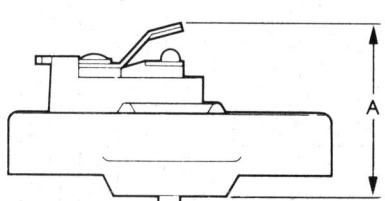

FIG.4.3. DISTRIBUTOR ROTOR—CONTACT SPRING HEIGHT

A = 1.38 - 1.44 inch (35.0 - 37.0 mm)

FIG.4.1. COMPONENT PARTS OF DISTRIBUTOR

1 Distributor cap	19 Vacuum advance unit
2 Rotor	20 Screw
3 Rotor securing screw	21 Base
4 Lockwasher	22 Cap clip
5 Mainshaft	23 Spring pin
6 Bob weights	24 Drive gear
7 Bob weight spring	25 Gear retaining pin
8 Cam assembly	26 Suction pipe
9 Retainer clip	27 Gasket (early fitment
10 Contact points	only)
11 Insulator clip	28 Securing screw
12 Contacts locking screw	29 Coil and bracket
13 Condenser bracket	30 Mounting screw
14 Condenser fixing screw	31 Plain washer
15 LT lead and grommet	32 Lockwasher
16 Earth lead	33 HT lead
17 Contact breaker plate	34 Seal
18 Felt washer	35 Seal

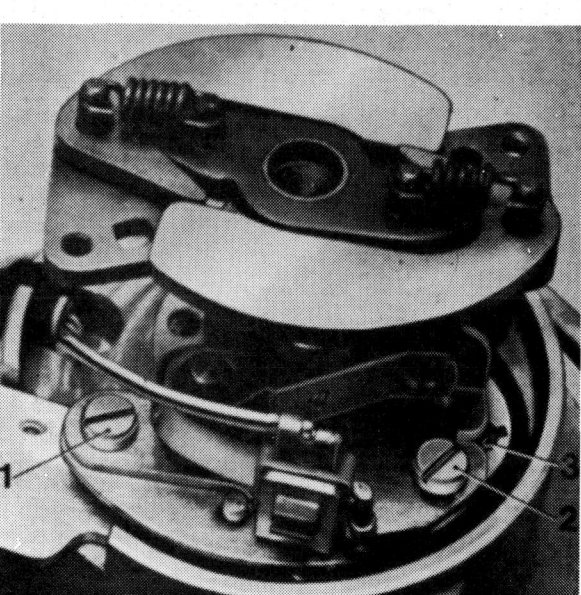

FIG.4.4. CONTACT BREAKER POINTS—ROTOR REMOVED

1 Points assembly fixing screw
2 Points assembly fixing screw
3 Screwdriver adjustment slot

7 It is necessary to remove completely the built up deposits, but not necessary to rub the pitted point right down to the stage where all the pitting has disappeared, although obviously if this is done it will prolong the time before the operation of refacing the points has to be repeated.

8 Thoroughly clean the points before refitting them. Locate the fixed contact plate over the base of the pivot pin and then fix the moving contact into position so that the end of the spring fits over the centre boss of the nylon insulator lug ((Fig.4.5). Refit the two fixing screws.

9 Press in the condenser and coil lead tags to the nylon insulator lug. The contact breaker points gap should now be reset as described in Section 3.

10 Refit the rotor and finally the distributor cap.

5 Condenser - removal, testing and replacement

1 The purpose of the condenser (sometimes known as a capacitor) is to ensure that when the contact breaker points open there is no arcing across them which would cause rapid deterioration of the points and inefficient operation of the ignition system.

2 The condenser is fitted in parallel with the contact breaker points. If it develops a short circuit is will cause complete ignition system failure as the points will be prevented from interrupting the low tension circuit.

3 If the engine becomes difficult to start or begins to misfire whilst running and the contact breaker points show signs of excessive burning, then the condition of the condenser must be suspect. A further test can be made by separating the points by hand with the ignition switched on. If this is accompanied by a bright spark at the contact breaker points it is indicative that the condenser has failed.

4 Without special test equipment the only sure way to diagnose condenser trouble is to replace a suspected unit with a new one and note if there is any improvement.

5 To remove the condenser from the distributor, first remove the rotor arm as described in Section 2. Carefully pull out the condenser head lip from the nylon insulator where it fits behind the contact point spring and ignition coil LT wire terminal.

6 Undo and remove the condenser mounting bracket securing screw, withdraw the black earth lead terminal and then lift away the condenser.

7 Refitting the condenser is the reverse sequence to removal. Take particular care that the condenser wire cannot short circuit against any portion of the contact breaker point assembly.

6 Distributor - removal and replacement

1 To remove the distributor, first mark the HT leads so that they may be refitted to the correct spark plugs upon replacement. Detach the leads from the spark plugs.

2 Pull off the plastic cover and release the HT lead from the centre of the ignition coil by pulling sharply.

3 Pull off the vacuum hose from the vacuum unit on the side of the distributor.

4 Detach the low tension wire from the ignition coil.

5 It is not possible to remove and replace the distributor without having to reset the ignition timing. Removal and replacement is therefore dealt with in Section 8. 'Ignition timing'

6 The distributor is held in place by three bolts and plain washers through slotted holes in the base flange. When these bolts have been removed the distributor can be lifted straight out.

7 Replacement of the distributor must follow the sequence as described in Section 8. ·

7 Distributor - dismantling and reassembly

1 Before a distributor is dismantled the following points should

be noted:

a) If the shaft bushes are worn a complete base assembly must be obtained as bushes are not supplied separately by Vauxhall.

b) With the exception of the rotor and contact breaker points other parts may not be readily obtainable. It is very important to be quite sure of the type of distributor fitted before changing weights, springs or mainshaft cam. The specifications at the beginning of this chapter indicate the types available. The distributor for use on the 1759cc engine can be identified by a green tag on the low tension wire, whilst that for use on the 2279cc engine is marked with a blue plastic tape tag.

c) If the distributor is seriously worn it may be more satisfactory in the long run to change the whole unit for a new one.

2 Begin dismantling by removing the rotor, contact breaker points and condenser as previously described in Sections 4 and 5.

3 Carefully remove the circlip at the top end of the mainshaft and detach the contact breaker points mounting plate from the base assembly (Fig.4.6).

4 Using a suitable diameter parallel pin punch carefully tap out the spring pin that secures the drive gear to the mainshaft (Fig.4.7).

5 If items are to be replaced take care to note the numbers stamped on them which identify the type for each engine. Additionally the mainshaft may be identified by the number 081 (1759cc engine) or 064 (2279cc engine) stamped on the plate. Cams are identified by the number 27 (1759cc engine) or 25 (2279cc engine) stamped on the underside of the cam base plate. Advance weights used are all stamped with the number 53. The advance weight springs are the same for both distributors and are identified by blue and black paint marks at the end of the spring (Fig.4.8).

6 When reassembling the distributor make sure the felt oil retainer engages correctly in the slot in the main base before replacing the contact breaker plate. Soak the felt in Castrol GTX before refitting (Fig.4.9).

7 If a new drive shaft is to be fitted the gear pin hole will need to be drilled using a 0.125 in (3.175 mm) diameter drill. It should be arranged so that the angle between the centre line of any gear tooth and the centre line of the drive slot is 70° as shown in Fig.4.10. Also ensure that there is an end float of 0.085 - 0.175 in (2.16 - 4.44 mm).

8 Always smear a little Castrol LM Grease on the link end of the vacuum control arm before reconnecting. Also lubricate the distributor drive gear with a little graphite grease.

8 Ignition timing

1 The procedure for setting the ignition timing is described from the point of installing the distributor. If the distributor has not been removed and the timing is known to be in need only of an adjustment, then the procedure leading up to this stage can be ignored. Only the final setting of the opening of the points gap is necessary.

2 With the distributor removed rotate the crankshaft until No. 1 piston is on the compression stroke (removal of No. 1 spark plug and a thumb over the spark plug hole will ensure compression is felt). Continue to rotate the crankshaft until the 9° BTDC mark on the engine front cover. is aligned with the crankshaft pulley mark. (Fig.4.11).

3 Using a pair of pointed pliers move the oil pump tongue to the position shown in Fig.4.12

4 Prepare the mating faces of the distributor body flange and the oil pump flange by cleaning them thoroughly and applying a thin coat of Hylomar SQ 32/M jointing compound to the oil pump flange.

5 Hold the distributor over the installation position with the vacuum unit facing towards the fuel pump and the rotor contact at the 11 o'clock position as seen when looking down on the distributor from the side of the engine (see Fig.4.13)

6 Lower the distributor into position and it should be noted that as the gear helix engages the rotor moves round clockwise to

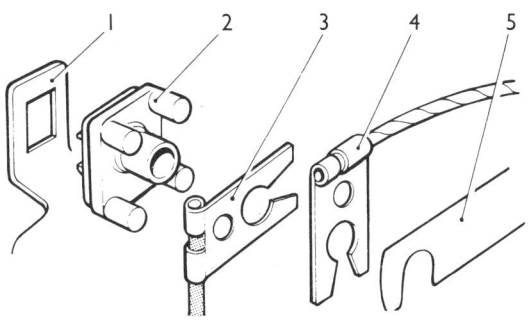

FIG.4.5. CORRECT ASSEMBLY ORDER OF CONTACT BREAKER POINTS & CONDENSER LEADS

1 Base plate lug
2 Insulator/connector
3 Condenser wire
4 LT wire from ignition coil
5 Contact breaker point spring

Fig.4.6. Location of circlip retaining contact breaker points mounting plate

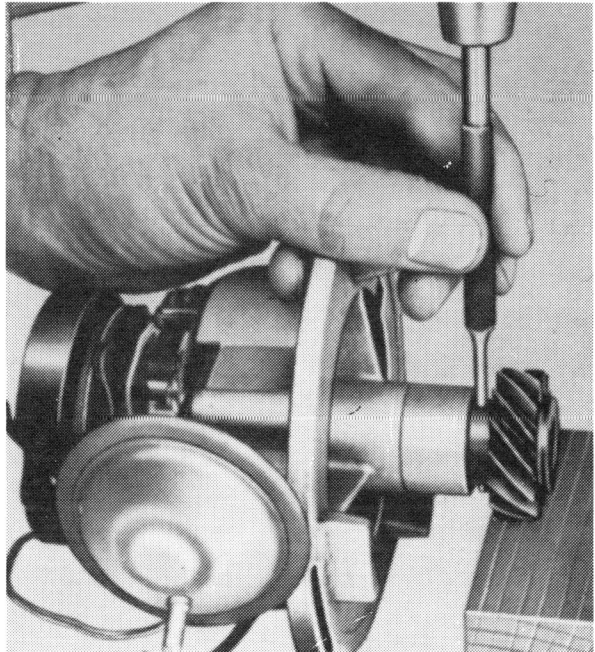

Fig.4.7. Use of parallel pin punch to drift out skew gear spring pin

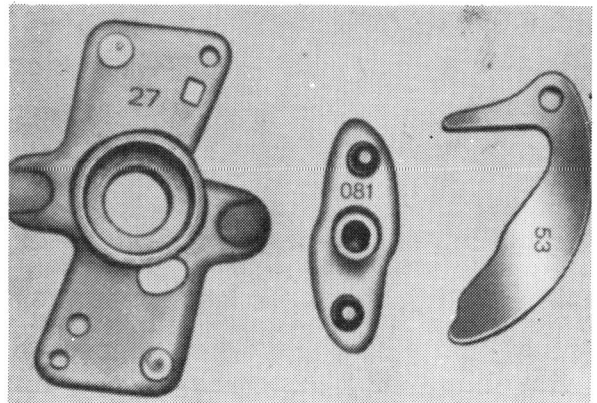

Fig.4.8. Distributor component identification numbers

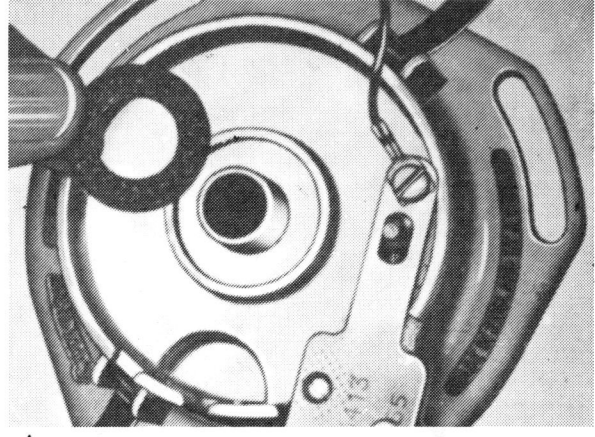

Fig.4.9. Refitting felt lubricator to slotted base

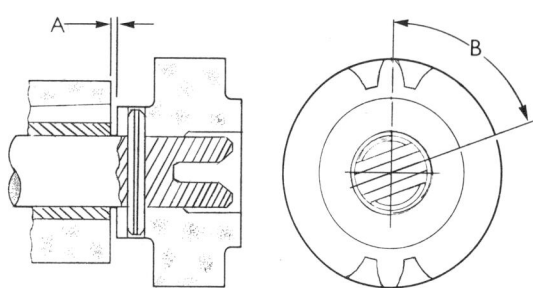

FIG.4.10. DISTRIBUTOR MAINSHAFT DRIVE GEAR PINNED POSITION

A End float 0.085 - 0.175 in (2.16 - 4.44 mm)
B Pin position to slot - 70

FIG.4.11. IGNITION TIMING MARKS

1 Notch in crankshaft pulley
2 9° mark on drive belt cover

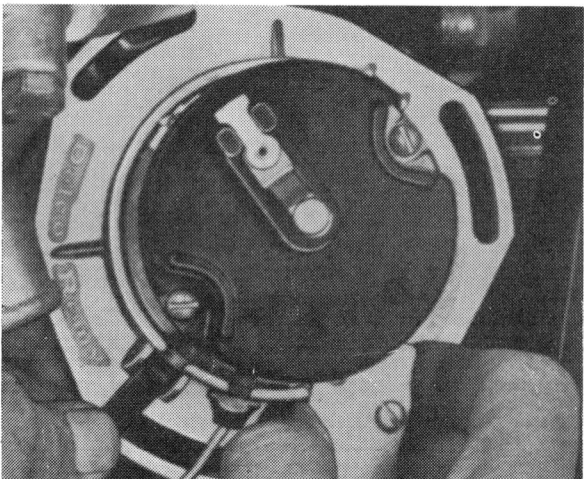

Fig.4.12. Position of oil pump tongue

Fig.4.13. Rotor in the 11 o'clock position ready for refitting distributor

the 12 o'clock position as shown in Fig.4.14 . The mounting bolt holes should now be in the centre of the flange slots.

7 If an error has been made withdraw the distributor and repeat the procedure. Should the distributor body not go right down easily it is an indication that the oil pump drive shaft is not correclty aligned. Refer to Fig.4.12.

8 Replace the three distributor securing bolts and plain washers but do not fully tighten yet.

9 Refer to Section 3, paragraph 6 onwards and reset the contact breaker points to the correct gap.

10 Carefully turn the distributor anti clockwise until the contact breaker points are closed. Now turn the distributor body clockwise until the contact breaker points are just about to open. This can be accurately gauged if a 12 volt, 6 watt bulb is connected in parallel with the contact breaker points. Switch on the ignition and when the points open the bulb will light.

11 Tighten the three distributor securing bolts.

12 If a stroboscopic light is used for a final static ignition setting, remove the lead from No. 1 spark plug and connect up the strobe light, one wire to the spark plug and the other to the plug lead. With the engine idling as slowly as possible shine the light on to the engine front cover mark and it will be noted that the crankshaft pulley mark should appear stationary opposite to the front cover 9° mark.

13 If the engine speed is increased, then the effect of the vacuum and centrifugal advance controls can be seen and in fact, measured to some extent, in so far as the distance between the two crankcase timing markers represent 9° of crankshaft revolution.

9 Spark plugs and leads

1 The correct functioning of the spark plugs is vital for the correct running and efficient operation of the engine. The spark plugs fitted as standard are as listed in the specifications at the beginning of this chapter.

2 At intervals of 3,000 miles (4,800 Km) the spark plugs must be removed, examined and cleaned. If worn excessively they must be renewed. This cleaning frequency may seem high to some owners but experience has shown that it is well worth the short time involved. The condition of the spark plug will also tell much about the overall condition of the engine.

3 If the insulator nose of the spark plug is clean and white, with no deposits, this is indicative of a weak mixture, or too hot a plug. (A hot plug transfers heat away from the electrode slowly - a cold plug transfers it away quickly).

4 If the tip and insulator nose is covered with sooty black deposits, then this is indicative that the mixture is too rich. Should the plug be black and oily, then it is likely that the engine is fairly worn, as well as the mixture being rich.

5 If the insulator nose is covered with a light tan to greyish brown deposit, then the mixture is correct and it is likely that the engine is in good condition.

6 If there are any traces of long brown tapering stains on the outside of the white portion of the spark plug, then the plug will have to be renewed, as this shows that there is a faulty joint between the plug body and the insulator, and pressure is being allowed to leak past.

7 Spark plugs should be cleaned by a sand blasting machine, which will free them from carbon more thoroughly than cleaning by hand. The machine will also test the condition of the spark plugs under pressure conditions. Any plug that fails to spark at the recommended pressure should be discarded.

8 The spark plug gap is of considerable importance, as, if it is too large, or too small the size of the spark and its efficiency will be seriously impaired. The spark plug gap should be set to:

Normal running	0.030 inch (0.75 mm)
Running in	0.026 inch (0.65 mm)

9 To reset the gap, measure the gap with a feeler gauge and then using a special spark plug resetting tool bend the outer plug

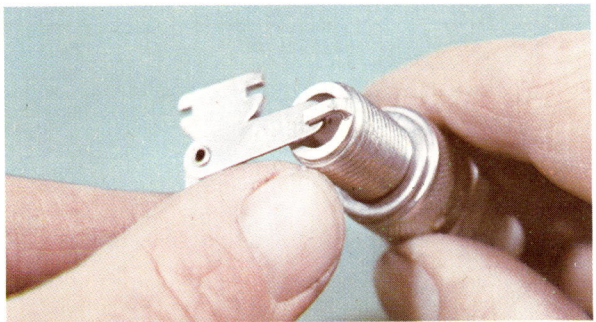

Measuring plug gap. A feeler gauge of the correct size (see ignition system specifications) should have a slight 'drag' when slid between the electrodes. Adjust gap if necessary

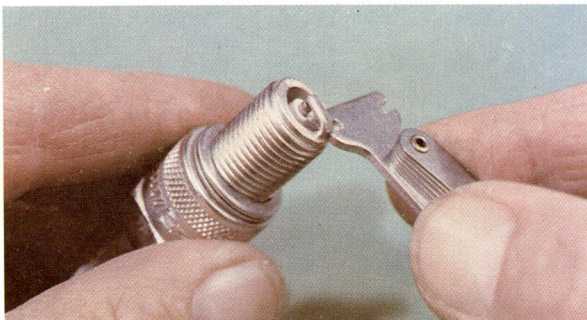

Adjusting plug gap. The plug gap is adjusted by bending the earth electrode inwards, or outwards, as necessary until the correct clearance is obtained. Note the use of the correct tool

Normal. Grey-brown deposits lightly coated core nose. Gap increasing by around 0.001 in (0.025 mm) per 1000 miles (1600 km). Plugs ideally suited to engine and engine in good condition

Carbon fouling. Dry, black, sooty deposits. Will cause weak spark and eventually misfire. Fault: over-rich fuel mixture. Check: carburettor mixture settings, float level and jet sizes; choke operation and cleanliness of air filter. Plugs can be re-used after cleaning

Oil fouling. Wet, oily deposits. Will cause weak spark and eventually misfire. Fault: worn bores/piston rings or valve guides; sometimes occurs (temporarily) during running-in period. Plugs can be re-used after thorough cleaning

Overheating. Electrodes have glazed appearance, core nose very white - few deposits. Fault: plug overheating. Check: plug value, ignition timing, fuel octane rating (too low) and fuel mixture (too weak). Discard plugs and cure fault immediately

Electrode damage. Electrodes burned away; core nose has burned, glazed appearance. Fault: initial pre-ignition. Check: as for 'Overheating' but may be more severe. Discard plugs and remedy fault before piston or valve damage occurs

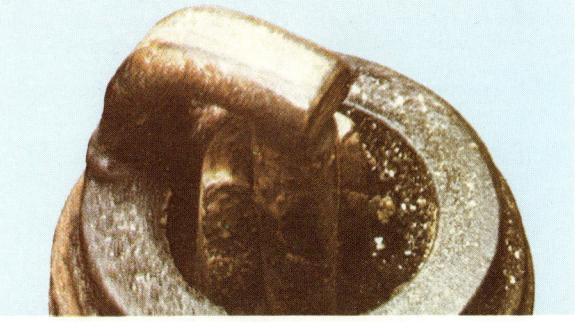

Split core nose (may appear initially as a crack). Damage is self-evident, but cracks will only show after cleaning. Fault: pre-ignition or wrong gap-setting technique. Check: ignition timing, cooling system, fuel octane rating (too low) and fuel mixture (too weak). Discard plugs, rectify fault immediately

electrode until the correct gap is obtained. The centre electrode must not be bent as it will crack the insulation resulting in plug failure.

10 When refitting the spark plugs it is important that the tapered contact seats of the plugs and cylinder head are clean and undamaged.

11 The spark plugs must not be overtightened. As they are a different size from most other common spark plugs (5/8 AF) it is worthwhile obtaining the correct size socket and extension bar to fit a torque wrench. Always tighten the spark plugs to a torque wrench setting of 15 lb ft (2.07 Kg m).

12 The plug leads require no routine maintenance other than being kept clean and wiped over regularly. At intervals of 6,000 miles (9660 Km) thoroughly inspect the leds for signs of deterioration or loose connections. Rectify as necessary.

10 Ignition system - fault symptoms

There are two main symptoms indicating ignition faults. Either the engine will not start or fire, or the engine is difficult to start and misfires. If it is a regular misfire i.e. the engine is only running on two or three cylinders, the fault is almost sure to be in the secondary or high tension circuit. If the misfiring is intermittent, the fault could be in either the high or low tension circuits. If the engine stops suddenly, or will not start at all, it is likely that the fault is in the low tension circuit. Loss of power and overheating apart from faulty carburation settings, are normally due to faults in the distributor, or incorrect ignition timing.

11 Fault diagnosis - engine fails to start

1 If the engine fails to start and it was running normally when it was last used, first check that there is fuel in the petrol tank. If the engine turns over normally on the starter motor and the battery is evidently well charged, then the fault may be in either the high or low tension circuits. First check the HT circuit. NOTE. If the battery is known to be fully charged, the ignition light comes on, and the starter motor fails to turn the engine, CHECK THE TIGHTNESS OF THE LEADS ON THE BATTERY TERMINALS and also the secureness of the earth lead to its CONNECTION TO THE BODY. It is quite common for the leads to have worked loose, even if they look and feel relatively secure. If one of the battery terminal posts gets very hot when trying to operate the starter motor this is a sure indication of a faulty connection to that terminal.

2 One of the commonest reasons for bad starting is wet or damp spark plug leads and distributor. Remove the distributor cap. If condensation is visible internally, dry the cap with a rag and also wipe over the leads. Replace the cap. Also wipe the top of the ignition coil.

3 If the engine still fails to start, check that current is reaching the plugs by disconnecting each plug lead in turn at the spark plug end, and holding the end of the cable about 3/16 inch (4.8 mm) away from the cylinder block. Spin the engine on the starter motor.

4 Sparking between the end of the cable and the cylinder block should be fairly strong with a regular blue spark. Hold the lead with rubber or plastic gloves to avoid electric shocks. If current is reaching the spark plugs, then remove them and clean. Regap them to the specified clearance and see specifications. The engine should now start.

5 If there is no spark at the plug leads take off the HT lead from the centre of the distributor cap and hold it to the cylinder block as before. Spin the engine as before, when a rapid succession of blue sparks between the end of the lead and the block indicate that the ignition coil is in order, and that the distributor cap is cracked, the rotor faulty, or the carbon brush in the top of the distributor cap is not making good contact with the spring on the rotor. Possibly the contact breaker points are burnt, pitted or dirty. If the points are in bad shape, clean and

reset them as described in Section 4.

6 If there are no sparks from the end of the lead from the ignition coil, then check the connections of the lead to the coil and distributor cap, and if they are in order, check out the low tension circuit starting with the battery.

7 Switch on the ignition and turn the crankshaft so that the contact breaker points have fully opened. They will either be a contact breaker points have fully opened. Then with either a 20v voltmeter or a bulb and two lengths of wire check that open current is flowing along the low tension wire to the ignition coil terminal SW or + by putting the test wire ends on the aforementioned terminal and earth. No reading indicates a break in the supply from the ignition switch. Check the connections at the switch to see if any are loose. Refit them. A reading shows a faulty coil or condenser or broken lead between the coil and distributor.

8 Detach the condenser wire from the points assembly and with the points open, test between the moving point and earth. If there now is a reading, then the fault is in the condenser. Fit a new one as described in Section 5.

9 With no reading from the moving contact breaker point to earth, take a reading between earth and the CB or - terminal of the coil. A reading here shows a broken wire which will need to be replaced between the coil and distributor. No reading confirms that the coil has failed and must be renewed. Remember to refit the condenser wire to the points assembly. For these tests it is sufficient to separate the points with a piece of dry paper while testing with the points open.

10 Models covered by this manual are fitted with a device which boosts the output from the ignition coil when the starter motor is operated. (When the starter motor is operated the battery voltage tends to drop due to the load placed on it). Quite simply, the coil is rated for a continuous 6 volt supply. As the vehicle system is 12 volts a resistor is fitted into the LT supply to the coil so that under normal operating conditions the coil only receives a 6 volt supply. However, when the starter is operated the system voltage drops as previously described. In addition to the normal LT feed to the coil therefore an additional feed is taken from the starter solenoid switch direct to the coil. This feed only operates when the starter solenoid terminals are closed i.e. when the starter is turning. Consequently for a brief time when the voltage drops from 12 to about 8 volts this is fed direct to the 6 volt coil providing a temporary starting voltage boost. Certain checks are necessary to ensure that:

a) The starter feed is functioning properly - otherwise only about 2 volts would reach the coil on starting.

b) The resistor is in good order - otherwise either 12 or 0 volts may reach the coil. The tests detailed below are clarified by reference to the wiring connections given in Fig.4.15 and Fig.4.16

A1 To check the current supply to the coil through the resistor wire, disconnect the white/yellow resistor wire and connect it to earth via a voltmeter. With the contact breaker points closed and the ignition switched on the reading should be at least 8 volts. If not then there is a fault in the wire or the starter solenoid switch, (Fig. 4.15A).

A2 With the white/yellow resistor wire reconnected, and the voltmeter connected as far as the previous test, there should be a reading of approximately 5 volts with the ignition switched on and the points closed. (Fig. 4.15B).

B1 To check the primary (LT) coil winding, contact breaker points and condenser, connect the voltmeter to the CB or - terminal (white/black wire) of the coil leaving both coil wires connected. Switch on the ignition with the contact breaker points open. The voltage should be approximately 12 volts (ie battery voltage). If the reading is very low or zero then there is a fault in the coil primary winding or a short circuit at the contact breaker points or condenser (Fig. 4.16).

B2 With the same connections, close the contact breaker points. With the ignition still on the reading should be between 0 and 0.2 volts. Should the reading be greater then the contact breaker points are dirty,

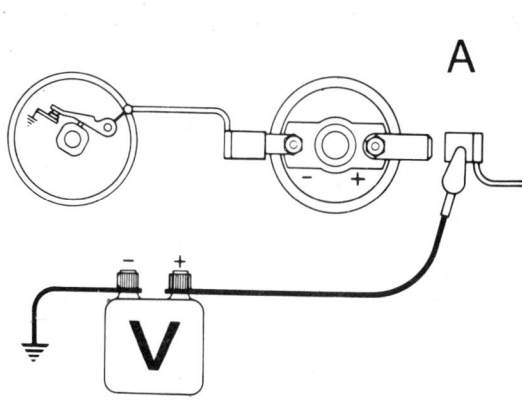

A

Fig.4.14. New position of rotor with distributor correctly fitted

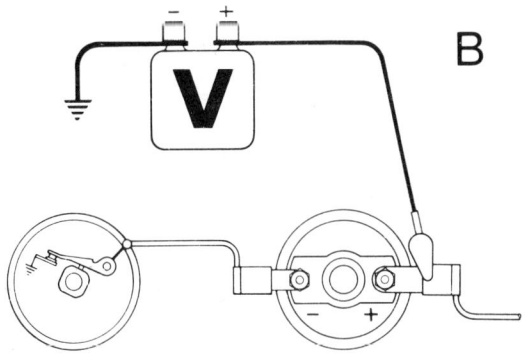

B

Fig 4.15. Resistor cable test

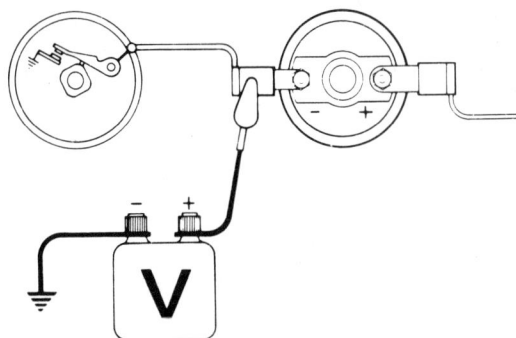

Fig.4.16. LT circuit test connections

12 Fault diagnosis - engine misfires

1   If the engine misfires regularly, run it at a fast idling speed and short out each of the spark plugs in turn by placing a screwdriver across from the plug terminal to the cylinder. Ensure that the screwdriver has a clean and dry wooden or plastic insulated handle.

2   No difference in engine running will be noticed when the plug in the defective cylinder is short circuited. Short circuiting the working plugs will accentuate the misfire.

3   Remove the plug lead from the end of the defective plug and hold it about 3/16 inch (4.8 mm) from the cylinder block. Restart the engine. If the sparking is fairly strong and regular the fault must lie in the spark plug.

4   The spark plug may be loose, the insulation may be cracked or the points may have burnt away giving too wide a gap for the spark to jump when under pressure conditions. Worse still, one of the points may have broken off. Either renew the plug, or clean it, reset the gap and then test it.

5   If there is no spark at the end of the plug lead, or if it is weak and intermittent, check the ignition lead from the distributor to the plug. If the insulation has deteriorated renew the lead. Check the connections at the distributor cap.

6   If there is still no spark, examine the distributor cap carefully for tracking. This can be recognised by a very thin black line running between two or more electrodes, or between an electrode and some other part of the distributor. These lines are paths which now conduct electricity across the cap thus letting it run to earth. Also check the top of the coil for the same symptoms.

7   Apart from the ignition timing being incorrect, other causes of misfiring have already been dealt with under the section dealing with failure of the engine to start.

8   If the ignition timing is too far retarded, it should be noted that the engine will tend to overheat, and there will be quite a noticeable drop in power. If the engine is overheating and the power is down, and the ignition timing is correct then the carburettor should be checked, as it is likely that this is where the fault lies. See Chapter 3 for further details.

Chapter 5 Clutch and actuating mechanism

Contents

Specifications

Make:		Victor	Borg and Beck
		VX 4/90	Laycock
Type:		Diaphragm spring	
Clutch identification	Victor	Brown paint on diaphragm	
	VX 4/90	Orange paint on cover	
Disc identification	Victor (1759 cc)	Light grey/violet hub springs	
	(2279 cc)	White/light green hub springs	
	VX 4/90	Green paint on hub	
Disc diameter	Victor de luxe	8.03 in (204 mm)	
	Victor SL	8.5 in (215.9 mm)	
	VX 4/90	8.44 in (214.4 mm)	
Number of springs		6	
Actuating arm free travel		0.20 in (5 mm)	
Pedal shaft diameter		0.589 - 0.591 in (14.96 - 15.00 mm)	
Pedal shaft clearance in bush		0.002 - 0.006 in (0.05 - 0.16 mm)	
Pedal load		17 lb (7.7 kg)	

Torque wrench settings:

Clutch cover to flywheel bolts (dry threads)	14 lb ft	1.94 kg m

1 General description

The clutch comprises an integral pressure plate and diaphragm spring assembly with a single dry plate friction disc between the pressure plate assembly and the flywheel.

The bellhousing on the gearbox encloses the whole unit but only the top half of the bellhousing bolts to the engine. Consequently there is a semi-circular steel plate bolted to the lower half of the bellhousing to act as a cover.

The clutch is operated mechanically by a Bowden cable direct from the clutch pedal. This actuates a clutch release lever and thrust bearing, the lever pivoting on a ball pin inside the bellhousing and projecting through an aperture in the bell housing opposite the ball pin. Adjustment of free play is effected at the end of the cable where it is attached to the clutch operating lever.

2 Clutch cable - removal and replacement

1 Release the actuating arm return spring from the bracket on the gearbox (photo).
2 Undo and remove the locknut, adjustment nut, plain washer, pressure pad, insulator, and slotted washer from the threaded end of the cable (Fig.5.3 and photos).
3 Draw the cable out through the hole in the bellhousing and recover the rubber insulator (photo).

4 Uncover the pedal mounting bracket inside the car and unhook the inner cable from the forked end of the clutch pedal. This is shown in Fig.5.5 .
5 Withdraw the clip securing the outer cable to the support bracket and recover the grommet.
6 Pull the cable out from inside the engine compartment and unclip it from the sump before lifting away from the car (photo).
7 Refitting the clutch cable assembly is the reverse sequence. The following additional points should be noted:
a) Fit the pedal end of the cable first and apply a little Castrol LM Grease to the cable eye and pedal hook.
b) Adjust the release arm clearance and refit the return spring as described in Section 3.

3 Clutch - adjustment

1 The free play in the clutch pedal cannot be determined accurately from the pedal. It is necessary to check the degree of movement of the actuating arm as shown in Fig.5.4 .
2 To measure the gap the return spring is first unhooked from the arm.
3 Move the actuating arm until it can be felt to be up against the clutch. Using a rule measure the movement from this position to the fully released position. This should be 0.20 in (5 mm).
4 To adjust the actuating arm movement slacken the locknut

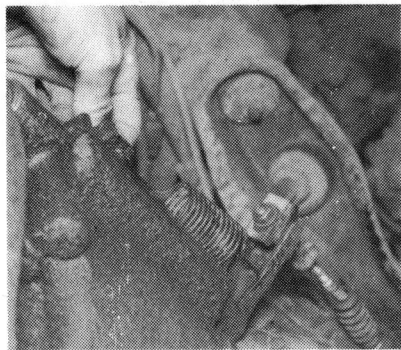

2.1. Detaching the clutch cable return spring

2.2A. Releasing locknut

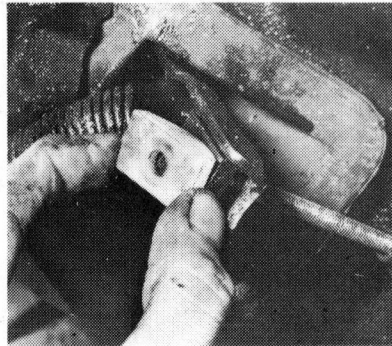

2.2B. Lifting away pressure pad

2.2C. Drawing off rubber sleeve

2.3 The clutch cable may now be drawn forwards

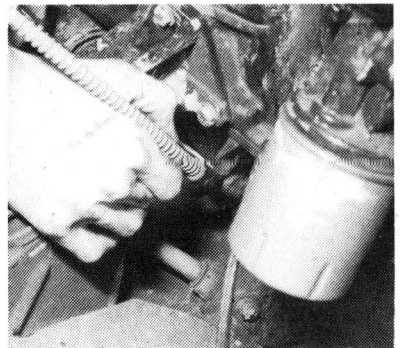

2.6 Removing cable from sump clip

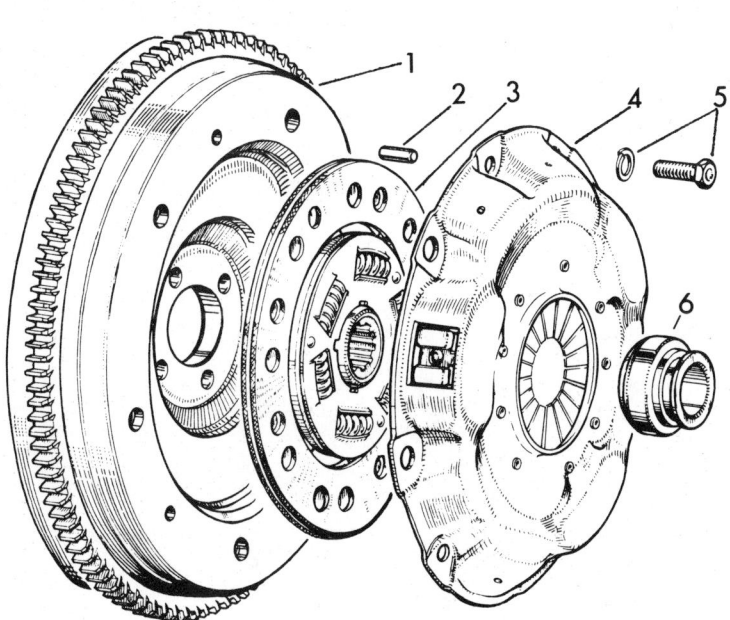

FIG.5.1. THE CLUTCH ASSEMBLY

1 Flywheel	3 Friction disc
2 Dowel	4 Pressure plate assembly

5 Pressure plate assembly securing bolt and spring washer

6 Thrust release bearing

A

B

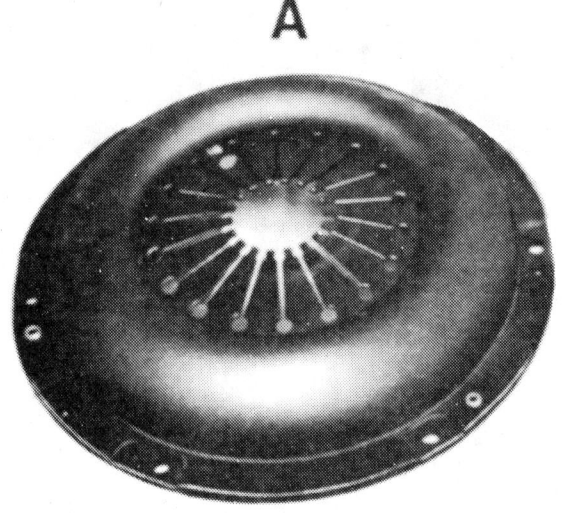
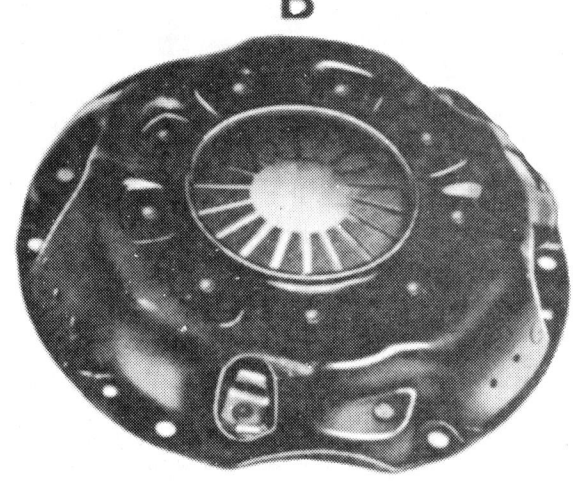

FIG.5.2. ALTERNATIVE CLUTCH ASSEMBLIES

A Laycock
B Borg and Beck

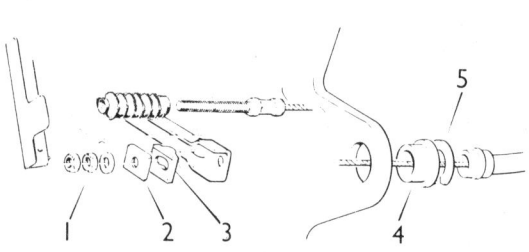

FIG.5.3. CLUTCH CABLE - ACTUATING ARM END

1 Adjustment nut
2 Pressure pad
3 Insulator

4 Rubber insulator
5 Slotted washer

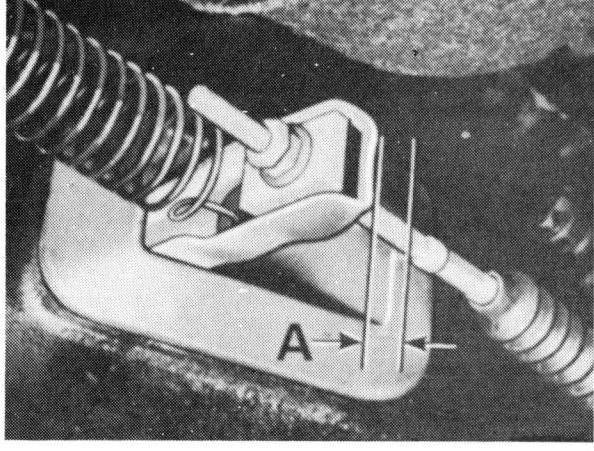

FIG.5.4. CLUTCH RELEASE BEARING ACTUATING ARM
FREE TRAVEL

A = 0.2 inch (5 mm)

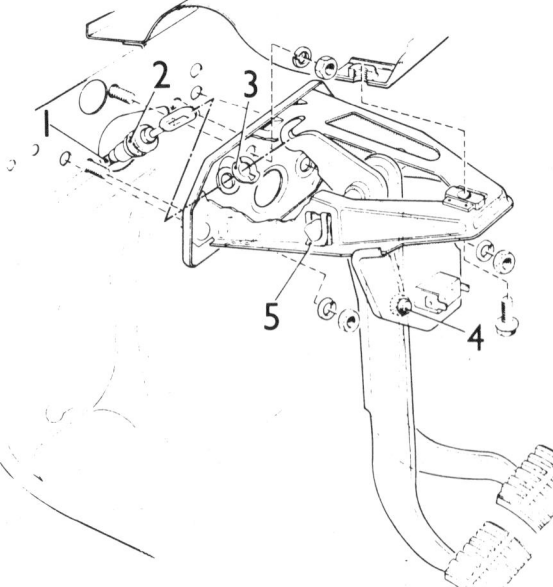

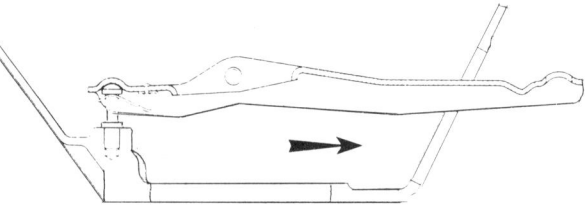

Fig.5.6. Clutch actuating arm. Cross section view to show pivot
pin and clip. Pull in direction of arrow to remove arm

FIG.5.5. CLUTCH PEDAL AND MOUNTING BRACKET

1 Clutch outer cable
2 Grommet
3 Clip

4 Rubber buffer
5 Spring clip

and screw the adjusting nut in or out until the correct movement is obtained. Tighten the locknut and refit the spring (Fig.5.3)).

5 Too little or no movement will wear out the thrust race prematurely. If badly adjusted this way clutch slip could occur. Too great a movement will result in excessive pedal movement before the clutch disengages.

6 If the return spring is broken or left disconnected it will be immediately apparent by looseness in the pedal at the top end of its travel. The clutch will work but the actuating arm will rattle and cause wear on the thrust bearing also.

4 Clutch pedal and shaft - removal and replacement

1 The clutch pedal has a single bush and is carried, together with the brake pedal and a spacer sleeve on a single shaft. This shaft is held in the support by one spring clip fitted at either end. To prevent noise after pedal operation a rubber buffer located in the pedal stop bracket cushions the return of the pedal.

2 Release the actuating arm return spring from the bracket on the gearbox.

3 Slacken the cable locknut and adjustment nut at the actuating arm.

4 Detach the cable from the hooked end of the clutch pedal.

5 Using a screwdriver carefully ease off the left hand pedal shaft retaining spring clip and push the shaft rightwards until the clutch pedal is free.

6 Check the degree of wear in the pedal bush which if worn may be pressed out and a new one fitted. In some instances where the new bush is tight on the shaft it will be necessary to ream out the bush until the specified clearance is obtained.

7 Refitting the pedal and pedal shaft is the reverse sequence to removal. Lubricate the pedal shaft with a little Castrol LM Grease. It will be necessary to adjust the clutch as described in Section 3.

5 Clutch assembly - removal and inspection (Borg and Beck)

1 Remove the gearbox as described in Chapter 6.

2 To remove the clutch bellhousing the engine may need to be lowered to facilitate access to the two top bolts on the left-hand side. Alternatively a cranked spanner, or socket wrench and universal joint, can be used.

3 If the engine is not being removed then disconnect the

exhaust downpipe from the manifold and the clutch operating cable from the actuating arm.

4 Grasp the end of the actuating arm and firmly pull in the direction shown in Fig.5.6 . This will release the inner end of the actuating arm from the ball pin. Lift the actuating arm and rubber grommet from the side of the clutch housing.

5 The right hand engine mounting bracket must next be unbolted from the engine. Suitably support the weight of the engine - preferably by a sling from above. If supported from underneath remember that it has to be lowered and swung to one side.

6 Detach the positive and negative terminals from the battery and then the cables from the starter motor.

7 Undo and remove the two bolts and spring washers that secure the starter motor to the clutch housing and crankcase. Lift away the starter motor.

8 Undo and remove the remaining bolts and spring washers that secure the bellhousing and draw rearwards from the dowels located on either side of the crankcase. (Fig.5.7) . Lift away the bellhousing.

9 Mark the relative position of the clutch cover and flywheel.

10 Slacken off the bolts holding the clutch cover to the flywheel in a progressive and diagonal manner. This keeps the pressure even all round the diaphragm spring and prevents distortion. When all the pressure on the bolts has been released remove the bolts and spring washers. Lift the cover off the dowel pegs and take it off together with the friction disc which is fitted between it and the flywheel. Note which way round the friction disc is fitted.

11 Thoroughly clean all parts by wiping with a rag to remove any dust.

12 Examine the clutch disc friction lining for wear, loose or broken springs and rivets. The linings must be proud of the rivets and light in appearance, with the material structure visible. If it is dark in appearance, further investigation is necessary as it is a sign of oil contamination caused by oil leaking past the crankshaft rear seal.

13 Check the machined faces of the flywheel and pressure plate for signs of grooving. If evident, new parts should be fitted. Inspect the pressure plate for signs of hair line cracks usually caused by overheating due to clutch slip.

14 Inspect the diaphragm spring for signs of cracking, wear at the centre or overheating, and if evident a new unit must be fitted.

15 Fit the disc to the gearbox input shaft, and check that it is free to slide up and down the splines without signs of binding.

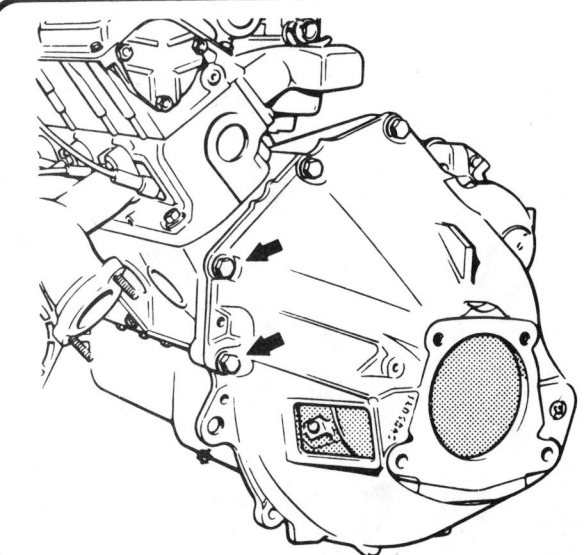

Fig.5.7. Clutch housing. To remove bolts (arrowed) the engine may need to be lowered and moved to one side

Fig.5.8. Location of clutch housing locating dowels

6 Clutch assembly - removal and inspection (Laycock)

1 VX 4/90 models are fitted with the Laycock type clutch assembly. Removal and inspection is basically identical to that described in Section 5. However, unlike the Borg and Beck clutch assembly it may be dismantled and certain parts renewed.

2 It will be observed that the cover and driving plate are secured by rivets and these must be removed first by drilling. It is not necessary for rivets to be refitted during reassembly.

3 To separate the pressure plate from the driving plate remove the diaphragm spring retaining ring using a screwdriver.

4 Lift away the four anti-rattle springs (Fig.5.9) .

5 Using a scriber or file mark the driving plate, pressure plate and diaphragm spring and then separate the parts (Fig.5.10).

6 Upon reassembly apply a little Castrol MS3 Grease to the sides of the pressure plate lugs: fulcrum points for the diaphragm spring on the pressure plate, driving plate and cover.

7 Line up the previously made marks making sure the depressions in the cover and driving plate coincide as one of them is offset.

8 Make sure the retaining ring is replaced with the flat sections under the pressure plate lugs and the curved sections against the edge of the diaphragm spring.

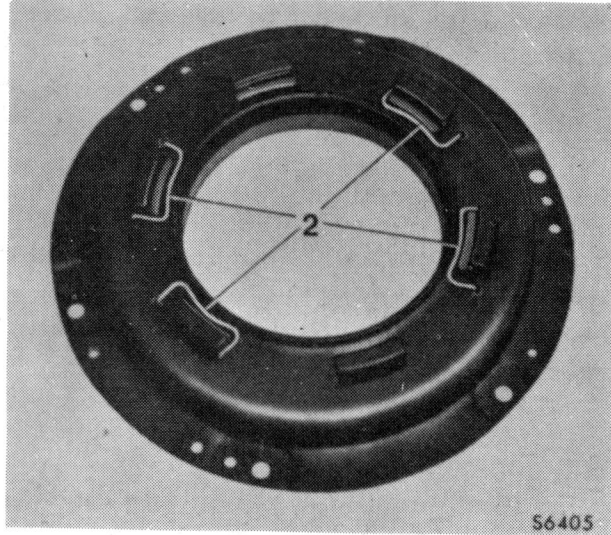

Fig.5.9. Location of anti-rattle springs

7 Clutch assembly - replacement

1 Replacement of the clutch cover and friction disc is the reverse sequence to removal but is not quite so straightforward as the following paragraphs will indicate.

2 If the clutch assembly has been removed from the engine with the engine out of the car, it is a relatively easy matter to line up the hub of the friction disc with the centre of the cover and flywheel. The cover and friction disc are refitted onto the flywheel with the holes in the cover fitting over the three dowels on the flywheel. The friction disc is supported with a finger while this is being done (photo).

3 Note that the Borg and Beck friction disc is mounted with the longer hub of the boss towards the flywheel, wherease the Laycock disc is fitted the other way round (see Fig.5.11) Usually a replacement disc is marked 'flywheel side' to prevent a mistake being made (photo).

4 Refit the cover mounting bolts and spring washers and screw up finger tight just sufficiently to grip the friction disc. Then set the friction disc in position so that the hub is exactly concentric with the centre of the flywheel and cover assembly. An easy way of doing this is to make a temporary mandrel using a bar from a socket set which should fit fairly closely in the flywheel bush. Wrap a few turns of adhesive tape round the bar near the end which will make a snug fit inside the splined boss of the friction plates. Use this as a centering device. It is most important to get this right when refitting the clutch to the flywheel when the engine is still in the car. This is to prevent any difficulty or possible damage when refitting the gearbox. (photo).

5 Tighten up the cover bolts in a diagonal and progressive manner to maintain an even pressure. Finally tighten the bolts to a torque wrench setting of 14 lb ft (1.94 Kg m). For this to be accurate the bolts must be clean and dry.

6 Replace the bellhousing and then move the engine back to its original position on its mounting bracket (photo). Finally replace the gearbox and reconnect the propeller shaft as described in Chapter 7.

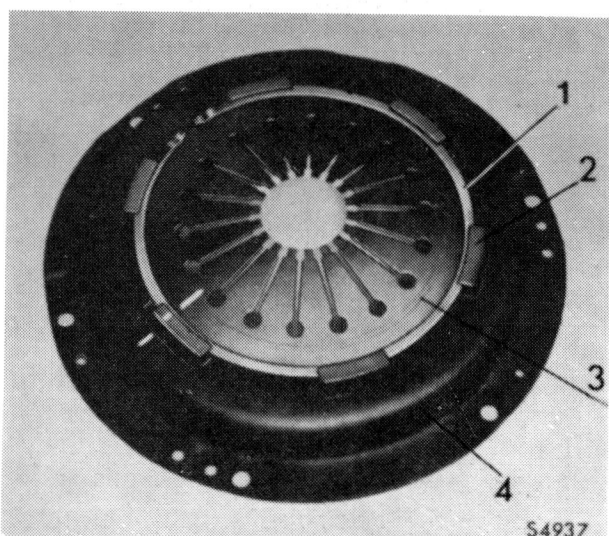

FIG.5.10. LAYCOCK CLUTCH ASSEMBLY

1 Retaining ring   3 Diaphragm spring
2 Pressure plate   4 Driving plate

8 Clutch actuating lever and thrust release bearing - removal, inspection and replacement

1 Refer to Chapter 6 and remove the gearbox.

2 Disconnect the clutch operating cable from the actuating arm as described in Section 2 paragraphs 1 - 3 inclusive.

3 Grasp the end of the actuating arm and firmly pull: this will release the inner end of the actuating arm from the ball pin

Fig.5.11. The larger side of the hub must face away from the flywheel on Laycock friction disc

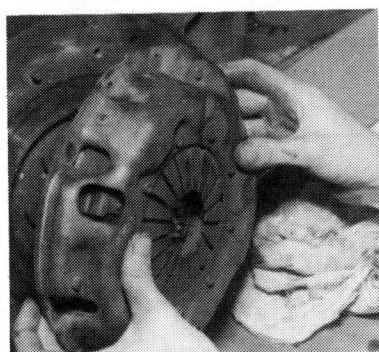

7.2. Positioning driven plate and clutch cover together onto the flywheel

7.3 New clutch driven plate in relation to flywheel

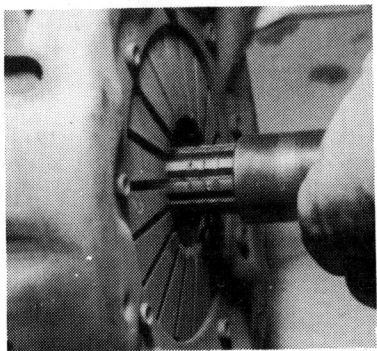

7.4. Centering the clutch driven plate by using an old gearbox input shaft

7.6. Offering up the bellhousing to the engine cylinder block. Note lower cover plate resting behind flywheel

8.3. View through rear of bellhousing of clutch actuating lever being pulled out

(Fig.5.6) . Lift the actuating arm and rubber grommet from the side of the clutch housing (photo).

4   The clutch release bearing may now be taken off.

5   If the bellhousing is removed inspect the pivot ballpin for signs of wear and flats. If necessary it can be removed by gripping with a mole wrench and tapping out. A new one may be driven in using a soft faced hammer.

6   If the release bearing is obviously worn and is noisy it should be replaced. Do not clean the release bearing in any oil solvent liquid as the races have been loaded with grease during assembly and such cleaning would wash it out.

7   Refit the actuating arm and release bearing in the reverse sequence to removal. It is important that the radiused face of the thrust bearing faces towards the clutch.

8   Smear a little Castrol LM Grease onto the clutch actuating arm ball pin head.

9   Make sure that the retaining spring clip on the inner end of the actuating arm fastens securely over the head of the ball pivot pin.

10   Refit the gearbox as described in Chapter 6 and then adjust the clutch as described in Section 3.

9   Clutch pilot bush - renewal

1   In the centre of the flywheel is a bushed hole in which runs the spigot at the front of the gearbox input shaft. If this bush is badly worn the clutch operation will be unsatisfactory.

2   It is difficult to judge the condition of the bush unless a bar of exactly the same diameter as the spigot is available. With the engine removed from the car it is possible to measure it but once again unless the gearbox is also removed it is impossible to check the fit of the two parts concerned.

3   The old bush can be removed by finding a bolt which can be forced into the soft metal of the bush. Fit a nut spacer tube having a larger diameter than the bush and packing washers on the bolt. Force the bolt into the bush and then draw out the bush by tightening the nut.

4   Replacement of the bush is best done using a suitable diameter stepped mandrel which will ensure that it is not distorted or damaged when being driven in. It is most important that the shaft is an easy fit in the bush on reassembly.

see page 92 for ''Fault Diagnosis''

10   Fault diagnosis

Symptom	Reason/s	Remedy
Judder when taking up drive	Loose engine or gearbox mountings or over flexible mountings	Check and tighten all mounting bolts and replace any 'soft' or broken mountings.
	Badly worn friction surfaces or friction disc contaminated with oil carbon deposit	Remove clutch assembly and replace parts as required. Rectify any oil leakage points which may have caused contamination.
	Worn splines in the friction plate hub or on the gearbox input shaft	Renew friction disc and/or input shaft.
	Propeller shaft or rear axle mounting faults	Examine propeller shaft universal joints and rear axle to suspension attachment points.
Clutch spin (or failure to disengage) so that gears cannot be meshed	Clutch actuating cable clearance from fork too great	Adjust clearance.
	Clutch friction disc sticking (usually apparent after standing idle for some length of time)	As temporary remedy engage top gear, apply handbrake, depress clutch and start engine. (If very badly stuck engine will not turn). When running rev up engine and slip clutch until disengagement is normally possible. Renew friction plate at earliest opportunity.
	Damaged or misaligned pressure plate assembly	Replace pressure plate assembly.
Clutch slip - (increase in engine speed does not result in increase in car speed - especially on hills)	Clutch actuating cable clearance from fork too small resulting in partially disengaged clutch at all times	Adjust clearance.
	Clutch friction surfaces worn out (beyond further adjustment of operating cable) or clutch surfaces oil soaked	Replace friction disc and remedy source of oil leakage.

Chapter 6 Gearbox and automatic transmission

Contents

Specifications

Manual transmission:

No of gears	4 forward 1 reverse
Type	Helical cut constant mesh with straight cut reverse gear. Synchromesh on all forward gears.
Change mechanism	Floor mounted, remote lever
Oil capacity	2.4 pints (1.4 litres)
with overdrive	3.1 pints (1.8 litres)

Ratios:

First	3.3 : 1
Second	2.141 : 1
Third	1.362 : 1
Fourth	1 : 1
Reverse	3.064 : 1
Overdrive - third	1.100 : 1
fourth	0.778 : 1

Mainshaft:

Diameter	1.4738 - 1.4744 in	(37.43 - 37.45 mm)
Gear clearance on shaft	0.0016 - 0.0032 in	(0.04 - 0.08 mm)
First speed gear and sleeve		
Diameter	1.3484 - 1.3490 in	(34.25 - 34.26 mm)
Gear clearance on shaft	0.0020 - 0.0041 in	(0.05 - 0.10 mm)

Layshaft gear:

Overall length	7.141 - 7.144 in	(181.39 - 181.46 mm)
Thrust washer thickness	0.0615 - 0.0635 in	(1.56 - 1.61 mm)
End float in casing	0.0048 - 0.0177 in	(0.12 - 0.45 mm)

Reverse pinion:

Shaft diameter	0.7790 - 0.7795 in	(19.79 - 19.80 mm)
Clearance on shaft	0.0025 - 0.0040 in	(0.06 - 0.10 mm)

Speedometer gears:

Teeth in drive gear	

5

Axle ratio	Tyre size	Teeth on driven gear	Housing colour
10/39	6.40S - 13	16	Natural
10/39	175SR - 13	16	Natural
10/41	6.40S - 13	17	Natural
10/41	175SR - 13	17	Natural
11/41	6.40S - 13	15	Natural
11/41	175SR - 13	16	Natural
11/34	185/70HR - 14	13	Blue
11/38	185/70HR - 14	14	Natural

Circlips and shims available thicknesses

Circlips: ... ...
0.059 - 0.061 in	(1.499 - 1.549 mm)
0,062 - 0.064 in	(1.575 - 1.626 mm)
0.065 - 0.067 in	(1.651 - 1.702 mm)
0.068 - 0.070 in	(1.727 - 1.778 mm)
0.071 - 0.073 in	(1.803 - 1.854 mm)
0.074 - 0.076 in	(1.879 - 1.930 mm)
0.077 - 0.079 in	(1.956 - 2.007 mm)

Shims: ... ...
0.003 in	(0.0762 mm)
0.005 in	(0.1270 mm)
0.010 in	(0.254 mm)

Overdrive:

Make	Laycock - de Normanville Type J	
Hydraulic pressure		
Residual	30 lb sq in	(2.11 kg sq cm)
Operating	450 - 490 lb sq in	(31.62 - 33.71 kg sq cm)
Operating pistons		
Diameter	1.2489 - 1.2496 in	(31.72 - 31.74 mm)
Clearance in bore	0.0004 - 0.0023 in	(0.01 - 0.06 mm)
Clutch springs		
Force at 1.67 in (42.5 mm)	110 - 116 lb	(49 - 52.2 kg)

Oil pump:

Pump plunger diameter	0.4996 - 0.500 in	(12.69 - 12.70 mm)
Plunger clearance in body	0.0003 - 0.0013 in	(0.01 - 0.03 mm)
Pump eccentric diameter	1.459 - 1.460 in	(37.06 - 37.08 mm)
Strap clearance on eccentric	0.001 - 0.003 in	(0.03 - 0.08 mm)

Speedometer gears:

Axle ratio	Tyre size	Teeth on driving gear	Teeth on driven gear
10/39	6.40S - 13	6	20
10/39	175SR - 13	6	20
10/41	6.40S - 13	5	17
10/41	175SR - 13	5	17
11/38	185/70HR - 14	6	17
11/41	185/70HR - 14	6	19

Automatic transmission:

Type	GM 3 speed	
Gear ratio		
1st	2.4 : 1	
2nd	1.48 : 1	
3rd	1 : 1	
Reverse	1.92 : 1	
Oil capacity - total from dry	9 pints (5.114 litres)	
refill	4.5 pints (2.557 litres)	
Torque converter diameter	9.00 in (228.6 mm)	
Stall speed	2100 - 2150 rpm	
Approximate change speeds in 'D' range		

	Change	Speed
Minimum throttle	1 - 2	10 mph
	2 - 3	12 mph
Closed throttle	3 - 2	10 mph
	2 - 1	8 mph
90% throttle	1 - 2	32 mph
	2 - 3	43 mph
Full throttle	1 - 2	35 mph
	2 - 3	58 mph
	3 - 2	52 mph
	3 - 1	32 mph

Torque wrench settings:

	lb ft	kg m
"Overdrive"		
Relief valve plug	16	2.21
Pump plug	16	2.21
Pressure filter plug	16	2.21
"Automatic transmission"		
Flexplate to crankshaft bolts	25	3.4
Torque converter to flexplate bolt	42	5.81
Converter housing to transmission bolts	25	3.4
Transmission sump to case bolts	7	1.0
Cooler pipe adaptors to transmission case	12	1.6
Transmission selector lever nut	8	1.11

1 General description

The manual gearbox fitted to models covered by this manual have four forward speeds and all have synchromesh action. Gear selection is from a lever mounted on the rear cover and connected to the transmission striking lever shaft by a mechanical linkage.

The front of the mainshaft is supported by needle rollers located in the main drive pinion (input shaft) and the rear by a ball bearing in the rear cover. The mainshaft first speed gear is bushed and operates on a sleeve which is pressed on the mainshaft whilst the second and third speed gears operate directly on the mainshaft journals. The rear of the main drive pinion is supported in a ball bearing in the front cover and the front by a spigot engaged in a bearing in the end of the crankshaft.

The layshaft gear runs in needle roller bearings at either end of the stationary layshaft. The reverse gear is of the sliding pinion type and has a groove in the hub into which the reverse striking fork engages.

Gear selection is by means of two striking forks which are secured to rods positioned longitudinally in the gearbox casing. Mounted transversely below the rods is the striking lever shaft. A striking lever is secured to each end of the shaft and engages in a slot in each striking fork rod.

When reverse gear is to be selected the shaft moves across beyond the first and second gear position until the lower end of the third and fourth striking lever engages with the reverse shift fork mounted in the bottom cover. The reverse pinion is then moved into engagement with the gear on the first and second clutch and the layshaft gear by a rotating movement of the striking lever.

2 Gearbox - removal

1 If overdrive is fitted read the overdrive removal and replacement section before commencing work. Jack up the car in the centre of the right hand body side frame member, and then support the car at the front and rear of this side member using axle stands. If a pit is used this is not necessary, of course. If wheel ramps are used put them at the front and rear wheels on the same side of the car. In this way access to the gearbox and rear of the propeller shaft is equally satisfactory. Check the wheels remaining on the ground. Drain the gearbox oil.

2 Disconnect the propeller shaft flange bolts at the rear axle as described in Chapter 7. Lower the rear to the ground but before drawing the front end from the gearbox extension housing (or overdrive) obtain a plastic bag and strong rubber band to put over the end of the extension casing to catch any remaining oil.

3 Draw the front end of the propeller shaft out of the gearbox and secure the plastic bag over the end of the gearbox (or overdrive).

4 Release the gear change lever boot from the lip around the edge of the gear change lever aperture and slide the boot up the gear lever. Untie the lace in the gear change lever aperture and push down the cover. Using a screwdriver release the 'E' clip from the groove in the pivot pin and withdraw the pin.

5 If a centre console is fitted this must be removed first by undoing and removing the four self tapping screws that secure the insert to the console and then the four self tapping screws that secure the console to the body panel.

6 Disconnect the speedometer cable by undoing the knurled retainer round the end of the outer cable on the right hand side of the rear extension. Where applicable, disconnect the reverse light switch leads from the left-hand side of the gearbox and the overdrive switch from the right-hand side.

7 Unhook the clutch operating lever return spring from the bracket bolted to the side of the casing. If the clutch is to be dismantled and/or the engine removed disconnect the clutch cable from the actuating arm.

8 Undo and remove the two lower bolts that secure the gearbox to the clutch housing. These bolts fit from inside the housing into the gearbox and access to them is through the lower apertures in the housing. Use a cranked ring spanner to loosen and remove them.

9 Support the edge of the clutch housing with a jack in preparation for removing the gearbox support crossmember.

10 Mark the crossmember so as to prevent confusion as to which way round it goes on replacement.

11 Undo and remove the two bolts, spring washer and spacer from the ends of the crossmember.

12 Undo and remove the nut and shakeproof washer that secures the centre of the crossmember to the gearbox mounting. Lift away the crossmember.

13 Carefully lower the jack under the bellhousing just sufficient to permit access to the two bolts which secure the top of the gearbox casing to the bellhousing. These bolt through the lugs in the gearbox into the bellhousing and are easily undone using a socket and extension bar. Even when all four bolts are removed, the gearbox should not fall; it must still be supported as a safety precaution.

14 Carefully draw the gearbox rearwards whilst supporting it well so it does not drop and then take it out from under the car. When overdrive is fitted it is very heavy.

96

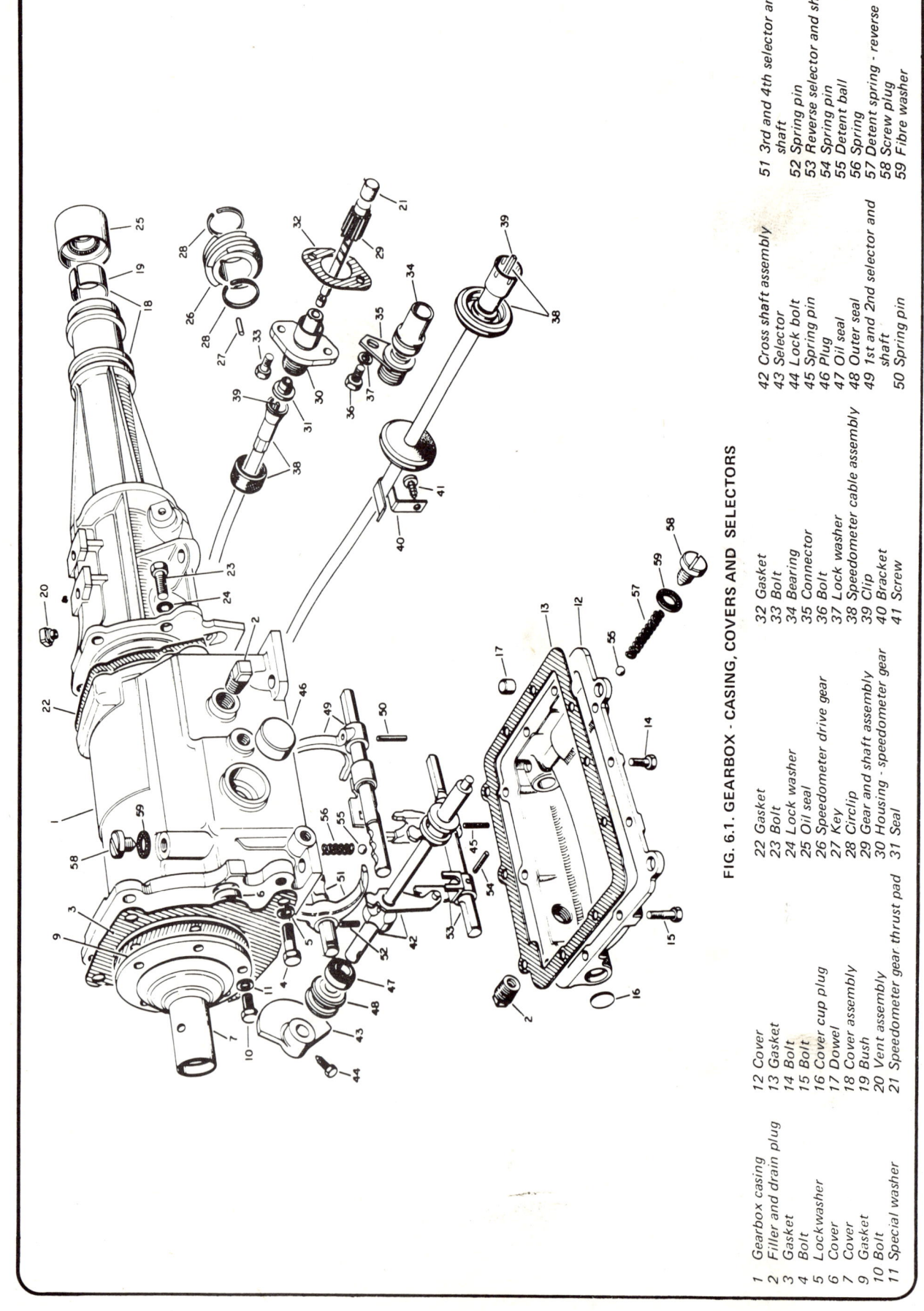

FIG. 6.1. GEARBOX - CASING, COVERS AND SELECTORS

1 Gearbox casing	12 Cover	22 Gasket	32 Gasket	42 Cross shaft assembly	51 3rd and 4th selector and shaft
2 Filler and drain plug	13 Gasket	23 Bolt	33 Bolt	43 Selector	52 Spring pin
3 Gasket	14 Bolt	24 Lock washer	34 Bearing	44 Lock bolt	53 Reverse selector and shaft
4 Bolt	15 Bolt	25 Oil seal	35 Connector	45 Spring pin	54 Spring pin
5 Lockwasher	16 Cover cup plug	26 Speedometer drive gear	36 Bolt	46 Plug	55 Detent ball
6 Cover	17 Dowel	27 Key	37 Lock washer	47 Oil seal	56 Spring
7 Cover	18 Cover assembly	28 Circlip	38 Speedometer cable assembly	48 Outer seal	57 Detent spring - reverse
9 Gasket	19 Bush	29 Gear and shaft assembly	39 Clip	49 1st and 2nd selector and shaft	58 Screw plug
10 Bolt	20 Vent assembly	30 Housing - speedometer gear	40 Bracket	50 Spring pin	59 Fibre washer
11 Special washer	21 Speedometer gear thrust pad	31 Seal	41 Screw		

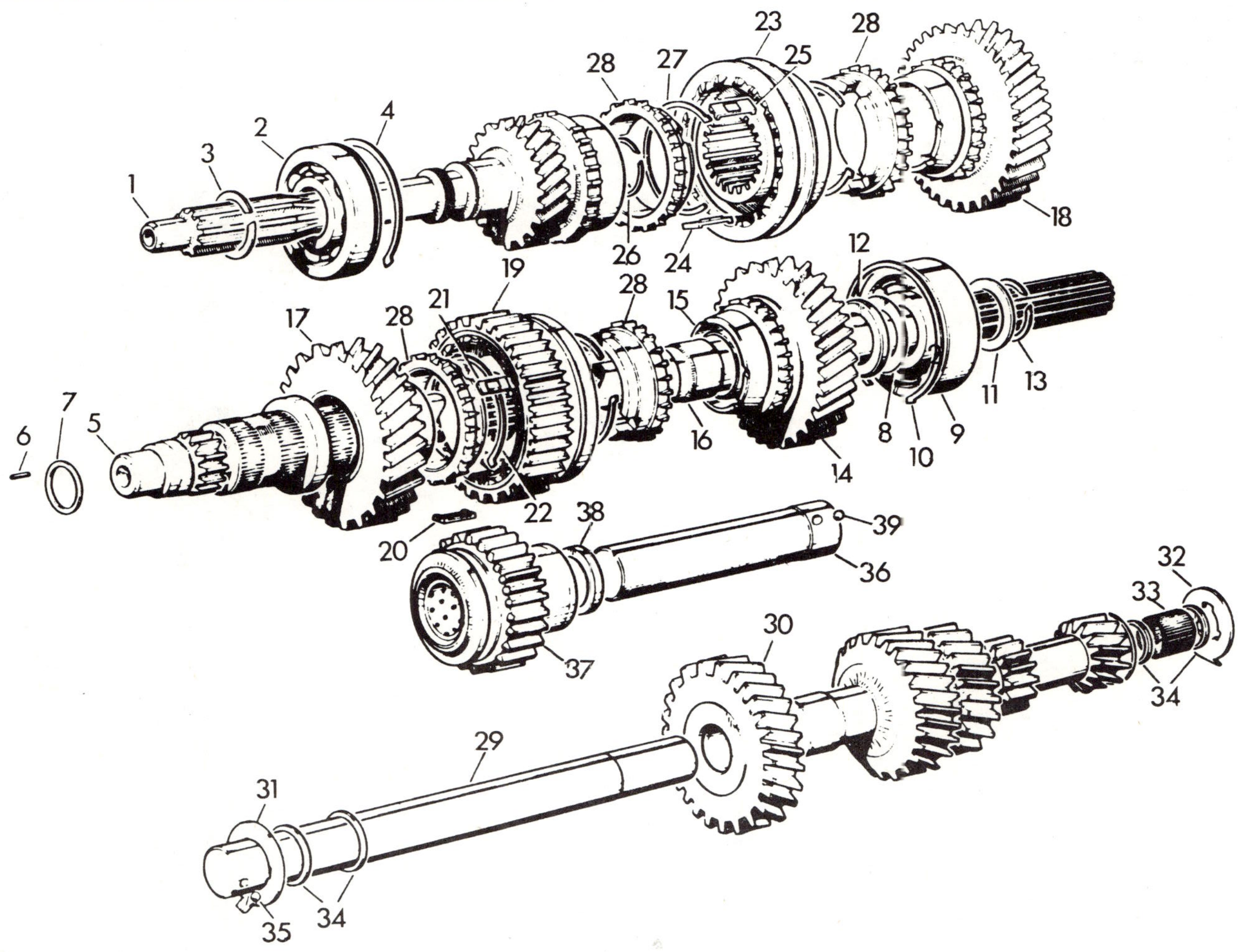

FIG. 6.2. GEARBOX - INTERNAL SHAFTS AND GEARS

1 Input shaft	8 Mainshaft shim	15 First gear bush	21 Sliding key
2 Bearing - input shaft	9 Mainshaft bearing	16 First gear sleeve	22 Spring
3 Circlip	10 Circlip - bearing rear cover	17 Second gear	23 3rd/4th synchro hub
4 Circlip	11 Thrust washer	18 Third gear	24 Sliding key
5 Mainshaft	12 Thrust washer	19 1st/2nd synchro hub	25 Sliding key
6 Needle roller	13 Circlip - selective	and reverse gear	26 Spring
7 Spacer ring	14 First gear	20 Sliding key - slotted	27 Circlip - selective

28 Synchro ring	35 Shaft locking ball
29 Layshaft	36 Reverse pinion shaft
30 Lay gear	37 Reverse pinion
31 Thrust washer - front	38 Spacer
32 Thrust washer - rear	39 Shaft locking ball
33 Needle roller	
34 Spacer rings	

3 Gearbox - dismantling

1 Place the complete unit on a firm bench or table and ensure that you have the following tools (in addition to the normal range of spanners etc.,) available:-

a) Good quality circlip pliers, 2 pairs, 1 expanding and 1 contracting.
b) Copper head mallet, at least 2 lb.
c) Drifts, steel 3/8 inch and brass 3/8 inch.
d) Small containers for needle rollers.
e) Engineer's vice mounted on firm bench.
f) Method of heating, such as blow lamp or butagas stove.

Any attempt to dismantle the gearbox without the foregoing is not necessarily impossible, but will certainly be very difficult and inconvenient resulting in possible injury or damage.
Read the whole of this section before starting work.
Take care not to let the synchro hub assemblies come apart before you want them to. It accelerates wear if the splines of hub and sleeve are changed in relation to each other. As a precaution it is advisable to make a line-up mark with a dab of paint.
Before finally going ahead with dismantling first ascertain the availability of spare parts - particularly shims and selective circlips which could be difficult.
2 Remove the gear change mechanism by undoing the securing clips which locate the pins in both the selector shaft and control rod.
3 Undo and remove the two bolts and spring washers that secure the gear lever carrier to the top of the extension housing or overdrive unit.
4 Remove the flexible mounting from the underside of the extension housing or overdrive unit.
5 Refer to Section 18 and remove the overdrive unit from the adaptor at the rear of the gearbox.
6 Undo and remove the ten bolts and spring washers that secure the cover plate to the gearbox body.
7 Undo the bolts that secure the rear extension (or overdrive adaptor) to the gear casing. Turn it until the rear end of the layshaft is exposed.
8 Using a suitable diameter drift and working from the rear, drive the shaft out through the front of the casing. Note there is a locking ball bearing in a recess in the front end of this shaft to stop it rotating when fitted to the casing. Take care not to lose it.
9 When the layshaft has been removed carefully drift up the laygear, keeping it horizontal. Remove the needle rollers and spacers from each end.
10 Recover the thrust washers from each end of the casing round the layshaft openings.
11 The selector striking levers are held to the cross shaft by tubular spring pins. These are driven downwards with a suitable diameter parallel pin punch just far enough to release the levers on the shaft. Manoeuvre the shaft to the most advantageous position for driving out. If driven too far they can jam against the side of the casing.
12 Draw out the cross shaft and lift out the striking levers.
13 The selector forks are also held by spring pins to their respective rails. These should also be driven out, using a parallel pin punch, sufficiently to prevent jamming against the side of the casing.
14 The detent ball bearings and springs for the selector rails are contained in recesses in the casing side. Remove the screwed plug with a wide blade screwdriver to release the springs and ball bearings.
15 Once again, rotate the rear cover so as to expose the ends of the selector fork rails which are then drifted out from the rear to the front of the casing. Take care to watch that the forks do not jam while the rails are being drifted out through them.
16 Drift out the reverse pinion shaft next otherwise the mainshaft cannot be removed. Note there is a spacer collar between the rear face of the pinion and the casing.
17 Withdraw the mainshaft and rear cover assembly from the casing. Collect up the needle rollers from the counterbore of the input shaft - also the spacer ring.
18 Undo and remove the five bolts and spring washers that hold the input shaft bearing cover to the front of the casing. Withdraw the input shaft assembly.
19 Should it be necessary to remove the reverse gear selector fork and striking fork, first drift out the spring pins by working through the drain plug hole. Before driving out the shaft remove the detent spring and ball bearing by undoing the screwed plug in the housing.
20 The gearbox main casing is now stripped out. Thoroughly flush out the interior of the casing with paraffin and wipe clean with a non fluffy rag.

4 Mainshaft - dismantling

1 The mainshaft is held into the extension cover by a circlip behind the main bearing. The bearing is also a tight fit and to avoid damage the cover should be warmed over a suitable heat source first. Remove the rubber mounting block before holding the cover over a naked flame. Contract the circlip to release it from the bore of the casing, support the casing against the vice jaws and drive the shaft out from the rear with a soft faced mallet.
2 Remove the speedometer driven gear and spindle by undoing the two set screws, marking the position of the flat on the housing relative to the cover, and lifting it out.
3 With long nosed pliers remove the circlip inside the extension cover which retains the bearing.
4 Warm the extension cover over a heat source such as a butane gas camping stove and then clamp the flange in a vice.
5 Tap the tail end of the protruding mainshaft with a hammer and block of wood to drive the shaft and bearing out of the cover.
6 Without the services of a press it is essential to have an assistant when dismantling the shaft. The synchro hubs, gear sleeve and bearing are very tightly fitted and considerable force must be carefully applied to get them off.
7 Starting with the rear end of the shaft remove the circlips retaining the speedometer drive worm gear and drive off the gear with a suitable drift. It is keyed to the shaft with a small barrel key which should not be lost.
8 Remove the circlip on the shaft which retains the bearing by its inner race.
9 Support the front face of 1st gear over the jaws of the vice adjusting the jaw width to give maximum support to the gear without touching the gears below because the gear is next to the bearing.
10 With one person holding the assembly firmly, the rear end of the shaft needs firm striking with a heavy soft headed mallet. The shaft will be driven out through the gears.
11 Repeat this operation with the front face of the 2nd gear supported over the vice jaws in order to drive the shaft out through 2nd gear, 1st/2nd synchro hub and the centre sleeve on which 1st gear revolves.
12 Take note of the thrust washer and any shims fitted between the bearing and adjacent gear/hub.
13 The rear end of the shaft now being clear up to the shoulder remove the circlip from the opposite end which retains the 3rd/4th speed synchro hub in position.
14 Support the rear face of 3rd gear over the vice jaws and drive the nose of the shaft down through the gear and 3rd/4th synchro hub assembly. With the exception of the hub assemblies (dealt with in a later section), the mainshaft is now dismantled.

5 Input shaft - dismantling

1 The shaft and bearing are retained in the front cover by a circlip which also locks into a groove in the bearing outer race.

2   Grip the cover sleeve with the gear upwards and expand the circlip sufficiently to clear the groove in the bearing. At the same time tap the end of the shaft on the bench or a solid wood block to move it out of the casing.

3   To get the bearing off the shaft grip the shaft across the covered jaws of the vice at a place clear of the splines and drift the bearing down off it.

6   Synchro hubs - dismantling and inspection

1   Synchro hubs are only too easy to dismantle - just push the centre out and the whole thing flies apart. The point is to prevent this happening before you are ready. Do not dismantle the hubs without reason and do not mix up the parts of the two hubs.

2   The most important check to make is for any backlash in the splines between the outer sleeve and inner hub. If any is noticeable the whole assembly must be renewed.

3   Mark the hub and sleeve so that you may reassemble them on the same splines. With the hub and sleeve separated the teeth at the ends of the splines which engage with corresponding teeth of the gear wheels must be checked for damage or wear.

4   Do not confuse the keystone shape at the ends of the teeth with wear. This shape matches the gear teeth shape and it is a design characteristic to minimise jump out tendencies.(Fig.6.3)

5   If the synchronising cones are being renewed it is sensible also to renew the sliding keys and springs which hold them in position.

7   Synchro hubs - reassembly

1   The hub assemblies are not interchangeable so must be re-assembled with their original or identical new parts.

2   The pips on the sliding keys are offset and must be assembled to both hubs so that the offset is towards the spigoted end of the hub.

3   One slotted key is assembled to each hub for locating the turned out end of the key spring.

4   It should be noted that the third and fourth clutch keys are shorter then the first and second clutch keys.

5   The turned out end of each spring must locate in the slotted key and be assembled to the hub in an anti clockwise direction as viewed from either side of the hub.

8   Gearbox components - inspection

1   It is assumed that the gearbox has been dismantled for reasons of excessive noise, lack of synchromesh on certain gears or for failure to stay in gear. If anything more drastic than this (total failure, seizure or gear case cracked) it would be better to leave well alone and look for a replacement, either secondhand or exchange unit.

2   Examine all gears for excessively worn, chipped or damaged teeth. Any such gears should be replaced.

3   Check all synchromesh rings for wear on the bearing surfaces, which normally have clear machined oil reservoir lines in them. If these are smooth or obviously uneven, replacement is essential. Also, when the rings are fitted to their gears - as they would be when in operation - there should be no rock. This would signify ovality, or lack of concentricity. One of the most satisfactory ways of checking is by comparing the fit of a new ring with an old one on the gearwheel cone.

    The teeth and cut outs in the synchro rings also wear, and for this reason also it is unwise not to fit new ones when the opportunity avails.

4   All ball race bearings should be checked for chatter and roughness after they have been flushed out. It is advisable to replace these anyway even though they may not appear too badly worn.

5   Circlips which are all important in locating bearings, gears

Fig. 6.3. Synchromesh hub outer sleeve
Illustration showing 'Keystone' shape of engagement dogs on all hubs

and hubs should also be checked to ensure that they are undistorted and undamaged. In any case a selection of new circlips of varying thicknesses should be obtained to componcato for variations in new components fitted, or wear in old ones. The specifications indicate what is available.

6   The thrust washers at the ends of the laygear should also be replaced, as they will almost certainly have worn if the gearbox is of any age.

7   Needle roller bearings between the input shaft and mainshaft and in the laygear are usually found in good order, but if in any doubt replace the needles as necessary.

8   For details of inspection of the synchro hub assemblies refer to Secion 6.

9   Input shaft - reassembly

1   The bearing can be driven onto the shaft with a piece of tube with an inside diameter of 1.125 in (28.575 mm) which will go over the shaft and butt against the inner race of the bearing. Do not drive the bearing on by the outer race. The circlip groove is off centre of the bearing and it should be nearest the gear on the shaft.

2   Make sure the bearing is driven fully up to the gear.

3   Put the circlip into the housing, expanding it with circlip pliers and then put the shaft and bearing in. Tap the shaft down so that the bearing first goes through the circlip and then make sure it is driven in far enough for the circlip to engage the groove.

10 Mainshaft - reassembly

1   Start with the tail end of the mainshaft and first place 2nd gear (the middle sized one of the three loose gears you have) onto the shaft with the gear teeth next to the shoulder of the shaft.

2   Place a synchro ring over the gearwheel cone.

3   Put the 1st/2nd gear synchro hub assembly (the one with the straight cut teeth on the outer sleeve) onto the shaft so that the teeth of the sleeve are nearest to the gear already fitted (photo).

4   The hub centre will need driving onto splines. A piece of 1.125 in (28.575 mm) internal diameter tube is ideal for this as it will be necessary to drive only the hub centre. It is also necessary to make sure that the cut outs in the synchro ring engage with the sliding keys in the hub when it is driven fully home. If you do not have a long enough piece of tube even then, use a drift or support the hub centre across the vice jaws and drive the shaft into it with a soft mallet (photo).

5   The hub sleeve for first gear is also a drive fit and goes on next. It helps, to heat it up. It is important to make sure that the edges of this sleeve are not nicked, burred or spread in the process of fitting. If two people are available it can be done with

the vice jaw method. Make sure it butts tight up to the hub of the synchro assembly (photos).

6　Fit a synchro ring into the hub assembly, lining up the cut outs with the sliding keys.

7　Place 1st gear (the largest) onto the shaft with the cone section fitting into the synchro ring (photo).

8　Fit the large thrust washer.

9　At this stage it is theoretically necessary to check the measurement from the front face of the shoulder on which 3rd gear runs to the rear face of the thrust washer just fitted. This is because the longitudinal position of the mainshaft in the casing is controlled by the position of the rear bearing which goes on next. The measurement referred to should be between 5.781 - 5.783 in (147.837 - 147.888 mm). The design is such that shims need adding between the thrust washer and bearing to make up the correct distance.

10　Provided that only the bearing and synchro rings have been renewed one may replace the shims originally fitted without trepidation. If the synchro hub assembly and gears have been renewed then the shim thickness may need altering. For this, a large caliper gauge will need to be acquired to carry out the necessary measurement. Shim thickness can then be calculated. Available shims are listed in the specifications (photo).

11　With the thrust washer and shims in position the rear bearing is driven onto the shaft in the same way as the hubs. Replace the large circlip behind the bearing first - otherwise it will have to be spread excessively in order to get it in position afterwards. Be careful not to trap the shim in the circlip groove while the bearing is driven on (photo).

12　Having ensured that the bearing is driven fully up to the shims and thrust washer, fit the thrust collar and circlip in the shaft groove behind the bearing inner race. This is where a circlip of a different thickness may need selecting. Too thick a circlip will not go in, and too thin a circlip will allow the bearing to creep fractionally along the shaft until it butts up against the circlip. Select one which is a snug fit (photos).

13　The speedometer drive gear is next fitted to the main shaft. Line up the keyway first. Here again the correct thickness of the circlip on each side of the gear will prevent movement of the gear on the shaft (photos).

14　Turning to the front of the shaft fit third gear (the only loose gear left) onto the nose with the flat side up against the shoulder (photo).

15　Place a synchro ring over the gear cone and put the 3rd/4th hub assembly onto the shaft with the selector fork groove in the sleeve towards the front of the shaft. This hub will need driving on in the same way as the other end; once again the sliding keys must line up and fit into the synchro ring cut outs. Make sure that the hub assembly is driven on fully up to the third gear (photos).

16　Select a circlip which is a tight fit in the groove to retain the hub assembly on the shaft (photo).

17　Before fitting the mainshaft back into the rear extension cover fit a new rear oil seal. The old one can be taken out by clamping it in the vice and pulling the casing out (photo).

18　Carefully tap the new seal into position keeping it square and undistorted. Soak the felt ring with oil (NB, this job can be done with the gearbox installed and propeller shaft removed) (photo).

19　Warm the extension housing so that the main bearing on the shaft will enter easily (photo).

20　When the bearing is in position make sure that the retaining circlip fits the housing groove properly (photo).

21　Fit the gearbox mounting to the extension cover ensuring it is the correct way round.

11 Gearbox - reassembly

1　Make sure the mating faces of the casing and rear extension cover are clean, fit a new gasket in position and place the main-shaft assembly into the casing. Do not replace any bolts yet (photo).

10.3　2nd gear, synchro ring and 1st/2nd gear synchro hub being put into the rear end of the mainshaft.

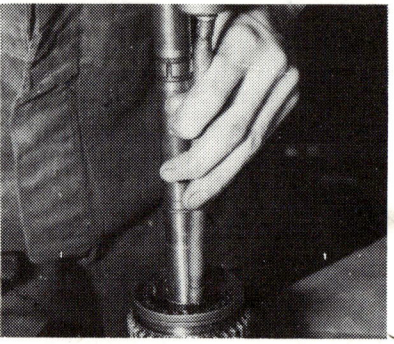

10.4　Driving lst/2nd gear synchro hub onto the shaft splines

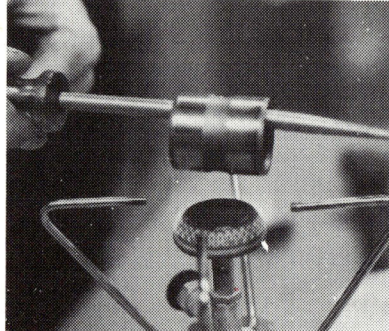

10.5a　Heating 1st gear hub sleeve

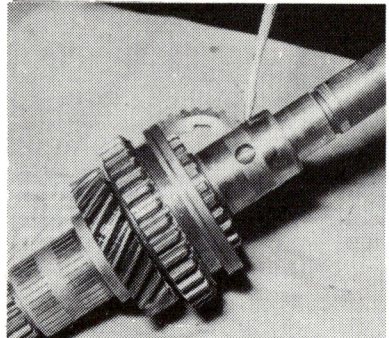

10.5b　Showing the hubsleeve position on the shaft butted up to the synchro hub assembly

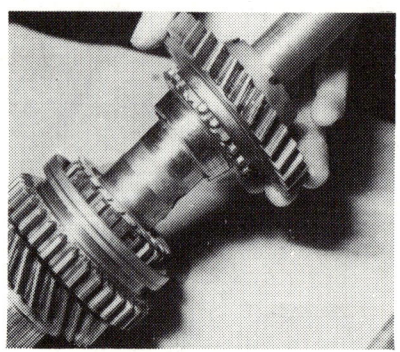

10.7　Fitting first gear. Note that the synchro ring is in position in the synchro hub.

10.10　Placing the thrust washer and shim in position.

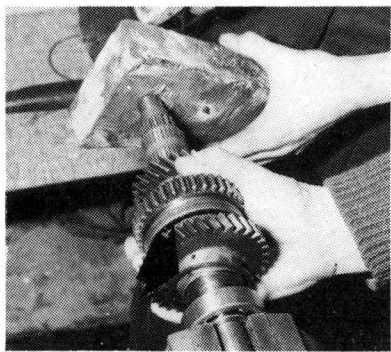

10.11 Driving the bearing onto the shaft. Note the large circlip between the bearing and gear (arrowed)

10.12a Rear thrust collar being fitted

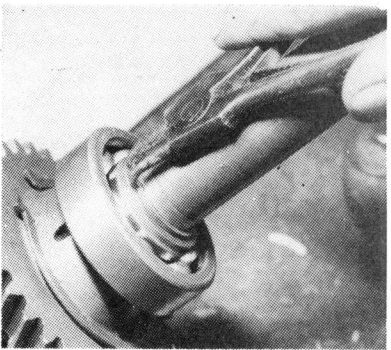

10.12b Circlip being fitted

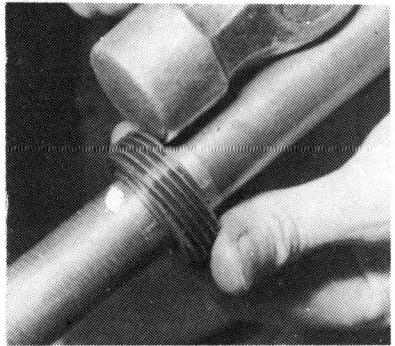

10.13a Tapping the speedometer drive gear up to one circlip

10.13b Fitting the second circlip

10.14 Fitting 3rd gear to the front of the shaft

10.15a Placing the synchro ring and 3rd/4th hub onto the front of the mainshaft

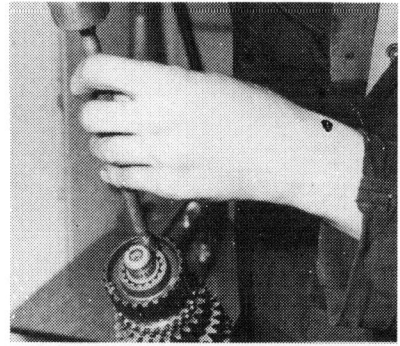

10.15b Driving hub onto the splines The outer sleeve has not yet been assembled to the hub

10.16 Fitting the circlip to retain 3rd/4th synchro hub

10.17 Pulling off the rear extension cover oil seal

10.18 Fitting a new rear extension oil seal

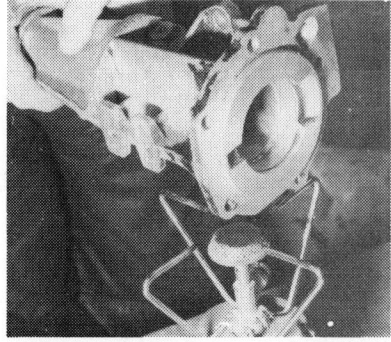

10.19 Warming the rear extension cover prior to fitting the mainshaft assembly into it

2 Rotate the cover (or overdrive adaptor) until the reverse pinion shaft hole is clear. Put the locking ball into the recess in the reverse pinion shaft and then guide the plain end into the casing.

3 Put the spacer ring over the shaft followed by the pinion. The pinion teeth chamfered ends should face the front of the casing (photo).

4 Rotate the shaft so that the locking ball lines up with the notch in the casing and then drive it fully home until the end is flush with the casing (photo).

5 Fit the rear cover bolts but do not tighten them up fully at this stage. On units with overdrive do not forget to fit the inhibitor switch mounting bracket.

6 The 24 needle rollers should next be prepared for fitting to the input shaft onto the nose of the mainshaft. This can be done by either fitting them in the counterbore of the input shaft or around the nose of the mainshaft. (The latter method is less likely to cause dislodging of the needles on assembly). Use a little grease - not too much, to hold the needles in position (photo).

7 The spacer must be installed correctly. It is positioned at the mainshaft end of the needle rollers.

8 Check the input shaft mating surfaces on the cover and casing, and position a new gasket on the flange.

9 Fit a synchro ring (the remaining one) into the 3rd/4th synchro hub so that the cut outs engage the sliding keys.

10 Fit the input shaft into the casing so that the counterbore engages over the nose of the mainshaft without dislodging the needle rollers (photo).

11 Replace the front cover bolts, but do not tighten them fully at this stage.

12 The selector forks and rails are fitted next. It is best to have new cylindrical pins to secure the forks to the shaft. In subsequent paragraphs remember that you are working with the gearbox inverted so references to the left and right side are based on the bore being the proper way up and looking from rear to

front.

13 First/second selector fork has legs of unequal length and the rail is fitted from the front of the casing. The striking lug is fitted to the rail with the jaw for the lever towards the casing front.

14 Place the rail into the casing from the front on the left side. The three detent grooves are at the front end of the shaft and face the top of the casing when finally positioned.

15 Pass the shaft through the striking lug.

16 Fit the selector fork into the 1st/2nd selector hub groove with the recessed face of the fork facing the front of the casing.

17 Pass the rail through the fork base and tap it home as far as it will go. The front end will come clear of the front of the casing (photo).

18 Pin the striking lug and selector fork to the rail using a flat nosed punch to fit the pins (photo).

19 The 3rd/4th selector fork rail is fitted on the other side of the casing. The selector fork should be fitted into the groove in the outer sleeve of the 3rd/4th gear hub with the recessed face facing the front of the casing like the other.

20 No separate striking lug is fitted on this rail. There is a cut out in the rail itself.

21 Pin the fork to the rail so that the cut out faces the interior of the casing (photo).

22 The cross shaft and striking levers are next assembled.

23 A conventional lip type seal is fitted into the casing for the right hand end of the shaft. This should be prised out and renewed while the opportunity presents itself. Lubricate the new seal lip with molybdenum paste or grease and drive it in open side first until it butts up against the shouldered recess in the casing (photos).

24 Insert the cross shaft, spigot end first into the casing from the right hand side.

25 Take up the striking lever which has two legs - one long - and put the shaft through it so that the long leg points to the bottom of the bore and the boss faces the side of the casing (photo).

10.20 Fitting the mainshaft bearing circlip into the rear cover.

11.1 Replacing the mainshaft into the gearbox casing

11.3 Assembling the reverse pinion and shaft

11.4 Reverse pinion shaft showing locking ball joint being driven fully home

11.6 Fitting needle rollers in input shaft counterbore

11.10 Replacing the input shaft into the casing. In this instance the synchro ring is fitted on the gear cover rather than in the synchro hub on the mainshaft

11.17 First/second gear selector rail with the fork and lug not yet pinned into position The front of the casing is to the left of the photo

11.18 Pinning the 1st/2nd selector fork to the rail

11.21 Pinning the fork to the rail

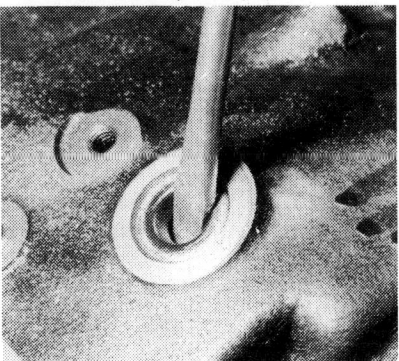

11.23A Prising out the old seal

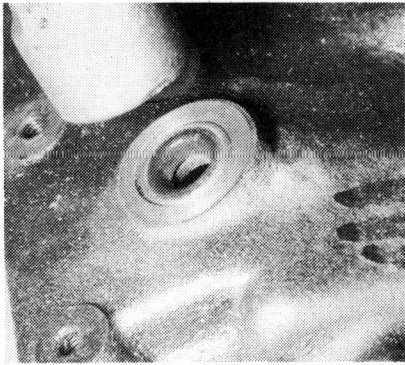

11.23b Fitting a new seal for the cross shaft in the right hand side of the casing

11.25 Striking lever in correct position relative to 3rd/4th selector fork rail (before cross shaft has been put through it)

11.26 Striking lever in correct position relative to 1st/2nd selector fork rail (before shaft has been put through it)

11.28a Placing the pin in position on the striking lever

11.28b Pinning the striking lever to the cross shaft

11.31 Lay gear first thrust washer in position

11.32 Levering the lay gear into the casing.

11.33 Fitting the layshaft

26 Pass the shaft next through the other striking lever, the leg pointing to the top of the box and the boss facing the side of the casing (photo).

27 Manoeuvre both levers to line up with the holes in the shaft making sure that the set screw recess on the right hand end of the shaft faces the front of the casing. If this is not done correctly the operating lever on the end of the shaft cannot be clamped on in the correct position.

28 Refit the spring pins to lock the striking levers to the shaft (photos).

29 The laygear is fitted next. The front end has 26 needle rollers and the rear 25. Each set has a spacer ring at each end. Put the needles and spacers in position using grease to prevent them dropping out.

30 Fit the thrust washers into the casing with the dimpled faces facing inwards. The washer with the flat edge goes at the rear with the edge in line with the casing edge.

31 The circular front washer is positioned so that the tab engages in the groove (photo).

32 Carefully lower the laygear into the casing (large gear to the front) taking care not to disturb the thrust washers or needle rollers. Line up the holes of the casing and the gear (photo).

33 Put the locking ball in the recess of the layshaft and introduce the plain end of the layshaft from the front of the casing end into the gear without upsetting the needle rollers (photo).

34 Tap it gently through the gear. The hole at the other end of the casing will be covered by the rear cover flange so as to ensure that the needle rollers are not disturbed, the bolts can be removed and the cover rotated to expose the hole. If the hold is left covered make sure that the cover bolts are not fully tightened. If they are, air may be trapped which could prevent the shaft being driven fully home.

35 Turn the shaft to line up the locking ball with the recess at the front of the casing and drive the shaft fully home.

36 At this stage rotate the mainshaft to ensure that everything revolves freely and smoothly.

37 Fully tighten the input shaft flange bolts and rear cover bolts and check once again that the shafts revolve freely.

38 Drive in the two cups that seal the selector fork rail holes in the front of the casing. They should be driven in open end first, just flush with the casing (photo).

39 Refit the detent balls, springs and screwed plugs into each side of the casing (photo).

40 The cover incorporates the reverse selector fork and rail. Having made sure that the mating surfaces are clean, fit a new gasket and replace the cover so that the fork engages the groove in the reverse gear pinion (photo).

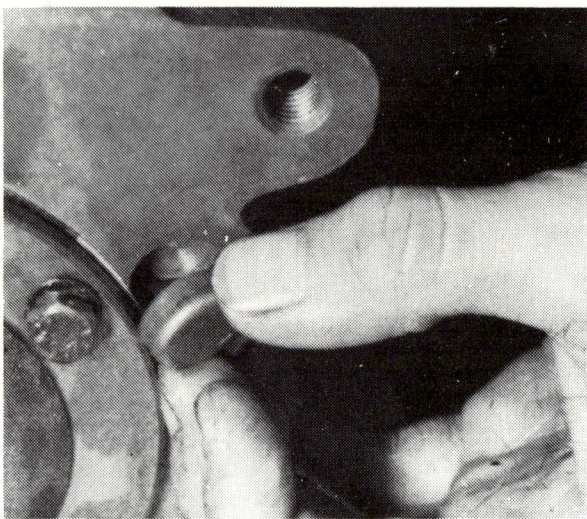

11.38 Fitting the selector fork rail blanking plugs to the front of the casing

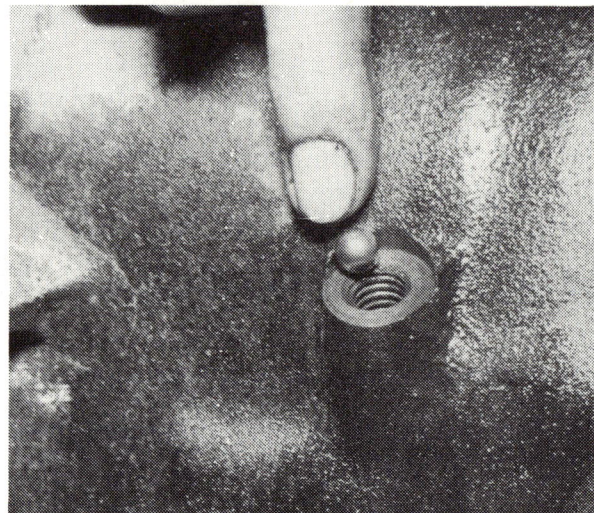

11.39 Replacing the detent ball (Prior to spring and flag) in the casing

11.40 Refitting the cover plate and reverse selector rail. Note fork which will engage the pinion groove

11.41 Tightening gear casing cover bolts.

41 Replace the cover bolts and tighten them. (photo)
42 Refit the detent ball and spring followed by the screwed plug into the cover if they have been taken out.
43 Fit the speedometer driven gear not forgetting the thrust pad, a new seal (with circular spring on the small inner lip) and the housing (photo). The housing should have been marked on removal. If not, then the position of the flat on the housing depends on the number of teeth on the gear. Fig.6.5 shows the flat position for the various numbers of teeth.

12 Gearbox - replacement

1 Replacement of the gearbox is a reversal of the removal procedure but certain matters have to be remembered.
2 The change mechanism should be assembled and fitted, and all gears engaged before reinstallation.
3 If you have overhauled the gearbox do not neglect the change mechanism as it is subject to wear and this results in a sloppy change action.
4 The clutch actuating lever is fitted by a spring clip to a ball ended stud in the bellhousing. Make sure this is fitted correctly as the gearbox input shaft has be be passed through the thrust bearing when the gearbox is replaced.
5 Do not forget to fit a new gasket between the gearbox face and the bellhousing. Hold it in position with some grease during assembly. Do not use sealing compound.
6 Make sure that the rear mounting and crossmember are fitted the correct way round.

13 Extension housing oil seal - removal and refitting

1 Refer to Chapter 7 and remove the propeller shaft.
2 Using a chisel shown in Fig.6.4 knock off the old oil seal and casing.
3 The new seal and casing assembly may now be refitted using a suitable diameter drift.
4 Before refitting the propeller shaft smear the lip of the seal with a little Castrol LM Grease to ensure the seal fine lip is not damaged. Check that the propeller shaft sleeve is free from burrs and scores.

11.43 Fitting speedometer driven gear and spindle with the housing

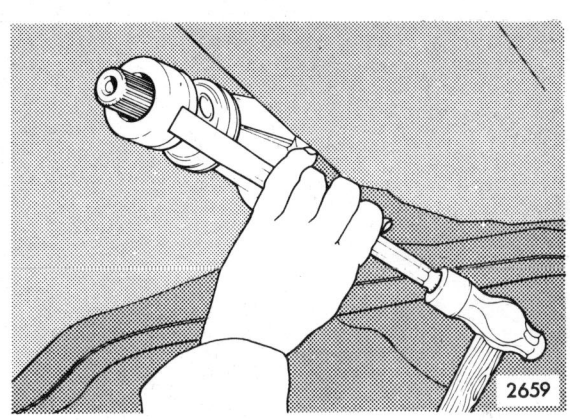

Fig. 6.4. Removal of oil seal and casing

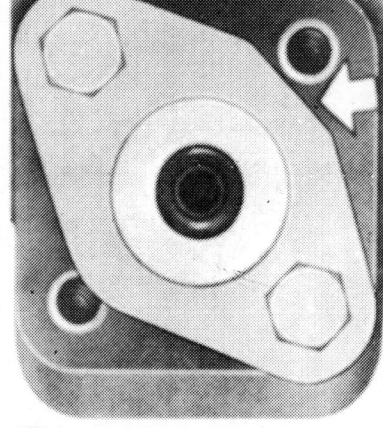

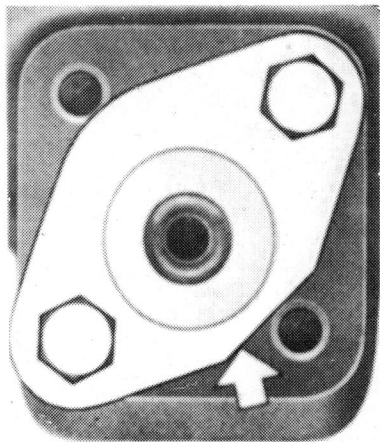

FIG.6.5. SPEEDOMETER GEAR HOUSING

A 13, 14, 15 and 16 Tooth gears   B 17 Tooth gears   C 19 and 20 Tooth gears

14 Gearchange mechanism

Upon reference to Fig.6.6 it will be seen that the gear shift upper lever (11) is pinned to a finger (2) which is able to pivot in an intermediate lever (1). The intermediate lever pivots on a bush (8) which is pressed into a carrier bracket (7), this being bolted to the transmission extension housing. The intermediate lever outer leg is extended downwards and is connected to the quadrant shaped striking lever shaft coupling (6) by a control rod (5). The spherical end of the finger engages in the intermediate lever pivot shaft (10) which runs in the carrier bracket bush and is loaded by a spring and pad (9) in the centre of the shaft.

A selector bar (4) engages in a grooved adjuster (3) in the lever pivot shaft and connects the pivot shaft to the striking lever shaft coupling.

The forward or rearward movement of the upper lever is transmitted through the intermediate lever to the control rod. Sideways movement of the upper lever is transmitted through the finger and intermediate pivot shaft to the selector bar.

A safety device is incorporated in the gear change lever system whereby it is not possible to accidently engage reverse. This is made possible by a stepped abutment (3), Fig.6.7, in the housing (2) at the lower end of the upper lever contacting a corresponding step (4) on the intermediate lever.

To engage reverse the abutment is lifted by a cable (1) which passes through the centre of the gear change lever and connected to a lift collar at the top of the lever. It is possible to fit a new cable once the gear change lever assembly has been removed from the car.

To remove the gear change lever assembly first release the plastic boot from the lip around the edge of the gear change lever aperture and slide the boot up the gear lever. Untie the lace in the gear change lever aperture and push down the cover. Using a screwdriver release the 'E' clip from the groove in the pivot pin and withdraw the pin (Fig.6.8).

If a centre console is fitted this must be removed first by undoing and removing the four self tapping screws that secure the insert to the console, and then the four self tapping screws that secure the cowl to the body panel ((Fig.6.9)).

If it is necessary to gain access to the reverse gear abutment override cable pull off the lever knob, lift away the spring and then undo the grub screw located in the lever collar (Fig.6.10). Before withdrawing the cable from the lower end of the lever, drift out the spring pin that secures the gear shift finger and stepped abutment (Fig.6.11).

Note that on overdrive models, the lever knob also includes the overdrive switch and is threaded to the lever shroud. The knob may be unscrewed once the top of the knob has been prised off and the wires detached from the switch.

When reassembling the retainer (see arrow Fig.6 12) it must be located between the lift collar spring and the wires to prevent the wires being chafed. Before screwing on the knob coat the threads with Loctite Grade 'C' to prevent the knob rotating and twisting the cables.

When the gear change lever has been refitted check that the selector bar is fully engaged in the groove of the adjuster before assembling the retainer. If necessary a bend can be introduced in the bar to provide full engagement.

When the gear change upper lever is fitted to the intermediate lever, adjust the cable length so that there is a clearance 'A' (Fig.6.13) between the underside of the abutment and the top of the intermediate lever of 0.02 - 0.04 in (0.5 - 1.0 mm). Engage 1st and 2nd gear and set the adjuster bolt in the lever pivot shaft so that clearance 'B' is 0.012 - 0.020 in (0.3 - 0.5 mm).

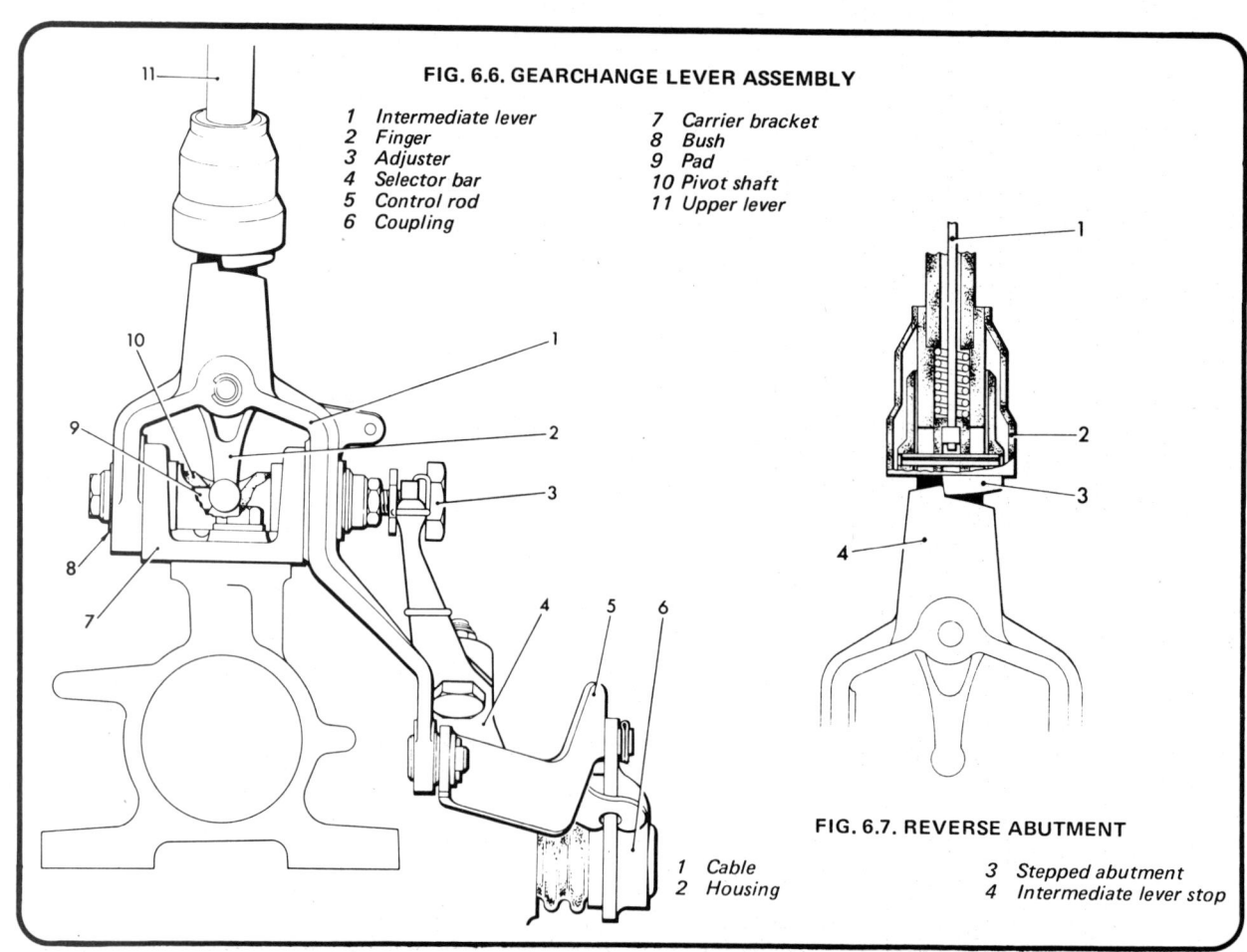

FIG. 6.6. GEARCHANGE LEVER ASSEMBLY

1 Intermediate lever
2 Finger
3 Adjuster
4 Selector bar
5 Control rod
6 Coupling
7 Carrier bracket
8 Bush
9 Pad
10 Pivot shaft
11 Upper lever

FIG. 6.7. REVERSE ABUTMENT

1 Cable
2 Housing
3 Stepped abutment
4 Intermediate lever stop

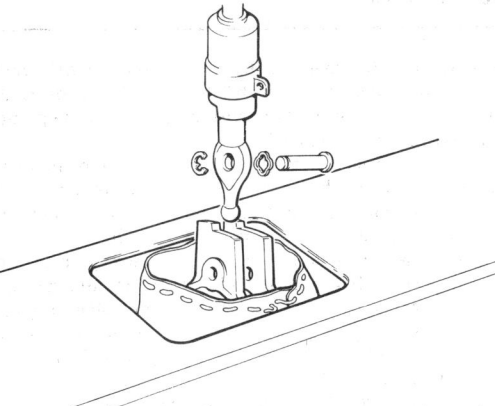

Fig. 6.8. Gear change lever pivot pin assembly

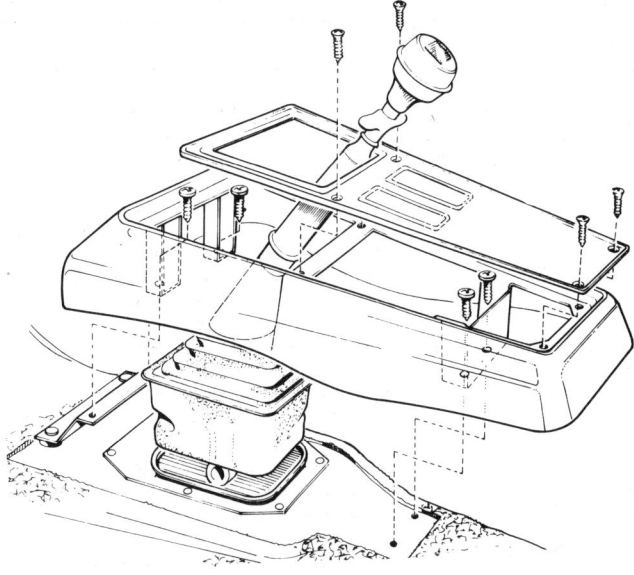

Fig. 6.9. Gear change lever console assembly

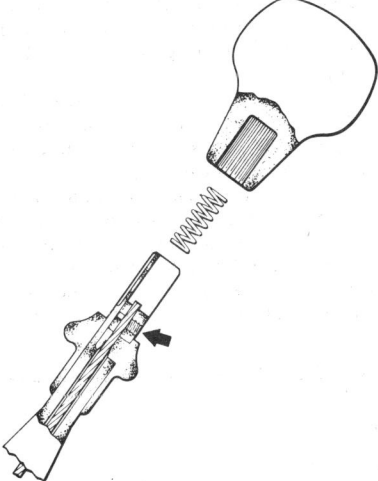

Fig. 6.10. Grab screw location in lever collar

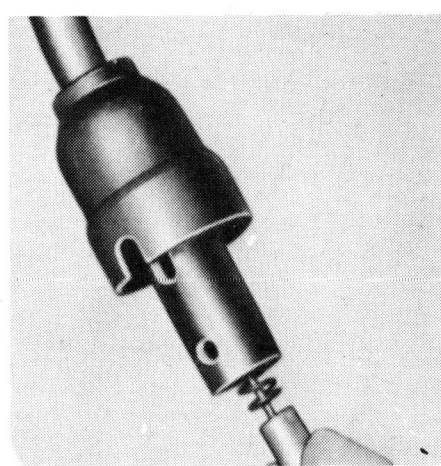

Fig. 6.11. Drawing reverse selection cable downwards through gear change lever

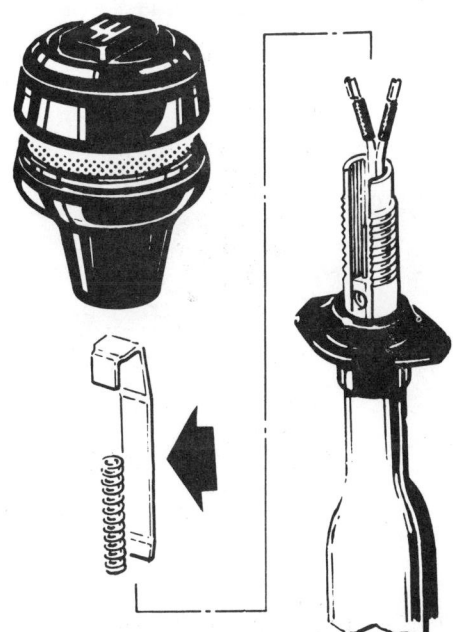

Fig. 6.12. Gear change lever knob assembly (overdrive models)

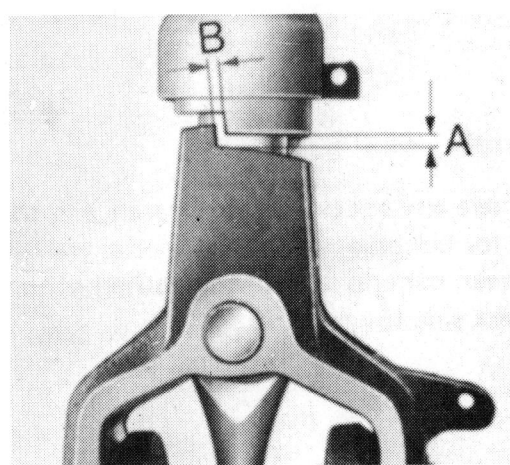

FIG. 6.13. GEAR CHANGE LEVER CABLE ADJUSTMENT

A = 0.02 - 0.04 inch (0.5 - 1.0 mm)
B = 0.012 - 0.020 inch (0.3 - 0.5 mm)

15   Fault diagnosis

NOTE: It is sometimes difficult to decide whether it is worthwhile removing and dismantling the gearbox for a fault which may be nothing more than a minor irritant. Gearboxes which howl, or where the synchromesh can be 'beaten' by a quick gear change, may continue to perform for a long time in this state. A worn gearbox usually needs a complete rebuild to eliminate noise because the various gears, if re-aligned on new bearings will continue to howl when different wearing surfaces are presented to each other.

The decision to overhaul, therefore, must be considered with regard to time and money available, relative to the degree of noise or malfunction that the driver has to suffer.

Symptom	Reason/s	Remedy
Ineffective synchromesh	Worn baulk rings or synchro hubs	Dismantle and renew.
Jumps out of one or more gears (on drive or over-run)	Weak detent springs or worn selector forks or worn gears	Dismantle and renew. (Detent balls and springs can be renewed without dismantling the gearbox).
Noisy, rough, whining and vibration	Worn bearings and/or laygear thrust washers (initially) resulting in extended wear generally due to play and backlash	Dismantle and renew.
Noisy and difficult engagement of gears	Clutch fault	Examine clutch operation.

16 Overdrive - general description

An overdrive unit is fitted as a factory optional extra to those vehicles with a manual gearbox only. It is attached to the rear of the gearbox and takes the form of a hydraulically operated epicyclic gear. Overdrive operates on third and top gears to provide fast cruising at lower engine revolutions. The overdrive is engaged or disengaged by a driver controlled switch which controls an electric solenoid mounted on the overdrive unit. A further switch called an inhibitor switch is included in the electrical circuit to prevent accidental engagement of the overdrive in reverse, first or second gears.

The overdrive unit is designed to be engaged or disengaged when engine power is being transmitted through the power line and without the use of the clutch pedal at any throttle opening or road speed. It is important that the overdrive is not dis-engaged at high road speeds as this will cause excessively high engine speeds.

It will be seen from Fig.6.14 that overdrive gears are epicyclic and comprise a central sunwheel which is in mesh with three planet wheels. These three gears are also in mesh with an internally toothed annulus. The planet carrier is splined to the input shaft which is, in fact the mainshaft of the manual gearbox. The annulus is an integral part of the output shaft.

When the overdrive is disengaged the engine torque is transmitted from the input shaft (A) Fig 6.14, to the inner member of an uni-directional clutch (N) and then onto the outer member of the clutch (C) via rollers (B) which are driven up inclined faces and wedge or lock the inner and outer members. The outer members of the clutch (C) form part of the combined annulus (H) and the output shaft (D). Thus, as the gear train is not operative the drive is direct through the overdrive unit.

Mounted on the externally splined extension shaft (F) of the

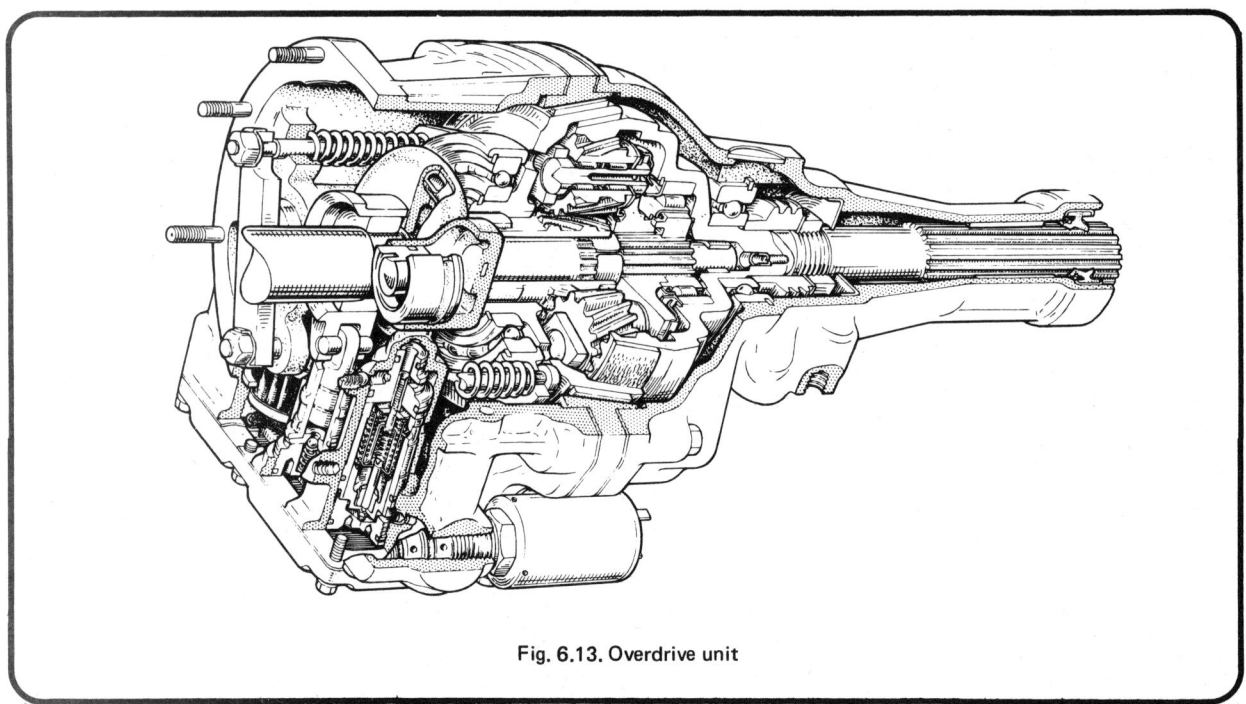

Fig. 6.13. Overdrive unit

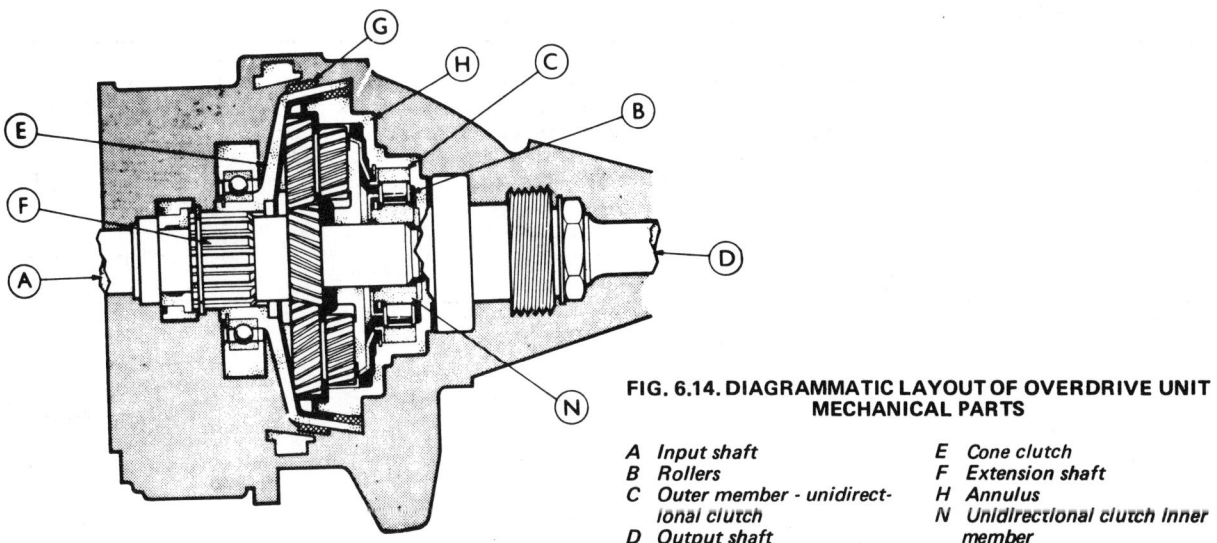

FIG. 6.14. DIAGRAMMATIC LAYOUT OF OVERDRIVE UNIT MECHANICAL PARTS

A	Input shaft	E	Cone clutch
B	Rollers	F	Extension shaft
C	Outer member - unidirect-	H	Annulus
	ional clutch	N	Unidirectional clutch inner
D	Output shaft		member

sun gear is a cone clutch (E) and this is pressed onto the annulus by a number of springs which press against the overdrive unit casing. The spring pressure is transmitted to the clutch member by a thrust ring and ball bearing, so causing the inner friction lining of the cone clutch to be in contact with the outer cone of the annulus (H) and rotate with the annulus whilst the springs and thrust rings remain stationary.

As the sunwheel is splined to the clutch member, the whole gear train is locked together so permitting overrun and engine torque in reverse gear to be transmitted through the overdrive unit. Also an additional load is imparted to the clutch during overrun and reverse conditions by the sun wheel, which, due to the special helix angle of the gear teeth, thrusts rearwards and has for its reaction member the cone clutch.

When the overdrive unit is engaged, the cone clutch takes up a new position, whereby it is no longer in contact with the annulus, but has now moved forward, so that the outer friction lining is in contact with the brake ring which is part of the overdrive unit casing. The sunwheel to which the clutch is attached is now held still. The planet carrier rotates with the input shaft (A) and the three planet wheels are caused to rotate about their own axis and drive the annulus at a greater speed than the input shaft. This is made possible because the uni-directional clutch outer member can overrun the inner member. Hydraulic pressure generated by a pump in the overdrive unit acts on two pistons when a little valve is opened and moves the cone clutch in a forward direction. The little valve is controlled by the solenoid which is operated by the driver using an electric switch. This hydraulic pressure is sufficiently light to overcome the spring pressure that holds the clutch member onto the annulus and causes the clutch to engage with the brake ring and hold the sunwheel at rest. As the overdrive unit is attached to the rear of the gearbox, it is able to share the oil in the gearbox. The cam operated plunger pump draws the oil from the overdrive oil sump and via drillings, passes it to the two operating piston chambers, the ball type operating valve and the pressure relief valve. Oil is also passed to the various other parts of the overdrive unit for lubrication purposes.

When the driver moves the overdrive switch to the 'engaged' position current passes to the solenoid and causes the operating valve to close. Pressure built up in the hydraulic system causes the two pistons to move against the action of the springs which hold the sliding member onto the annulus. Therefore, the sliding member is moved into contact with the brake ring.

Oil is then continued to be pumped into the hydraulic operating system so compressing the modulator springs that are inside the pistons resulting in a cushioning effect by the progressive application of the load between the sliding member and the brake ring. As the sunwheel is now in a locked condition and the planet gears are free to revolve, the overdrive condition is in existence. Any further delivery of oil will open the pressure relief valve which will allow oil to pass to the various components for lubrication purposes and then return to the overdrive oil sump.

When the driver moves the overdrive switch to the 'disengaged' position, current will cease to flow to the solenoid and the operating valve ball will be unsealed by hydraulic pressure so uncovering the exhaust port. The spring load on the sliding member will force oil to pass from the piston chambers whilst, at the same time, oil will continue to be pumped into the circuit and with the two circuits connected allowing mixing of the two oil flows, causing action against each other, and will control the movement of the sliding member. The sliding member is, therefore, disengaged from the brake ring and this time engaged with the annulus at a controlled rate. The oil flow will then pass through the exhaust port and provide lubrication for the various internal parts.

17 Overdrive - precautions

1 Overdrive units are robust and well engineered, and provided they are not abused will last as long as the rest of the transmission without trouble.

2 If there are any indications that some part of the system is not functioning properly then checks should be immediate. If left, serious damage will result with more expensive repairs resulting.

3 Do not engage the overdrive when accelerating fiercely. It will function but it imposes unnecessary strain.

4 Remember that it should only operate on 3rd and 4th gears. If it should start operating on 1st and 2nd (if tried) something is wrong with the inhibitor switch circuit. This means that reverse might be engaged with overdrive accidentally in operation. The unit would be ruined.

5 Be a little more fussy about the gearbox oil level. Oil cleanliness is more important also as any metal particles can upset the pressure system. There is an oil filter incorporated in the unit.

6 If the overdrive does not disengage the car must not be reversed - either under its own power or otherwise. Damage would result. (The same applies in rare circumstances such as coming to a halt going up hill with overdrive engaged and then letting it run back).

7 Overdrive should not engage at all with the ignition switched off.

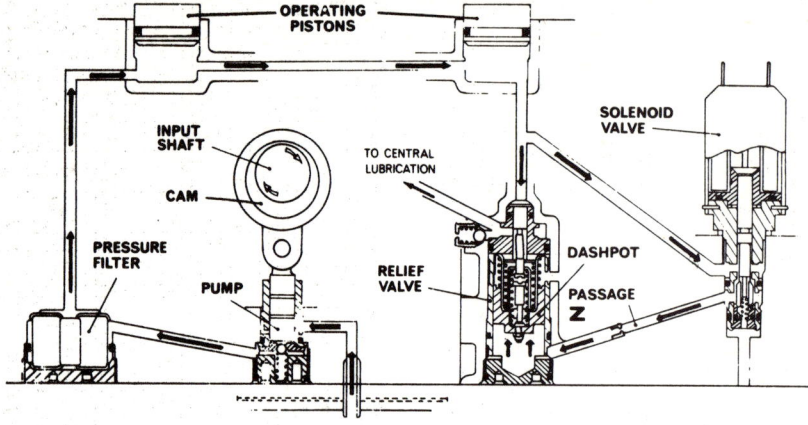

Fig. 6.15. Hydraulic circuit - overdrive conditions

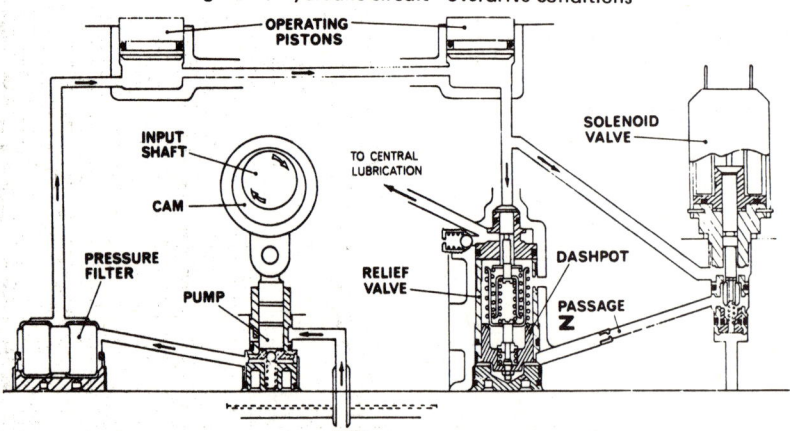

Fig. 6.16. Hydraulic circuit - direct drive condition

18 Overdrive - maintenance

If it works satisfactorily leave it alone. The only possible exception to this is the cleaning of the oil filter.

As Vauxhall routine servicing procedures no longer provide for periodic changing of the gearbox oil (it will presumably last as long as the gearbox!), it is possible that the filter will gradually become choked. (If there was nothing in the oil to choke it there would be no point in fitting a filter).

Access to the filter for cleaning is dealt with in Section 23.

19 Overdrive unit - removal and replacement

1 It is most important that the overdrive is in 'free' state before removal. If it was in a drive situation the splines on the uni-directional clutch and planet carrier will be loaded on to the gearbox output shaft and prevent the unit from being drawn off. So drive the car in 3rd or top in overdrive and whilst in gear depress the clutch and disengage the overdrive. Do not use the overdrive again before removal.

2 Drain the oil from the gearbox and overdrive sump. Take off the propeller shaft as described in Chapter 7 and disconnect the leads to the overdrive solenoid.

3 Undo the nuts securing it to the overdrive adaptor.

4 Draw the unit off the gearbox.

5 Replacement is a reversal of the removal procedure. It helps if the high point of the eccentric on the gearbox shaft (which drives the overdrive pump) is facing downwards when the unit is fitted (Fig.6.17).

6 If you are unable to measure exactly the three pints of oil needed for refilling the transmission make sure that you check the level after the overdrive unit has been used.

Fig.6.17 Eccentric on gearbox mainshaft

20 Overdrive - dismantling, overhaul and reassembly

1 Refer to Fig.6.21 which shows all the components of the overdrive unit.

2 Using a screwdriver or small chisel, bend back the tab washers that lock the four nuts that secure the operating piston bridge pieces and undo the four nuts. Lift away the four nuts and tab washers followed by the two bridge pieces.

3 Undo and remove the six nuts that secure the main casing to the rear casing in a progressive manner as these two parts will be under the influence of the clutch return spring pressure. Note

the position of the copper washers which fit on the two studs at the top of the casing.

4 The main casing complete with brake ring can now be separated from the rear casing.

5 Lift out the sliding member assembly complete with the sunwheel followed by the planet carrier assembly. This should be done with care as it is easy to accidentally damage the oil catcher which is located under the planet carrier assembly.

6 To dismantle the main casing and brake ring first tap the brake ring from its spigot in the main casing using a suitable drift.

7 Using a pair of pliers carefully remove the two operating pistons.

8 Undo and remove the six bolts and spring washers securing the sump to the main casing. Lift away the sump, gasket and suction filter.

9 To remove the relief valve and dashpot assembly a special tool is now necessary. It has a part number of L354, (Fig.6.18). Remove the relief valve and then withdraw the dashpot piston complete with its component springs and cap, followed by the residual pressure spring. It should be noted that this spring is the only loose spring in the general assembly.

10 The relief valve piston assembly can now be withdrawn by pulling down carefully using a pair of pliers.

11 A further special tool is required to remove the relief valve.

Using tool number L401 (Fig.6.19) inserted into the now exposed relief valve, bore and withdraw the relief valve together with the dashpot sleeve. Take great care not to damage these parts during removal.

12 Using tool number L354 undo and remove the pump plug taking care not to lose the non-return valve spring and ball bearing.

13 The pump valve seat can now be withdrawn. The pump body will be held in position by its 'O' ring so to remove this hook a piece of wire into the inlet port and draw the assembly downwards.

14. To remove the pressure filter use tool number L401 and unscrew the pressure filter base plug. The filter element will be released with the plug. Note the aluminium washer which locates on the shoulder in the filter bore.

15 Using a 1 in (25 mm) A/F open ended spanner unscrew the solenoid control valve. Do not use a wrench on the cylindrical body as it will be irrepairably damaged.

16 With a screwdriver carefully remove the circlip from the sunwheel extension and lift out the sunwheel.

17 Again using a screwdriver remove the circlip from its groove on the cone clutch hub and tap the clutch from the thrust ring bearing with a soft faced hammer.

18 If necessary the bearing may be removed from its housing using a vice and suitable packing. It will be necessary to remove the larger circlip which retains it before removal commences.

19 Reverse spline type overdrive. For fixed flange type proceed to paragraph 26. Using a screwdriver remove the circlip which retains the uni-directional clutch. Lift away the oil thrower.

20 Place tool number L178 (Fig.6.20) over the now exposed uni-directional clutch and lift the inner member complete with rollers into the special tool. Lift away the bronze thrust washer.

21 Withdraw the speedometer driven gear and bearing.

22 To remove the annulus, first drive a centre punch into the welch plug located at the top of the rear casing and lever it out.

23 Using a pair of circlip pliers expand the circlip which secures the annulus bearing.

24 Place the rear casing carefully over supports and with a light blow from a soft faced hammer on the end of the annulus, drive

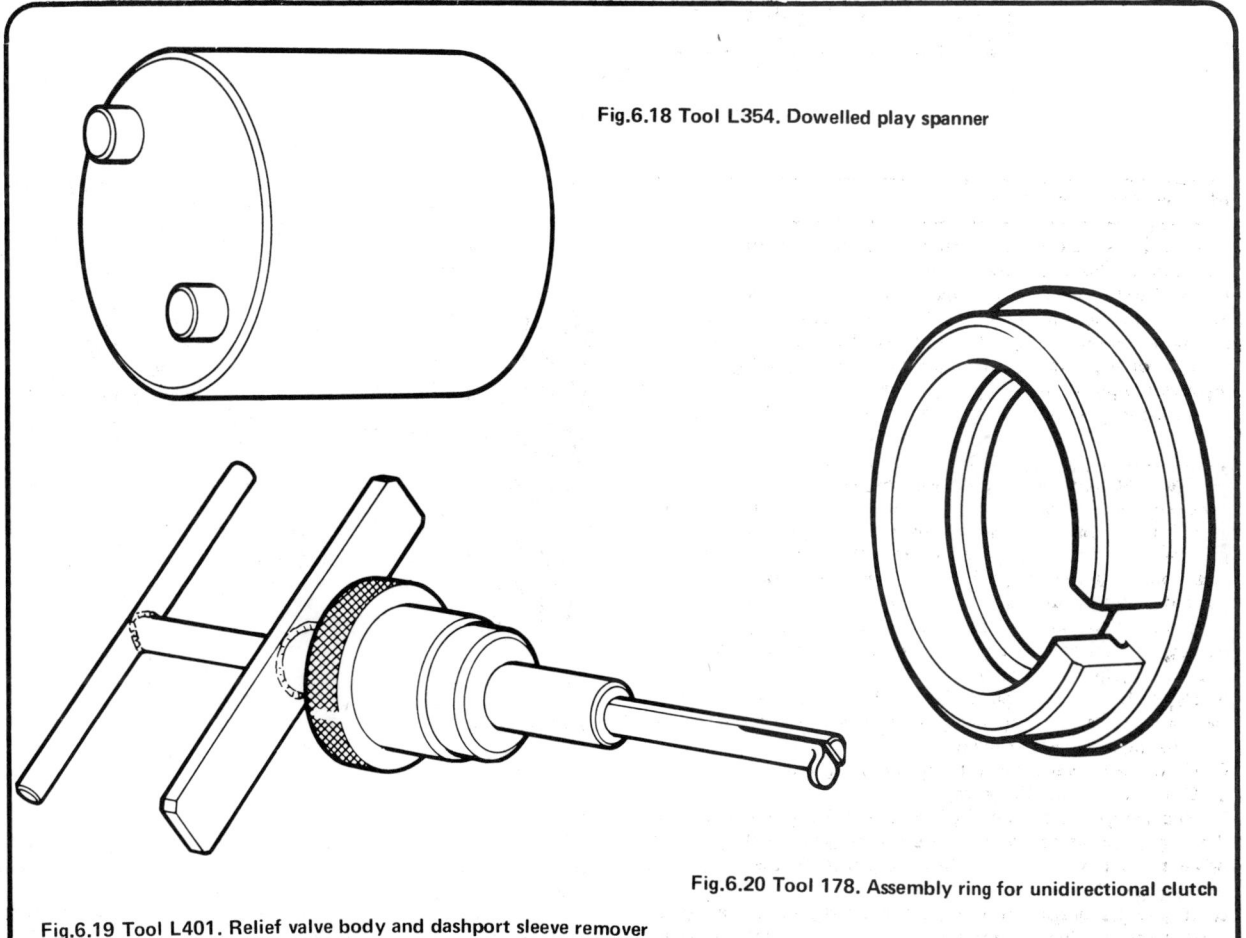

Fig.6.18 Tool L354. Dowelled play spanner

Fig.6.20 Tool 178. Assembly ring for unidirectional clutch

Fig.6.19 Tool L401. Relief valve body and dashport sleeve remover

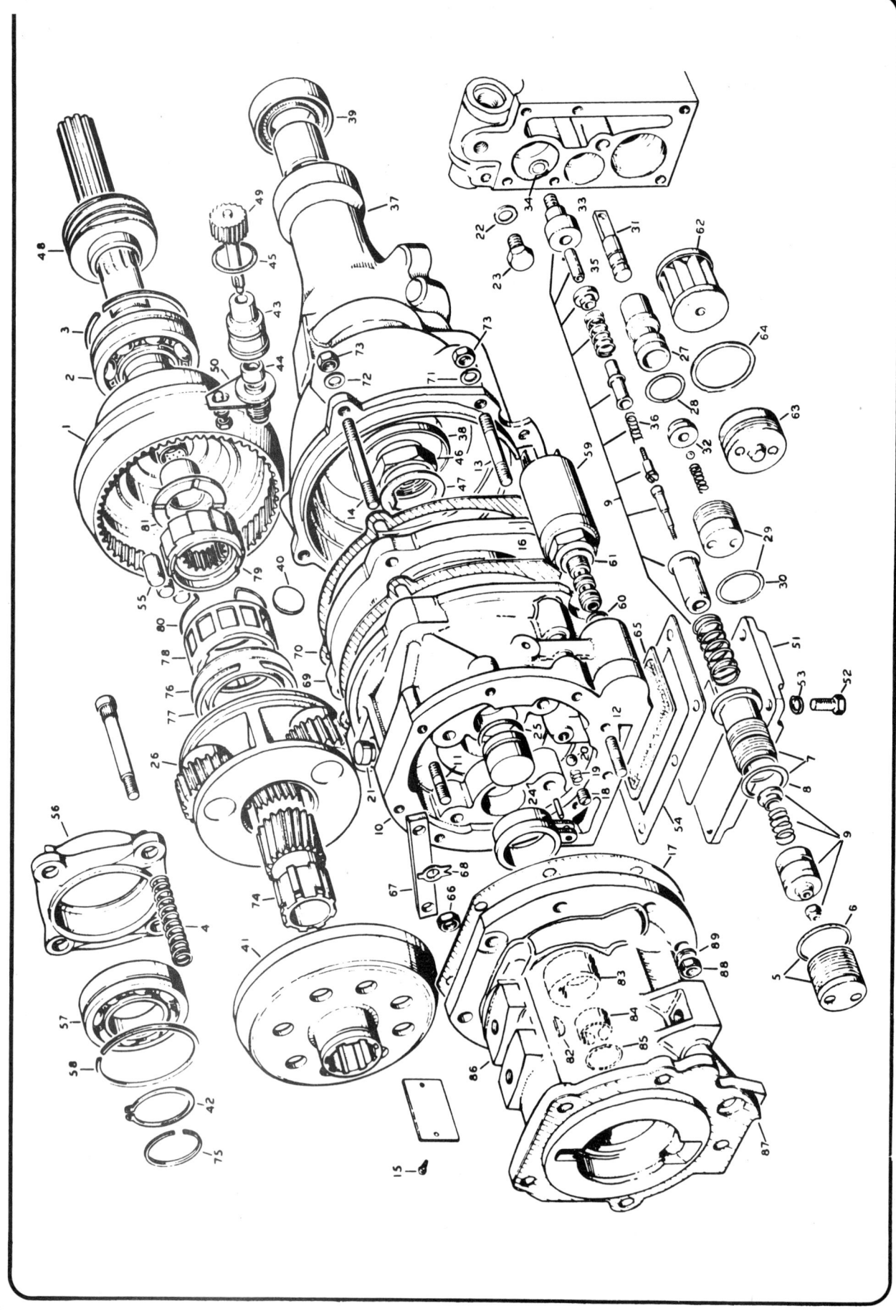

FIG. 6.21. LAYCOCK TYPE J OVERDRIVE - COMPONENTS

1 Annulus assembly	16 Gasket	31 Pump plunger	46 Locking nut	61 Copper washer	76 Oil thrower
2 Ball bearing	17 Gasket	32 Non-return valve	47 Tab washer	62 Pressure filter	77 Clip
3 Circlip	18 Relief valve plug	33 Relief valve body	48 Driving gear	63 Plug	78 Freewheel cage
4 Clutch spring	19 Relief valve spring	34 'O' ring	49 Pinion	64 Washer	79 Freewheel inner
5 Dashpot plug	20 Valve ball	35 Relief valve piston	50 Connection	65 Suction filter	80 Spring
6 'O' ring	21 Breather	36 Piston spring	51 Sump	66 Bridge piece nut	81 Thrust washer
7 Dashpot sleeve	22 Washer	37 Rear casing	52 Setscrew	67 Bridge piece	82 Woodruff key
8 'O' ring	23 Plug	38 Rear casing weir	53 Spring washer	68 Tab washer	83 Cam (as gearbox mainshaft)
9 Dashpot piston assembly	24 Operating piston	39 Oil seal	54 Gasket	69 Brake ring	84 Spring ring
10 Main casing	25 'O' ring	40 Welch plug	55 Steel rollers	70 Gasket	85 Circlip
11 Adaptor stud	26 Planet carrier	41 Sliding clutch	56 Thrust bearing housing	71 Spring washer	86 Adaptor
12 Adaptor stud	27 Pump body	42 Circlip	57 Thrust bearing	72 Copper washer	87 Gasket
13 Rear casing stud	28 'O' ring	43 Speedo bearing	58 Circlip	73 Nut	88 Nut
14 Rear casing stud	29 Pump plug	44 Oil seal	59 Solenoid valve	74 Sunwheel	89 Lockwasher
15 Screw	30 'O' ring	45 'O' ring	60 'O' ring	75 Circlip	

the annulus complete with bearing downwards from the rear casing.

24 Undo and remove the nut that secures the speedometer driving gear and with the aid of a universal puller withdraw the ball race.

26 If the fixed flange type overdrive is fitted first remove the uni-directional clutch as described in paragraphs 19 and 20.

27 Remove the speedometer driven gear.

28 Undo and remove the coupling flange nut and washers and withdraw the flange using a universal puller.

29 Remove the annulus as described in paragraph 24. The front bearing speedometer driving gear and spacer will also be withdrawn with the annulus. The rear bearing and oil seal will remain in position in the rear casing and these may be drifted out using a suitable soft metal drift.

30 The overdrive unit is now fully dismantled and may be inspected for wear.

31 Inspect the teeth and cone surface of the annulus for wear. Check that the uni-directional clutch rollers are not chipped and that the inner and outer members are free from damage.

32 Examine the spring and cage for distortion. Check that the lubrication part at the rear of the annulus is clear.

33 Inspect the rear casing bush and oil seal for wear or damage.

34 Examine the clutch linings on the sliding member for signs of excessive wear or overheating. Should there be signs of these conditions the whole sliding member assembly must be renewed. It is not possible to fit new linings as these are precision machined after bonding.

35 Make sure that the ball race rotates smoothly as this can be a source of noise when the car is running in direct gear.

36 Inspect the clutch return springs for any signs of distortion, damage or loss of springiness.

37 Check the sunwheel teeth for signs of wear or damage.

38 Inspect the main casing for cracks or damage. Examine the operating cylinder bores for scores or wear. Check the operating pistons for wear and replace the sealing rings if there is any sign of damage.

39 Check the pump plunger assembly and ensure that the strap is a good fit on the mainshaft cam and that there is no excess play between the plunger and strap.

40 Should the pump plunger assembly be worn or damaged this must be replaced as a complete assembly.

41 With the non-return valve assembly clean, inspect the ball and valve seat, also the 'O' rings for signs of damage.

42 Check the relief valve and dashpot assembly for wear. The pistons must move freely in their respective housing. Ensure that the rings are in good order.

43 Do not dismantle the dashpot and relief valve piston assemblies otherwise the predetermined spring pressures will be disturbed.

44 Finally examine the 'O' rings on the solenoid valve for damage; if evident they should be renewed together with sealing washers.

45 Clean the sump filter in petrol and if any particles are stuck in the gauze rub with an old toothbrush. Wipe the magnetic plug free of any metallic particles.

46 Reassembly of the unit can commence after any damaged or worn parts have been exchanged and new gaskets and seals obtained. Do not use jointing compound during assembly.

47 Reverse spline type overdrive. For fixed flange type proceed to paragraph 55. Fit a new annulus ball race and then position the speedometer driving gear so that the plain portion is facing the ball race. Secure with the nut and a new locking washer. Tighten the nut to a torque wrench setting of 50 - 60 lb ft (6.910 - 8.28 Kg.m).

48 Place the ball race circlip in the rear casing and expand using a pair of circlip pliers.

49 Press the annulus through the circlip and into the casing until the bearing is fully home and the circlip is located in its groove. This must be done carefully so that the rear bush and oil seal are not damaged.

50 Fit a new welch plug and secure by striking lightly in the centre with a suitable size flat faced punch.

51 Next position the spring and inner member of the uni-directional clutch into the cage, locating the spring so that the cage is spring loaded in an anti-clockwise direction when viewed from the front.

52 Place this assembly onto tool L178 with the open side of the cage uppermost and feed the clutch is a clockwise direction until all the rollers are in place. Refit the bronze thrust washer in the recess in the annulus.

53 Transfer the uni-directional clutch assembly from the special assembly tool into its outer member in the annulus.

54 Refit the oil thrower and secure with the circlip. Check that the clutch rotates in an anti clockwise direction only.

55 With fixed flange type, place the speedometer driving gear in the rear casing with its plain boss facing the front bearing. Note that the speedometer driving gear cannot be fitted from the rear of the casing.

56 Press the front bearing into the rear casing making sure that its outer track abuts against the shoulder in the casing.

57 Place the annulus with the inner face resting on a suitable packing piece. Using a piece of tube of suitable diameter press the front bearing together with the rear casing and speedometer driving gear onto the annulus until the bearing abuts on the locating shoulder. Fit the spacer onto the annulus.

58 Using the same piece of tube press the rear bearing onto the annulus and into the rear casing simultaneously. Finally press on the coupling flange and secure with the washer and self locking nut. Tighten to a torque wrench setting of 80 - 130 lb ft (11.00 - 17.12 Kg m).

59 Both models; to assemble the clutch sliding member assembly fit the ball race into its housing and secure with the large circlip.

60 Place the assembly onto the hub of the cone clutch and fit the circlip into its groove.

61 Insert the sunwheel into the hub and refit the circlip onto the sunwheel extension.

62 Place a new gasket into the main casing and fit the brake ring ensuring it is fully home on its spigot location.

63 Before refitting the relief valve and dashpot assembly ensure that all component parts are clean and lightly oiled. Insert the relief body in the bore, and using the relief valve outer sleeve push it fully home. Note the end with the 'O' ring is nearest to the outside of the casing.

65 Next place the relief valve spring and piston assembly into the dashpot cup taking care that the ends of the residual pressure spring are correctly located.

66 Place these parts in the relief valve outer sleeve whilst at the same time engaging the relief valve piston in its housing.

67 Finally fit the base plug and tighten flush with the housing to a torque wrench setting of 16 lb ft (2.2 Kg m).

68 Place the pump non return valve spring in the non-return plug and then place the ball on the spring.

69 The non return seat can now be located on the ball and the complete assembly screwed into the main casing using tool L354. Tighten to a torque wrench setting of 16 lb ft (2.2 Kg m).

70 Refit the pressure filter and new aluminium washer. Tighten the plug to a torque wrench setting of 16 lb ft (2.2 Kg m).

71 Refit the overdrive sump, suction filter and gasket and secure with the six bolts and spring washers.

72 Refit the solenoid control valve and tighten firmly using an open ended spanner.

73 Mount the rear casing assembly vertically in a bench vice and insert the planet carrier assembly. The gears may be meshed in any position.

74 Place the sliding member assembly complete with clutch non return springs onto the cone of the annulus, at the same time engaging the sunwheel with the planet gears. Fit the brake ring into its spigot in the tail casing using a new joint washer on both sides.

75 Position the main casing assembly onto the thrust housing pins, at the same time centering the studs in the brake ring.

76 Fit the two operating piston bridge pieces and secure with the four nuts and new tab washers.

77 Fit the six nuts which secure the rear and main casing assemblies, ensuring that the two copper washers are correctly located on the two top studs. It will be observed that as the nuts are tightened the clutch return spring pressure will be felt.

78 The unit is now ready for refitting to the gearbox as described in Section 19, paragraphs 5 and 6 inclusive.

21 Solenoid control valve - removal and refitting

1 The solenoid and operating valve are a self contained factory sealed unit (Fig.6.21A)

2 Disconnect the two terminals at the rear of the solenoid noting which way round the cables are fitted.

3 Using a 1 in (25 mm) open ended spanner unscrew the assembly. Do not use a wrench around the cylindrical body of the solenoid valve otherwise it will be severely damaged.

4 To test the solenoid connect up to a 12 volt battery and ammeter. The solenoid should require approximately 2 amps.

5 Check that the plunger in the valve moves forwards when the solenoid is energised and is returned to its direct drive position by spring pressure when de-energised.

6 It should be noted that this type of solenoid does not operate with a click as observed in other types of overdrive.

7 Inspect the 'O' rings on the solenoid valve for damage and if necessary renew them together with a sealing washer.

8 If it is necessary to clean the operating valve, immerse this part of the solenoid valve only in paraffin until the valve is clean.

9 If the solenoid proves to be faulty it should be renewed as a complete unit.

10 Refitting is the reverse sequence to removal.

22 Relief valve and dashpot assembly - removal and refitting

1 For this a special tool L354 is necessary to remove the relief valve plug. If the vehicle has been recently used take care to avoid burns from hot oil which will be released.

2 Undo and remove the six bolts and spring washers securing the overdrive sump oil gauze filter. Lift away the sump joint washer and gauze filter.

3 Lift out the dashpot piston complete with its component springs and cup followed by the residual pressure spring.

4 The relief valve piston assembly may now be withdrawn by carefully pulling down with a pair of pliers. The components are shown in Fig.6.22.

5 Another special tool is required, part number L401 which should be inserted into the now exposed relief valve bore. Withdraw the relief valve together with the dashpot sleeve taking extreme care not to damage the valve bore.

6 Do not attempt to dismantle the dashpot and relief valve piston assemblies otherwise the pre-determined spring pressures will be disturbed.

7 Inspect the pistons and ensure that they move freely in their respective housings. Make sure the 'O' rings are not damaged.

8 Before assembly make sure all components are clean and lightly oiled.

9 Insert the relief body in the bore and using the relief valve outer sleeve push fully home.

10 It should be noted that the end with the 'O' ring is nearest the outside of the main casing.

11 Next position the relief valve spring and piston into the dashpot cup taking care that both ends of the residual pressure spring are correctly located. Carefully position these components in the relief valve outer sleeve at the same time engaging the relief valve piston in its housing. Fit the base plug and tighten flush with the main housing to a torque wrench setting of 16 lb ft (2.2 Kg m).

12 Refit the filter, gasket and sump and secure with the six bolts and spring washers.

23 Pump non-return valve - removal and refitting

1 For removal a special tool L354 is necessary to remove the

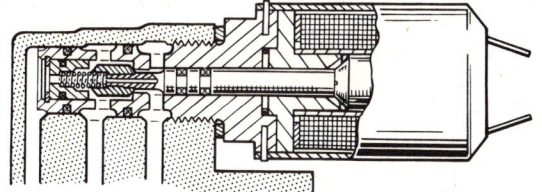

 6.21A Solenoid control valve

FIG.6.22 RELIEF VALVE AND DASHPOT ASSEMBLY

1 Mainshaft lubrication passage
2 Relief valve
3 Residual pressure spring
4 Relief valve spring
5 Control orifice
6 Threaded plug
7 Dashpot
8 Dashpot
9 Spill port

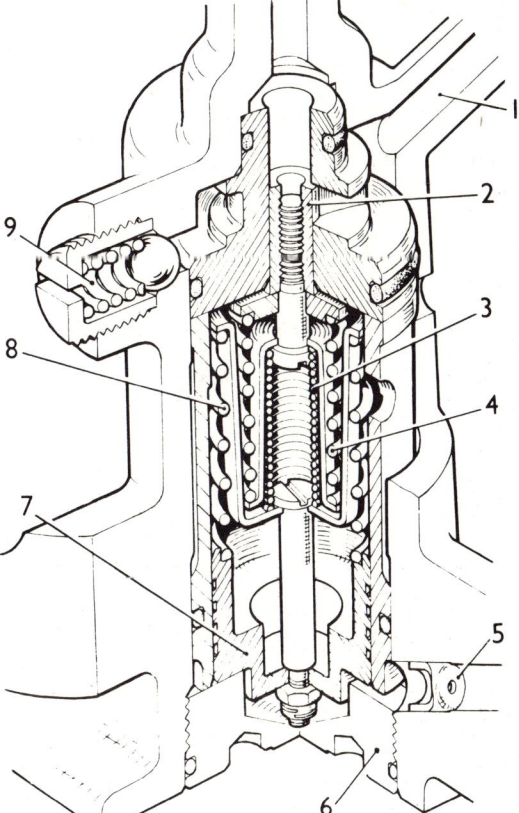

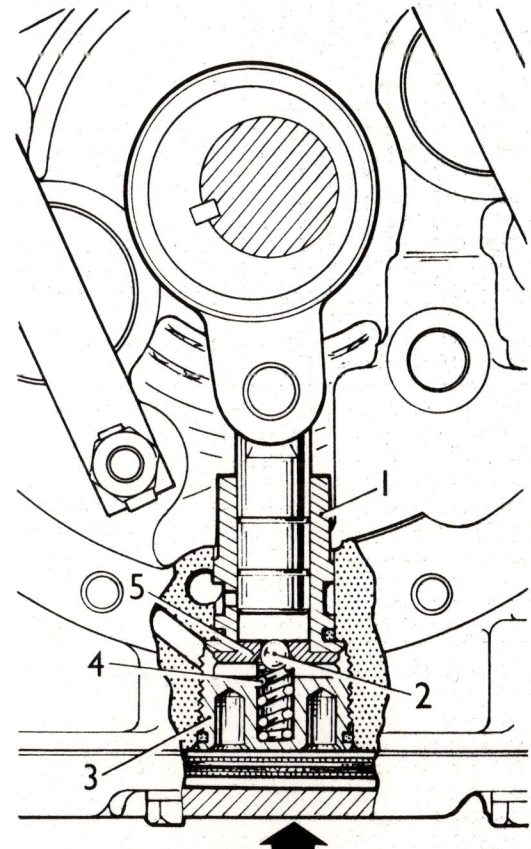

 FIG.6.23 PUMP NON-RETURN VALVE

1 Pump body
2 Steel ball
3 Threaded plug
4 Spring
5 Seating

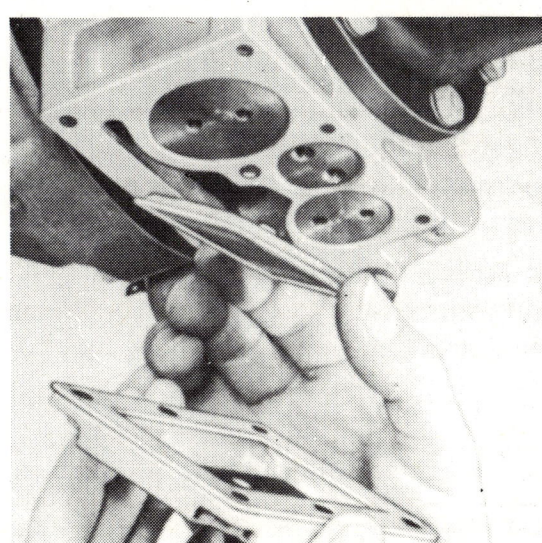

Fig.6.24 Filter removal

pump plug. If the vehicle has been recently used take care to avoid burns from hot oil which will be released.

2 Undo and remove the six bolts and spring washers securing the overdrive sump and gauze filter. Lift away the sump, joint washer and gauze filter (Fig.6.24)

3 Using tool L354 remove the pump plug taking care not to lose the return valve spring and ball. The pump valve seat can now be lifted away.

4 The pump body will be held in position by its 'O' ring. Should it be necessary to remove this rotate the propeller shaft until the pump plunger is at the top of its stroke.

5 Next carefully withdraw the pump body by hooking a piece of wire into the now exposed inlet port.

6 Carefully clean and then inspect the non return valve ball and valve seat and make sure that the 'O' rings are not damaged. Fit new 'O' rings if necessary.

7 To refit the non return valve assembly, first place the spring in the non return valve plug, then position the ball on the spring.

8 The non return valve seat can now be located on the ball and the complete assembly screwed into the main case using tool L354. Tighten to a torque wrench setting of 16 lb ft (2.2 Kg m).

9 Refit the suction filter, sump gasket and sump and secure with the six bolts and spring washers.

24 Pressure filter - removal and refitting

1 For removal a special tool L354 is necessary to remove the pump plug. If the vehicle has been recently used take care to avoid burns from hot oil which will be released.

2 Undo and remove the six bolts and spring washers securing the overdrive sump and gauze filter. Lift away the sump, joint washer and gauze filter.

3 Using tool L354 remove the pressure filter base plug.

4 The filter element will come away with the plug. Note the aluminium washer which locates on the shoulder in the filter bore.

5 Remove any dirt and thoroughly wash the element in petrol or paraffin.

6 Refitting is the reverse sequence to removal. Always fit a new aluminium washer. Tighten the plug to a torque wrench setting of 16 lb ft (2.2 Kg m).

25 Overdrive - fault diagnosis

(This is a cumulative diagnosis sequence. There are four faults mentioned. Each fault has a list of checks and remedies listed in order of their likelihood which should be strictly followed. After each check is undertaken if the fault does not disappear go on to the next check).

26 Overdrive does not engage

1 Check oil level - top up if necessary.

2 Check electrical circuit to solenoid. Rectify break if necessary.

3 Remove to check operation of the solenoid valve. Renew if inoperative.

4 Check hydraulic pressure with pressure gauge (20 psi at 25 mph). If incorrect clean blocked filters. If clean check the pump non return valve seat for clogging and pitting. Renew if dirty or damaged. If satisfactory check relief valve for sticking piston. Renew assembly if piston will not free.

5 Remove overdrive for specialist inspection.

27 Overdrive does not disengage

Special note: If in this condition DO NOT REVERSE THE VEHICLE. It will damage the overdrive beyond repair.

1 Check electrical system for closed circuit and open if necessary.

2 Remove solenoid control valve and check for seized plunger. If seized replace total valve.

3 Check residual pressure with a pressure gauge (20 psi max.). If incorrect check relief valve for sticking piston. If clean check control orifice for blocking, otherwise renew parts.

4 Check cone clutch for sticking. If sticking, free by tapping brake ring with soft faced hammer.

5 Remove overdrive for specialist inspection.

28 Overdrive slips in engagement

Carry out first four checks under "does not engage". If they prove satisfactory:

1 Remove overdrive and check for worn and/or glazed clutch linings or a mechanical obstruction of the cone clutch.

2 Remove overdrive for further specialist inspection.

29 Overdrive disengagement slow and/or freewheeling on over-run

1 Check the relief valve for sticking piston. If sticking free off defective parts or renew total relief valve assembly.

2 Check solenoid for sticking or blocked control valve. Clean and free off valve or renew solenoid assembly.

3 Check restrictor orifice for partial blockage. Clean orifice.

4 Remove overdrive for further specialist inspection.

30 Automatic transmission - description

The automatic transmission replaces the conventional clutch and gearbox, and occupies the same space in the same way being bolted onto the rear of the engine. It comprises two basic parts - the torque converter and the three speed epicyclic gearbox.

The torque converter is a form of oil operated turbine which transmits the engine power from a multi bladed rotor (the pump) directly connected to the crankshaft to another multibladed rotor (the turbine) directly connected to the input shaft of the transmission. At low engine revolutions, the oil driven by the pump has little force imparted to it, so the turbine does not move. When the pump speed increases, so the force of the oil is transferred to the turbine.

An intermediate multibladed rotor (the stator) regulates the flow of oil back to the pump after it has done its work through the turbine.

The gearbox consists of a ravignaux planetary gear set in constant mesh and the selection of the gears is by braking one or more of the components of this gear set.

This braking is effected by one of the three servo operated multi plate clutches and a band literally a brake band, which can be applied to the outer ring gear of the set. The automatic operation of three clutches and the low speed band is the complicated part, involving a servo hydraulic pump system controlled by road speed, inlet manifold vacuum, and the position of the accelerator.

The capabilities of the automatic transmission are different from the manual system and in order that those unfamiliar with them may understand the difference, a full description of the function at starting, parking and stopping, in all of the five or six selector positions is given below.

'P' Park. In this position with the engine either stopped or running, no gears are 'engaged' and the gearbox output shaft is mechanically locked, which in effect means that the propeller shaft and rear axle are also locked. The car cannot be moved, therefore. The engine may be started in this position. In order to select the 'P' position, the selector lever button must be fully depressed. Do not select 'P' if the car is moving. Damage will result.

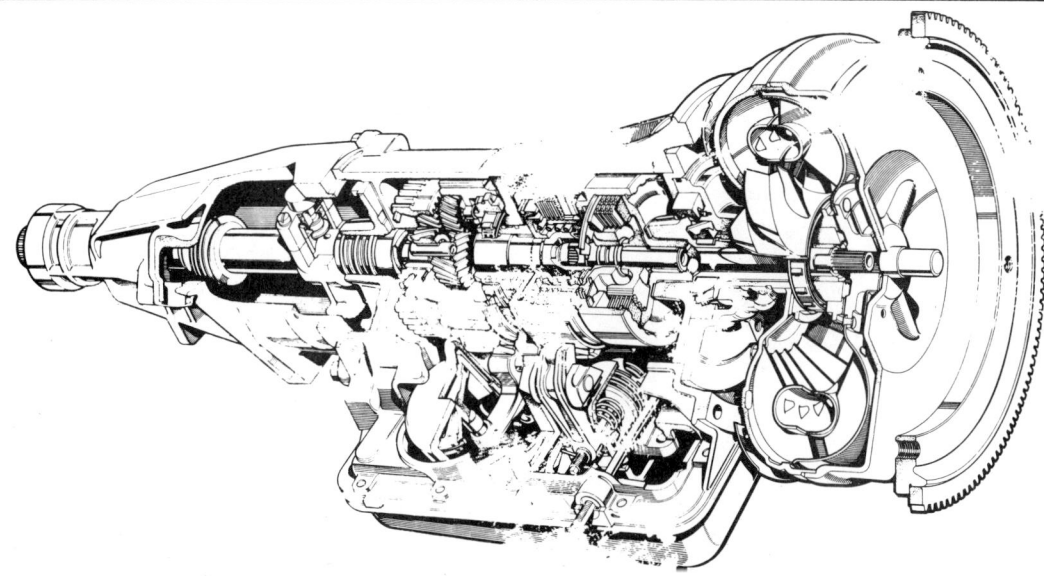

Fig.6.25 Automatic transmission assembly

'N' Neutral. The conditions for neutral are the same as for 'P' except that the gearbox output shaft is not mechanically locked. The car will, therefore, roll with the engine either running or stopped.

'R' Reverse. The button on the selector lever must be partially depressed to engage 'R'. In this position reverse gear is 'engaged'. If the engine is not running, it cannot be started unless the selector lever is moved to 'P' or 'N'. With the brakes applied the car will not move. With the brakes off, increase in engine speed will move the car backwards. When the engine speed is decreased, the engine will act as a brake through the transmission. If the car is standing with the brakes off, it may roll at low engine speed in either direction. Reverse should not normally be selected whilst the car is moving.

'D' Drive. The selector position for normal driving requirements. In this position first gear is initially 'engaged' but, at low engine speed with the brakes off, the car may roll in either direction. The engine cannot be started in this position. With the engine speed increased, the car will move forward in low gear.

When the speed and load conditions are right, the transmission will automatically move to second gear 'engagement' and then subsequently to top gear. When speed decreases, the gears will automatically shift back down as far as first, again according to speed and load situation.

The engine does not act as a brake or overrun in any of the three speeds in the 'D' position.

'I' Intermediate. To select this position the lever button must be partially depressed. When selected, the automatic transmission will operate as in 'D' except that it will not move up out of 2nd. It should not be used in excess of 60 mph.

It is possible to change to 'I' when the vehicle is moving. It will immediately put the vehicle in 2nd gear until speed or throttle position may cause it to change down to first. The intermediate range is normally used in traffic or on uphill sections where one would tend to get a lot of changing going on between 2nd and top if in the 'D' position. Although there is no overrun braking in 1st gear, there is on 2nd gear in the 'I' position.

'L' Low. To select this position, the selector lever button is fully depressed. This position should not be selected above 35 mph. It would normally be used to provide engine braking on steep downhill sections of road, or to avoid unnecessary changing between 1st and 2nd in dense traffic or on continuous slow uphill climbs.

As implied the engine acts as a brake on overrun in this range.

Some points to bear in mind in the operation of automatic transmission are:
a) It is possible to obtain a quick change down to provide instant acceleration by depressing the accelerator fully. This change will not take place, however, if the vehicle is already in excess of the maximum speed of the gear below.
b) Where continuous engine braking on overrun is wanted 'L' or 'I' ranges must be selected. It follows, therefore, that when shifting into these ranges when on the move, engine braking will take place if the car speed is high. On slippery surfaces the possibility of skids occuring must, therefore, be considered due to the sudden braking effect on the rear wheels.
c) It is not possible to push or tow-start the car.
d) If the car is to be towed for any reason, the speed must be kept below 30 mph and the selector be put in 'N'. Not more than 30 miles should be covered. If there is a suspected fault in the transmission, the car should not be towed at all unless the propeller shaft is disconnected or the driving wheels raised to prevent the transmission being ruined.
e) Cars fitted with automatic transmission are also fitted with automatic chokes on the carburettor so that the engine speed is suitably governed until it is warmed up. There will be a tendency to a faster tickover and subsequent 'creep' when in any of the driving ranges, until the engine is fully warm. Engine tuning and smooth running is much more significant where automatic transmission is fitted.
f) Transmission fluid normally heats up in use. Severe or abusive use, or failure to keep cooling areas clean, can cause overheating and damage.

31 Automatic transmission - fluid level

1 The total capacity of the system is 9 pints (5.114 litres). A dipstick is provided in the filler pipe which is located on the right hand side and projects into the engine compartment at the rear of the engine (Fig.6.26).
2 To check the fluid level, the engine and transmission should be fully warmed up to normal working temperature. With the car stationary on level ground, engine ticking over at idling speed and the selector lever in 'P' or 'N' remove the dipstick, clean it off, replace and remove again to note the level. The level must be kept between the 'Full' and 'Add' marks. From 'Add' to 'Full' calls for 1 pint. Do not overfill or foaming and loss of fluid may

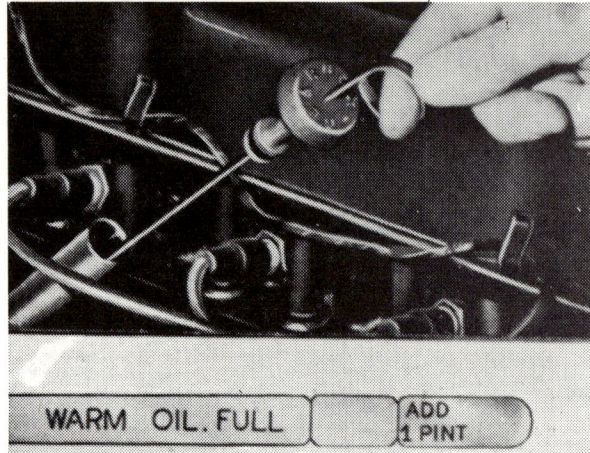

Fig.6.26 Automatic transmission - fluid level dipstick

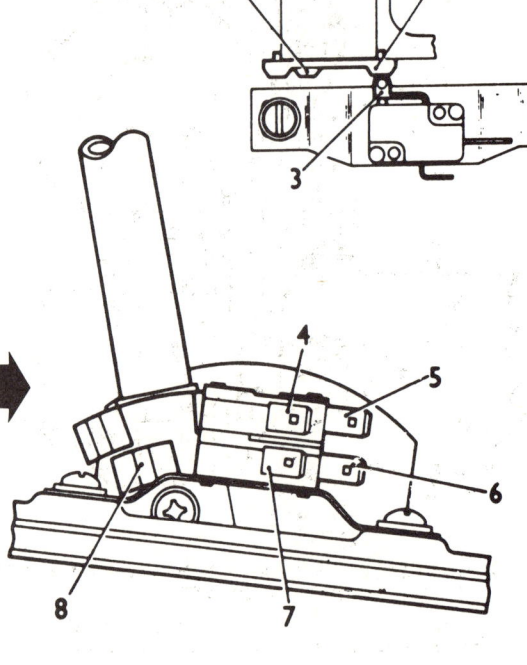

FIG.6.27 AUTOMATIC TRANSMISSION – STARTER INHIBITOR AND REVERSE LAMP SWITCH

1   Neutral cam
2   Park cam
3   Switch roller upper
4   Red/White connector
    (starter inhibitor)
5   Yellow/White connector

    (starter inhibitor)
6   Green/Brown connector
    (reverse lamp)
7   Green connector (reverse
    lamp)

Position switch so that cams (1 and 2) operate switch lever in neutral and park positions.

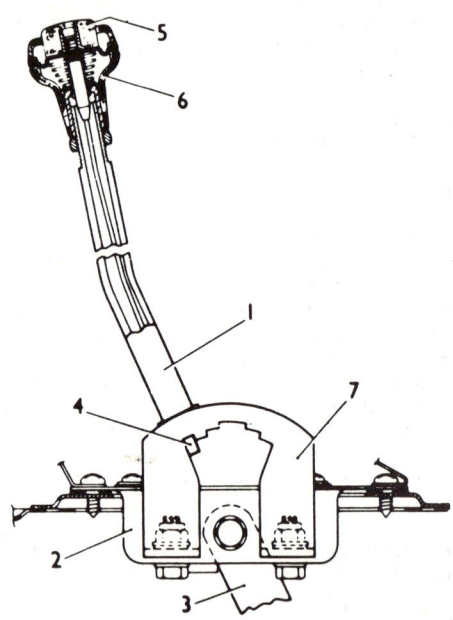

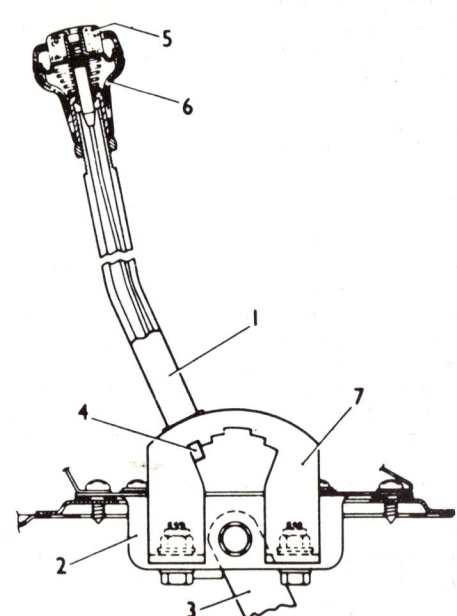

FIG.6.28 AUTOMATIC TRANSMISSION – SELECTOR LEVER LONGITUDINAL CROSS SECTION

1   Selector lever
2   Housing
3   Lower lever
4   Plunger pawl

5   Push button
6   Grip
7   Selector plate

FIG.6.29 AUTOMATIC TRANSMISSION – SELECTOR LEVER LATERAL CROSS SECTION

1   Selector lever and pivot
    shaft
2   Lower lever
3   Pivot shaft bushes

4   Pivot shaft locking nut
5   Selector plate
6   Locking ring and grip

Dimension A = 0.24 inch with plunger up and selector lever in 'P' position.

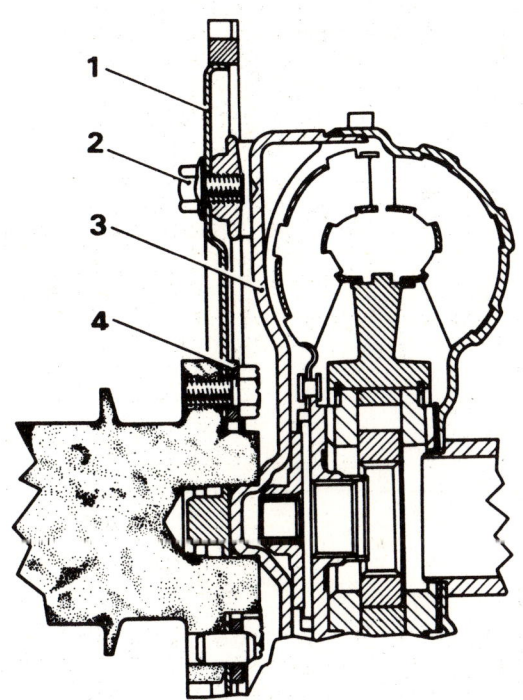

FIG.6.30 AUTOMATIC TRANSMISSION — COUPLING TO ENGINE FLEXPLATE

1 Flexplate	3 Torque converter
2 Flexplate to converter bolts	4 Distance plate

occur. Use only the proper fluid for topping up the transmission (Castrol TQ Dexron 'R') and under no circumstances should additives of any kind be mixed with it.

3 It is generally best to check the level after a normal run, otherwise, it is difficult to judge the correct working temperature. If starting from cold, then it will be necessary to select a drive range, apply brakes (driver in the driving seat for safety) and run the engine at a fast idle for no more than two minutes.

32 Automatic transmission - adjustments and attention

1 Automatic transmission systems are sophisticated and complicated and require specialist tools, experience and skill if they are to be properly set up. As they tend to be the exception rather than the rule on anything other than large vehicles, it follows that the availability of the tools and frequency of experienced mechanics is rare. Non-professional experience is rarer still. Consequently the owner is not advised to tamper with his unit himself.

2 A cross section of the selector lever mechanism and starter inhibitor switch is given so that adjustment can be made to ensure that the operation of the selector lever button and the safety start cut out are correct. It should not be possible to start the engine when the selector lever is in the 'D', 'I', 'L', or 'R' positions. Similarly it should only be possible to select 'L' or 'P' when the selector button is fully depressed, and 'I' and 'R' when it is partially depressed.

3 Details are given in the next Section on how to remove the

transmission unit but, it must be emphasised that, full testing can only be carried out when it is installed. Thus removal and replacement should only be carried out when it is known that the unit is beyond repair in its installed position.

4 The test which the owner may carry out, if he suspects that there is either slip or otherwise, is the stall test. However, it will be necessary for a tachometer to be fitted to the engine. With the transmission fully warmed up, apply the brakes fully (chock the wheels too for safety), engage a drive range and press the accelerator to the floor. The engine speed should settle at 2100 - 2150 rpm. Do not maintain the test for more than 10 seconds or overheating will result. If the engine rpm are too high then the torque converter oil supply should be suspect, and then the low band servo in the transmission itself. If the rpm are too low then the engine is not delivering full power or the torque converter unit is faulty.

5 The lower part of the torque converter housing is fitted with a perforated metal cover to permit cooling air into the housing. It is important to keep this clean as any restriction could result in overheating and loss of efficiency and damage.

33 Automatic transmission - removal and replacement

1 Before making any attempt to remove the transmission, make sure your reasons are valid. In other words get expert diagnosis first if transmission malfunctioning is the reason.

2 If you are removing the engine from a car with automatic transmission, the two should be separated at the flexplate which connects the crankshaft to the torque converter. Do not try and separate the torque converter from the gearbox.

3 All the normal precautions for gearbox removal as described in Section 2, should be taken. It must be remembered that they are heavier than conventional gearboxes - approximately 110 lbs and therefore, adequate support must be provided.

4 Proceed to remove the crossmember support after having first slackened the transmission brace bolts at the sump bracket, and moving the starter as far forward as possible to clear the starter teeth on the flexplate rim.

5 If an oil cooler is fitted it will be necessary to drain the oil out so that the cooler tubes may be disconnected from the transmission. Make sure the unions are perfectly clean first and seal the holes suitably to stop dirt entering. The combined filler/dipstick tube must be removed taking the same precautions.

6 The three bolts which hold the flexplate to the torque converter are accessible as soon as the semicircular sheet steel plate across the bottom half of the casing has been removed. These three bolts must be removed before the main housing bolts securing the transmission to the engine are undone, otherwise, a strain could be put on the flexplate which would distort.

7 Once the flexplate bolts are removed, the casing bolts can come out with the whole unit properly supported. The transmission is then drawn a little to the rear and lowered in the normal way.

8 If the flexplate is to be renewed, it may be unbolted from the crankshaft flange. Seal the bolts on replacement as for the flywheel.

9 When replacing the transmission, proceed in the reverse order or removal. Line up the painted balance marks on torque converter and flexplate. When tightening the transmission brace, tighten the bolts on the torque converter housing first and then those on the sump bracket.

Chapter 7 Propeller shaft

Contents

Specifications

Propeller shaft:

Make	Hardy Spicer or BRD
Type	Tubular
Diameter - Victor	3.00 in (76.2 mm)
VX 4/90	2.75 in (69.85 mm)

Universal joints:

Make	Hardy Spicer or BRD
Type	Tubular
Number of rollers to each bearing	34

Sliding sleeve:

Diameter - Manual transmission and overdrive	1.374 - 1.375 in	(34.90 - 34.92 mm)
Automatic	1.502 - 1.503 in	(38.15 - 38.17 mm)
Clearance in transmission rear cover	0.002 - 0.005 in	(0.05 - 0.12 mm)

Shaft identification colours:

1759 cc standard	Yellow - Yellow - Yellow
1759 cc with heavy duty axle	Yellow - Yellow - Blue
1759 cc + overdrive	Yellow - Red - Blue
1759 cc + automatic transmission	Yellow - Green - Blue
2279 cc standard	Yellow - Yellow - Blue
2279 cc + overdrive	Yellow - Red - Blue
2279 cc + automatic transmission	Yellow - Green - Blue

Torque wrench settings:

Coupling flange bolts	18 lb ft	(2.49 kg m)

1 General description

The drive from the gearbox to the rear axle is via the propeller shaft which is, in fact, a tube. Due to the variety of angles caused by the up and down motion of the rear axle in relation to the gearbox, universal joints are fitted to each end of the shaft to convey the drive through the constantly varying angles. As the movement also increases and decreases the distance between the rear axle and the gearbox, the forward end of the propeller shaft is a splined sleeve which is a sliding fit over the rear of the gearbox splined mainshaft. The splined sleeve runs in an oil seal in the gearbox mainshaft rear cover, and is supported with the mainshaft on the gearbox rear bearing. The splines are lubricated by oil in the rear cover coming from the gearbox.

The universal joints each comprise a four way trunnion, or 'spider', each leg or which runs in a needle roller bearing race, pre-loaded with grease and fitted into the bearing journal yokes of the sliding sleeve and propeller shaft and flange.

2 Propeller shaft - removal and replacement

1 Jack up the rear of the car and support on firmly based axle stands.

2 The rear of the propeller shaft is connected to the rear axle pinion by a flange held by four nuts and bolts. Mark the position of both flanges relative to each other, and then undo the bolts.

3 Move the propeller shaft forwards to disengage it from the pinion flange and then lower it to the ground.

4 Draw the other end of the propeller shaft, that is the splined sleeve, out of the rear of the gearbox rear cover. The shaft is then clear for removal from the underside of the car.

5 Place a container under the gearbox rear cover opening so as to catch any oil which will certainly come out.

6 Refitting the propeller shaft is the reverse sequence to removal, but the following additional points should be noted.

a) Ensure that the mating marks on the propeller shaft and differential pinion flanges are lined up.

b) Tighten the flange retaining nuts to a torque wrench setting of 18 lb ft (2.49 Kg m).

3 Universal joints - inspection and repair

1 Wear in the needle roller bearings is characterised by vibration in the transmission, 'clonks' on taking up the drive and in extreme cases of lack in lubrication, metallic squeaking, and

ultimately grating and shrieking sounds as the bearings break up.

2   It is easy to check if the needle roller bearings are worn, with the propeller shaft in position, by trying to turn the shaft with one hand, the other hand holding the rear axle flange. Any movement between the propeller shaft and the flange is indicative of considerable wear. If worn, the old bearings and spiders will have to be discarded and a repair kit, comprising new universal joint spiders, bearings and oil seals purchased.

3   It is important to note that unlike the older types of propeller shaft where the universal joint bearings were held in position with circlips this propeller shaft has the edge of each yoke staked or peened. Therefore this job should not be taken lightly; it may be well worth while to purchase a replacement shaft.

4   The front needle roller bearings should be tested for wear using the same principle described in paragraph 2.

5   To test the splined coupling for wear lift the end of the shaft and note any movement in the splines.

4   Universal joints - dismantling

1   Before beginning dismantling make sure that a repair kit is to hand as there may be a delay in obtaining this kit - not every Vauxhall garage holds this in stock.

2   Clean away all traces of dirt and grease from the universal joint yoke. Using a very small and sharp chisel remove the metal that has formed a lip over the bearing cup faces by peening. This will take time and require great care.

3   Hold the propeller shaft and using a soft faced hammer tap the universal joint yoke so as to remove the bearing cups by 'shock' action.

4   Remove all four bearing cups in the manner described and then free the propeller shaft from the spider.

5   Universal joints - reassembly

1   Thoroughly clean out the yokes and journals.

2   Fit new oil seals and retainers on the spider journals, place the spider on the propeller shaft yoke and assemble the needle rollers into the bearing cups retaining them with some thick grease.

3   Fill each bearing cup about 1/3 full with Castrol LM Grease. Also fill the grease holes in the journal spider with grease taking care that all air bubbles are eliminated.

4   Refit the bearing cups on the spider and tap the bearings home so that they lie squarely in position.

5   Using a centre punch peen over the end of the bearing cup bores to stop the cups from working out.

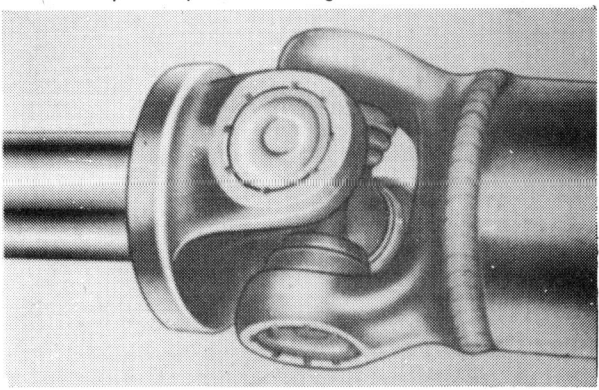

FIG.7.1 UNIVERSAL JOINT – GEARBOX END

Note staking used to retain bearing instead of circlip. Some Hardy Spicer universal joints may still use circlips.

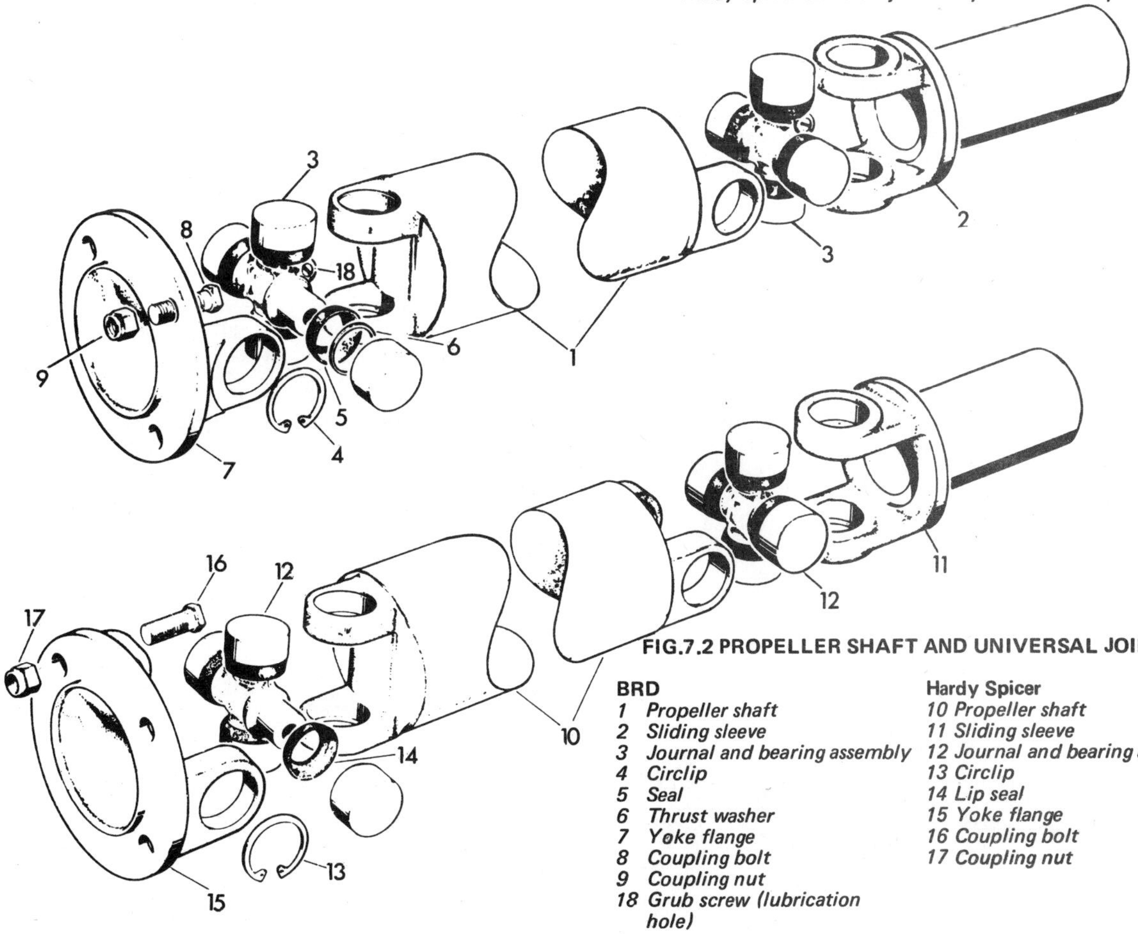

FIG.7.2 PROPELLER SHAFT AND UNIVERSAL JOINTS

BRD	Hardy Spicer
1 Propeller shaft	10 Propeller shaft
2 Sliding sleeve	11 Sliding sleeve
3 Journal and bearing assembly	12 Journal and bearing assembly
4 Circlip	13 Circlip
5 Seal	14 Lip seal
6 Thrust washer	15 Yoke flange
7 Yoke flange	16 Coupling bolt
8 Coupling bolt	17 Coupling nut
9 Coupling nut	
18 Grub screw (lubrication hole)	

Chapter 8 Rear axle

Contents

Specifications

Type:	Semi floating hypoid	
Ratios:		
1800 saloon	3.9 : 1	
1800 estate	4.1 : 1	
2300 SL saloon, estate and V X 4/90	3.7 : 1	
Oil capacity	2.5 pints (1.42 litres)	
Pinion bearing pre-load		
New bearings	10 - 15 lb in	(11.4 - 17.15 kg cm)
Used bearings	8 - 12 lb in	(9.0 - 13.72 kg cm)
Differential		
Pinion shaft diameter	0.6242 - 0.6248 in	(15.85 - 15.87 mm)
Pinion clearance on shaft	0.0027 - 0.0053 in	(0.07 - 0.13 mm)
Side bearing pre-load		
New bearings	3 lb in	(3.4 kg cm)
Used bearings	1 lb in	(1.14 kg cm)
Permissible run out of differential case flange (max)	0.001 in	(0.03 mm)
Crownwheel and pinion backlash	0.005 - 0.007 in	(0.13 - 0.18 mm)
Crownwheel run out (max)	0.002 in	(0.06 mm)
Interference fit of differential bearings in housing	+0.0007 to −0.0005 in	(+0.1778 to −0.127 mm)
Interference fit of differential bearings on differential		
housing	0.0014 - 0.0025 in	(0.0508 - 0.0762 mm)
Pinion depth adjustment shims	0.003, 0.005, 0.010 in	(0.0762, 0.1270, 0.254 mm)
Radial clearance of differential side gears in housing bore	0.002 - 0.005 in	(0.0508 - 0.127 mm)
Interference fit of pinion shaft in differential housing	+0.0013 to −0.0003 in	(+0.0508 to −0.0076 mm)
Differential bearing adjustment, available spacers	0.100, 0.101 in available; shims 0.003 in	(2.54, 2.794 mm) (0.076 mm)
Interference fit of pinion rear bearing in housing	0.0003 - 0.0012 in	(0.0076 - 0.0305 mm)
Fit of pinion rear bearing on pinion shaft	0.0003 - 0.0012 in	(0.0076 - 0.0305 mm)
Interference fit of pinion front bearing in housing	0.0003 - 0.0019 in	(0.0076 - 0.050 mm)
Fit of pinion front bearing on pinion shaft	+0.002 to −0.007 in	(+0.0508 to −0.01778 mm)
Interference fit of rear wheel bearings in axle tube	+0.0006 to 0.0005 in	(+0.01524 to 0.01270 mm)
Wheel bearing bore diameter in rear axle tube	2.4404 - 2.4410 in	(61.976 - 62.001 mm)
Interference fit to wheel bearing on axle shaft	0.0006 - 0.0016 in	(0.01524 - 0.04064 mm)

Torque wrench settings:

	lb ft	kg m
Differential bearing cap bolts	24	3.3
Crownwheel gear bolts	38	5.6
Axle shaft bearing retainer nuts	20	2.77
Wheel nuts	82	11.2
Axle shaft bearing retainer nuts	12	1.6
Pinion/coupling flange nut	75	10.2
Flange/propeller shaft bolts	18	2.49

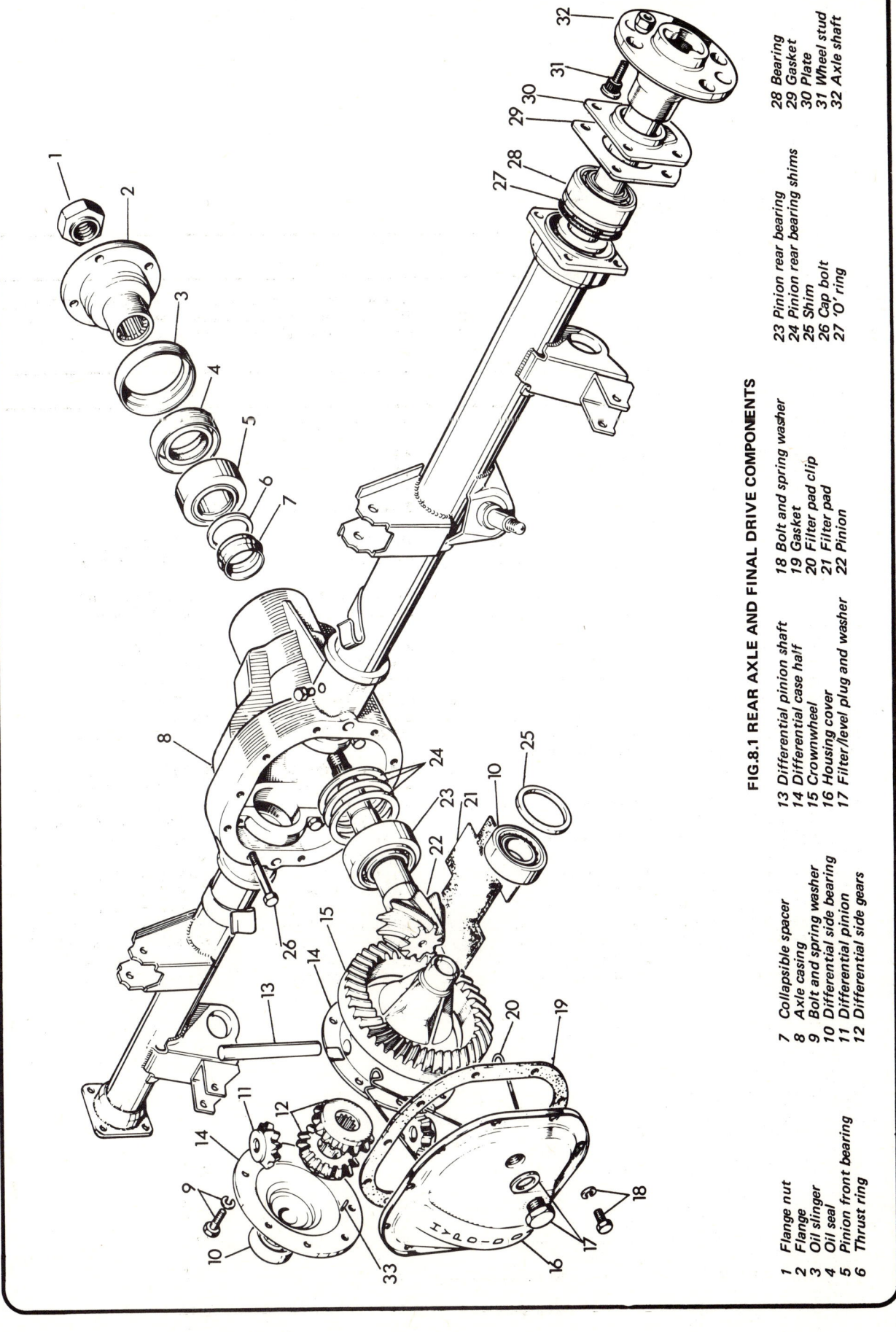

FIG. 8.1 REAR AXLE AND FINAL DRIVE COMPONENTS

1 Flange nut	7 Collapsible spacer	13 Differential pinion shaft	18 Bolt and spring washer	23 Pinion rear bearing
2 Flange	8 Axle casing	14 Differential case half	19 Gasket	24 Pinion rear bearing shims
3 Oil slinger	9 Bolt and spring washer	15 Crownwheel	20 Filter pad clip	25 Shim
4 Oil seal	10 Differential side bearing	16 Housing cover	21 Filter pad	26 Cap bolt
5 Pinion front bearing	11 Differential pinion	17 Filter/level plug and washer	22 Pinion	27 'O' ring
6 Thrust ring	12 Differential side gears			28 Bearing
				29 Gasket
				30 Plate
				31 Wheel stud
				32 Axle shaft

1 General description

The rear axle is of the semi-floating type with a hypoid final drive. The pinion is underhung and located within the final drive housing.

The rear axle casing assembly is located on the body main horizontudinal members by means of four arms, two each side located above and below the casing. These are longitudinal in position and their attachment points comprise steel bolts passing through rubber mounting bushes on hanger brackets which are an integral part of the axle casing.

A transverse panhard rod between an anchorage on the left hand side of the underbody and a bracket on the right hand side axle casing controls lateral movement.

The crownwheel and pinion assembly is supported in the axle housing by two taper roller bearings which are secured by end caps and bolts. Precise location is determined by positioning shims at the outer face of the bearing outer track.

The pinion runs in two pre-loaded taper roller bearings. The pinion is held in correct location to the crownwheel by shims located between the front face of the rear bearing outer track and the abutment face in the axle housing.

An oil seal is pressed into the end of the pinion housing to retain the lubricating oil.

2 Rear axle - removal and replacement

1 Remove the rear wheel trims and slacken the wheel nuts.

2 Chock the front wheels, jack up the rear of the car and support on firmly based axle stands located under the underbody longitudinal members in front of the suspension lower arms. Remove the road wheels.

3 Mark the mating flanges of the propeller shaft and rear axle pinion with a scriber or file. Detach the propeller shaft by undoing and removing the four retaining nuts and bolts.

Tie it in position to one side rather than lower it to the ground which would possibly impose a strain and cause damage to the gearbox extension housing bush and oil seal.

4 Refer to Chapter 9 and detach the handbrake cable from the rear brake units and rear axle casing.

5 Refer to Chapter 9 and detach the brake hydraulic flexible hose at the end of the main feed pipe adjacent to the rear axle.

6 Undo and remove the nut and bolt that secures the lower end of each shock absorber to the suspension lower arm mounting bracket on the axle housing. Contract the shock absorbers.

7 Support the weight of the rear axle assembly and first slacken the lower arm mounting bolt nuts at the rear axle. This will relieve spring pressure on the bushes. Now remove each mounting bolt and swing each lower arm down. Place a jack under the lower arm to take the weight of spring. Lift away the spring and seats and place to one side having noted their locations so that they are not inverted or fitted to the wrong side on replacement.

8 Undo and remove each shorter upper arm securing nut and bolt at the rear axle top bracket.

9 Disconnect the transverse panhard rod from the axle bracket by undoing and removing the retaining nut and plain washer. Pull the panhard rod downwards.

10 On VX 4/90 models there is a load conscious pressure

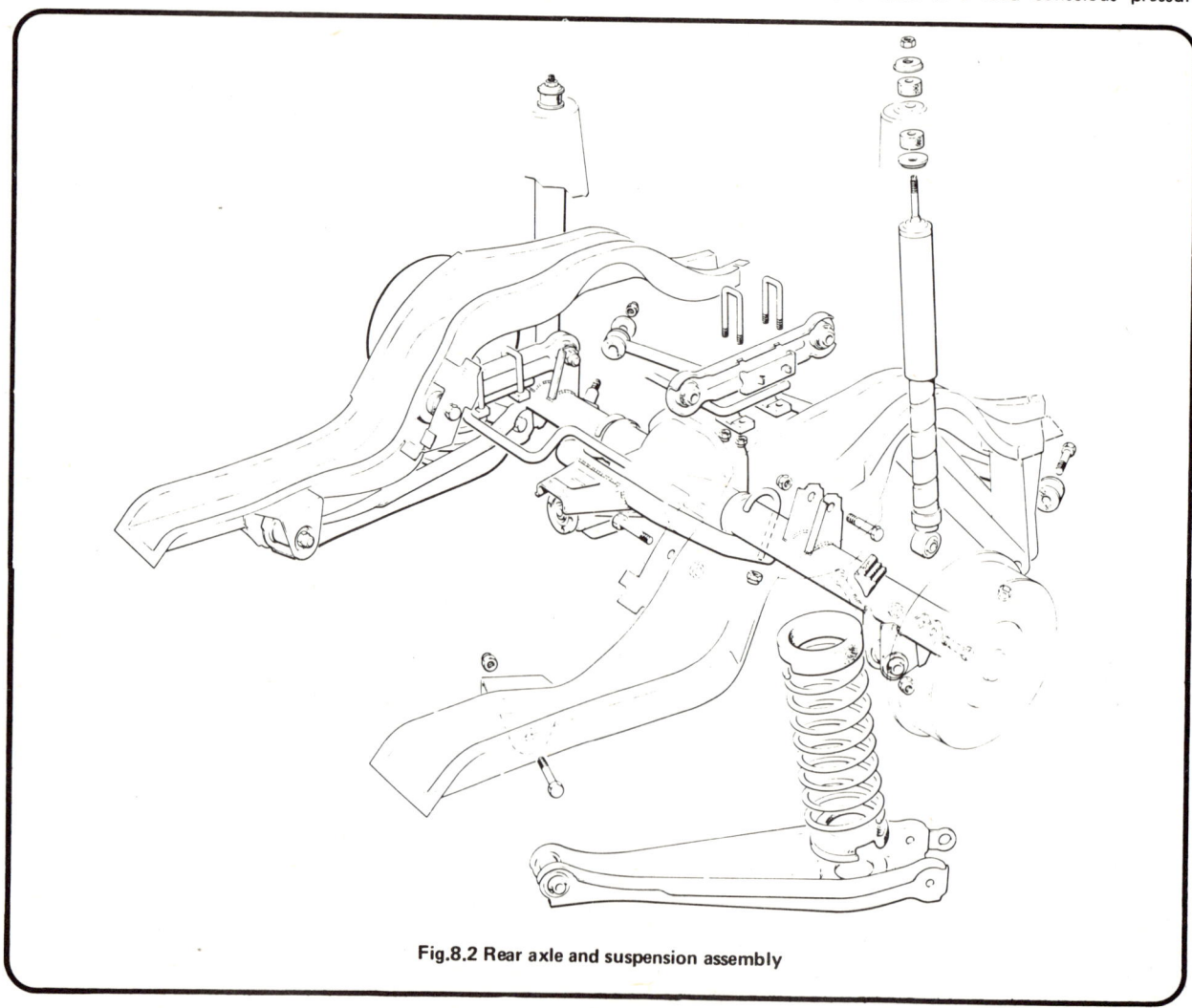

Fig.8.2 Rear axle and suspension assembly

reducing valve assembly and this must be detached. However, further information will be found in Chapter 9.

11 The whole axle assembly should now be completely free of the body and it may be drawn rearwards from under the car.

12 Refitting the rear axle assembly is the reverse sequence to removal. It will be necessary to bleed the brake hydraulic system and reset the load conscious pressure reducing valve assembly (if fitted) as described in Chapter 9.

3 Axle shafts - removal and replacement

1 Each axle shaft is supported by a ball race integral with a lip type oil seal to prevent loss of oil. Additionally there is a sealing ring in the outer track to prevent loss of oil between the bearing and axle housing. The axle shaft bearing is held in position on the shaft by a shrunk on ring. When obtaining a new axle shaft it should be noted that the left hand shaft is 3.33 in (84.5 mm) shorter than the right hand shaft and therefore not interchangeable. Also different diameter axle shafts are used between VX 4/90 saloon and the estate models and the Victor saloon.

2 To remove the axle shaft first remove the relevant wheel trim and slacken the wheel nuts.

3 Jack up and support the side of the axle from which the axle shaft will be removed. Remove the wheel. NOTE. If both axle shafts are to be removed and the car is jacked up level, oil may run out of the axle tubes. Precautions must be taken to prevent it running over the brake linings. The safest way is to remove the brake shoes as described in Chapter 9.

4 Chock the front wheels and release the handbrake. The composite brake drums (cast iron rim and pressed steel web) are located on the axle shaft spigot and retained by two spring clips. Release these clips on the wheel studs and withdraw the brake drum.

5 Using a socket through the holes in the shaft flange undo and remove the axle shaft retainer plate securing self lock nuts.

6 The shaft assembly may now be withdrawn and inspected. If the bearing is a tight fit in the housing a slide hammer will be required. Do not use levers as they can distort the brake flange plate (Fig.8.4).

7 Carefully inspect the differential engagement splines for wear, and also the bearing integral oil seal. If the oil seal shows any signs of failure it should be replaced together with the bearing as these two parts are not available individually.

8 Refitting of the axle shaft is a straightforward reversal of the removal procedure. The following additional points should however be noted:

a) Make sure that the cutaway in the bearing retainer plate gasket is aligned with the drain hole and also that the drain hole is clear of obstruction (Fig.8.5)

b) Ensure that the sealing ring in the bearing outer track is located correctly in the bearing groove and then smear both sealing ring and housing bore with a little oil. This will allow easy refitting without damage (Fig.8.6 and 8.7)

c) Smear the axle shaft with oil to prevent rusting.

d) Tighten the bearing retainer plate nuts to a torque wrench setting of 20 lb ft (2.77 Kg m).

e) Adjust the brakes as described in Chapter 9.

4 Axle shaft bearing and oil seal - removal and replacement

If it is decided after inspection (see Section 3) to renew the bearing and oil seal assembly proceed as follows:

1 Using a sharp chisel, chisel out the bearing retaining ring to facilitate removal.

2 Normally a press is required to ease the bearing from the axle shaft, but as the bearing will be discarded the following method of removal may be used:

a) Firmly clamp the bearing in a large vice so that the axle shaft is parallel with the jaws.

b) Now using a soft faced hammer on the splined end of the axle shaft, drive it back through the bearing and retainer. NOTE:

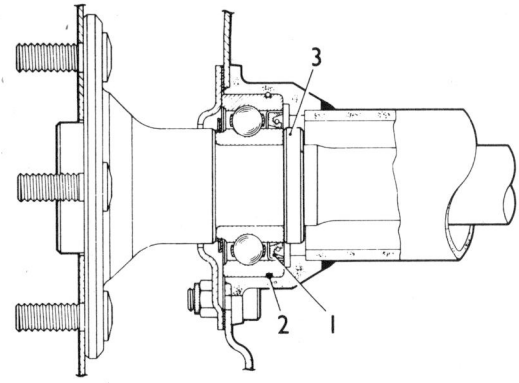

FIG. 8.3 CROSS SECTION OF AXLE SHAFT AND BEARING ASSEMBLY

1 Lip type oil seal   *3 Retainer ring*
2 Sealing ring

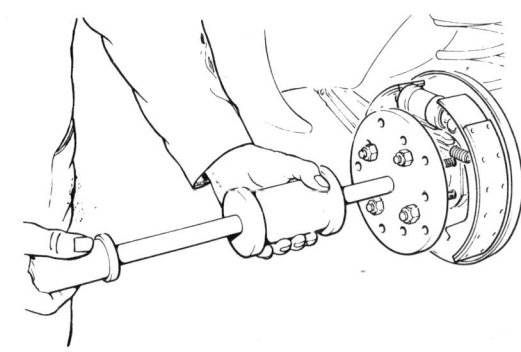

Fig.8.4 Use of slide hammer to remove axle shaft assembly

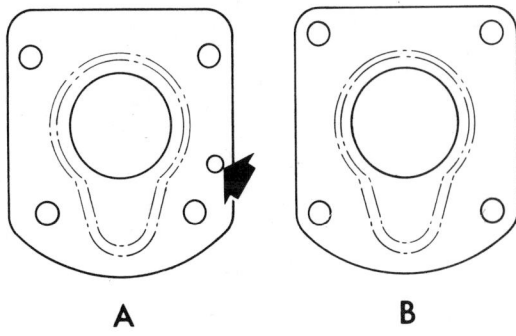

A   **B**

FIG.8.5 BEARING RETAINER PLATES

A Victor saloon models
B Victor estate and VX 4/90 models

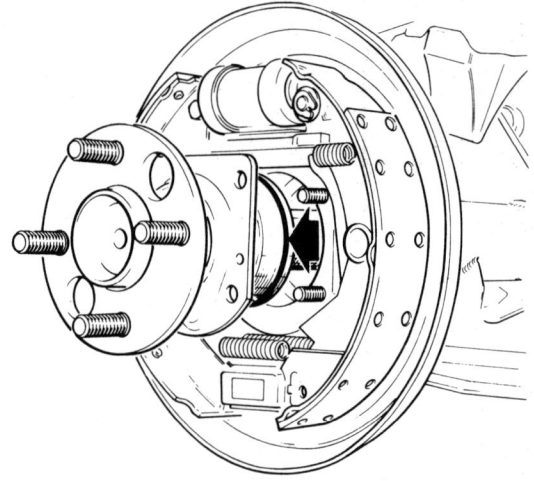

Fig.8.6 'O' ring seal located in bearing outer track

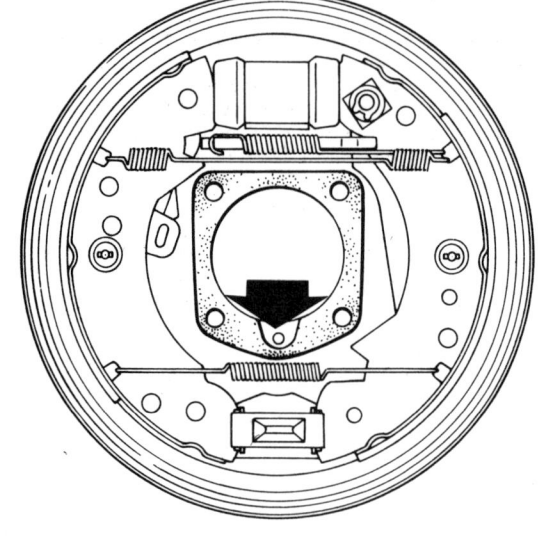

Fig.8.7 Oil drain hole (arrowed)

Fig. 8.8 Fitting bearing retaining ring with suitable diameter tube

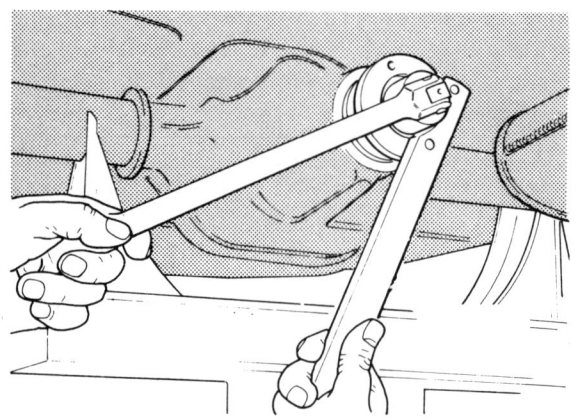

Fig.8.9 Holding pinion flange and slackening nut

Fig.8.10 Staking nut to slot in pinion

A piece of wood MUST be interposed between the hammer and axle shaft.

3 Care must be taken when ordering new bearings as the axle shaft diameters differ between the VX 4/90 and the estate models and the Victor saloons. Also should the bearing retainer plate require renewal these are not interchangeable.

4 Refit the bearing retainer, lubricate the new bearing inner track bore and push the bearing down the axle shaft as far as it will go by hand. Make sure that the integral oil seal is facing towards the splines. Now drive the bearing right home against the shaft shoulder using a piece of steel tubing of a suitable length and diameter. Note that the tubing must only contact the bearing inner track, not the bearing cage or outer track.

5 Using the flame of a gas stove, blow lamp or other suitable means carefully heat the retainer ring to a dark blue colour and quickly slide into position on the shaft. Push on the retainer with the steel tube until it has cooled sufficiently to grip the axle shaft (Fig.8.8).

6 Refitting the axle shaft is described in Section 3.

7 If a new axle shaft is being fitted it will be necessary to fit new wheel bolts. All models have four wheel bolts with the exception of VX 4/90 models which have five. The old bolts may be drifted out. New bolts can be drawn into position using a spacer and wheel retaining nut.

5 Pinion oil seal - removal and replacement

If oil is leaking from the pinion end of the axle casing it is an indication that the oil seal requires renewal.

1 Chock the front wheels, jack up the rear of the car and support on firmly based axle stands.

2 Refer to Section 2, paragraphs 2 and 3 and detach the propeller shaft from the pinion flange.

3 The pinion flange nut will now be exposed and, where it is staked into the slot in the pinion, should be tapped back with a centre punch.

4 In order to hold the flange when undoing the nut, it will be necessary to make up a piece of flat bar with two holes at one end which can be bolted to the flange. Alternatively a large wrench can be used to hold the flange (Fig.8.9).

5 Using a socket undo the flange retaining nut. Mark the relative position of the flange and pinion shaft so that the flange may be fitted in its original position.

6 Remove the flange by tapping or if very tight use a universal puller and suitable thrust pad.

7 The oil seal may now be removed using a pointed punch or screwdriver and a hammer.

8 A new oil seal should be obtained and soaked in oil for a few minutes.

9 Before refitting the new seal, grind a slot 180° away from, but similar to, the existing slot in the pinion shaft, so as to provide a new location for staking.

10 Fit the new seal with the lip facing into the casing. Using a suitable diameter tube tap in the seal until it either contacts the shoulder in the axle housing or seal case is flush with the end of the housing - whichever occurs first.

11 Smear a little oil onto the lip of the seal and flange sleeve and carefully ease the flange into position. Do not forget to align the originally made marks.

12 Refit the coupling flange nut and tighten until the original nut staking and pinion shaft slot are aligned. Do not overtighten the nut as this alignment is essential to restore correct pinion bearing pre-load otherwise wear and noise will result.

13 Finally, stake the nut rim into the pinion slot and reconnect the propeller shaft (Fig.8.10). Check the level of oil and top up if necessary with Castrol Hypoy.

6 Pinion, crownwheel and differential - overhaul

1 This chapter has so far described how to replace bearings and oilseals for the axle shafts and the pinion oil seal, as these are considered to be within the average owner drivers competence and facilities. It is not recommended that owners go into the more complicated problems of pinion to crownwheel settings, differential gear settings, differential side bearing replacement, or pinion bearing replacement.

2 If, however, an owner feels he has the competence and an exceptionally good tool kit full overhaul details are given. Read the whole section through first. Make a list of tools and spares probably required and investigate their availability.

3 Remove the rear axle from the car and then the axle shafts from the rear axle as described in Sections 2 and 3.

4 Place the axle assembly on the edge of a bench or suitably supported on the floor and thoroughly clean the exterior.

5 Undo and remove the ten bolts and spring washers that secure the rear cover plate to the axle casing. Place a container under the centre of the rear axle and remove the cover plate and gasket. Allow the oil to drain into the container.

6 Undo and remove the two bolts that secure each differential side bearing cap to the axle casing. Carefully lift away each end cap noting the 'X' marks on the right hand cap and housing adjacent to the cap (Fig.8.13).

7 Place a bar under one of the differential case bolts and lever the casing and crownwheel assembly from the axle casing.

8 Carefully lift away the spacers and shims from each side of the housing and keep in their respective sets as they will probably be used again. Also note from which side they came.

9 Refer to Section 5 and remove the pinion flange and oil seal.

10 Using a soft faced hammer at the front of the housing carefully tap out the pinion assembly. Recover the collapsible spacer and inner bearing assembly. The collapsible spacer must be discarded and a new one obtained (Fig.8.12).

11 The pinion head bearing may be removed using a universal puller with long legs. Lift the pinion head shims away from behind the pinion head.

12 Using a tapered soft metal drift, carefully drift out the pinion outer bearing cups. Recover any shims between the outer bearing cups and the casing.

13 The crownwheel and differential assembly may now be dismantled. Undo and remove the bolts and spring washers that secure the crownwheel to the differential case. Mark the relative position of the crownwheel and differential case halves so that they may be refitted in their original positions. Tap off the crownwheel using a soft faced hammer. Part the two halves of the differential case.

14 Place the large half of the differential case vertically in a vice and with a parallel pin punch tap out the dowel peg locking the differential pinion shaft to the casing. Now tap out the differential pinion shaft. The differential side gears and pinions may now be lifted from the differential case half. Note their locations so that they may be refitted in their original positions and also recover any hemispherical shaped thrust gears

15 If the side bearings are to be renewed, draw them off the differential case with a universal puller and suitable thrust block

16 Dismantling is now complete. Thoroughly wash all parts in petrol or paraffin and wipe dry using a clean non fluffy rag.

17 Lightly lubricate the bearings and reassemble. Test for signs of roughness by rotating the inner and outer tracks. Check the rollers for signs of pitting, wear or excessive looseness in their cage. Inspect any thrust washers for signs of excessive wear. Check for signs of wear on the differential pinion shaft and gears. Any parts that show signs of wear must be renewed.

18 The crownwheel and pinion must only be replaced as a matched pair. The pair number is etched on the outer face of the crownwheel and the forward face of the pinion.

19 If it is found that only one of the differential bearings is worn, both bearings must be renewed. Likewise if one pinion bearing is worn, both pinion bearings must be renewed.

20 Make sure that the breather in the axle casing is clean and that the cap can be rotated freely.

21 To reassemble first fit the differential bearing cones to the differential case using a piece of tube of suitable diameter.

22 During reassembly well lubricate all moving parts with

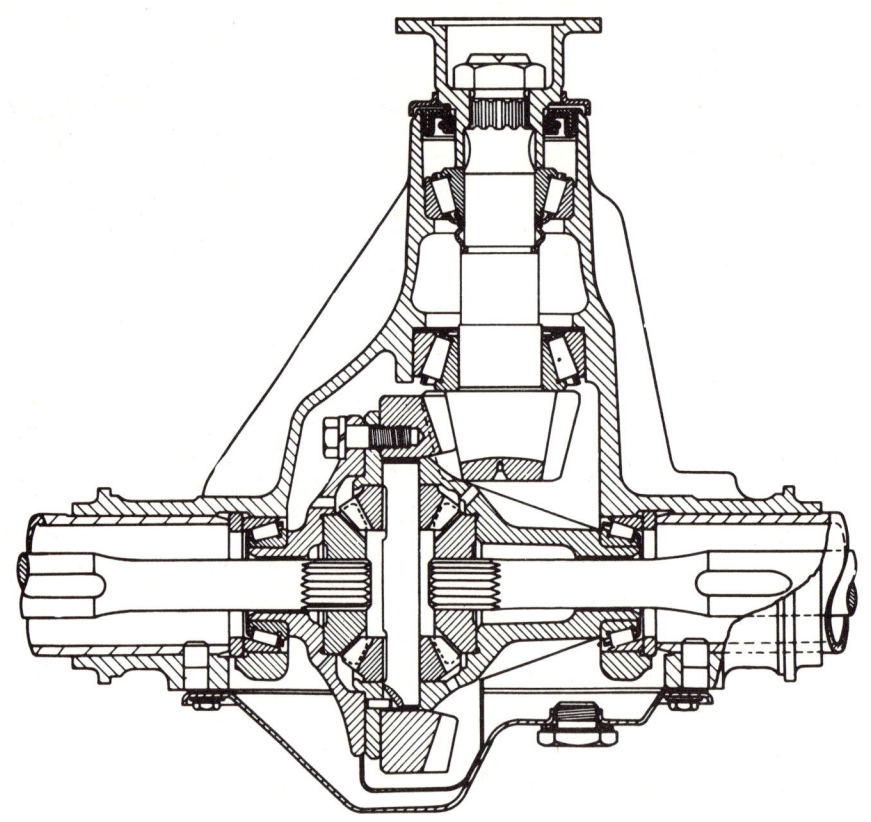

Fig.8.11 Cross section view of final drive

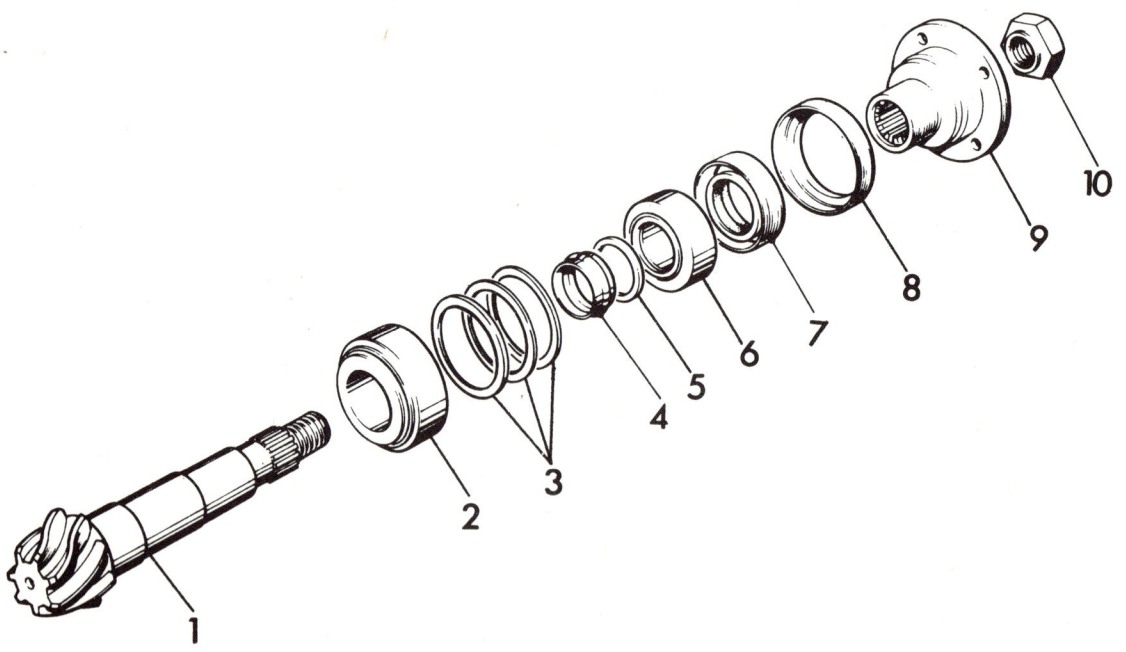

FIG.8.12 PINION ASSEMBLY COMPONENTS

1 Pinion
2 Pinion rear bearing
3 Shims
4 Collapsible spacer
5 Thrust rings
6 Pinion front bearing
7 Lip type oil seal
8 Oil slinger
9 Pinion flange
10 Nut

Castrol Hypoy.

23 Place, preferably new, thrust washers behind the two pinions and position in the differential case halves.

24 Fit the spacers to the side gears and refit to the differential case half.

25 Slide in the pinion gear shaft taking care to line up the retaining pin hole in the casing. Do not replace the retaining pin yet.

26 Using a feeler gauge behind each side gear spacer check the clearance between each of them and the casing half. This should be 0.002 - 0.005 in (0.0508 - 0.127 mm) with no gear backlash evident.

27 Increase or decrease the spacer thickness accordingly. Spacers are available in seven thickness with a total range from 0.019 - 0.033 in (0.483 - 0.838 mm) inclusive. It is permissible for the spacers used on each side to be of different thicknesses if necessary. When tolerances are correct fit a new shaft retaining pin and lock by peening.

28 Warm up the crownwheel on a hot plate and fit to the differential case half. To assist alignment of the bolt holes make up two guide studs (old bolts with the heads cut off) and screw into two opposite bolt holes in the gear. If the original crownwheel is being refitted do not forget to align   the previously made marks.

29 Draw the crownwheel on with the mounting bolts and spring washers and tighten in a diagonal and progressive manner to a final torque wrench setting of 38 lb ft (5.6 Kg m).

30 The lateral location of the differential case assembly in the axle casing is controlled by spacers and shims. These also determine the side bearing pre-load and are available in two thicknesses of spacer VIZ. 0.100 and 0.101 in (2.54 and 2.794 mm), and shims of 0.003 in (0.0762 mm). These cover from 0.100 in (2.54 mm) upwards, therefore, in steps of 0.001 in (0.0254 mm) using two spacers for each bearing and the requiste shims (Fig.8.14).

31 Fit the differential case into the housing complete with side bearings and then select four spacers and the appropriate number of shims which will remove all the end float between the bearing outer tracks and the ends of the axle housing tubes.

32 Lift out the differential casing and place to one side. Divide the spacers and shims equally into two packs, ie two spacers for each side with the necessary shims. Fit one pack on one side of the housing, making sure that any shims are sandwiched between the spacers and that the spacer chamfers are facing outwards.

33 Add one extra shim of 0.003 inch (0.0762 mm) to the second pack, arranging the pack in the same manner as for the first one. Place the pack at the other end of the axle housing aperture, fit the differential casing into the housing once more. This time a little pressure will be needed to fit the assembly into position and care must be taken to ensure the side bearings do not tilt and jam.

34 Using a soft faced hammer lightly tap the axle housing near the bearings and rotate the assembly so that the bearings will settle properly. Next replace the bearing caps in their correct positions and tighten the bolts to a torque wrench setting of 24 lb ft (3.3 Kg m).

35 The bearing pre-load can now be checked by measuring the torque resistance at the periphery of the crownwheel. This is simply done by tying a piece of string around the crownwheel and measuring the turning resistance with a spring balance. If the reading is outside the limits - new bearings 3 lb in (3.4 Kg cm) - old bearings 1 lb in (1.14 Kg cm) then the unit must be removed and the shim thicknesses adjusted accordingly (Fig.8.15).

36 Check that the runout of the crownwheel rear face does not exceed 0.002 in (0.06 mm) using a dial indicator gauge. If it does, it indicates that dirt or burrs may have affected its location when being assembled to the differential case (Fig.8.xx).

37 Once the differential assembly has been satisfactorily fitted and checked remove it once more, keeping the shims and spacers carefully for final assembly.

38 Fitting of the pinion is a little more difficult and there are the factors which determine the initial selection of the pinion spacers and shims to control the relative mesh of the crownwheel

Fig.8.13 Differential side bearing cap identification

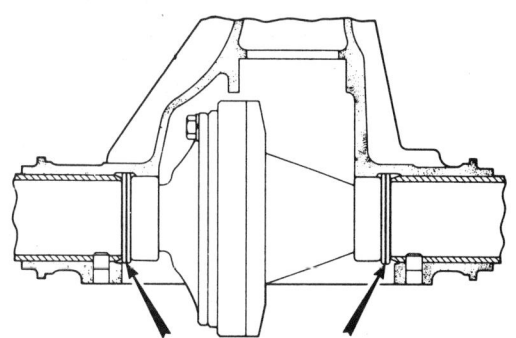

Fig.8.14 Location of differential case assembly spacers and shims

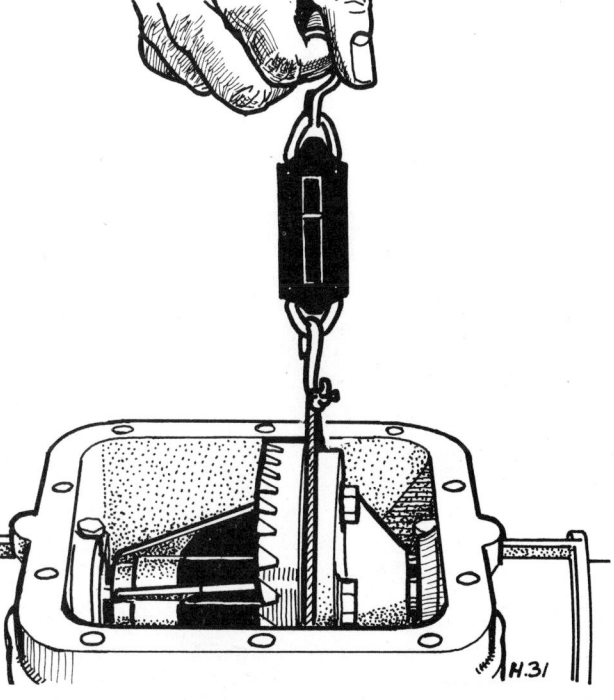

Fig.8.15 Measurement of turning resistance

and pinion. These are:

a) The pinion bearing correction - being the variance from the maximum of 0.9626 in (24.46 mm) thickness of the pinion rear bearing - is determined by measuring the actual thickness of the rear pinion bearing with a micrometer.

b) The pinion meshing correction - being the deviation from the nominal depth of the bearing adjustment face in relation to the centre line of the crownwheel axis. This figure is stamped on the axle housing rear face at the top - the single figure represents thousandths of an inch.

39 The calculation of the pinion spacer/shims required is best indicated using an example: To retain accuracy Imperial units must be used.

Pinion rear bearing maximum thickness	0.9626 inch
Pinion rear bearing actual thickness	0.9590 inch
Difference (Pinion bearing correction)	0.0036 inch
Axle housing correction '3'	0.0030 inch
Pinion meshing correction '5'	0.0050 inch
Total shim thickness required	0.0116 inch

Shims are available in three thicknesses, 0.003, 0.005 and 0.010 inch (0.0762, 0.1270, 0.254 mm). The nearest thousandth of an inch is taken. So here one would have four shims of 0.003 inch (0.0762 mm) making a total of 0.012 inch (0.3048 mm).

From experience it is better to select the larger thickness in this case as this will reduce the backlash fractionally rather than to increase it.

40 Having checked each shim and spacer with a micrometer the shims should be placed on the pinion head rear bearing abutment face in the axle housing (Fig.8.16).

41 The pinion rear bearing outer race should next be fitted to the axle housing using a tube of suitable diameter. Follow this with the front bearing outer track.

42 Having fitted the pinion rear bearing inner race to the shaft

then fit a new compressible spacer and bearing washer over the shaft. Place the shaft into the axle housing.

43 Next place the front bearing inner race over the shaft and whilst supporting the end of the pinion, tap it home on the shaft using a suitable diameter tube.

44 All is now set to apply the pinion bearing pre-load. Well lubricate the pinion and pinion shaft threads with Castrol Hypoy and carefully fit the coupling flange and new nut.

45 The coupling flange nut should now be tightened progressively to compress the compressible spacer whilst making a frequent check with a spring balance until the specified bearing pre-load as given in the specifications at the beginning of this chapter is achieved.

46 Should the pre-load limit be exceeded due to overtightening of the nut, the compressible spacer must be discarded and a new one fitted.

47 Refit the filter pad and retainer to the bottom of the axle housing. The differential case assembly together with the selected shims and spacers should now be fitted to the axle housing. Should there be an odd number of shims the greater number must be put between the right hand pair of spacers.

48 Now is the time to check the backlash between the crownwheel and pinion. Using a dial indicator gauge or feeler gauges determine the total backlash which should be between 0.005 - 0.007 inch (0.13 - 0.18 mm)

49 Should adjustment be necessary remove the shims behind the differential bearings once the caps have been removed and fit different thickness shims. It should be noted that a movement of 0.002 in (0.05 mm) shim thickness from one differential bearing to the other will vary the backlash by approximately 0.002 in (0.05 mm).

50 Refit the bearing caps and tighten the bolts to a torque wrench setting of 24 lb ft (3.3 Kg m).

51 A final test for correct pinion/crownwheel location can be carried out by applying a load to the crownwheel and driving it by turning the pinion so that marks will be made on the teeth. Use engineers blue to emphasise the marks (Fig.8.17).

52 When all is well lubricate and fit a new oil seal with the lip facing inwards. Using a suitable diameter tube tap in the seal until it either contacts the shoulder in the axle housing or seal case is flush with the end of the housing - whichever occurs first.

53 Smear a little oil on the lip of the seal and flange sleeve and carefully ease the flange into position.

54 Refit the coupling flange nut and tighten until the required pre-load is obtained. Stake the nut rim into the pinion slot (Fig.8.10).

55 Fit a new rear cover plate gasket and replace the rear cover. Secure in position with the twelve bolts and spring washers and tighten in a diagonal and progressive manner.

56 Refit the axle shafts as described in Section 3.

57 Refit the rear axle as described in Section 2. Refill the rear axle with 2.5 pints (1.42 litres) of Castrol Hypoy.

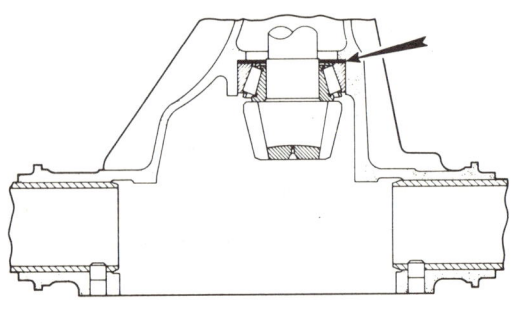

Fig.8.16 Location of pinion head adjustment shims

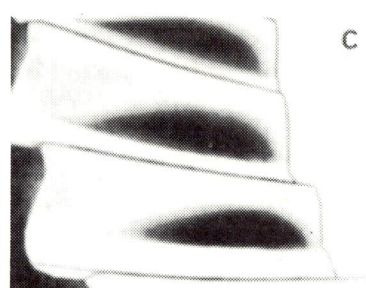

FIG.8.17 TOOTH CONTACT MARKS

A Correct
B Pinion too far out of en-   gagement. Increase pinion   C Pinion too far into mesh.   shim thickness.
                                 rear bearing shim thickness   Decrease pinion rear bearing

Chapter 9 Braking system

Contents

Specifications

Type:	Lockheed disc brakes at front, drum brakes at rear. Cable operated handbrake to rear wheel. Tandem master cylinder. Servo assisted.	
Total swept area		
Victor	281.2 sq in (1814 sq cm)	
VX 4/90	316.1 sq in (2043 sq cm)	
Front - disc		
Disc diameter		
Victor...	9.38 in	(238 mm)
VX 4/90	10.74 in	(272.7 mm)
Permissible run-out	0.004 in	(0.1 mm)
Minimum pad thickness	0.06 in	(1.5 mm)
Brake disc thickness	0.375 - 0.380 in	(9.525 - 9.625 mm)
Rear - drum:		
Type	Manual or automatic adjusters	
Drum size	9 in x 1.75 in	(229 x 44 mm)
Diameter after refacing (max)	9.06 in (230 mm)	
Run-out of drum braking surface checked on axle shaft (max)	0.004 in (0.1 mm)	
Minimum lining thickness	See text	
Master cylinder:		
Type	Tandem	
Bore	0.75 in	(19.05 mm)
Piston travel	1.38 in	(35.05 mm)
Brake pedal:		
Pressure	70 lb (31.5 kg)	
Pedal travel (correctly adjusted)	4.50 in (114 mm)	
Shaft diameter	0.589 - 0.591 in	(14.96 - 15.00 mm)
Clearance in bush	0.002 - 0.006 in	(0.05 - 0.16 mm)
Handbrake:		
Pressure	50 lb (22.5 kg)	
Lever travel (correctly adjusted)		
Dash mounted	12 - 14 notches	
Floor mounted	8 - 10 notches	

Servo unit:

Type	Direct acting
Diaphragm effective diameter	5.5 in (139.7 mm)
Boost ratio	2.2 : 1

Warning lamp actuator:

Operating pressure	70 lb (31.5 kg)

Torque wrench settings:

	lb ft	kg m
Brake caliper bolts	37	5.1
Brake caliper to steering knuckle bolts	33	4.6
Brake disc to hub bolts:		
4 bolt fitting	14	1.94
5 bolt fitting	30	4.15
Pressure reducing valve spring arm pivot nut and bolt	39	5.398

1 General description

Models covered by this manual are fitted with disc brakes at the front and drum brakes at the rear. They are operated by hydraulic pressure created in the master cylinder when the brake pedal is depressed. This pressure is transferred to the respective wheel cylinder or caliper cylinders by a system of metal and flexible pipes and hoses.

The tandem master cylinder is divided into two parts whereby the hydraulic system to the front wheels is not interconnected to that of the rear wheels. This means that if one brake line should fail there will still be braking effort on two wheels.

The drum brakes are of the internally expanding type with the shoes and linings moving outwards into contact with the rotating brake drum. The brake units are fitted with one wheel cylinder so enabling a one leading, one trailing shoe arrangement to be used. The term 'leading shoe' means that the leading edge of one shoe is moved into contact with the rotating drum by the wheel cylinder and   a self servo or wrapping action of the brake shoe tends to pull it on further, thereby giving braking assistance.

The handbrake operates on the rear brakes only using a system of links and cables.

The front disc brakes fitted are of the conventional fixed caliper design. Each half of the caliper contains a piston which operates in a bore both being interconnected so that under hydraulic pressure these pistons move towards each other. By this action they clamp the rotational movement of the disc. Special seals are fitted between the piston and bore and these seals return to their natural shape and draw the pistons back slightly so giving a running clearance between the pads and disc. As the pads wear, the piston is able to slide through the seal so allowing wear to be taken up.

The front disc brakes are self adjusting as also are some drum brakes. Other drum brakes have to be adjusted manually.

A brake servo unit is fitted as standard and this is fitted between the brake pedal and master cylinder and adds to the pressure on the master cylinder pushrod when the brake pedal is being depressed.

On VX 4/90 models a load conscious pressure reducing valve is incorporated in the rear brake system.

2 Drum brake - adjustment

This section is only applicable to models fitted with manual adjustable brakes and are identifiable by square headed adjusters at the rear of the backplate beneath the handbrake cable.

If the pedal travel becomes noticeably excessive before the brake operates and presuming that the pedal pressure is still firm and hard when pressure is applied, then the brake shoes need adjustment. This will be necessary, on average, every 3,000 miles (4,800 Km).

2 Chock the front wheels, jack up the rear of the car and support on firmly based axle stands. Release the handbrake.

3 Turn the adjuster clockwise until the brake shoes lock the wheel. Then back off the adjuster two notches. Rotate the wheel to ensure that the shoes are not binding on the drum. The rear wheels will not turn without resistance because of the differential gear so do not confuse this turning resistance with brake drag. Repeat the adjustment process for the second rear wheel (photo).

4 It is often possible that a little shoe rubbing can be detected after the adjuster has been slackened off the required two notches. Provided the degree of drag in such instances is negligible, ignore it. The shoes will bed down into their new positions on the drums after a mile or two. If there is serious binding after the adjusters have been slackened off two or more notches it will be necessary to remove the drum and examine the shoes and drums further.

3 Disc brakes - adjustment

Disc brakes are fitted to the front wheels only and do not require external adjustment. Regularly inspect the pad thickness as described in Section 8 and if worn fit new pads.

4 Bleeding the hydraulic system

1 The system should need bleeding only when some part of it has been dismantled which would allow air into the hydraulic circuit, or if the reservoir level has been allowed to drop so far that air has entered the master cylinder. If the vehicle has been left standing unused for any length of time it is possible also that air bubbles may have developed in the system due to the air absorbing nature of hydraulic fluid. Bleed nipples are found on each of the front wheels calipers and one only for the rear brakes to be found on the left hand backplate (photo). The hydraulic line goes through the right hand rear cylinder en route to the left rear cylinder.

2 Ensure that a supply of clean non aerated fluid of the correct specification is to hand in order to replenish the reservoir during the bleeding process. It is necessary to have someone available to help, as one person has to pump the brake pedal while the other attends to the bleed nipple. The reservoir level has also to be continually watched and replenished. Fluid bled out must not be reused. A clean clear glass jar and a 12 inch (305 mm) length of 0.125 inch (3.175 mm) internal diameter rubber tube that will fit tightly over the bleed nipples is also required.

3 With the engine switched off depress the brake pedal six

2.3 Removal of dust cap from adjuster

4.1 Brake bleed nipple

times to make sure that there is no residual vacuum in the servo unit.

4   It is recommended that the rear brakes are bled first, then the left hand front and finally the right hand front.

5   Put a little hydraulic fluid in the bottom of the glass jar. Clean the bleed nipple and fit the tube onto the nipple and place the other end in the jar so that it is under the surface of the fluid. Keep it under the surface throughout the bleeding operation.

6   Unscrew the bleed screw half a turn and request the assistant to depress and release the brake pedal in short sharp bursts. Short sharp strokes are far better as they will force any air bubbles along the line with the fluid rather than pump the fluid past them. It is not essential to remove all the air first time. If the whole system has to be bled, attend to each wheel for three or four complete pedal strokes and then repeat the process. On the second time around operate the pedal sharply in the same way until no bubbles come out of the pipe into the jar. With the brake pedal in the fully depressed position tighten the bleed screw. Do not forget to keep the reservoir topped up throughout.

7   When all wheels have been bled satisfactorily re-adjust the shoe clearance as described in Section 2.

8   If the reason for bleeding has been a repair to a pipe or cylinder near a wheel then it should be normally necessary to bleed only the wheel of the line in question - PROVIDED that no fluid has been allowed to drain out of the disconnected line. If in any doubt bleed the whole system.

9   Depress the brake pedal which should offer a firm resistance with no trace of sponginess. The pedal should not continue to go down under sustained pressure. If it does there is a leak or the master cylinder seals have badly worn.

5   Rear drum brake shoes - inspection, removal and refitting

1   Check the front wheels, apply the handbrake, jack up the rear of the car and support on firmly based axle stands. Remove the wheel.

2   Back off the brake shoe adjusters by turning in an anti-clockwise direction - manual adjustment rear brakes only. This is to provide clearance so allowing brake drum removal.

3   The composite brake drum (cast iron rim and pressed steel web) is located on the axle shaft spigot and retained by two spring clips. Release these clips on the wheel studs and withdraw the brake drum. If it is tight it may be tapped outwards using a soft faced hammer on the outer circumference (photos).

4   Examine the friction surface on the interior of the drum.

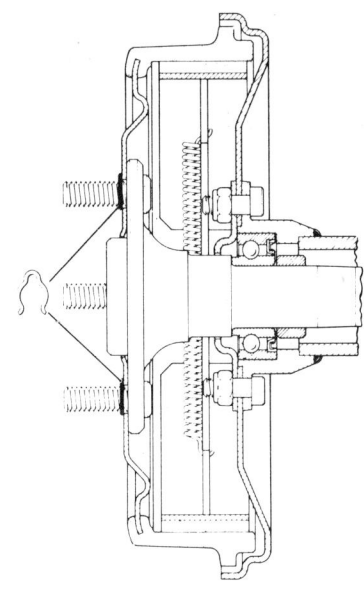

Fig.9.1 Cross section view through rear brake assembly

Normally this should be completely smooth and bright. Remove any dust with a dry cloth and examine the surface for any score marks or blemishes. Very light hairline scores running around the surface area are not serious but indicate that the shoes may be wearing or grit and dirt has found its way into the drum at some time. If there are signs of deep scoring the drum needs reconditioning or replacement. As reconditioning will probably cost as much as a new drum, and certainly more than a good second-hand one (obtained from car breakers), it is not recommended.

5   Inspect the drum stud holes for concentricity. If they are oval the drum must be discarded and a new one obtained.

6   Examine the brake shoes for signs of oil contamination, deep scoring, or overall wear of the friction material. Deep scoring will be immediately apparent and will relate to any scoring in the drum. Oil contamination is evident where there are hard black shiny patches on the linings caused by the heat generated in braking which carbonises any oil that may have reached them. As a temporary measure, these areas can be rasped down but it is far better to replace the shoe. Normal wear can be judged by the depth of the rivet heads from the surface of the linings. If this is 0.025 inch (0.65 mm) or less, the linings should be renewed.

5.3a Drum retaining clip removal

5.3b Removal of brake drum

5.7a Turning slotted washer with plier

5.7b Lifting away pin from backplate

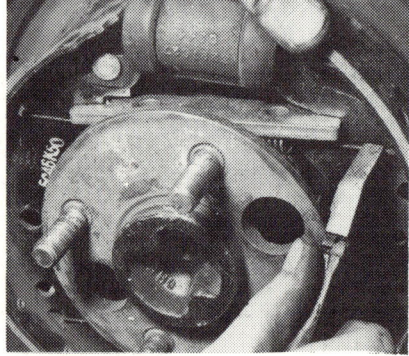

5.8a Releasing upper spring tension

5.8b Lifting away brake shoe

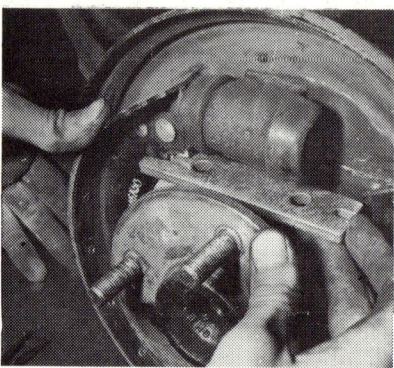

5.8c Recovering upper link

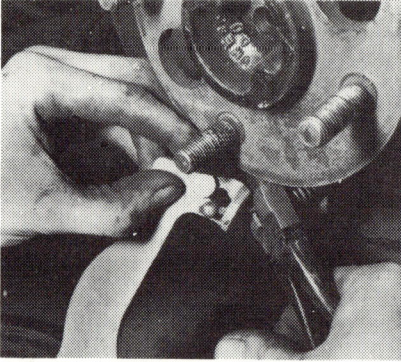

5.11a Handbrake cable ball end

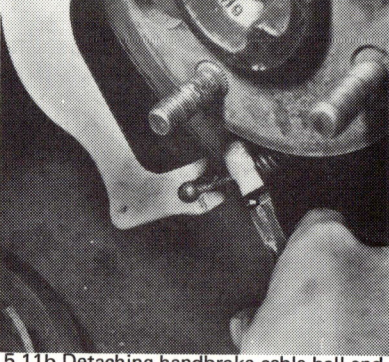

5.11b Detaching handbrake cable ball end from linkage

With the bonded linings the minimum lining thickness is 0.0625 inch (1.6 mm).

7 With a pair of pliers turn the slotted washer on the pin so that it comes off the end of the pin. The spring, pin and washers can then be removed (photos)

8 Release the forward shoe first by levering it away from the adjuster with a screwdriver. Once this spring tension is released it will be quite easy to remove the shoes and springs. Make a special note of the location of the springs in the shoe webs and which way round they fit (photos).

9 As soon as the shoes are removed make sure that the hydraulic cylinder pistons are prevented from coming out of the cylinders by tying wire or string around the cylinder.

10 With automatic adjuster, it will be necessary to detach the ratchet plate and spring assembly from the shoe web if new shoes are to be fitted. Release the spring clip and lift away the plain washer, spring plate washer and draw the ratchet plate peg through the web.

11 With manual adjustment brakes, using a pair of pliers compress the handbrake cable return spring and detach the handbrake cable ball end from the linkage on the rear shoes, at the same time recovering the cable locking disc (photos)

12 Refitting the brake shoes and drum assembly is the reverse sequence to removal but the following additional points must be noted:

a) Automatic adjuster: The brake shoe operating lever should be assembled with the pin head against the ratchet plate and the spring plate washer between the shoe web and plain washer (Fig.9.2) .

b) Smear the ratchet plate pin, brake shoe operating lever pin and contact pads on the flange plate with Castrol PH Grease.

c) Always handle the brake shoes with clean hands. Even a small oil or grease deposit could affect their performance.

d) If any shoe requires replacement it means that all shoes at the rear must be replaced together. Anything less can only lead to dangerous braking characteristics and uneconomical wear. All brake shoes are interchangeable.

13 Refit the drums to the wheels from which they came and secure with two spring clips.

14 In the case of manual adjustment brakes, refer to Section 2 and adjust the shoe to drum clearance.

15 In the case of automatic adjuster brakes, pull on and then release the handbrake several times so as to set the ratchet plate.

6 Rear brake shoes adjuster - removal and refitting

1 Should it be necessary to remove the brake adjuster first remove the road wheel, brake drum and brake shoes as described in Section 5.

2 Undo and remove the two adjuster retaining nuts and spring washers. The adjuster can now be lifted away from the back-plate.

3 Remove the rubber dust shield and check that the adjuster wedge can be screwed both in and out to its fullest extent without showing signs of tightness (Fig.9.4).

4 Lift away the two adjuster links and thoroughly clean the adjuster assembly. Inspect the adjuster body and the two links for signs of excessive wear or corrosion. Obtain new parts as necessary.

5 Lightly smear the adjuster links with Castrol PH Grease and reassemble. Double check correct operation by holding the two links between the fingers and rotating the adjuster wedge whereupon the links should move out together.

6 Refitting is the reverse sequence to removal.

7 Rear drum brake backplate - removal and refitting

1 Refer to Chpater 8, Section 3 and remove the axle shaft.

2 Wipe the top of the brake master cylinder reservoir and unscrew the cap. Place a piece of thin polythene sheet over the reservoir neck and refit the cap. This will prevent hydraulic fluid syphoning out during subsequent operations.

3 Using an open ended spanner disconnect the brake pipe from the rear of the wheel cylinder.

4 Remove the axle shaft from the rear axle assembly as described in Chapter 8.

5 The brake backplate assembly may now be lifted from the rear axle casing.

6 Refitting is the reverse sequence to removal. Tighten the axle shaft bearing retainer nuts to a torque wrench setting of 12 lb ft (1.6 Kg m).

8 Front disc brake caliper pad - removal and refitting

1 The thickness of the pads can be visually checked by jacking up the front of the car and supporting on firmly based axle stands. Remove the road wheel.

2 The pads may now be seen sandwiched between the disc and caliper body. If the thickness of the friction lining is less than 0.060 in (1.5 mm) the pads must be renewed. Sometimes the pads wear unevenly, but if one of a pair is below the minimum thickness the pair must be renewed. As a general rule pads on both front wheels should be renewed even if only one side needs it.

3 Wipe the top of the reservoir and unscrew the cap. Carefully syphon out some of the hydraulic fluid so preventing the fluid overflowing when the level rises as the pistons are pushed back for fitting new pads.

4 To remove the pads first straighten the two split pin ears and withdraw the pins. Lift out the spring retaining plate (photo).

5 Apply pressure to the faces of the old pads with the fingers so pressing the pistons behind the back into the caliper body. Then lift out the pads and any anti-squeal shims (photo).

6 Using a soft brush remove traces of dust from the caliper. Refer to Fig.9.6 and check that the relieved section of the piston is correctly located. If not carefully rotate the piston

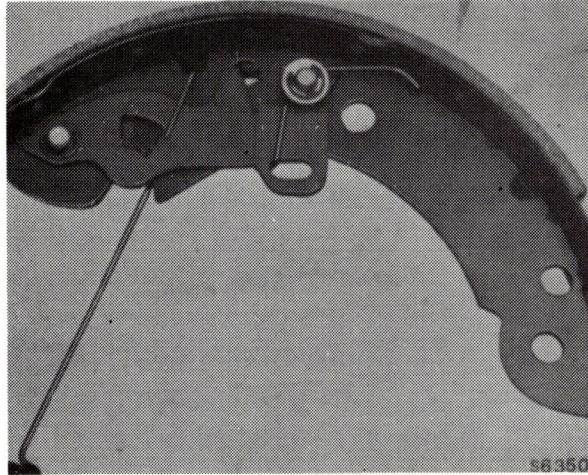

Fig.9.2 Hooked end return spring retaining ratchet plate in position against shoe web (automatic adjuster type)

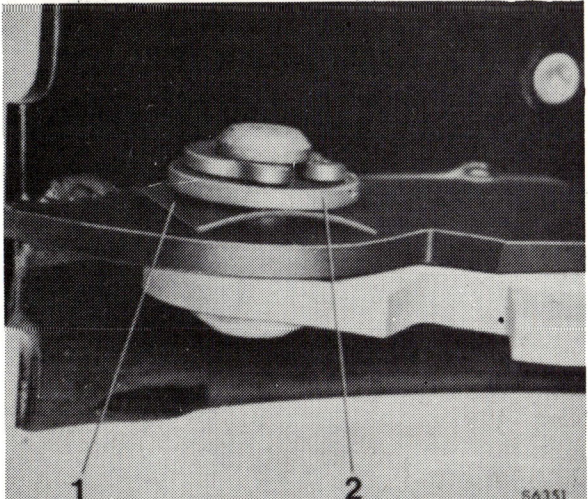

FIG.9.3 BRAKE SHOE OPERATING LEVER ASSEMBLED WITH PIN HEAD AGAINST LEVER AND SPRING PLATE BETWEEN SHOE WEB AND PLAIN WASHER

1 Spring plate   2 Plain washer

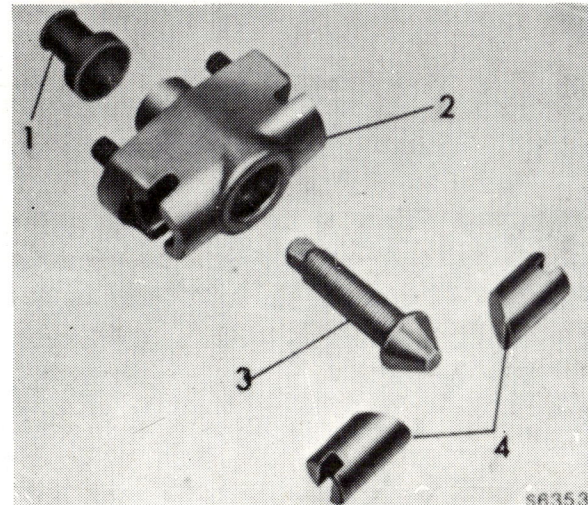

FIG.9.4 REAR BRAKE SHOE ADJUSTER

1 Dust shield   3 Adjuster wedge
2 Body   4 Adjuster link

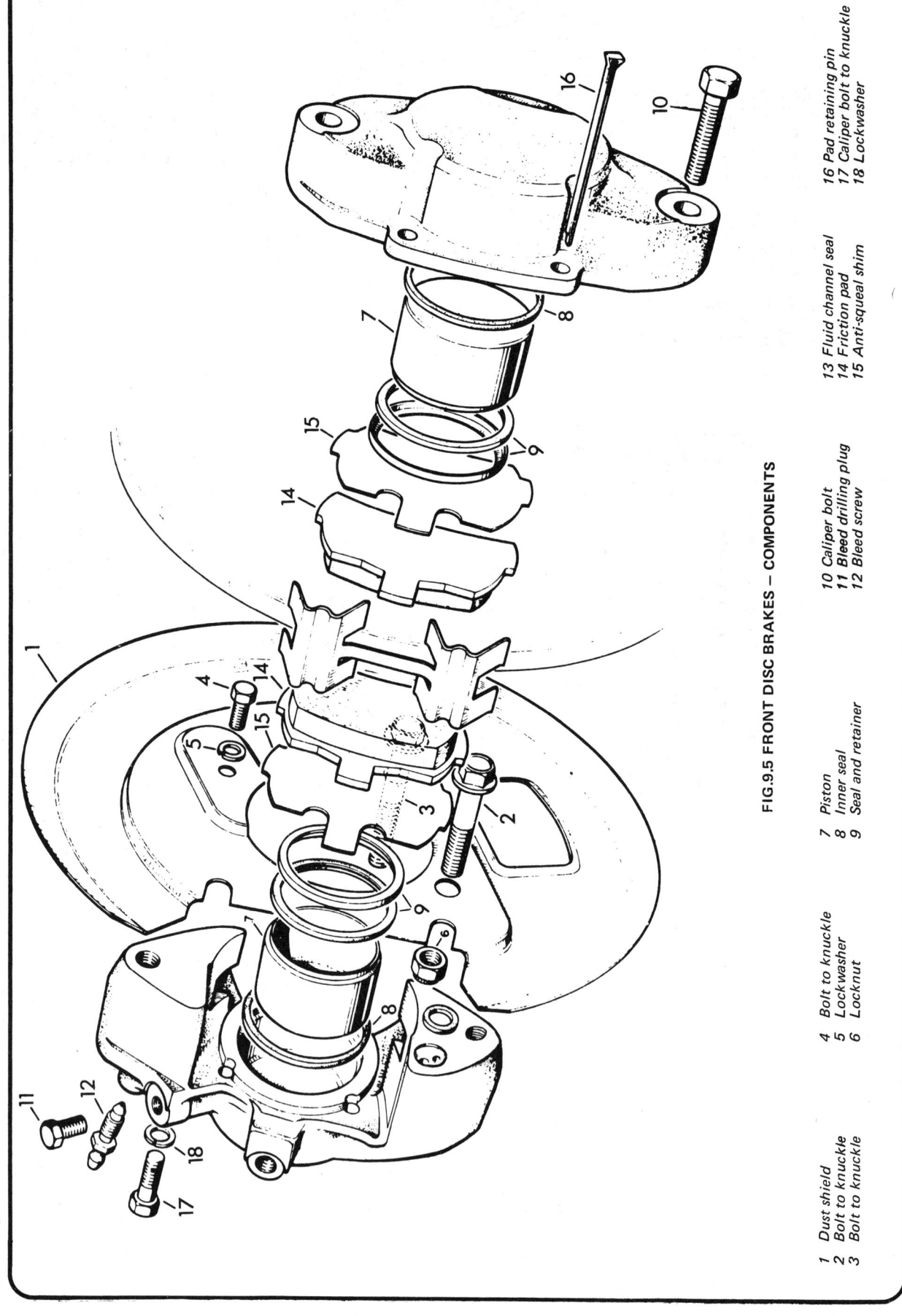

FIG.9.5 FRONT DISC BRAKES – COMPONENTS

1 Dust shield
2 Bolt to knuckle
3 Bolt to knuckle

4 Bolt to knuckle
5 Lockwasher
6 Locknut

7 Piston
8 Inner seal
9 Seal and retainer

10 Caliper bolt
11 Bleed drilling plug
12 Bleed screw

13 Fluid channel seal
14 Friction pad
15 Anti-squeal shim

16 Pad retaining pin
17 Caliper bolt to knuckle
18 Lockwasher

8.4a Straightening split pin ready for removal

8.4b Withdrawing split pin from caliper body

8.4c Lifting away spring retaining plate

8.5 Lifting away pad and anti-squeal shim

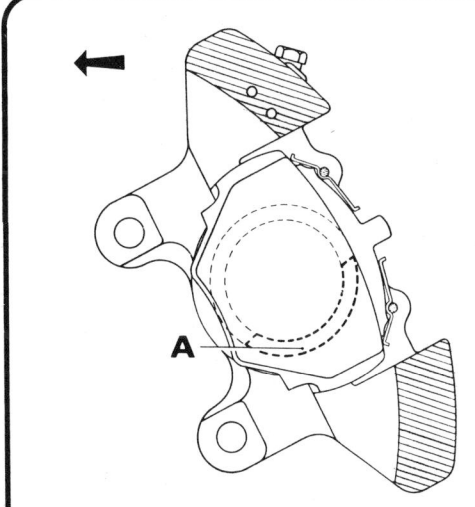

Fig.9.6 The relieved section of piston 'A' must be located in this position before refitting piston

A

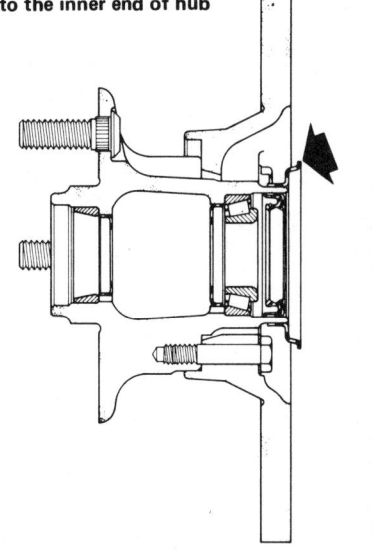

Fig.9.7 Arrow showing shield pressed onto the inner end of hub

using a screwdriver.

7   Refit new pads and shims (if fitted) also if the old ones show signs of distortion or deterioration.

8   Refitting the pads is now the reverse sequence to removal. The following additional points should be noted:

a) If it is suspected that air has entered the system it must be bled as described in Section 4.

b) Top up the reservoir fluid level and depress the brake pedal several times to settle the pads. Recheck the hydraulic fluid level.

9   Front brake disc - removal and refitting

1   Chock the rear wheels, apply the handbrake, jack up the front of the car and support on firmly based axle stands. Remove the road wheel.

2   Refer to Section 14 of this chapter and detach the caliper assembly. There is no need to undo the hydraulic hose but hang the caliper on wire or string so as not to strain the hose.

3   Using a wide blade screwdriver ease off the hub grease cap.

4   Straighten the hub nut locking split pin and withdraw the split pin. Lift away the nut retainer. Undo and remove the nut and washer.

5   Withdraw the complete front hub assembly from the spindle.

6   To separate the hub from the disc first ease the sheet metal shield from the inner end of the hub (Victor models). This prevents the ingress of water and mud (Fig.9.7) .

7   Mark the relative position of the hub and disc. Undo and remove the four/five bolts securing the hub to the disc and separate the two parts.

8   Should the disc surfaces be grooved and a new disc not readily obtainable it is permissible to have the two faces ground by an engineering works. See the specifications for the minimum disc thickness. Score marks are not serious provided that they are concentric but not excessively deep. It is however, far better to fit a new disc rather than to regrind the original one.

9   To refit the disc to the hub make sure that the mating faces are very clean and then line up the previously made alignment marks if the original parts are to be used. Secure with the four/five bolts which should be tightened in a progressive and diagonal manner to a final torque wrench setting of 14 lb ft (1.94 Kg m) - four bolt fitting, or 30 lb ft (4.15 Kg m) - five bolt fitting.

10 Refit the sheet metal shield to the inner end of the hub so that the flat surface of the shield is in line with the end face of the hub.

11 Refitting is now the reverse sequence to removal, but the following additional points should be noted.

a) Before refitting the caliper check the disc run out with a dial indicator gauge or feeler gauges located 0.70 in (20 mm) from the circumference of the disc. The run out must not exceed 0.004 in (0.1 mm). If necessary remove the disc and check for dirt on the mating faces. Should these be clean reposition the disc on the hub. If this does not cure the trouble fit a new disc

b) The hub bearing end float must be adjusted as described in Chapter 11.

10   Master cylinder - removal and refitting

1   Wipe the top of the master cylinder reservoir and unscrew the filler cap. Place a piece of polythene sheeting over filler neck and refit the cap. This will prevent syphoning of the hydraulic fluid during subsequent operations.

2   Wipe the arms around the union on the master cylinder body and then undo and detach the hydraulic pipes from their unions on the master cylinder body. Also detach the low brake pressure warning light cable (if fitted).

3   Undo and remove the two nuts and spring washers that secure the tandem master cylinder to the servo unit and lift away the master cylinder.

4   Refitting the tandem master cylinder is the reverse sequence

to removal. It will be necessary to bleed the brake hydraulic system as described in Section 4.

11   Master cylinder - dismantling - and reassembly

1   The component parts are shown in Fig.9.8x.

2   Prior to dismantling wipe the exterior of the master cylinder clean of dirt. Undo and remove the two bolts that secure the plastic reservoir to the master cylinder body. Recover the two rubber seals.

3   On master cylinders fitted with a low brake pressure warning light switch unscrew the switch and lift away together with the 'O' ring seal.

4   Unscrew and remove the pressure differential chamber plug and seal from the rear end of the master cylinder.

5   Plug the rear brake pipe connections and the control switch thread bore and remove the two pressure differential pistons and springs using an air jet on the front reservoir connection.

6   Remove the piston springs and seals.

7   Using a clean metal rod of suitable diameter depress the primary piston until it reaches the stop so that the pressure of the secondary piston is removed from the stop screw.

8   Unscrew the stop screw and remove the sealing washer. Release the pressure on the piston.

9   Lightly depress the primary piston again to relieve the pressure on the circlip located on the bore at the flanged end of the cylinder. With a pair of pointed pliers remove the circlip taking care not to scratch the finely finished bore.

10 Lift away the stop washer, and withdraw the primary piston assembly.

11 Withdraw the intermediate spring from the cylinder bore. Note which way round the primary piston seals are fitted and remove the seals from the piston.

12 The secondary piston assembly may now be removed by lightly tapping the master cylinder against a wooden base.

13 Withdraw the second spring from the cylinder bore. Note which way round the secondary piston seals are fitted and remove the seals from the piston.

14 Thoroughly wash all parts in either methylated spirits or clean approved hydraulic fluid and place in order ready for inspection.

15 Examine the bore of the master cylinder carefully for any signs of scoring, ridges or corrosion, and if it is found to be smooth all over, new seals can be fitted. If there is any doubt as to the condition of the bore, then a new cylinder must be fitted.

16 If examination of the seals shows them to be apparently oversize or very loose on their seats, suspect oil contamination in the system. Oil will swell these rubber seals, and if one is found to be swollen it is reasonable to assume that all seals in the braking system will require attention.

17 Before reassembly again wash all parts in methylated spirits or clean approved hydraulic fluid. Do not use any other type of oil or cleaning fluid or the seals will be damaged.

18 Commence reassembling by lubricating the bores with clean hydraulic fluid.

19 Smear the new secondary piston seals with hydraulic fluid and fit these to the secondary piston. Make sure that they are fitted the correct way round.

20 Smear the new primary piston seals with hydraulic fluid and fit these to the primary pistons. Make sure that they are fitted the correct way round.

21 Position the master cylinder between soft faces and clamp in a vice in such a manner that the main bore is inclined with the open end downwards.

22 Insert the spring and then the secondary piston assembly, second spring and the primary pistons assembly. To avoid any damage to the cup seals a flattened needle should be passed around the lip of each seal to assist entry into the cylinder bore.

23 Reposition the master cylinder so that it is now vertical with the open end upwards and place the top washer in position. Depress the primary piston slightly and fit the circlip.

24 Next fully depress the primary piston and fit the stop screw

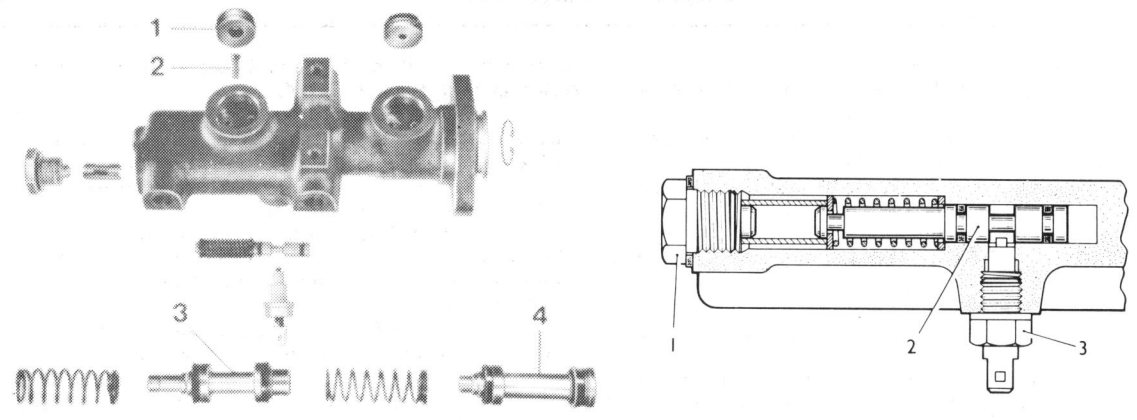

FIG.9.8 MASTER CYLINDER — MAJOR COMPONENTS

1   Reservoir seal   3   Secondary piston
2   Stop pin   4   Primary piston

FIG. 9.9 PRESSURE WARNING LAMP ACTUATION PISTON AND SWITCH

1   Plug   3   Actuation switch
2   Actuation piston

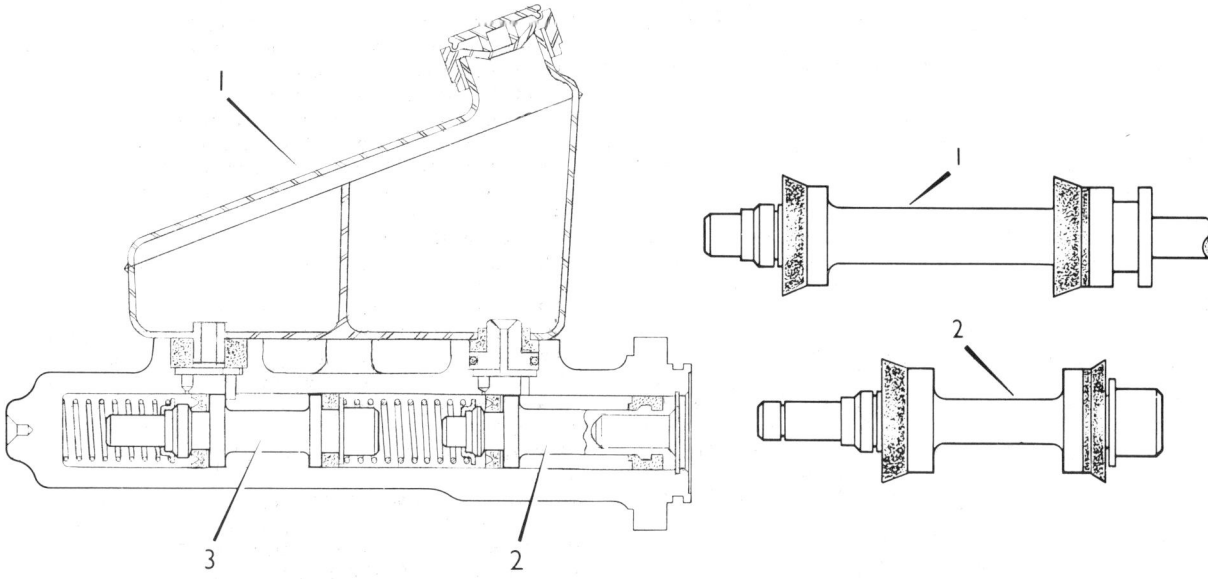

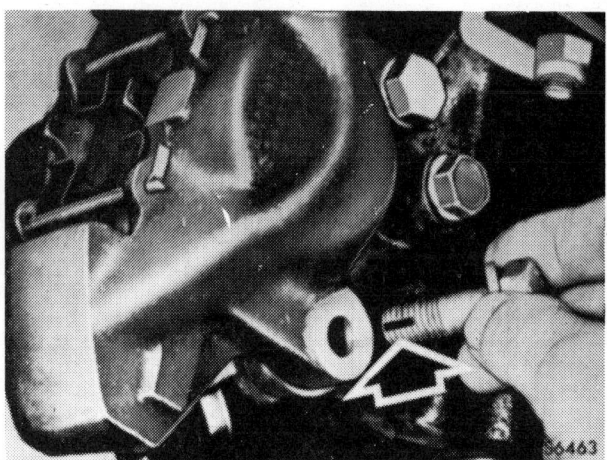

FIG. 9.10 CROSS SECTION THROUGH MASTER CYLINDER

1   Reservoir   3   Secondary piston
2   Primary piston

FIG. 9.11   DETAIL   OF   SEAL   ASSEMBLY   TO   PISTONS

1   Primary piston   2   Secondary piston

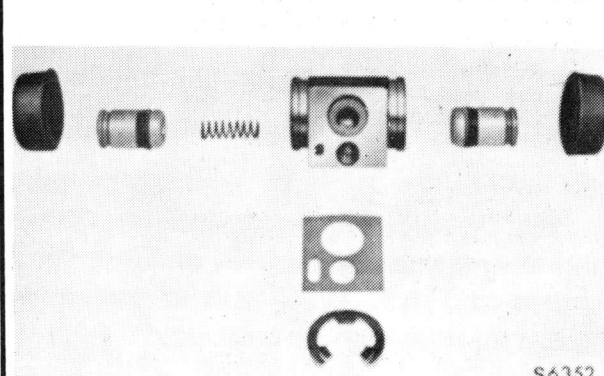

Fig. 9.12 Components of drum brake wheel cylinder

Fig. 9.13 Special bolts used to secure caliper to steering knuckle

with a new sealing washer. Tighten the stop screw to a torque wrench setting of 4.3 - 7.0 lb ft (0.6 - 1.0 Kg m).

25 For models fitted with the low brake pressure warning light, lubricate and fit new seals to the pressure differential pistons and fit the spring, two pistons, second spring and the differential pressure plug fitted with a new sealing washer. Tighten the plug to a torque wrench setting of 10.9 to 13.7 lb ft (1.5 - 1.9 Kg m).

26 Fit new reservoir seals and then the plastic reservoir. Secure with two bolts. Reassembly is now complete.

12 Rear drum brake wheel cylinder - removal and refitting

1 If hydraulic fluid is leaking from the brake wheel cylinder, it will be necessary to dismantle it and replace the seal.

2 Refer to Section 5, and remove the brake drum and brake shoes.

3 Wipe the top of the brake master cylinder reservoir and unscrew the cap. Place a piece of polythene sheet over the top of the reservoir and replace the cap. This is to prevent hydraulic fluid syphoning out during subsequent operations.

4 Using an open ended spanner carefully unscrew the hydraulic pipe connections to the rear of the wheel cylinder.

5 If the left hand cylinder is to be removed also remove the bleed screw which is located below the wheel cylinder.

6 If the right hand cylinder is to be removed also detach the bridge feed pipe.

7 Using a screwdriver carefully ease off the 'E' clip that holds the wheel cylinder to the backplate. Push the wheel cylinder through the backplate and lift away. Recover the gasket.

8 Refitting the wheel cylinder is the reverse sequence to removal. Take care to ensure that the 'E' clip correctly locates in its groove in the master cylinder. Make sure that the gasket is correctly located over the boss and dowel before refitting.

13 Rear drum brake wheel cylinder - overhaul

1 Ease off the rubber dust cover that protects the open ends of the cylinder bore.

2 Withdraw the pistons from the wheel cylinder body followed by the spring.

3 Using fingers only carefully remove the piston seal from the piston noting which way round it is fitted. (Do not use a screwdriver as this could scratch the piston).

4 Inspect the inside of the cylinder for score marks caused by impurities in the hydraulic fluid. If any are found the cylinder will require renewal. NOTE: If the wheel cylinder is to be renewed always ensure that the replacement is exactly similar to the one removed.

5 If the cylinder is sound, thoroughly clean it out with fresh hydraulic fluid.

6 The old rubber seals will probably be swollen and visibly worn so they must be discarded. Smear each new rubber seal with hydraulic fluid and fit it to the piston so that the flat surface is towards the piston.

7 Fit the spring into the cylinder bore followed by the two pistons taking care to make sure that the fine edge lip does not roll or become trapped.

8 Refit the dust covers engaging the lip with the groove in the outer surface, of the wheel cylinder body.

14 Front disc brake caliper - removal and refitting

1 If the caliper pistons are suspected of malfuntioning or leaking hydraulic fluid, chock the rear wheels, jack up the front of the car and support on firmly based stands. Remove the road wheel.

2 Examine for fluid leaks and if these are apparent it will be necessary to remove the caliper and proceed as described from paragraph 4 onwards.

3 If there are no signs of leaking ask someone to depress the brake pedal and watch how the two disc pads come up to the disc. One may move very slowly or not at all, in which case it will be necessary to remove the caliper and proceed further.

4 Remove the disc pads and shims (if fitted) as described in Section 8.

5 Wipe the top of the master cylinder reservoir, remove the cap and place a piece of polythene sheet over the filler neck. Refit the cap.

6 Using an open ended spanner undo and remove the hydraulic pipe union nut from the rear of the caliper body.

7 Undo and remove the two bolts that secure the caliper to the steering knuckle. Do NOT undo the bolts which clamp the two halves of the caliper together. These bolts must be renewed on refitting as they have special nylon inserts.(Fig.9.13)

8 Lift the caliper from engagement with the disc.

9 Refitting the caliper is the reverse sequence to removal. In addition:

a) The two caliper securing bolts should be tightened to a torque wrench setting of 37 lb ft (5.1 Kg m).

b) Bleed the brake hydraulic system as described in Section 4.

c) Depress the brake pedal several times to reset the pads in their correct operating position.

15 Front disc brake caliper - overhaul

1 Clean the exterior of the caliper assembly and then temporarily reconnect the caliper to the hydraulic system and support its weight. Do not allow the caliper to hang on the hydraulic pipe. Using a small G clamp hold the piston in the mounting half of the caliper. Carefully depress the footbrake pedal with the bleed nipple open so as to bleed the system and then close the nipple. Depress the footbrake again and this will push the piston in the rim half of the caliper outwards. Ease the rubber piston cover out of the grooves in the piston and caliper body. Remove the piston covers (Fig.9.5).

2 Continue to depress the brake pedal and eject the rim half piston. It is advisable to have a container or tray available to catch any hydraulic fluid once the piston is removed.

3 Using a tapered wooden rod or an old plastic knitting needle carefully extract the fluid seal from its bore in the caliper half.

4 Remove the G clamp from the mounting half piston. Temporarily refit the rim half piston and repeat the operations in paragraphs 1 - 3 of this section.

5 Thoroughly clean the internal parts of the caliper using methylated spirits. Any other fluid cleaner will damage the internal seals between the two halves of the caliper. DO NOT SEPARATE THE TWO HALVES OF THE CALIPER.

6 Inspect the caliper bores and pistons for signs of scoring. If evident, a new assembly should be obtained.

7 To reassemble the caliper first wet a new piston seal with approved brake fluid and carefully insert it into its groove in the rim half of the caliper seating, ensuring that it is correctly fitted.

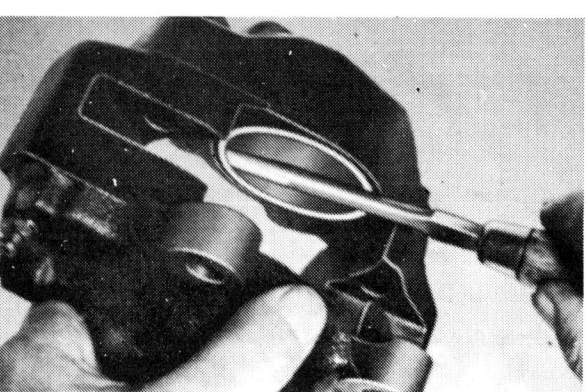

Fig. 9.14 Removal of retainer using screwdriver

Refit the dust cover into its special groove in the cylinder.

8　Release the bleed screw in the caliper one complete turn. Coat the side of the piston with hydraulic fluid and with it positioned squarely in the top of the cylinder bore ease the piston in until approximately 0.3125 in (7.938 mm) is left protruding. Engage the outer lip of the dust cover in the piston groove and push the piston into the cylinder as far as it will go. Turn the piston until the relieved section is located as shown in Fig.9.6　Fit the dust cover retaining ring.

9　Repeat the operations in paragraphs 7 and 8 for the mounting half of the caliper.

10 The pads and anti-squeal shims (if fitted) may be refitted either now or when the caliper has been refitted. See Section 8 for full information. Do not forget to bleed the hydraulic system as described in Section 4.

16　Handbrake cable - adjustment

1　When the handbrake is correctly adjusted an effort of 50 lb (22.5 Kg) when applied to the hand control or mid way along the handgrip of the floor mounted lever type should move the hand control 12 - 14 notches or raise the lever 8 - 10 notches.

2　Under normal operating conditions the handbrake should not require separate adjustment as it is automatically adjusted with the rear brakes. However, after a while the cables will stretch, necessitating separate adjustment.

3　Manual adjustment rear brakes. Refer to Section 2 and adjust the rear brake.

4　Refer to Fig.9.15 and temporarily detach the two cable return springs from the rear cable anchor bracket.

5　Slacken the cable adjustment sleeves locknut and then rotate the sleeves whilst at the same time holding the intermediate cable ends until cable slackness is eliminated. Tighten the locknuts and reconnect the two cable return springs.

17　Handbrake underbody cables - removal and refitting

1　The layout used for the floor mounted handbrake system is shown in Fig.9.16 and rearwards of the pulley wheel type equaliser is also similar to the twist release handbrake as used in cars fitted with bench seats.

2　The system comprises a pulley type equaliser and a clevis to which is attached　the front cable. The ends of the intermediate cable are threaded and screwed into adjusting sleeves on the rear inner cables.

　　The rear outer cables are anchored to a body mounted bracket and to the rear axle by two clips.

Intermediate cable

1　To remove the intermediate cable first detach the cable return springs from the rear cable anchor bracket (Fig.9.15).

2　Release the locknuts and unscrew the adjusting sleeves from the ends of the intermediate cable.

3　Expand the pins of the intermediate cable guide by drifting through the guide. Detach the cable from the guide.

4　Release the front cable from the equaliser pulley clevis.

5　Refitting the intermediate cable is the reverse sequence to removal. Refer to Section 16 and adjust the cable tension.

6　After adjustment apply Castrol LM Grease liberally on the cable in the area around the cable guide.

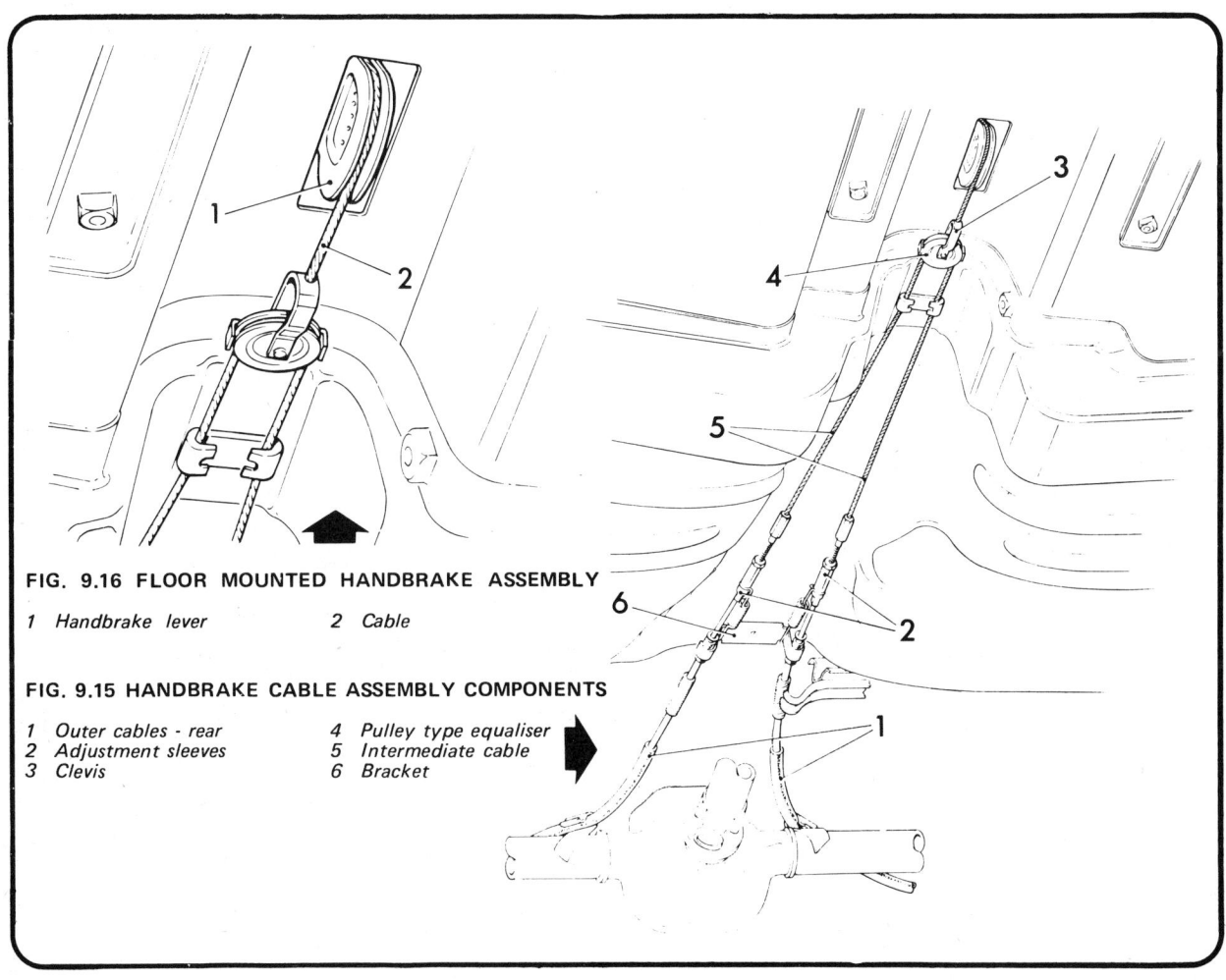

FIG. 9.16 FLOOR MOUNTED HANDBRAKE ASSEMBLY

1　Handbrake lever　　　　*2　Cable*

FIG. 9.15 HANDBRAKE CABLE ASSEMBLY COMPONENTS

1　Outer cables - rear　　　*4　Pulley type equaliser*
2　Adjustment sleeves　　　*5　Intermediate cable*
3　Clevis　　　　　　　　*6　Bracket*

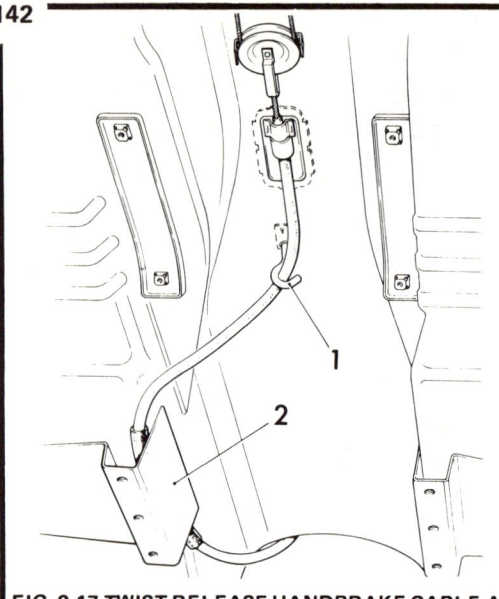

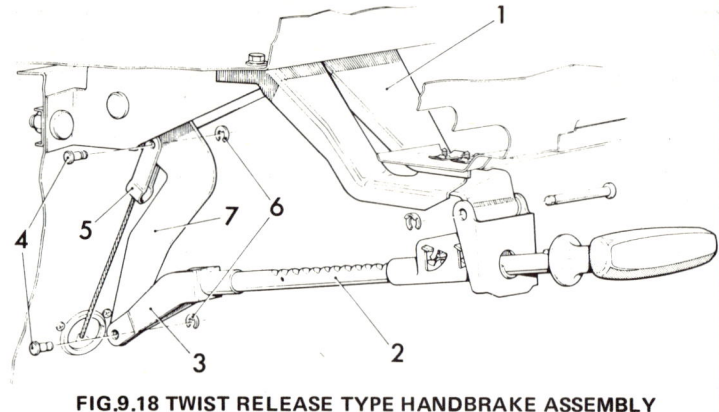

FIG. 9.18 TWIST RELEASE TYPE HANDBRAKE ASSEMBLY

1	Bracket	5	Clevis
2	Control rod	6	'E' clip
3	Clevis	7	Bush assembly
4	Pin		

FIG. 9.17 TWIST RELEASE HANDBRAKE CABLE ASSEMBLY LAYOUT

1	Guide	2	Body bracket

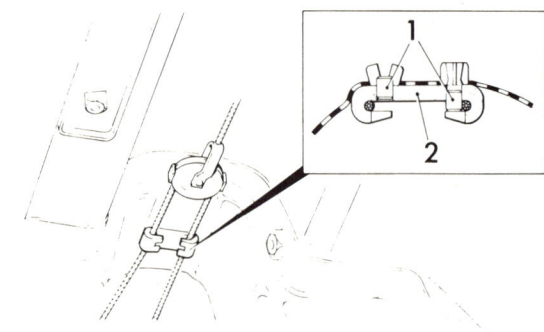

FIG. 9.20 INTERMEDIATE CABLE GUIDE

1	Pins	2	Cable guide

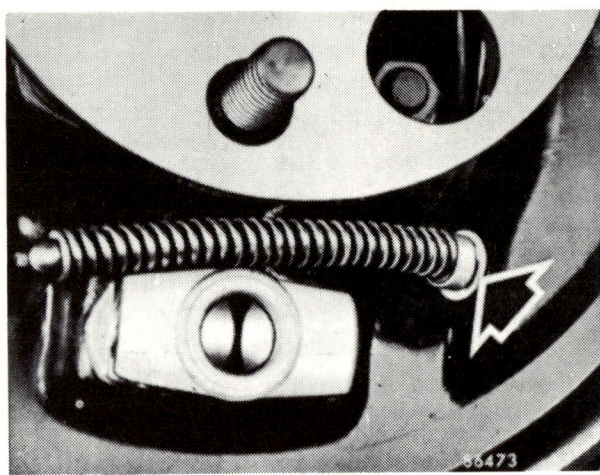
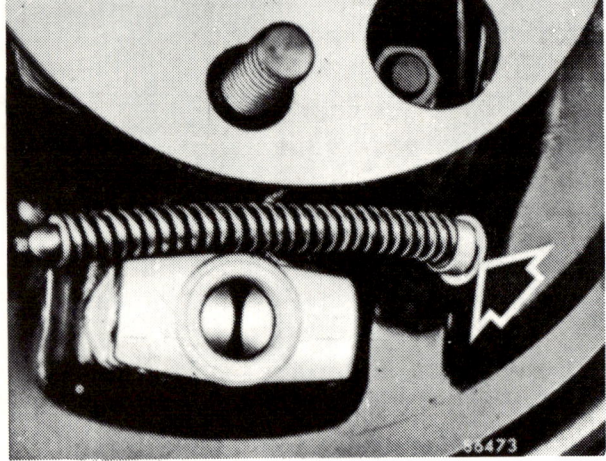

Fig. 9.19 Handbrake cable retaining 'E' clip

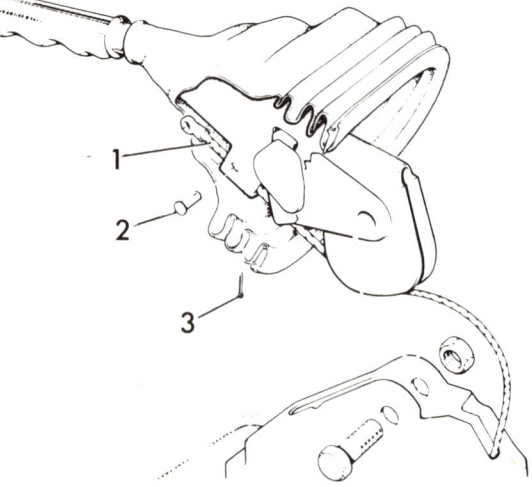

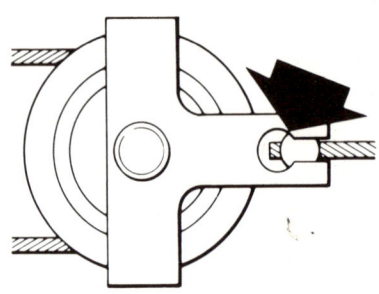

Fig. 9.21 The slotted hole (arrowed) in equaliser must be fitted uppermost

FIG. 9.22 FLOOR MOUNTED TYPE HANDBRAKE ASSEMBLY

1	Short cable	3	Split pin
2	Clevis pin		

Rear cable

1 Detach the cable return springs from the rear cable anchor bracket.

2 Release the locknut and unscrew the adjusting sleeves from the ends of the intermediate cable.

3 Refer to Section 5 and remove the rear brake drums and shoes. This will give access to the 'E' clip, on the inside of the back plate. (Fig.9.19).

4 Detach the cable from the body mounted bracket and rear axle clips.

5 Refitting the rear cable is the reverse sequence to removal. Refer to Section 16 and adjust the cable tension. Take great care to ensure that the forward end of the outer cable casing is fully engaged in the anchor bracket and each adjusting sleeve is screwed onto the intermediate cable ends by an equal amount.

---

18 Handbrake lever assembly - removal and refitting

Twist release type

1 The layout of the twist release type handbrake assembly as located under the instrument panel is shown in Fig.9.18 .

2 To remove the control assembly first detach the 'E' clip from the clevis pin located at the lower end of the lever and bush assembly.

3 Again using a screwdriver detach the 'E' clip from the long clevis pin at the handle end of the mounting bracket.

4 Withdraw the clevis pin and lift away the handle and ratchet assembly.

5 Should it be necessary to remove the front cable first detach it from the clevis pin at the upper end of the lever and bush assembly by removing the 'E' clip from the end of the clevis pin and withdrawing the pin.

6 Detach the inner cable from the clevis on the pulley type equaliser located under the body, release the outer casing from the dash panel by removing the two screws and then draw the cable assembly through the bulkhead.

7 Refitting in both cases is the reverse sequence to removal but the following additional points should be noted:

a) When refitting a new front cable make sure that the cable is located between the front right hand bracket for the engine rear support crossmember and also hooked over the guide near to the equaliser.

b) Lubricate all moving parts with Castrol LM Grease.

Floor mounted lever type

1 The layout of the floor mounted lever type handbrake assembly is shown in Fig.9.22.

2 To remove the assembly ease the rubber gaiter up the lever until the pivot bolt is accessible.

3 Undo and remove the nut and pivot bolt and draw the lever upwards.

4 Straighten the ears of the split pin locking the front cable retaining clevis pin, withdraw the split pin and remove the clevis pin.

5 Should it be necessary to remove the front cable detach it from the clevis on the pulley type equaliser located under the body.

6 Refitting is the reverse sequence to removal but the following additional points should be noted:

a) Make sure that the cable is correctly seating in the groove of the handbrake lever.

b) Lubricate all moving parts with Castrol LM Grease.

c) When refitting the handbrake lever make sure that the tag on the ratchet plate is located BELOW the edge of the mounting plate.

---

19 Brake pedal assembly - removal and refitting

1 Upon reference to Fig.9.23 it will be seen that the brake pedal has a single bush and is carried, together with the clutch pedal and a spacer sleeve on a single shaft. This shaft is held in

the support by one spring clip fitted at either end. To prevent noise after pedal operation a rubber located in the pedal stop bracket cushions the return of the pedal.

2 Release the return spring from the pedal.

3 Using a screwdriver draw the spring clip from the clevis pin that attaches the servo unit actuating rod to the pedal. Withdraw the clevis pin.

4 Again using a screwdriver carefully ease off the right hand pedal shaft retaining spring clip and push the shaft leftwards until the brake pedal is free.

5 Check the degree of wear in the pedal bush which if worn may be pressed out and a new one fitted. In some instances where a new bush is tight on the shaft it will be necessary to ream out the bush until the specified clearance is obtained.

6 Refitting the pedal and pedal shaft is the reverse sequence to removal. Lubricate the pedal shaft with a little Castrol LM Grease.

---

20 Vacuum servo unit - general description

A vacuum servo unit is fitted into the brake hydraulic circuit in series with the master cylinder to provide 'power' assistance to the driver when the brake pedal is depressed.

The unit operates by vacuum obtained from the inlet manifold and comprises basically a booster diaphragm and a non return valve.

The servo unit and hydraulic master cylinder are connected together so that the servo unit piston rod acts as the master cylinder pushrod. The driver's braking effort is transmitted through another pushrod to the servo unit piston which does not fit tightly into the cylinder but has a strong diaphragm to keep its edges in constant contact with the cylinder wall. This ensures that the air under vacuum pressure created in the inlet manifold of the engine provides servo assistance. During periods when the brake pedal is not in use, the controls open a passage to the rear chamber so placing it under vacuum. When the brake pedal is depressed, the vacuum passage to the rear chamber is cut off and the chamber opened to atmospheric pressure. The consequent rush of air pushes the servo piston forward in the vacuum chamber and operates the main pushrod to the master cylinder. The controls are designed so that assistance is given under all conditions and, when the brakes are not required, vacuum in the rear chamber is established when the brake pedal is released. All air from the atmosphere entering the rear chamber is passed through a small air filter.

---

21 Brake servo unit - removal and replacement

1 Refer to Section 10 and remove the brake master cylinder.

2 Slacken the hose clip and detach the vacuum hose from the connector on the non-return valve.

3 Straighten the ears of the split pin retaining the servo to the brake pedal pushrod clevis pin. Extract the split pin, lift away the plain washer and withdraw the clevis pin.

4 Undo and remove the four nuts and spring washers that secure the servo unit to the mounting bracket. Lift away the servo unit.

5 Refitting the servo unit is the reverse sequence to removal. It is important that the brake hydraulic system be completely bled as described in Section 4.

---

22 Vacuum servo unit - overhaul

Thoroughly clean the outside of the unit with a stiff brush and wipe with a non fluffy rag. It cannot be too strongly emphasised that cleanliness is important when working on the servo. Before any attempt be made to dismantle, refer to Fig.9.24 where it will be seen that two items of equipment are required. Firstly, a base plate must be made to enable the unit to be safely held in a vice. Secondly, a lever must be made similar

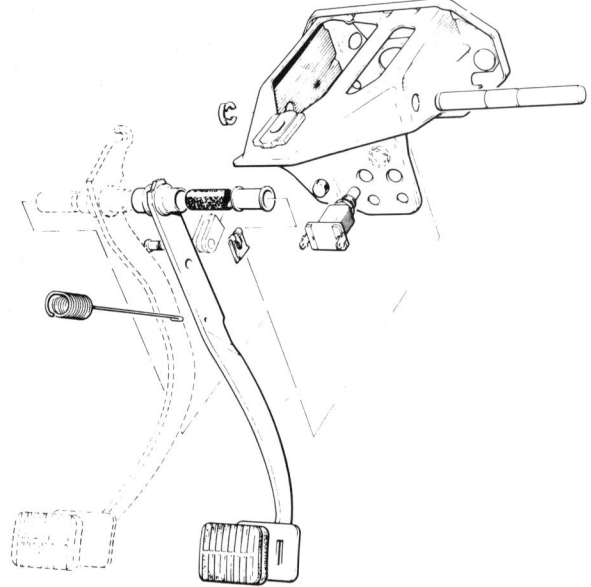

Fig.9.23 Brake pedal assembly

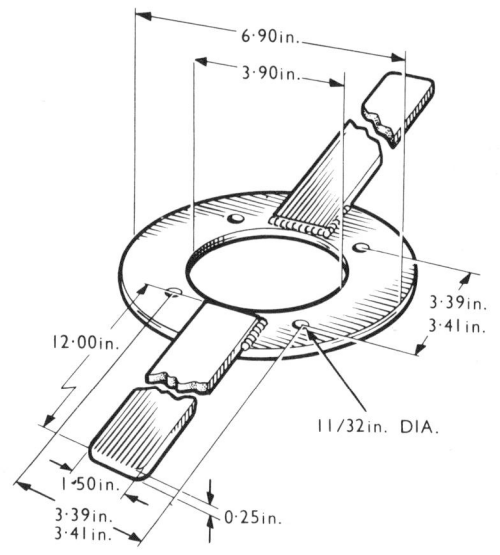

Fig.9.25 Vacuum servo unit air filter assembly

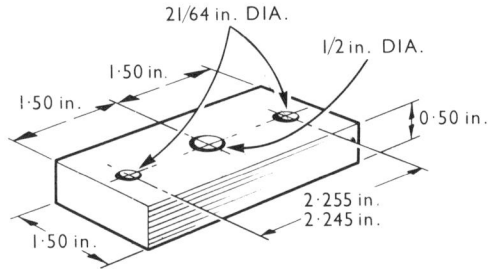

Fig.9.24 Two special tools necessary to strip servo unit

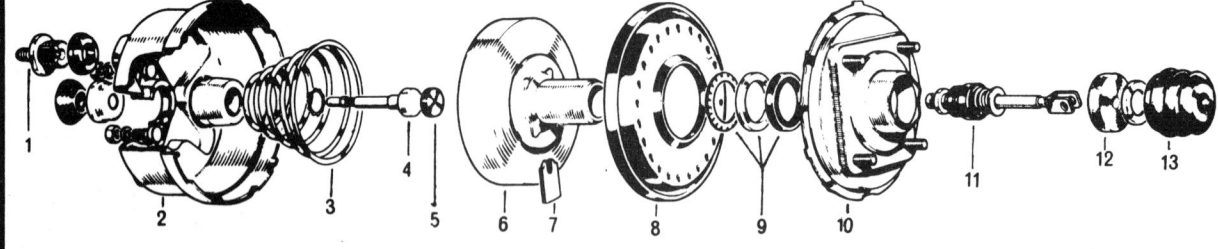

FIG.9.26 SERVO UNIT – EXPLODED VIEW

1 *Suction pipe union and non-return valve*	4 *Piston rod*	8 *Diaphragm*	11 *Pushrod assembly*
	5 *Seal*	9 *Seal assembly*	12 *Filter*
2 *Body shell*	6 *Piston*	10 *End cover*	13 *Pushrod and filter cover*
3 *Return spring*	7 *Piston rod locking plate*		

to the form shown. Without these items it is impossible to dismantle satisfactorily.

To dismantle the unit proceed as follows:

1 Refer to Fig.9.26 and, using a file or scriber, mark a line across the two halves of the unit to act as a datum for alignment.
2 Fit the previously made box plate into a firm vice and attach the unit to the plate using the master cylinder studs.
3 Fit the lever to the four studs on the rear shell as shown in Fig.9.24.
4 Use a piece of long rubber hose and connect one end to the adaptor on the engine inlet manifold and the other end to the non-return valve. Start the engine and this will create a vacuum in the unit so drawing the two halves together.
5 Rotate the lever in an anti-clockwise direction until the front shell indentations are in line with the recesses in the rim of the rear shell. Then press the lever assembly down firmly whilst an assistant stops the engine and quickly removes the vacuum pipe from the inlet manifold connector. Depress the operating rod so as to release the vacuum, whereupon the front and rear halves should part. If necessary, use a soft faced hammer and lightly tap the front half to break the bond.
6 Lift away the rear shell followed by the diaphragm return spring, the dust cover, end cap and the filter. Also withdraw the diaphragm. Press down the valve rod and shake out the valve retaining plate. Then separate the valve rod assembly from the diaphragm plate.
7 Gently ease the spring washer from the diaphragm plate and withdraw the pushrod and reaction disc.
8 The seal and plate assembly in the end of the front shell are a press fit. It is recommended that, unless the seal is to be renewed, they be left in situ.
9 Thoroughly clean all parts in Girling Cleaning Fluid and wipe dry using a non-fluffy rag. Inspect all parts for signs of damage, stripped threads etc, and obtain new parts as necessary. All seals should be renewed and for this a 'Major Repair Kit' should be purchased. This kit will also contain two separate greases which must be used as directed and not interchanged.
10 To reassemble first smear the seal and bearing with grease numbered 64949008 and refit the rear shell positioning it so that the flat face of the seal is towards the bearing. Press into position and refit the retainer.
11 Lightly smear the disc and hydraulic pushrod with grease number 64949008. Refit the reaction disc and pushrod to the diaphragm plate and press in the large spring washer. The small spring washer supplied in the 'Major Repair Kit' is not required. It is important that the length of the pushrod is not altered in any way as any attempt to move the adjustment bolt will strip the threads. If a new hydraulic pushrod has been required, the length will have to be reset. Details of this operation are given at the end of this section.
12 Lightly smear the outer diameter of the diaphragm plate neck and the bearing surfaces of the valve plunger with grease number 64949008. Carefully fit the valve rod assembly into the neck of the diaphragm and fit with the retaining plate.
13 Fit the diaphragm into position and also the non-return valve to the front shell. Next smear the seal and plate assembly with grease numbered 64949008 and press into the front shell with the plate facing inwards.
14 Fit the front shell to the box plate and the lever to the rear shell. Reconnect the vacuum hose to the non-return valve and the adaptor on the engine inlet manifold. Position the diaphragm return spring in the front shell. Lightly smear the outer head of the diaphragm with grease numbered 64949009 and locate the diaphragm assembly in the rear shell. Position the rear shell assembly on the return spring and line up the previously made scriber marks.
15 The assistant should start the engine. Watching one's fingers very carefully, press the two halves of the unit together and, using the lever tool, turn clockwise to lock the two halves together. Stop the engine and disconnect the hose.
16 Press a new filter into the neck of the diaphragm plate, refit the end cap and position the dust cover onto the special lugs of the rear shell.

17 Hydraulic pushrod adjustment only applies if a new pushrod has been fitted. It will be seen from Fig.9.26 that there is a bolt screwed into the end of the pushrod. The amount of protrusion has to be adjusted in the following manner: remove the bolt and coat the threaded portion with Loctite Grade B. Reconnect the vacuum hose to the adaptor on the inlet valve and non-return valve. Start the engine and screw the prepared bolt into the end of the pushrod. Adjust the position of the bolt head so that it is 0.011 to 0.061 inch below the face of the front shell. Leave the unit for a minimum of 24 hours to allow the Loctite to set hard.
18 Refit the servo unit to the car as described in the previous section. To test the servo unit for correct operation after overhaul, first start the engine and run for a minimum period of two minutes and then switch off. Wait for ten minutes and apply the footbrake very carefully, listening for the rush of air into the servo unit. This will indicate that vacuum was retained and, therefore, operating correctly.

23 Vacuum servo unit - air filter renewal

Pull back the servo unit dust cover located as shown in Fig.9.25 and ease off the end cap. Cut and remove the old filter. To fit a new filter, cut it diagonally to the centre hole and then fit it over the pushrod and into the housing. Replace the end cap and dust cover.

24 Load conscious pressure reducing valve - removal, refitting and adjustment

1 A load conscious pressure reducing valve is fitted to VX 4/90 models and is inserted in the rear brake hydraulic pipe. Upon reference to Fig.9.28 it will be seen that the valve is located forward of the rear axle and secured to the underframe.

The valve metering plunger is actuated by a spring arm which is attached to the rear axle casing via a connecting link. The function of the valve is to prevent the rear brakes locking before the front brakes under heavy braking conditions by controlling the hydraulic pressure passed to the rear brakes.
2 To check the operation, the use of a brake retardation meter (as used by most garages) is necessary, so unless the meter can be borrowed this check must be left to the garage.
3 Select a straight road with a clean dry tarmac surface for a test run. A retardation of at least 19 ft/ sec^2 (5.8m/sec2)) must be obtained without locking the rear wheels.
4 Under heavy braking conditions in excess of the figures quoted in paragraph 3 the rear wheels must NOT lock before the front wheels.
5 If the conditions described in paragraphs 3 and 4 cannot be met it is an indication that either the valve metering plunger adjustment screw requires adjustment or a new valve is needed.
6 To remove the valve and spring arm assembly first wipe the top of the brake master cylinder and unscrew the cap. Place some polythene sheet over the filler neck and refit the cap. This prevents syphoning out of the hydraulic fluid during subsequent operations.
7 Wipe the area around the two hydraulic pipe unions on the side of the valve body and with an open ended spanner undo the two union nuts.
8 Undo and remove the two nuts and spring washers that secure the pressure valve mounting bracket to the underbody.
9 Detach the connecting link from the spring arm and lift away from the underside of the body. The valve may now be detached from the mounting bracket once the securing bolt has been removed.
10 Refitting the valve and spring arm is the reverse sequence to removal. It will be necessary to bleed the brake hydraulic system as described in Section 4.
11 Adjustment requires the use of a special setting link and this operation must be left to the local Vauxhall agent.

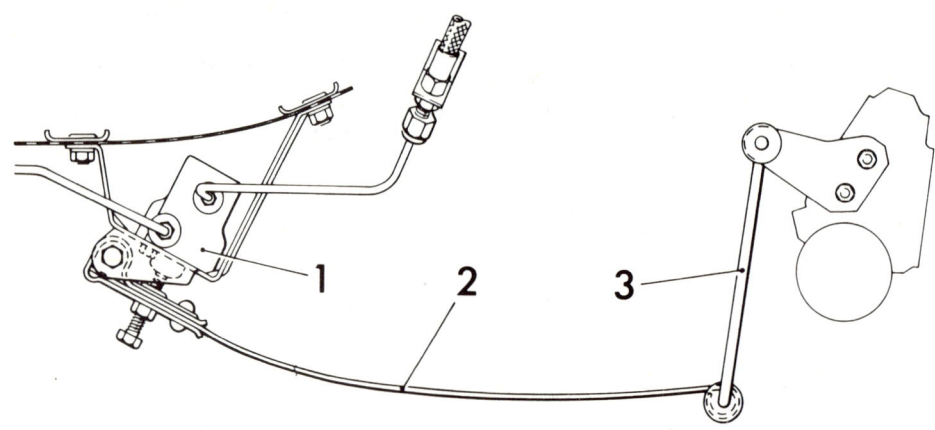

FIG.9.27 LOAD CONSCIOUS PRESSURE REDUCING VALVE

1   Valve   2   Spring arm   3   Connecting link

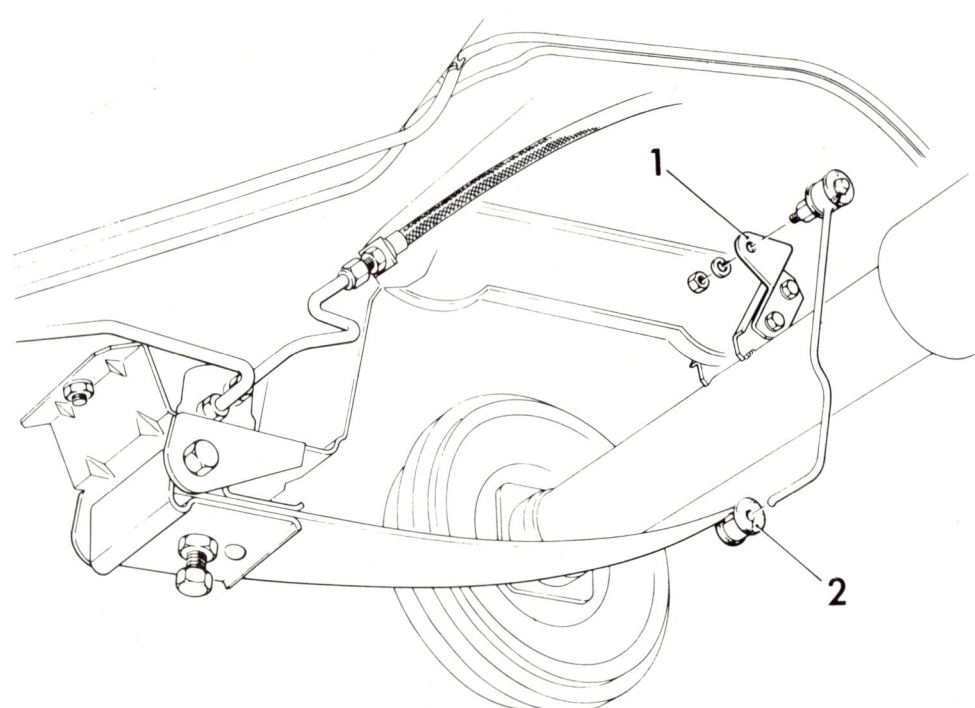

FIG.9.28 SPRING ARM REAR ATTACHMENTS

1   Axle tube bracket   2   Spring arm bush

---

25 Brake pressure warning light switch - operation check

This switch is located in the lower end of the master cylinder between the primary and secondary pistons. It is operated by a spring loaded double ended piston housed in a separate bore in the master cylinder body (Fig.9.9).

Should the line pressure in the front or rear braking system drop the double ended piston will move from its central position and make contact with the switch. The warning light bulb will come on. The only time when the warning light should be on, although no fault in the hydraulic system, is when the ignition is on and the handbrake applied.

To check the operation of the switch and piston proceed as follows:-

1   Switch off the ignition and depress the brake pedal several times to evacuate the servo unit.

2   Chock the front wheels, switch on the ignition and release the handbrake. Open the rear brake bleed screw and depress the brake pedal. The light should come on. Leave the pedal depressed and close the bleed screw.

3   Repeat the instructions given in paragraph 2 for the front brakes.

4   Should the warning light fail to come on test the bulb and if satisfactory, the switch and piston must be removed and checked. See Section 11 for further information.

26   Fault diagnosis

Before diagnosing faults from the following chart check that any braking irregularities are not caused by:—

1 Uneven and incorrect tyre pressures.
2 Incorrect 'mix' of radial and cross-ply tyres.
3 Wear in the steering mechanism.
4 Defects in the suspension and dampers.
5 Misalignment of the body frame.

NOTE: For vehicles fitted with disc brakes at the front the references in the chart to front wheel shoe adjustments do not apply. The 'Reason/s' referring to hydraulic system faults or wear to the friction material of the linings still apply, however. Disc pads also come in different material and references to variations are also relevant.

Symptoms	Reason/s	Remedy
Pedal travels a long way before the brakes operate	Brake shoes set too far from the drums	Adjust the brake shoes to the drums.
Stopping ability poor, even though pedal pressure is firm	Linings and/or drums badly worn or scored	Dismantle, inspect and renew as required.
	Failure of one circuit in the dual hydraulic system (where fitted)	Check both circuits for hydraulic leaks and repair.
	One or more wheel hydraulic cylinders seized, resulting in some brake shoes not pressing against the drums (or pads against disc)	Dismantle and inspect wheel cylinders. Renew as necessary.
	Brake linings contaminated with oil	Renew linings and repair source of oil contamination.
	Wrong type of linings fitted (too hard)	Verify type of material which is correct for the car, and fit it.
	Brake shoes wrongly assembled	Check for correct assembly.
	Servo unit not functioning (disc brakes)	Check and repair as necessary.
Car veers to one side when the brakes are applied	Brake pads or linings on one side are contaminated with oil	Renew pads or linings and stop oil leak.
	Hydraulic wheel cylinder(s) on one side partially or fully seized	Inspect wheel cylinders for correct operation and renew as necessary.
	A mixture of lining materials fitted between sides	Standardise on types of linings fitted.
	Unequal wear between sides caused by partially seized wheel cylinders	Check wheel cylinders and renew linings and drums as required.
Pedal feels spongy when the brakes are applied	Air is present in the hydraulic system	Bleed the hydraulic system and check for any signs of leakage.
Pedal feels springy when the brakes are applied	Brake linings not bedded into the drums (after fitting new ones)	Allow time for new linings to bed in after which it will certainly be necessary to adjust the shoes to the drums as pedal travel will have increased.
	Master cylinder or brake backplate mounting bolts loose	Retighten mounting bolts.
	Severe wear in brake drums causing distortion when brakes are applied	Renew drums and linings.
Pedal travels right down with little or no resistance and brakes are virtually non-operative. (With dual braking systems this would be extraordinary as both systems would have to fail at the same time)	Leak in hydraulic systems resulting in lack of pressure for operating wheel cylinders	Examine the whole of the hydraulic system and locate and repair source of leaks. Test after repairing each and every leak source.
	If no signs of leakage are apparent, the master cylinder internal seals are failing to sustain pressure	Overhaul master cylinder. If indications are that seals have failed for reasons other than wear all the wheel cylinder seals should be checked also and the system completely replenished with the correct fluid.
Binding, juddering, overheating	One or a combination of causes given in the foregoing sections	Complete and systematic inspection of the whole braking system.

Chapter 10 Electrical system

Contents

Specifications

Battery

Standard	Exide 6VTAZ 9BR or Lucas BH9 - 38 amp/hrs at 20 hr rate
Heavy duty	Exide 6VTA 11BR or Lucas D11/13 - 55 amp/hrs at 20 hr rate
Earth	Negative

Alternators

	Lucas 15ACR	17ACR	Delco-Remy DN460
Type	Lucas 15ACR	17ACR	Delco-Remy DN460
Voltage	12	12	12
Output	28 amps	36 amps	28 and 35 amps
Field resistance ($\pm$ 5%)	4.3 ohms	4.16 ohms	—
Brushes - minimum length	0.20 in (5 mm)	0.20 in (5 mm)	—
Brush spring pressure	7 - 10 oz	7 - 10 oz	—
Regulator (incorporated)	8 TR		

Starter motors

	Lucas	3M 100/PE	
Make	Lucas	3M 100/PE	
Types	M35 J/1	M35 G/PE	M35 J/PE
Brush length (minimum)	0.38 in (9.5 mm)	.38 in (9.5 mm)	.38 in (9.5 mm)
Brush spring tension new brushes	28 oz	25 oz	28 oz
Commutator diameter minimum	—	1.422 in (36 mm)	—
Commutator thickness minimum	.080 in (2 mm)	0.14 in (3.5 mm)	.080 in (2 mm)
Armature shaft end float maximum	.010 in (0.25 mm)	0.010 in (0.25 mm)	.010 in (0.25 mm)
Pinion to thrust collar			

clearance	—	.005 - .010 in	(0.127 — 0.254 mm)

Solenoid switch test data

series winding resistance	—	0.25 - 0.27 ohms	.21 - .25 ohms
shunt winding resistance	—	0.76 - 0.80 ohms	.9 - 1.1 ohms
Starter test data	—		—
Free running current	65 amps at 8000 —10000 rpm	65 amps at 6000 —10000 rpm	65 amps at 8000
Lock torque	7 lb ft at 350— 375 amps	16 lb ft at 545— amps	7 lb ft at 350— 375 amps

Windscreen wiper motor:

Make	Delco-Remy
Total light running current consumption	
High speed	5 amp
Low speed	2.5 amp
Wiper arm spring tension	24 oz.

Fuses:

Four **35** amp fuses are housed in a block on the bulkhead

Numbers **2** and **3** fuses are fed via the key start switch and number **4** via the lighting circuit. The four fuses cover the circuits not protected by the thermal circuit breaker.

No. 1	Horns, front interior light, head lamp flasher. (Electric clock and hazard warning system if fitted).
No. 2	Stop lamps, turn signal lamps and warning lamps, oil and alternator warning lamps, voltage stabilizer, fuel and temperature gauges, fan motor. (reverse lamps, rear window demister, tachometer, battery condition meter, overdrive circuit, if fitted).
No. 3	Windscreen wipers. (electric screen washer, radio, cigar lighter, if fitted).
No. 4	Instrument lamps, side and rear lamps, number plate lights, fog lamps, luggage compartment lamp. (Interior lamp estate cars).

Bulbs:

Lamp	Watts
Head - Victor	
Right drive	75/60
Head - VX 4/90	
Right drive:	
Inner lamp (main beam)	*45/40
Outer lamp (dual beam)	75/60
Side - Victor	
Right drive	5
Side - VX 4/90	4
Tail/stop	5/21
Turn signal	21
Side repeater	5
Number plate	4
Reverse	21
Fog	55
Interior	10
Speedometer	5
Tachometer - VX 4/90	5
Temperature and fuel gauges	
Victor	5
VX 4/90	3
Ignition warning	3
Oil pressure warning	3
Turning signal indicator	3
Oil pressure gauge) VX 4/90	
Battery condition meter)	3
Clock)	
Heater controls - Victor	3
Brake pressure warning	1,5
Main beam warning	1,5
Windshield wash control) Victor	
Choke control)	1,5
Automatic transmission selector	2
Heater controls - VX 4/90	2
Rear window demist warning	2
Clock - Victor	2
Cigarette lighter	2
Lighting switch	†3

*45 watt filament only used †24 volt bulb

1 General description

The electrical system is of the 12 volt type and the major components comprise, a 12 volt battery of which the negative terminal is earthed, an alternator which is fitted to the front left hand side of the engine and is driven from the pulley on the front of the crankshaft, and a starter motor which is mounted on the rear right hand side of the engine.

The battery supplies a steady amount of current for the ignition, lighting and other electrical circuits, and provides a reserve of electricity when the current consumed by the electrical equipment exceeds that being produced by the alternator. Further information on the alternator will be found in Section 6.

When fitting electrical accessories to cars with a negative earth system it is important, if they contain silicone diodes or transistors, that they are connected correctly, otherwise serious damage may result to the component concerned. Items such as radios, tape recorders, electronic tachometer, automatic dipping, parking lamp and anti-dazzle mirrors should all be checked for correct polarity.

It is important that the battery is always disconnected if the battery is to be boost charged or if any body and most mechanical repairs are to be carried out, using electric arc welding equipment. Serious damage can be caused to the more delicate instruments, specially those containing semi-conductors.

2 Battery - removal and replacement

1 The battery is on a special carrier fitted on the right hand wing valance of the engine compartment. It should be removed once every three months for cleaning and testing. Disconnect the positive and then the negative leads from the battery terminals by slackening the clamp retaining nuts and bolts or by unscrewing the retaining screws if terminal caps are fitted instead of clamps.
2 Unscrew the clamp bar retaining wing nuts and lower the clamp bar to the side of the battery. Carefully lift the battery from its carrier. Hold the battery vertical to ensure that none of the electrolyte is spilled.
3 Replacement is a direct reversal of this procedure. NOTE: Replace the negative lead before the positive lead and smear the terminals with petroleum jelly (vaseline) to prevent corrosion. NEVER use an ordinary grease as applied to other parts of the car.

3 Battery - maintenance and inspection

1 Normal weekly battery maintenance consists of checking the electrolyte level of each cell to ensure that the separators are covered by ¼ inch of electrolyte. If the level has fallen, top up the battery using distilled water only. Do not overfill. If a battery is overfilled or any electrolyte spilled, immediately wipe away the excess as electrolyte attacks and corrodes any metal it comes into contact with very rapidly.
2 As well as keeping the terminals clean and covered with petroleum jelly, the top of the battery, and especially the top of the cells, should be kept clean and dry. This helps prevent corrosion and ensures that the battery does not become partially discharged by leakage through dampness and dirt.
3 Once every three months, remove the battery and inspect the battery securing bolts, the battery clamp plate, tray and battery leads for corrosion (white fluffy deposits on the metal which are brittle to touch). If any corrosion is found, clean off the deposits with ammonia and paint over the clean metal with an anti-rust/anti-acid paint.
4 At the same time inspect the battery case for cracks. If a crack is found, clean and plug it with one of the proprietary compounds marketed by firms, such as Holts, for this purpose. If leakage through the crack has been excessive then it will be necessary to refill the appropriate cell with fresh electrolyte as

detailed later. Cracks are frequently caused to the top of the battery cases by pouring in distilled water in the middle of winter AFTER instead of BEFORE a run. This gives the water no chance to mix with the electrolyte and so the former freezes and splits the battery case.
5 If topping up the battery becomes excessive and the case has been inspected for cracks that could cause leakage, but none are found, the battery is being overcharged and the voltage regulator will have to be checked and reset.
6 With the battery on the bench at the three monthly interval check, measure its specific gravity with a hydrometer to determine the state of charge and condition of the electrolyte. There should be very little variation between the different cells and if a variation in excess of .025 is present it will be due to either:
a) Loss of electrolyte from the battery at some time caused by spillage or a leak, resulting in a drop in the specific gravity of the electrolyte when the deficiency was replaced with distilled water instead of fresh electrolyte.
b) An internal short circuit caused by buckling of the plates or a similar malady pointing to the likelihood of total battery failure in the near future.
7 The specific gravity of the electrolyte for fully charged conditions at the electrolyte temperature indicated, is listed in Table A. The specific gravity of a fully discharged battery at different temperatures of the electrolyte is given in Table B.

TABLE A

Specific gravity - battery fully charged

1.268 at 100°F or 38°C electrolyte temperature
1.272 at 90°F or 32°C electrolyte temperature
1.276 at 80°F or 27°C electrolyte temperature
1.280 at 70°F or 21°C electrolyte temperature
1.284 at 60°F or 16°C electrolyte temperature
1.288 at 50°F or 10°C electrolyte temperature
1.292 at 40°F or 4°C electrolyte temperature
1.296 at 30°F or -1.5°C electrolyte temperature

TABLE B

Specific gravity - battery fully discharged

1.098 at 100°F or 38°C electrolyte temperature
1.102 at 90°F or 32°C electrolyte temperature
1.106 at 80°F or 27°C electrolyte temperature
1.110 at 70°F or 21°C electrolyte temperature
1.114 at 60°F or 16°C electrolyte temperature
1.118 at 50°F or 10°C electrolyte temperature
1.122 at 40°F or 4°C electrolyte temperature
1.126 at 30°F or -1.5°C electrolyte temperature

4 Battery electrolyte replenishment

1 If the battery is in a fully charged state and one of the cells maintains a specific gravity reading which is .025 or more lower than the others, and a check of each cell has been made with a voltage meter to check for short circuits (a four to seven second test should give a steady reading of between 1.2 to 1.8 volts), then it is likely that electrolyte has been lost from the cell with the low reading at some time.
2 Top the cell up with a solution of 1 part sulphuric acid to 2.5 parts of water. If the cell is already fully topped up draw some electrolyte out of it with a pipette.
3 When mixing the sulphuric acid and water NEVER ADD WATER TO SULPHURIC ACID — always pour the acid slowly onto the water in a glass container. IF WATER IS ADDED TO SULPHURIC ACID IT WILL EXPLODE.
4 Continue to top up the cell with the freshly made electrolyte and then recharge the battery and check the hydrometer readings.

5 Battery charging

1 In winter time when heavy demand is placed upon the battery, such as when starting from cold, and much electrical equipment is continually in use, it is a good idea occasionally to have the battery fully charged from an external source at the rate of 3.5 to 4 amps.

2 Continue to charge the battery at this rate until no further rise in specific gravity is noted over a four hour period.

3 Alternatively, a trickle charger, charging at the rate of 1.5 amps can be safely used overnight.

4 Specially rapid 'boost' charges which are claimed to restore the power of the battery in 1 to 2 hours are most dangerous as they can cause serious damage to the battery plates through overheating.

5 While charging the battery note that the temperature of the electrolyte should never exceed 100°F.

6 Alternators - general description

1 More and more cars are being fitted with alternators in place of the more well known dynamo and models covered by this manual are no exception. They provide a higher output for lower weight and are able to cope with the full electrical loads at low revolutions.

2 Basically the alternator, as the name implies, generates alternating current rather than direct current. This current is rectified (by diodes) into direct current so that it can be stored by the battery. The transistorised regulators are self limiting in current output so they control only voltage.

3 Apart from the renewal of the rotor slip ring brushes and rotor shaft bearings, there are no other parts which need periodic inspection. All other items are sealed assemblies and must be replaced if indications are that they are faulty.

7 Alternators - safety precautions

If there are indications that the charging system is malfunctioning in any way, care must be taken to diagnose faults properly, otherwise damage of a serious and expensive nature may occur to parts which are in fact quite serviceable.

The following basic requirements must be observed at all times, therefore, if damage is to be prevented.

1 ALL alternator systems use a NEGATIVE earth. Even the simple mistake of connecting a battery the wrong way round could burn out the alternator diodes in a few seconds.

2 Before disconnecting any wires in the system the engine and ignition circuits should be switched off. This will minimise accidental short circuits.

3 The alternator must NEVER be run with the output wire disconnected.

4 Always disconnect the battery from the car's electrical system if an outside charging source is being used.

5 Do not use test wire connections that could move accidentally and short circuit against nearby terminals. Short circuits will not blow fuses - they will blow diodes or transistors.

6 Always disconnect the battery cables and alternator output wires before any electric welding work is done on the car body.

8 Lucas 15 ACR or 17 ACR alternator systems - fault diagnosis

1 It is essential that when a fault occurs the correct procedure

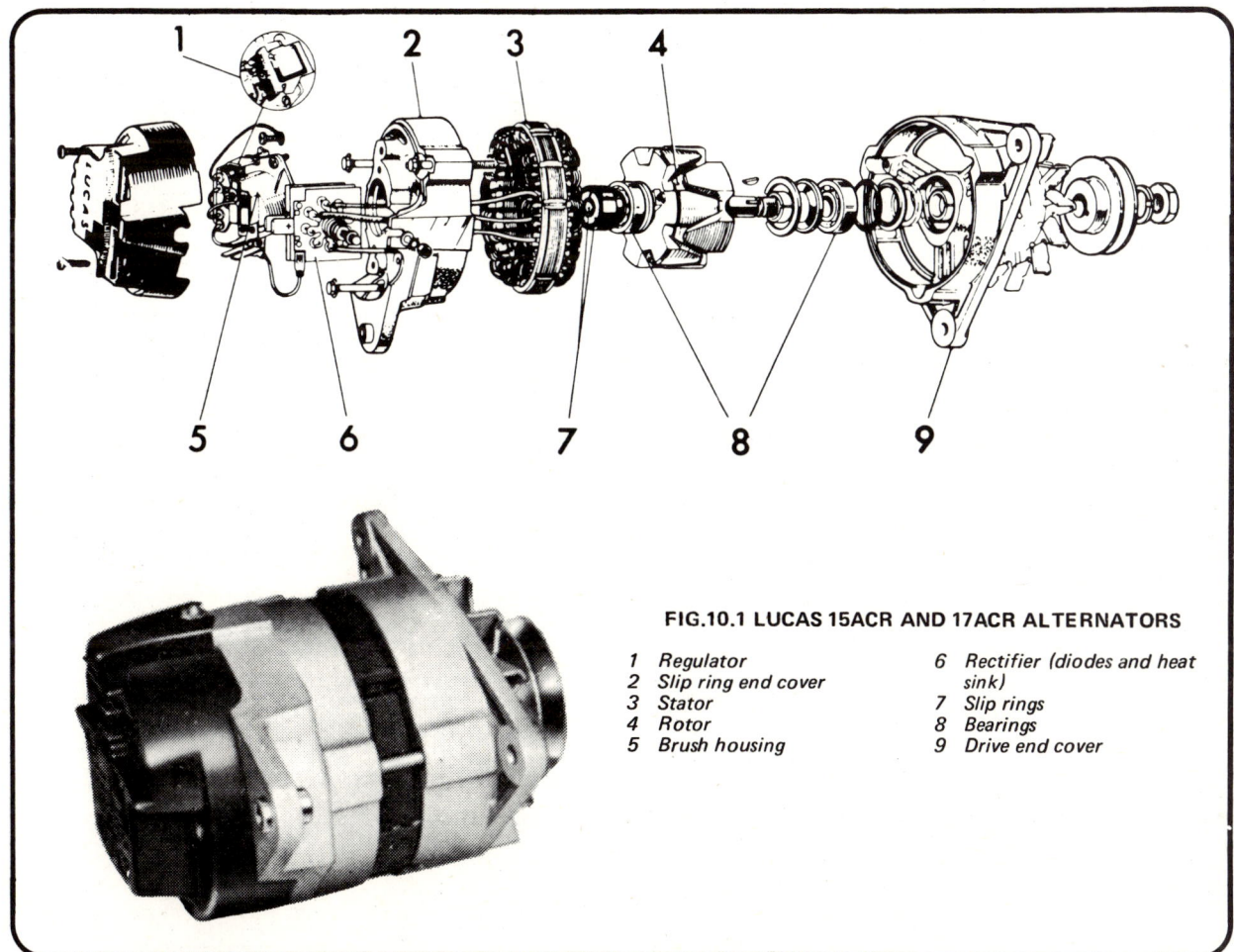

FIG.10.1 LUCAS 15ACR AND 17ACR ALTERNATORS

1 Regulator
2 Slip ring end cover
3 Stator
4 Rotor
5 Brush housing
6 Rectifier (diodes and heat sink)
7 Slip rings
8 Bearings
9 Drive end cover

152

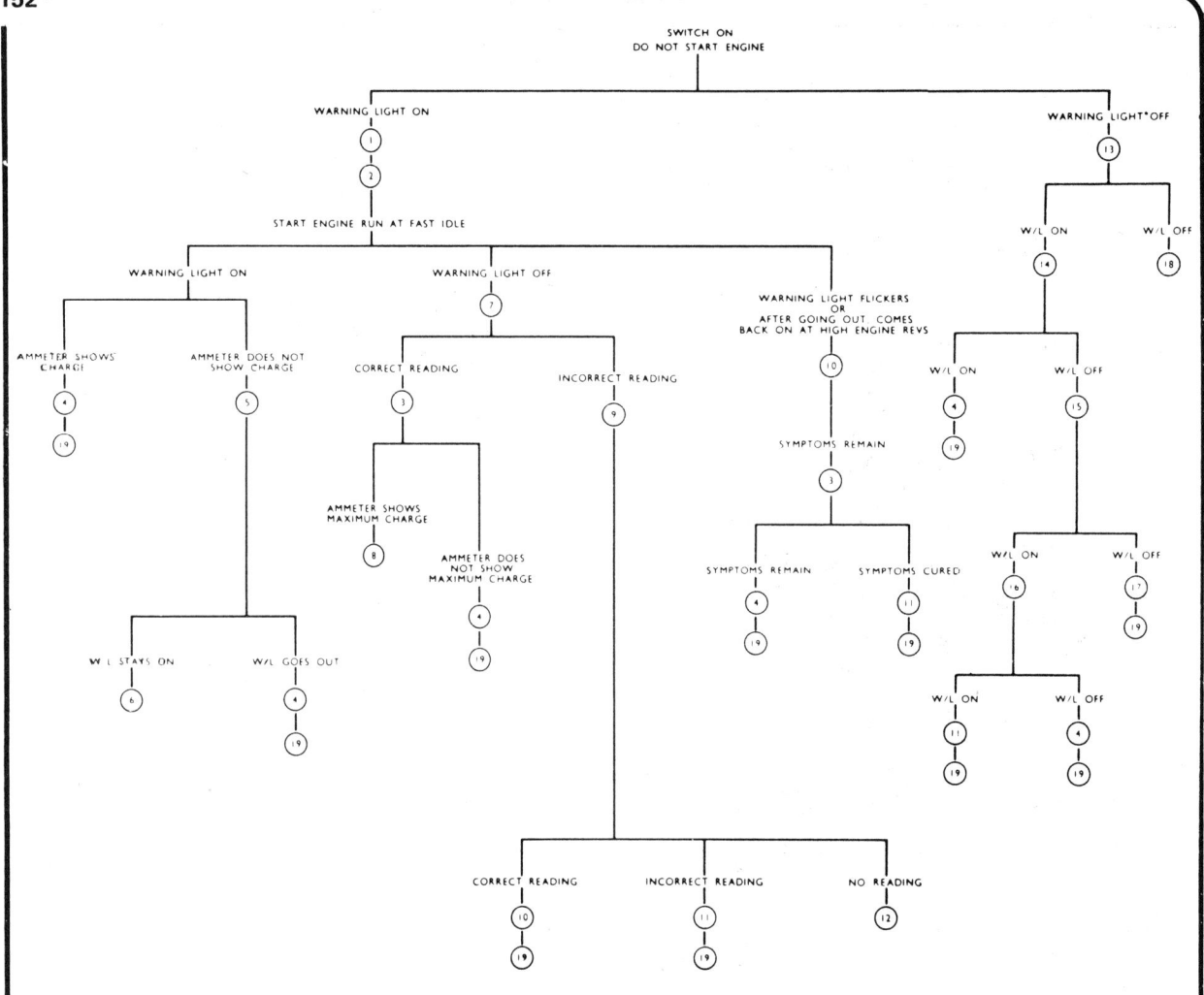

FIG.10.2 LUCAS 15/17 ACR ALTERNATOR SYSTEM — FAULT DIAGNOSIS CHART

1 Check fan belt(s) for tension and condition.
2 Disconnect main output connector and auxiliary connector. Install slave wire with a male Lucar terminal and a female Lucar terminal between alternator negative terminal and socket. Connect ammeter between alternator positive terminal and socket removed from this terminal. Reconnect auxiliary connector.
3 Remove rear cover from alternator. Re-install auxiliary connector, slave and ammeter wires. Bridge outer brush contact strip to ground. Adjust engine speed to give maximum output.
4 Install new or repair alternator.
5 Remove connector from field and sensing terminals (IND and B+). 'Switch On' but do not start engine.
6 Check for short circuit in wire between alternator indicator terminal and warning light bulb.
7 Connect voltmeter between battery positive and negative terminals; increase speed to approximately 1500 rpm. Voltmeter should read 14.1 to 14.5 volts, ammeter reading 7.5 amp maximum. Higher amperage which would probably give lower voltage readings could indicate need to recharge battery before continuing with test.
8 If fan belt tension and condition are satisfactory, faulty battery or overloaded system is indicated. Comparison should be made between electrical loading and alternator output. 15ACR: 28 amp. 17ACR: 36 amp.
9 Remove voltmeter from battery and connect it between battery sensing terminal on alternator (B+) and ground (this should be made between electrical loading and alternator output. 15ACR: 28 amp. 17ACR: 36 amp.
10 Check battery terminals, ground strap connections, and wiring between battery and alternator for poor connection and resistive circuits.
11 Install new 8TR regulator.
12 Check wire from alternator B+ to starter solenoid for continuity.
13 Remove connector from alternator indicator socket and bridge double wires (brown/yellow 9/.012 in) connector to ground.
14 Remove rear cover from alternator, re-install socket connectors. Disconnect yellow wire from field diode heat sink.
15 Reconnect yellow wire to field diode heat sink. Connect slave wire between outer brush contact strip and ground.
16 Disconnect slave wire from outer brush contact strip and connect between inner brush contact strip and ground.
17 Check connecting wire between indicator and field terminals in socket connector for continuity.
18 Check warning lamp bulb. Check bulb-holder for loose connection. Check wire (brown/yellow) between alternator indicator terminal, warning lamp bulb and key-start switch for continuity. Note: warning lamp bulb must be 12 volt 2.2 watt.
19 Check that charging system operates satisfactorily by connecting voltmeter across battery terminals and ammeter in series with alternator output circuit. Impose approximate 28 amp (15ACR) or 36 amp (17ACR) load on battery, start engine and increase engine speed until ammeter reads maximum charge, 28 amp and 36 amp respectively. Remove load from battery. Ammeter should then drop slowly back to show trickle charge. Voltmeter should show 14.1 to 14.5 volts.

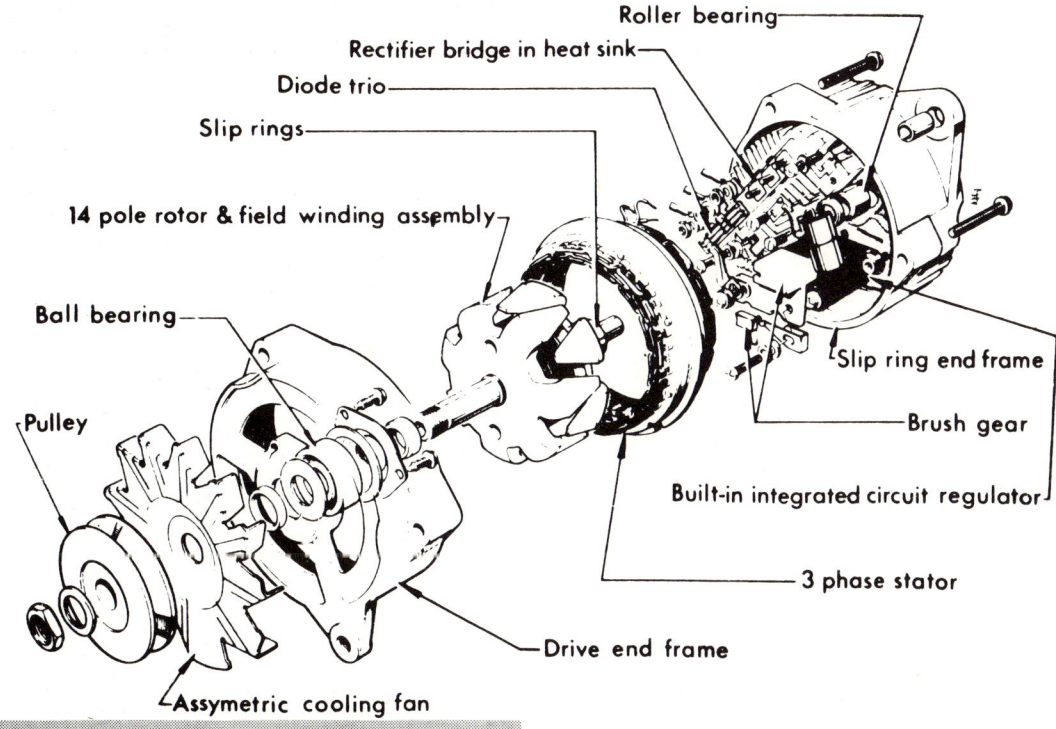

Roller bearing

Rectifier bridge in heat sink

Diode trio

Slip rings

14 pole rotor & field winding assembly

Ball bearing

Pulley

Slip ring end frame

Brush gear

Built-in integrated circuit regulator

3 phase stator

Drive end frame

Assymetric cooling fan

S 5642

Fig.10.3 AC – Delco 'Delcotron' DN 460 Alternator - exploded illustration

which you know is equipped to deal with this make of alternator.

10 Alternators - removal, replacement and belt adjustment

1 Details of the procedure to be followed when removing, replacing and adjusting the alternator position are given in Chapter 2.
2 The only points to note are that for alternators the rear mounting lug is fitted with a split sliding bush. This enables the bolts to be tightened without imposing any strain on the alloy mounting lugs. The front bolt should always be tightened first.
3 If the alternator is levered to tighten the fan belt avoid any strain against the fragile end casing.
4 Electrical connections are through two multi-socket connectors.

11 Alternators - dismantling and inspection

1 If tests indicate that the alternator is faulty it is possible that the slip ring brushes and slip ring may be the cause.
2 Alternators require the unsoldering of the stator connections to get at the brushes and slip ring and this is not recommended. If the diodes to which they are attached are overheated they could be damaged.
3 Therefore, we do not recommend dismantling as a general principle, as more damage could be caused to the system - not just the alternator, if a mistake is made.
4 When an alternator is diagnosed as unserviceable it should only be as a result of a thorough check of the complete system. If this is not done a new unit could be completely ruined immediately following installation if something is also at fault elsewhere.

is followed to diagnose it. If it is not, the likelihood of damage is high. The safety precautions as described in Section 12 should always be observed.
2 No proper diagnosis is possible without an ammeter (0—100 amps range) a voltmeter (0—50 volts range) and a test lamp (12v 6 watt) being available. If you are unable to acquire these then leave the circuit checking to a competent electrician.
3 Check the obvious first, ie battery, battery terminals, fan belt tension and disconnected wires.
4 Follow the line of diagnosis as shown in Fig.10.2 and the accompanying table.

9 AC Delco alternators - fault diagnosis

Fault diagnosis procedure for this type is not readily translatable into 'Do-it-yourself' terms. If a fault develops it is recommended that proper checks are made by a service station

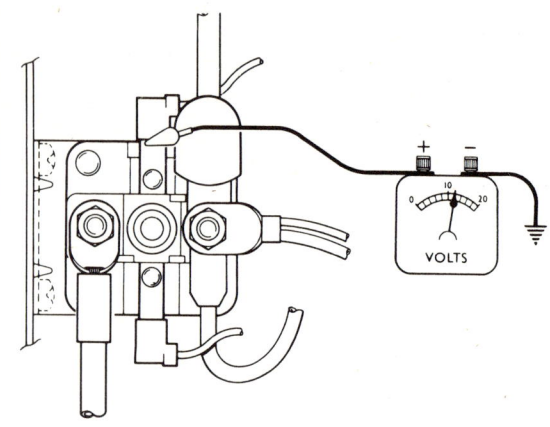

Fig. 10.4 Starter motor (Inertia) connection for feed to solenoid check

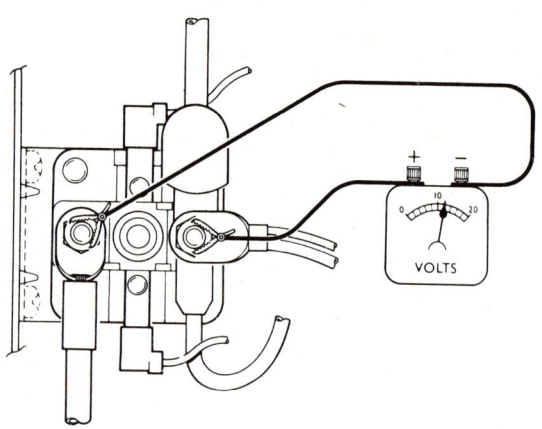

Fig. 10.5 Starter motor (Inertia) connection for solenoid main contact check

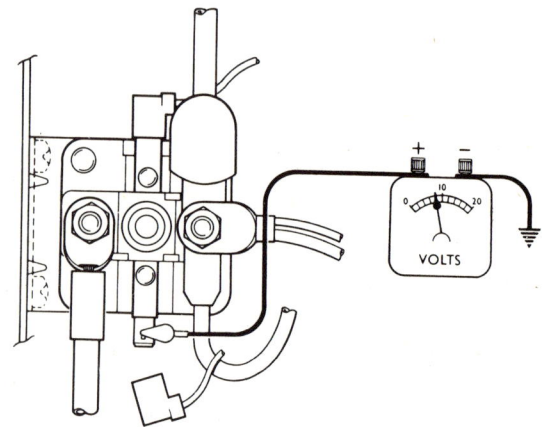

Fig. 10.6 Starter motor (Inertia) connection for cold start feed to coil check

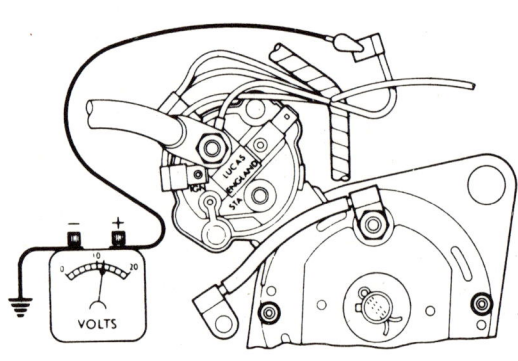

Fig. 10.7 Starter motor (pre-engaged) connection for feed to solenoid check

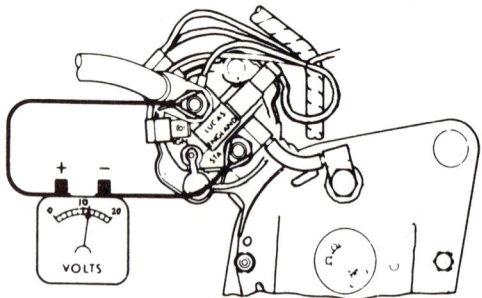

Fig. 10.8 Starter motor (pre-engaged) connection for solenoid main contact check

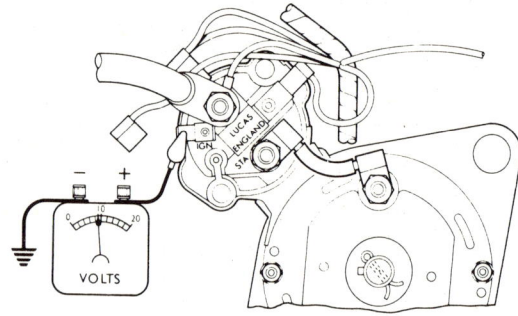

Fig. 10.9 Starter motor (pre-engaged) connection for cold start feed to coil check

12 Starter motor - testing in the car

1 If the starter motor fails to operate then check the condition of the battery by turning on the headlamps. If they glow brightly for several seconds and then gradually dim, the battery is in an uncharged condition.

2 If the headlamps glow brightly and continue to glow, and it is obvious that the battery is in good condition, then check the tightness of the battery wiring connections (and in particular the earth lead from the battery terminal to its connection on the bodyframe). Check the tightness of the connections at the relay switch and at the starter motor.

3 If the starter motor still fails to turn the fault lies in the wiring, the solenoid switch or the motor itself. The following procedure will determine where the fault lies: (To prevent inadvertent starting of the engine remove the HT lead from the coil).

4 Connect a voltmeter (or 12 volt bulb) to the terminal on the solenoid to which the white/red wire is connected (Fig.10.4) . If there is no reading (12 volts) when the starter switch is operated, there is a fault in the starter switch or white/red wire.

5 If the previous test is favourable connect voltmeter (or 12 volt bulb) to the two main terminals as shown in Fig.10.5 . A 12 volt reading should be obtained (without touching the starter switch). If the starter switch is operated the reading should fall to zero (bulb goes out). If it does not the solenoid switch needs renewal.

6 The remaining terminal on the solenoid switch, to which the white/blue lead is attached, is the cold start feed to the coil which directs current to the coil only when the solenoid is operating. It can be tested by connecting a voltmeter (or 12v bulb) to the terminal, after disconnecting the lead, as shown in Fig.10.6 . When the starter is operated there should be a 9v reading at least (bulb glows). If not there must be a fault in the internal solenoid connection.

7 On pre-engaged starters the solenoid switch is mounted directly on top of the starter motor. For these units the procedure is as follows:-

8 Disconnect the white/red wire from the solenoid and connect the voltmeter (or bulb) from the wire to earth. When the key start switch is operated the voltage should read 12v. Otherwise the wiring or start switch is faulty (Fig.10.7) .

9 Connect the voltmeter across the two main terminals of the solenoid and a 12v reading should be given. When the key start is operated the voltage should drop to zero. If otherwise, the solenoid needs renewal (Fig.10.8) .

10 To check the cold start feed to the coil, disconnect the white/blue wire from the 'IGN' terminal and connect the voltmeter from the terminal to earth. When the start switch is operated the reading should be at least 9 volts (Fig.10.9) .

11 On either type of starter a solenoid fault confined to the non-functioning of the coil feed wire does not necessarily mean that the car will not start, although difficulty will certainly occur in cold weather or if the battery charge is low.

12 NOTE: When a new or reconditioned engine has been fitted it will be initially very stiff to turn. This could result in a very rapid discharge of the battery and slow turning of the engine before the engine has been successfully started. It is always advisable to have an additional battery available (in someone elses car perhaps) with a pair of jumper leads so that the extra power is available when it is really needed.

13 If the starter motor is the faulty item it must be removed from the car for inspection. Make sure that it is not merely jammed. This can be ascertained by putting a spanner on the square end of the shaft which protrudes. If it turns easily the starter is free. Otherwise use the spanner to turn the shaft in either direction until it is completely free. This latter facility applies only to inertia type starters.

13 Starter motor - M35J/1 - removal and replacement

1 Disconnect the battery earth lead from the negative terminal.

2 Remove the cable from the starter terminal at rear of motor.

3 Remove the two bolts and spring washers that secure the starter motor to the clutch housing and lift out the starter and spacer plate, (if fitted).

4 Refitting is the reverse sequence to removal.

14 Starter motor M35J/1 - dismantling and reassembly

1 With the starter motor on the bench, first mark the relative positions of the starter motor body to the two end brackets (Fig.10.10)

2 Undo and remove the two screws and spring washers securing the drive end bracket to the body. The drive end bracket, complete with armature and drive, may now be drawn forwards from the starter motor body.

3 Lift away the thrust washer from the commutator end of the armature shaft.

4 Undo and remove the two screws securing the commutator end bracket to the starter motor body. The commutator end bracket may now be drawn back about an inch allowing sufficient access so as to disengage the field bushes from the bracket. Once these are free, the end bracket may now be completely removed.

5 With the motor stripped, the brushes and brush gear may be inspected. To check the brush spring tension, fit a new brush into each holder in turn, and using an accurate spring balance, push the brush on the balance tray until the brush protrudes approximately 1/16 inch from the holder. Make a note of the reading which should be approximately 28 ounces. If the spring pressures vary considerably the commutator end bracket must be renewed as a complete assembly.

6 Inspect the brushes for wear and fit a new brush which is nearing the minimum length of 3/8 inch. To renew the end bracket brushes, cut the brush cables from the terminal posts and, with a small file or hacksaw, slot the head of the terminal posts to a sufficient depth to accommodate the new leads. Solder the new brush leads to the posts.

7 To renew the field winding brushes, cut the brush leads approximately ¼ inch from the field winding junction and carefully solder the new brush leads to the remaining stumps, making sure that the insulation sleeves provide adequate cover.

8 If the commutator surface is dirty or blackened, clean it with a petrol dampened rag. Carefully examine the commutator for signs of excessive wear, burning or pitting. If evident it may be reconditioned by having it skimmed at the local engineering works or Vauxhall dealer who possesses a centre lathe. The thickness of the commutator must not be less than 0.08 inch. For minor reconditioning, the commutator may be polished with glass paper. DO NOT UNDERCUT THE MICA INSULATORS BETWEEN THE COMMUTATOR SEGMENTS.

9 With the starter motor dimantled, test the field coils for open circuit. Connect a 12 volt battery with a 12 volt bulb in one of the leads between each of the field brushes and a clean part of the body. The lamp will light if continuity is satisfactory between the brushes, windings and body connection.

10 Replacement of the field coils calls for the use of a wheel operated screwdriver, a soldering iron, caulking and riveting operations and is beyond the scope of the majority of owners. The starter motor body should be taken to an automobile electrical engineering works for new field coils to be fitted. Alternatively purchase an exchange Lucas starter motor.

11 Check the condition of the bushes and they should be renewed when they are sufficiently worn to allow visible side movement of the armature shaft.

12 To renew the commutator end bracket bush, drill out the rivets securing the brush box moulding and remove the moulding, bearing seal retaining plate and felt washer seal.

13 Screw in a ½ inch tap and withdraw the bush with the tap.

156

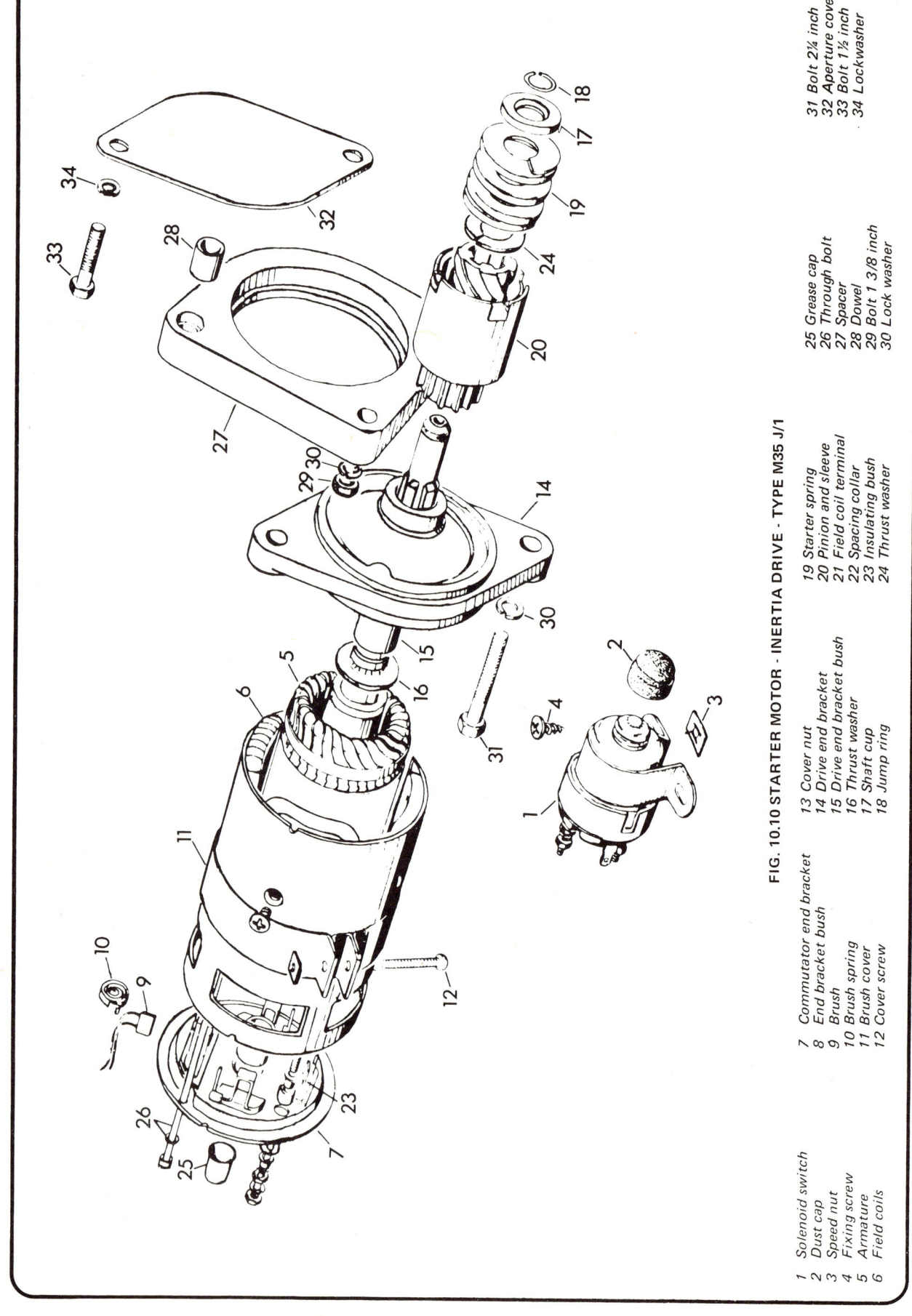

FIG. 10.10 STARTER MOTOR - INERTIA DRIVE - TYPE M35 J/1

1 Solenoid switch	13 Cover nut	25 Grease cap
2 Dust cap	14 Drive end bracket	26 Through bolt
3 Speed nut	15 Drive end bracket bush	27 Spacer
4 Fixing screw	16 Thrust washer	28 Dowel
5 Armature	17 Shaft cup	29 Bolt 1 3/8 inch
6 Field coils	18 Jump ring	30 Lock washer
7 Commutator end bracket	19 Starter spring	31 Bolt 2¼ inch
8 End bracket bush	20 Pinion and sleeve	32 Aperture cover
9 Brush	21 Field coil terminal	33 Bolt 1½ inch
10 Brush spring	22 Spacing collar	34 Lockwasher
11 Brush cover	23 Insulating bush	
12 Cover screw	24 Thrust washer	

14 As the bush is of the phospher bronze type it is essential that it is allowed to stand in engine oil for at least 24 hours before fitment. Alternatively soak in oil at 100°C for 2 hours.

15 Using a suitable diameter drift, drive the new bush into position. Do not ream the bush as its self lubricating properties will be impaired.

16 To remove the drive end bracket bush it will be necessary to remove the drive gear as described in paragraphs 18 and 19.

17 Using a suitable diameter drift remove the old bush and fit a new one as described in paragraphs 14 and 15.

18 To dismantle the starter motor drive, first use a press to push the retainer clear of the circlip which can then be removed. Lift away the retainer and main spring.

19 Slide off the remaining parts with a rotary action of the armature shaft.

20 It is most important that the drive gear is completely free from oil, grease and dirt. With the drive gear removed, clean all parts thoroughly in paraffin. UNDER NO CIRCUMSTANCES OIL THE DRIVE COMPONENTS. Lubrication of the drive components could easily cause the pinion to stick.

21 Reassembly of the starter motor drive is the reverse sequence to dismantling. Use a press to compress the spring and retainer sufficiently to allow a new circlip to be fitted to its groove on the shaft. Remove the drive from the press.

22 Reassembly of the starter motor is the reverse sequence to dismantling.

15 Starter motor 3M100/PE and M35J/PE - removal and replacement

Removal is basically identical to that as described in Section 13 with the exception that care must be taken to note the cable connections at the rear of the solenoid before they are detached.

16 Starter motor 3M100/PE - dismantling and reassembly

1 Undo and remove the nut and spring washer that secures the connecting link between the solenoid and starter motor at the solenoid 'STA' terminal. Carefully ease the connecting link out of engagement of the terminal post on the solenoid (Fig.10.11)

2 Undo and remove the two nuts and spring washers that secure the solenoid to the drive end bracket.

3 Carefully ease the solenoid back from the drive end bracket, lift the solenoid plunger and return spring from the engagement lever, and completely remove the solenoid.

4 Recover the shaped rubber block that is placed between the solenoid and starter motor body.

5 Carefully remove the end cap seal from the commutator end cover.

6 Ease the armature shaft retaining ring (spire nut) from the armature shaft. NOTE: The retaining ring must not be reused, but a new one obtained ready for fitting.

7 Undo and remove the two long through bolts and spring washers.

8 Detach the commutator end cover from the yoke, at the same time disengaging the filed brushes from the brush box moulding.

9 Lift away the thrust washer from the armature shaft.

10 The starter motor body may now be lifted from the armature and drive end assembly.

11 Ease the retaining ring (spire nut) from the engagement lever pivot pin. NOTE: The retaining ring must not be reused, but a new one obtained ready for fitting.

12 Using a parallel pin punch of suitable size, remove the pivot pin from the engagement lever and drive end bracket.

13 Carefully move the thrust collar clear of the jump ring, and slide the jump ring from the armature shaft.

14 Slide off the thrust collar, and finally remove the roller clutch drive and engagement lever assembly from the armature shaft.

15 For inspection and servicing information of the brush gear, commutator, and armature refer to Section 14, paragraphs 5 and 8 inclusive.

16 To test the field coils refer to Section 14, paragraphs 9 and 10.

17 Check the condition of the bushes and if they show signs of wear remove the old ones and fit new as described in Section 14, paragraphs 11 to 17. Disregard the reference in paragraph 16 to

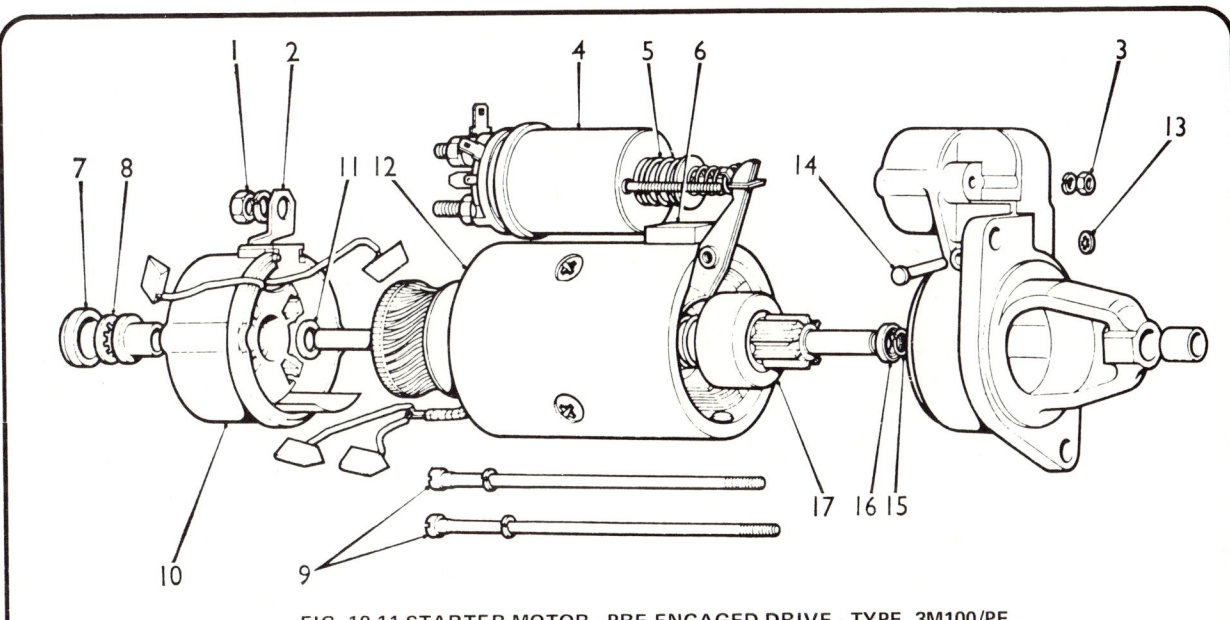

FIG. 10.11 STARTER MOTOR - PRE-ENGAGED DRIVE - TYPE 3M100/PE

1	Connecting link securing nut	5	Solenoid plunger and return spring	9	Through bolts	13	Retaining ring (spire nut)
2	Connecting link	6	Rubber block	10	Commutator end cover	14	Pivot pin
3	Solenoid to drive end bracket securing nut	7	End cap seal	11	Thrust washer	15	Thrust collar jump ring
4	Solenoid	8	Armature shaft retaining ring	12	Yoke	16	Thrust collar
						17	Roller clutch drive

158

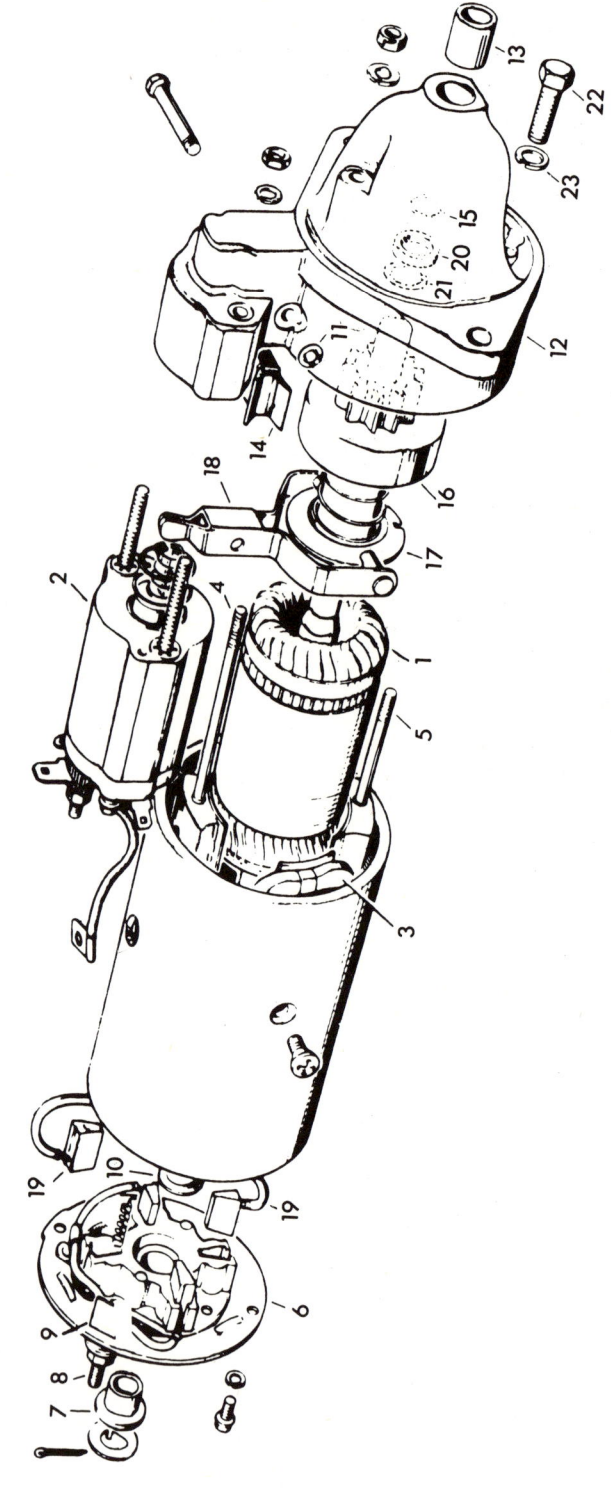

FIG. 10.12 STARTER MOTOR - PRE-ENGAGED DRIVE TYPE - TYPE M35J/PE

1 Armature
2 Solenoid
3 Field coil
4 Pole piece and long stud

5 Pole piece and short stud
6 Commutator end bracket bush
7 Commutator end bracket bush
8 Field terminal

9 Terminal insulating bush
10 Thrust plate
11 Pivot pin retaining clip
12 Drive end bracket

13 End bracket bush
14 Grommet
15 Jump ring
16 Roller clutch drive

17 Bearing bush
18 Lever and pivot assembly
19 Brush
20 Thrust collar

21 Shim
22 Fixing bolt
23 Lock washer

the removal of the drive gear as this will have already been done.

18 Whilst the motor is apart, check the operation of the drive clutch. It must provide instantaneous take up of the drive in one direction and rotate easily and smoothly in the opposite direction.

19 Make sure that the drive moves smoothly on the armature shaft splines without binding or sticking.

20 Reassembling the starter motor is the reverse sequence to dismantling. The following additional points should be noted:

21 When assembling the drive end bracket always use a new retaining ring (spire nut) to secure the engagement lever pivot pin.

22 Make sure that the internal thrust washer is fitted to the commutator end of the armature shaft before the armature end cover is fitted.

23 Always use a new retaining ring (spire nut) onto the armature shaft to maximum clearance of 0.010 inch between the retaining ring and the bearing shoulder. This will be the armature end float.

24 Tighten the through bolts to a torque wrench setting of 8 lb ft and the nuts securing the solenoid to the drive bracket to 4.5 lb ft.

17 Starter motor M35J/PE - dismantling and reassembly

1 Detach the heavy duty cable, linking the solenoid STA terminal to the starter motor terminal by undoing and removing the securing nuts and washers (Fig.10.12).

2 Undo and remove the two nuts and spring washers securing the solenoid to the drive end bracket.

3 Carefully withdraw the solenoid coil unit from the drive end bracket.

4 Lift off the solenoid plunger and return spring from the engagement lever.

5 Remove the rubber sealing block from the drive end bracket.

6 Remove the retaining ring (spire nut) from the engagement lever pivot pin and withdraw the pin.

7 Unscrew and remove the two drive end bracket securing nuts and spring washers and withdraw the bracket.

8 Lift away the engagement lever from the drive operating plate.

9 Extract the split pin from the end of the armature and remove the shim washers and thrust plate from the commutator end of the armature shaft.

10 Remove the armature, together with its internal thrust washer.

11 Withdraw the thrust washer from the armature.

12 Undo and remove the two screws securing the commutator end bracket to the starter motor body.

13 Carefully detach the end bracket from the yoke, at the same time disengaging the field brushes from the brush gear. Lift away the end bracket.

14 Move the thrust collar clear of the jump ring, and then remove the jump ring. Withdraw the drive assembly from the armature shaft.

15 Inspection and renovation is basically the same as for the Lucas 3M100/PE starter motor and full information will be found in Section 16. The following necessitated by the fitting of the solenoid coil should be noted:

16 If a bush is worn, so allowing excessive side movement of the armature shaft, the bush must be renewed. Drift out the old bush with a piece of suitable diameter rod, preferably with a shoulder on it to stop the bush collapsing.

17 Soak a new bush in engine oil for 24 hours of if time does not permit, heat in an oil bath at 100°C for two hours prior to fitting.

18 As new bushes must not be reamed after fitting it must be pressed into position using a small mandrel of the same diameter as the bush and with a shoulder on it. Place the bush on the mandrel and press into position using a bench vice.

19 Use a test light and battery to test the coninuity of the coil windings between terminal STA and a good earth point on the solenoid body. If the light fails to come on, the solenoid should be renewed.

20 To test the solenoid contacts for correct opening and closing, connect a 12 volt battery and a 60 watt test light between the main unmarked Lucar terminal and the STA terminal. The light should not come on.

21 Energise the solenoid with a separate 12 volt supply connected to the small unmarked Lucar terminal and a good earth on the solenoid body.

22 As the coil is energised the solenoid should be heard to operate and the test lamp should light with full brilliance.

23 The contacts may only be renewed as a set, ie moving and fixed contacts. The fixed contacts are part of the moulded cover.

24 To fit a new set of contacts, first undo and remove the moulded cover securing screws.

25 Unsolder the coil connections from the cover terminals.

26 Lift away the cover and moving contact assembly.

27 Fit a new cover and moving contact assembly, soldering the connections to the cover terminals.

28 Refit the moulded cover securing screws.

29 Whilst the motor is apart, check the operation of the drive clutch. It must provide instantaneous take up of the drive in one direction and rotate easily and smoothly in the opposite direction.

30 Make sure that the drive moves smoothly on the armature shaft splines without binding or sticking.

31 Reassembly of the starter motor is the reverse sequence to dismantling. The following additional points should be noted:

32 When assembling the drive, always use a new retaining ring (spire nut) to secure the engagement lever pivot pin.

33 Make sure that the internal thrust washer is fitted to the commutator end of the armature shaft before the armature is fitted.

34 Make sure that the thrust washers and plate are assembled in the correct order and are prevented from rotating separately by engaging the collar pin with the locking piece on the thrust plate.

18 Fuses, thermal circuit breaker and fusible link

1 The fuse block is mounted on the right hand side of the bulkhead and access is gained to it once the bonnet is open. Four 35 amp fuses are used and protect the circuits as listed in the specifications at the beginning of the chapter.

2 If any of the fuses should blow check the circuits on that fuse, trace and rectify the fault before renewing the fuse.

3 A thermal type circuit breaker is inserted in the circuit between the lighting switch and headlamps to provide an individual protection to the headlamps. It is a self centred unit and screwed to a bracket located under the instrument panel adjacent to the bulkhead connector. The unit comprises a bi-metal strip and a pair of contacts. For inspection it has a detachable cover.

4 If operation of the circuit breaker is suspect it may be tested using a battery, ammeter and variable resistance, in series with the circuit breaker. The contacts should remain closed with a current of 25 amps but should open within 30 to 180 seconds at 20°C with a current of 33 amps. Do not bend the bi-metal strip or clean contacts. If the test results obtained are not within the limits the unit must be renewed (Fig.10.15).

5 A fusible link as shown in Fig.10.16 is connected into the main battery feed circuit between the bulkhead connector and a terminal block on the battery tray and is designed to protect the complete system with the exception of the starter. It comprises a length of copper wire which is designed to burn out in the event of a heavy overload such as caused by a short circuit. It is specially insulated so that the outer cable will not break up or burn during fusing.

19 Flasher circuit - fault tracing and rectification

1 The flasher signal unit is one of two types; Lucas which has a

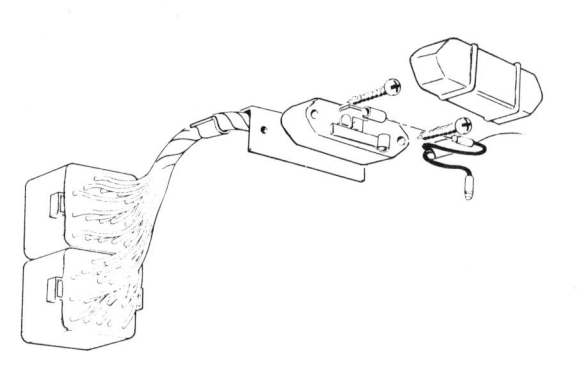

Fig. 10.14 Thermal circuit breaker

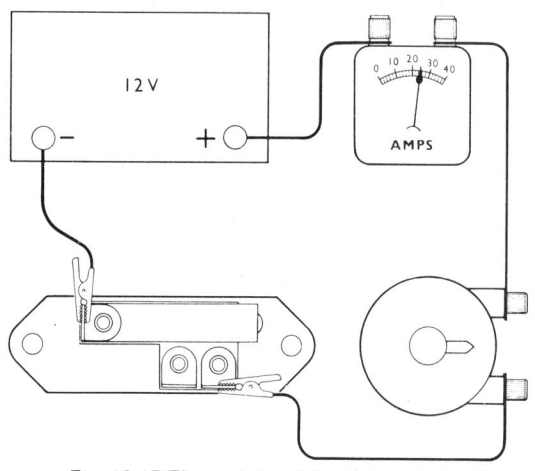

Fig. 10.15 Thermal circuit breaker test circuit

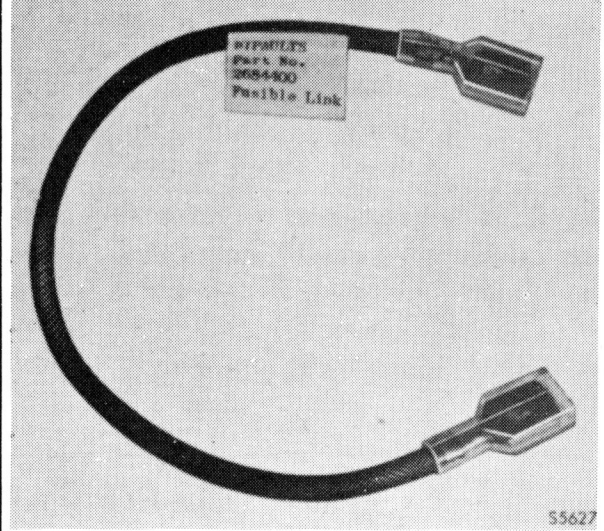

Fig. 10.16 Fusible link

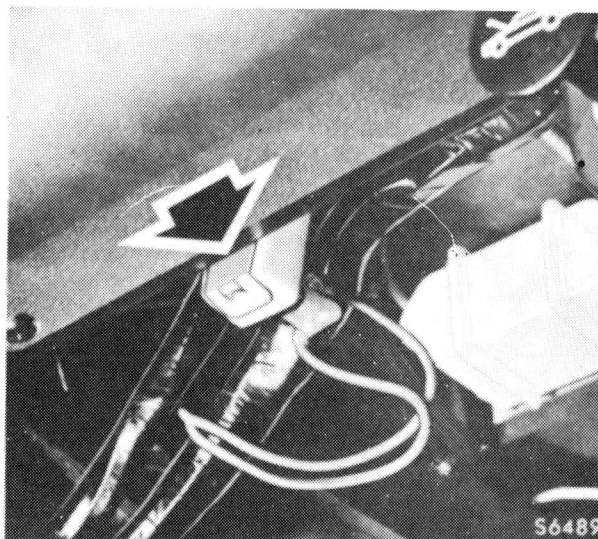

Fig. 10.17 Flasher unit location under instrument panel (arrowed)

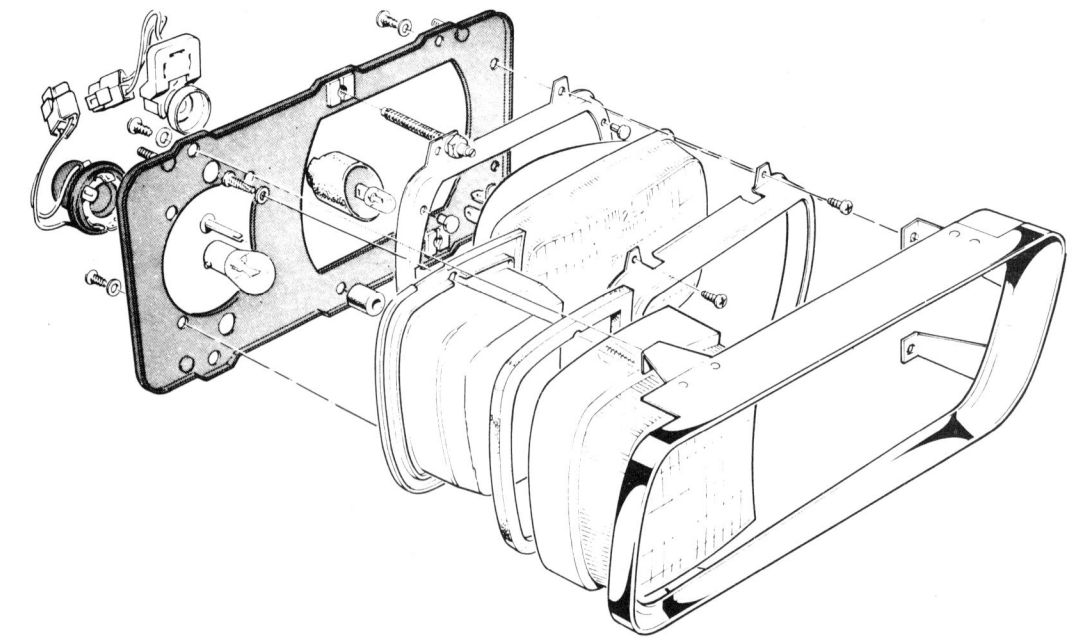

Fig. 10.18 Victor headlight and direction indicator light assembly

rectangular shape or Magnatex which is cylindrical. The unit is clipped to the bottom edge of the instrument panel adjacent to the steering column (Fig.10.17).

2   One direction indicator bulb defective. The other bulb on the same side and the respective warning light bulb will remain on - without flashing - and no audible warning from the unit when the switch is operated.

3   Both direction indicator bulbs defective. The warning light bulb will remain on - without flashing - and no audible warning from the unit when the switch is operated.

4   Warning light bulb defective. The direction indicator bulbs will flash at a slightly lower frequency and audible warning remain operative.

20 Horn - fault tracing and rectification

1   If the horn works badly or fails completely, check the wiring to it for short circuits and loose connections. Check that the horn is firmly secured and that there is nothing lying on the horn body.

2   If the horn still does not work or operates incorrectly check with a test lamp that current is reaching the horn when the control is operated.

3   The horn adjusting screw is located in the back of the horn body. To adjust it turn it anti clockwise until nothing is heard and then turn it clockwise until the horn just starts to operate. Then turn another ¼ turn clockwise.

21 Headlights - removal and replacement

The Victor models are fitted with two rectangular headlights of the sealed beam type whereas VX 4/90 models use a four lamp system comprising twin square headlights of the pre-focus type. All four light units have twin filament bulbs but only the main filament is used on the inner lights, these being of a different wattage to the outer lamps. In addition, the outer lights incorporate a bulb shield fitted inside the light unit.

Victor

1   To remove the headlight unit first open the bonnet and then undo and remove the four nuts and washers that secure the complete headlight assembly to the front panel.

2   Detach the connectors to the rear of the light unit. Also withdraw the sidelight and direction indicator bulb holders. The complete headlight assembly may now be drawn forwards from the front of the car.

3   To gain access to the sealed beam unit undo and remove the four screws that secure the rim. Lift away the rim and sealed beam unit.

4   Take care of the rubber plugs on which the light unit seats and make sure that they are correctly located when refitting.

5   Refitting the light unit is the reverse sequence to removal.

VX 4/90

1   To gain access to the rectangular headlight units undo and remove the five screws that secure the surround to the rear of the front panel.

2   Ease the stay out of the plastic support and then detach the unit from the beam setting screws and the opposite stay from the underneath spring.

3   Refitting the light unit is the reverse sequence to removal.

22 Headlight alignment

1   Headlight beam adjustment is best carried out using proper optical alignment equipment. This is particularly so with VX 4/90 models. However, if the lights are seriously out adjustment can be carried out using the slotted screws at the rear of the mountings.

2   The main beam of the rectangular lights and the outer lights of the twin light system does not have a well defined spot of light intensity at the centre due to the masking effect of the shielded dip filament. These lights must be aimed on the dipped beam.

3   The light pattern of the dipped beam for the right hand lamp is assymetrical as shown in Fig.10.20. The pattern for a left hand

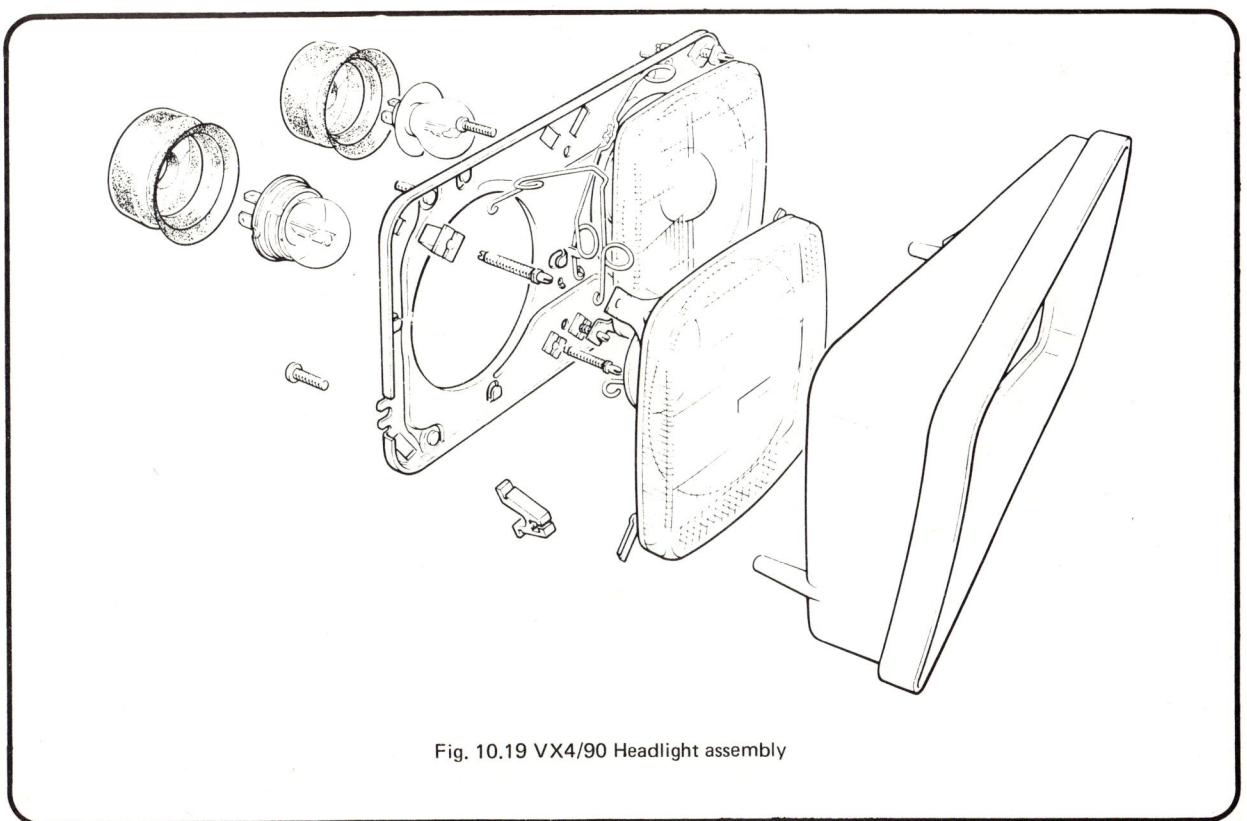

Fig. 10.19 VX4/90 Headlight assembly

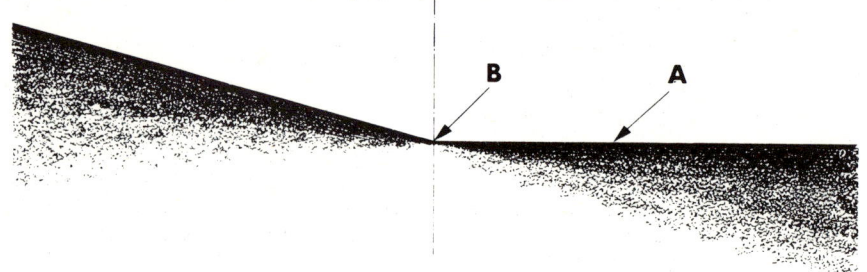

Fig. 10.20 Headlight beam adjustment pattern

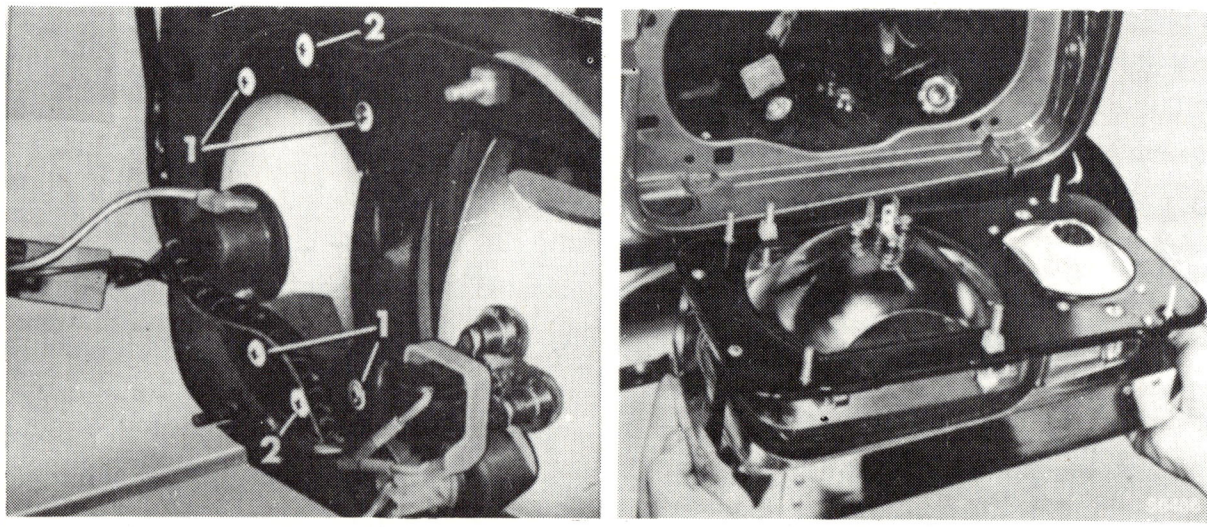

Fig. 10.21 Victor front direction indicator light attachment

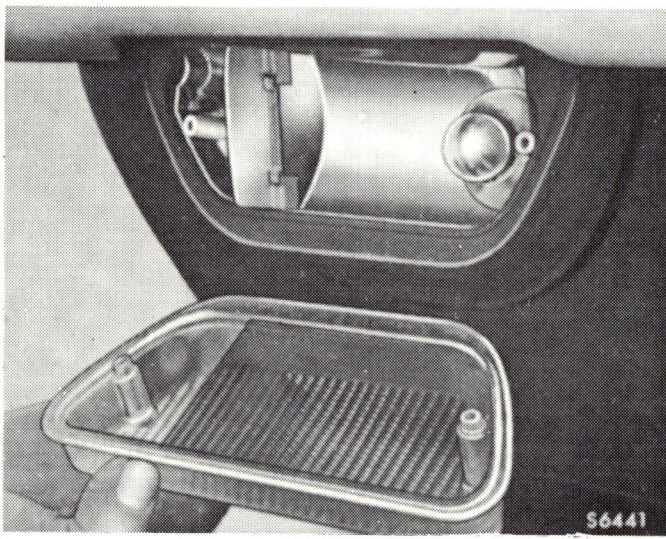

Fig. 10.22 VX4/90 front direction indicator and side light lens removal

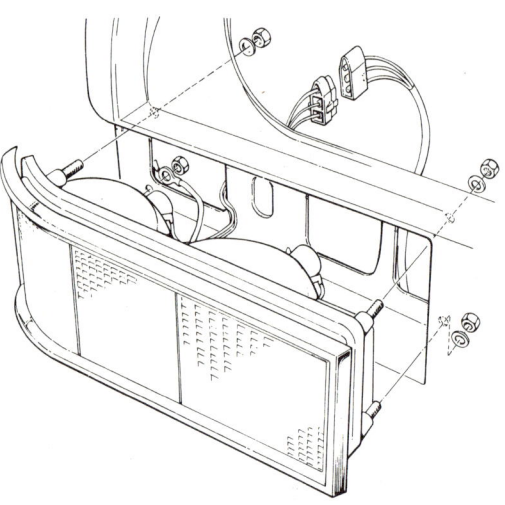

Fig. 10.23 Rear light cluster

light is similar but reversed. The lights must be aimed so that the horizontal portion of the beam 'A' is ¾° down.

4   For right hand drive lights the junction of the sloping and horizontal areas of the beam 'B' must be at the light vertical centre line or slightly to the left of the point. This junction must not occur to the right of the light centre line because it will cause dazzle to oncoming traffic.

5   When setting left hand lights the junction of the sloping and horizontal areas of the beam must be slightly to the right of the light centre line. If twin light systems are being set the inner (main beam) light must be set so that the beam is ½° down with no lateral deflection.

23 Front direction indicator lights

Victor

1   The lights are secured to the headlight mounting plate by four screws.

2   The lens is attached to the light body by two screws one each at the top and bottom. The bulb itself is carried in a push in type holder which may be detached by pulling rearwards.

VX 4/90

1   The complete light unit is secured to the front end panel by three studs and nuts. The side light section is outermost of the direction indicator bulb.

2   To fit a new bulb undo and remove the two screws that secure the lens to the light assembly. Lift away the plastic lens (Fig.10.22)

24 Front side lights

Victor

To renew a bulb, working inside the engine compartment draw the headlight unit terminal block rearwards. This will also release the side light holder as well.

VX 4/90

The procedure for renewing the bulb is identical to that for the front direction indicator light. For further information see Section 23.

25 Rear light cluster

1   The rear light cluster incorporates the direction indicator bulb, stop/tail bulb, reflex reflector and a compartment for a reverse light. For safety reasons the outermost bulb compartment (direction indicator) is of the semi-wrap round type thus being visible from the side of the car (Fig.10.23).

The complete light assembly is secured to the rear panel by four nuts and plain washers. Removal necessitates first undoing the two screws securing the protective cover and then unscrewing the four nuts and detaching the multi pin connector inside the luggage compartment. Draw the light assembly forwards and recover the foam type seal.

To gain access to an individual bulb unscrew the four self tapping screws that secure the lens to the main body. Lift away the lens and foam type seal.

26 Rear number plate light

The rear number plate lights are attached to the rear panel by two screws. On estate car models these are accessible from inside the luggage compartment once the floor panel has been removed. On saloon models the screws are accessible from inside the luggage compartment.

To gain access to the bulb, remove the one screw that secures the light rim and lens. Lift away the rim, lens and rubber seal.

27 Windscreen washer - fault finding

1   If the windscreen washers do not work when pumped, first check that there is water in the washer reservoir and that the jets in the discharge nozzles are clear (clear them with a pin).

2   Examine the water pipe connections at all junctions to ensure they are firmly fitted.

3   If there is still no jet from the screen nozzle detach the pipes from the pump unit and remove the unit from the dashboard with the wiper switch.

4   Submerge the inlet union of the pump in a bowl of water and operate the pump. Water should come from the outlet under reasonable pressure. Then operate the pump with the outlet only

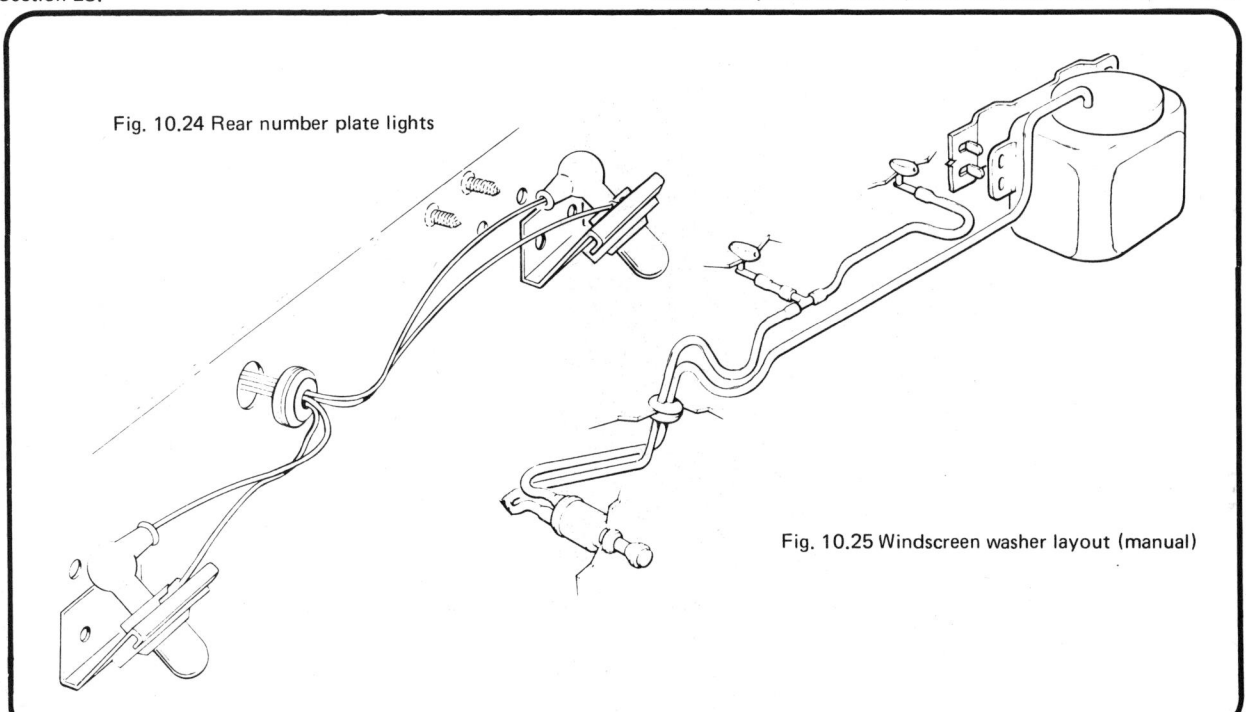

Fig. 10.24 Rear number plate lights

Fig. 10.25 Windscreen washer layout (manual)

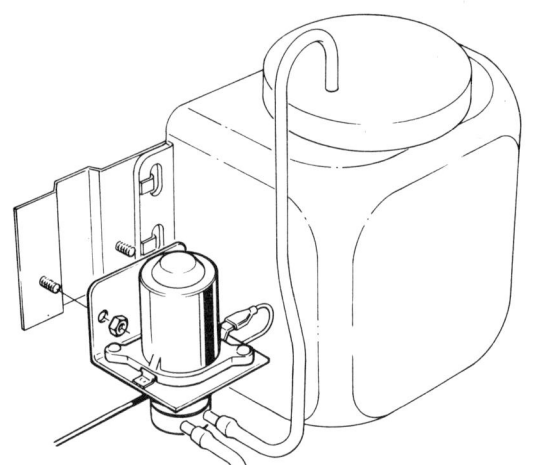

Fig. 10.26 Location of electrically operated windscreen washer pump

FIG. 10.27 WINDSCREEN WASHER PUMP COMPONENTS (ELECTRIC)

1 Cover   3 Impeller
2 Seal

under water, when bubbles will come out. After a few strokes in this manner release the plunger and lift the outlet out of the water. If, on operating the pump again, some water comes from the unit then it means that the non-return valves inside are not functioning properly and the unit should be renewed. If the pump is satisfactory then the only possible faults can be in the suction or delivery pipes, unions or nozzles all of which must be carefully examined for splits, links, blockages or leaking connections.

5 Some models have an electrically driven washer pump and it is mounted on an extension of the reservoir mounting bracket. It is operated from the wiper switch mounted on the steering column and controlled by raising the switch lever towards the steering wheel against spring pressure.

6 Fig.10.27 shows an exploded view of the pump assembly. It is possible to renew a worn impeller by removing the end cover and seal.

28 Windscreen wipers - fault finding

1 If the wipers do not operate when they are switched on first check the No.3 fuse. If this is sound then there is either an open circuit in the wiring or switch, the wiper motor is faulty, or the pivot or linkages may be binding.

2 If the wipers work intermittently then suspect either a short circuit in the motor or dirty electrical connection. Alternatively the armature shaft and float adjustment may be too tight or the wiper linkage may be binding.

3 Should the wipers not stop when they are turned off there must be a short circuit in the switch, wiring or park segment in the motor.

29 Windscreen wiper arms - removal and replacement

1 Before removing a wiper arm, turn the windscreen wiper switch on and off to ensure the arms are in their normal parked position with the arm to blade connection approximately 1.20 in (30 mm) from the lower windscreen glass moulding.

2 To remove the arm, pivot the arm back and pull the wiper arm head off the splined drive, at the same time easing back the clip with a screwdriver.

3 When replacing an arm, place it so it is in the correct relative parked position and then press the arm head onto the splined drive until the retaining clip clicks into place.

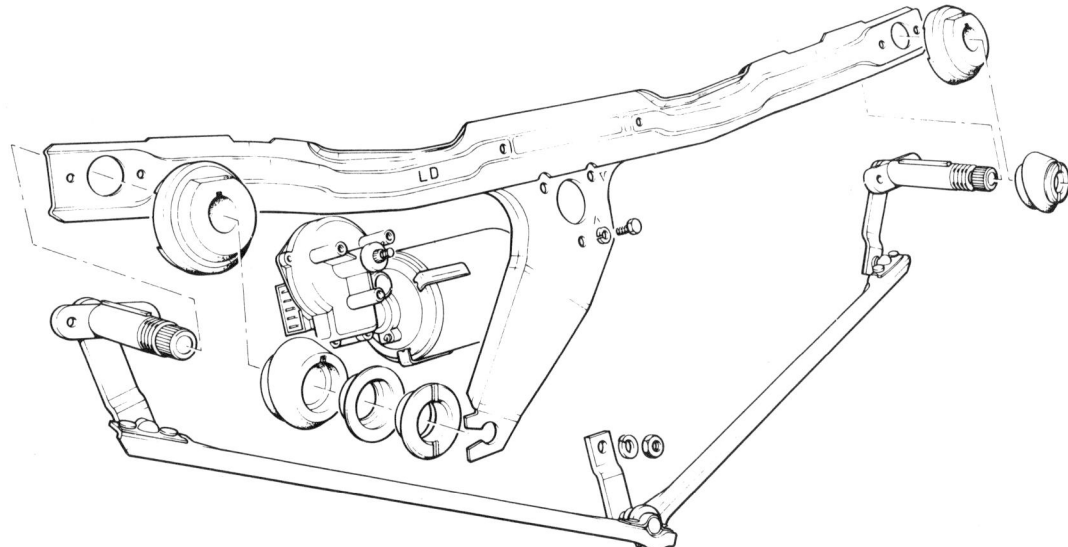

Fig. 10.28 Windscreen wiper assembly

4 If blade judder occurs when the blade is moving downwards the arm should be twisted in a clockwise direction when looking along the arm towards the centre of the windscreen. Reverse this instruction for judder on the upward stroke. Always carry out these adjustments with the screen wet.

30 Windscreen wiper assembly - removal and replacement

1 Refer to Section 29 and remove the wiper arms and blades.
2 Undo and remove the two screws and plain washers that secure the water deflector to the scuttle. Lift away the deflector.
3 Make a note of the electric cable connections to the ventilation fan and motor. Release these connectors.
4 Undo and remove the two most readily accessible motor attaching screws and then withdraw the forked end of the third bracket from the rubber grommet.
5 The wiper assembly may now be detached by unscrewing the nuts from the pivot housings. These are shaped nuts and require a tubular tool as shown in Fig.10.28. Lift away the nuts and rubber escutcheons together with their sleeve inserts. The unit may now be pulled down and tilted so as to clear the scuttle. Detach the electric cable connection and then lift away the complete assembly.
6 Refitting the wiper motor and linkage assembly is the reverse sequence to removal. Lubricate all moving parts with Castrol GTX.

31 Windscreen wiper motor - dismantling, inspection and re-assembly

The only repair which can be effectively undertaken by the do-it-yourself mechanic to the wiper motor is brush replacement. Anything more serious than this will mean either exchanging the complete motor or having a repair done by an automobile electrician. Spare part availability is really the problem.

1 The wiper motor may be detached from the mounting bracket once the assembly has been removed from the car as described in Section 30.
2 Undo and remove the nut and shakeproof washer that secures the crank arm to the cross shaft. Detach the crank arm. Next undo and remove the three bolts and spring washers that secure the motor to the mounting bracket.
3 Wipe the exterior of the motor free of dust and dirt and then using a screwdriver ease the clips from the slots in the frame.
4 Draw the end frame from the gear housing. The armature will be left assembled to the housing.
5 Undo and remove the four screws that secure the cover to the gear housing. Lift away the cover.
6 The main gear and cross shaft may now be lifted from the gear housing.
7 Hook the brush leads over the tags on the brush holder so maintaining the brushes in a retracted position. This will make removal of the armature easier.
8 Slacken the bearing retainer nut and withdraw the armature and bearing from the gear housing.
9 Undo and remove the small crosshead screws that hold the brush plate to the gear housing. Lift away the brush plate together with brushes and leads.
10 The armature shaft and cross shaft bushes are not serviced separately. The gear housing however, is serviced complete with bushes and the end frame is serviced as an assembly with magnets and bush.
11 The cross shaft and gear also the brushes, leads and gear housing cover are serviced as an assembly.
12 Reassembling the motor is the reverse sequence to removal but the following additional points should be noted.
a) Before refitting the cross shaft, pack the space between the bushes and also half fill the housing with Castrol LM Grease.
b) Smear the thrust washer at the inner end of the cross shaft, and the bearing surface in the gear housing cover with Castrol

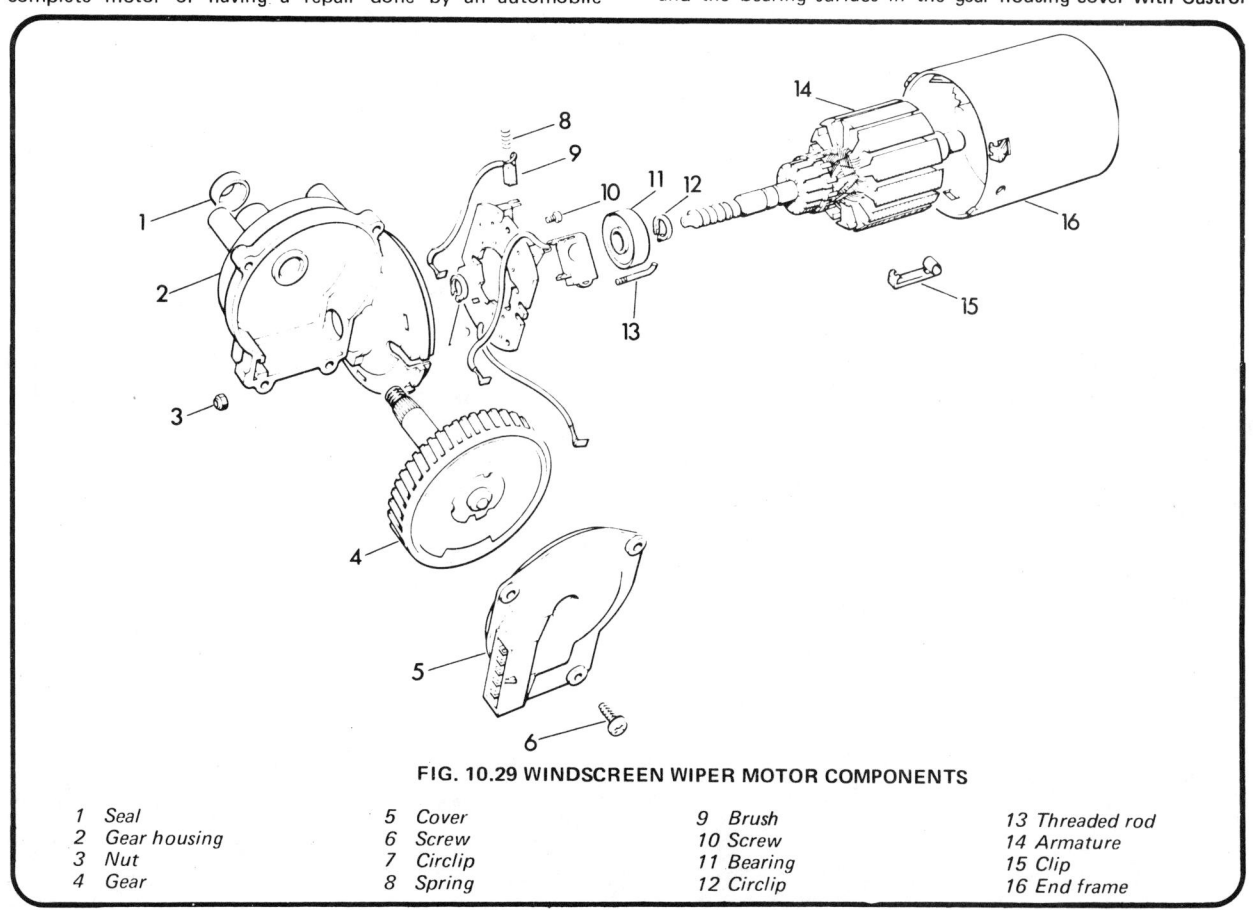

FIG. 10.29 WINDSCREEN WIPER MOTOR COMPONENTS

1 Seal	5 Cover	9 Brush	13 Threaded rod
2 Gear housing	6 Screw	10 Screw	14 Armature
3 Nut	7 Circlip	11 Bearing	15 Clip
4 Gear	8 Spring	12 Circlip	16 End frame

LM Grease.

c) The brushes must be retracted before the armature is inserted into the gear housing. The brush leads can then be unhooked thereby returning the brushes to their normal operating position before the end frame is replaced.

d) Make sure that the 'L' shaped bearing retainer is positioned on the bearing outer race before tightening.

13 The motor may now be tested for correct operation. For information the terminals are numbered as follows to correspond to a standard European wiring system.

31b	Black	Motor earth and earth for self park switch (non adjustable).
53	Red	Motor - low speed.
53b	Blue	Motor - high speed.
53a	No visible wire	Feed for self park switch.
53e	No visible wire	Current reversal feed for self park switch.

14 **Test A.** Motor. Connect the motor in circuit with a 12 volt battery and ammeter as shown in Fig.10.30. Connect the battery negative lead to terminal '31 b' and positive lead to terminal '53' for low speed operation check. Connect positive lead to terminal '53 b' for high speed operation check. The current consumption should be as given in Specifications at the beginning of this chapter after 5 - 10 minutes running.

15 **Test B.** Self park. Connect the motor in circuit with a 12 volt battery and ammeter as shown in Fig.10.31 Connect battery positive lead to terminal '53' and '53 a' and the negative to terminal '31 b'. Detach the lead from terminal '53'. The shaft should rotate a maximum of one revolution before stopping.

16 Before refitting the motor set the motor to the parked position. (Test B connections).

17 Fit the crank so that it lies horizontally between the two marks stamped on the mounting bracket.

32 Instrument facia - Victor - removal and refitting

The instruments are mounted in a detachable facia which is secured to the instrument panel by self tapping screws. Also fitted to the facia are the direction indicator warning lights, illumination lights for fan switch, panel lamp rheostat, rear window demist switch, windscreen washer and choke controls. Apertures for the heater and ventilation controls and for the drivers face level vent are also included.

A magnetic type speedometer is fitted and it houses the main beam warning light. An instrument assembly incorporates the fuel and water temperature gauges, ignition, oil and brake pressure warning lights. To remove the instrument facia proceed

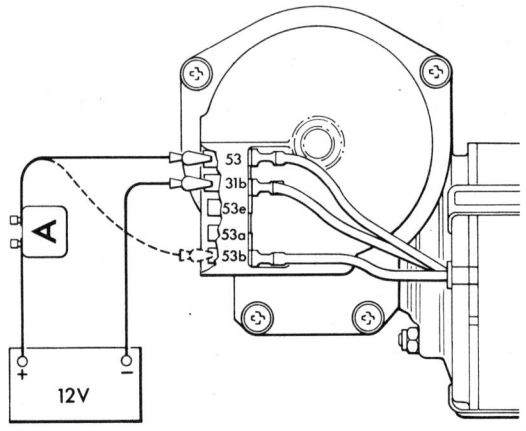

Fig. 10.30 Windscreen wiper motor test A

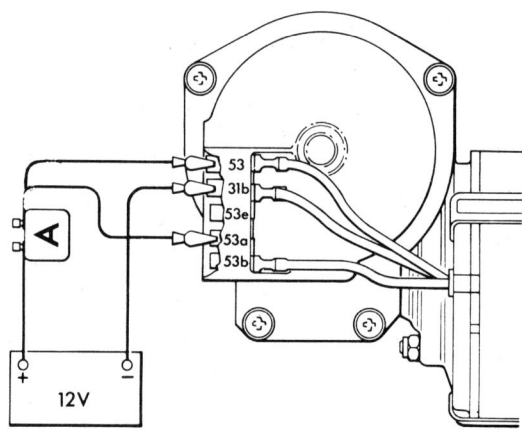

Fig. 10.31 Windscreen wiper motor test B

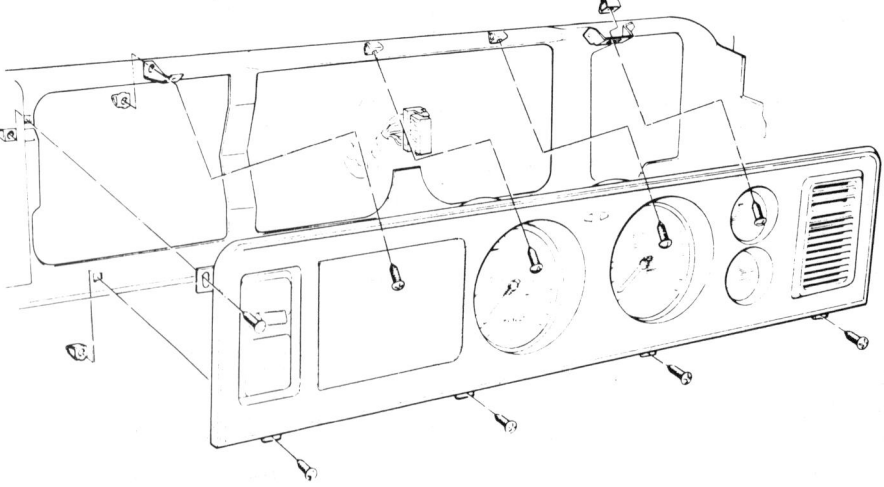

Fig. 10.32 Instrument facia attachment screw locations

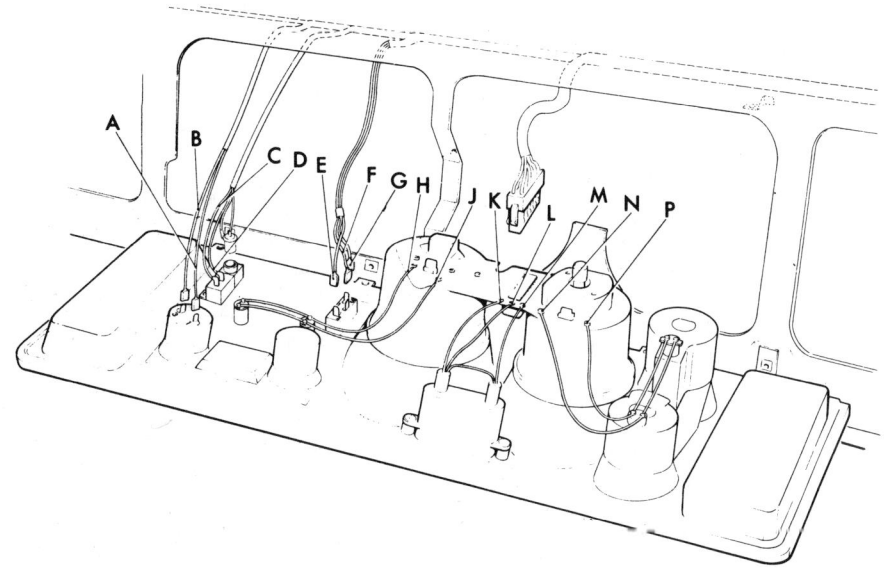

FIG. 10.33 VICTOR INSTRUMENT WIRING

A Red (terminal 1)
B Red/brown (terminal 3)
C Green/yellow
D Green
E Green/yellow (terminal 2)
F Green (terminal 1)
G Green/slate (terminal 3)

H Black
J Red/brown
K Green/red
L Black
M Green/white
N Black
P Red/brown

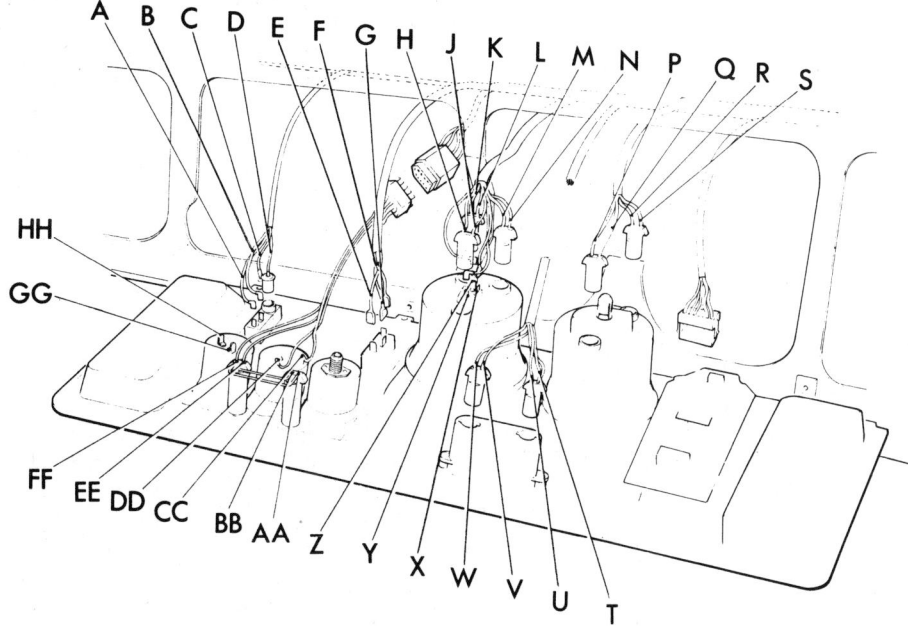

FIG. 10.34 VX4/90 INSTRUMENT WIRING

A	Green	J	Black	S	Black	AA	Red
B	White/black	K	Brown/yellow	T	Black	BB	Black
C	Black	L	Green	U	Green/white	CC	Purple
D	White/black	M	Green	V	Green/red	DD	Black
E	Green/yellow	N	White/brown	W	Black	EE	Red
F	Green/slate	P	Black	X	White/slate	FF	Black
G	Green	Q	Red/brown	Y	Black	GG	Black
H	Red/brown	R	Blue/white	Z	Green	HH	Brown

as follows:
1 Undo and remove the nine screws located as shown in Fig.10.32.
2 Refer to Chapter 3 and detach the manual choke control from the carburettor.
3 Working at the rear of the speedometer lead depress the clip that retains the speedometer cable and draw the complete facia forwards. Detach the electric cable terminal connector.
4 Refitting the facia is the reverse sequence to removal. Fig.10.33 shows the correct locations of the terminal connectors. When refitting the cable to the speedometer head simply push and the spring clip will automatically engage with the cable ferrule.

33 Instrument facia - VX 4/90 - removal and refitting

The instrument facia is equipped with a magnetic type speedometer which also incorporates an odometer trip as well as the main beam and brake pressure warning lights. An electronically operated tachometer houses the ignition and the oil pressure warning lights. Individual temperature gauges are mounted in the facia and a battery condition meter, electric clock and an oil pressure gauge are incorporated in the heater control facia. To remove the instrument facia proceed as follows:
1 Detach the odometer trip control from the instrument panel. from the instrument panel.
2 Refer to Section 35 and remove the heater control facia.
3 Undo and remove the nine screws that secure the instrument facia, located as shown in Fig.10.32
4 Refer to Chapter 3 and detach the manual choke control from the carburettor.
5 Working at the rear of the speedometer head depress the clip that retains the speedometer cable and draw the complete facia forwards. Detach the electric cable terminal connectors and bulb holders.
6 Refitting is the reverse sequence to removal. Fig.10.34 shows the correct locations of the terminal connectors and bulb holders.
7 When refitting the cable to the speedometer lead simply push and the spring clip will automatically engage with the cable ferrule.

34 Instrument facia light bulbs - renewal

1 Refer to Section 32 (Victor) or 33 (VX 4/90) and remove the instrument facia.
2 The bulbs used are of the push in or bayonet type with wedge base capless type bulbs. Before purchasing a new bulb determine which type is used.
3 The bulb holders located in the printed circuit must be detached by hand and not a screwdriver otherwise the circuit may be damaged.
4 Access to the illumination bulbs for the switches and/or instruments mounted on the heater control facia can be gained once the facia is detached from the instrument facia as described in Section 35.

35 Heater control facia - removal and refitting

The heater control facia is a separate panel and is secured to the instrument facia by a single screw at the top and two spring clips at the bottom. These engage in lugs on the instrument facia. Beside the apertures for the heater controls it is possible to fit switches for the ventilation fan and rear window demister if switches have to be fitted. Victor models have a panel light rheostat and provision is made for an electric clock and fog light switch.

VX 4/90 models have a battery condition meter, electric clock and oil pressure gauge fitted.

To remove the heater control facia proceed as follows:
1 Pull off the heater control knobs and then undo and remove the one retaining screw.
2 Draw the facia forwards by a sufficient amount to gain access to the wiring and bulb holders. Note the electric cable connections and detach.
3 VX 4/90 models. Detach the oil gauge pressure pipe.
4 The facia may now be lifted away from the instrument facia.
5 Refitting the heater control facia is the reverse sequence to removal.

36 Voltage stabilizer

The voltage stabilizer is a sealed unit which supplies current to the fuel and water temperature gauges at a constant voltage thereby preventing fluctuations in readings caused by variations in battery voltage.
To remove the voltage stabilizer proceed as follows:

Victor models
The unit is plugged into the printed circuit and slots in the instrument assembly. Remove the instrument facia as described in Section 32. The unit may now be detached from the printed circuit by pulling. Do not use a screwdriver to lever it from the printed circuit (Fig.10.37).
Refitting is the reverse sequence to removal.

VX 4/90 models
The unit is plugged into terminal sockets which are attached to the printed circuit and fuel and temperature gauge backplate. Remove the instrument facia as described in Section 33. The unit may now be detached from the circuit by pulling. Do not use a screwdriver to lever it from the printed circuit.
Refitting is the reverse sequence to removal.

Testing voltage stabilizer
1 Remove the stabilizer as previously described.
2 Refer to Fig. 10.35 and connect to a voltmeter and 12 volt battery in the manner shown.
3 It should be observed that there are regular pulsations of the voltmeter needle and the reading between maximum and minimum be 10 volts.
4 Should no reading or inaccurate reading or a constant battery voltage without pulsations be obtained the unit should be renewed.

37 Printed circuit - Victor - removal and replacement

The printed circuit is attached to the rear of the speedometer and combined instrument bodies. There is a multi-pin socket connector on the wiring harness and a voltage stabilizer plug into the circuit in addition to the instrument and warning lights. The temperature and fuel gauges are connected to the circuit by means of their securing nuts and studs. To remove the printed circuit proceed as follows:
1 Refer to Section 32 and remove the instrument facia.
2 Detach the bulb holders and voltage stabilizer from the printed circuit. Also the electric cables.
3 Undo and remove the nuts from the gauge mounted studs and lift away the printed circuit.
4 Refitting the printed circuit is the reverse sequence to removal. Refer to Fig.10.35 for information on the correct cable and bulb locations.

38 Printed circuit - VX 4/90 - removal and replacement

The printed circuit is mounted on the fuel and temperature gauge backplate and is riveted to this plate, together with the three sockets for the voltage stabilizer A multi pin socket

169

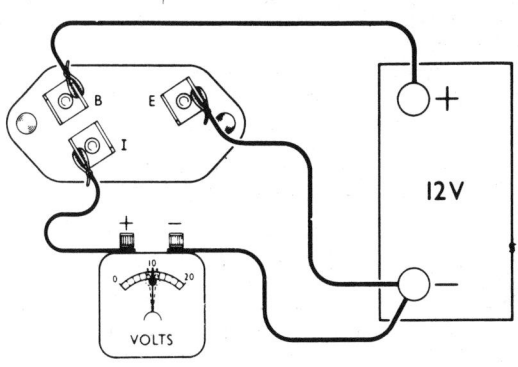

Fig. 10.35 Odometer trip control

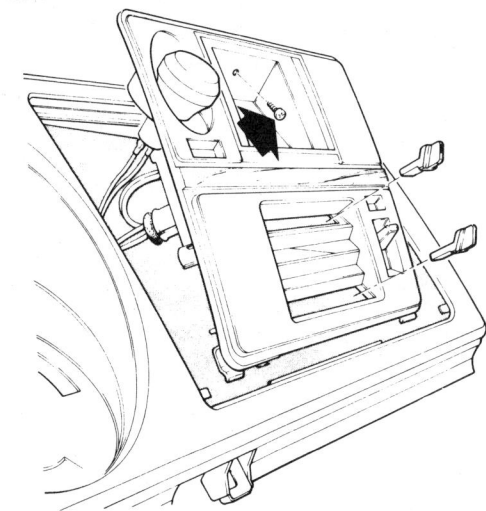

Fig. 10.36 Heater control fascia (arrow shows retaining screw

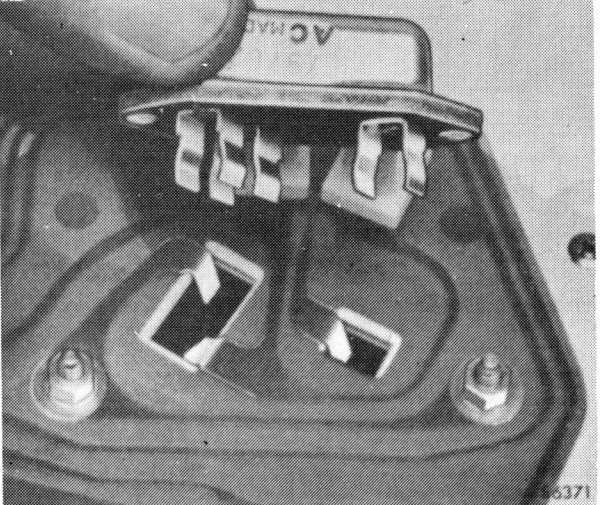

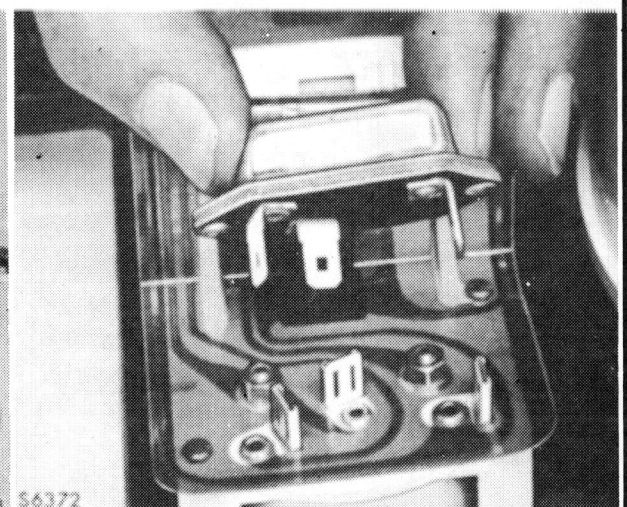

Victor models

FIG. 10.37 VOLTAGE STABILIZER

VX4/90 models

Fig. 10.38 Printed circuit - Victor models

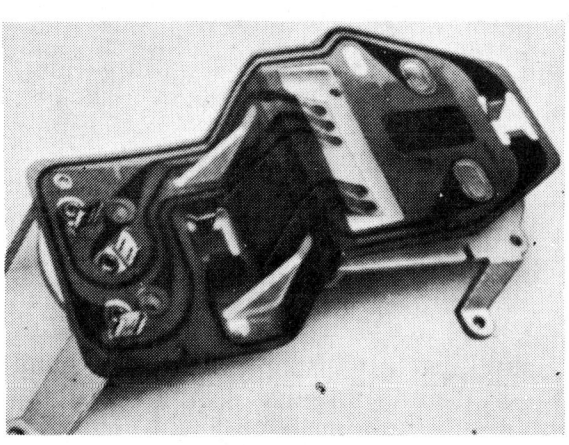

Fig. 10.39 Printed circuit - VX4/90 models

connector is on the wiring harness as well as the fuel and temperature gauge lights which plug into the circuit.

To remove the printed circuit proceed as follows:

1 Refer to Section 3 and remove the instrument facia.

2 Undo and remove the four screws that secure the fuel and temperature gauge assembly to the facia. Lift away the gauge assembly.

3 Undo and remove the four screws that secure the fuel and temperature gauge casings to the backplate.

4 Undo and remove the two nuts and plain washers that secure each gauge to the backplate. Carefully lift away the gauges.

5 The printed circuit and backplate are serviced as an assembly so this is as far as it is necessary to go for dismantling.

6 Refitting is the reverse sequence to removal. Refer to Fig.10.34 for information on the correct cable and bulb connections.

39 Speedometer head and cable - removal and replacement

The speedometer is attached to the rear of the instrument facia by three screws so commence removal by referring to Section 32 (Victor) or Section 33 (VX 4/90) and remove the instrument facia. Then proceed as follows:

1 Withdraw the bulb holders from the speedometer casing backplate.

2 **Victor models.** Refer to Section 37 and remove the printed circuit.

3 **VX 4/90 models.** Unscrew the trip reset cable from the speedometer.

4 Undo and remove the three screws that secure the speedometer backplate to the casing. Withdraw the backplate and speedometer head.

5 If necessary undo the two screws and shakeproof washers that secure the speedometer head to the backplate.

6 Refitting is the reverse sequence to removal. When refitting the speedometer lead to the backplate make sure that the slot in the cable retaining clip engages with the spigot on the speedometer head body. Refer to Fig.10.33 (Victor) or Fig.10.34 (VX 4/90) for information on the correct cable and bulb connections.

Speedometer cable

To remove the speedometer cable proceed as follows:

1 Working under the car detach the cable from the right hand side of the transmission unit by unscrewing the knurled nut and drawing the cable assembly from the transmission unit.

2 Working behind the speedometer head, depress the spring clip and pull the speedometer cable from the speedometer head.

3 Detach the cable rubber grommets from the body and withdraw the cable from the body.

4 Refitting the speedometer cable is the reverse sequence to removal. When fitting the cable to the speedometer head simply push and the spring clip will automatically engage with the cable ferrule.

40 Tachometer - removal and replacement

1 Refer to Section 33 and remove the instrument facia.

2 Undo and remove the three screws that secure the backplate and tachometer to the casing. Withdraw the backplate and tachometer from the casing (Fig.10.41)

3 If necessary undo the three nuts and plain washers that secure the tachometer to the backplate.

4 Refitting the tachometer is the reverse sequence to removal. Refer to Fig.10.34 for information on the correct cable and bulb connections.

41 Fuel and temperature gauges - testing

1 Switch on the ignition and wait at least 1 minute. If one gauge operates it is reasonably safe to assume that the voltage

stabilizer is operating correctly.

2 If neither gauge operates the voltage stabilizer may be checked as described in Section 36.

3 To determine if the gauge sender unit is faulty, first detach the wire from the sender unit and with the ignition switched on earth the cable. The gauge needle should now move slowly to the 'H' (HOT) or 'F' (FULL) sector in the appropriate gauge.

4 To check the gauge and wiring circuit, withdraw the instrument facia from the instrument panel as described in Section 32 (Victor) or 33 (VX 4/90).

5 Shut the sender unit terminal on the gauge to earth. The needle should give the same reading as described in paragraph 3. On Victor models the sender terminals are the ones nearest the top of the instrument and on VX 4/90 models the sender terminals are those on the right hand side. Rectify the fault as necessary.

42 Fuel and temperature gauges - removal and replacement

Victor

1 Refer to Section 32 and remove the instrument facia.

2 Refer to Section 37 and detach the printed circuit.

3 Undo and remove the three screws that secure the backplate to the casing. Carefully withdraw the backplate and gauges (Fig.10.42).

4 Using a pair of pliers squeeze the peg shank and withdraw the three pegs that secure the mask supports to the backplate. Lift away the backplate and gauges.

5 The gauges may now be lifted away from the backplate.

6 Refitting is the reverse sequence to removal. Refer to Fig.10.33 for information on the correct cable and bulb connections.

VX 4/90

1 Refer to Section 3 and remove the instrument facia.

2 Refer to Section 38 and detach the printed circuit from the gauges.

3 Refitting is the reverse sequence to removal. Refer to Fig.10.34 for information on the correct cable and bulb connections.

43 Battery condition meter, clock and oil pressure gauge - removal and replacement

1 Refer to Section 35 and remove the heater control facia.

2 Remove the knob from the clock hands control and then undo and remove the four screws that secure the instrument assembly to the heater control facia.

3 Undo and remove the four screws that secure the instruments to the housing. Separate the instruments from the housing (Fig.10.44).

4 To remove either the battery condition meter or the oil pressure gauge undo and remove the two securing nuts and terminal blades (battery condition meter) or the two screws (oil pressure gauges).

5. To remove the clock first prise off the hands with a pair of tweezers and then undo and remove the two screws that secure the face to the casing.

6 Release the three pins that secure the clock to the casing. Note that the dished washer between the clock and the facing is fitted with the concave side towards the casing.

7 Refitting the instruments is the reverse sequence to removal. It is preferable that new fixing springs are used.

44 Windscreen wiper and direction indicator switch - removal and replacement

1 Refer to Chapter 11, Section 23 and remove the steering wheel and steering column canopy.

2 Disconnect the multi pin socket connectors from the wiring

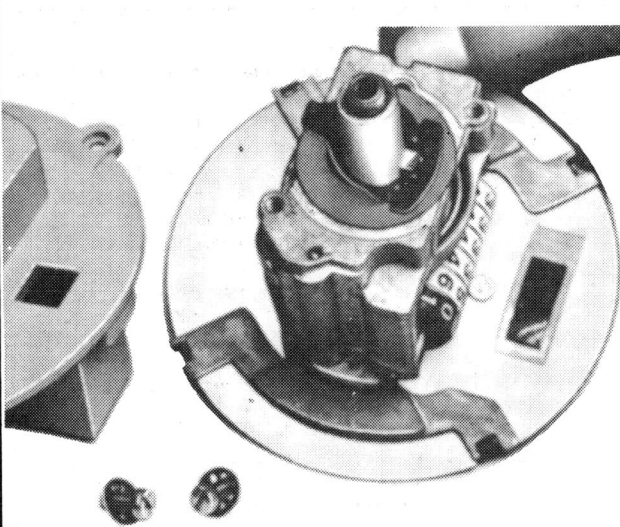

Fig. 10.40 Speedometer head and back plate

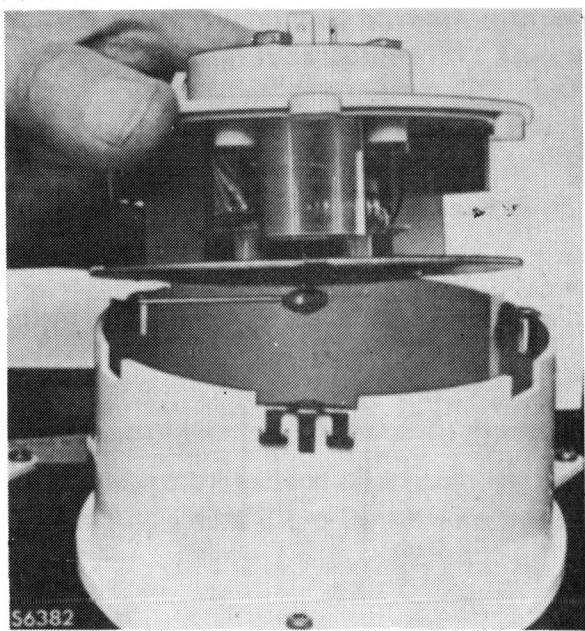

Fig. 10.41 Lifting tachometer from casing

Fig. 10.42 Fuel and temperature gauge assembly (Victor models)

Fig. 10.43 Fuel and temperature gauge removal (VX4/90 models)

Fig. 10.44 'Three instrument' cluster housing removal (VX4/90 models)

Fig. 10.45 Correct windscreen wiper and direction indicator switch fitment to column

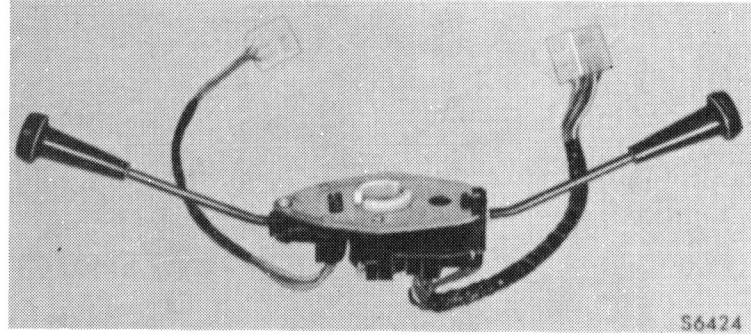

Fig. 10.46 Windscreen wiper and direction indicator switch assembly

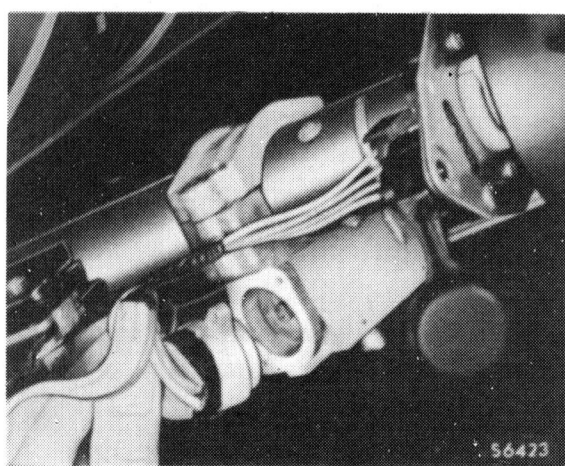

Fig. 10.47 Key start switch removal

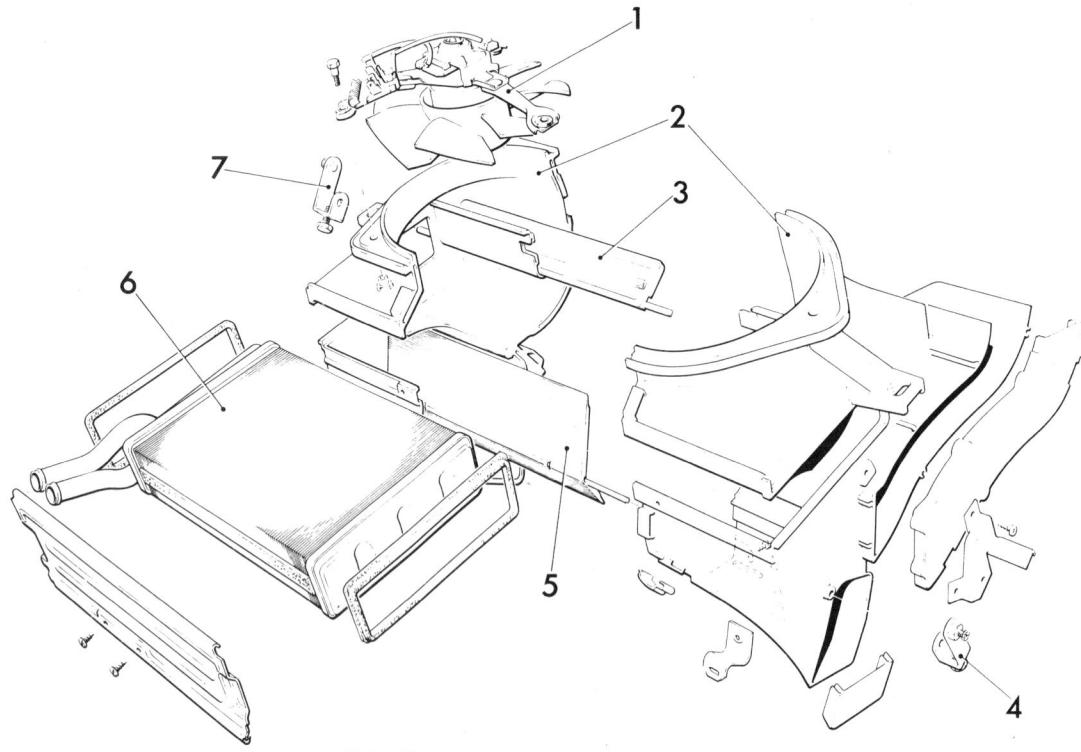

FIG. 10.48 HEATER AND VENTILATOR ASSEMBLY

1	Motor and fan	3	Mixing flap	5	Air distribution flap
2	Casing	4	Lever - distribution flap	6	Radiator

7 Lever - air mix flap

harness.

3 Slacken the combined switch clamp screw and carefully withdraw the switch assembly.

4 The direction indicator switch and wiper switch is serviced complete with the mounting plate and striker bush as an assembly. Do not attempt to remove the direction indicator switch from the plate as the interior of the switch will separate into its component parts (Fig.10.46).

5 The wiper switch is also serviced as a separate item. This switch may be detached from the mounting plate by drilling out the rivets and then unscrewing the cross head screw. The new switch may be secured by small nuts and bolts and the cross head screw.

6 Should it be necessary to gain access to the horn push contacts the end cap may be carefully prised off using a blunt knife blade.

7 Refitting is the reverse sequence to removal. Correctly locate the switch by lining up the raised peg with the recess in the outer column as shown in Fig.10.45.

45 Key start switch - removal and replacement

1 Undo and remove the seven screws that secure the steering column lower canopy and lift away the lower canopy

2 Disconnect the multi pin socket connector at the switch wiring harness and then undo and remove the two retaining screws that hold the switch to the lock body.

3 Refitting the switch and canopy is the reverse sequence to removal.

46 Switches - general - removal and replacement

Lighting switch

1 Undo and remove the screws that secure the lower canopy half.

2 Disconnect the multi pin socket connector at the switch wiring harness and then undo and remove the switch retaining screws.

3 Refitting the switch is the reverse sequence to removal. The terminals on the switch are identified by numbers and the wiring connections are as follows:

    1 Blue.   2 Brown.   3 Red with green tracer.

Ventilation fan and backlight demist switches

1 Refer to Section 35 and remove the heater facia panel.

2 Make a note of the electrical cable connections at the rear of the switch and then detach the terminal connectors.

3 Undo and remove the two switch securing self tapping screws. Lift away the switch.

4 Refitting is the reverse sequence to removal.

Instrument light switch or rheostat
Victor

1 Using a small screwdriver depress the plunger that locks the knob onto the switch shaft. Pull off the knob.

2 Refer to Section 35 and remove the heater facia panel.

3 Using a pair of pliers carefully unscrew the switch securing nut. Lift away the switch.

VX 4/90

4 Using a small screwdriver depress the plunger which locks the knob onto the rheostat shaft. Pull off the knob.

5. Using a pair of pliers carefully unscrew the switch securing nut. The plain washer and escutcheon may then be removed and finally the rheostat withdranw from behind the instrument panel.

6 Make a note of the electrical cable connections to the base of the rheostat and detach the terminal connectors.

7 Refitting in both cases is the reverse sequence to removal.

Interior light door switch

1 Using a small screwdriver undo and remove the screw that

secures the switch flange to the pillar.

2 Draw the switch forwards and detach the cable connector. Take care that it does not slip back into the pillar. Should this happen, the trim will have to be removed.

3 Refitting is the reverse sequence to removal. Lightly lubricate the switch plunger with Castrol GTX.

Stop light switch

The stop light switch is retained in position on the brake pedal support bracket by two nuts threaded on the switch body. Removal is simply a matter of detaching the two cable connectors and unscrewing the locknut. Refitting the switch is basically identical to the reverse sequence to removal. The position must be adjusted so that the switch contacts have just parked as the pedal rests in the off position.

Handbrake lever switch

On models with a dash mounted handbrake lever a switch is located on the brake operating lever support bracket and retained in position with two bolts. With the floor mounted type handbrake lever the switch is mounted on the transmission tunnel and accessible once the lever boot has been detached.

Reverse light switch - manual transmission

1 The switch is of the plunger type and screwed into a housing which is attached to the side of the gearbox casing by a plate and two bolts. The switch is operated by the striking lever shaft and requires no adjustment.

2 To remove the switch undo and remove the bolts and spring washers that secure the plate to the gearbox. Detach the electric cable terminal connectors and lift away the switch and housing.

3 The switch can now be unscrewed from the housing.

4 Refitting is the reverse sequence to removal. Make sure that when fitting the switch to the housing the sealing washer is correctly located. Also before refitting the housing check that the 'O' ring is in position on the housing.

Reverse light and starter inhibitor switches - automatic transmission

Two switches and the operating cam are attached to a bracket which is secured to the selector lever housing by two nuts. The cam is actuated by a pin on the side of the selector lever. The inhibitor switch is the one nearer to the front of the car. To allow adjustment clearance holes are provided in the switch bracket.

1 To gain access to the switches undo and remove the three screws that secure the console to the lever bracket.

2 To adjust the position of the switches move the selector lever to the 'N' position and check that the plunger is in alignment with the cutaway in the top of the selector plate.

3 Slacken the two nuts that secure the switch bracket and slide the bracket until the line on the cam is in alignment with the line on the setting aperture on the switch bracket. Retighten the nuts.

4 Check that the starter motor does not operate when 'D', 'I' 'L' or 'R' is selected. Ensure that the roller on the reverse light switch is depressed by the cam when 'R' is selected.

5 Should the switches have been removed the cable connections are as follows:

Inhibitor switch	White/red. and white/yellow.
Reverse light switch	Green. and green/brown.

47 Ventilator and heater assembly

The ventilator and heater assembly comprise a motor and fan (1) (Fig.10.48) radiator matrix (6), air mixing flap (3) and air distribution flap (5), all mounted in two halves of a casing (2) which are clipped together with small spring clips.

The air distribution flap is cable operated by a lever (4) which is attached to the spindle. The lever (7) is operated by a cable from the water valve in the engine compartment and controls movement of the air mixing flap.

To remove the assembly proceed as follows:

1 Make a note of the electric cable connections to the ventilation fan and motor. Release these connectors.

2 Refer to Chapter 2 and drain the cooling system.

3 Undo and remove the two screws and plain washers that secure the fan motor water deflector. Lift away the deflector.

4 Refer to Chapter 12 and remove the parcel shelf, instrument panel long lower cover and the cover support.

5 Carefully ease the demister ducts from the connecting sleeves.

6 Undo and remove the two nuts and plain washers that secure the assembly to the upper dash panel and then the one screw to the floor mounted bracket.

7 Very carefully lift away the heater assembly.

8 Refitting is the reverse sequence to removal. Refill the cooling system as described in Chapter 2.

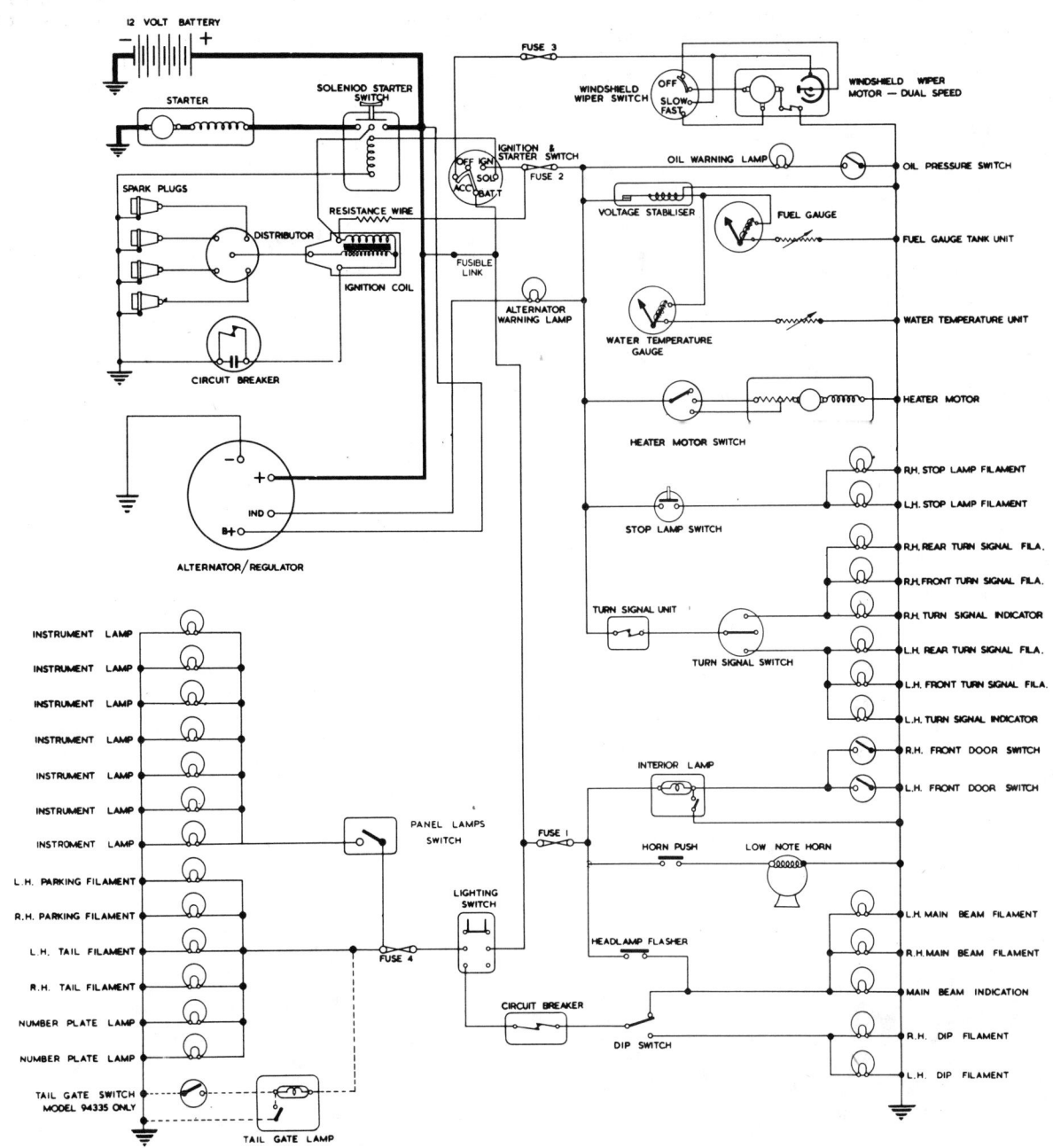

Theoretical Wiring Diagram - Victor de luxe

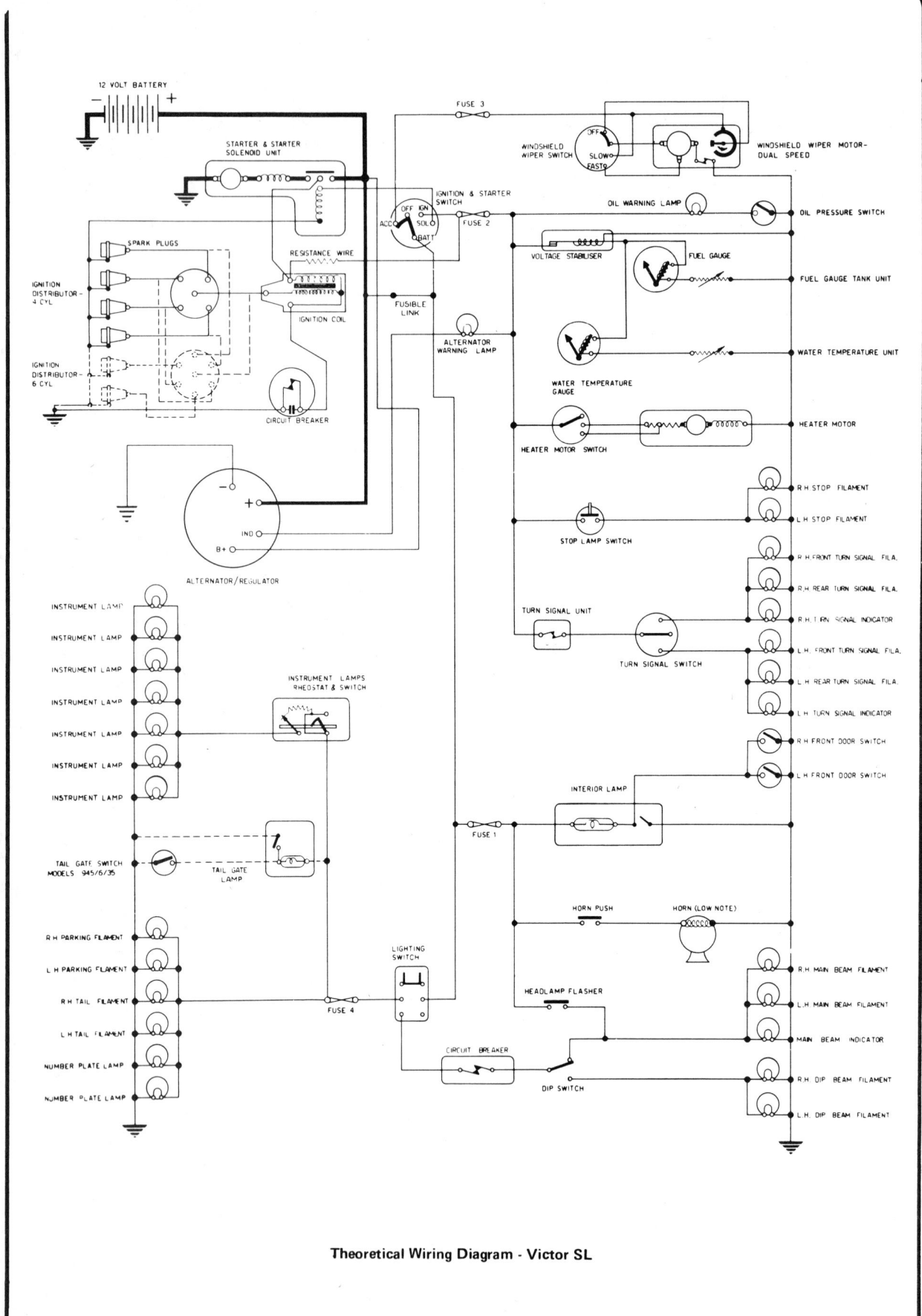

Theoretical Wiring Diagram - Victor SL

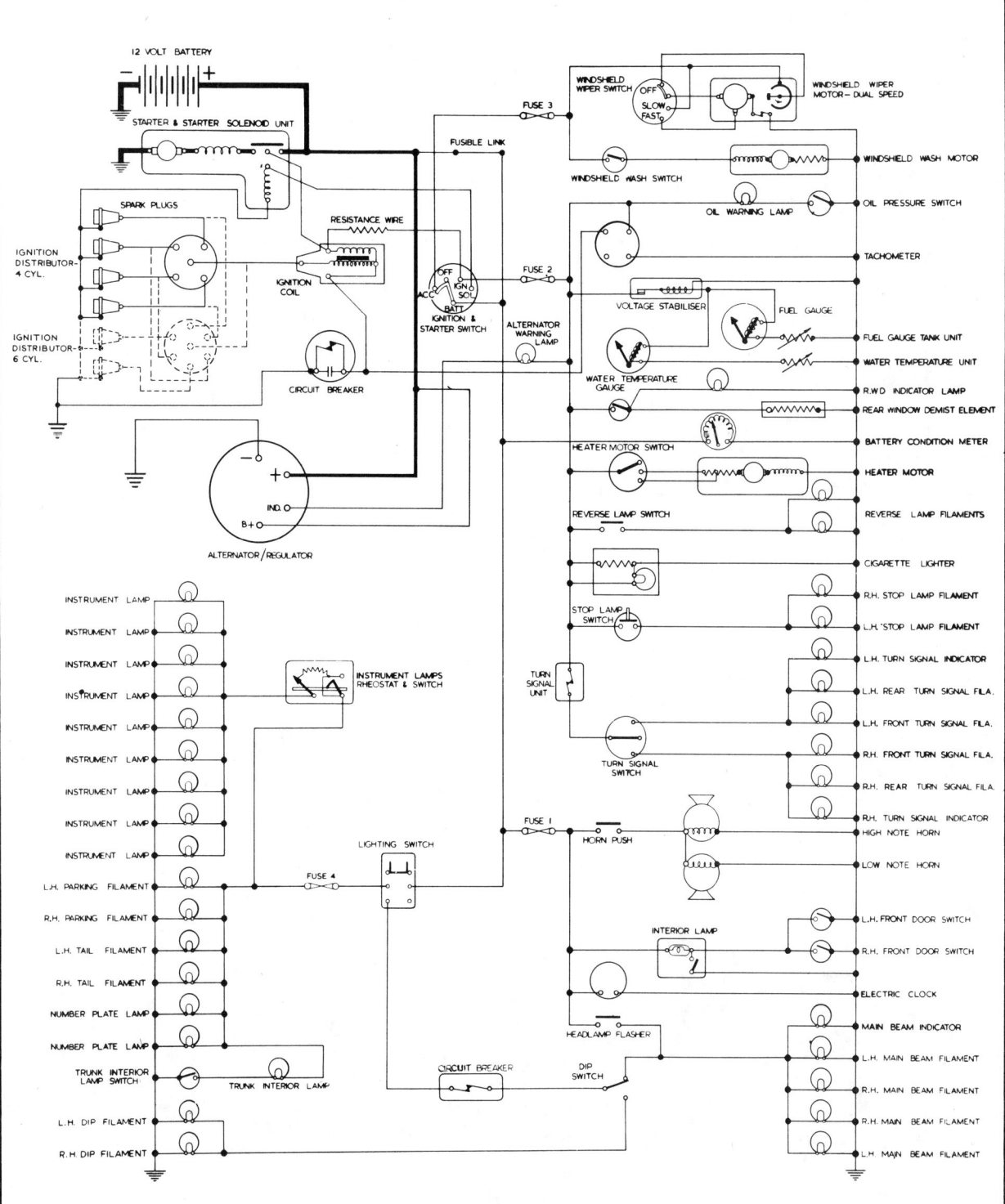

Theoretical Wiring Diagram - VX4/90

VICTOR

VX 4/90

PARKING BRAKE SWITCH

PRESSURE DIFFERENTIAL WARNING SWITCH

PARKING BRAKE SWITCH

PRESSURE DIFFERENTIAL WARNING SWITCH

WARNING LAMP

G1

G1

FUSE 2   E4

FUSE 3   G2

BRAKE PRESSURE WARNING LAMP

CIGARETTE LIGHTER

CIGARETTE LIGHTER

FUSE 3   G3
FUSE 4   J5

TO WINDSHIELD WIPER SWITCH

WINDSHIELD WASH MOTOR

WINDSHIELD WASH SWITCH

FUSE 3   G5

ELECTRIC WINDSHIELD WASH-VICTOR

R.H. INDICATOR LAMP

R.H. FRONT TURN SIGNAL LAMP

RH REAR TURN SIGNAL LAMP

L.H. INDICATOR LAMP

L.H. FRONT TURN SIGNAL LAMP

L.H. REAR TURN SIGNAL LAMP

HAZARD WARNING SWITCH

TURN SIGNAL SWITCH

HAZARD WARNING UNIT

TURN SIGNAL UNIT

FUSE1   C3
FUSE 2   E5

HAZARD WARNING SYSTEM

TO BE USED IN CONJUNCTION WITH ACCESSORY WIRING DIAGRAM & 12 VOLT ALTERNATOR SYSTEM THEORETICAL WIRING DIAGRAMS

FUSE1
C4

HORN PUSH

F4

LOW NOTE HORN

HIGH NOTE HORN

TWIN HORNS-VICTOR DE LUXE

REVERSE LAMP

REVERSE LAMP

REVERSE LAMP SWITCH

FUSE 2   E2

REVERSE LAMPS

IGNITION WARNING LAMP

TO BATTERY - ALTERNATOR - IGNITION SW. (BATT)

TO IGNITION SW. (SOL)

TO IGNITION COIL +

STARTER & STARTER SOLENOID UNIT

FUSE   B5

PRE-ENGAGED STARTER-VICTOR DE LUXE

DEMIST ELEMENT

WARNING LAMP

DEMIST SWITCH

FUSE 2   E3

REAR WINDOW DEMIST

E2   FUSE 2

D5   FUSE 2

F5   FUSE 3

ACC IGN SOL
OFF BATT
IGNITION SWITCH

INHIBITOR & REVERSE LAMP SWITCH

TO REVERSE LAMPS

B5

STARTER & STARTER SOLENOID

TO IGNITION COIL

TO BATTERY

AUTOMATIC TRANSMISSION

Theoretical Wiring Diagram - Optional Equipment

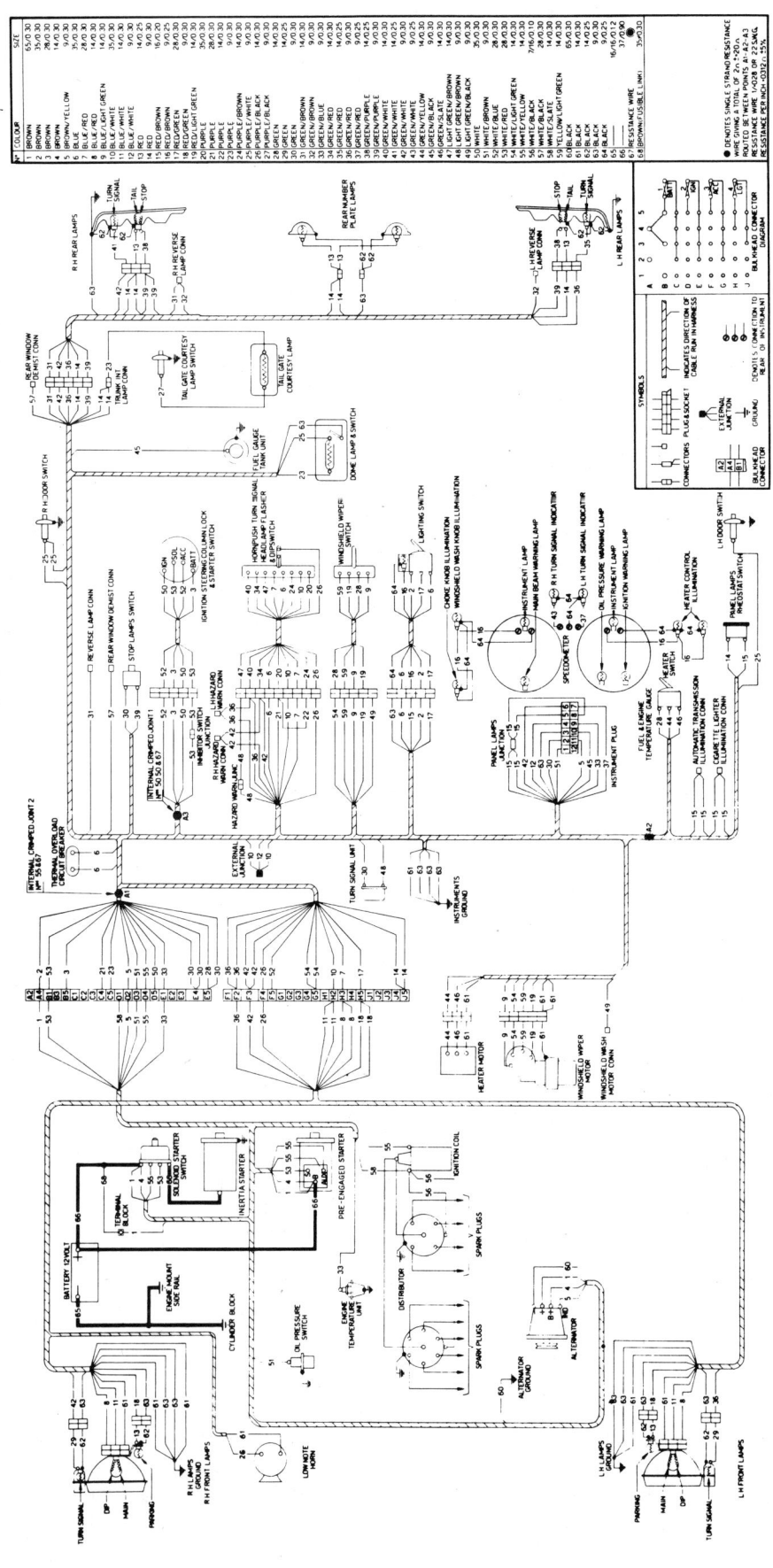

Physical Wiring Diagram - Victor de luxe and SL

Physical Wiring Diagram - VX4/90

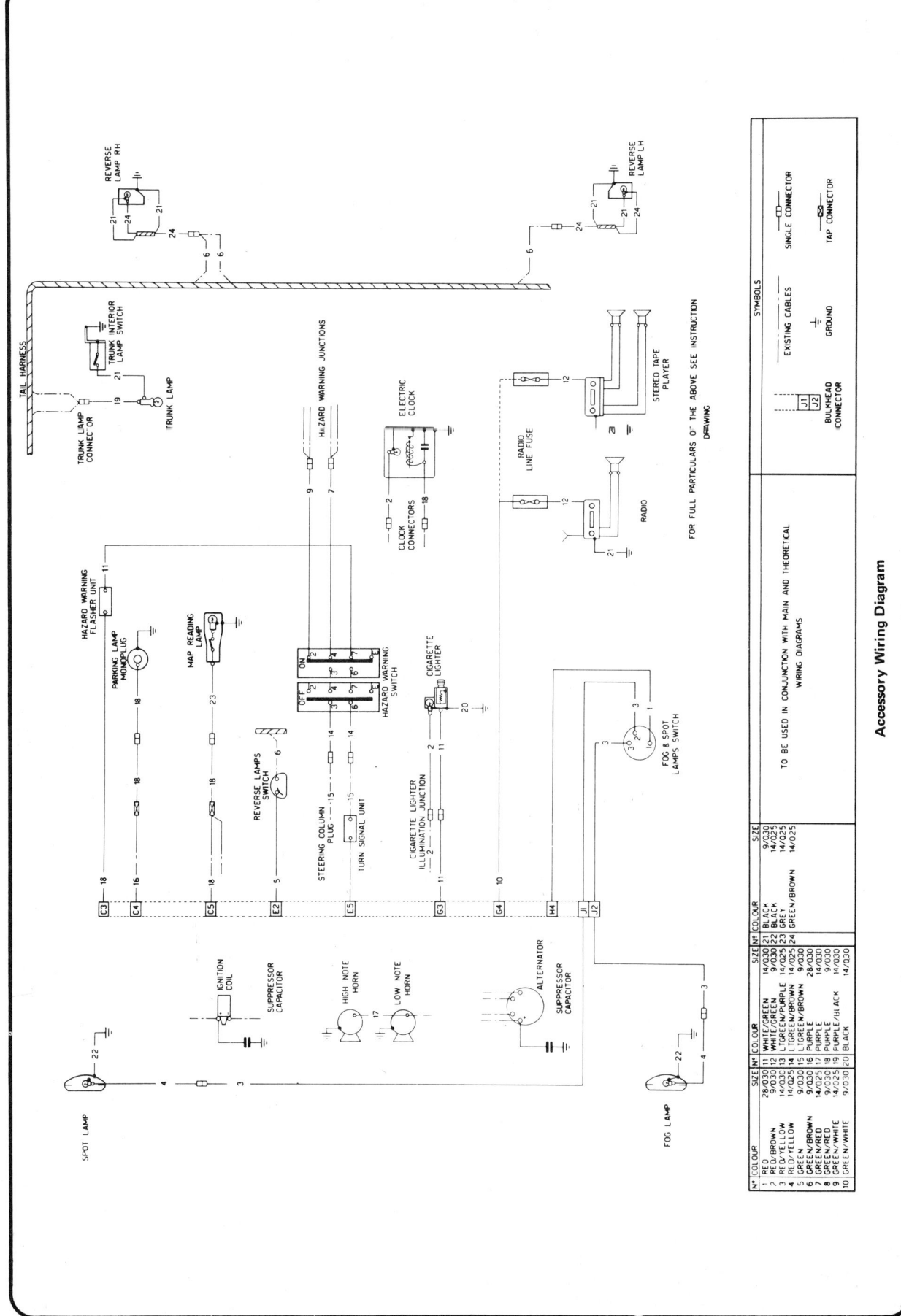

Accessory Wiring Diagram

Chapter 11 Suspension and steering

Contents

Specifications

Front suspension:

Type ... ... Independent, coil springs with short upper and long lower arm. Double acting telescopic shock absorbers and stabilizer bar.

Rear suspension:

Type ... ... Coil springs, with upper and lower arms, telescopic shock absorbers and Panhard rod. Rear stabilizer bar fitted to Victor SL and 4 x 4/90 models.

Steering:

Make	Cam gears or Burman	
Type	Rack and pinion	
Oil capacity	0.25 pint (0.17 litre)	
Rack diameter:		
Burman	0.979 - 0.980 in	(24.87 - 24.90 mm)
Cam gears	0.982 - 0.984 in	(24.95 - 25.00 mm)
Clearance in support bush	0.001 - 0.003 in	(0.03 - 0.08 mm)
Steering gear pre-load (max)	12 lb in (13.72 kg cm)	
Effort to move tie rods radially	2 - 4 lb (0.9 - 1.8 kg), to be applied at inner end of thread.	

Steering geometry :

Castor:
  Check ... ... * 15' negative to 1° 45' negative
  Reset ... ... † 45' negative ± 30'
Camber:
  Check ... ... * 45' positive to 45' negative
  Reset ... ... † Zero ± 45'
King pin inclination:
  Check ... ... * 7° to 9°
  Reset ... ... † 8° ± 45'
Front wheel alignment :
  Check ... ... 0.02 – 0.18 in (0.5 – 4.5 mm) toe-in at wheel rims
  Reset 0.10 ± 0.04 in (2.5 ± 1 mm) toe-in at wheel rims

* To be within 1° side for side
† To be within 45' side for side

Wheels and tyres:

Type ... ... Steel disc 4 or 5 stud fixing
Size:
  Victor ... ... 5J x 13

  VX 4/90 ... ... 6J x 14

Tyre size:
Victor saloon ... ...   6.405 x 13 4 ply
Victor estate ... ...   6.405 x 13 6 ply
VX 4/90 ... ...   185/70 HR - 14
Tyre pressures:
All models: Front ...   . 24 psi/1.69 kg.cm^2
Rear ...   . 28 psi/1.97 kg.cm^2

For heavily laden vehicles increase the rear tyre pressures
to: Cars ...   . 30 psi/2.11 kg.cm^2
Estates ...   . 33 psi/2.32 kg.cm^2
The figures given are for original equipment only. Consult the tyre manufacturer for different fitment.

Torque wrench settings:

Front suspension	lb ft	kg m
Upper arm fulcrum bolts	80	11.06
Lower arm fulcrum bolts	80	11.06
Axle upper mounting bolts	48	6.6
Axle upper mounting lower retaining bolt	45	6.22
Axle lower mounting bolts	38	5.26
Axle lower mounting retaining nuts	48	6.6
Upper ball joint retaining nuts	20	2.77
Stabilizer bar to link retaining nuts	11	1.53
Stabilizer link to lower arm retaining nuts	38	5.26
Stabilizer bar mounting bolts	38	5.26
Shock absorber upper mounting bolts	80	11.06
Shock absorber lower mounting bolts	95	13
Rear suspension		
Panhard rod to body mounting bolt	80	11.06
Panhard rod to axle retaining nut	38	5.26
Lower arm to axle mounting bolt	80	11.06
Lower arm to body mounting bolts	68	9.3
Upper arm to body mounting bolts	38	5.26
Upper arm to axle mounting bolts	45	6.22
Shock absorber lower mounting nuts	38	5.26
Steering		
Steering wheel nut	45	6.22
Steering column support bracket bolts	25	3.4
Steering column lower mounting nuts	9	1.2
Steering intermediate shaft to steering shaft nut	18	2.49
Flexible coupling to intermediate shaft and lower flange nuts	18	2.49
Flexible coupling cotter nut	7	1.0
Steering gear to crossmember nuts	35	4.8
Wheel nuts	48	6.6

1 General description

The component parts of the front suspension assembly are shown in Fig.11.1 and upon inspection it will be seen that one long and one short arm are attached at their inner ends to a crossmember. This is in turn bolted to the underbody side members. Located between the lower long arm and the crossmember is a coil spring in which is placed a double action telescopic shock absorber.

Ball joints are attached to the outer suspension arms and on these is carried the steering knuckle.

A stabilizer bar (anti-roll bar) is attached between the lower arms and the underbody.

To control excessive movement of the suspension arms a rubber bump stop is mounted on the upper arm and makes contact with the crossmember.

The front hubs are mounted on taper roller bearings located on the steering knuckle spindle.

Each rear suspension assembly incorporates upper and lower arms, coil spring, a double acting telescopic damper and a Panhard rod which controls lateral movement. Rubber bump stops are mounted onto the underbody side members and also at the centre of the rear floor panel. A rear stabilizer/anti-roll bar is fitted to all except the Victor de luxe model. It is located between the suspension upper arms.

The steering is rack and pinion of conventional design and the product of either of two manufacturers is fitted, namely Burman or Cam gears. These are identified by the manufacturers name cast on to the bottom of the gear housing. The assembly comprises a housing and rack and pinion and is supported in rubber mountings on the front of the axle crossmember. The rack is mounted in one end of the housing by a bush, and at the other by a spring loaded adjustable yoke which also maintains engagement with the pinion. The pinion is mounted between ball thrust bearings, the pre-loading of which is also adjustable. The inner ends of the steering tie rods are attached to the rack by adjustable ball joints.

The steering column is of the safety type. A lattice work section in the tube will collapse on impact and the shaft is telescopic, held in position by plastic injections for normal use. The steering column is mounted on brackets attached to the lower and upper dash panels.

A new type of steering column lock is fitted which makes it a two handed operation to remove the ignition key but - much more important - the risk of inadvertently locking the steering whilst in motion is eliminated.

2 Front hub bearings - removal and replacement

1 Chock the rear wheels, apply the handbrake, jack up the front of the car and support on firmly based axle stands. Remove the road wheel.

2 Refer to Chapter 9, Section 14, and remove the caliper assembly.

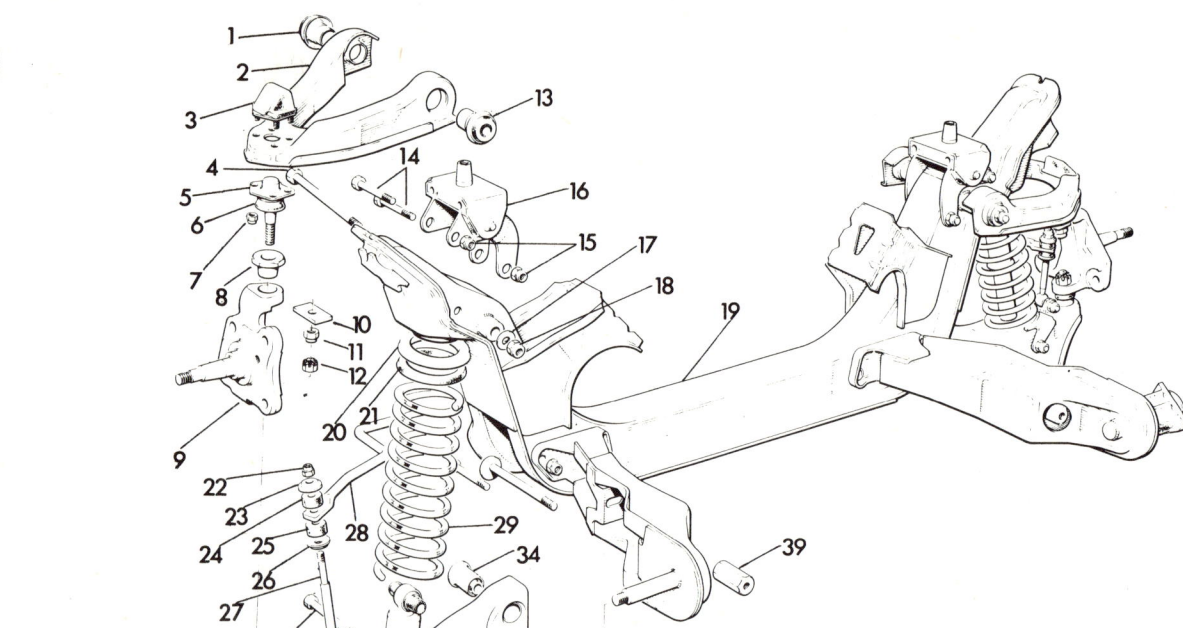

FIG. 11.1 FRONT SUSPENSION ASSEMBLY

1 Front bush	11 Nut	21 Rubber insert	31 Lower ball joint
2 Upper suspension arm	12 Castellated nut	22 Nut	32 Shock absorber
3 Rebound rubber	13 Rear bush	23 Shaped washer	33 Lower suspension arm
4 Fulcrum bolt	14 Bolts	24 Bush	34 Front bush
5 Upper ball joint seat	15 Nuts	25 Bush	35 Rear bush
6 Upper ball joint	16 Mounting	26 Shaped washer	36 Suspension mounting rubber
7 Nut	17 Plain washer	27 Link	37 Plain washer
8 Bush	18 Nut	28 Stabilizer bar	38 Nut
9 Swivel pin	19 Front axle	29 Spring	39 Special nut
10 Pad	20 Spring metal seat	30 Bolt	

3 Using a wide blade screwdriver ease off the hub grease cap.

4 Straighten the hub nut locking split pin and withdraw the split pin. Lift away the nut retainer. Undo and remove the nut and washers.

5 Withdraw the complete front hub assembly from the spindle. Recover the outer tapered bearing.

6. Upon reference to Fig.11.1 it will be seen that the two different types of hub and disc assemblies are used on Victor and VX4/90 models.

7 To separate the hub from the disc first ease the sheet metal shield from the inner end of the hub (Victor models). This prevents the ingress of water and mud.

8 Mark the relative position of the hub and disc. Undo and remove the four/five bolts securing the hub to the disc and separate the two parts.

9 From the back of the hub assembly carefully prise out the grease seal noting which way round it is fitted. Lift away the inner tapered bearing.

10 Carefully clean out the hub and wash the bearings with petrol making sure that no grease or oil is allowed to get onto the brake disc (if still fitted).

11 Using a soft metal drift carefully remove the inner and outer bearing cups.

12 Thoroughly examine the rollers, cages and cups for signs of

wear. If in doubt obtain new sets of bearings. Wear can be detected by running perfectly clean, lightly oiled bearings in their cups and feeling for traces of roughness. Blue discolouration indicates overheating, but brown discolouration will only be lubricant stain and is not to be taken as an adverse indication.

13 To fit new cups make sure they are the right way round and using metal tubes of suitable diameter carefully drift them into position.

14 Pack the cone and roller assembly with Castrol LM Grease working the grease well into the cage and rollers. NOTE: leave the hub and grease seal empty to allow for subsequent expansion of the grease.

15 To reassemble the hub, first fit the inner bearing and then gently tap the grease seal back into the hub. A new seal must always be used as during removal it will probably be damaged. The lip must face inwards to the hub.

16 To adjust the hub bearings tighten the nut using a box spanner and bar, whilst the road wheel is being turned (Fig.11.3). When the nut is tight stop the wheel rotating, slacken off the nut and then tighten hand tight using the box spanner. Finally assemble the nut retainer so that two of its slots are in alignment with the pin hole. Lock the nut with a new split pin.

17 Refit the brake caliper if this has not already been done.

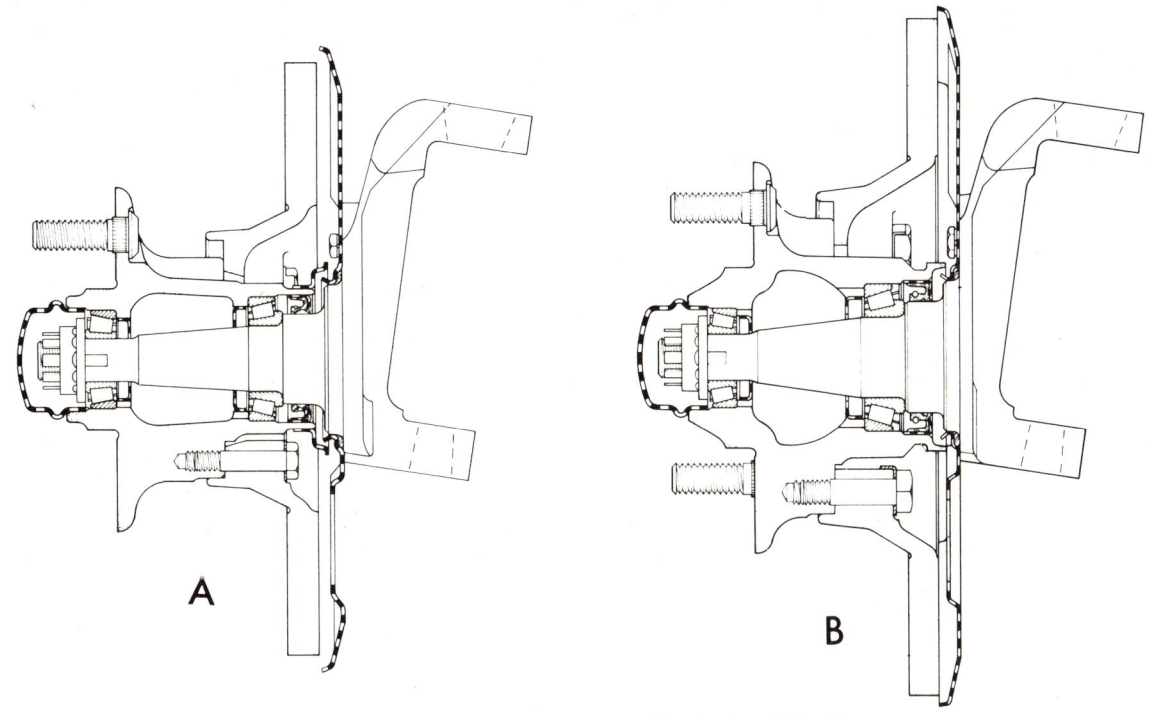

FIG. 11.2 CROSS SECTIONAL VIEW OF FRONT HUBS

A   Victor models
B   VX4/90 models

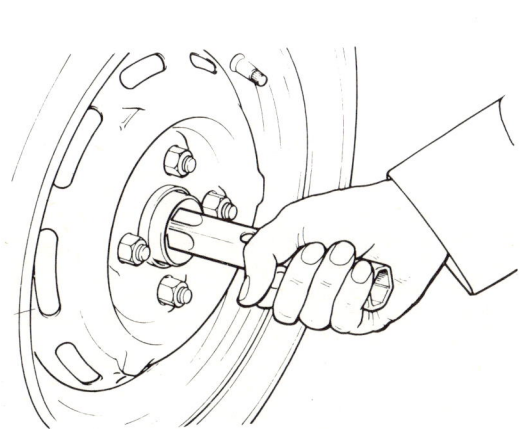

Fig. 11.3 Using box spanner to tighten hub bearing nut

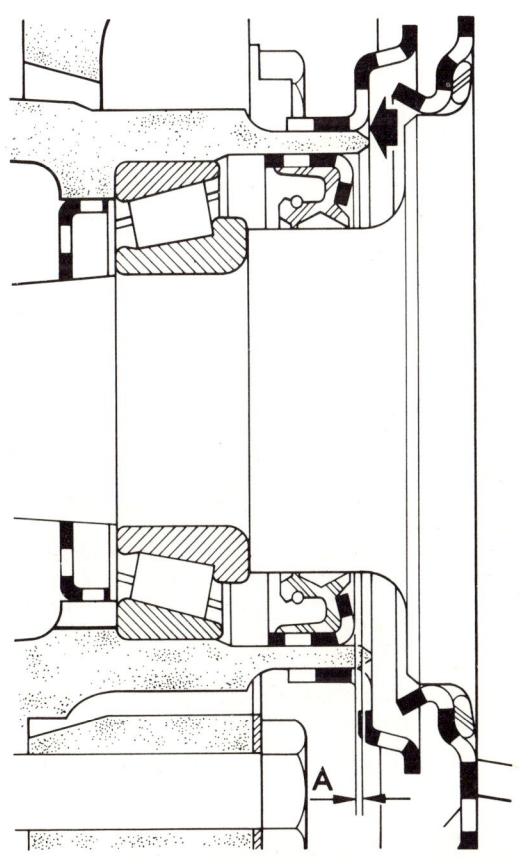

**FIG. 11.4 FRONT HUB GREASE SEAL ARRANGEMENT
(VICTOR MODELS)**

A   =   0.06 inch (1.5 mm)

3 Stabilizer bar - removal and replacement

1 Chock the rear wheels, jack up the front of the car and support on firmly based stands.
2 Undo and remove the two bolts and spring washers that secure the metal straps and insulator rubbers to the front underbody.
3 Undo and remove the self locking nuts and bushes that secure the ends of the stabilizer bar to the links. Lift away the stabilizer bar.
4 Refitting the stabilizer bar is the reverse sequence to removal. All attachments must be tightened to the specified torque wrench setting when the weight of the car is on the tyres.

4 Front shock absorber - removal and replacement

1 Removal of the shock absorbers is made easier with the special Vauxhall tool to compress the spring but is not essential.
2 Chock the rear wheels and jack up the front of the car. Place a support under the suspension lower arm and lower front of the car until the spring is partially compressed.
3 Undo and remove the upper and lower mounting self lock bolts and nuts and carefully tap out the two bolts. Lift away the shock absorber assembly.
4 The shock absorber mounting bushes may be removed separately if required.
5 Examine the shock absorber for signs of damage to the body, distorted piston rod or hydraulic leakage. If evident a new unit should be fitted.
6 To test for damping efficiency, hold the unit in the vertical position and gradually extend and contract the unit between its maximum and minimum limits ten times. It should be apparent that there is equal resistance in both directions of movement. If this is not so a new unit should be fitted. Always renew shock absorbers in pairs.
7 When refitting the shock absorber it will be found necessary for the front axle crossmember to support the weight of the car. This will ensure that the holes in the crossmember and engine mounting bracket are aligned so that the shock absorber upper mounting bolt may be inserted easily. Tighten the mounting bolts to a torque wrench setting of 80 lb ft (11.06 Kg m).

5 Front spring - removal and replacement

1 Before beginning work it is important that a Vauxhall spring compressor is to hand or a spring retainer is made up from three lengths of steel bar with the ends hooked over. See also paragraph 6 and Fig.11.8.
2 Chock the rear wheels, jack up the front of the car and support the body on firmly based stands. Remove the wheel.
3 Slacken the suspension arm fulcrum bolt nuts but do not completely remove yet.
4 Undo and remove the nut securing the stabilizer bar link to the bracket on the lower arm. Detach the link from the bracket.
5 Refer to Section 4, and remove the shock absorber as described in paragraphs 2 and 3. As the car is already on stands a jack may be used to take the weight of the suspension arm by compressing the coil spring slightly.
6 Raise the jack under the lower suspension arm until the coil spring is at least three quarters compressed and then fit the three lengths of steel bar so that eight spring coils are kept compressed. If this condition is not achieved it will not be possible to withdraw the spring.
7 Undo and remove the nut securing the lower arm ball joint to the steering knuckle. Using a universal ball joint separator, detach the ball joint from the steering knuckle.
8 Using a piece of wire tie the upper suspension arm up so that it is on the bump stop seat on the front axle.
9 Carefully lower the jack under the lower suspension arm and lift away the coil spring assembly. Recover the rubber insulation

from the top end of the coil spring.
10 If a new coil spring is to be fitted it will need to be compressed and retained before it can be fitted. Use a long high tensile steel bolt and end pads to compress the spring or take it, together with the old one, to the local Vauxhall garage and have them transfer the steel bars to the new spring using a special compressor.
11 Refitting the coil spring is the reverse sequence to removal, but the following additional points should be noted:
a) If one coil spring is to be renewed always renew the other one as well as the apparently satisfactory one will probably have settled slightly ' over a period of time.
b) Make sure that the rubber insulator is in good condition and that it is assembled to the top end of the spring before lining up the spring onto the lower arm seating.
c) Before reconnecting the ball joint to the steering knuckle always wipe away all traces of grease from the tapers.
d) The suspension arm fulcrum bolt nuts must be tightened to the recommended torque wrench setting when the weight of the car is on the tyres.

6 Steering arm - removal and replacement

1 Chock the rear wheels, jack up the front of the car and support on firmly based stands.
2 Undo and remove the tie rod ball joint retaining nut and then using a universal ball joint separator detach the ball joint from the steering arm.
3 Refer to Chapter 9 and detach the caliper from the steering knuckle. It is not necessary to disconnect the hose but to hang the caliper out of the way on a piece of string or wire.
4 Refer to Section 2 and remove the front hub assembly.
5 Undo and remove the two bolts that secure the steering arm to the steering knuckle. Note that the longer bolt is rearmost.
6 Refitting the steering arm is the reverse sequence to removal but the following additional points should be noted:
a) Always use new steering arm retaining bolts as they have a nylon insert in the threads.
b) Adjust the front hub bearings as described in Section 2.
c) Before reconnecting the ball joint make sure that all traces of grease have been removed from the tapers.
d) Check the front wheel alignment Further information will be found in Section 21.

7 Steering knuckle - removal and replacement

1 Chock the rear wheels, jack up the front of the car and support on firmly based stands located under the body.
2 Place a jack under the lower suspension arm and partially compress the spring.
3 Undo and remove the nut securing the steering arm ball joint and then with a universal ball joint separator detach the ball joint from the steering arm.
4 Refer to Chapter 9 and detach the flexible hose from the caliper.
5 Undo and remove the lower ball joint to knuckle securing nut and using a universal ball joint separator detach the lower ball joint from the knuckle.
6 Before disconnecting the upper suspension arm from the knuckle mark the knuckle adjacent to the notch on the camber eccentric adjuster. This will eliminate the need to reset the camber angle after reassembly (Fig.11.9) .
7 Undo and remove the nut and plate securing the ball joint to the upper suspension arm and then disconnect the steering knuckle from the ball joint by striking with a hammer.
hammer.
8 Refitting the steering knuckle is the reverse sequence to removal but the following additional points should be noted:
a) Before reconnecting any ball joint make sure that all traces of grease have been removed from the tapers.
b) Always use a new sealing ring between the shield and knuckle mating faces.

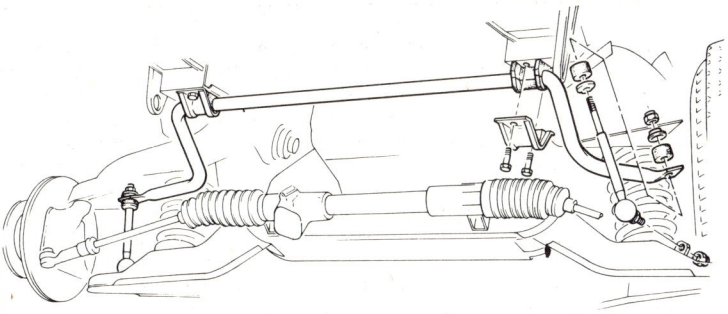

Fig. 11.5 Front suspension stabilizer bar

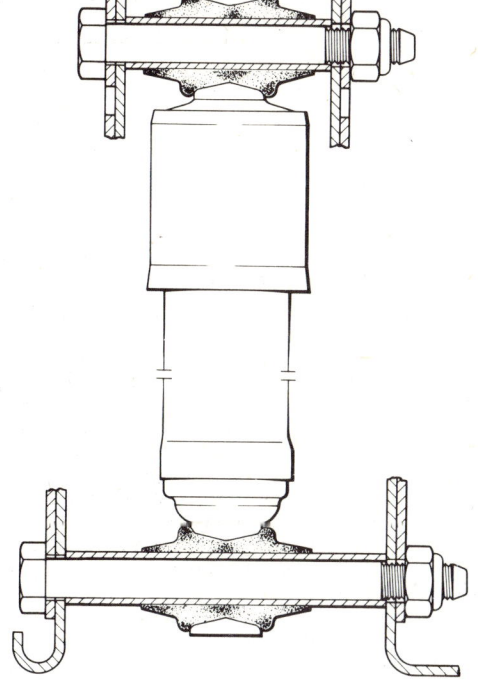

Fig. 11.6 Front suspension shock absorber and mountings

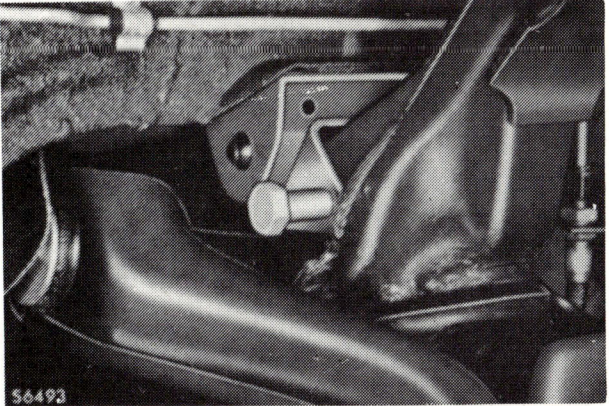

Fig. 11.7 Front shock absorber upper mounting attachment

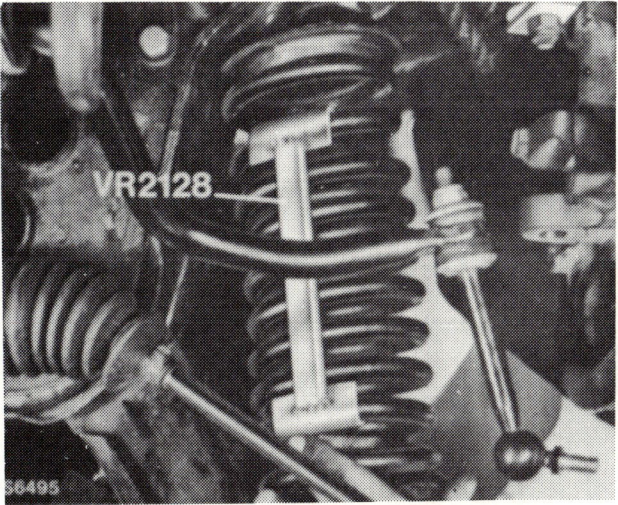

Fig. 11.8 Front suspension coil spring retainer

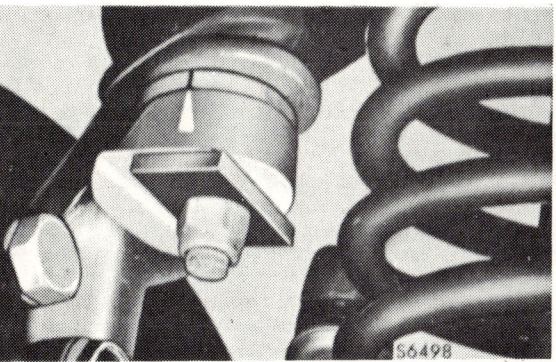

Fig. 11.9 Camber eccentric adjuster mark

c) If a new knuckle is fitted the steering geometry must be checked and adjusted as necessary. Reset the camber eccentric adjuster to its original position as noted during dismantling.

8 Suspension arm ball joints - removal and replacement

To check for wear in the ball joints jack up the front of the car and support under the lower suspension arms. Rock the wheel whilst holding the upper and lower joints in turn. If any slackness of the ball is felt in its seating the joint as a whole must be renewed. Also if the rubber boot has split or chafed the joint must be renewed as the rubber boot is not serviced separately.
1 Refer to Section 7 and remove the steering knuckle.
2 To remove the upper ball joint undo and remove the nuts that secure the bump stop and ball joint to the upper suspension arm. Lift away the upper ball joint assembly (Fig.11.11).
3 To remove the lower ball joint requires the use of some metal tubes, thick washers and a high tensile steel nut and bolt to draw out the ball joint from the lower suspension arm. It is splined externally so that when initially pressed into the lower suspension arm corresponding splines are broached in the reinforcing ring welded into the suspension arm aperture.
4 Refitting the ball joints is the reverse sequence to removal but the following additional points should be noted:-
a) Make sure that the notch in the eccentric adjuster coincides with the mark made on the steering knuckle (Fig.11.9).
b) Check that there is no distortion of the rubber boot.
c) The suspension upper arm fulcrum bolt nut must be tightened to the specified torque wrench with the weight of the car on the tyres.
d) If new ball joints have been fitted always check the steering geometry. Further information will be found in Section 21.

9 Suspension lower arm (front) - removal and replacement

1 Refer to Section 5 and remove the front spring assembly.
2 Fully remove the suspension arm fulcrum bolt nuts and carefully tap through the two bolts. To facilitate removal of the front bolt from the left hand suspension arm turn the steering to the right hand lock and vice versa for the right hand suspension arm.
3 It is possible to fit new rubber bushes using a press or vice and suitable diameter tubes. However, if the suspension arm is damaged a new one may be obtained and this will be fitted with bushes and ball joint.
4 Refitting the suspension lower arm is the reverse sequence to removal, but the following additional points should be noted:-
a) Make sure that the ball pin and steering knuckle tapers are clear and free of grease.
b) Tighten the upper and lower fulcrum bolt nuts to the specified torque wrench setting when the weight of the car is on the tyres.
c) Check and adjust the steering geometry. Further information will be found in Section 21.

10 Suspension upper arm (front)- removal and replacement

To gain access to the suspension upper arm the front axle must be removed. Because of the work involved it is recommended that the opportunity be taken to overhaul the complete axle assembly. Without the correct coil spring compressor the coil springs should be removed with the axle still on the car as described in Section 5, and then proceed as follows:
1 Refer to Section 7 and detach the steering knuckle from the suspension upper arm.
2 Undo and remove the nut that secures the suspension upper arm fulcrum bolt and withdraw the bolt. Lift away the plain washers and then the suspension upper arm.
3 If it is necessary to remove the ball joint undo and remove the four nuts that secure the bump stop and ball joint to the

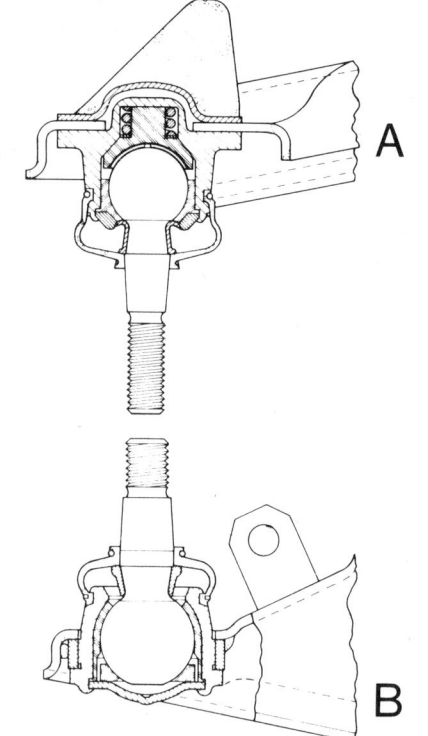

FIG. 11.10 SUSPENSION ARM BALL JOINTS

A   Upper
B   Lower

Fig. 11.11 Upper ball joint mounting to suspension arm

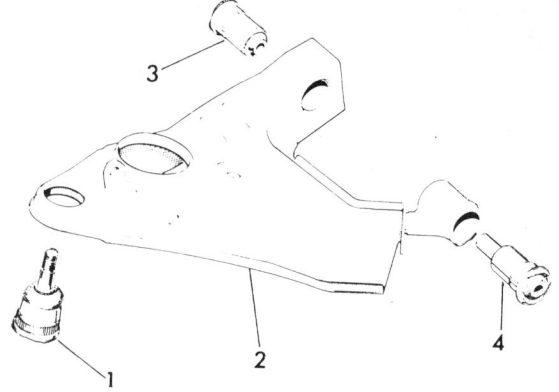

FIG. 11.12 FRONT SUSPENSION LOWER ARM

1 Lower ball joint assembly   3 Front bush
2 Lower arm   4 Rear bush

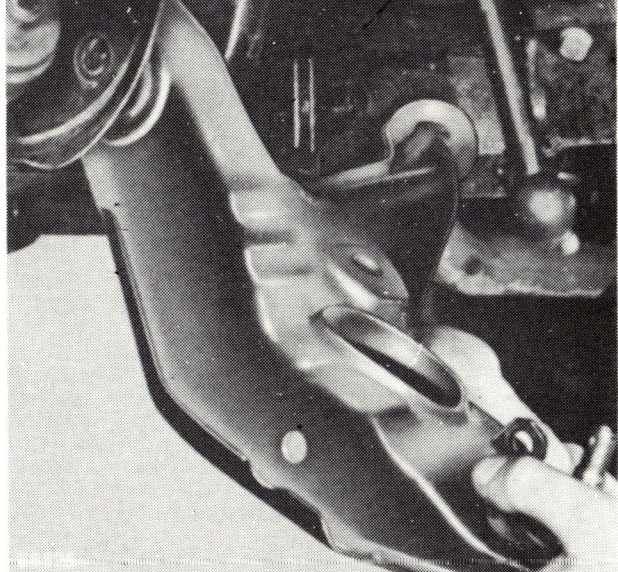

Fig. 11.13 Lifting away front suspension lower arm

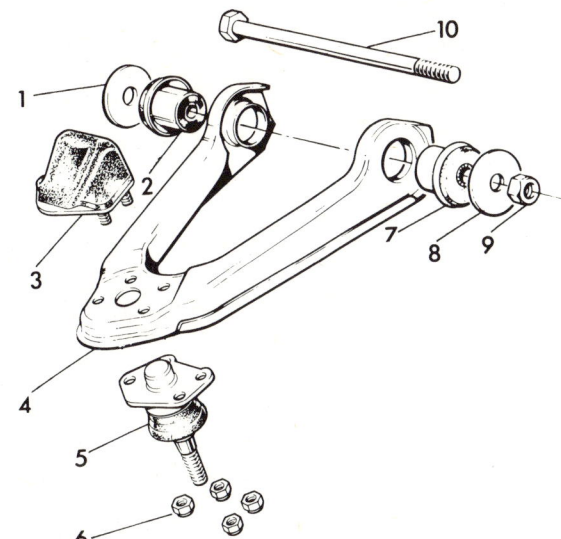

FIG. 11.14 FRONT SUSPENSION UPPER ARM

1	Plain washer - bolt head end	6	Balljoint securing nuts
2	Front bush	7	Rear bush
3	Rebound rubber	8	Plain washer - nut end
4	Upper rubber	9	Nut
5	Upper ball joint	10	Fulcrum bolt

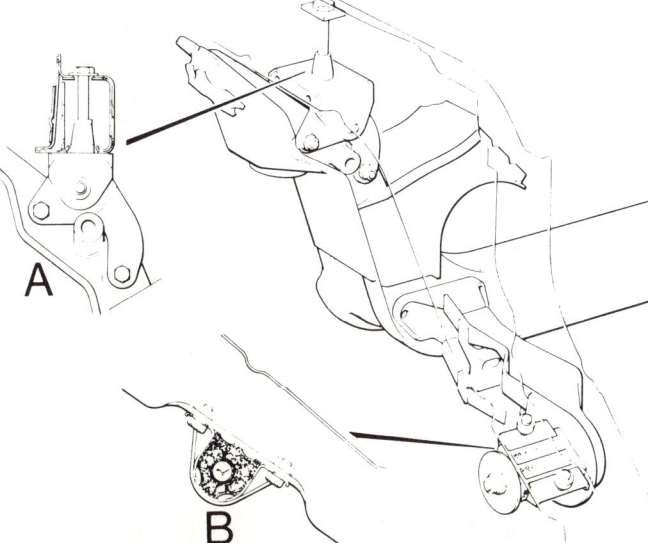

FIG. 11.15 FRONT AXLE MOUNTINGS

A	Upper mounting
B	Lower mounting

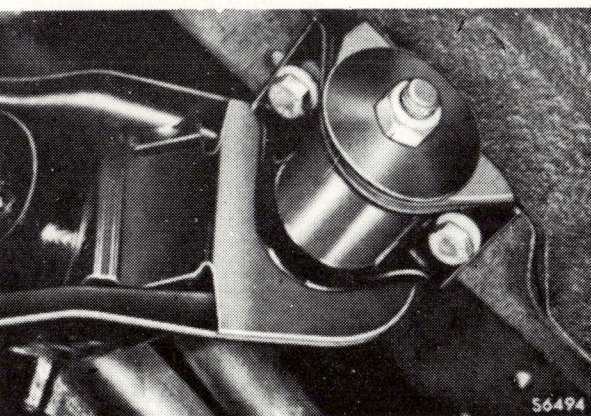

Fig. 11.16 Front axle lower mounting

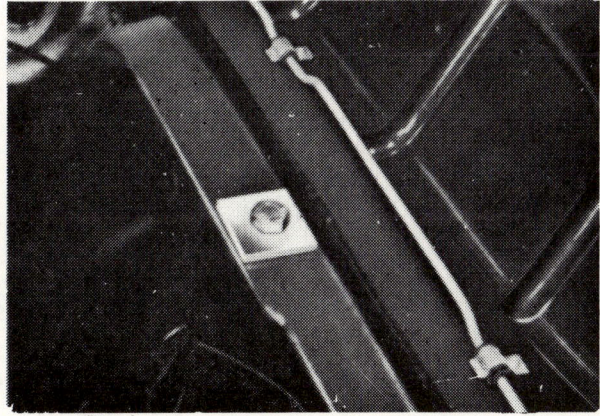

Fig. 11.17 Axle mounting to side member

upper arm and lift away the ball joint.

4 To renew the bushes use a selection of tubes, washers and a high tensile steel nut and bolt to draw out the old bush and insert a new one.

5 Refitting the upper suspension arm is the reverse sequence to removal. Tighten the fulcrum bolt nut to the specified torque wrench setting when the weight of the car is on the tyres.

11 Front axle - removal, inspection and replacement

1 Refer to Section 25 and remove the steering intermediate shaft and coupling to avoid damage to the plastic injections in the steering shaft.

2 Chock the rear wheels, jack up the front of the car and support the body on firmly based stands. Remove the wheels.

3 Using suitable blocks support the weight of the engine under the sump, and also the front axle assembly.

4 Undo and remove the nut and spring washer that secures each engine mounting to the axle.

5 Next undo and remove the bolts and packing washers that secure the axle upper mountings to the side members. These are accessible from within the engine compartment (Fig.11.17).

6 Detach the brake hydraulic pipes as described in Chapter 9.

7 Lower the front axle assembly and draw from under the car.

8 If the car has been in an accident or violently 'kerbed' the front axle should be checked at the locations shown in Fig.11.18. Do not attempt to straighten the axle if bent but always renew.

9 Refitting the front axle is the reverse sequence to removal but the following additional points should be noted:

a) Tighten the suspension arm fulcrum bolt nuts to the specified torque wrench setting when the weight of the car is on the tyres.

b) Check and adjust the steering geometry as necessary. Further information will be found in Section 21.

12 Panhard rod - removal and replacement

1 Chock the front wheels, jack up the rear of the car and support the body on firmly based axle stands.

2 Jack up the axle until the Panhard rod is horizontal.

3 Undo and remove the securing nut and bolt from each end of the Panhard rod and lift away the rod (Fig.11.19)

4 Note that both ends of the rod are rubber bushed. The end which is secured to the underbody also has an internal sleeve.

5 The bushes may be renewed using a vice and suitable diameter tubes. Always dip the new bushes in a concentrated soap solution before refitting.

6 Refitting the Panhard rod is the reverse sequence to removal. Tighten the mounting nuts and bolt to the specified torque wrench setting.

13 Rear shock absorber - removal and replacement

1 Chock the front wheels, jack up the rear of the car and support the axle on firmly based axle stands.

2 **Saloon models.** Remove the plastic cup from the shock absorber upper mounting located in the luggage compartment. Undo and remove the securing nut, shaped washer, rubber bush and second shaped washer.

3 **Estate models.** Remove the luggage compartment floor panel to give access to the upper mounting. For this it is necessary to remove the fourteen screws that secure the edge of the floor carpet to enable the carpet to be pulled back to expose the six floor retaining screws and washers. Remove the mounting nut, washers and rubber bush in the order described in paragraph 2.

4 **Saloon models.** Undo and remove the lower mounting nut and bolt and lift away the shock absorber. Note that the lower

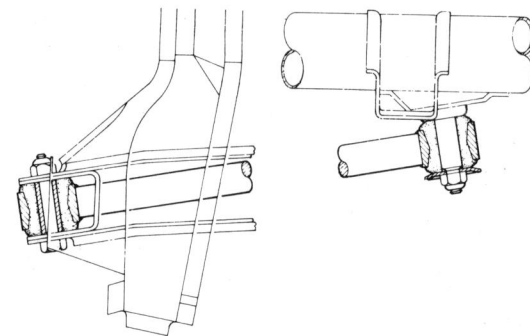

Fig. 11.19 Panhard rod attachments

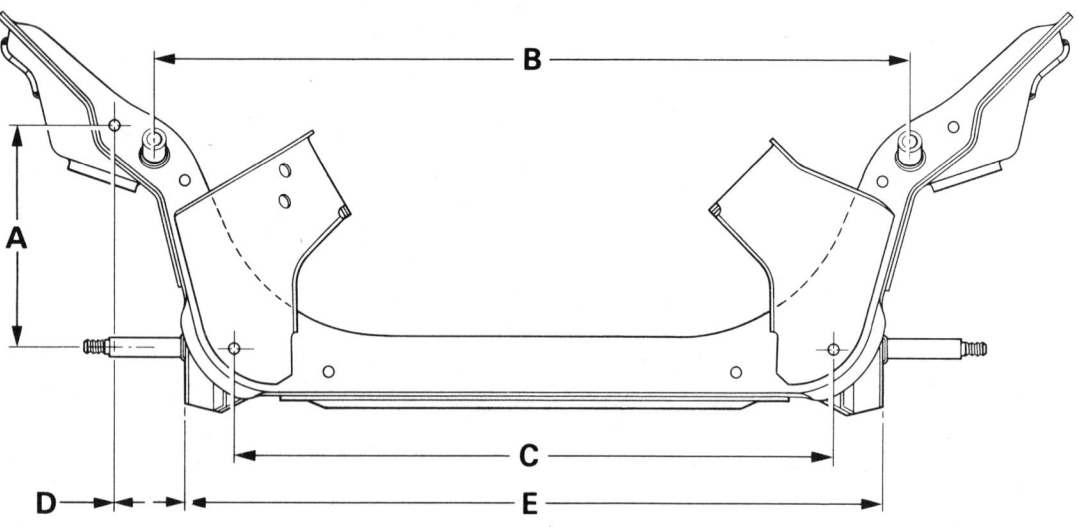

FIG. 11.18 FRONT AXLE - MAJOR DIMENSIONS

A 8.90 inch (226 mm)   C 24.90 inch (632 mm)
B 31.50 inch (800 mm)   D 5.00 inch (127 mm)
          E 29.00 inch (738 mm)

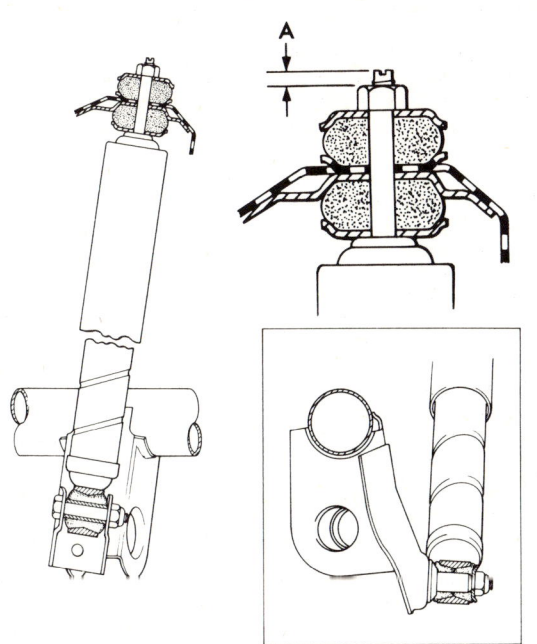

Fig. 11.21 Rear shock absorber upper mounting

Fig. 11.20 Rear shock absorber and mountings. Upper insert
A = 0.040 inch (10 mm)

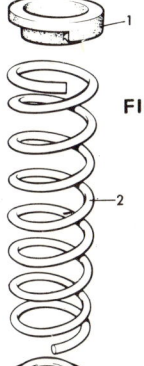

FIG. 11.22 REAR SPRING AND SEATS

1 Upper seat
2 Coil spring
3 Lower seat

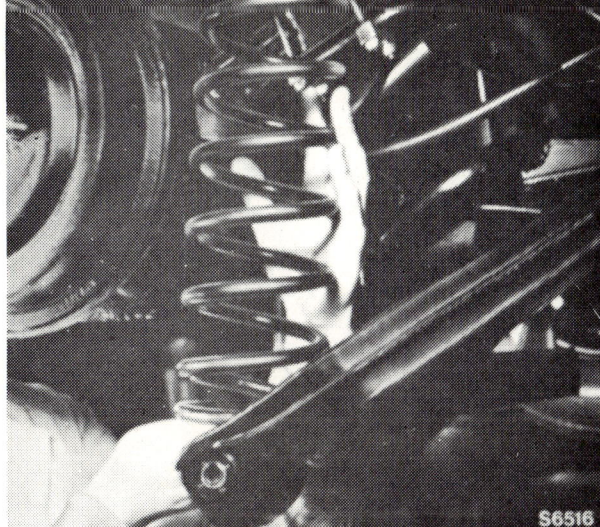

Fig. 11.23 Lifting away rear suspension spring

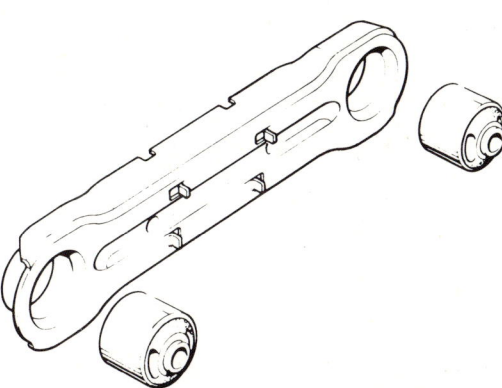

Fig. 11.24 Rear suspension upper arm and bushes

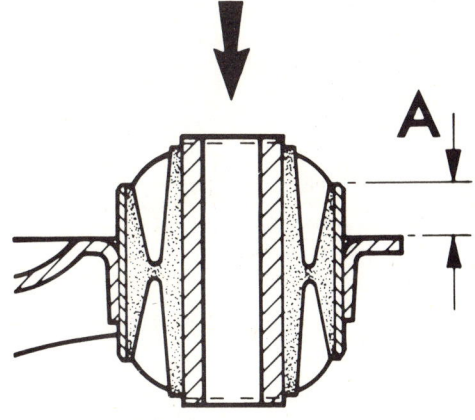

**FIG. 11.25 CORRECT FITMENT OF REAR SUSPENSION
UPPER ARM BUSH**

A = 0.36 inch (9.0 mm)

mounting comprises a single bush and sleeve.

5 **Estate models.** Undo and remove the lower mounting nut and ease the shock absorber from the stud. Lift away the shock absorber. Note that the lower mounting comprises two tapered rubber bushes and washer.

6 Examine the shock absorber for signs of damage to the body, distorted piston rod or hydraulic leakage. If evident, a new unit should be fitted.

7 To test for damping efficiency, hold the unit in the vertical position and gradually extend and contract the unit between its maximum and minimum limit ten times. It should be apparent that there is equal resistance in both directions of movement. If this is not so, a new unit should be fitted. Always renew shock absorbers in pairs.

8 Refitting the shock absorber is the reverse sequence to removal. Make sure that the upper mounting bushes and shaped washers are located correctly. Tighten the upper mounting nuts until the top of the stud protrudes by 0.040 inch (10 mm), (Fig.11.20)

14 Rear spring - removal and replacement

1 Chock the front wheels, jack up the rear of the car and support the body on firmly based stands. Support the axle using a garage hydraulic jack. Remove the road wheels.

2 Refer to Section 13, and remove the shock absorber mounting.

3 Slacken the lower arm mounting bolt nuts and carefully lower the axle as far as possible without straining the brake flexible hydraulic hose. This will relieve the spring load.

4 Undo and remove the lower arm rear mounting bolt and swing down the lower arm. Lift away the spring and its rubber seatings.

5 Before refitting the spring make sure that the spring seat is correctly positioned in the lower arm. Position the upper spring seat in the spring so that the step in the seat is in contact with the end of the coil spring.

6 If it is found necessary to renew one spring then the spring on the other side must also be renewed as it will have settled slightly over a period of time.

15 Rear stabilizer bar - removal and replacement

1 Chock the front wheels, jack up the rear of the car and support on firmly based axle stands.

2 Undo and remove the four nuts that secure the 'U' bolts to the upper arms. Lift away the blocks, 'U' bolts and reinforcing plate located on the outer side of each upper arm.

3 Refitting is the reverse sequence to removal.

16 Suspension upper arm (rear) - removal and replacement

1 Refer to Section 15 and remove the stabilizer bar (if fitted).

2 Mark one end of the arm before removal to ensure correct refitting.

3 Undo and remove the fulcrum nuts and bolts and lift away the suspension arm.

4 The bushes may be removed using a bench vice and suitable diameter tubes. When refitting lubricate with a concentrated soap solution and insert until the outer sleeve reaches the position 'A' (Fig.11.25)

5 If a new upper arm has been obtained, refer to Fig.11.xx to ensure it is fitted the right way round. The arm must be fitted with the open side towards the outside of the car.

6 Before fully tightening the mounting nuts and bolts allow the weight of the car to rest on the tyres.

17 Suspension lower arm (rear) - removal and replacement

1 Refer to Section 14 and remove the rear spring.

2 Undo and remove the fulcrum nut and bolt and lift away the lower suspension arm.

3 The front bush may be removed using a bench vice and suitable diameter tubes. When refitting lubricate the outer sleeve with a little castor oil and then insert so that the flange on the outer sleeve is in contact with the arm.

4 To remove the rear bush use suitable diameter tubes, thick washers, a high tensile steel bolt and washer to draw out the bush. When refitting lubricate the outer sleeve with a little castor oil and draw the bush into position so that its flange contacts the inner side of the bracket on the axle tube.

5 Before fully tightening the mounting nuts and bolts allow the weight of the car to rest on the tyres.

18 Steering mechanism - inspection

1 The steering mechanism is uncomplicated and easy to check. As the statutory test for vehicles more than three years old pays. particular attention to it, the owner can save himself a lot of trouble by regular examination, apart from, of course, keeping check on his own safety.

2 Assuming that the suspension joints and bushes and front wheel bearings have been checked and found in order the steering check involves tracing the amount of lost motion between the rim of steering wheel and the road wheels. If the rim of the steering wheel can be moved more than 1 to 2 inches at its periphery with no sign of movement at either or both of the front wheels it may be assumed that there is wear at some point. If there are signs of lost motion, jack up the car at the front and support it under the front crossmember so that both wheels hang free.

3 Grip each wheel in turn and rock it in the direction it would move when steering. It will be possible to feel any play. Check first for any sign of lateral play in the ball joints which connect the tie rods from the steering gear to the steering arms on the wheel hubs. This is the more common area for wear to occur and if any is apparent the ball joints must be renewed. The joints are spring loaded up and down so they can move in this plane, but not without considerable pressure. If the socket moves easily then the joint needs renewal.

4 Finally, if play still exists it must be in the steering gear itself. This is more serious (and expensive). If either of the rubber boots at each end of the gear housing is damaged, resulting in loss of oil from the unit then various bearings and teeth on the rack and pinion may have been severely worn. In such cases renewal of the complete steering gear assembly may be necessary. Certainly adjustments will be required.

19 Steering gear - examination, adjustment, removal and replacement

1 Assuming that all ball joints and front wheel bearings are in order, it may be necessary to remove and replace, or renovate, the steering gear if there is excessive play between the steering shaft and the steering tie-rods. This can be checked by gripping the inner end of both the rods in turn near the rubber boot, and getting someone to rock the steering wheel. If the wheel moves more than 0.625 of a revolution (11¼% in either direction) without moving the steering tie rod, then the wear is sufficient to justify overhaul. If the rubber boots have leaked oil they will also need renewal, and, in order to do this and effectively refill the unit with the proper oil, it is easiest in the long run to remove the assembly from the car.

2 To remove the steering gear from the car first disconnect the lower half of the flexible coupling flange from the pinion shaft by extracting the cotter pin from the flange. This item can be a very tight fit and may call for an extraction tool or some form of

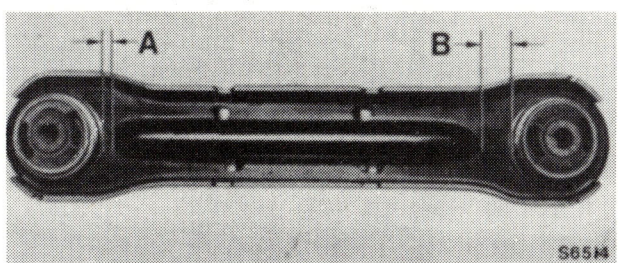

FIG. 11.26 REAR SUSPENSION UPPER ARM FITTING

A   Front end
B   Rear end

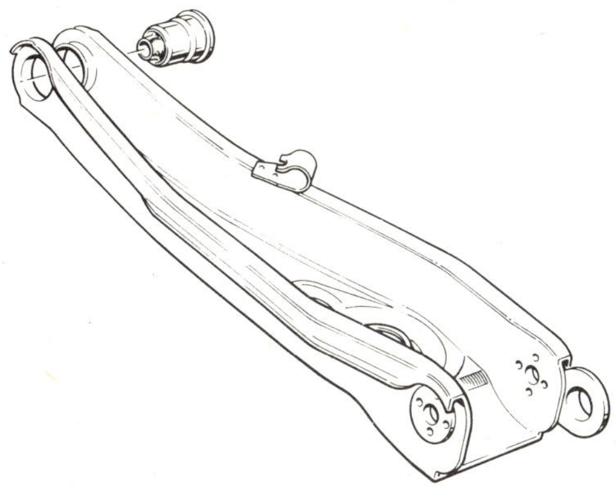

Fig. 11.27 Rear suspension lower arm

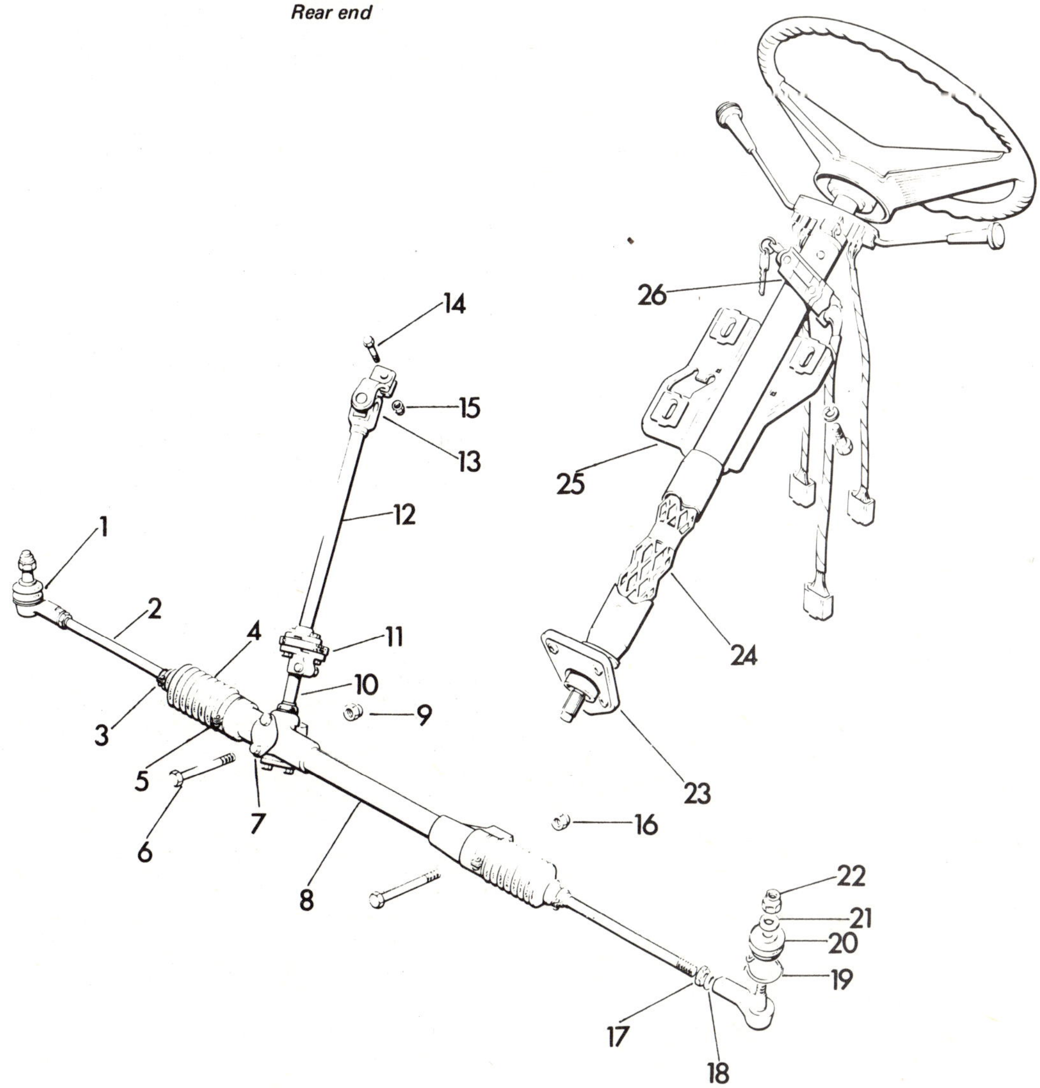

FIG. 11.28 STEERING SYSTEM LAYOUT

1 Ball joint	7 End cover	13 Upper coupling	20 Boot
2 Track rod	8 Rack body	14 Bolt	21 Retainer
3 Clip	9 Nut	15 Nut	22 Nut
4 Gaiter	10 Pinion	16 Nut	23 Lower retaining bracket
5 Clip	11 Lower coupling	17 Locknut	24 Collapsible shaft
6 Securing bolt	12 Intermediate shaft	18 Shakeproof washer	25 Upper retaining bracket
		19 Circlip	26 Steering lock

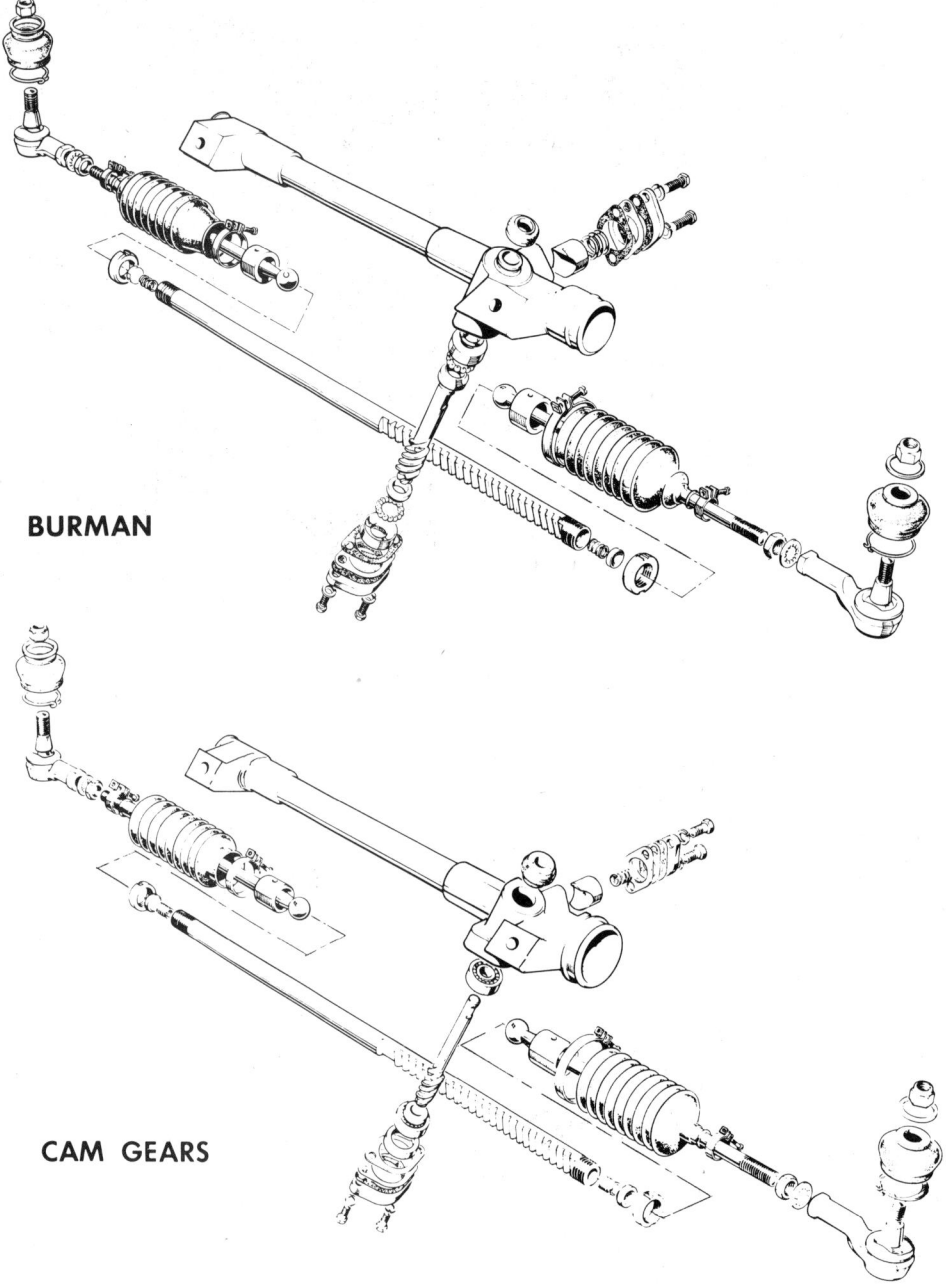

BURMAN

CAM GEARS

Fig. 11.29 Two types of steering assembly fitted

'G' clamp. Then disconnect both tie rod outer ball joints from the steering arms as described in Section 6. The three mounting bolts holding the assembly to the front crossmember may then be removed and the unit taken off. Take care of the washers and shims behind each bolt.

3 If it is necessary to replace only the rubber boots and refill the assembly with lubricant remove both outer ball joints from the tie rods together with the locknuts, having noted their original position carefully. Slacken off the boot retaining clips noting their position in relation to the assembly housing. If the steering arms are dirty, clean them thoroughly and slide off the old boots.

4 Refit the clips to new boots and slide them onto the rods. Tighten the clips in position on one boot only. Stand the unit on end, refill the housing with 0.25 pint (0.14 litre).

Castrol Hypoy 90 - no more - and then refit the other boot and lighten the chips

5 It is possible to alleviate some of the play in the gear (between rack and pinion) by checking that the yoke pre-load is correct.

6 Remove the yoke cover plate and remove the shims and spring followed by the yoke.

7 Replace the yoke and cover without the spring or any shims and lightly tighten the bolts.

8 Measure the gap between the cover and the housing with a feeler gauge (Fig.11.31). The thickness of the shims should be the gap measurement plus 0.0005 - 0.0030 inch (0.0127 - 0.0762 mm) on Burman units or plus 0.0005 - 0.0060 inch (0.0127 - 0.1524 mm) on Cam Gear units. Make up the shim packs accordingly. Note that on Cam gears only one gasket is used between

FIG. 11.30 STEERING ASSEMBLY IDENTIFICATION

Top   Burman
Bottom   Cam Gears

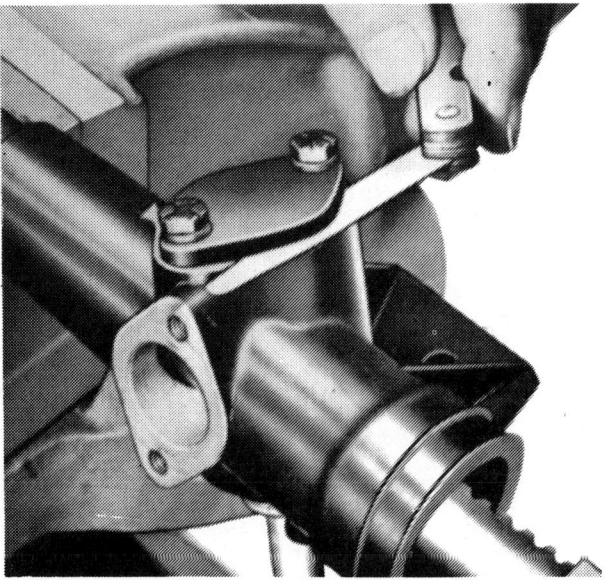

Fig. 11.31 Measurement of gap between cover and housing

Fig. 11.32 Measurement of pinion turning torque

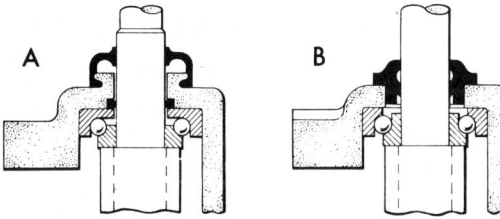

FIG. 11.33 PINION OIL SEAL ARRANGEMENT

A   Burman
B   Cam Gear

the shim pack and the cover whereas on Burman units there is a gasket on each side of every shim. Gasket thickness must be included in the total shim pack dimensions. Adjust the shim required to give a turning torque on the pinion of 12 lb in (13.72 Kg cm) (Fig.11.32).

9 Similarly, any sign of end float and slackness in the pinion shaft may be taken up by moving the cover opposite the pinion extension and reducing the thickness of the shims behind the cover accordingly. In this case the shims should be 0.001 - 0.005 in (0.0254 - 0.127 mm) LESS than the measured clearance between the cover and housing. The same remarks as regard gaskets apply.

10 It must be emphasised that the adjustments mentioned in the previous paragraphs are not sufficient to compensate for extreme wear. Before making them therefore, it must be decided wether the wear apparent is beyond adjustment, or sufficient to warrent adjustment anyway.

11 Any play in the tie rod INNER ball joints may be adjusted but involves drilling and repinning the joint and this calls for precision work.

12 Replacement of the assembly is a reversal of the procedure as described in paragraph 2. Make sure the assembly is centralised

Fig. 11.34 Steering joint pin

on the steering lock before attaching the pinion shaft to the steering column. Due to some problems of distortion in the steering gear casing later models are fitted with special washers on the outer mounting bolts between the housing and front axle. The centre point is then shimmed between casing and axle to take up any clearance. The two outer bolts are then tightened to 19 lb ft (2.53 Kg m) the centre bolt, last, to 9 lb ft (2.1 Kg m).
13 The front wheel toe in should then be checked with proper equipment.

20 Steering tie rods outer half joints - removal and replacement

1 The removal of the ball joints is necessary if they are to be renewed, or if the rubber boots on the steering gear are being renewed.
2 It is not necessary to jack the car up but the increase in height above ground level may make it more convenient to do so.
3 Slacken the self locking nut, completely remove it to clear the threads, and replace it after oiling them until the head of the nut is level with the end of the stud. This will protect the threads in subsequent operations if the same joint is being replaced.
4 If a claw clamp is being used to 'break' the taper of the joint pin from the steering arm, the joint may be disconnected without further ado.
5 If no claw clamp is available and it is necessary to strike the pin out, it is essential to provide a really firm support under the steering arm first. A firm tap with a normal weight hammer is all that is then necessary to move the pin out of the steering arm. Another way is to strike one side of the arm whilst holding the head of another hammer against the opposite side. This tends to 'squeeze' the taper pin out.
6 If the nut now turns the pin when trying to remove it, (despite the precaution taken in paragraph 3) jam the pin back in to the arm with the jack to hold it whilst the nut is removed. If difficulty is experienced with a joint being renewed then cut it off.
7 Once the ball joint is clear, slacken the locknut on the rod but leave it at its original position. The joint may then be removed and a new one fitted by screwing it up as far as the locknut. The pin should point upwards and then be fitted into the steering arm.
8 As the nut is self locking it will be necessary to prevent the pin turning whilst tightening it. This can be done by putting a jack under the joint so that the weight of the wheel rests on the taper.
9 Tighten the locknut on the tie rod.
10 It is advisable to have the front wheel alignment checked as soon as possible.

21 Steering geometry - checking and adjustment

1 Unless the front axle and suspension has been damaged the castor angle, camber angle and steering pivot angles will not alter, provided, of course, that the suspension ball joints and wishbones fulcrum pin bushes are not worn in any way.
2 The toe in of the front wheels is a measurement which may vary more frequently and could pass unnoticed, if, for example, a steering tie rod was bent. When fitting new tie rod ball joints, for example, it will always be necessary to reset the toe in.
3 Indications of incorrect wheel alignment (toe in) are uneven tyre wear on the front tyres and erratic steering particularly when turning. To check toe in accurately needs optical aligning equipment, so get a garage to do it. Ensure that they examine the tie rod for straightness and all ball joints and wheel bearings at the same time, if you have not done so yourself.

22 Steering wheel - removal and replacement

1 The steering wheel is located on splines to the column shaft and secured by a nut.
2 First remove the centre pad by undoing the two screws on the underside of the spoke.
3 Undo the nut with a tubular spanner and then mark the relative position of the wheel to the shaft by making two marks with a centre punch. Then pull the wheel off.
4 The hub incorporates the direction indicator cancelling sleeve which must be prised out if it is being transferred to a new wheel.
5 Replacement is a straightforward reverseal of the removal procedure, but make sure that the cancelling sleeve is replaced correctly with the tags in the proper holes (Fig.11.35).
6 If the wheel and shaft were not marked then set the road wheels straight ahead and replace the wheel with main spoke horizontal and dividing spoke pointing down. The combined switch and horn push should not be at a left or right turn position when this is done.
7 Tighten the steering wheel retaining nut to a torque wrench setting of 45 lb ft (6.22 Kg m).

23 Steering column canopy - removal and replacement

The steering column canopy comprises two halves which are held together by self tapping screws. The lower half of the canopy is secured to the steering column by three screws located as shown in Fig.11.35 (arrowed).

The canopy cannot be removed without first removing the steering wheel as described in Section 22. Also the steering column lock and key assembly must be removed for the upper half to be removed.

24 Steering column lock - removal and replacement

1 A steering column lock is fitted to some cars and it is secured by two special bolts with heads that are broken off on installation for security purposes. To remove the lock and switch assembly, drill a 1/8 inch hole into each bolt using a good sharp high speed drill and then extract the bolts with a proper screw extractor. The bolts are very hard so the drill will need sharpening for each one.
2 When fitting the lock, special break head bolts should be used once again. Make sure the lock and switch are fully tested before finally breaking the bolt heads off.(Fig.11.37)

25 Steering intermediate shaft and coupling - removal and replacement

1 The main steering shaft is connected to the steering box pinion shaft by an intermediate shaft. The upper end of the shaft is connected by a splined universal joint. The lower end has a flexible coupling, the lower flange being secured to the pinion by a cotter.
2 To remove the shaft and coupling take out both upper and lower cotters and slide the shaft downwards until the upper universal joint is disengaged. Then take the shaft off.
3 If the shaft does not move easily do not strike it in any way as this could damage the collapsible section in the upper column. Twist the section to loosen it if necessary.
4 If the flexible coupling is being put on a new shaft, clamp it with a hose clip to stress the rubber before taking it off the shaft (Fig.11.36). This assists installation.
5 New couplings are supplied with a retention band fitted which should be cut off after installation.
6 When refitting the shaft and coupling first set the road wheels and steering wheel in the straight ahead position. Install the upper cotter (for clamp bolt) just to ensure correct axial alignment and then fit the lower one. Tighten them to the correct torque of 7 lb ft (1.0 Kg m), or cotter nuts or 14 lb ft (1.94 Kg m) for a clamp bolt nut.

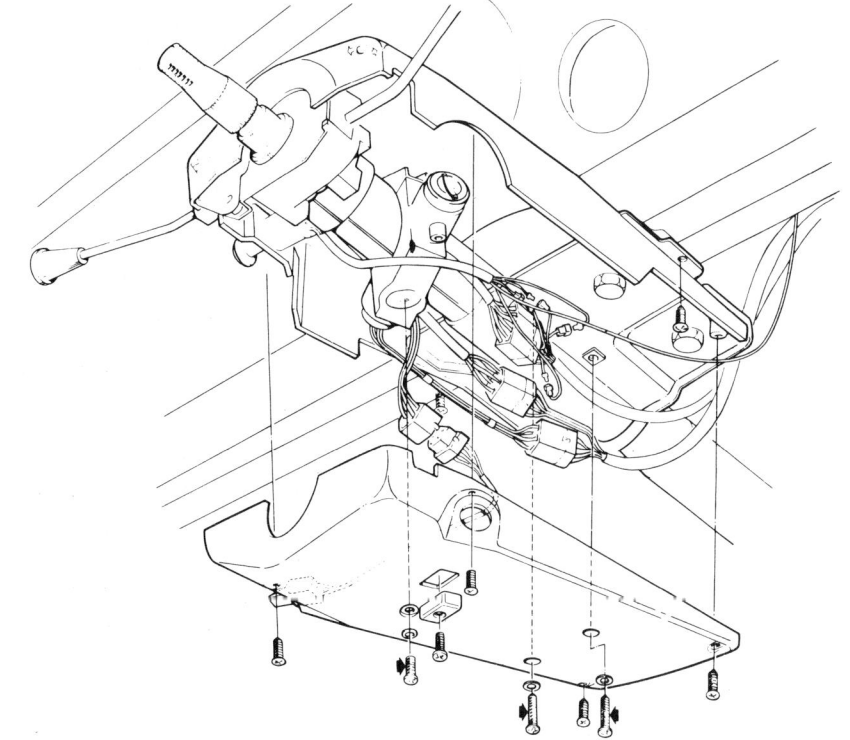

Fig. 11.35 Steering column canopy attachments

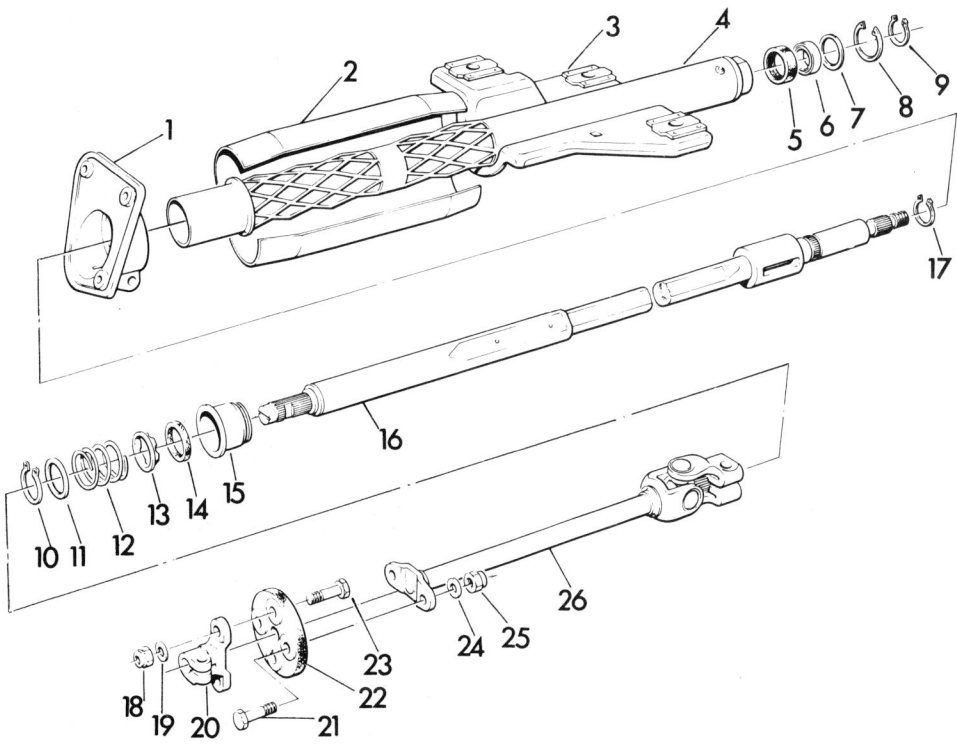

FIG. 11.36 STEERING COLUMN INTERMEDIATE SHAFT AND COUPLING

1 Lower bracket	7 Retainer	13 Spring seat	20 Coupling flange
2 Cover	8 Circlip	14 Seal	21 Bolt
3 Upper bracket	9 Circlip	15 Seal housing	22 Coupling
4 Outer column	10 Circlip	16 Inner column	23 Bolt
5 Rubber sleeve	11 Retainer washer	17 Circlip	24 Washer
6 Bearing	12 Spring	18 Nut	25 Nut
		19 Washer	26 Intermediate shaft

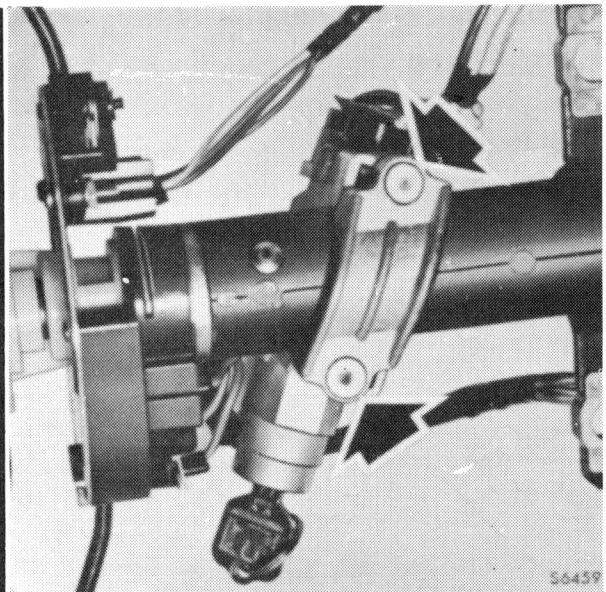

Fig. 11.37 Steering lock shear bolts (arrowed)

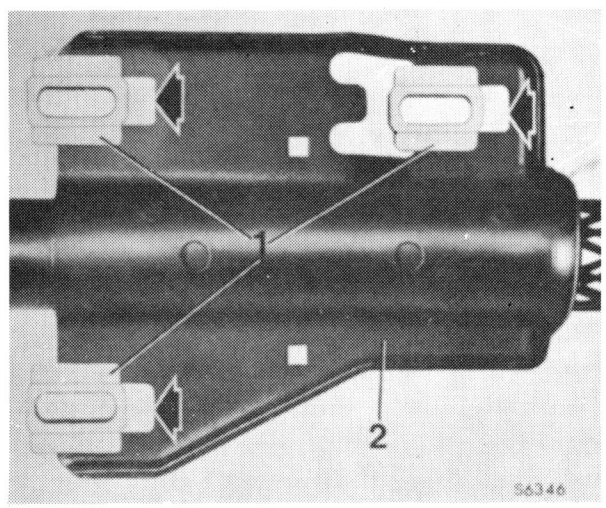

FIG. 11.38 STEERING COLUMN UPPER MOUNTING BRACKET

1 Plastic pad   2 Bracket

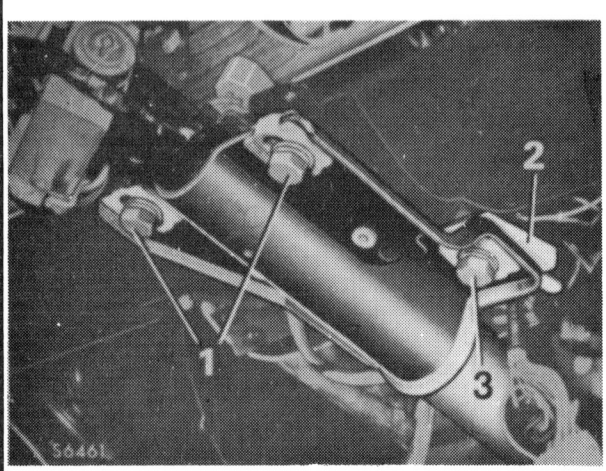

FIG. 11.39 LOWER MOUNTING AND WEDGE

1 Securing bolts   3 Lower securing bolt
2 Wedge

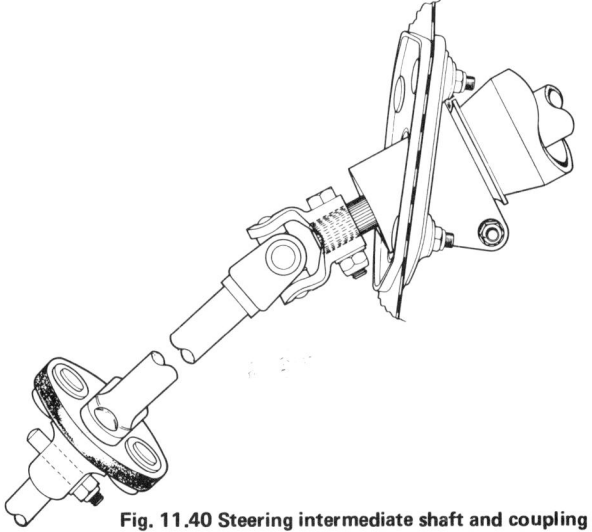

Fig. 11.40 Steering intermediate shaft and coupling

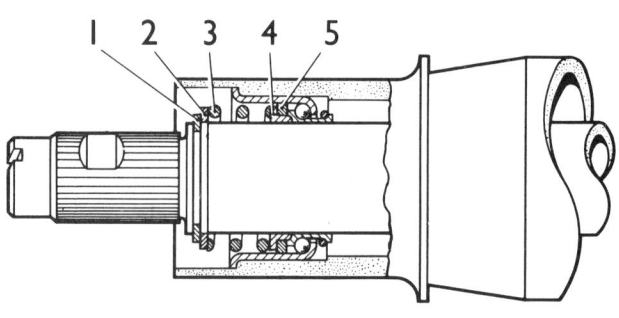

FIG. 11.41 STEERING SHAFT AND COLUMN LOWER
BEARING

1 Circlip   4 Spring seat
2 Retainer washer   5 Seal
3 Spring

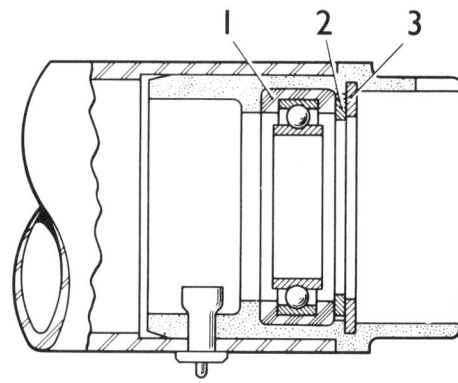

FIG. 11.42 STEERING SHAFT AND COLUMN UPPER
BEARING

1 Rubber sleeve and   2 Retaining washer
   bearing   3 Circlip

26 Steering column - upper mounting bracket and upper bearing - inspection and repair

1 The steering column assembly is designed to collapse under impact to lessen the risk of injury to the driver. The column has a section of expanded metal and the steering shaft is telescopic. The telescoping halves are maintained in their normal position by a plastic substance injected between them which shears on impact. The same applies to the three sections of gear shift tube. It is most important that the assembly and its components are handled with care. Any damage to any of these sections means that the whole column will have to be renewed.

2 The column and mounting bracket may be examined in position. The upper mounting bracket has plastic mounting pads for the three bolts which will shear on impact.

If there are any visible gaps between the bracket and pads then this means that the pads have sheared (Fig.11.38). The column lattice work section will bulge and buckle on impact and this can be confirmed if the overall length of the section has decreased (Fig.11.36)

3 If the bearing needs renewal the whole upper housing must be renewed as the bearing is not supplied separately.

4 The upper housing is retained by three screws. It may be drawn off after removing the screws and the bearing circlip washer and shims. If the housing is a little stiff, do not hammer it or you may damage the columns. It may be necessary to obtain a suitable puller.

27 Steering column assembly - removal and replacement

1 Refer to Section 23 and remove the steering column canopy.

2 Release the intermediate shaft for the steering shaft by removing the cotter and then slacken the clamp bolt from the column lower mounting bracket.

3 Undo and remove the steering column bracket securing bolts and lift away the column assembly. Recover the wedge from the lower mounting bolt.

4 To refit first remove the cotter from the flexible coupling lower flange and slide the intermediate shaft downwards.

5 Fit the column lower mounting clamp bolt from the right hand side.

6 Make sure that the steering column lower mounting is securely attached before lowering the column into position.

7 Tighten the column upper mounting brackets to the specified torque wrench setting and then insert the wedge as far up as possible between the mounting bracket using finger pressure only. Tighten the one mounting bracket lower bolt to the specified torque wrench setting (Fig.11.39).

8 Tighten the column lower mounting clamp bolt, the intermediate shaft universal coupling clamp bolt and the flexible coupling lower flange cotter nut to the specified torque wrench settings

9 Refit the canopy which is the reverse sequence to removal.

28 Wheels and tyres

1 To provide equal, and obtain maximum wear from all the tyres they should be rotated on the car at intervals of 6000 miles (10000 km) to the following pattern:

Spare to offside rear.
Offside rear to nearside front.
Nearside front to nearside rear.
Nearside rear to offside front.
Offside front to spare.

Wheels should be rebalanced when this is done. However, some owners baulk at the prospect of having to buy five new tyres all at once and tend to let two run on and replace a pair only. The new pair should always be fitted to the front wheels, as these are the most important from the safety aspect of steering and braking.

2 Never mix tyres of a radial and crossply construction on the same car, as the basic design differences can cause unusual and, in certain conditions, very dangerous handling and braking characteristics. If an emergency should force the use of two different types, make sure the radials are on the rear wheels and drive particularly carefully. If three of the five wheels are fitted with radial tyres then make sure that no more than two radial are in use on the car (and those at the rear). Rationalise the tyres at the earliest possible opportunity.

3 Wheels are normally not subject to servicing problems, but when tyres are renewed or changed the wheels should be balanced to reduce vibration and wear. If a wheel is suspected of damage - caused by hitting a kerb or pot hole which could distort it out of true, change it and have it checked for balance and true running at the earliest opportunity.

4 When fitting wheels do not overtighten the nuts. The maximum possible manual torque applied by the manufacturers wheel brace is adequate. It also prevents excessive struggle when the same wheel brace has to be used in emergency to remove the wheels.

29 Fault diagnosis

Before diagnosing faults from the following chart, check that any irregularities are not caused by:

1 Binding brakes
2 Incorrect 'mix' of radial and cross-ply tyres
3 Incorrect tyre pressures
4 Misalignment of the body frame or rear axle

Symptom	Reason/s	Remedy
Steering wheel can be moved considerably before any sign of movement of the wheels is apparent	Wear in the steering linkage, gear and column coupling	Check movement in all joints and steering gear and overhaul and renew as required.
Vehicle difficult to steer in a consistent straight line - wandering	As above	As above.
	Wheel alignment incorrect (indicated by excessive or uneven tyre wear)	Check wheel alignment.
	Front wheel hub bearings loose or worn	Adjust or renew as necessary.
	Worn ball joints on track rods or suspension arms	Renew as necessary.
Steering stiff and heavy	Incorrect wheel alignment (indicated by excessive or uneven tyre wear)	Check wheel alignment.
	Excessive wear or seizure in one or more of the ball joints in the steering linkage or suspension arms	Renew as necessary or grease the suspension unit ball joints.
	Excessive wear in the steering gear unit	Adjust if possible or renew.
Wheel wobble and vibration	Road wheels out of balance	Balance wheels.
	Road wheels buckled	Check for damage.
	Wheel alignment incorrect	Check wheel alignment
	Wear in the steering linkage, suspension arm ball joints or suspension arm pivot bushes	Check and renew as necessary.
	Broken front spring	Check and renew as necessary.
Excessive pitching and rolling on corners and during braking	Defective dampers and/or broken spring	Check and renew as necessary.

Chapter 12 Bodywork and underframe

Contents

1 General description

The combined body and underframe is of all steel welded construction. This makes a very strong and torsionally rigid shell.

The models covered by this manual all show the same basic shape, but offer a widely varying choice of performance and luxury. They are readily distinguished from each other in their appearance by contrasting grilles, headlamp arrangements and brightwork.

For corrosion prevention, in addition to the factory applied complete underbody seal the new body is protected by a seven stage phosphate anti-rust process. After being phosphate coated - inside and out - the body is submerged above waist level in a deep tank of anti-rust primer. A red oxide primer surfacer is then applied to the inside of the sill panels and underside of the body, and two coats are sprayed on the body exterior in readiness for four coats of a new formula acrylic lacquer. This gives improved protection against paint chipping and surface distortion and a high degree of gloss retention.

A highly protective aluminised wax is pumped inside the body sills and before leaving the assembly line, the entire underside of the car, including mechanical components, is sprayed with a lanolin wax.

The front seats are upholstered in Ambla and have 7 inches (178 mm) fore and aft movement and built into their backrests is the ability to absorb impact in the event of an accident. Reclining front seats are standard on VX 4/90 models.

On Victor models two large circular dials are recessed in the facia which is black on de luxe and wood grained on SL models. The facia on VX 4/90 models is finished in brushed aluminium and houses the two large circular dials and two separate smaller ones. The heater controls are mounted centrally.

For safety the window glass is deeper than usual and combined with slender pillars gives good all round visibility. The door frames and centre pillar are made in one piece as also is the windscreen frame. Roof braces are built in for strength and safety. The shaping of the body sides has been designed to allow a very strong box section along the whole underbody and the doors are heavily reinforced.

With silence in mind, the smooth projection free body shape soft rubber seals to snug fitting doors and full width door glasses in tight clinging sides are all designed to defeat wind noise. The liberal use of insulation material and isolation of the suspension from the body by big bushings and mountings play a big part in keeping road noise out.

On estate models the tailgate is counterbalanced by telescopic tubular stays and opens through an extremely wide angle to give full height and width.

2 Maintenance - body exterior

1 The general condition of a car's bodywork is the one thing that significantly affects its value. Maintenance is easy but needs to be regular and particular. Neglect, particularly after minor damage, can lead quickly to a further deterioration and costly repair bills. It is important also to keep watch on those parts of the car not immediately visible, for instance the underside, inside all the wheel arches and the lower part of the engine compartment. The rear of the front wheel arches consists of a detachable panel held by three screws. Make sure that this panel is intact otherwise the aperture behind will fill up with debris. If your car is not fitted with mud flaps at the front, it is strongly recommended that they are installed. Vauxhall agents will supply them made to measure for the car at a very fair price. These protect the door undersills.

2 The basic maintenance routine for the bodywork is washing preferably with a lot of water, from a hose. This will remove all the loose solids which may have stuck to the car. It is important to flush these off in such a way as to prevent grit from scratching the finish. The wheel arches and underbody need washing in the same way to remove any accumulated mud which will retain moisture and tend to encourage rust. Paradoxically enough, the best time to clean the underbody and wheel arches is in wet weather when the mud is thoroughly wet and soft. In very wet weather the underbody is usually cleaned of large accumulations automatically and this is a good time for inspection.

3 Periodically it is a good idea to have the whole of the underside of the car steam cleaned, engine compartment included, so that a thorough inspection can be carried out to see what minor repairs and renovations are necessary. Steam cleaning is available at many garages and is necessary for removal of accumulations of oily grime which sometimes cakes thick in certain areas near the

engine, gearbox and back axle. If steam facilities are not available, there are one or two excellent grease solvents available which can be brush applied. The dirt can then be simply hosed off.

4   After washing paintwork, wipe it off with a chamois leather to give an unspotted clear finish. A coat of clear protective wax polish will give added protection against chemical pollutants in the air. If the paintwork sheen has dulled or oxidised, use a cleaner/polisher combination to restore the brilliance of the shine. This requires a little more effort, but is usually caused because regular washing has been neglected. Always check that door and ventilator opening drain holes and pipes are completely clear so that water can drain out. Bright work should be treated the same way as paintwork. Windscreens and windows can be kept clear of the smeary film if a little ammonia is added to the water. If they are scratched, a good rub with a proprietary metal polish will often clear them. Never use any form of wax or chromium polish on glass.

3   Maintenance - interior

1   Mats and carpets should be brushed or vacuum cleaned regularly to keep them free of grit. If they are badly stained remove them from the car for scrubbing or sponging and make quite sure they are dry before replacement. Seats and interior trim panels can be kept clean by a wipe over with a damp cloth. If they do become stained (which can be more apparent on light coloured upholstery) use a little detergent and a soft nail brush to scour the grime out of the grain of the material. Do not forget to keep the head lining clean in the same way as the upholstery. When using liquid cleaners inside the car do not over wet the surfaces being cleaned. Excessive damp could get into the seams and padded interior causing stains, offensive odours or even rot. If the inside of the car gets wet accidentally it is worthwhile taking some trouble to dry it out properly, particularly where carpets are involved. Do NOT leave oil or electric heaters inside the car for this purpose.

4   Minor repairs to bodywork

1   A car which does not suffer some minor damage to the bodywork from time to time is the exception rather than the rule. Even presuming the gatepost is never scraped or the door opened against a wall or high kerb, there is always the likelihood of gravel and grit being thrown up and chipping the surface, particularly at the lower edges of the doors and wings.

2   If the damage is merely a paint scrape which has not reached the metal base, delay is not critical, but where bare metal is exposed action must be taken immediately before rust sets in.

3   The average owner will normally keep the following 'first aid' materials available which can give a professional finish for minor jobs:

a)   A resin based filler paste.
b)   Matched paint either in an aerosol can or 'touch up' tin.
c)   Fine cutting paste.
d)   Medium and fine grade wet and dry abrasive paper.

4   Where the damage is superficial (ie not down to the bare metal and not dented), fill the scratch or chip with sufficient filler to smooth the area, rub down with paper and apply the matching paint.

5   Where the bodywork is scratched down to the metal, but not dented, clean the metal surface thoroughly and apply a suitable metal primer first, such as red lead. Fill up the scratch as necessary with filler and rub down with wet and dry paper. Apply the matching colour paint.

6   If more than one coat of colour is required rub down each coat with cutting paste before applying the next.

7   If the bodywork is dented, first beat out the dent as near as possible to conform with the original contour. Avoid using steel

hammers - use hardwood mallets or similar and always support the back of the panel being beaten with a hardwood or metal 'dolly'. In areas where severe creasing and buckling has occurred it will be virtually impossible to reform the metal to the original shape. In such instances a decision should be made whether or not to cut out the damaged piece or attempt to re-contour over it with filler paste. In large areas where the metal panel is seriously damaged or rusted, the repair is to be considered major and it is often better to replace a panel or sill section with the appropriate part supplied as a spare. When using filler paste in largish quantities, make sure the directions are carefully followed. It is false economy to try and rush the job, as the correct hardening time must be allowed between stages or before finishing. With thick application the filler usually has to be applied in layers - allowing time for each layer to harden. Sometimes the original paint colour will have faded and it will be difficult to obtain an exact colour match. In such instances it is a good scheme to select a complete panel such as a door, or boot lid, and spray the whole panel. Differences will be less apparent where there are obvious divisions between the original and resprayed areas.

5   Major repairs to bodywork

1   Where serious damage has occurred or large areas need renewal due to neglect, it means certainly that completely new sections or panels will need welding in and this is best left to professionals. If the damage is due to impact it will also be necessary to completely check the alignment of the bodyshell structure. Due to the principle of construction, the strength and shape of the whole can be affected by damage to a part. In such instances the services of a Vauxhall agent with specialist checking jigs are essential. If a body is left mis-aligned, it is first of all dangerous as the car will not handle properly - and secondly, uneven stresses will be imposed on the steering, engine and transmission, causing abnormal wear or complete failure. Tyre wear will also be excessive.

6   Front and rear bumpers - removal and replacement

1   The front bumper is mounted on brackets which are bolted to the engine mounting side rail closing plate and also at each end to the front wings (Fig.12.1).

2   The rear bumper is mounted on brackets bolted to the rear end panel and rear quarter panels. To gain access to the bumper bolts on estate models the luggage compartment floor must be removed (Fig.12.2).

3   When removing a bumper take it off by undoing the bolts holding the brackets to the bodywork, then if necessary detach the brackets from the bumper.

4   Replacement is a reversal of the removal procedure. It is necessary to use sealing putty (Bostik No 5) round the bolt holes in the rear panels to keep water from entering the luggage compartment.

7   Windscreen - removal and replacement

1   The windscreen is either toughened or laminated glass and each type can be identified by the manufacturers symbol etched on the glass.

2   If you are unfortunate enough to have a windscreen shatter fitting a replacement windscreen is one of the few jobs that the average owner is advised to leave to a body repair specialist, but for the owner who wishes to do the job himself the following instructions are given:

3   Remove the wiper arms from their spindles using a screwdriver to lift the retaining clip from the spindle and pull away.

4   Place a thick blanket on the bonnet and wings so protecting the paintwork.

5   **Toughened glass windscreen.** Moving to the inside of the

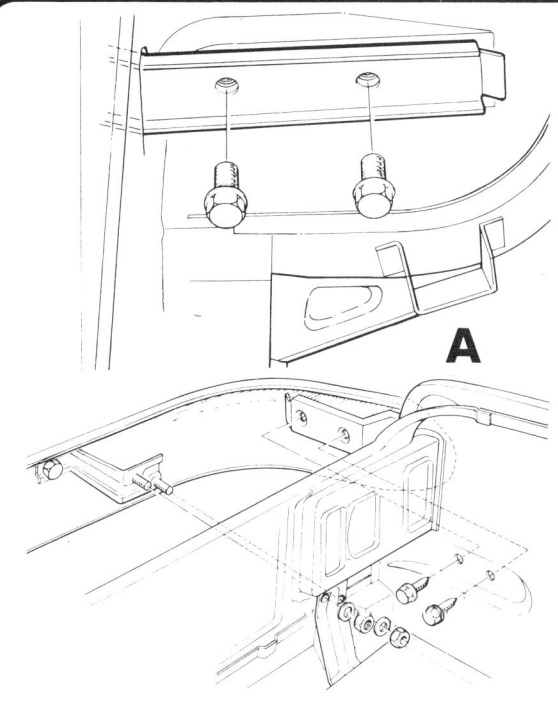

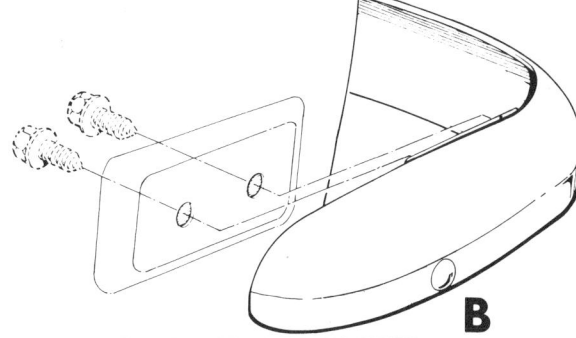

FIG. 12.1 FRONT BUMPER ATTACHMENTS

A   Front bumper bracket
B   Bumper attachment to front wing

Fig. 12.2 Rear bumper attachments

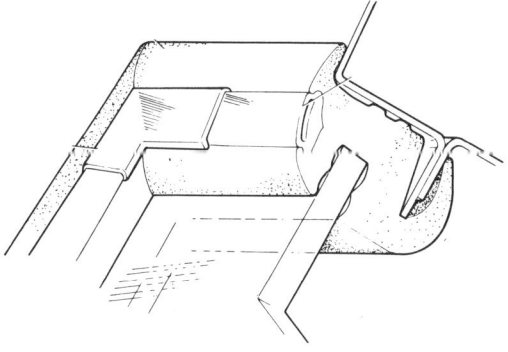

Fig. 12.3 Cross section through glazing channel

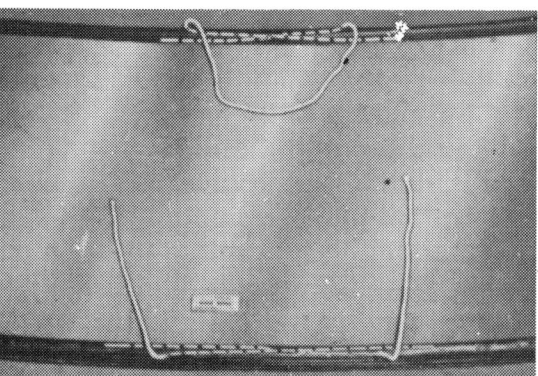

Fig. 12.4 Draw cord correctly fitted in glazing channel

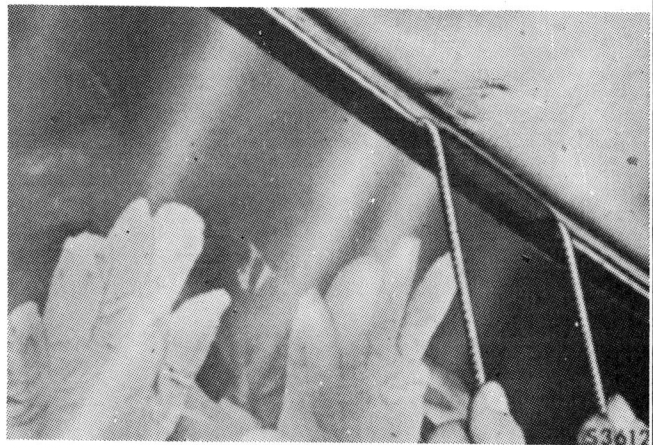

Fig. 12.5 Pulling draw cord so easing lip of glazing channel over aperture flange

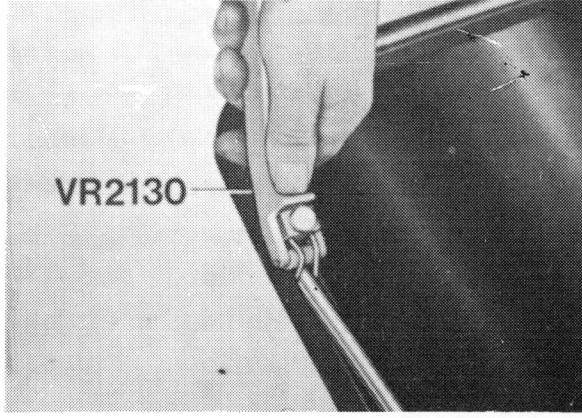

VR2130

Fig. 12.6 Fitting glazing insert

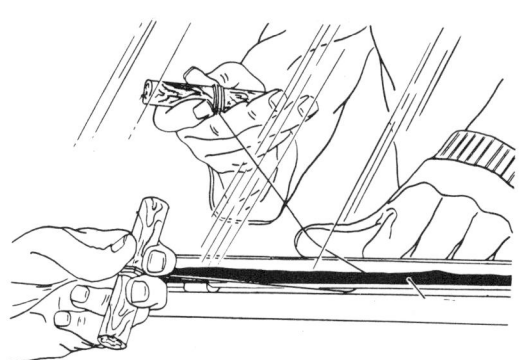

Fig. 12.7 Pulling wire through rear quarter glass adhesive

and with an assistant outside ready to catch the glass as it is released, push on the glass with the palms of the hands placed at one of the top corners. Whilst this is being done ease the lip of the weatherstrip over its body retaining lip until the glass and weatherstrip are clear. This is, of course not applicable if the glass has shattered. Remove the rubber weatherstrip from the glass or the remains of the glass from the weatherstrip channel.

6   **Laminated glass windscreen.** Remove the glazing channel insert and cut away the channel lip on the outer side of the glass (Fig.12.3) . Carefully push the glass outwards away from the channel. Do not thump on the glass as this could fracture the glass.

7   Now is the time to remove all pieces of glass if the screen has shattered. Use a vacuum cleaner to extract as much as possible. Switch on the heater boost motor and adjust the controls to 'screen defrost' but watch out for flying pieces of glass which might be blown out of the ducting.

8   Carefully inspect the rubber surround for signs of splitting or deterioration. Clean all traces of sealing compound from the weatherstrip and windscreen aperture.

9   To refit the glass insert a piece of strong thin cord around the securing lip groove of the glazing channel leaving a loop at the top of the glass. The cord should be crossed in the channel groove where the loop is formed and also where the cord ends meet the bottom of the glass as shown in Fig.12.4 .

10 Apply sealing compound all round the base of the body flange.

11 With the glass placed central in the body aperture, apply light pressure to the outside of the glass. Lift the lip of the glazing channel over the aperture bottom flange by pulling the cord to within 6.00 inch (150 mm) of each corner (Fig.12.5)

12 Make sure that the glass is still central in the aperture before repeating the procedure to the top of the glass and also before refitting the side sections.

13 After installing the glass carefully inject sealing compound between the outside of the glass and glazing channel.

14 The windscreen glazing insert is in four pieces. A shaped tool is now required to fit the insert. Full details of this are shown in Fig.12.6 and a handyman can make up something similar.

15 Soak the aperture in concentrated soap solution to prevent tearing of the channel lips. Refit the inserts and check that they are seating correctly.

16 Finally fit an escutcheon over each corner joint and then the wiper arms and blades.

8   Backlight - removal and replacement

The backlight is of toughened glass and on some models incorporates a 'hot line' system for demisting. Whenever the glass is cleared care must be taken not to scratch the printed circuit on the glass inner surface. Should the printed circuit be damaged it can be repaired using a high conductivity paint. Before removing the glass disconnect the wires from the terminals at each side of the glass and then follow the instructions given in section 7 for toughened glass.

9   Rear quarter window glass (Estate car) - removal and replacement

The quarter window glass is bonded into the body apertures and for refitting a special kit is required.

1   To remove an undamaged glass, first remove the reveal mouldings with a screwdriver then push one end of the special steel wire through the adhesive and attach the ends to wooden handles.

2   Using a steady pull draw the wire sideways through the adhesive until the glass is free. Do not use a sawing action as the wire will overheat and break (Fig.12.7) .

3   Clean off all adhesive from the body flange and glass using Bostik thinners.

4   Clean the new glass to ensure there are no traces of oil or

moisture which will prevent the new adhesive bonding.

5   Check that the reveal moulding attaching clips are tight and undamaged. If any clips are damaged or distorted these must be renewed (Fig.12.8).

6   Inspect the paintwork around the rebate or flange and if chipped it should be touched up with a matt black paint. Allow the paint to dry.

7   Brush a light coat of adhesive primer onto the flange and around the edge of glass approximately 0.50 inch (12 mm) in width. Do not allow the primer to contact polished surface of the paintwork. Allow the primer to dry.

8   Fit some small taper wedges to the lower aperture to obtain correct height of glass.

9   With the glass resting on the spacers centralise the glass in the aperture and attach a piece of masking tape from the lower edge of the glass to the body. Cut through the masking tape at the gap between the glass and body so as to provide a reference point when the glass is finally fitted. Remove the glass again.

10 Apply adhesive strip around the aperture flange making sure that the joints are well made.

11 Refit the glass to the aperture and carefully press at the sealer contact surface to ensure a good seal.

12 Touch up any weak points with a Bostik sealer and finally refit the reveal mouldings. These must be assembled before replacing on the clips.

10 Radiator grille - removal and replacement

Victor

The radiator grille is one pressing and is removed by undoing the four screws located at the top and a further two at the bottom. It may now be lifted away from the front of the car (Fig.12.10) .

VX 4/90

The radiator grille comprises a frame and plastic insert. The frame is secured to the front end panel by four screws located at the top and a further two at the bottom and is removed by undoing these six screws (Fig.12.9). The assembly may now be lifted away from the front of the car. To separate the plastic insert from the frame drill out the four 'pop' rivets. Refitting in both cases is the reverse sequence to removal.

11 Front wing - removal and replacement

1   Remove the four headlamp surround securing screws which are accessible from within the engine compartment. Lift away the headlamp surround.

2   Using a screwdriver carefully remove the scuttle side trim.

3   Refer to Fig.12.11 and undo and remove the fourteen screws that secure the wing to the body. Note the one screw, depicted by an arrow, attaches the rear of the wing at the bottom.

4   Clean down the wing and mating face of the body and if rust is evident, remove and touch up the paintwork.

5   Apply sealing putty (Bostik No 5) to the wing contact areas and then offer up the new wing. Secure with the fourteen screws. The wiring harness which is clipped to the inner wing panel should be released in case it is damaged when refitting the top securing screws.

6   Remove all traces of old sealant. Pack sealant around the two rear securing screws to prevent water ingress.

12 Bonnet - removal and replacement

1   Open the bonnet and hold open using the bonnet stay. To act as a datum for refitting, mark the position of the hinges on the bonnet using a soft pencil.

2   With the assistance of a second person hold the bonnet in the open position and release the stay. Undo and remove the two bolts and washers that hold each bonnet hinge to the bonnet.

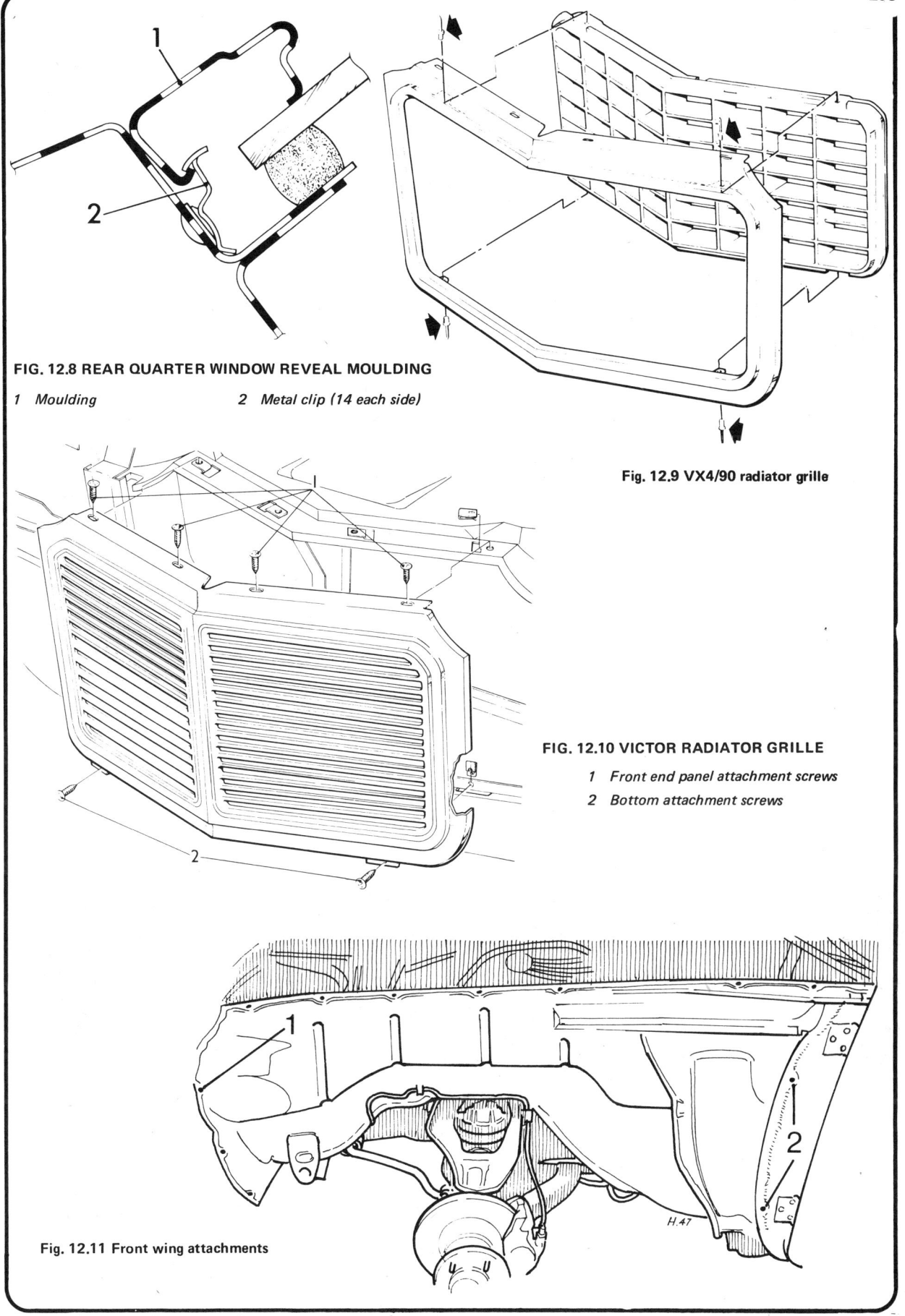

FIG. 12.8 REAR QUARTER WINDOW REVEAL MOULDING

1   Moulding   2   Metal clip (14 each side)

Fig. 12.9 VX4/90 radiator grille

FIG. 12.10 VICTOR RADIATOR GRILLE

1   Front end panel attachment screws
2   Bottom attachment screws

Fig. 12.11 Front wing attachments

H.47

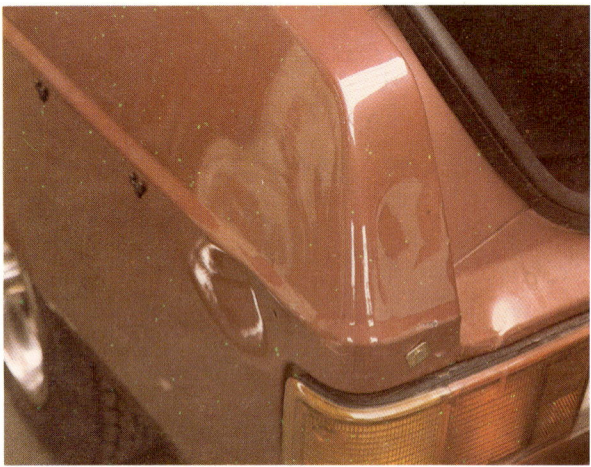

This sequence of photographs deals with the repair of the dent and scratch (above rear lamp) shown in this photo. The procedure will be similar for the repair of a hole. It should be noted that the procedures given here are simplified - more explicit instructions will be found in the text

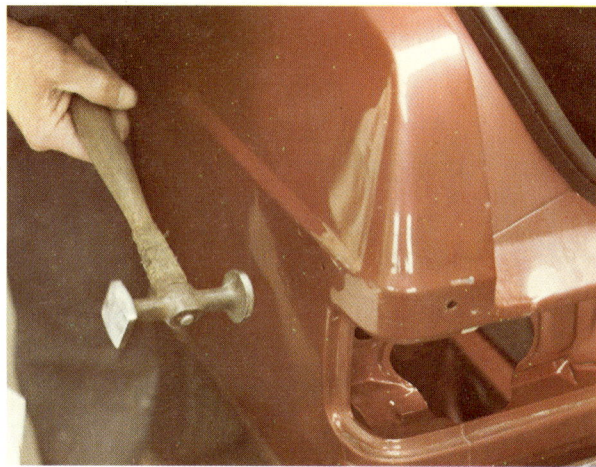

In the case of a dent the first job - after removing surrounding trim - is to hammer out the dent where access is possible. This will minimise filling. Here, the large dent having been hammered out, the damaged area is being made slightly concave

Now all paint must be removed from the damaged area, by rubbing with coarse abrasive paper. Alternatively, a wire brush or abrasive pad can be used in a power drill. Where the repair area meets good paintwork, the edge pf the paintwork should be 'feathered', using a finer grade of abrasive paper

In the case of a hole caused by rusting, all damaged sheet-metal should be cut away before proceeding to this stage. Here, the damaged area is being treated with rust remover and inhibitor before being filled

Mix the body filler according to its manufacturer's instructions. In the case of corrosion damage, it will be necessary to block off any large holes before filling - this can be done with zinc gauze or aluminium tape. Make sure the area is absolutely clean before ...

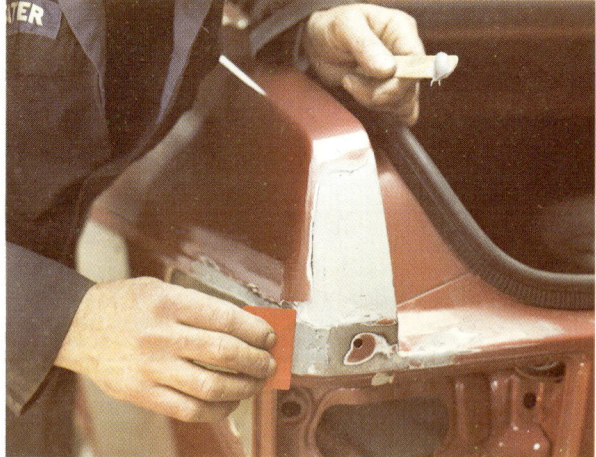

... applying the filler. Filler should be applied with a flexible applicator, as shown, for best results: the wooden spatula being used for confined areas. Apply thin layers of filler at 20-minute intervals, until the surface of the filler is slightly proud of the surrounding bodywork

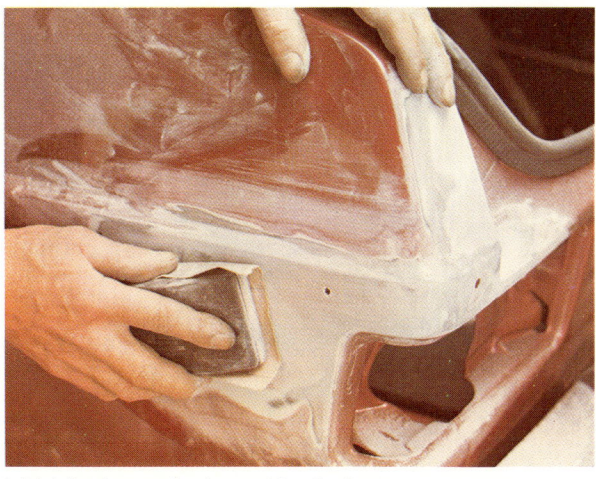

Initial shaping can be done with a Surform plane or Dreadnought file. Then, using progressively finer grades of wet-and-dry paper, wrapped around a sanding block, and copious amounts of clean water, rub-down the filler until really smooth and flat. Again, feather the edges of adjoining paintwork

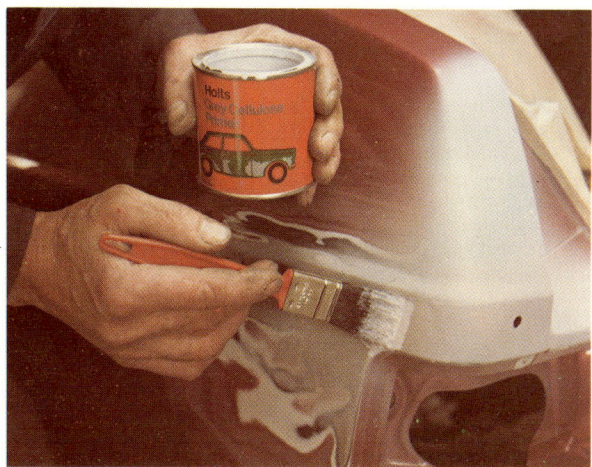

The whole repair area can now be sprayed or brush-painted with primer. If spraying, ensure adjoining areas are protected from over-spray. Note that at least one-inch of the surrounding sound paintwork should be coated with primer. Primer has a 'thick' consistency, so will fill small imperfections

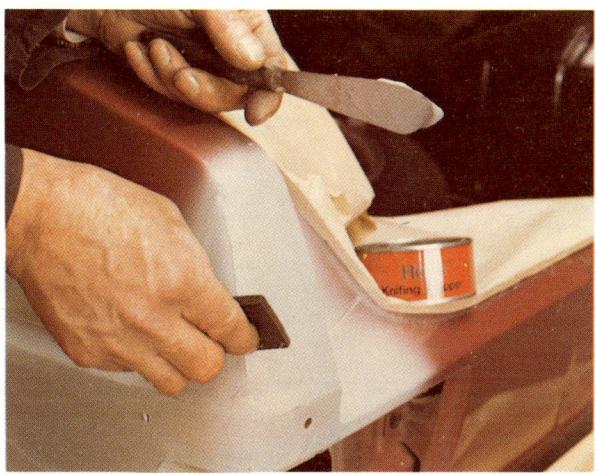

Again, using plenty of water, rub down the primer with a fine grade of wet-and-dry paper (400 grade is probably best) until it is really smooth and well blended into the surrounding paint-work. Any remaining imperfections can now be filled by carefully applied knifing stopper paste

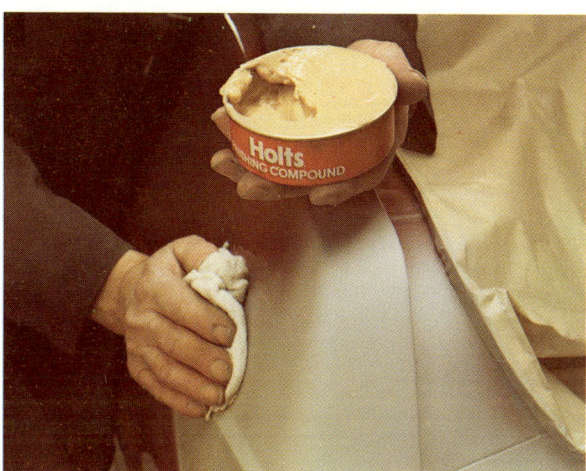

When the stopper has hardened, rub-down the repair area again before applying the final coat of primer. Before rubbing-down this last coat of primer, ensure the repair area is blemish-free - use more stopper if necessary. To ensure that the surface of the primer is really smooth use some finishing compound

The top coat can now be applied. When working out of doors, pick a dry, warm and wind-free day. Ensure surrounding areas are protected from over-spray. Agitate the aerosol thoroughly, then spray the centre of the repair area, working outwards with a circular motion. Apply the paint as several thin coats.

After a period of about two-weeks, which the paint needs to harden fully, the surface of the repaired area can be 'cut' with a mild cutting compound prior to wax polishing. When carrying out bodywork repairs, remember that the quality of the finished job is proportional to the time and effort expended

Lift away the bonnet taking care not to scratch the top of the wings.

3   Lean the bonnet up against a wall suitably padded to stop scratching the paint.

4   The bonnet hinges are welded to the upper dash panel and if renewal is necessary this must be left to a body repair shop.

5   Refitting the bonnet is the reverse sequence to removal, any adjustment necessary can be made either at the hinges or the bonnet catches. Lubricate the hinge pivots with Castrol GTX.

13 Bonnet lock and cable - removal and replacement

1   To detach the cable from the lock, release the outer cable securing clip with a screwdriver. Carefully ease the inner cable nipple from the slot in the lock release lever (Fig.12.12).

2   Refer to Section 10 and remove the radiator grille.

3   To remove the lock undo and remove the three securing nuts and washers. Lift away the lock assembly (Fig.12.13).

4   To release the bonnet lock control slacken the locknut at the rear of the sleeve (Fig.12.14).

5   Move the outer cable sleeve across the mounting bracket to the larger hole and pull the cable assembly through the bracket.

6   Refitting the lock or cable is the reverse sequence to removal. Lubricate the cable with Castrol GTX and the lock contact surfaces with Castrol LM Grease.

14 Bonnet lock - adjustment

1   Should it be necessary to adjust the bonnet catch first slacken the locknut securing the shaft in position.

2   Using a wide blade screwdriver, screw the shaft inwards or outwards and tighten the locknut once the correct position has been obtained (Fig.12.15).

3   Test the adjustment by opening and closing the bonnet several times. Lubricate the contact surfaces with Castrol LM Grease.

15 Boot lid - removal and replacement

1   Open the boot lid and using a soft pencil mark the outline of the hinges or the lid to act as a datum for refitting.

2   With the assistance of a second person hold the boot lid in the open position and then release the two bolts and spring washers to each hinge (Fig.12.16).

3   Lift away the boot lid taking care to recover any wedges fitted to the front end of the hinge arms.

4   Refitting the boot lid is the reverse sequence to removal. If necessary wedges may be removed or fitted to the front end of the hinge arms to raise or lower the front of the boot lid. Do not fit more than two wedges to one hinge.

5   Upon inspection of the hinge assembly it will be seen that the hinge pivots are riveted to a support panel. The full length torque rod for either side hinge operates on the hinge arm and is anchored in one of three positions - the centre one is normally used. To remove a torque rod, carefully detach the hooked end and allow to move to the released position. An anti-rattle pad is wrapped around the centre of the torque rods. When refitting a torque rod lubricate the friction surfaces with Castrol LM Grease.

16 Boot lid lock and striker - removal and replacement

1   The key type lock is secured to the boot lid by a shaped spring retainer. Working through the hole in the lid inner panel carefully slide the retainer sideways towards the lock thereby detaching it from the lock (Fig.12.17).

2   Draw the lock through its aperture in the boot lid outer panel.

3   Should it be necessary to dismantle the key lock refer to Fig.12.18 and remove the lock support and nut. Next detach the lock lever. Release the spring and lift away the extension from the body. Finally insert the key and draw out the lock barrel (Fig.12.18).

4   When reassembling the lock barrel lubricate with a non greasy lubricant such as Duckhams WD 40. Lubricate the friction surfaces of the extension and body with Castrol LM Grease.

5   The extension must be fitted on the body so that the spring anchor lugs are each diametrically opposed. Also the lock lever must be fitted the correct way round as shown in Fig.12.19.

6   To remove the boot lid latch undo and remove the securing screws and lift away through the aperture in the lid inner panel. This can only be done once the key lock has been removed (Fig.12.20)

7   Upon refitting lubricate the friction surfaces with Castrol LM Grease.

8   To remove the latch assembly undo and remove the retaining clip securing bolt and washer. Lift away the latch, clip bolt and washer (Fig.12.21)

9   Refitting is the reverse sequence to removal. Any adjustment necessary may be made until the boot lid closes under a firm hand pressure.

17 Front and rear door - removal and replacement

1   Disconnect the door check link by tapping out the rivet on the door pillar. Detach the link and place a screwdriver or bent metal bar through link hole so that it does not drop inside the door (Fig.12.22).

2   Using a pencil accurately mark the outline of the hinge relative to the door to assist refitting - a little difficult for the front door due to inaccessibility. It is desirable to have an assistant to take the weight of the door once the two hinges have been released.

3   Remove the bolts that hold the hinges to the pillars and lift away the door assembly. The front door hinge bolts may present a little difficulty but can be done using a ring spanner. For storage it is best to stand the door on an old blanket and allow it to lean against a wall also suitably padded at the top to stop scratching.

4   Refitting the door is the reverse sequence to removal. To enable the door to fit in the aperture to be adjusted shims can be inserted between the hinge flap and door pillar (Fig.12.23).

18 Front door - dismantling and reassembly

1   The door trim panels are complete with an integral armrest which incorporates a door pull. The trim is hung over the top edge of the door inner panel and secured with screws and clips.

2   Refer to Fig.12.24 and undo and remove the two screws and shaped washers.

3   Undo and remove the one screw located inside the door pull recess.

4   Using a screwdriver or knife carefully ease the remote control escutcheon away from the door trim panel.

5   Again using a screwdriver push the spring retainer from the rear of the handle hub and draw the handle from the regulator shaft.

6   Unscrew the inside lock button and then remove the ash tray. Unscrew the ash tray housing retaining screw and lift away the housing.

7   Ease the trim panel away from the door using a wide bladed screwdriver behind the spring clips located as shown in Fig.12.24.

8   A polythene water deflector is attached to the door inner panel by adhesive around the sides and inserted into the lower slot in the door.

9   To remove the door lock remote control undo and remove the two securing screws. Detach the control rod and lift away the control assembly (Fig.12.25).

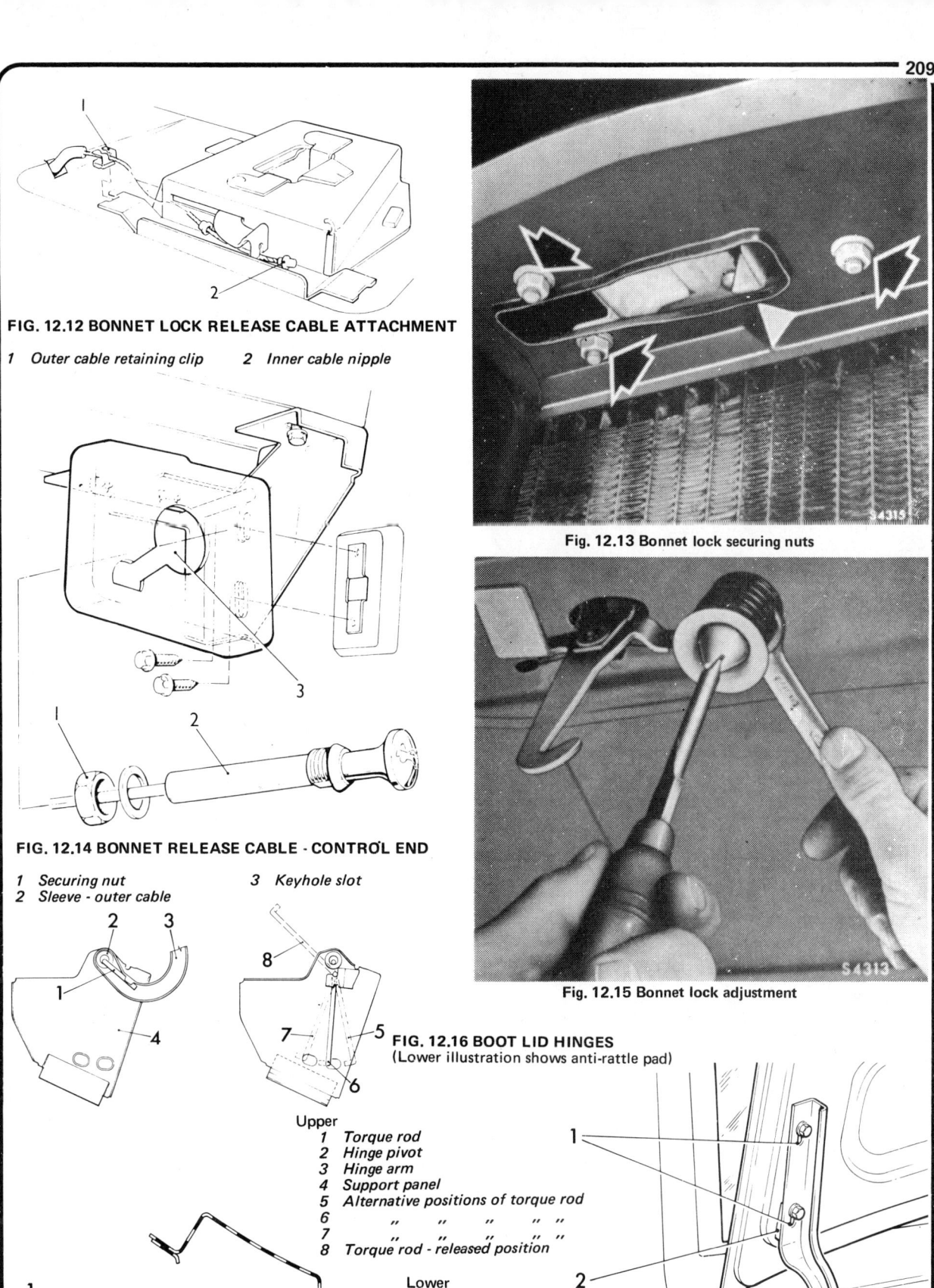

FIG. 12.12 BONNET LOCK RELEASE CABLE ATTACHMENT

1   Outer cable retaining clip   2   Inner cable nipple

FIG. 12.13 Bonnet lock securing nuts

FIG. 12.14 BONNET RELEASE CABLE - CONTROL END

1   Securing nut   3   Keyhole slot
2   Sleeve - outer cable

Fig. 12.15 Bonnet lock adjustment

FIG. 12.16 BOOT LID HINGES
(Lower illustration shows anti-rattle pad)

Upper
1   Torque rod
2   Hinge pivot
3   Hinge arm
4   Support panel
5   Alternative positions of torque rod
6   "   "   "   "   "
7   "   "   "   "   "
8   Torque rod - "released" position "

Lower
1   Anti-rattle pad
2   Torque rods

Right
1   Securing bolts
2   Wedge

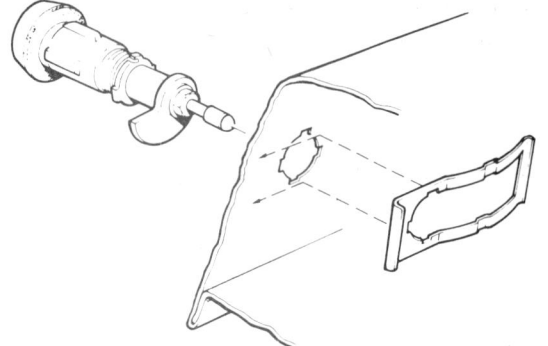

Fig. 12.17 Boot lid key lock and retainer

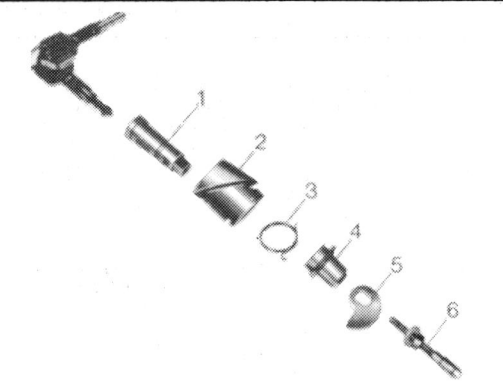

FIG. 12.18 BOOT LID KEY LOCK COMPONENTS

1	Lock barrel	4	Extension
2	Body	5	Lock lever
3	Spring	6	Lock support and nut

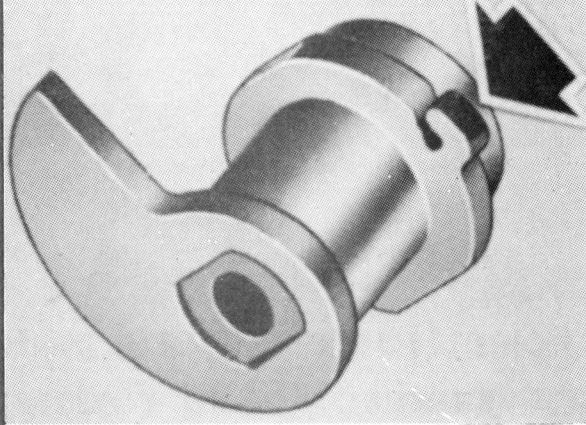

Fig. 12.19 Correct fitting position of lock lever relative to extension lug

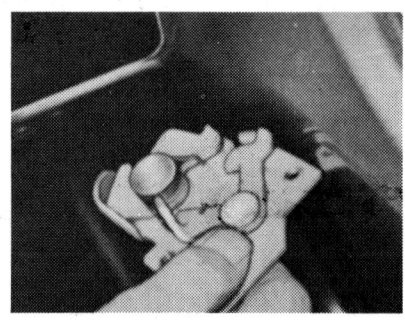

Fig. 12.20 Lifting away boot lid latch

Fig. 12.21 Boot lid latch striker adjustment

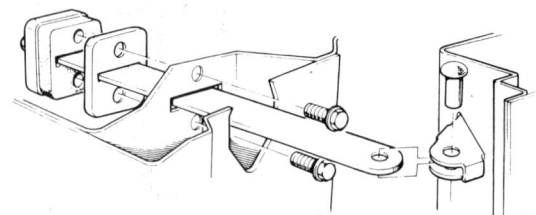

Fig. 12.22 Door check link assembly

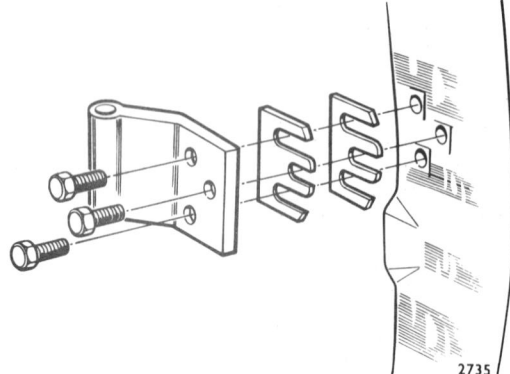

Fig. 12.23 Door hinge half and adjustment shims

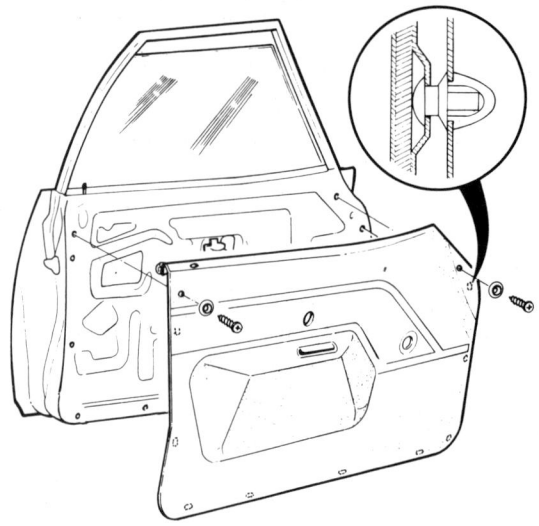

Fig. 12.24 Front door trim attachment points

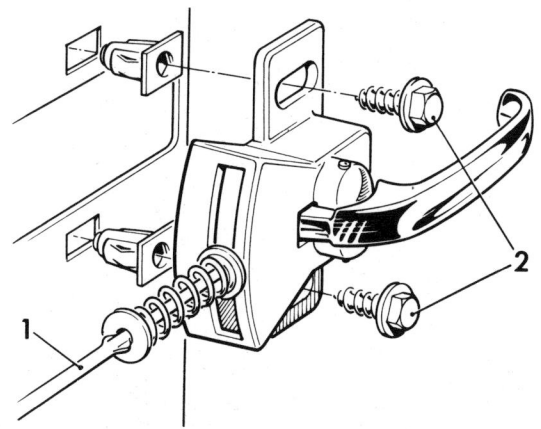

FIG. 12.25 DOOR LOCK REMOTE CONTROL

1   Rod - control to lock   2   Securing screws

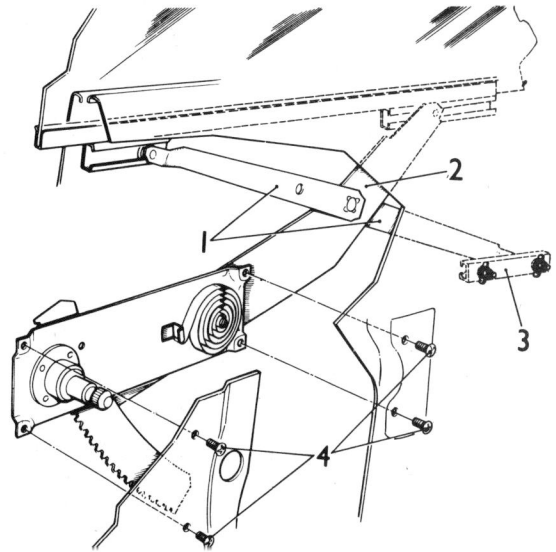

**FIG. 12.26 FRONT DOOR WINDOW REGULATOR
ASSEMBLY**

1   Balance arm   3   Adjustable support channel
2   Main arm   4   Attachment screws

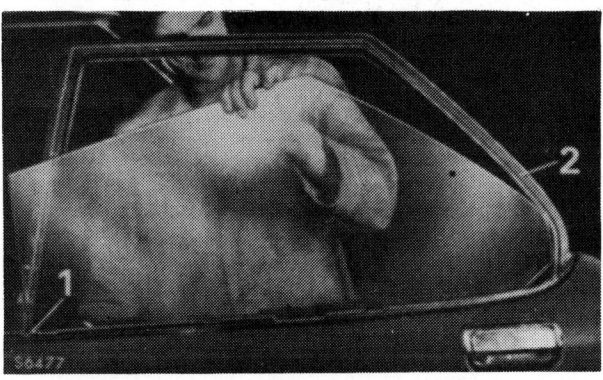

FIG. 12.27 LIFTING AWAY DOOR GLASS

1   Recess   2   Front channel

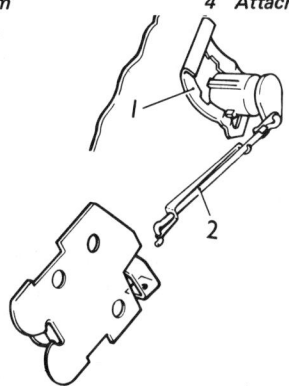

FIG. 12.28 TURN BUTTON RETAINER PLATE AND LATCH

1   Plate   2   Connecting rod

10 To remove the window regulator assembly first wind up the door window glass. Undo and remove the four screws located as shown in Fig.12.26.

11 Detach the balance arms from the glass carrier and lift away the assembly through the largest door aperture. It will assist if the glass is propped up using a piece of wood.

12 To remove the glass tilt the rear downwards and lift through the aperture (Fig.12.27).

13 The outside key lock is secured to the door by a shaped spring retainer. To remove the lock push the retainer towards the lock and then unhook the control rod from the lock lever (Fig.12.28). Lift away the door glass still in position.

14 To remove the outside handle undo and remove the two securing nuts, then detach the handle from the control rod and lift away the exterior handle and its gasket. This operation can be carried out with the door glass still in position.

15 To remove the lock and catch assembly first detach the three operating rods and then undo and remove the lock retaining screws. Lift away the lock assembly.

16 The parts are then ready for inspection and refitting should the window winder or door lock mechanism prove to be faulty, the complete unit must be renewed as individual service parts are not available.

17 Refitting the door parts is the reverse sequence to removal. Well lubricate all moving parts.

19 Rear door – dismantling and reassembly

The components of the rear door are basically identical to those fitted to the front door. The exceptions are shown in Figs.12.34 to 12.37

20 Tailgate latch, turn button and striker (estate models)

The estate tailgate latch is similar to the boot lid latch. A turn button incorporates a latch release plate which is connected to the latch by a rod as shown in Fig.12.38

The latch may be removed after pushing the turn button retainer plate towards the turn button and releasing the turn button from the connecting rod.

To remove the lock barrel and extension (Fig.12.40) release the circlip and detach the lock lever. Release the spring and withdraw the lock barrel and turn button from the body. Next push the keep segment out of the trim button and withdraw the lock barrel.

Using a small screwdriver depress the spring loaded plunger in the end of the lock barrel to remove the barrel extension.

When reassembling the lock barrel, lubricate with a non greasy lubricant such as Duckhams WD - 40. Lubricate the

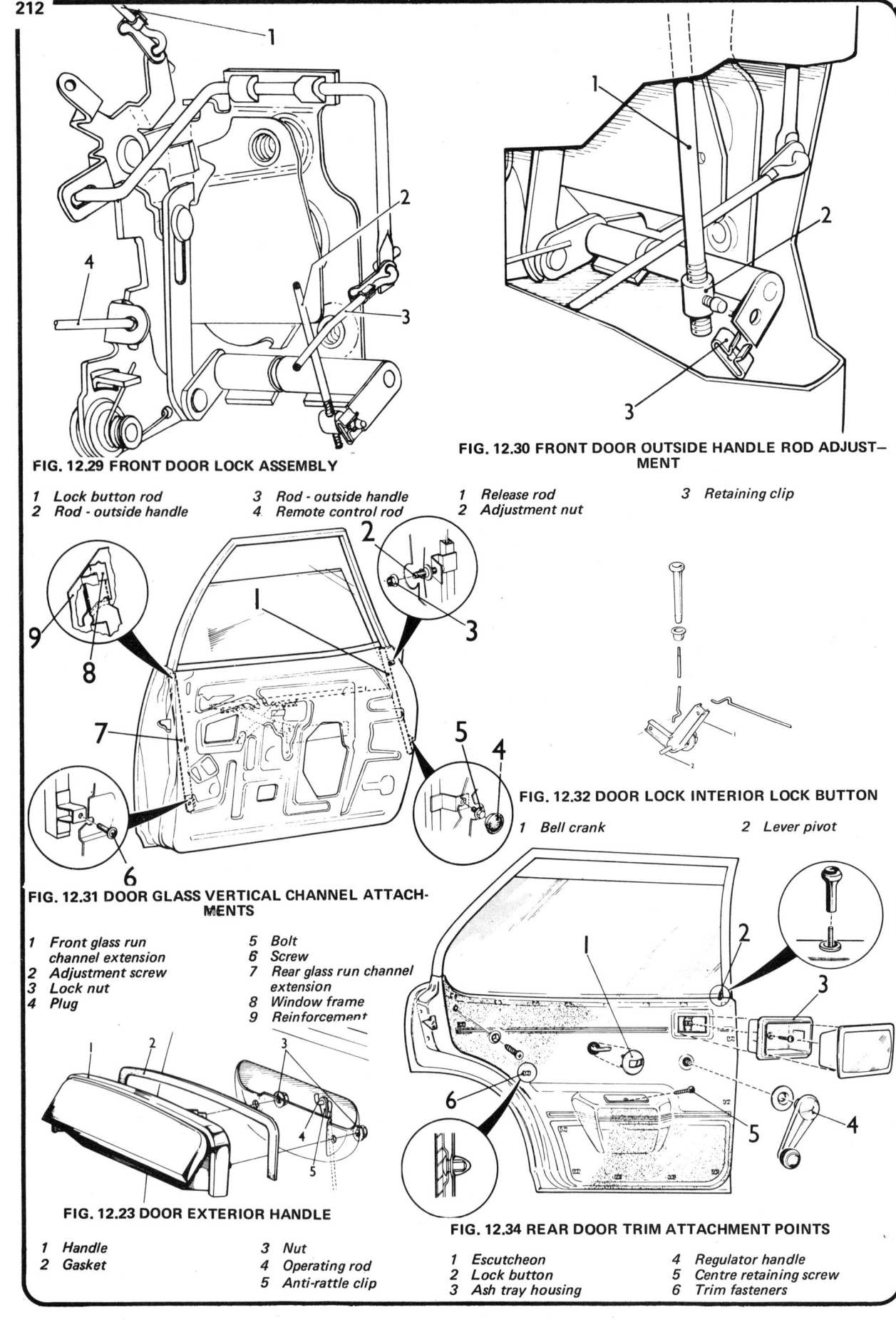

FIG. 12.29 FRONT DOOR LOCK ASSEMBLY

1 Lock button rod   3 Rod - outside handle
2 Rod - outside handle   4. Remote control rod

FIG. 12.30 FRONT DOOR OUTSIDE HANDLE ROD ADJUST—MENT

1 Release rod   3 Retaining clip
2 Adjustment nut

FIG. 12.31 DOOR GLASS VERTICAL CHANNEL ATTACH-MENTS

1 Front glass run   5 Bolt
   channel extension   6 Screw
2 Adjustment screw   7 Rear glass run channel
3 Lock nut   extension
4 Plug   8 Window frame
                            9 Reinforcement

FIG. 12.32 DOOR LOCK INTERIOR LOCK BUTTON

1 Bell crank   2 Lever pivot

FIG. 12.23 DOOR EXTERIOR HANDLE

1 Handle   3 Nut
2 Gasket   4 Operating rod
                            5 Anti-rattle clip

FIG. 12.34 REAR DOOR TRIM ATTACHMENT POINTS

1 Escutcheon   4 Regulator handle
2 Lock button   5 Centre retaining screw
3 Ash tray housing   6 Trim fasteners

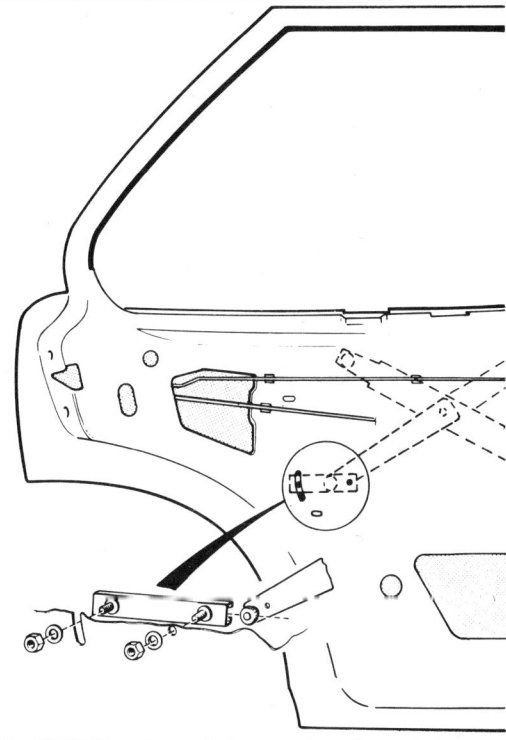

Fig. 12.35 Rear door window regulator lower balance arm support

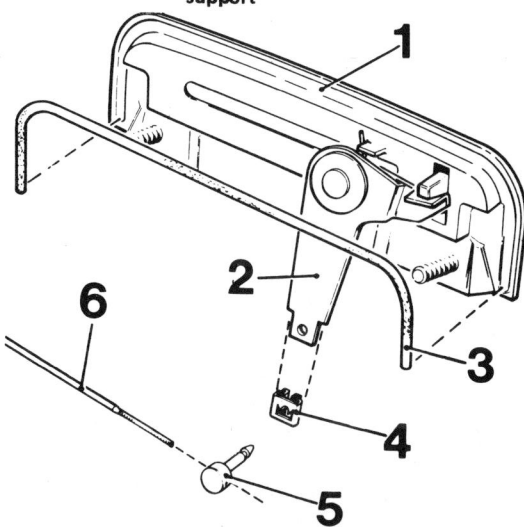

FIG. 12.37 REAR DOOR EXTENSION HANDLE

1 Exterior handle   4 Retaining clip
2 Handle lever   5 Adjustment nut
3 Gasket   6 Catch operating rod

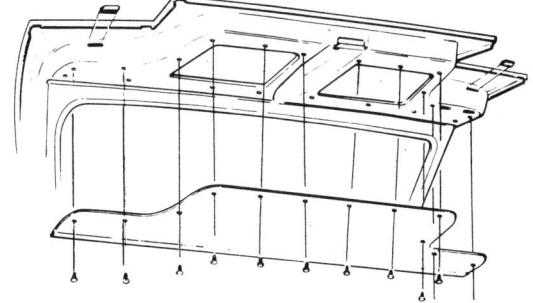

Fig. 12.39 Tailgate trim attachment points (estate models)

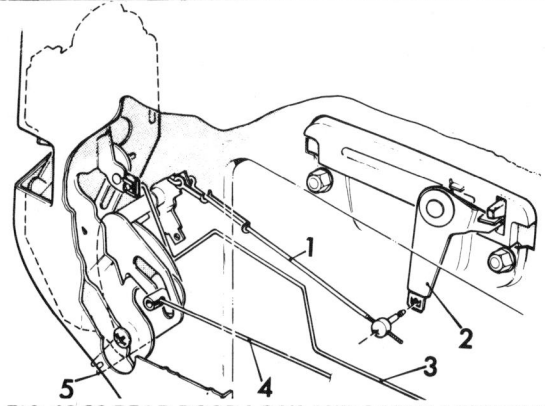

FIG. 12.36 REAR DOOR LOCK AND CATCH ASSEMBLY

1 Adjustable rod   4 Rod - remote control
2 Outside handle lever   5 Childs safety catch
3 Rod - lock button

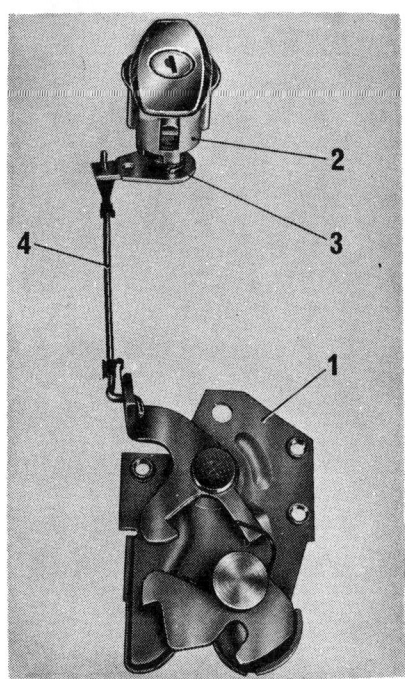

FIG. 12.38 TAILGATE LOCK ASSEMBLY

1 Latch   3 Latch release plate
2 Turn button   4 Rod

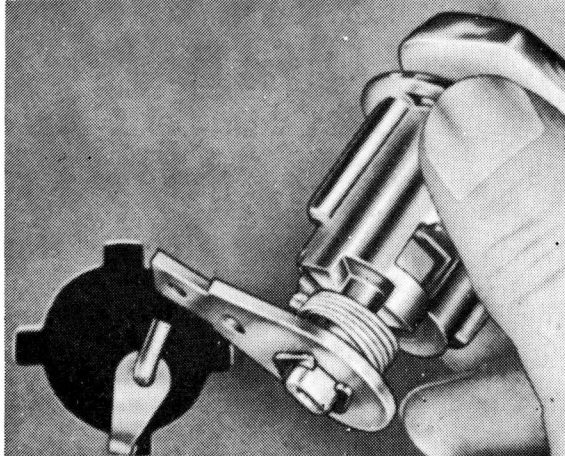

Fig. 12.40 Engagement end of rod in latch release plate hole

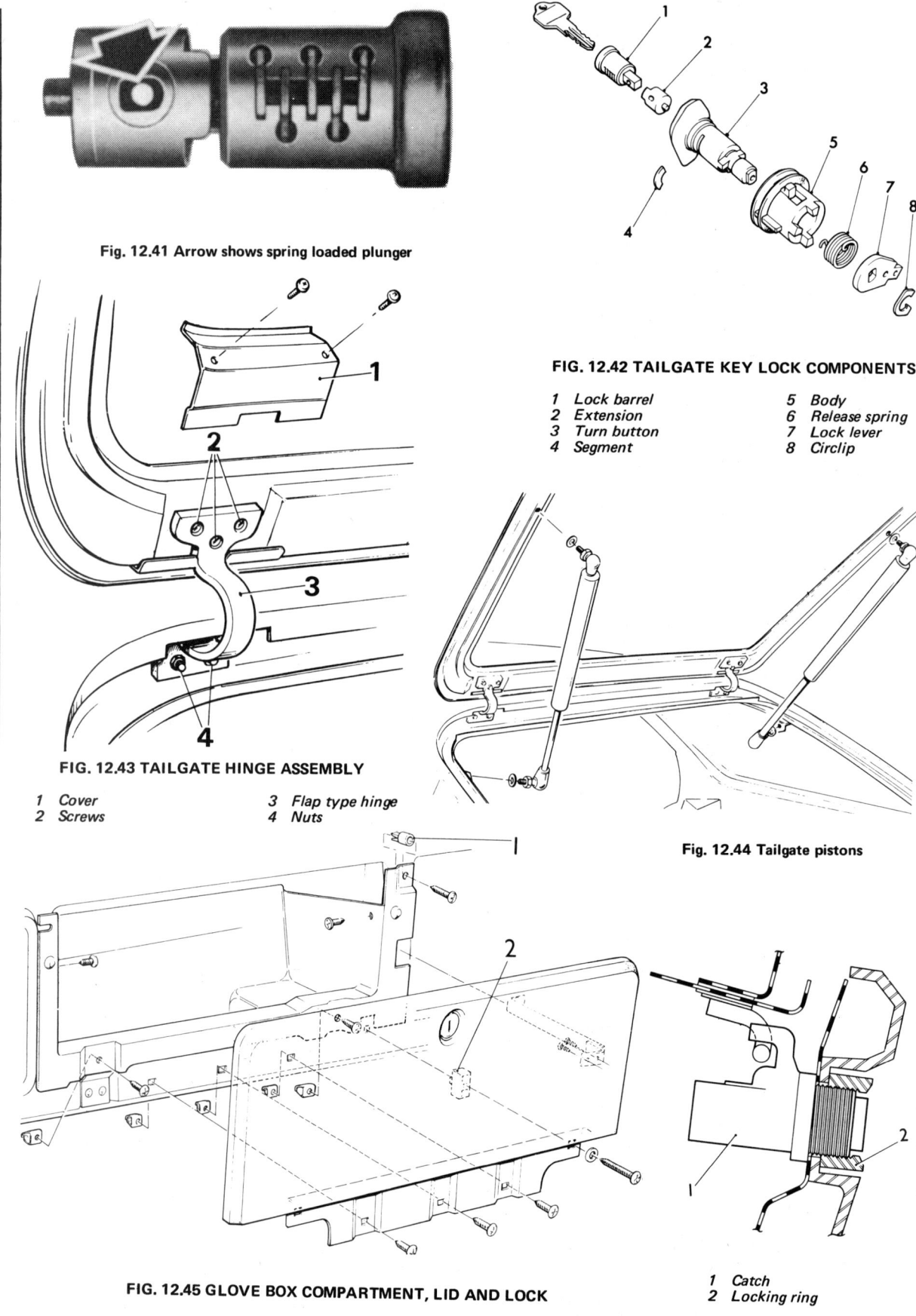

Fig. 12.41 Arrow shows spring loaded plunger

FIG. 12.42 TAILGATE KEY LOCK COMPONENTS

1	Lock barrel	5	Body
2	Extension	6	Release spring
3	Turn button	7	Lock lever
4	Segment	8	Circlip

FIG. 12.43 TAILGATE HINGE ASSEMBLY

1	Cover	3	Flap type hinge
2	Screws	4	Nuts

Fig. 12.44 Tailgate pistons

FIG. 12.45 GLOVE BOX COMPARTMENT, LID AND LOCK

1 Spacer nut (upper)   2 Spacer nut (lower)

1 Catch
2 Locking ring

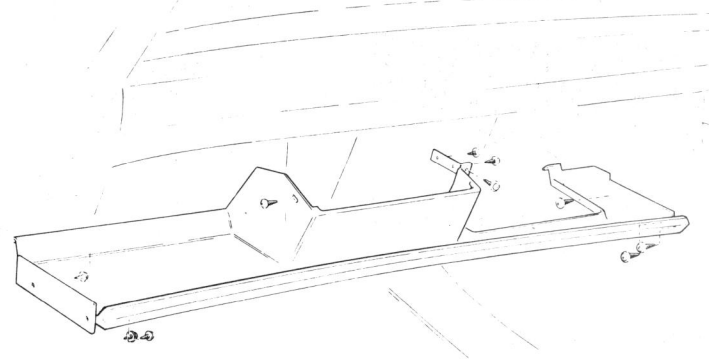

Fig. 12.46 Front parcel shelf attachments

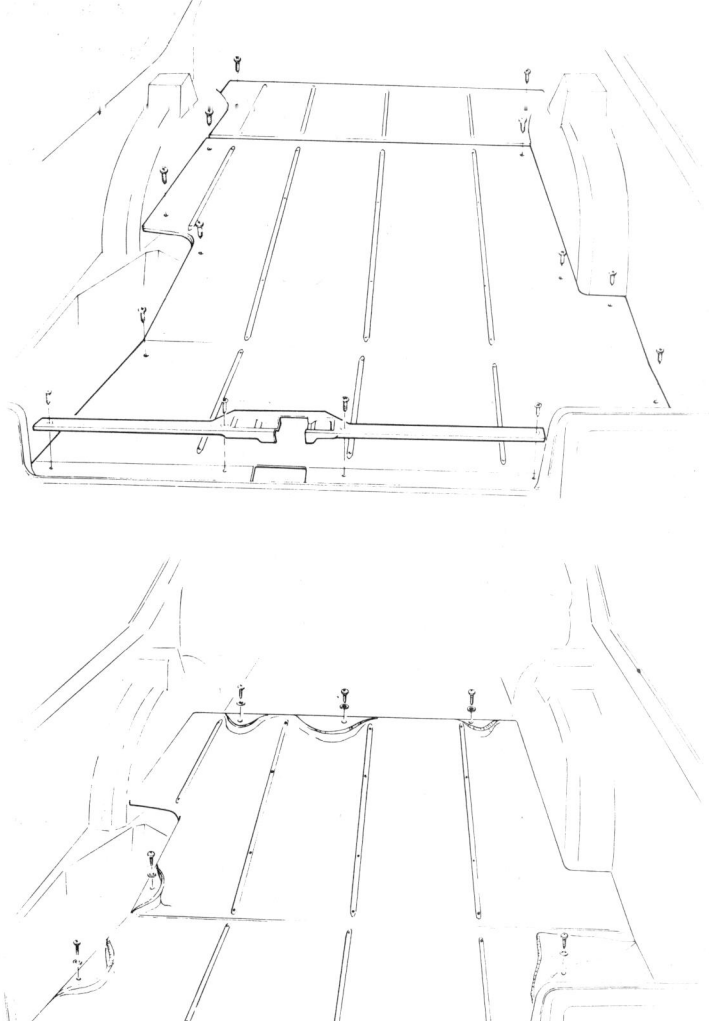

FIG. 12.47 LUGGAGE COMPARTMENT CARPET AND FLOOR ATTACHMENTS

A   Carpet attachment
B   Floor panel attachment

friction surfaces of latch and rods with Castrol LM Grease. The end of the rod must be engaged in the latch release plate hole furthermost from the turn button.

21 Tailgate hinges and stays - removal and replacement

The tailgate is mounted on two flap type hinges as shown in Fig.12.43 They are attached to the roof hinge rail by two nuts and studs and three screws to the door inner panel. A trim cover is fitted over each hinge and retained with two screws.

Two hold open pistons are fitted to the rear door to assist in opening and then holding open. They are mounted on ball joints which are screwed into the body aperture and door inner panel. When refitting they must be placed so that the ball joint at the cylinder end is attached to the door. WARNING: On no account must the piston be dismantled as it contains gas at a high pressure.

22 Glovebox - removal and replacement

1 Refer to Section 24 and remove the long lower instrument panel cover.
2 To remove the glove box lid undo and remove the four screws. Note that one screw is longer than the rest. Lift away the lid.
3 To remove the glove box undo and remove the two screws located inside the box and then the three screws around the edge. However before the two lower screws can be withdrawn with the lid still in place it is necessary to remove the two screws securing the stay to the lid.
4 Refitting is the reverse sequence but the following additional points should be noted:

a) When refitting the glove box to the instrument panel the spacer nut (1) Fig.12.45 must be positioned between the glove box and instrument panel at the upper hole nearest the centre of the instrument panel.
b) When refitting the glove box lid the spacer nut must be positioned between the instrument panel and lid hinge plate in the hole nearest the centre of the instrument panel.

23 Front parcel shelf

The full width parcel shelf is secured with screws located at each end and also at each side of the centre section. Once these have been removed the parcel shelf may be drawn rearwards and through the passenger door aperture.

24 Instrument panel covers

The three covers are held in position by self tapping screws.
To remove the instrument panel upper cover it is necessary to detach the instrument facia, glove box and striker support brackets. The five retaining nuts are then accessible.

25 Luggage compartment floor - Estate models

To remove the floor panel it is first necessary to remove the fourteen screws that secure the edge of the carpet to the floor. The floor may now be released by undoing and removing the six screws and washers. Lift one side of the panel up and draw the floor through the rear door aperture. Refitting the luggage compartment floor and carpeting is the reverse sequence to removal.

Chapter 13 Supplement

Contents

1 Introduction

In 1976 Vauxhall introduced the VX series. This new range of models has the same basic body shell and mechanical specification as the earlier FE series.

The purpose of this Supplement is to provide information on those aspects of the VX series which differ from the FE series. It also completes the information on the FE series — up until the time it was superseded by the VX series.

Each Section of this Supplement relates to one of the main Chapters elsewhere in this manual. The Sections are divided into sub-Sections (headed in italic type) and each one describes a procedure or component within the system or mechanism covered by the Section.

2 Specifications

Engine

Cylinder head (1976/77)
Minimum permissible depth of head after refacing
(camshaft housing face to bottom face, at valve guide centre
line)   ... ...   3.598 in (91.39 mm)

Cylinder block
Minimum permissible depth of block after refacing
(Top face to centre of main bearing housing)
    1759 cc engine   ... ...   8.567 in (217.6 mm)
    2279 cc engine   .. ..   8.552 in (217.2 mm)

Crankshaft and bearings
Rear main bearing width:
    Standard   ... ...   1.335—1.399 in (33.91—34.01 mm)
    0.010 in undersize   ... ...   1.340—1.344 in (34.04—34.14 mm)
    0.020 in undersize   ... ...   1.345—1.349 in (34.16—34.26 mm)
    0.040 in undersize   ... ...   1.350—1.354 in (34.29—34.39 mm)

Fuel system and carburation

Air cleaner (temperature-controlled type)
Type of element   ... ...   Paper (disposable)
Controlled air intake temperature:
    Early type   ... ... $18 \pm 8^\circ$C ($64.4 \pm 46.4^\circ$F)
    Later type   ... ... $29 \pm 4^\circ$C ($84.2 \pm 39.2^\circ$F)

Carburettor — Zenith 36IVE (1759cc engines)
Identification number:
    Manual transmission 3583B
    Automatic transmission 3584B
Choke Tube   ... ...   25 mm
Main jet
    Manual transmission   85
    Automatic transmission   75
Compensating jet
    Manual transmission   115
    Automatic transmission   125
Idling jet ... ...   See text
Pump jet   55
Part throttle air bleed screw   ... ...   1.9 mm
Needle valve   ... ...   2 mm
Needle valve washer thickness ... ...   2 mm
With carburettor cover inverted and needle valve on seating, the
distance between highest point of float and face of cover gasket
should be: ... ...   30.5—31.5 mm
Engine idling speed (Drive range selected on automatic transmission
models)   ... ...   725—775 rpm
Permissible exhaust CO at idling speed   ... ...   Refer to Chapter 3, Section 14

High altitude jet settings:

	Manual	Automatic
Main jet:		
5000—7000 ft (1500—2000 m)	82	72
7000—10 000 ft (2000—3000 m)	80	70
10 000—15 000 ft (3000—4500 m)	75	65
Compensating jet:		
5000—7000 ft (1500—2000 m)	—	122
7000—10 000 ft (2000—3000 m)	112	120
10 000—15 000 ft (3000—4500 m)	110	115

Carburettor — Zenith/Stromberg 175CD—2SE and 175CD—2SET
2279 cc engines — 1974/75 models
Identification number:
    Manual transmission 3592B
    Automatic transmission 3593B
Metering needle:
    Manual transmission   ... ...   BICY
    Automatic transmission   ... ...   BICU

Jet orifice ... ...   2.54 mm
Air valve spring identification colour ... ...   Red
Fast idle cam:
    Manual transmission   ... ...   D
    Automatic transmission C5
Cold start needle   ... ...   MI
Needle valve   ... ...   2 mm
Needle valve washer thickness ... ...   1.6 mm
With carburettor inverted and needle valve on seating, the distance
between highest point of float and face of body (gasket removed)
should be: ... ...   16—17mm
Engine idling speed (Drive range selected on automatic transmission
models)   ... ...   725—775 rpm
Permissible exhaust CO at idling speed   ... ...   Refer to Chapter 3, Section 23

2279 cc engine — 1974/75 VX 4/90 models

Identification number:
    Manual transmission 3599B
    Automatic transmission 3600B
Metering needle ... ...   AIDC
Jet orifice   ... ...   2.54 mm
Air valve spring identification colour ... ...   Blue
Fast idle cam:
    Manual transmission   ... ...   D
    Automatic transmission   ... ...   TI
Cold start needle 3M
Needle valve   ... ...   2 mm
Needle valve washer thickness ... ...   1.6 mm
With carburettor inverted and needle valve on seating, the distance
between highest point of floats and body face (gasket removed)
should be: ... ...   16—17mm
Engine idling speed (Drive range selected on automatic transmission
models)   ... ...   775—825 rpm
Permissible exhaust CO at idling speed   ... ...   Refer to Chapter 3, Section 23

1759 and 2279 cc engines — 1976/77 VX Series (except 4/90)

	Early models	Later models
Identification number:		
1759 cc engine		
Manual transmission	3844B	3934B
Automatic transmission	3845B	3935B
2279 engine		
Manual transmission	3846B	3936B
Automatic transmission	3847B	3937B
Metering needle:		
1759 cc engine	BIEF	
2279 cc engine	BIEG	
Jet orifice	2.6 mm	
Air valve spring identification colour	Blue	
Fast idle cam	C5	
Cold start needle:		
1759 cc engine	P2	
2279 cc engine	P3	
Needle valve	2 mm	
Needle valve washer thickness	1.6 mm	

With carburettor inverted and needle valve on its seat, the distance
between highest point of floats and body face (gasket removed)
should be: ... ...   16—17 mm
Engine idling speed (Drive range selected on automatic transmission
models)   ... ...   725—775 rpm

2279cc engine — 1977, 4/90 model (manual transmission)

Identification number 3906B
Metering needle ... ...   BIER
Jet orifice   ... ...   2.54 mm
Air valve spring identification colour ... ...   Blue
Fast idle cam   ... ...   D
Needle valve   ... ...   2 mm
Needle valve washer thickness ... ...   1.6 mm
With carburettor inverted and needle valve on its seat, the distance
between highest point of floats and body face (gasket removed)
should be: ... ...   16—17 mm
Engine idling speed ... ...   775—825 rpm

Ignition system

Spark plugs

Type	R41-5TS
Gap	0.030—0.040 in (0.76—1.0 mm)

Distributor (Early models)
Vacuum advance: 1759 and 2279 cc engines (1974 models)

Vacuum (in Hg)	Distributor degrees
5	0
10	4
20	6

Centrifugal advance: 1759 cc engine

Cut-in speed	300—400 rpm

Distributor rpm	Distributor degrees
200	0
600	1½—3½
800	3½—5½
1000	5½—7½
1500	7¾—9¾
1800 and over	9—11

Centrifugal advance: 2279cc engine (Victor)

Cut-in speed	375—525 rpm

Distributor rpm	Distributor degrees
375	0
525	0—2
600	1—3
900	4¾—6¾
1250	6¾—8¾
2000	9—11
2500	10½—12½
3000 and over	13½

Centrifugal advance: 2279 cc engine (VX 4/90)

Cut-in speed	350—550 rpm

Distributor rpm	Distributor degrees
300	0
700	3½—7½
850	7—8¾
1000	7½—9½
1500	9—11
1900 and over	10½—12½

Distributor (Later models)
Vacuum advance: 1759 cc (engine No. 3263015 on) and 2279 cc (engine No. 3262950 on) VX engines

Vacuum (in Hg)	Distributor degrees
4.4	0
5.6	0—2
8.0	4—5
9.7 and over	6½—8½

Vacuum advance: 2279 cc VX 4/90 engine

Vacuum (in Hg)	Distributor degrees
5	0
7	0—2¼
9	2¼—4½
11 and over	4—6

Centrifugal advance

Cut-in speed:	
1759 cc VX engine	350—550 rpm
2279 cc VX engine	550—675 rpm
2279 cc VX 4/90 engine	550—650 rpm

Distributor rpm			Distributor degrees		
1759 cc	**2279 cc**	**2279 cc (4/90)**	**1759 cc**	**2279 cc**	**2279 cc (4/90)**
350	500	500	0	0	0
550	700	700	0—4½	¼—2¼	1—3½
750	1000	850	4¼—8¼	4—6	4½—7
1000	1600	1000	7—9¼	8¼—10¼	5½—7½
1500	1850	1600	9¼—11¼	10—12	8½—10
2000	3000	1900	11¼—13¼	12	10—12
2500	—	3000	12½—14½		12

Cam dwell angle ... ...   49° — 51°

Gearbox and automatic transmission

FE Victor (later model) speedometer gears

Axle ratio	Tyre size	Teeth on driven gear
11/38	175SR—13	15
11/38	185/70SR—14	15
11/41	175SR—13	16
10/37	185/70SR—14	15

Overdrive operating pressure (later models)
1759 cc engine ... ...   320—350 lbf/in^2 (22.4—24.5 kgf/cm^2)
2279 cc engine ... ...   370—400 lbf/in^2 (25.9—28.0 kgf/cm^2)

Getrag 5-speed gearbox
Minimum width of selector fork flanges:
    1st/reverse and 2nd/3rd ... ...   0.230 in (5.85 mm)
    4th/5th ... ...   0.191 in (4.85 mm)
Reverse idler gear endfloat ... ...   0.004—0.008 in (0.1—0.2 mm)
Lubricant
    Type ... ...   SAE 90 EP (Castrol-Hypoy)
    Capacity ... ...   2.5 pints (1.4 litre)

Torque wrench settings	lbf ft	kgf m
Coupling flange nut	74	10
Layshaft 1st gear nut	44	6
Casing bolts	15	2
Gearchange support bracket bolts	30	4

Rear axle — VX 2300 and 4/90

Type ... ...   Semi-floating hypoid

Oil capacity ... ...   5.2 pts (2.95 litres)

Pinion bearing pre-load
    New bearings ... ...   4—8 lbf in (4.6—9.2 kgf cm)
    Used bearings ... ...   3—5 lbf in (3.4—5.7 kgf cm)

Differential
Pinion shaft diameter ... ...   0.6242—0.6248 in (15.85—15.87 mm)
Pinion clearance on shaft ... ...   0.0027—0.0053 in (0.07—0.13 mm)
Side bearing pre-load
    New bearings ... ...   3 lbf in (3.4 kgf cm)
    Used bearings ... ...   1 lbf in (1.14 kgf cm)
Permissible run-out of differential case flange ... ...   0.001 in (0.03 mm) maximum
Crownwheel and pinion backlash ... ...   0.006—0.008 in (0.15—0.20 mm)

Torque wrench setting	lbf ft	kgf cm
Differential bearing cap bolts	38	5.2
Axleshaft bearing retainer nuts	20	2.7
Coupling flange nut	100	13.8

Electrical system

Bulb — table for VX series

Component		Watts	Bulb type
Headlamp (except GLS models)	... ...	60/55	Quartz halogen H4
Headlamp, GLS models:			
Inner lamp (main beam)	... ...	55	Quartz halogen H1
Outer lamp (dual beam)	... ...	60/55	Quartz halogen H4
Sidelamp (except GLS)	... ...	4	Miniature centre contact
Sidelamp, GLS only	... ...	5	Wedge base, capless
Tail/stop lamp	... ...	21/5	Bayonet cap (offset pins)
Turn signal lamp	... ...	21	Centre contact
Fog lamp	... ...	55	Quartz halogen H3
Number plate lamp	... ...	5	Wedge base, capless
Interior lamp	... ...	10	Festoon
Instrument lamps	... ...	3	Wedge base, capless
Turn signal indicator lamp	... ...	3	Wedge base, capless
Oil pressure warning lamp	... ...	3	Wedge base, capless
Ignition warning lamp	... ...	3	Wedge base, capless
Main beam warning lamp	... ...	3	Wedge base, capless
Handbrake 'on' warning lamp	... ...	3	Wedge base, capless
Back window demist 'on' warning lamp	... ...	0.65(nom)	Lilliput edison screw
Hazard warning 'on' lamp	... ...	0.65(nom)	Lilliput edison screw
Heater fan 'on' lamp	... ...	0.65(nom)	Lilliput edison screw
Fog lamp 'on' lamp	... ...	0.65(nom)	Lilliput edison screw
Time clock lamp	... ...	2	Peanut
Heater controls lamp	... ...	2	Peanut
Automatic transmission lamp	... ...	2	Peanut
Lamp switches illumination lamp	... ...	0.03(amp)	Wedge base capless
Cigar lighter lamp	... ...	2.2	Miniature centre contact
Boot lamp	... ...	5	Small bayonet cap

3 Engine

Engine rear mounting

1   On later models the mounting is secured by a single bolt to a bracket attached to the transmission casing. A large washer is fitted beneath the mounting sleeve to restrict the upward movement of the transmission on rebound.

2   Hexagonal shaped washers must be positioned with two flats of the hexagon placed transversely across the car to ensure clearance of the crossmember channel on rebound.

3   On cars fitted with automatic transmission the bolts are located in the third hole of the bracket from the front.

4   On VX 4/90 models the rear crossmember rubber mounting

is secured to the mounting bracket by a single bolt. A large, shaped washer is fitted below the mounting (Fig. 13.2), and restricts upward movement of the transmission on rebound. When fitting the crossmember, ensure that the slotted end is on the left-hand side.

5   If fitting a new centre mounting to the crossmember ensure that the cut-out on the centre mounting is located towards the front of the car. (Fig.13.3)

Camshaft and auxiliary shaft drivebelt cover

6   On later engines a lower support bracket is fitted to improve the security of the camshaft and auxiliary shaft drivebelt cover. The bracket is fastened with pop-rivets to the cover and secured at the cylinder block by a 0.375 in UNF bolt using an existing threaded hole.

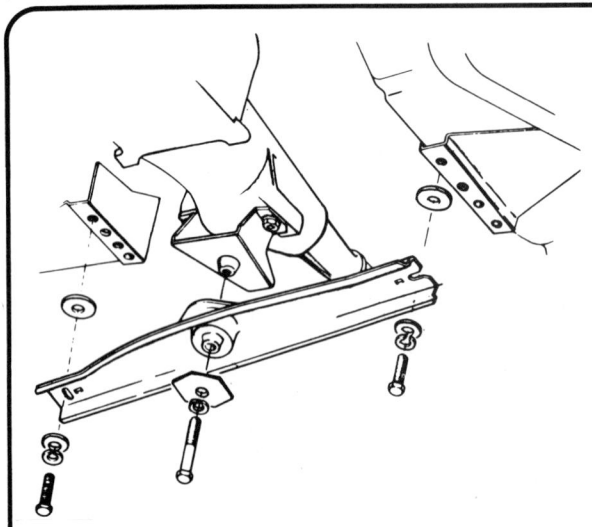

Fig. 13.1. Engine rear mounting—1800 and 2300 later models (Sec 3)

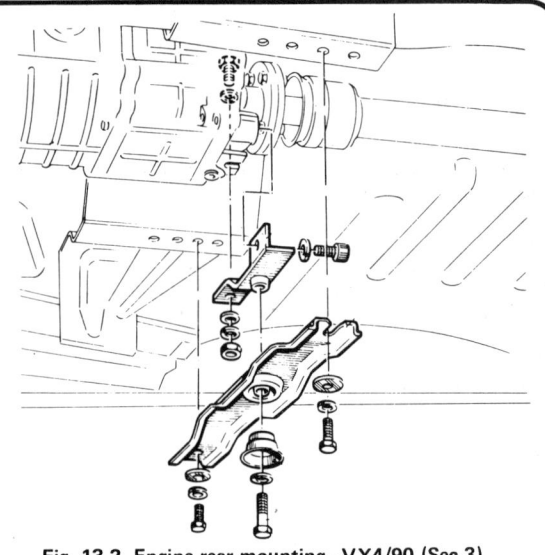

Fig. 13.2. Engine rear mounting—VX4/90 (Sec 3)

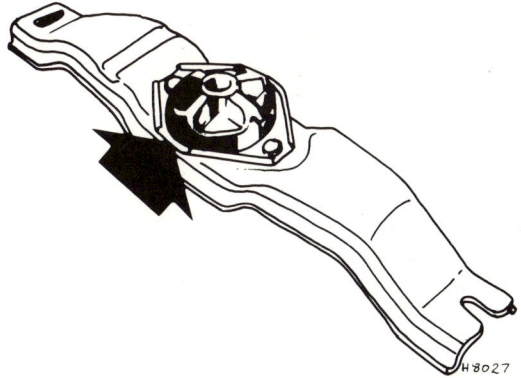

Fig. 13.3 Cut-out positioned towards front of car (Sec 3)

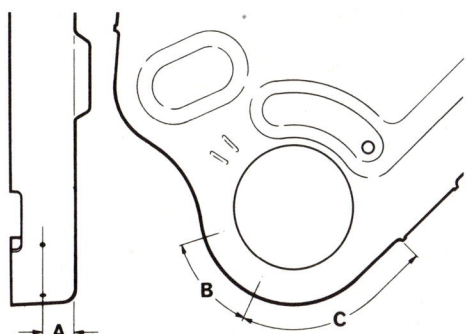

Fig. 13.4 Modifying the drivebelt cover (Sec 3)

A = 0.9 in (23 mm)   C = 4.88 in (123.8 mm)
B = 2.25 in (57.2 mm)

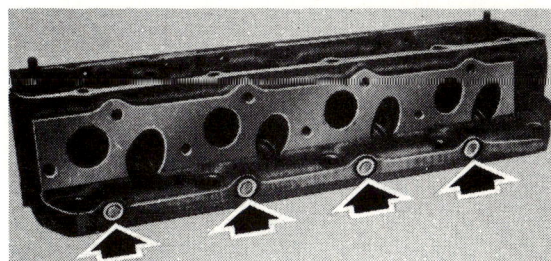

Fig. 13.5 Core plugs fitted to early type cylinder head (Sec 3)

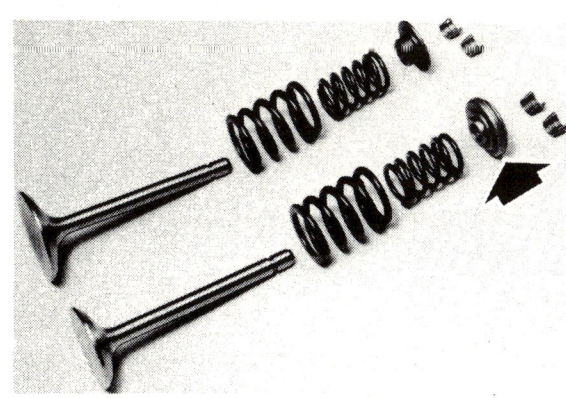

Fig. 13.6 Valve spring rotators (arrowed) (Sec 3)

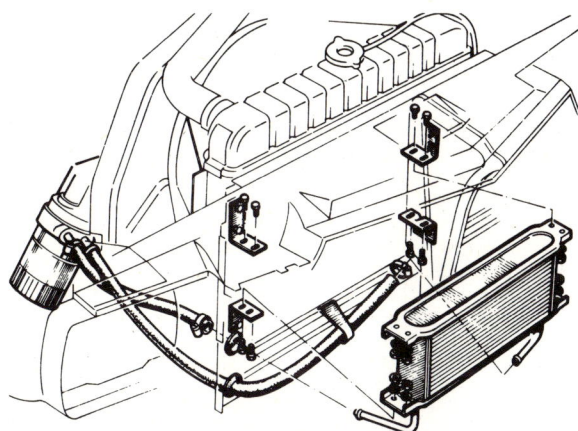

Fig. 13.7 Engine oil cooler — VX Series 4/90 (Sec 3)

7 Existing covers can be modified by drilling two 0.125 in (3.3 mm) holes, as shown in Fig.13.4, and attaching the bracket to the cover as described in paragraph 6.

Cylinder head
8 A new cylinder head is fitted to 1976/7 1759 and 2279 cc engines. It can be distinguished from earlier cylinder heads by the absence of core plugs which the early cylinder heads have as shown by the arrows in Fig.13.5.
9 On 1759 cc engines a new cylinder head gasket is used and the earlier type gasket cannot be used with the later type cylinder head.
10 On the later type cylinder heads the valve spring caps are replaced by valve rotators.

Engine oil cooler (VX series 4/90) — removal and refitting
11 VX 4/90 models equipped with an engine oil cooler have the cooler located between the radiator and the radiator grille. It is secured to four right-angled brackets, mounted on the front panel, by eight nuts and bolts.

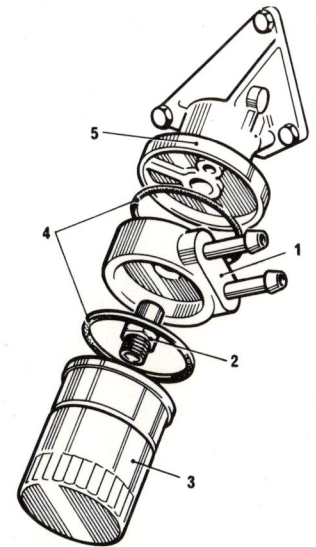

Fig. 13.8 Engine oil filter assembly — VX Series 4/90 (Sec 3)

1 Adaptor   4 Rubber sealing rings
2 Connector   5 Filter head
3 Oil filter

12 Oil travels to and from the oil cooler via hoses and an adaptor interposed between the filter head and the full-flow filter. The adaptor is secured to the filter head by a connector (Fig.13.8).

Two rubber sealing rings are used; one in a recess in the filter casing attachment face and the other in a recess in the adaptor top face.

13 Removal of the oil cooler is straightforward. Remove the radiator grille as described in Chapter 12. Place a suitable container under the oil cooler, disconnect the hoses and drain the oil. Undo and remove the attaching nuts and bolts and lift out the cooler.

14 Refitting is a reversal of the removal sequence. Do not forget to check the engine oil level and top up if necessary.

Flexplate distance plate

15 On later models fitted with automatic transmission a modified flexplate distance plate was introduced. The new distance plate is dished and of a larger diameter than the earlier type.

16 When fitting the flexplate and the distance plate on the crankshaft, locate the distance plate as shown in Fig.13.9 and tighten the bolts evenly to the specified torque.

17 It is recommended that whenever the opportunity arises the modified distance plate should be fitted in place of the earlier type.

Connecting rod assembly

18 In 1975 a strengthened connecting rod assembly was introduced. The new type of connecting rod has two oil discharge holes (Fig.13.10), and larger diameter cap securing bolts.

19 The larger diameter bolt does not have a shouldered shank and should be tightened to 58 lbf ft (8.0 kgf m).

4   Cooling system

Viscous coupling fan and water pump

1 Later models are equipped with a viscous coupling fan which is filled with oil and allows direct drive through the coupling to the fan up to engine speeds of approximately 1000 rpm. As the engine speed increases further, the drive through the coupling to the fan progressively decreases, and reduces fan noise, without impairing the efficiency of the cooling system.

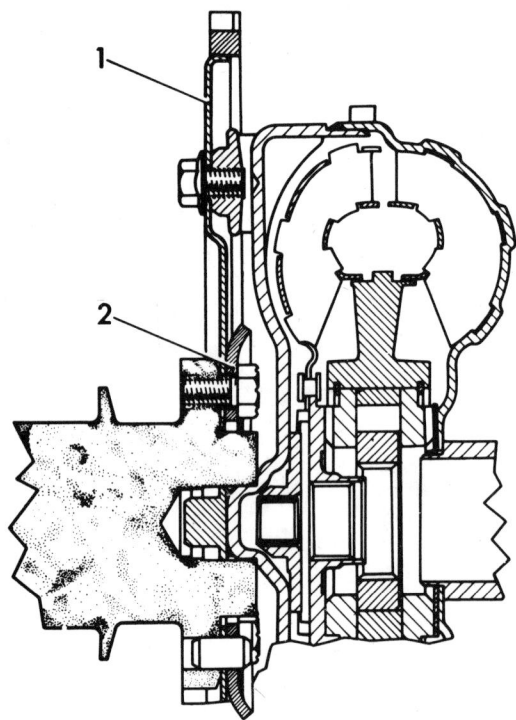

Fig. 13.9 Fitting the flex plate and distance plate (Sec 3)

1   Flex plate   2   Distance plate

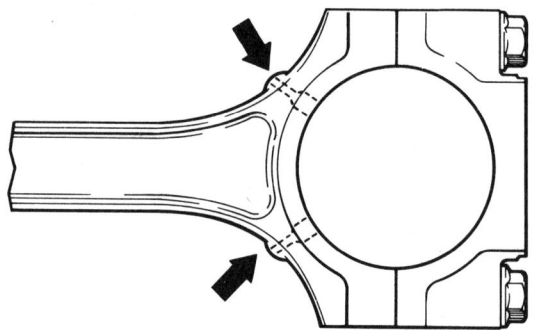

Fig.13.10 Later type connecting rod with two oil holes (Sec 3)

Fig.13.11 Exploded view of viscous coupling fan assembly (Sec 4)

2   The viscous coupling is bolted to the fan, which has five irregularly spaced blades, and the fan and coupling assembly is secured to the water pump flange by a centre bolt which has a left-hand thread.

3   If the fan and coupling assembly are to be separated for any reason, then the fan and coupling must be marked so that they can be reassembled in their original position. This is important as the assembly is a balanced unit.

4   The viscous coupling is a sealed unit and cannot be dismantled. If there are any signs of oil leaking past the seals, the fan and coupling assembly must be renewed complete.

5   When fitting the pulley flange to the water pump on engines equipped with a viscous coupling fan the pulley flange must be pressed onto the water pump shaft so that dimension 'A', (Fig.13.12) is 3.70 in (94 mm) and dimension 'B' 0.05 in (1.3 mm).

6   On later engines the water pump has a ceramic counterface located between the rotor and the seal. It should be fitted with its ceramic face towards the pump seal.

---

5   Fuel system and carburation

Temperature controlled air cleaner — description and checking

1   Models from 1974 onwards are fitted with a temperature controlled air cleaner, and comprise a paper type element, a temperature sensing unit, a vacuum motor and a control damper assembly. The purpose of this type of air cleaner is to maintain air passing into the carburettor intake at a constant temperature level which will permit the use of a weaker mixture and also eliminate icing of the carburettor.

2   The action of the sensor and control damper assembly regulates the intake of under-bonnet air and that drawn from a shroud covering the exhaust manifold so that a pre-determined air temperature level is maintained.

3   A fault in the sensor unit or vacuum motor will generally result in the control damper closing the hot air port and keeping the cold air port open. In warm weather this will probably go unnoticed. However, in cold weather, this fault may be indicated by a generally poor performance, hesitation, surge or stalling. If a weak mixture is indicated first check the air cleaner to ensure it functions correctly before checking the carburettor setting.

4   First check all hoses for correct routing. Check for kinked, blocked or damaged hoses. With the engine switched off check the position of the damper flap through the air cleaner intake using a mirror. The cold air port should be open, the hot air port should be closed. If the damper flap is not in this position, check the linkage for freedom of movement and adjust if necessary. For checking the vacuum motor a vacuum pump is required and this should be left to your local Vauxhall dealer.

5. An initial check of the sensor can be carried out by observing the position of the damper flap through the air cleaner intake (again using a mirror) before starting the engine. The cold air port should be fully open and the hot air port closed. Start the engine and run it at idling speed. Immediately after starting the engine check that the cold air port is closed and the hot air port is open. As the engine warms up check that the damper flap moves, partially opening the cold air port, and the air cleaner becomes warm when touched with a hand.

6   If the system fails to operate, as described in paragraph 5, it will be necessary to check the sensor against a thermometer as shown in Figs. 13.14, 13.15, 13.16, and 13.18. On later type air cleaners, an electric type thermometer is required because of the time delay in gaining access to read the ordinary type of thermometer. If the sensor is defective it cannot be adjusted and a new sensor unit must be fitted.

Temperature controlled air cleaner — renewal of vacuum motor and sensor unit

7   On early type air cleaners the vacuum motor is secured by a metal strap. One end is inserted in the intake tube and the other end is spot welded to the tube in three places (Fig.13.18). To remove the motor drill through the spot welds and release the strap, then unhook the diaphragm rod from the control damper and lift away the motor. When fitting the new motor use self-tapping screws to secure the motor in place of the spot welds. On later type air cleaners if the vacuum motor is defective, the motor and intake tube assembly must be renewed as a unit.

8   To remove the sensor unit, disconnect the vacuum hoses, lever off the retaining clip and lift away the sensor unit.

9   Refitting is a reversal of the removal sequence.

Fuel pump — general

10 On some types of fuel pump there is no diaphragm oil seal, retainer or fuel drain holes in the body. Fuel pumps with drain

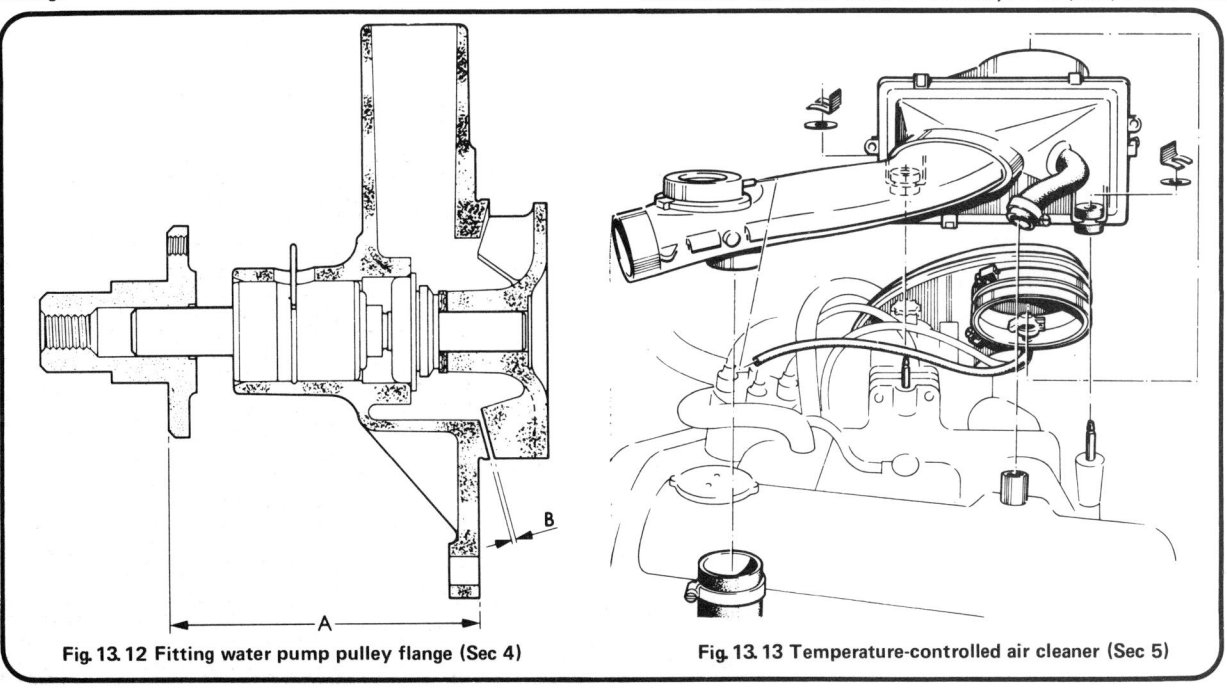

Fig. 13. 12 Fitting water pump pulley flange (Sec 4)   Fig. 13. 13 Temperature-controlled air cleaner (Sec 5)

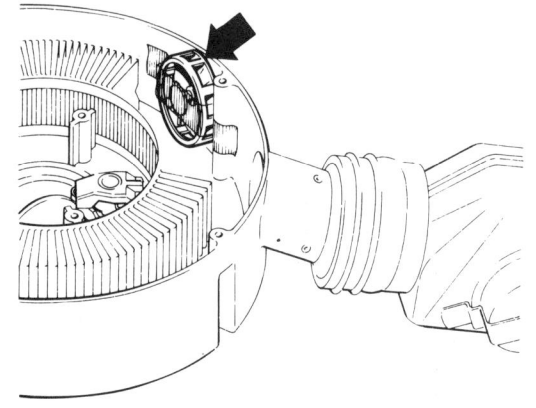

Fig. 13. 14 Position of thermometer on 1759cc engines (early type air cleaner) (Sec 5)

Fig. 13. 15 Position of thermometer on 2279cc engine (single carburettor) (Sec 5)

Fig. 13. 16 Position of thermometer on 2279cc engine (twin carburettors) (Sec 5)

Fig. 13. 17 Removing the vacuum motor — early type air cleaners (Sec 5)

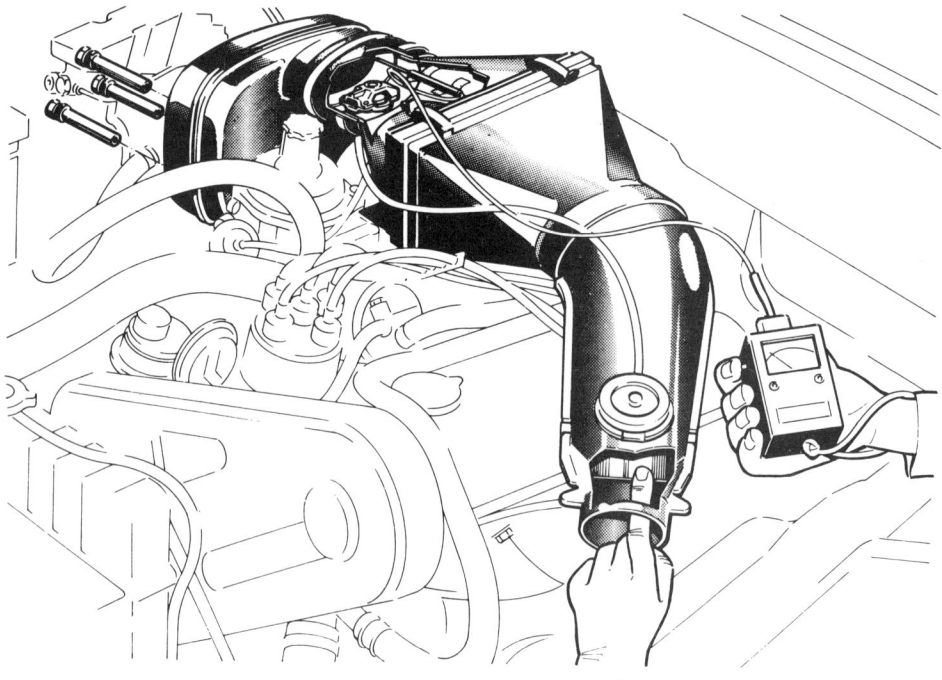

Fig. 13. 18 Using an electric-thermometer to check the sensor unit on later type air cleaner (Sec 5)

holes in the body must have a diaphragm oil seal and retainer fitted to prevent emission of crankcase vapours.

11 On later single carburettor engines a sealed fuel pump is fitted. Except for removing the top cover to gain access to the filter gauze, no other dismantling is possible. When refitting the filter gauze ensure that the four pegs on the filter are uppermost and that the top cover seats correctly on the sealing ring.

Zenith 36IVE carburettor — description

12 The Zenith 36IVE carburettor fitted to 1974/75 1759 cc engines is used on both manual and automatic transmission models. It is similar to the 36IVE carburettor described in Chapter 3 except for the following:

a) The float chamber is vented both internally and externally; the external vent having a plastic elbow vent (Fig. 13.20)

b) The acceleration pump connecting pin is fitted in the lower hole in the pump spindle lever on models with manual transmission, and in the upper hole on automatic transmission models

c) The idling jet is selectively fitted and should only be replaced by a jet of the same size within the range 47 to 53

d) A part-throttle air bleed screw is fitted

Zenith 36IVT carburettor — fast idle screw setting

13 Later engines fitted to models with automatic transmission have a different fast idle screw setting from that given in Chapter 3, Section 13.

14 With the carburettor removed from the engine, fully close the choke flap and adjust the fast idle screw against the top step of the fast idle cam to give a gap at the edge of the throttle flap of 1.4 mm. Use a No. 54 drill to ensure accuracy.

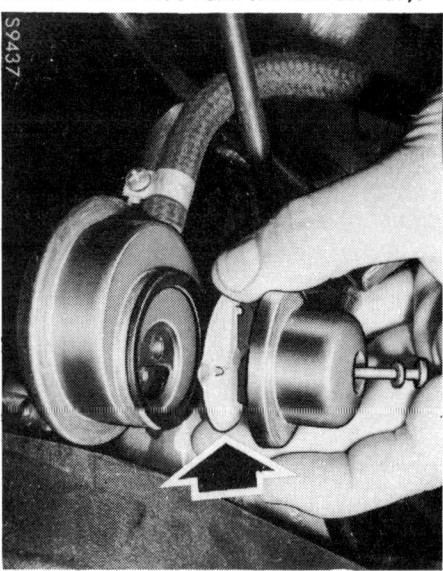

Fig. 13.19 Sealed type fuel pump with cover removed and filter gauge (arrowed) (Sec 5)

Fig. 13.20 External float chamber vent (Zenith 36IVE carburettor) Sec 5)

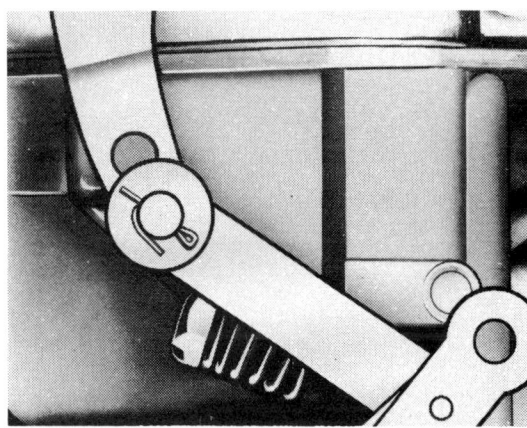

Fig. 13.21 Acceleration pump connecting pin (Zenith 36IVE carburettor) (Sec 5)

Fig. 13.22 Part throttle air bleed screw (Zenith 36IVE carburettor) (Sec 5)

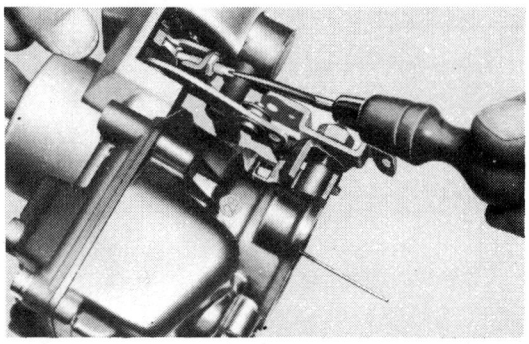

Fig. 13.23 Adjusting the fast idle screw setting (Zenith 36IVE carburettor) (Sec 5)

15 Earlier carburettors may be adjusted to this setting if the engine will not fast idle or stalls when cold.

Zenith/Stromberg 175CD–2SE and 175CD–2SET carburettors

16 1974/75 models with manual transmission are fitted with 175CD-2SE carburettor and automatic transmission models have the 175CD-2SET carburettor. All 1976/77 models, except VX 4/90 models (which have twin 175CD—2SE carburettors), have a 175CD—2SET carburettor fitted irrespective of which type of transmission is fitted.

17 The 175CD-2SE and 2SET carburettors are similar to the 175CD-2S and 2ST types respectively and can be serviced as described in Chapter 3 in conjunction with the following information:

    a) A different jet adjuster is fitted and is sealed with a nylon plug during manufacture. No attempt should be made to remove the nylon plug from the jet adjuster

    b) On later 175CD-2SET carburettors the float chamber housing is extended and a peg type wrench is required to rotate the jet adjuster. The Vauxhall wrench is shown in Fig.13.25. Note: The float chamber must be removed before withdrawing the jet adjuster

    c) The dome-shaped filter fitted to the fuel level needle valve cannot be dismantled from the needle valve assembly

    d) When fitting the jet assembly ensure that the nylon washer is located on the jet stem between the flange and plain washer. (Fig.13.26)

    e) Before fitting the float chamber, screw the jet adjuster fully into the carburettor body otherwise the float chamber may foul the shoulder on the jet adjuster before it seats on the carburettor body gasket.

Zenith/Stromberg 175CD-2SE and 175CD-2SET — adjustment

18 To initially set the jet adjuster, screw it fully home, then unscrew it two turns. Run the engine to obtain normal operating temperature.

19 Adjust the throttle stop screw to achieve the specified idling speed and rotate the jet adjuster until the engine runs smoothly.

20 The idling speed trimmer screw, located above the temperature compensator, regulates an air bleed into the mixing chamber and provides an idling speed fine mixture control. This screw must not be unscrewed more than four turns off its seat.

21 If further adjustment is necessary, set the idling speed trimming screw two turns off its seat and then re-adjust the jet adjuster.

22 On later carburettors the idling speed trimming screw is sealed with a nylon sleeve and soft metal cap. To gain access to the screw, pierce the cap and prise it from the nylon sleeve. Always fit a new soft metal cap after adjustment of the carburettor is complete.

23 On later single carburettor models the metering needle can be adjusted for height should it be necessary to disturb the manufacturer's setting. To reposition the metering needle in the air piston, slacken the securing screw (Fig.13.28), and rotate the adjusting screw using a suitable tool. Fig.13.29 shows the Vauxhall tool, but a tool can be made from a 9.5 mm bar or a 3/8 in bolt suitably polished to enter the piston guide tube.

24 On the 175CD-2SET single carburettor the clearance, dimension 'A' in Fig.13.30, between the fast idle screw and cam (on the base circle) should be 0.025 in (0.65 mm).

Throttle control linkage (VX 4/90)

25 The throttle cable on later FE series VX 4/90 cars, with automatic transmission, is routed via a bracket, (Fig.13.31), which

Fig. 13.26 Fitting the jet assembly (175CD—2SE and 2SET carburettor) (Sec 5)

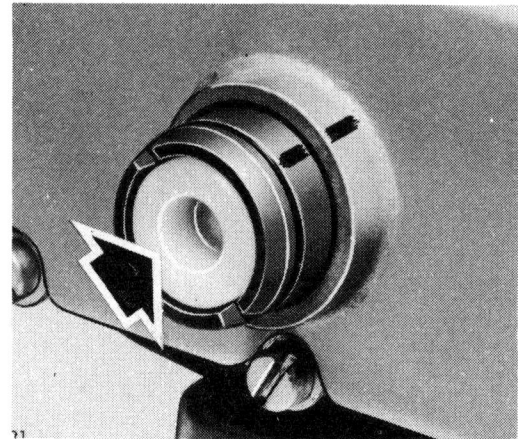

Fig. 13.24 Jet adjuster nylon plug (175CD—2SE and 2SET carburettors) (Sec 5)

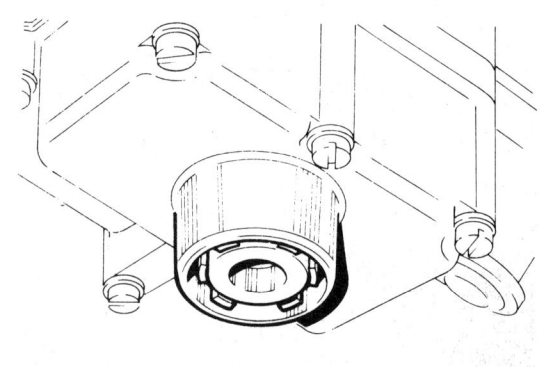

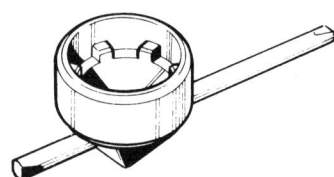

Fig. 13.25 Jet adjuster and wrench (later 175CD—2SET carburettor) (Sec 5)

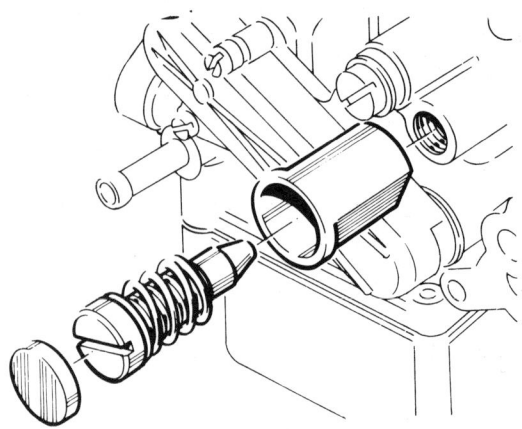

Fig. 13.27 Idle speed trimming screw and soft metal cap (Sec 5)

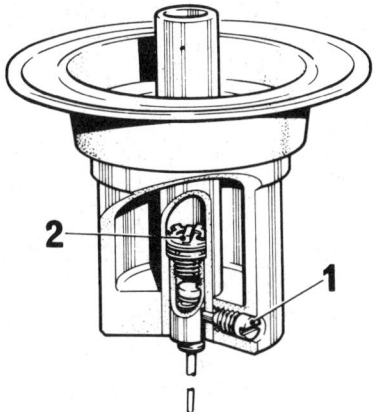

Fig. 13.28 Adjusting the metering needle position (later single carburettor engines) (Sec 5)

1 Securing screw 2 Adjusting screw

Fig. 13.30 Fast idle setting (175CD–2SET single carburettor engine) (Sec 5)

is secured to the intake manifold air balance tube. A new type of relay lever is fitted and is supported by a bracket attached to the manifold stabilizer bracket.

6 Ignition system

Distributor – 1759 and 2279 cc engines (1974 models)
1 With the introduction of hot air induction on 1974 models, the vacuum and centrifugal advance curves were changed. The revised data is given in the Specifications at the beginning of this Chapter.

Distributor cam lubricator
2 A distributor cam lubricator, consisting of a plastic foam wick, which is maintained in contact with the distributor cam by a nylon clip secured to the contact breaker plate, was introduced on 1759 cc and 2279 cc engines at engine Nos. 3098059 and 3097791 respectively.
3 The foam wick is initially impregnated with grease and oil must never be used as a substitute lubricant. At each servicing apply a lithium based grease very sparingly to the wick and work it well into the foam.
4 When the wick becomes contaminated with dirt renew the lubricator assembly. To remove the lubricator from the contact breaker plate, use a pair of long-nosed pliers to squeeze the legs of the retaining clip together and withdraw the lubricator. Fitting the new lubricator assembly is a reversal of the removal procedure.

Fig. 13.29 Metering needle adjusting tool (Sec 5)

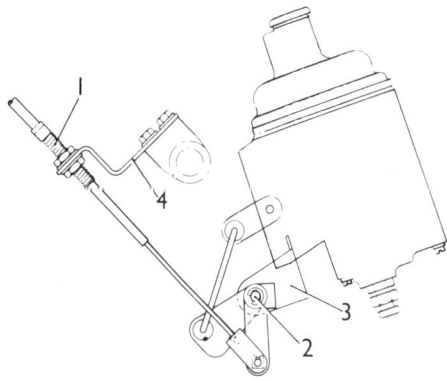

Fig. 13.31 Throttle control linkage – VX 4/0 (Sec 5)

1 Throttle cable 3 Bracket
2 Relay lever shaft 4 Bracket

Distributor cam dwell angle
5 The cam dwell angle on 1759 cc engines, No. 3263015 on and 2279 cc engines No. 3262950 on, is changed from 35°–37° to 49° – 51°. The contact breaker gap and ignition timing are unchanged.
6 The vacuum and centrifugal data is given in the Specifications at the beginning of this Chapter.

Spark plugs
7 The spark plugs, ACR41TS and R42TS, have been superseded by type R41–5TS for both 1759 cc and 2279 cc engines.
8 The gap of the R41–5TS spark plug is increased from 0.030 in (0.76 mm) to 0.040 in (1.0 mm) on engines from No.3276805 onwards.

Fig. 13.32 Removing the cam lubricator (Sec 6)

7   Clutch and actuating mechanism

1   On the VX series the clutch fork return spring is replaced by a torsion spring located on the pedal shaft (Fig.13.33), and a new clutch pedal is fitted.

2.   The torsion spring maintains tension on the clutch cable and there is no clutch fork free travel.

3   Clutch cable adjustment is correct when the clutch pedal is a-ligned with the brake pedal. Wear of the clutch causes the clutch pedal to move upwards and therefore out of alignment with the brake pedal. This indicates that the clutch cable requires adjust-ment. Adjust as necessary by loosening the locknut and rotating the adjusting nut. Tighten the locknut once adjustment is com-plete.

8   Gearbox and automatic transmission

Transmission/overdrive unit — draining the oil

1   On later models the gearbox drain plug is discontinued. In order to drain the gearbox it will be necessary to remove the bottom cover, in addition to the overdrive sump, to allow all the oil to drain completely.

Manual transmission — reverse pinion shaft

2   To improve the oil sealing of the gearbox a sealant is used on the end of the reverse pinion shaft. At assembly, after initial fitt-ing of the reverse pinion shaft, apply a sealant (Wellseal jointing compound is recommended) to the end of the shaft before it is driven fully home.

Selector lever, automatic transmission (later cars) — re-moval and refitting

3   On later cars a new selector lever, selector plate and housing

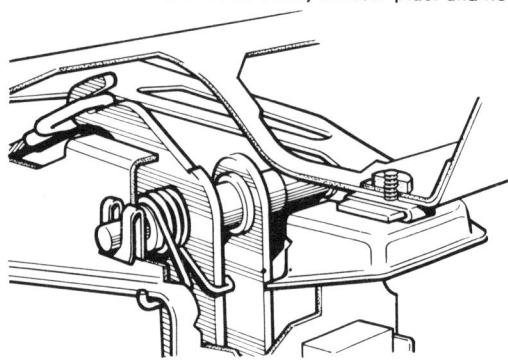

Fig. 13.33 Clutch pedal torsion spring (VX series) (Sec 7)

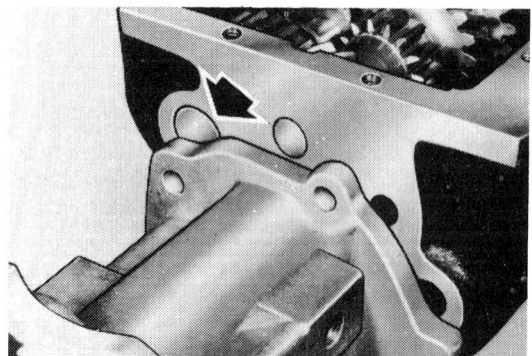

Fig. 13.34 Apply sealant to reverse pinion shaft (arrowed) (Sec 8)

assembly is fitted. The selector lever and pivot shaft can be lifted out from the housing after removing the switch bracket, selector plate and rollpin (Fig. 13.35).

4   Refitting is a reversal of the removal procedure. Always use a new rollpin.

Starter inhibitor and reverse lamp switches — automatic transmission

5   On VX and later FE models, the starter inhibitor and reverse lamp switches are operated by a cam and are attached to a brack-et secured to the selector lever housing by two nuts. The cam is operated by a pin on the side of the selector lever. The inhibitor switch is positioned towards the front of the car. Clearance holes are provided in the switch bracket to allow adjustment. The switches are accessible after removing the selector lever console.

6   To adjust the position of the switches, refer to Fig.13.36 and set the selector lever in 'N' (neutral), then check that the selector plunger (1) is in alignment with the cutaway (2) in the top of the selector plate.

7   Slacken the two nuts securing the switch bracket and slide the bracket until the line (3), scribed on the cam, is in alignment with alignment mark (4) on setting aperture on the switch bracket, then tighten nuts.

8   Check that the starter will not operate when 'D', 'I' (2), 'L' (I) or 'R' is selected. Check also that the roller on the reverse lamp switch is depressed by the cam when 'R' is selected.

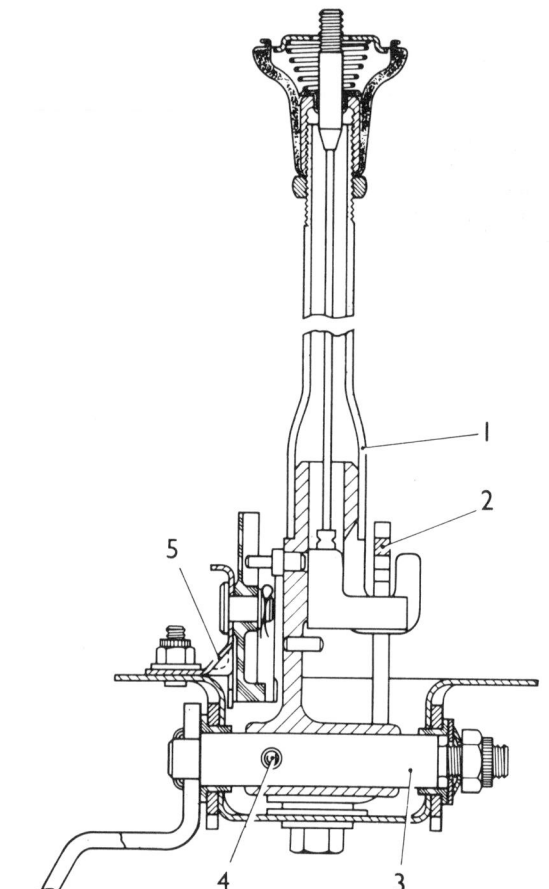

Fig. 13.35 Automatic transmission selector lever (later models)
(Sec 8)

1   *Selector lever*   4   *Roll pin*
2   *Selector plate*   5   *Switch bracket*
3   *Pivot shaft*

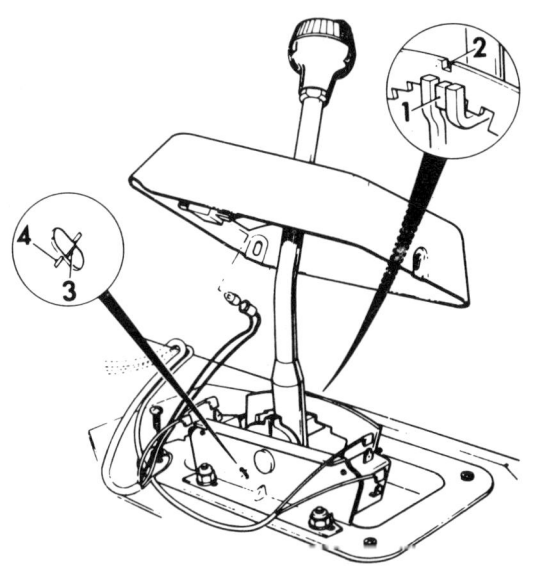

Fig. 13.36 Adjusting inhibitor and reverse lamp switches (Sec 8)

1 *Selector plunger*   3 *Line on cam*
2 *Selector plate cut-away*   4 *Line on switch bracket*

Getrag 5-speed gearbox — general description

The Getrag gearbox, introduced in 1977, has five forward gears and one reverse. Synchromesh is fitted to all forward gears. Gear selection is by means of a centrally located floor-type gearlever mounted on a bracket attached to the rear casing and connected to the selector shaft by a mechanical linkage.

A bearing supports the rear of the main drive pinion in the front casing and a spigot on the front of the pinion is located in a bearing in the end of the crankshaft.

The mainshaft runs in a roller bearing in the main drive pinion counterbore at the front end and in a ball bearing at the rear in the rear casing. All the mainshaft gears run on roller bearings. The synchromesh clutch assemblies are splined to the mainshaft between each pair of gears.

The front end of the layshaft runs in a ball bearing in the front casing and the rear end of the layshaft runs in a roller bearing in the intermediate casing. The reverse idler gear runs in two roller bearings on the stationary reverse idler gear shaft. The idler gear endfloat is adjusted by a selective thrust washer.

Gear selection is by means of three selector forks attached to three rods which are actuated by a single selector shaft.

Getrag gearbox — removal and refitting

9 Removal and refitting procedures are basically the same as described for the 4-speed gearbox in Chapter 6, Sections 2 and 12.

Getrag gearbox — dismantling

10 Before commencing any dismantling, read through the whole of this sub-section to ensure that the facilities to complete the job are at hand. It may be necessary to hire or borrow some of the tools and it is better to find this out before proceeding with any dismantling. Note that the mainshaft and layshaft gears (except reverse) are matched pairs and must not be renewed individually.
11 Dismantling of the gearbox can be carried out more easily if a simple holding bracket is fabricated from 1.0 x 0.2 in (25 x 5 mm) angle iron, to the dimensions shown in Fig. 13.37, which can be mounted in a vice.
12 If not already drained, drain the gearbox oil.
13 Remove the rear crossmember mounting bracket and all the casing securing bolts except the three shown by 'A' in Fig. 13.39. Use a suitable piece of tubing 2.6 in (66 mm) long (arrowed) when attaching the bracket to the gearbox and then mount the assembly in a vice.
14 Unscrew the reverse lamp switch from the rear casing.
15 Remove the front cover, gasket and shims then, using circlip pliers, remove the retaining circlip and selective washer from the main drive pinion. (Fig.13.40)

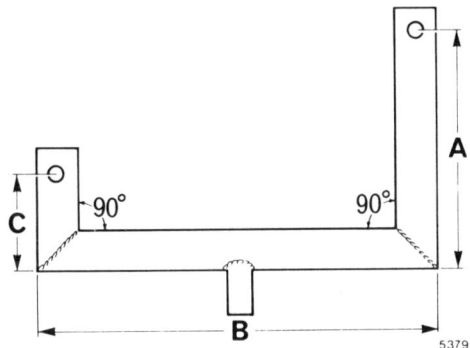

Fig. 13.37 Gearbox holding bracket dimensions (Sec 8)

A = 5.1 in (130 mm)   C = 2.3 in (59 mm)
B = 8.9 in (225 mm)

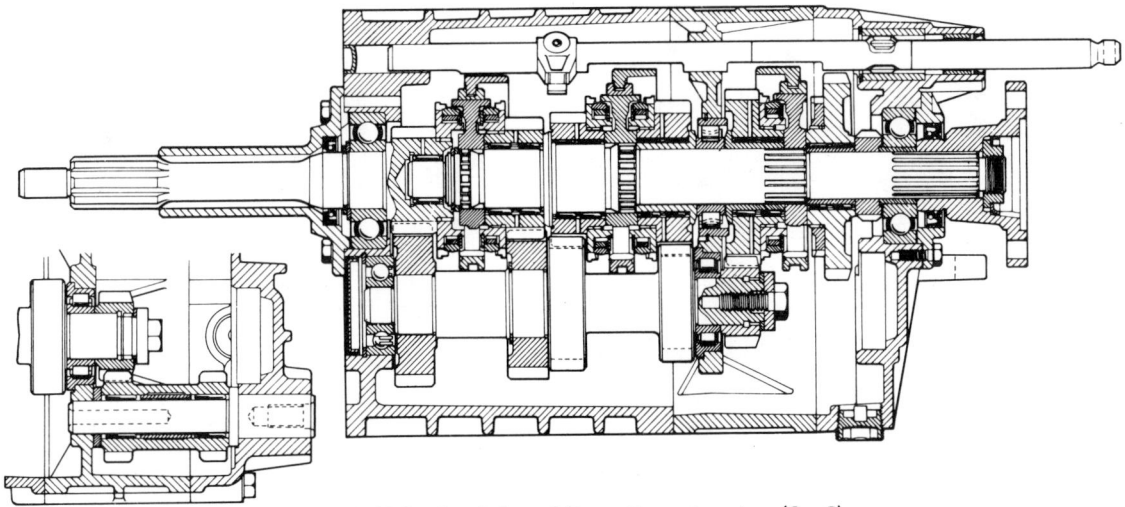

Fig. 13.38 Sectional view of Getrag 5-speed gearbox (Sec 8)

Fig. 13.39 Gearbox assembly mounted in vice (Sec 8)

Fig. 13.40 Removing circlip from the main drive pinion (Sec 8)

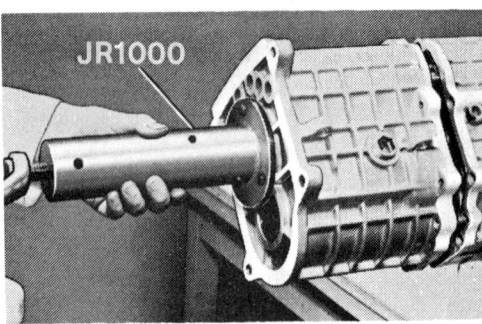

Fig. 13.41 Removing the front casing (Sec 8)

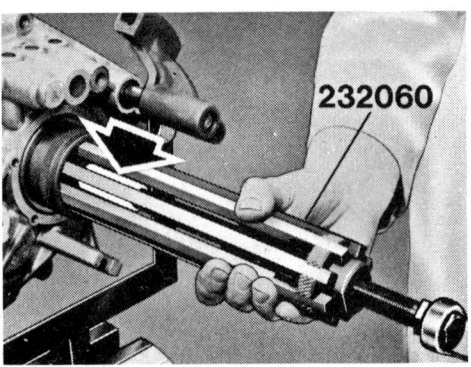

Fig. 13.42 Withdrawing the mainshaft rear bearing (Sec 8)

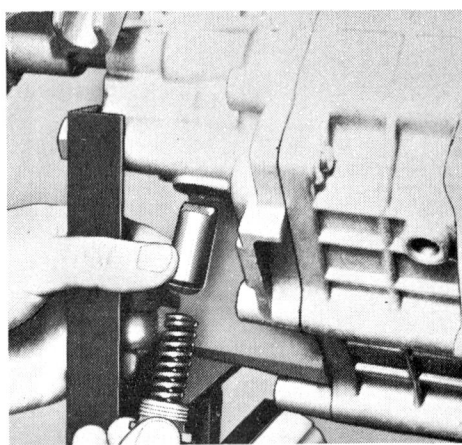

Fig. 13.43 Removing the selector shaft locking plunger (Sec 8)

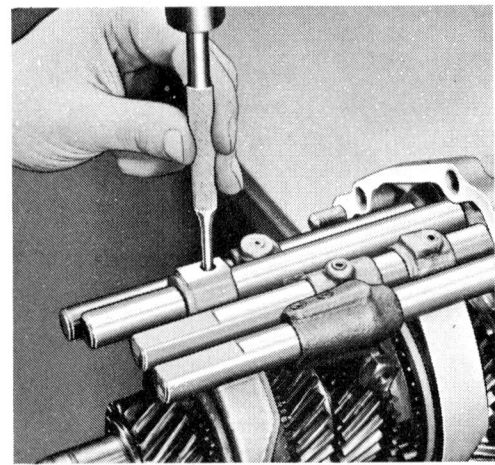

Fig. 13.44 Driving out the 4th/5th gear selector fork rollpin (Sec 8)

16 Remove the three remaining bolts securing the front casing. Using a suitable puller, attached to the casing with three front cover bolts, remove the front casing (Vauxhall tool No. JR 1000 is shown in Fig.13.41). Collect the shim from the end of the layshaft.

17 Using a suitable drift drive out the layshaft sealing plug and both bearings from the front casing.

18 Prise out the coupling flange securing nut lockplate, then lock the gearbox by engaging two gears at the same time and remove the coupling flange securing nut. Draw off the coupling flange using a universal puller.

19 Remove the rear cover, gasket and shims.

20 Using special tool, No. 232060 and spacer, arrowed in Fig. 13.42, withdraw the mainshaft rear bearing and shim.

21 Remove the retaining nut, spring and selector shaft locking plunger from the rear casing.

22 Remove the speedometer driven gear and housing.

23 Engage 5th gear, then drive out the rollpin securing the 4th/5th gear selector fork to the rod and withdraw the selector fork rod. Take care to collect the loose locking ball which may fall into the bottom of the casing.

24 Engage 3rd gear and remove the 2nd/3rd gear selector rod in

the same way as described for the 4th and 5th gear selector rod.

25 Using a suitable drift drive out the actuator securing pin and remove the actuator from the selector shaft.

26 Drive both locating dowels into the rear casing and withdraw the mainshaft, layshaft and intermediate casing from the rear casing.

27 Drive out the cup plugs from the selector rod bores then remove the locking and interlock balls and springs.

28 Remove the reverse idler gear and washer, then drive out the rollpin and remove the roller bearings and spacer.

29 Remove the retaining circlip and withdraw the selector shaft locking sleeve from the rear casing.

30 Drive out the selector shaft bush and seal.

31 Mount the intermediate casing in a vice fitted with soft jaws and remove the speedometer driving gear, reverse gear and roller bearing from the rear end of the mainshaft.

32 Using a suitable drift drive out the rollpins securing the 1st gear and reverse shift lug and withdraw the rod and fork assembly together with the clutch sliding sleeve.

33 Temporarily refit the coupling flange, engage 2nd gear and,

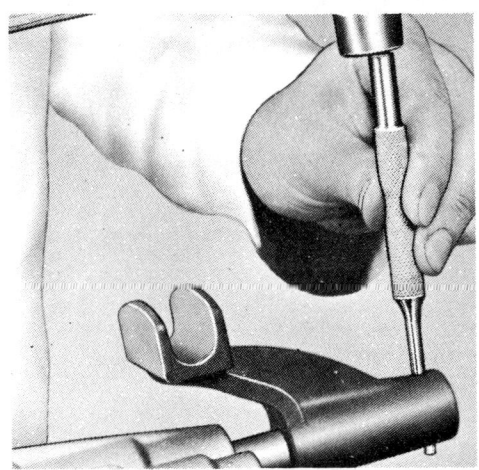

Fig. 13.45 Removing the actuator from the selector shaft (Sec 8)

Fig. 13.46 Withdrawing the mainshaft, layshaft and intermediate casing (Sec 8)

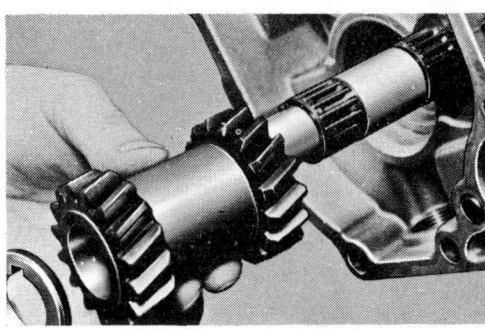

Fig. 13.47 Removing the reverse idler gear (Sec 8)

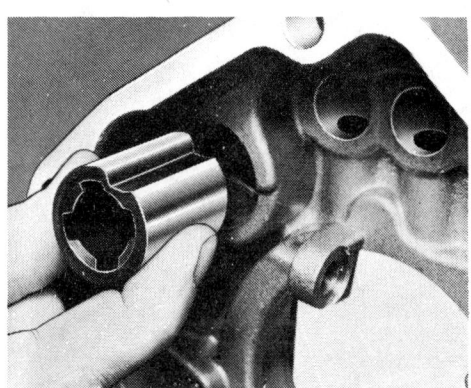

Fig. 13.48 Removing the selector shaft locking sleeve (Sec 8)

Fig. 13.49 Removing the speedometer gear and reverse gear from the mainshaft (Sec 8)

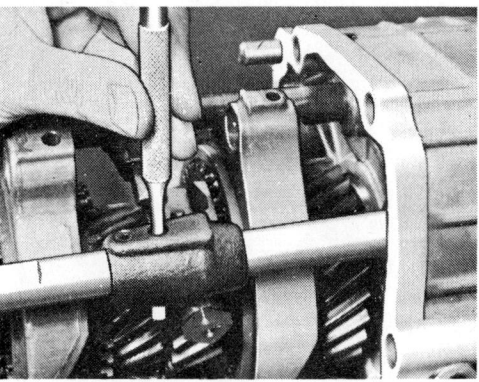

Fig. 13.50 Driving out the reverse shift lug rollpin (Sec 8)

using a suitable piece of bar together with two bolts fitted in the coupling flange to stop the flange from turning, remove the bolt securing the 1st gear to the layshaft. Carefully lever the gear off the end of the layshaft with two screwdrivers.

34 Drive out the selector shaft lug rollpin and withdraw the shaft.

35 Remove the reverse gear inner race, 1st gear and reverse clutch hub, 1st gear and roller bearing using a universal puller with the legs of the puller located behind 1st gear.

36 The mainshaft and layshaft assemblies can now be lifted out of the intermediate casing.

37 Remove the retaining keys from the mainshaft intermediate bearing outer race, then drive out the race and layshaft bearing towards the front.

38 Withdraw the main drive pinion, mainshaft spigot bearing and 4th/5th gear clutch sliding sleeve from the mainshaft.

39 Remove the spring, retaining ring and washer from the 4th/5th gear clutch hub and then lift off the 4th/5th gear clutch hub, 4th gear and roller bearing.

40 Press off the remaining gears, clutch assembly and bearings from the rear of the mainshaft.

Synchro assemblies — dismantling and inspection

41 Refer to Chapter 6, Sections 6 and 7 for information on the synchromesh assemblies.

42 Assemble the stops on 1st gear synchromesh assembly as shown arrowed in Fig. 13.53.

Gearbox components — inspection

43 Inspection of the gearbox components is basically the same as described in Chapter 6, Section 8, but the following points should be noted:

   a) *The mainshaft and layshaft gears (except reverse) are matched pairs and must not be renewed individually. 2nd and 3rd mainshaft gears are serviced as a set with the layshaft and must be renewed as a set*

   b) *Layshaft gears can be pressed off after removal of the 4th gear retaining circlip, but as they are a shrink fit and require heating to 100°C (212°F) when refitting them it is recommended that this job is left to your Vauxhall dealer*

   c) *If the layshaft rear bearing requires renewing, the inner race must be removed by splitting using a hammer and cold chisel*

   d) *Check that the thickness of the selector fork flanges are not less than that specified in the Specifications at the beginning of this Chapter*

   e) *Check that the breather in the top of the casing is clear*

Getrag gearbox — reassembly

44 Before assembly of mainshaft commences, the thickness of shims required between the intermediate bearing and the 1st gear inner race (arrowed in Fig.13.57) must be determined as follows:

Fig. 13.51 Lifting the mainshaft and layshaft assemblies out of the intermediate casing (Sec 8)

Fig. 13.52 Removing the retaining ring from the 4th/5th gear clutch hub (Sec 8)

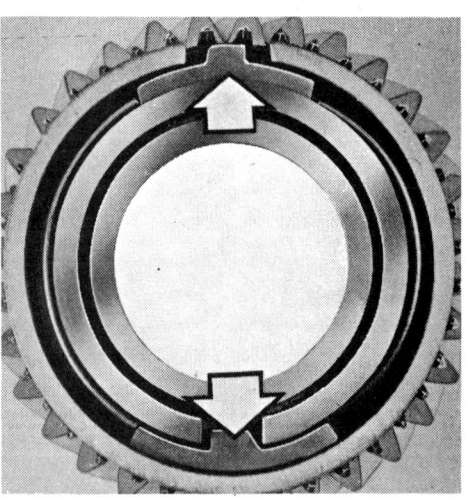

Fig. 13.53 Position of 1st gear synchro stops (Sec 8)

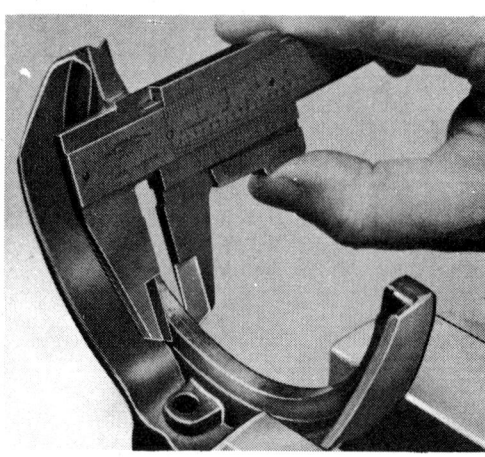

Fig. 13.54 Measuring the selector fork flanges (Sec 8)

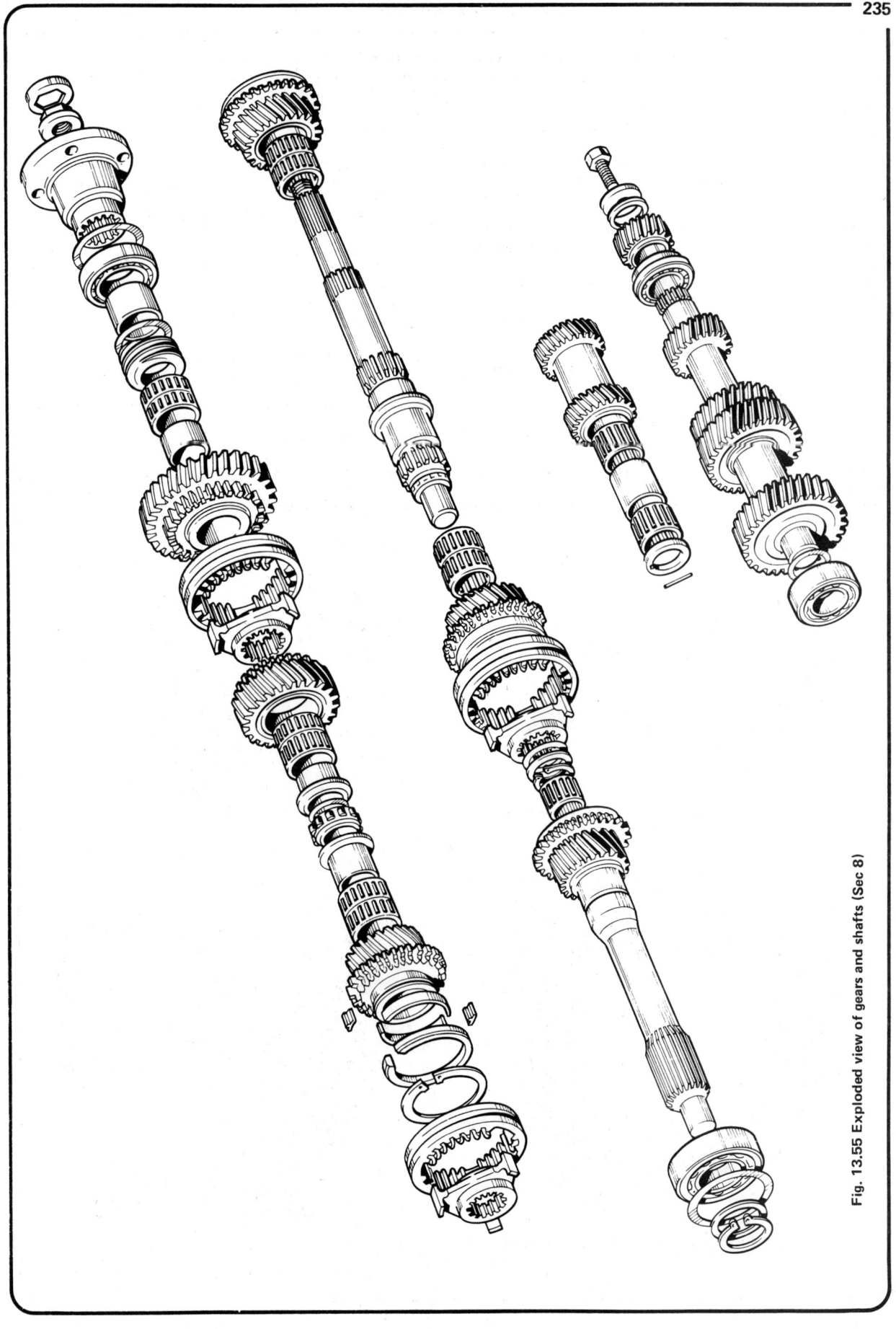

Fig. 13.55 Exploded view of gears and shafts (Sec 8)

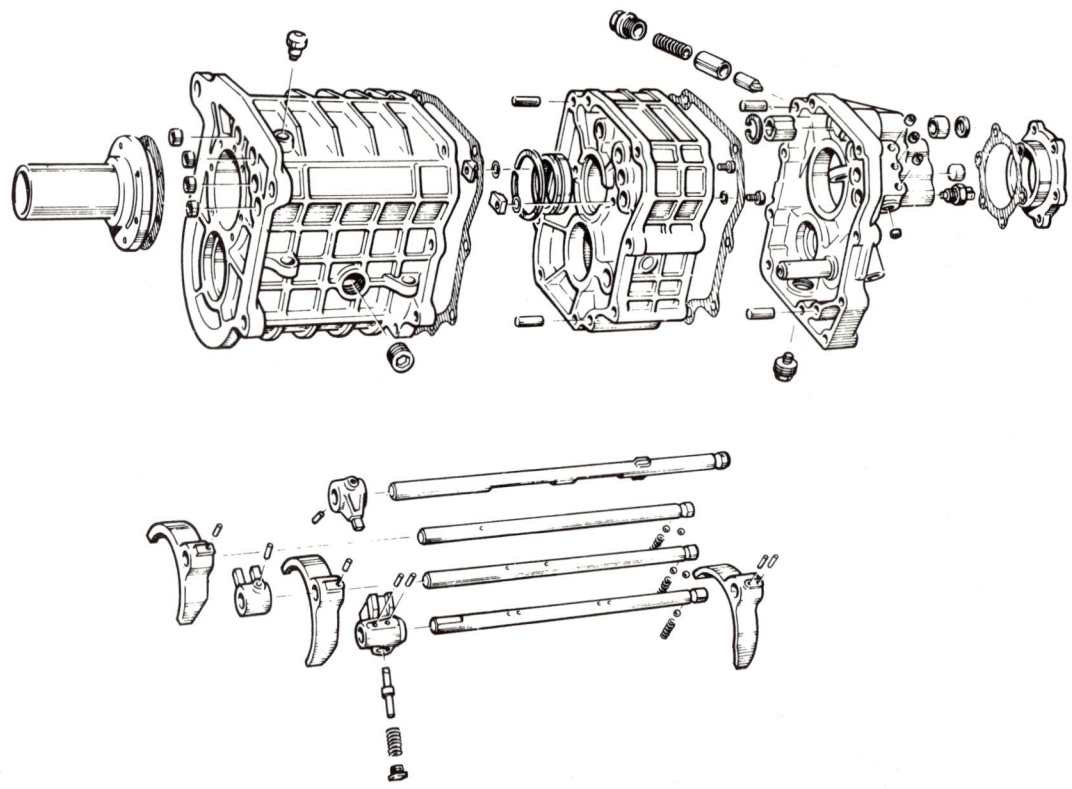

Fig. 13.56 Exploded view of casing and selector rods (Sec 8)

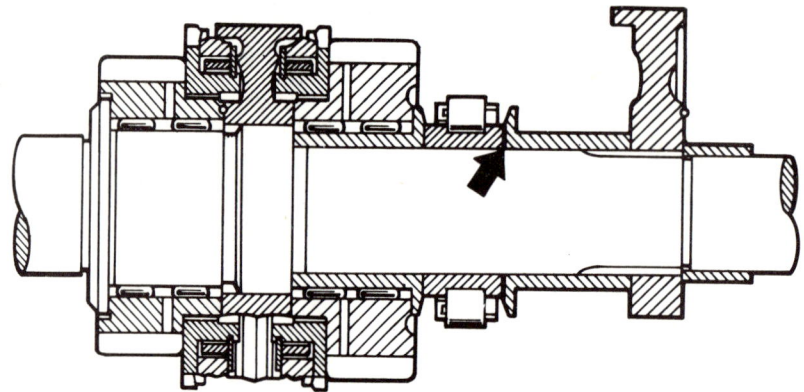

Fig. 13.57 Shims fitted between the mainshaft intermediate bearing and 1st gear inner race (Sec 8)

a) *Fit the 3rd gear on the mainshaft, with the dog teeth towards the rear, and then the 2nd/3rd gear clutch hub*

b) *Fit the roller bearing and inner race to the 2nd gear with the flanged end of the race opposite the dog teeth end of the gear and then press it onto the mainshaft*

c) *Press on the mainshaft intermediate bearing, then the 1st gear inner race (without shims) with the flange against the intermediate bearing*

d) *Fit the 1st gear and reverse clutch hub with the long leg, arrowed in Fig. 13.62, towards the front and then press on the reverse gear inner race*

e) *Measure the endfloat of the 1st gear and reverse clutch hub by inserting feeler gauges between the clutch hub and 1st gear inner race. Select shims which will eliminate endfloat or does not allow an endfloat of more than 0.004 in (0.09 mm)*

45 The mainshaft must now be dismantled (for the selected shims to be fitted in the position arrowed in Fig.13.57) and reassembled up to and including the fitting of the 1st gear inner race using the method described in the following paragraphs.

46 Fit the 2nd/3rd gear clutch sliding sleeve to the hub, retain the sleeve in position by engaging into 3rd gear and then press on the 2nd gear and inner race assembly.

47 Fit the selected thickness of shims and then the 1st gear inner race. Do not fit the 1st gear and reverse clutch hub or reverse gear inner race at this stage.

48 Fit the roller bearing, 4th gear and 4th/5th gear clutch hub on the front of the mainshaft with the dog teeth towards the front.

49 Fit the washer on the 4th/5th gear clutch hub and determine the number of shims required under the washer to eliminate endfloat (Fig.13.66)

Fig. 13.58 Fit the 3rd gear and 2nd/3rd gear clutch hub (Sec 8)

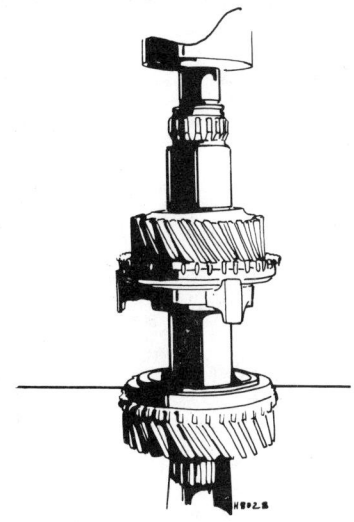

Fig. 13.59 Pressing on the 2nd gear (Sec 8)

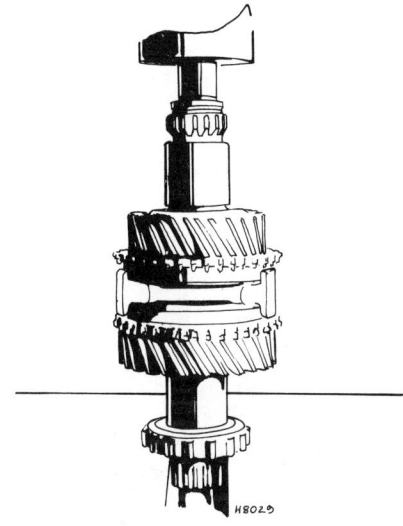

Fig. 13.60 Press the intermediate bearing onto the mainshaft (Sec 8)

Fig. 13.61 The 1st gear inner race is pressed on without shims (Sec 8)

Fig. 13.62 Fit the 1st gear and reverse clutch hub (Sec 8)

Fig. 13.63 Measuring the endfloat with feeler gauges (Sec 8)

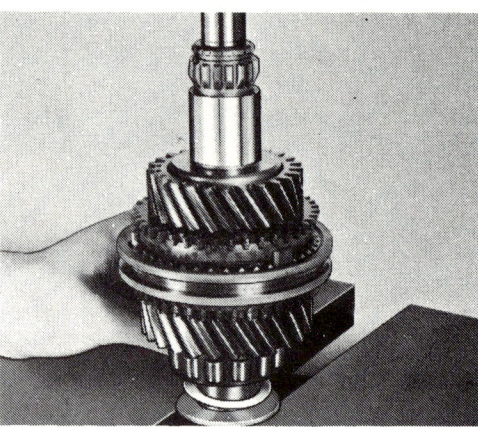

Fig. 13.64 Fit the selected shims and press on the 1st gear inner race (Sec 8)

Fig. 13.65 Fitting the 4th gear and 4th/5th gear clutch hub (Sec 8)

Fig. 13.66 Determining the number of shims to be fitted under the washer (Sec 8)

50 Fit the 4th/5th gear clutch sliding sleeve, mainshaft spigot bearing and main drive pinion to the mainshaft. (Fig.13.67)

51 Fit the reverse idler gear roller bearings and spacer, drive in the retaining rollpin, then fit the reverse idler gear and selective washer to the rear casing. Temporarily fit the intermediate casing to the rear casing, using a new gasket, and measure the endfloat of the idler gear with feeler gauges. Three thicknesses of selective washers are available for obtaining the specified endfloat. This will be found in the Specifications at the beginning of this Chapter. After obtaining the correct endfloat, remove the intermediate casing.

52 Fit the mainshaft intermediate bearing outer race and layshaft rear bearing into their bores in the intermediate casing and fit the mainshaft bearing outer race retaining keys. Should the retaining keys be angled as shown at 'B' in Fig.13.68, pack the space between the base of the key and casing with shims as shown at 'A'.

53 Fit the mainshaft and layshaft assemblies into the intermediate casing.

54 Fit the layshaft 1st gear with plain washer and bolt then, using feeler gauges, measure the gap between the washer and the gear (Fig. 13.70). Select shims, which are available in five thicknesses, to eliminate any endfloat.

55 When finally fitting the layshaft 1st gear, coat the threads of the retaining bolt with Loctite and tighten to the specified torque. Restrain the layshaft from turning by engaging 2nd gear and temporarily fitting the coupling flange as described in paragraph 33.

56 Fit the roller bearing, 1st gear and 1st and reverse gear clutch hub on the mainshaft with the dog teeth on the gear towards the rear and the long leg, arrowed in Fig. 13.71, of the hub towards the front.

57 Using a suitable piece of steel tubing, drive on the reverse gear inner race.

Fig. 13.67 Fitting the main drive pinion to the mainshaft (Sec 8)

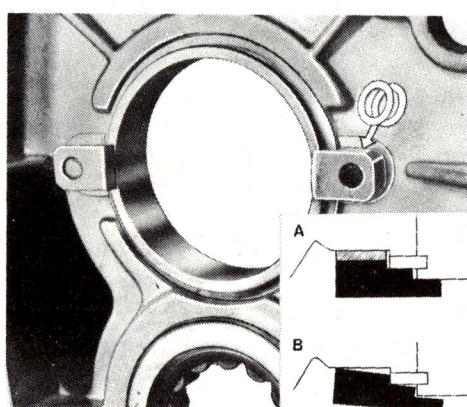

Fig. 13.68 Fitting the mainshaft intermediate bearing outer race into the intermediate casing (Sec 8)

58 Place the 4th/5th gear and 2nd/3rd gear selector forks in their respective sliding sleeves with the webs facing to the rear. (Fig. 13.73).
59 Fit the selector shaft and lug with chamfer (arrowed)

and position as shown in Fig. 13.74, then drive in the securing rollpin.
60 Assemble the sliding sleeve to the 1st gear and reverse selector fork, then fit the fork and rod assembly to the intermediate

Fig. 1369 Fitting the mainshaft and layshaft assemblies into the intermediate casing (Sec 8)

Fig. 13.70 Measuring the gap between the layshaft 1st gear and washer (Sec 8)

Fig. 13.71 Fitting the 1st gear and 1st gear and reverse clutch hub (Sec 8)

Fig. 13.72 Driving on the reverse gear inner race (Sec 8)

Fig. 13.73 The selector forks are fitted with the webs to the rear (Sec 8)

Fig 13.74 Fitting the selector shaft and lug (Sec 8)

casing with the sliding sleeve locating on the clutch hub.
61 Fit the 1st gear and reverse shift lug on the selector rod
and secure with rollpins.
62 Fit the roller bearing and reverse gear to the mainshaft
with the dog teeth towards the front.
63 Determine the thickness of shims (to ensure correct meshing
of the mainshaft and layshaft gears) to be fitted between the
mainshaft rear bearing and speedometer driving gear as follows:

    a) Temporarily fit the mainshaft rear bearing in the rear
       casing and then place the speedometer driving gear (with-
       out shims) on top of the bearing
    b) Using a depth gauge and straight edge, measure the
       distance from the joint face of the casing to the speedo-
       meter driving gear (Fig. 13.76). Select shims to obtain a
       dimension of 0.866—0.870 in (22.0—22.1 mm)
    c) Remove the speedometer driving gear and mainshaft
       rear bearing from the rear casing

64 Mount the rear casing in a vice with the holding bracket
and fit the selector shaft locking sleeve with the long side of the
groove (arrowed in Fig. 13.77) facing in a clockwise direction.
Fit the retaining circlip and position the sleeve as shown.
65 Fit the locking ball and spring in the 1st gear and reverse
selector bore. Stick a new gasket on the rear casing with a smear
of grease.

66 Depress the locking ball spring and fit the mainshaft, layshaft and intermediate casing assembly to the rear casing (Fig.
13.78). Tap the 1st gear and reverse selector rod into the
neutral position.
67 Drive both locating dowels into the intermediate casing.
68 Slide the 2nd/3rd gear selector rod through the selector
fork and into the casing as far as the locking ball bore. Fit the
interlock ball, spring and locking ball, then depress the locking
ball and push the 2nd/3rd gear selector rod to the neutral
position. Drive in the rollpin to secure the fork to the selector
rod.

Fig. 13.75 Fit the reverse gear on the mainshaft (Sec 8)

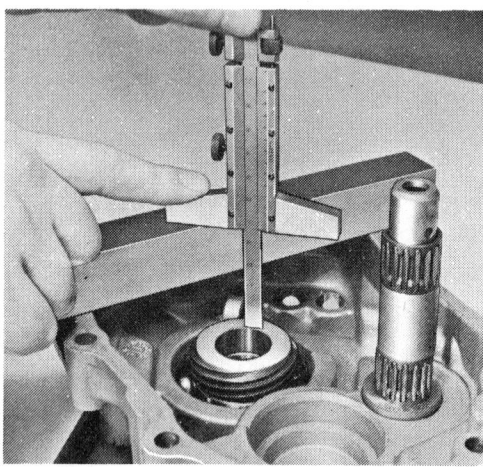

Fig. 13.76 Measuring the distance between the casing joint face
and the speedometer driving gear (Sec 8)

Fig. 13.77 Fitting the selector shaft locking sleeve (Sec 8)

Fig. 13.78 Depress the locking ball spring while fitting the mainshaft, layshaft and intermediate casing assembly to the rear case
(Sec 8)

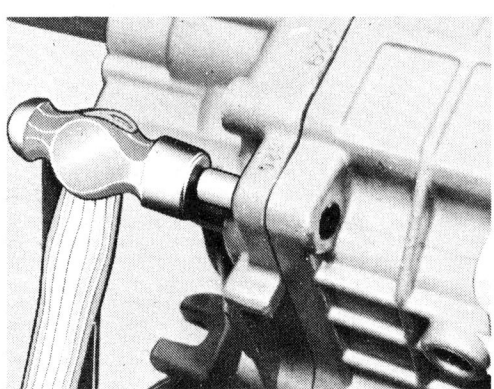

Fig. 13.79 Driving the locating dowels into the casing (Sec 8)

69 Fit the 4th/5th gear selector using the same procedure described in the previous paragraph. Do not forget to fit the interlock ball in the hole between the rod bores.

70 Fit the speedometer driving gear on the rear of the mainshaft with the counterbore to the rear, then stick the previously determined thickness of shims to the mainshaft rear bearing with grease (over the protruding sleeve) and drive the bearing into the casing with the shims towards the front. To ensure the bearing is fully home, temporarily fit the coupling flange and tighten the nut to the specified torque, then remove the coupling flange.

71 Determine the thickness of shims to be fitted between the mainshaft rear bearing and the shoulder on the rear cover as follows:

a) Tap the end of the mainshaft with a plastic hammer to ensure that the bearing is fully home in the casing

b) Measure the distance from the bearing face to the casing joint face with a depth gauge

c) Measure the distance from the shoulder on the rear cover to the joint face with a new gasket in position (Fig. 13.80)

d) The difference between the two measurements is the thickness of shims required between the bearing and the shoulder on the rear cover. Shims are available in two thicknesses

72 Stick the selected shims to the bearing face with a smear of grease. Lubricate the lip of the rear cover seal with gear oil and fit the rear cover, using a new gasket, to the casing. Fit the five securing bolts.

73 Fit the coupling flange and tighten the securing nut to the specified torque. Lock the nut with the locking plate.

74 Determine the thickness of shims to be fitted on the front end of the layshaft as follows:

a) Measure the distance between the machined shoulder on the front end of the layshaft and the joint face of the intermediate casing with a depth gauge

b) Fit the circlip, sealing plug and layshaft front bearing in the front casing. Position a new gasket on the front casing joint flange and, using a depth gauge and straight edge, measure the distance between the face of the layshaft front bearing inner race and the gasket

c) The difference between the two measurements, less 0.008 in (0.2 mm) to allow for permissible endfloat, is the thickness of shims to be fitted on the front end of the layshaft. Shims are available in two thicknesses

75 Fit the selected shims on the layshaft. Stick a new gasket on the joint flange of the intermediate casing with a smear of grease.

76 Press the main drive pinion bearing into the front casing.

77 Attach the special tool JR 1000 to the front casing with three front cover bolts and position the casing over the main drive pinion. Fit two short bars (arrowed in Fig. 13.82) through the tube and press on the front casing by rotating the tube counterclockwise with the tommy bar. Fit three securing bolts at 'A'. (Fig. 13.82).

78 Select a main drive pinion bearing washer of a thickness that eliminates endplay between the bearing and the retaining circlips. Washers are available in three thicknesses.

79 Fit the selected washer and retaining circlip.

80 Using a depth gauge, measure the distance between the face of the main drive pinion bearing and the joint face of the casing.

81 Fit a new gasket on the front cover and measure the distance between the shoulder on the front cover and the gasket face. The difference between the two measurements is the thickness of shims to be fitted between the bearing and the shoulder on the front cover. Shims are available in three thicknesses.

82 Stick the selected thickness of shims to the bearing face with grease, lubricate the lip of the oil seal with gear oil and fit the front cover, ensuring that the cut-out in the gasket is in alignment with the oil drain channel in the cover and that the channel

points towards the layshaft (Fig. 13.83).

83 Fit the gearchange actuator on the selector shaft and drive in the securing pin (Fig. 13.84)

84 Coat the reverse lamp switch threads with sealing compound and screw the switch into the rear casing (Fig. 13.85)

85 Coat the cup plugs with sealing compound and fit them in the selector rod bores.

86 Fit the other casing bolts, except the two top bolts which attach the gearchange support bracket to the casing, and tighten to the specified torque.

87 Fit the rear crossmember mounting bracket to the rear casing.

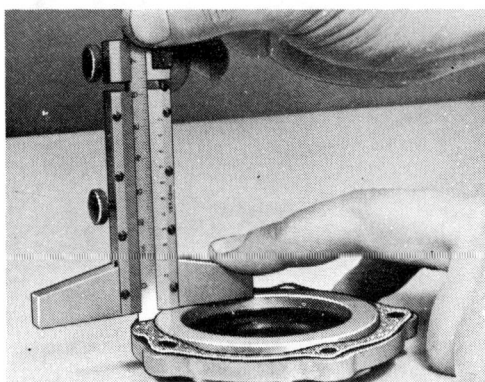

Fig. 13.80 Measuring the distance between the shoulder on the cover and the joint face (Sec 8)

Fig. 13.81 Fitting the selected shims on the layshaft (Sec 8)

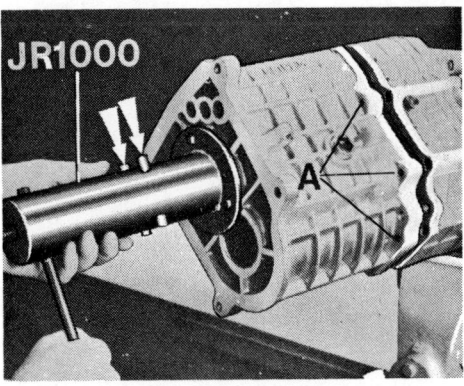

Fig. 13.82 Pressing on the front casing (Sec 8)

Fig. 13. 83 Cut-out in gasket aligned with oil drain channel (Sec 8)

9 Propeller shaft

General description

1 The propeller shaft described in Chapter 7 has been replaced by a twopiece shaft on later FE models. The rear end of the front shaft is carried in a rubber cushion bonded to a support.
2 The centre bearing support is secured directly to the underbody and the drive from the front shaft to the rear is transmitted through a constant velocity joint.
3 The constant velocity joint is a sealed assembly and no attempt should be made to dismantle it or to separate the two shafts.
4 Where renewal of the constant velocity joint, centre bearing or universal joint is indicated a completely new propeller shaft must be fitted.
5 With the introduction of the two-piece shaft the rear axle bump stop and bracket stopped being fitted.
6 On VX series models the propeller shaft is fitted with two constant velocity joints and a rear axle bump stop is fitted.

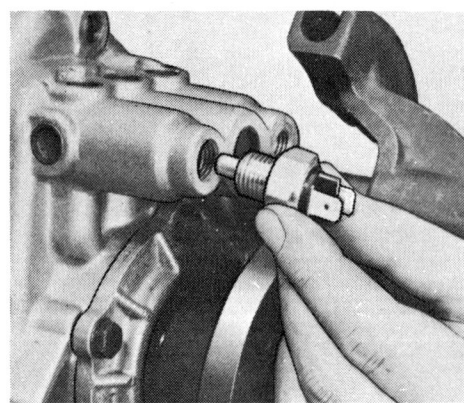

Fig. 13. 84 Driving in the gearchange actuator rollpin (Sec 8)

Fig. 13. 86 Propeller shaft centre bearing support (Sec 8)

Fig. 13. 85 Fitting the reverse lamp switch (Sec 8)

Fig. 13. 87 Propeller shaft rear constant velocity joint and rear axle bump stop — VX series (Sec 9)

10 Rear axle

oil, then fit the seal with the lip towards the casing so that dimension 'A' in Fig. 13.89 is 0.30 in (7.5 mm).

5 Fit the pinion shaft dust shield and drive it onto the shaft until dimension 'A' in Fig. 13.90 is 0.40 in (10 mm).

6 Refit the pinion flange as described in Chapter 8, Section 5.

VX series — general

1 The rear axle fitted to the VX series 1800 model is the same as that fitted to the FE series 1800. On the other VX series models a larger rear axle housing is used but overall the axle and differential unit is very similar to that fitted to the FE 4/90 model. It can be serviced in accordance with the procedures described in Chapter 8 and the Specifications at the beginning of this Chapter, except for the operations described in the following sub-sections.

Pinion oil seal — removal and refitting

2 Remove the pinion flange as described in Chapter 8, Section 5

3 Prise off the pinion shaft dust seal and remove the oil seal.

4 Before fitting the new oil seal, smear the lip of the seal with

Pinion, crownwheel and differential — overhaul

7 The overhaul of the pinion, crownwheel and differential on VX 2300 and 4/90 models is the same as that described in Chapter 8, Section 6, except for the following:

a) *After removing the pinion shaft flange, prise off the dust shield and then remove the oil seal, pinion bearing retaining nut and oil seal baffle*

b) *When calculating the thickness of the pinion spacer/ shims required, the pinion rear bearing maximum thickness of 1.1643 in must be taken into account*

c) *After fitting the pinion shaft front bearing inner race, fit the oil seal baffle, then the pinion bearing nut, and*

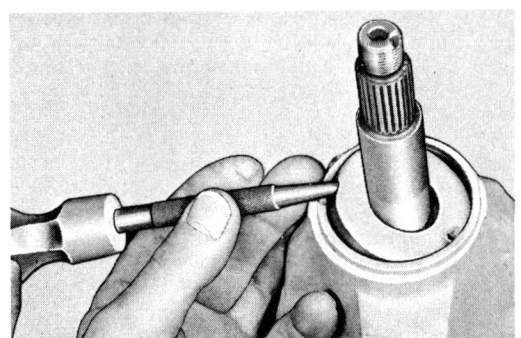

Fig. 13.88 Removing pinion shaft oil seal (Sec 10)

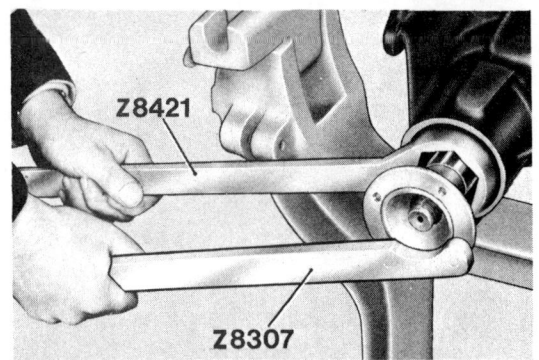

Fig. 13.91 Removing the pinion bearing retaining nut (Sec 10)

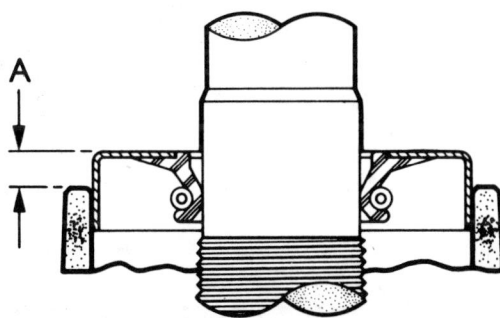

Fig. 13.89 Fitting the pinion shaft oil seal (Sec 10)

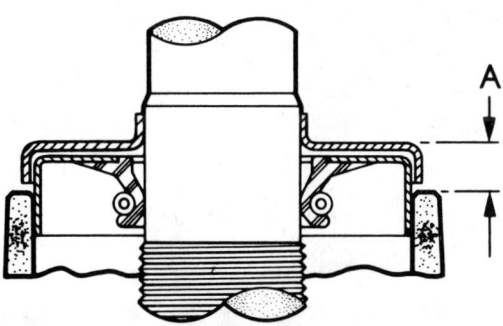

Fig. 13.90 Fitting the pinion shaft dust shield (Sec 10)

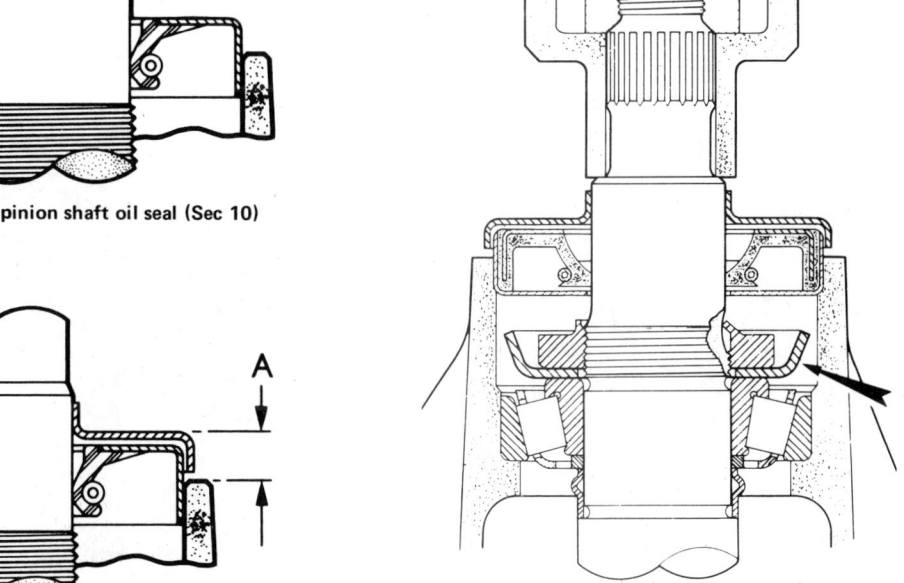

Fig. 13.92 The oil seal baffle is fitted between the retaining nut and the front bearing inner race (Sec 10)

tighten it progressively to compress the collapsible spacer, while checking the pre-load frequently with a spring balance, until the correct figure is reached as given in the Specifications at the beginning of this Chapter. Do not stake the nut at this stage.

    d) *After fitting the differential case assembly and adjusting the crownwheel to pinion backlash, stake the pinion shaft bearing nut and then fit the oil seal, dust shield and pinion flange*

Rear axle breather

8   On later models an improved venting for the rear axle is provided to prevent the entry of water through the breather.

9   The breather comprises a tube in the axle housing to which is secured a rubber hose which passes into the underbody side-member.

10   At service 'A' inspect the hose for cracks and damage and renew if there is any sign of deterioration.

Pinion shaft oil seal baffle

11   On later FE series and on VX 1800 models a pinion shaft oil seal baffle is fitted between the coupling flange and the front bearing inner race.

Fig. 13.93 Rear axle vent hose (later models) (Sec 10)

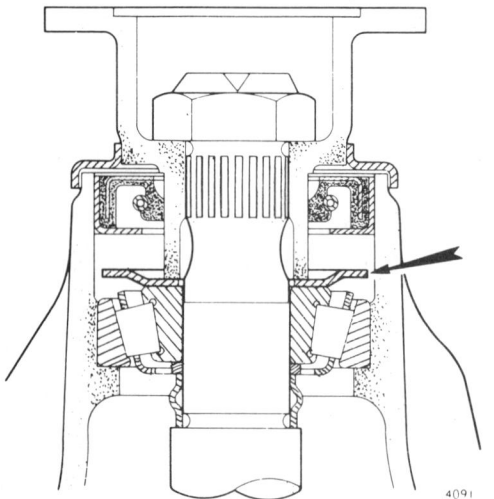

Fig. 13.94 Location of oil seal baffle on later FE series and on VX 1800 models (Sec 10)

11 Braking system

Brake pressure conscious reducing valve — description and renewal

1   On all models from Chassis No. DY 100101 a brake pressure conscious reducing valve is fitted and the load conscious brake pressure reducing valve on previous VX 4/90 models is discontinued.

2   The purpose of the valve is to prevent the rear brakes locking before the front ones under heavy braking conditions by controlling the hydraulic pressure passing to the rear brakes.

3   Fluid pressure to the front brake calipers passes through the valve ports 'B' and 'A' (refer to Fig. 13.95), and to the rear brakes through valve ports 'C' and 'D'. On increasing application of the footbrake, the front and rear brake line pressure increases at the same rate until the valve cut-in pressure is reached. Front brake line pressure continues to increase at the same rate but the valve reduces the rear brake line pressure to prevent the rear brakes locking before the front.

4   Should a failure occur in the new brake pressure line, full pressure will still be maintained to the front brakes or, if there is a failure of the front brake pressure line, the reducing characteristic of the valve is by-passed and full pressure is delivered to the rear brakes.

5   No attempt should be made to dismantle or adjust the valve, which is mounted on a bracket attached to the brake servo unit. If the valve is defective it must be renewed.

6   To remove the valve, first clean round the brake pipe unions, and then disconnect the pipes from the valve. Undo and remove the mounting bracket attachment nuts and lift the valve away from the brake servo unit. The valve can then be separated from the bracket.

7   Refitting is a reversal of the removal sequence. When connecting the brake pipe unions to the valve, ignore the arrows cast on the valve body and connect the pipes as shown in Fig. 13.95.

Parking brake rear cables — description and adjustment

8   On later models the forward end of the outer cables is insulated by a flanged rubber sleeve and washer (Fig. 13.96), and the ends of the anchor bracket are formed in a full circle around the insulating sleeve. The cable pull-off spring is attached to a cup washer.

9   The rear cable attaching brackets are bolted to the rear axle, and the cable and rubber insulator are retained by

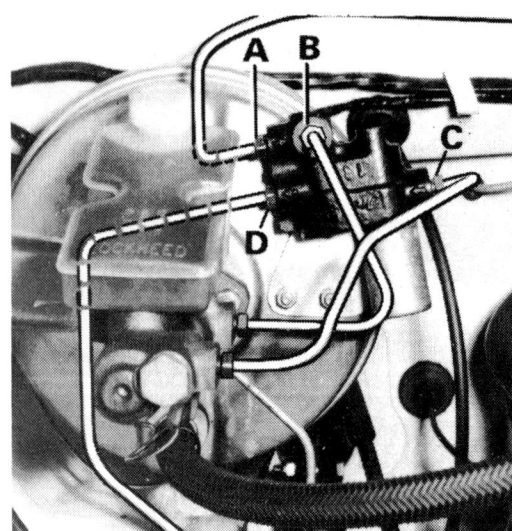

Fig. 13 95 Brake pressure conscious reducing valve location (Sec 11)

a clip. The upper end of the clip engages a slot in the bracket and the lower seal of the clip is slotted to receive the tag on the end of the bracket. The clip is then secured by bending the tag over the clip. (Fig. 13.97).

10 Before adjusting the cables ensure that the rear brakes are adjusted correctly. On models with self-adjusting rear brakes, apply the footbrake three or four times, with the engine running, to make sure that the brake adjustment is correct.

11 To adjust the rear cables, temporarily release the pull-off springs from the cup washers. Slacken the adjusting sleeve locknuts and rotate the sleeve counterclockwise, while holding the intermediate cable ends, to eliminate any slackness in the cables, without causing the brake shoes to bind on the brake drums. Tighten the locknuts and refit the springs in the cup washers.

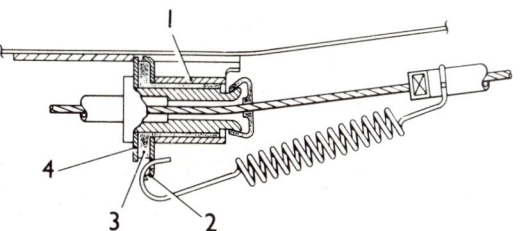

Fig. 13. 96 Parking brake rear cable anchorage (later models) (Sec 11)

1 Anchor bracket   3 Rubber sleeve
2 Cup washer   4 Washer

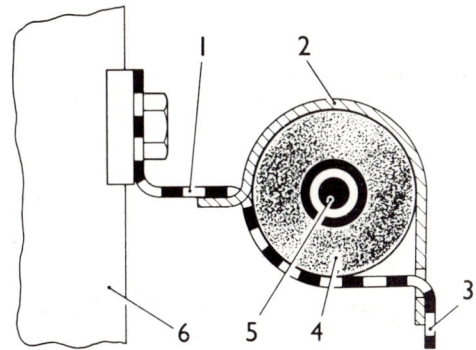

Fig. 13. 97 Rear cable attaching bracket (Sec 11)

1 Attaching bracket   4 Rubber insulator
2 Retaining clip   5 Cable
3 Tag   6 Rear axle

12 Electrical system

Fuses and fusible link — general

1 On models from Chassis No. DY 135432 the rating of No.2 fuse is increased from 35 amp, to 50 amp. The 50 amp fuse must not be used to replace any of the other circuit fuses. It may, however, be used to replace the No.2 fuse on earlier models fitted with a heated rear window.

2 Twin fusible links are connected into the main battery feed circuit on 1974 models in place of the single fusible link previously fitted. One of the links protects the lighting circuits whilst the other protects the remaining electrical systems with the exception of the starter motor circuit. **Note:** *The original single link has a greater capacity than one of the new links and must not be fitted in place of one of the twin links.*

Twin windtone-type horns — removal and refitting

3 Access to the horns for removal is gained by slackening the two radiator mounting nuts at the top and lifting the radiator slightly (to disengage the bottom mounting) and easing it rearwards. Sufficient movement is available without disconnecting the radiator hoses.

4 Remove the bolt securing the horns to the mounting bracket located between the radiator matrix and the radiator grille, disconnect the electrical connection and lift out the horns.

5 Refitting is a reversal of the removal sequence. Ensure that the radiator bottom mounting peg engages the hole in the front crossmember rubber buffer.

Headlamps — VX 1800 and 2300, and 1977 VX 4/90 models

6 The combined head and turn signal lamps have a plastic body with the lens secured to the body by a stainless steel rim. The headlamp reflector is attached to the three beam trim screws in the lamp body. The halogen bulb is retained in the

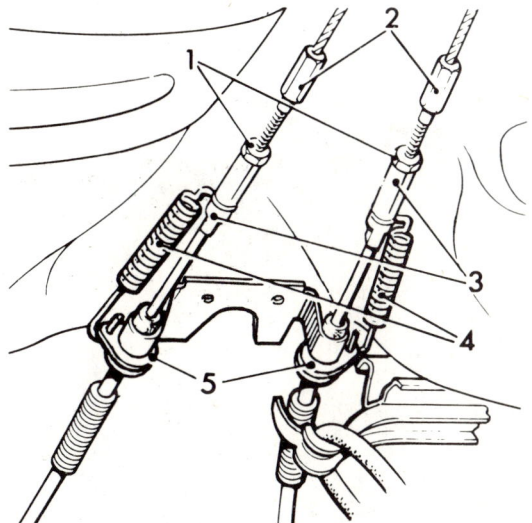

Fig. 13. 98 Adjusting parking brake rear cables (Sec 11)

1 Locknuts   3 Adjusting sleeves
2 Intermediate cables   4 Return springs
              5 Cup washers

Fig. 13. 99 Removing the twin windtone-type horns (Sec 12)

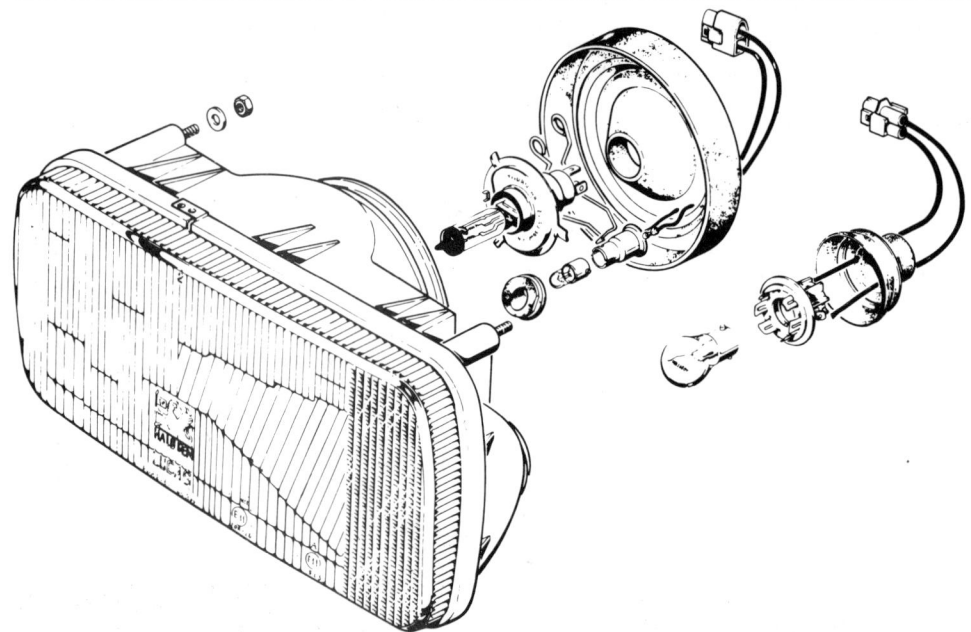

Fig. 13. 100 Headlamp assembly — VX 1800 and 2300 and 1977 VX 4/90 models (Sec 12)

reflector by a spring clip. A rubber grommet located in the reflector houses the sidelamp bulb holder.

7 A metal reflector for the turn signal lamp is secured in the plastic body which has four studs for attaching the lamp to the radiator panel.

8 To change the headlamp bulb, remove the rubber cover from the lamp body. Release the spring clip and withdraw the halogen bulb. Take care not to touch the glass of the bulb with bare fingers; always hold the bulb by the metal cap. If the glass of the bulb is touched with bare fingers it must be wiped with a cloth moistened in alcohol to prevent any fingerprints from burning into the glass.

9 The headlamp assembly can be removed after disconnecting

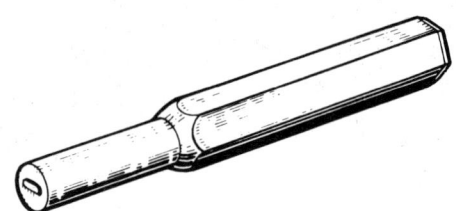

Fig. 13. 101 Headlight beam adjusting tool (Sec 12)

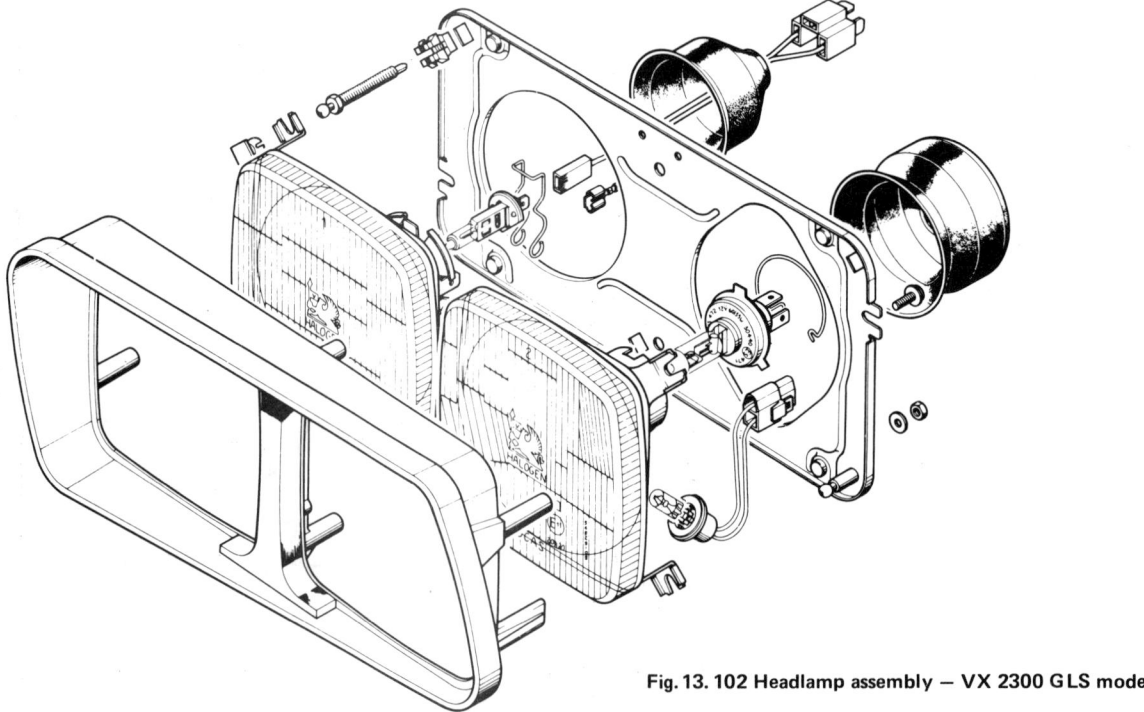

Fig. 13. 102 Headlamp assembly — VX 2300 GLS model (Sec 12)

the wiring and undoing the four nuts securing it to the studs on the radiator panel.

10 The headlamp beam adjusting screws have two flats formed on the head in place of the slotted type previously fitted. Fig. 13.101 shows a suitable type of adjusting tool.

Headlamps — VX 2300 GLS model

11 The VX 2300 GLS model has a four lamp system consisting of two sets of square halogen headlamps of the pre-focus type. The outer lamps incorporate a bulb shield for both high and low beams and have twin filament bulbs. A sidelamp bulb holder clips into an opening in the reflector. The inner lamps have single filament bulbs.

12 To renew a bulb, pull back the rubber boot and release the spring retaining clip, then remove the bulb. When handling a halogen bulb take care not to touch the glass with bare fingers. When fitting a bulb in the outer lamp ensure that the spring clip is located underneath the two spigots, 'A' in Fig. 13.104, and presses down on the three bulb holder spigots 'B'.

13 To remove a headlamp unit disconnect the wiring connector, remove the four nuts securing the mounting plate to the radiator

panel and withdraw the mounting plate and headlamp unit.

14 Remove the four attaching screws and separate the headlamp unit from the mounting plate.

15 Refitting is a reversal of the removal procedure. Do not forget to have the beam alignment checked.

Fog and front turn signal lamps — VX 2300 GLS and 1977 VX 4/90 models

16 The reflector of the halogen fog lamps is mounted on two pivots and rotation of an external knob adjusts the angle of the light beam.

17 Access to the bulb is obtained by removing the back cover, releasing the spring retaining clip and disconnecting the wire. Do not touch the bulb glass with bare fingers.

18 On VX 2300 GLS models the turn signal bulb holder is removed by pulling it from the reflector.

19 To remove the lamp, disconnect the wires at the plug and socket connector and also the earth wire inside the engine compartment. Remove the four screws securing the lamp to the lower valance panel, ease the lamp towards the outside of the

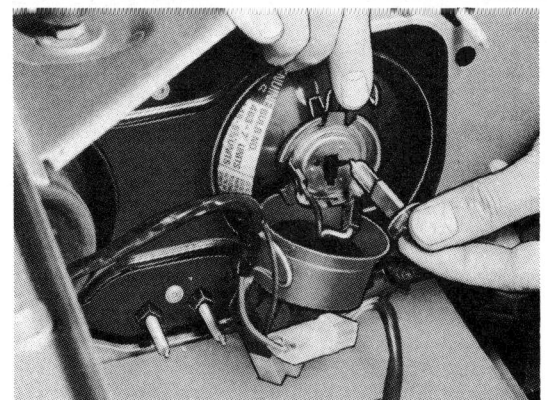

Fig. 13.103 Removing the halogen bulb — VX 2300 GLS model (Sec 12)

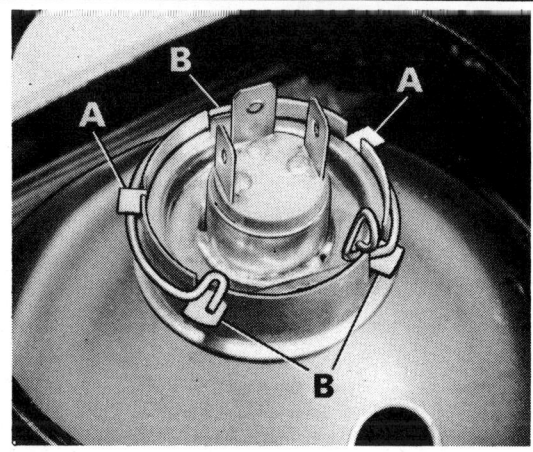

Fig. 13.104 Fitting the halogen bulb — VX 2300 GLS model

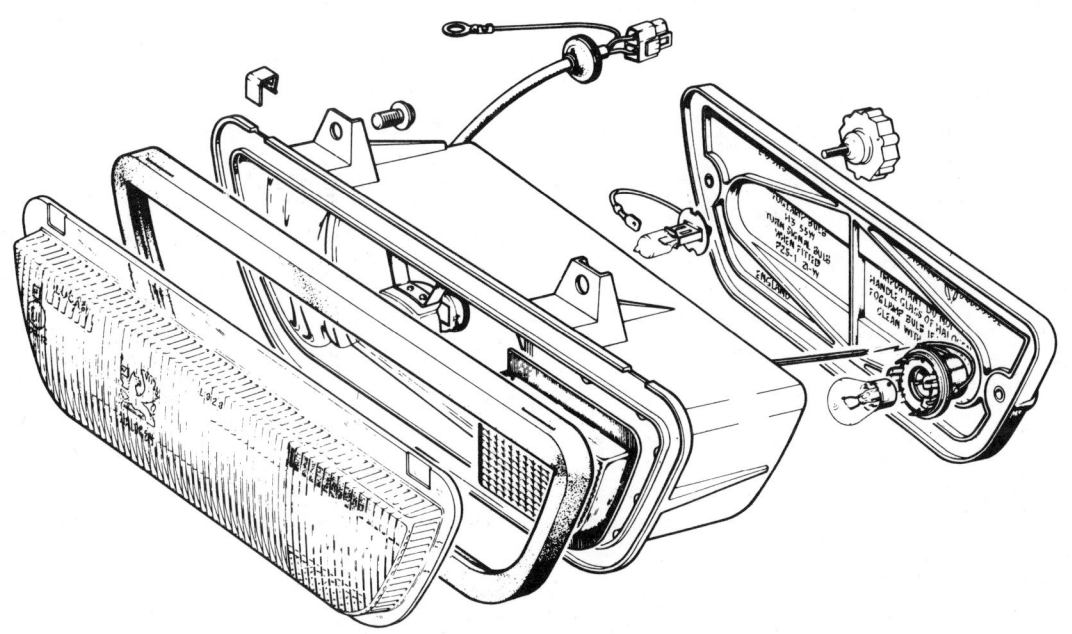

Fig. 13.105 Fog and front turn signal lamp — VX 2300 GLS and 1977 VX 4/90 models (Sec 12)

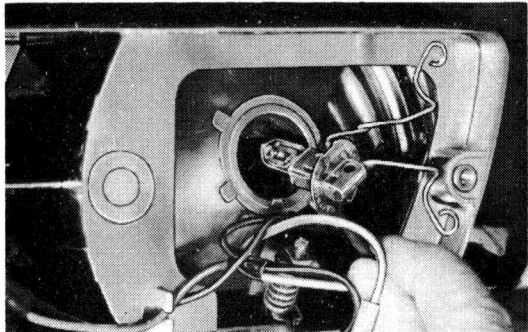

Fig. 13.106 Removing the halogen fog lamp bulb (Sec 12)

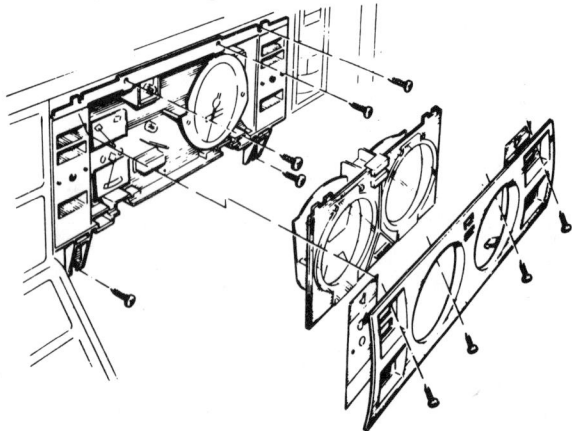

Fig. 13.107 Removing the instrument facia panel — VX 1800 and

Fig. 13.108 Warning light cowl securing screws (Sec 12)

wing and withdraw it.

20 The lamp lens and seal can be removed after prising off the three retaining clips.

21 Refitting the lamp is a reversal of the removal sequence but do ensure beforehand that the lens seal is in good condition and is seated correctly.

Rear number plate lamp — 1974 models

22 The single rear number plate lamp is secured to the rear panel with two screws.

23 To change the bulb remove the two lens securing screws, ease down the lens to free the spigot at the rear end from the body, and lift away the lens.

24 When refitting the lens make sure it is seated correctly on the neoprene gasket before tightening the securing screws.

Instrument and warning light bulbs (VX 1800 and 2300 models) — renewal

25 Refer to Fig. 13.107. Remove the four securing screws and

lift away the facia panel.

26 Withdraw the instrument lens from the two slots at the bottom of the instrument housing and remove the two warning lamp masks.

27 The warning light bulbs, located each side of the panel, are accessible after removing the two warning light cowls which are each secured by one screw, arrowed in Fig. 15.108.

28 Two of the three instrument illumination bulbs are now accessible. To renew the third bulb first remove the speedometer head.

Instrument and warning light bulbs (1977 VX 4/90 models) — renewal

29 Remove the four screws securing the instrument facia, pull off the speedometer trip knob and withdraw the instrument facia.

30 Withdraw the instrument lens frame from the two slots at the bottom of the instrument housing and lift out the lens frame.

31 The turn signal, brake pressure and oil pressure warning light bulbs can now be removed.

32 One of the instrument illumination bulbs and the alternator charge warning light bulb are accessible after removing the tachometer and withdrawing the lens housing.

33 The other two instrument illumination bulbs and the main beam warning light bulb are accessible after removing the speedometer and withdrawing the lens housing.

Instrument panel assembly (VX 2300 GLS and 1977 VX 4/90 models) — removal and refitting

34 Remove the steering column finisher and the canopy.

35 Remove the securing screws from the instrument panel side finisher and withdraw it from the slotted bracket.

36 Remove the three screws securing the top panel and ease it down slightly.

37 Remove the two screws securing the bottom of the instrument panel assembly and the three screws securing the top.

38 Ease out the instrument panel assembly and disconnect the speedometer cable. Unscrew the pipe union from the oil pressure gauge, disconnect the wiring harness plug and withdraw the assembly.

39 The fuel gauge, battery condition meter, temperature gauge, tachometer and voltage stabilizer can now be removed by undoing the securing screws.

40 Prise the nine clips, 'A' in Fig. 13.109, out of the printed circuit and instrument housing. Remove the three screws 'B' securing the stabilizer sockets. After removing the warning and illumination bulb holders the printed circuit can be withdrawn.

41 Refitting is a reversal of the removal procedure.

Instrument panel centre facia (1976/77 models) — removal and refitting

42 Remove the instrument panel assembly as described in paragraphs 34 to 41.

43 To gain access to the centre facia lower securing screws prise out the radio aperture blanking plate (if a radio is fitted, remove the radio), then remove the four securing screws.

44 Pull off the heater control knobs and remove the centre facia.

45 The electric clock is secured by two screws, arrowed in Fig. 13.110. The purple wire is connected to the positive (+) terminal and a push-in type holder houses the capless bulb.

46 The heater control illumination bulb is a peanut-sized bayonet type housed in a push-in holder.

47 Refitting the centre facia is a reversal of the removal procedure.

Lighting switch (1976/77 models) — removal and refitting

48 The switch is secured in the driver's lower control panel by a locking ring and the wiring harness is connected by a multi-pin plug and socket connector.

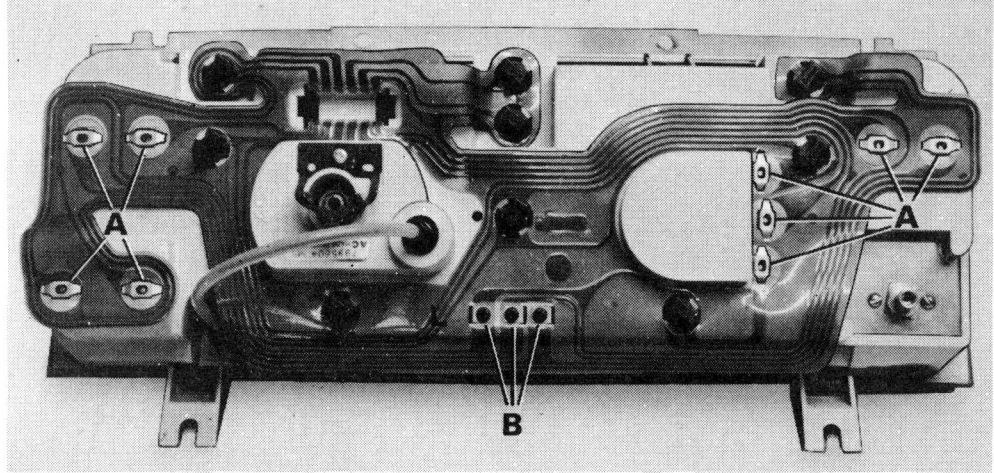

Fig. 13. 109 Removing the printed circuit — VX 2300 GLS and
1977 VX 4/90 models (Sec 12)

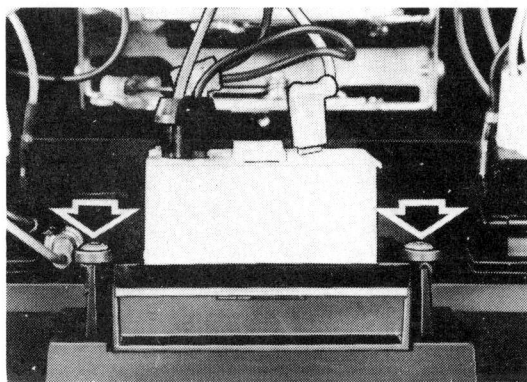

Fig. 13. 110 Removing the electric clock (Sec 12)

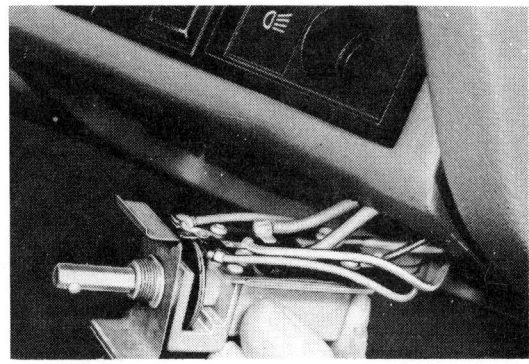

Fig. 13. 111 Fitting the lighting switch — 1976/77 models (Sec 12)

49 The switch knob can be withdrawn whilst depressing the spring plunger in the switch shaft.

50 Remove the locking ring, using an Allen key, and withdraw the switch from under the control panel after disconnecting the harness plug.

51 Refitting the switch is a reversal of the removal procedure. Ensure that the retaining clip is located correctly as shown in Fig. 13.111.

Rear window demist and fan switches — 1976/77 models

52 The switches are both of the rocker type and are retained in the centre facia by spring clips. A bulb illuminates a small lens on the end of the tumbler when the switch is in the 'ON' position. The switch wiring is connected by multi-sockets and by spade terminals at the sides.

53 To renew the bulb, which is an 0.65 watt Lilliput Edison screw type, prise off the switch tumbler when the switch is in the 'ON' position.

54 The switches can be removed, after detaching the centre facia and compressing the spring clips.

---

13 Suspension and steering

Front hub bearing (later models) — renewal

1 Steel inserts are used in the front hubs to retain the bearing lubricant. The inserts are located in the hub next to the inner edge of the bearing outer races.

2 To avoid damaging the inserts when removing a bearing outer race, both inserts should be drifted into the centre of the hub before removing the outer race.

3 When reassembling the hub each insert must be fitted before the bearing outer race. It should be fitted so that there is a clearance of 0.02 in (0.5 mm) between the flanged edge of the insert and the end face of the outer race, dimension 'A' in Fig. 13.112.

Stabilizer bar — refitting

4 To prevent overclamping of the insulator rubbers the front stabilizer bar link retaining nuts should be tightened so that the distance between the face of the cup washer and the end of the link, dimension 'A' in Fig. 13.113, is 0.66–0.70 in (17–18 mm).

Front suspension lower arms

5 Later models have a different front suspension lower arm and stabilizer bar link from those fitted on early models.

6 The later type suspension arm has a stabilizer link bracket different in shape from the earlier type.

7 The stabilizer link, 'A' in Fig. 13.114, used with the later arm has the ball-stud positioned at right-angles to the link, whereas the ball-stud of the early type link is positioned at 20° to the link.

8 The later type suspension arm and link can be fitted to early models provided they are used together.

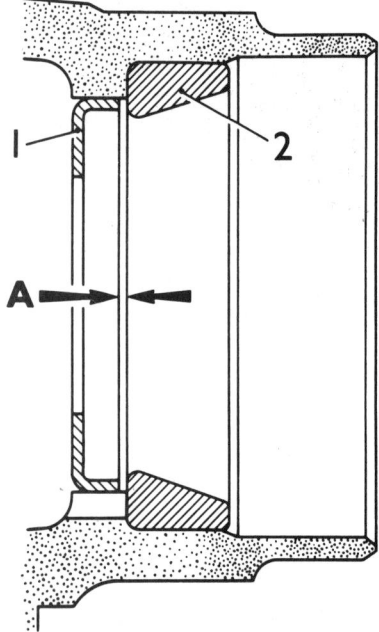

Fig. 13. 112 Location of front hub inserts (Sec 12)

1 Insert   2 Bearing outer race

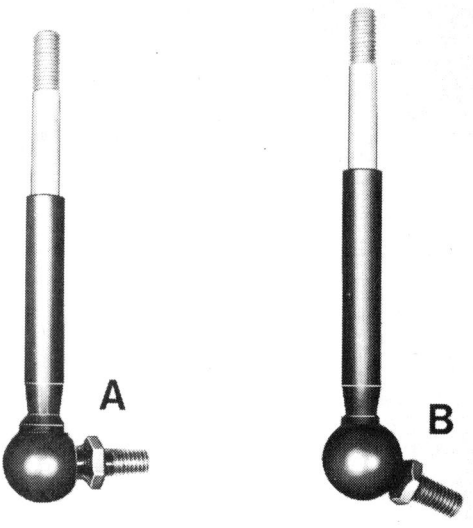

Fig. 13. 114 Stabilizer bar links (Sec 13)

A Later type   B Early type

Fig. 13. 113 Tightening stabilizer bar link retaining nuts (Sec 13)

Fig. 13. 115 Panhard rod mounting bolt cover (Sec 13)

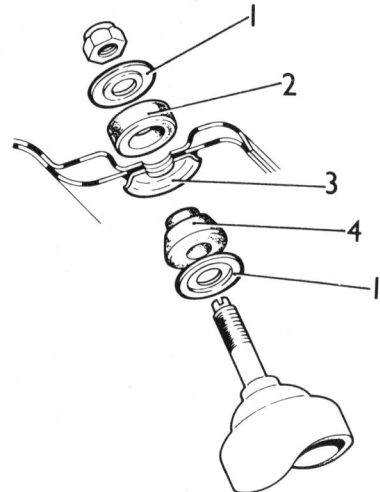

Fig. 13. 116 Rear shock absorber attachment (later Saloon models)
(Sec 13)

1 Dished washer   3 Cup washers
2 Upper bumper   4 Lower bumper

Panhard rod mounting bolt cover
9 The push-on type protection cap fitted over the right-hand
mounting bolt nut on early models is replaced by a bolt-on
cover. The cover has a larger contact area and is to prevent a
fuel tank rupture by the mounting bolt in the event of a rear-end
collision.
10 When fitting the cover, ensure that the rounded end is
uppermost before tightening the mounting bolt, then bend the
cover over the nut. (Fig. 13.115).

Rear shock absorber bushes and bumpers
11 The rear shock absorber upper and lower mountings on
later saloon models are similar to those fitted on the estate car
as described in Chapter 11, Section 13.

12 Dished washers and rubber bumpers are fitted at the stud end of the shock absorber. Cup washers are welded to the body.
13 The dished washers must be fitted with the raised side against the bumpers. The shock absorber upper nuts should be tightened until dimension 'A', in Fig. 13.117, is 0.40 in (10.0 mm).

Steering wheel — 1974 models

14 The steering wheel on later models has an adapter attached to the wheel by four screws, and a loose fitting plastic turn signal switch cancelling sleeve.
15 The sleeve has two dogs at one end for engagement with the turn signal switch and two grooves at the other end that engage corresponding dogs in the wheel boss. A coil spring is fitted between the sleeve and a shoulder in the steering shaft.
16 The steering wheel and adapter must not be separated. If defective, they must be renewed as an assembly.

Fig. 13.117 Fitting rear shock absorber (later Saloon models) (Sec 13)

14 Bodywork and underframe

Door trims and armrests

1 The armrests on Victor VX 1800 and VX 2300 models have door pulls similar to those described in Chapter 12. On FE VX 4/90 and VX 4/90 models, the armrest has an integral arm extending upwards and forwards which serves as a door pull.
2 Each armrest is secured by two screws and a key-type lug on the end of the extended arm.
3 To remove the armrest, undo the screws and lower the armrest to free the lug from its retaining slot in the door inner panel.
4 The padded trim is attached to the door inner panel as described in Chapter 12, except that the heads of the trim retainers are anchored in slotted holes in the trim panel.

Front wings — VX series

5 On VX series the front wing and inner wing panel are modified. The position of the wing-to-inner-wing panel securing bolt is shown arrowed in Fig. 13.118.
6 The modified parts can be fitted on FE series models but if fitting a front wing only, the securing bolt hole in the inner wing panel must be elongated so that it lines up with the bolt hole in the new wing.

Glove box — removal and refitting

7 On VX series models the glove box and lid are secured to the support by a plate and nuts (Fig. 13.119). Two wire stays support the lid when it is open.

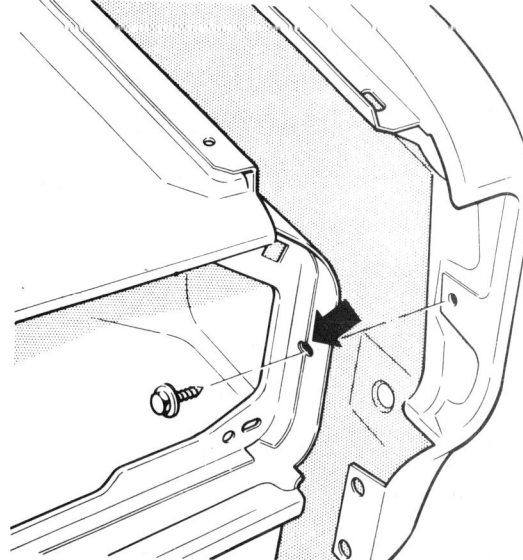

Fig. 13.118 Location of wing to inner wing panel securing bolt — VX series (Sec 14)

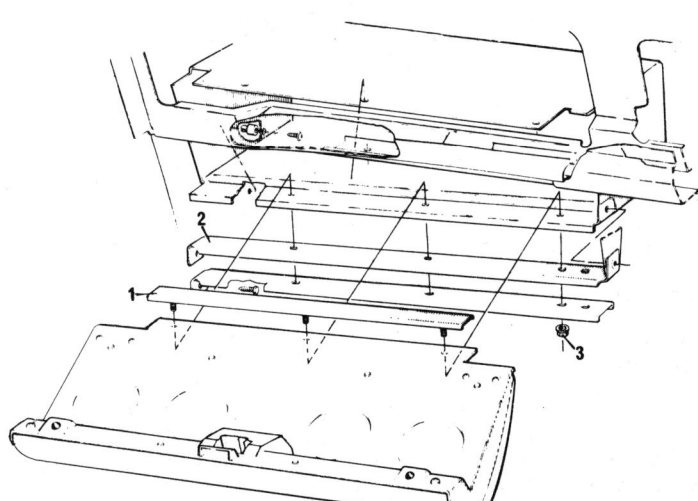

Fig. 13.119 Removing the glove box — VX series (Sec 14)

1 Support
2 Plate
3 Nuts

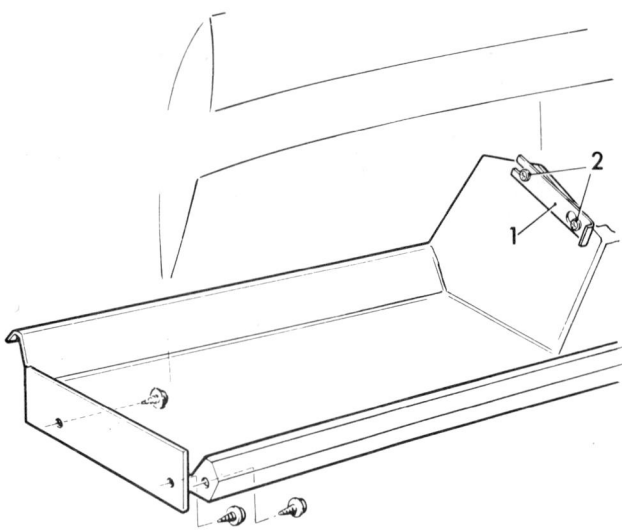

Fig. 13.120 Removing the parcel shelf (Sec 14)

1   Spring clip   2   Flanged spacer

8   A further five screws, three at the dash panel and one at each side, secure the glove box in position.

9   The glove box lid is in two parts, the inner panel being attached to the outer panel by twelve screws. The release catch and return spring are attached to the inner panel by a pin which is secured by a C-clip. The release catch handle is a push fit through the outer panel and must be released before removing the inner panel.

10   Refitting is a reversal of the removal sequence.

Front parcel shelf (later models) — removal and refitting

11   On later FE series models each side of the shelf centre section is retained by a spring clip, see Fig. 13.120, engaging flanged spacers which are secured to the instrument panel with screws.

12   Attachment of the parcel shelf to the side panels is unchanged and the shelf can be removed after withdrawing the clips and disengaging it from the spacers.

13   When refitting the parcel shelf, apply a sealant to the screw ends protruding under the wings.

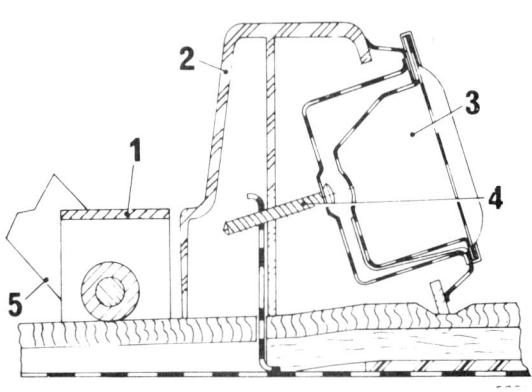

Fig. 13.121 Seat belt anchorage and ashtray housing (later FE series) (Sec 14)

1	Buckle support	4	Screws
2	Plastic housing	5	Seat belt buckles
3	Ashtray		

Seat belt anchorage and ash tray housing

14   On later FE models and on VX 1800 and VX 2300 models the seat belt buckles and buckle supports are partially enclosed in a plastic housing which incorporates an ash tray. (Fig. 13.121).

15   The housing can be removed after pulling out the ash tray and undoing the two securing screws.

16   When refitting the ash tray housing ensure that the tab is uppermost.

Centre console — VX series

17   The centre console is secured to the floor mounting and at the dash panel by four screws (two each end).

18   To remove the upper securing screws the radio aperture blanking plate, or radio (if fitted), must be removed first.

19   A centre console extension housing is fitted on VX 4/90 models. It is secured to the console and floor-panel by screws. The ash tray must be removed to gain access to the upper securing screws.

20   When removing the extension housing the seat belt buckles must be removed. Access to the buckle securing bolts can be gained by removing the blanking plugs in the housing.

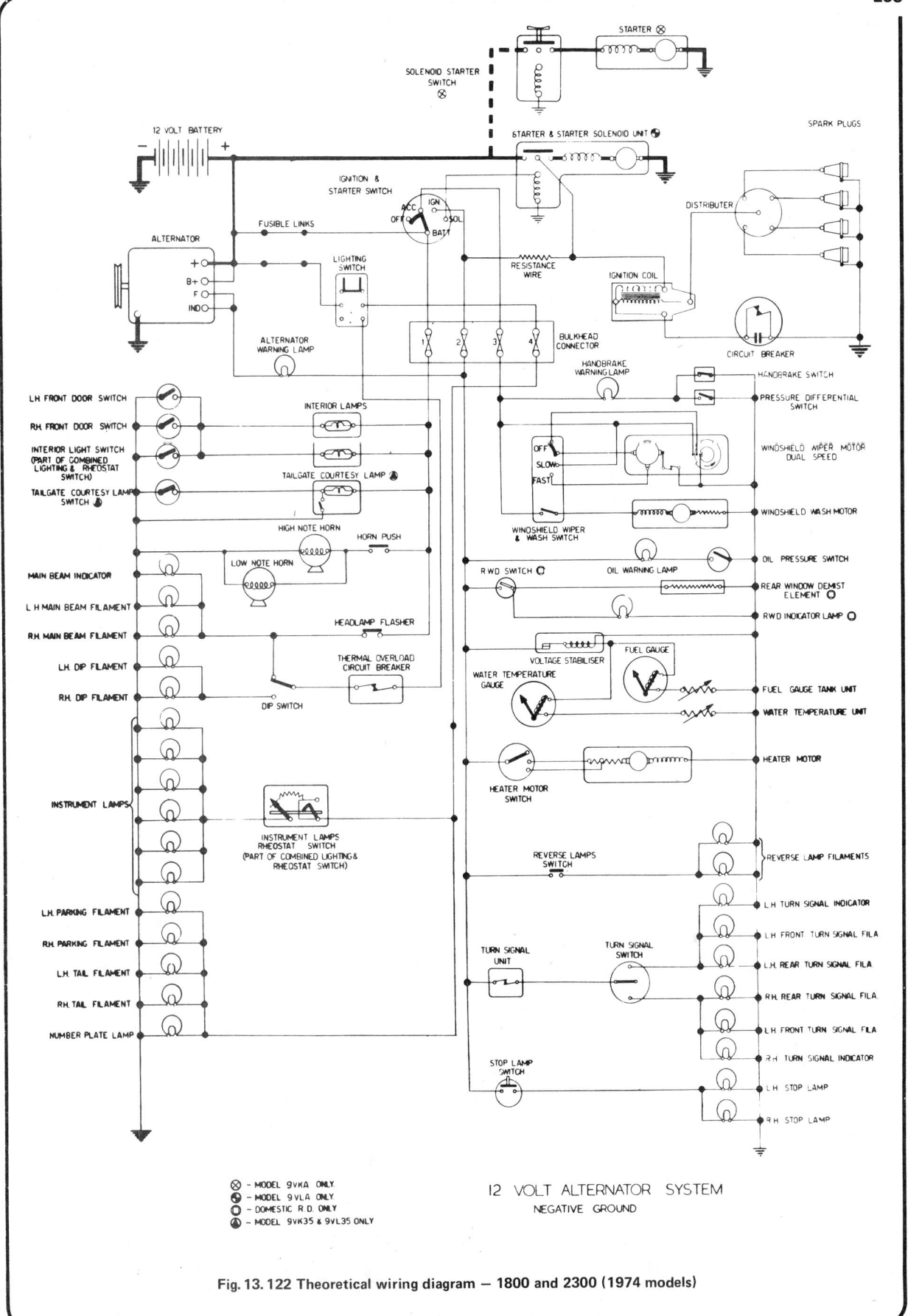

Fig. 13.122 Theoretical wiring diagram — 1800 and 2300 (1974 models)

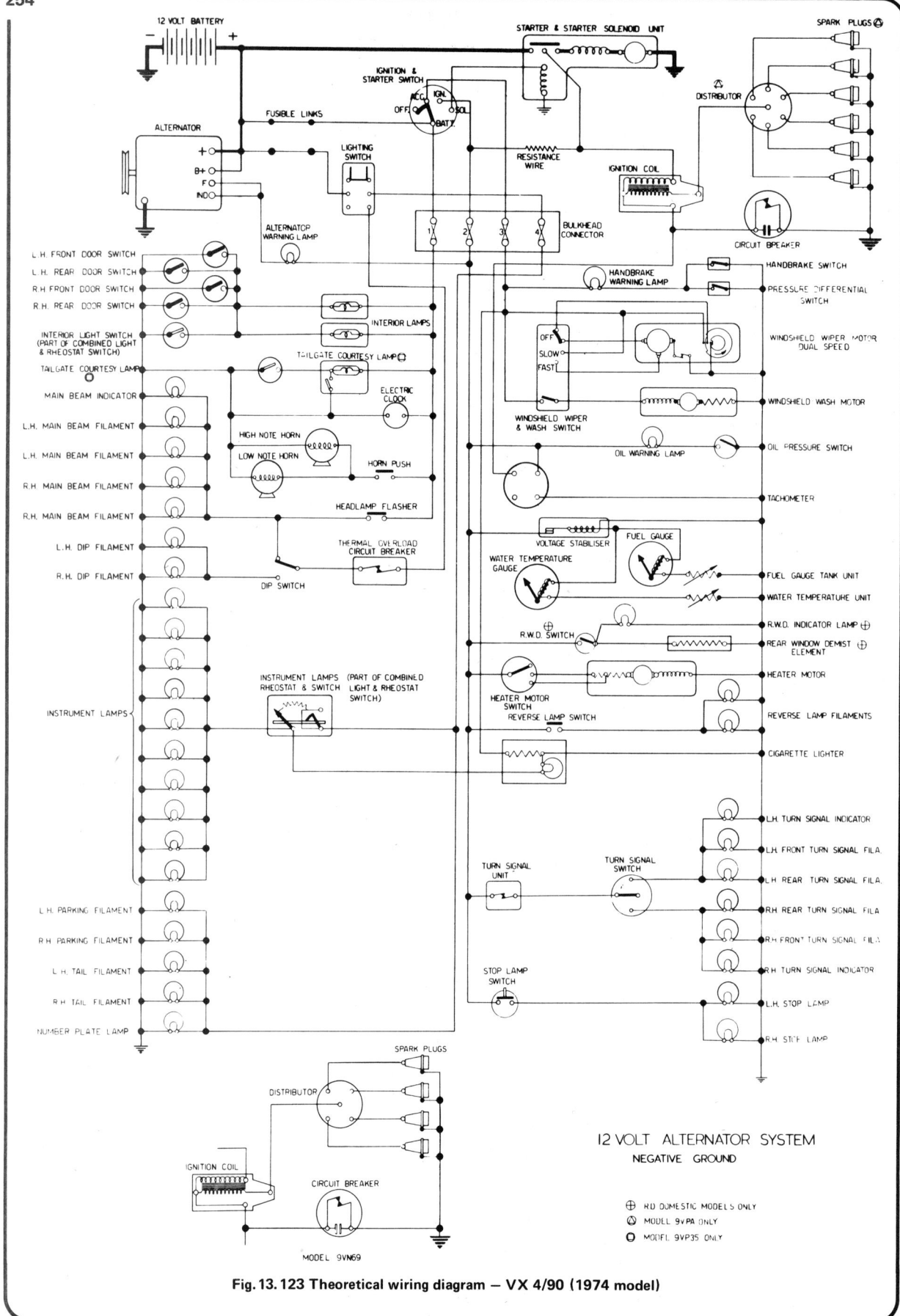

Fig. 13.123 Theoretical wiring diagram — VX 4/90 (1974 model)

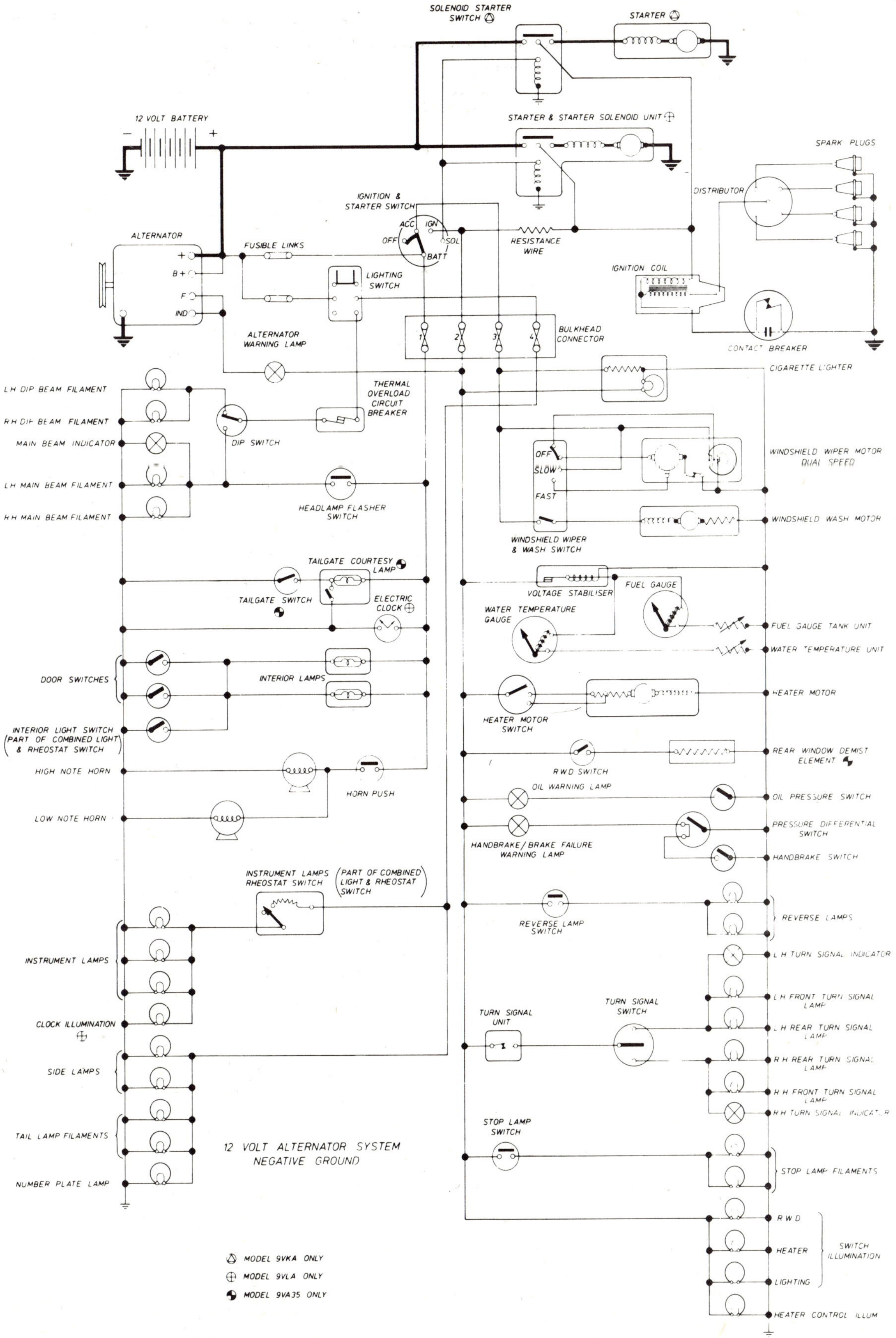

Fig. 13. 124 Theoretical wiring diagram — VX 1800 and VX 2300 (1976/77 models)

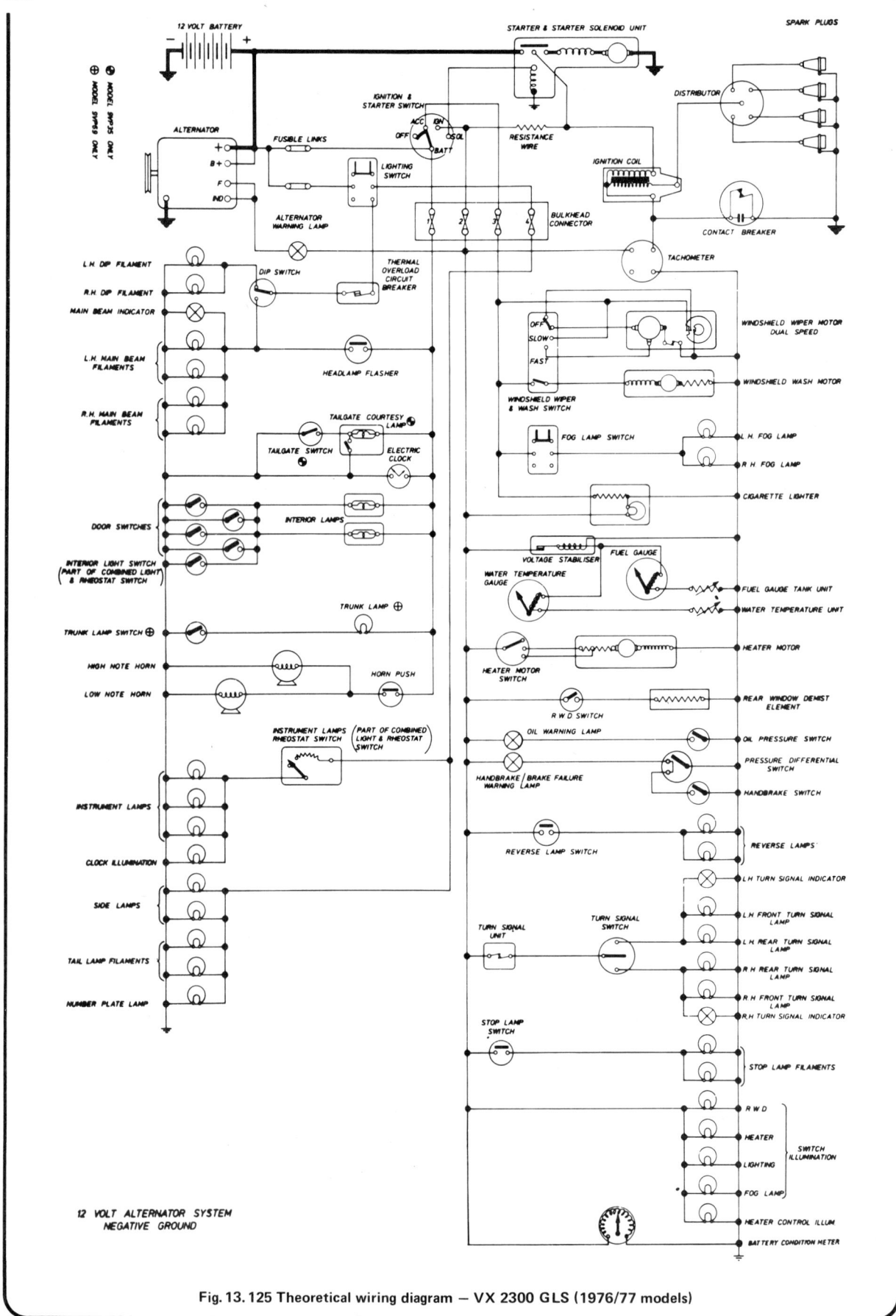

Fig. 13.125 Theoretical wiring diagram — VX 2300 GLS (1976/77 models)

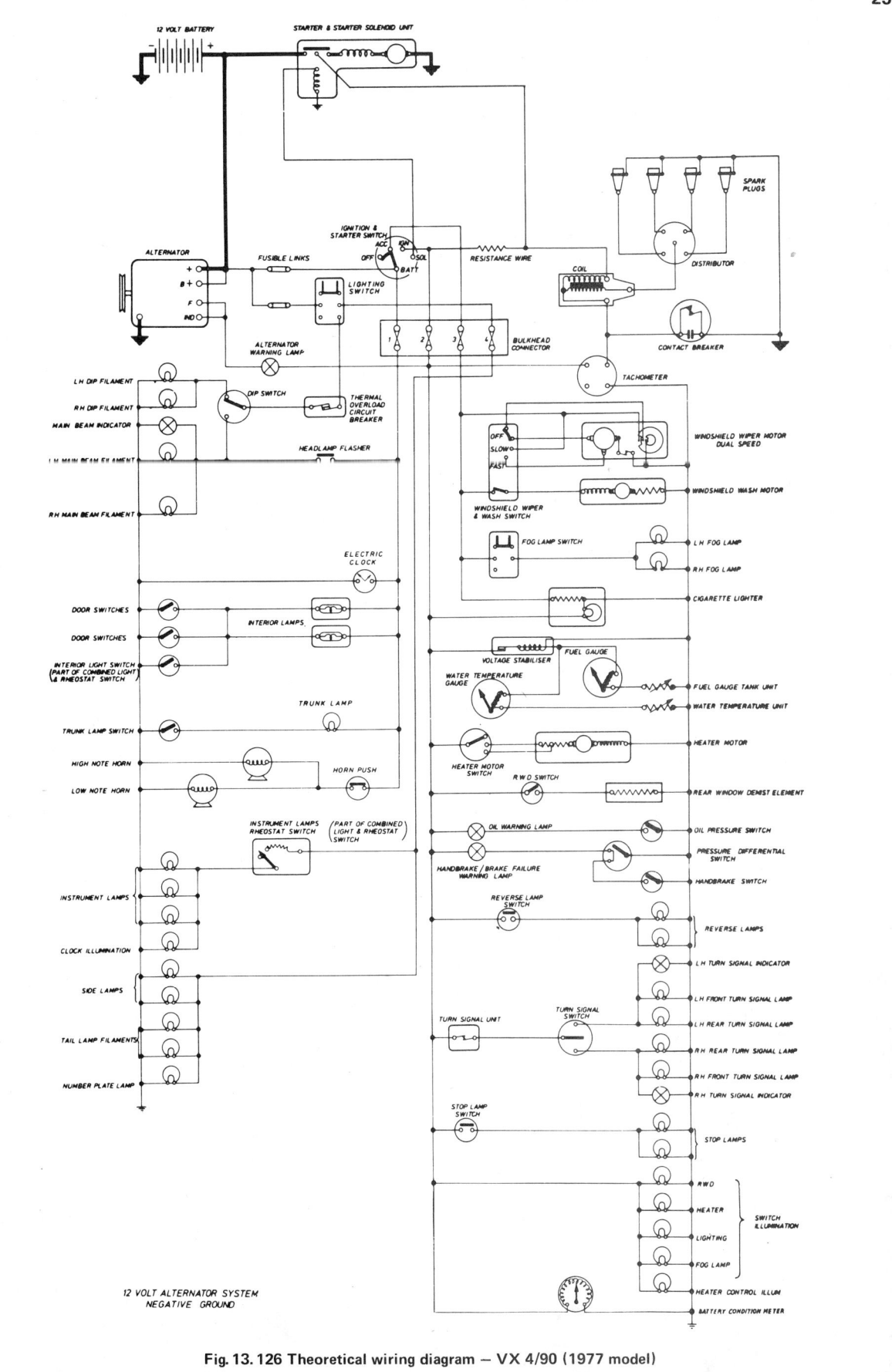

Fig. 13.126 Theoretical wiring diagram — VX 4/90 (1977 model)

Metric conversion tables

Inches	Decimals	Millimetres	Millimetres to Inches		Inches to Millimetres	
			mm	Inches	Inches	mm
1/64	0.015625	0.3969	0.01	0.00039	0.001	0.0254
1/32	0.03125	0.7937	0.02	0.00079	0.002	0.0508
3/64	0.046875	1.1906	0.03	0.00118	0.003	0.0762
1/16	0.0625	1.5875	0.04	0.00157	0.004	0.1016
5/64	0.078125	1.9844	0.05	0.00197	0.005	0.1270
3/32	0.09375	2.3812	0.06	0,00236	0.006	0.1524
7/64	0.109375	2.7781	0.07	0.00276	0.007	0.1778
1/8	0.125	3.1750	0.08	0.00315	0.008	0.2032
9/64	0.140625	3.5719	0.09	0.00354	0.009	0.2286
5/32	0.15625	3.9687	0.1	0.00394	0.01	0.254
11/64	0.171875	4.3656	0.2	0.00787	0.02	0.508
3/16	0.1875	4.7625	0.3	0.01181	0.03	0.762
13/64	0.203125	5.1594	0.4	0.01575	0.04	1.016
7/32	0.21875	5.5562	0.5	0.01969	0.05	1.270
15/64	0.234375	5.9531	0.6	0.02362	0.06	1.524
1/4	0.25	6.3500	0.7	0.02756	0.07	1.778
17/64	0.265625	6.7469	0.8	0.03150	0.08	2.032
9/32	0.28125	7.1437	0.9	0.03543	0.09	2.286
19/64	0.296875	7.5406	1	0.03937	0.1	2.54
5/16	0.3125	7.9375	2	0.07874	0.2	5.08
21/64	0.328125	8.3344	3	0.11811	0.3	7.62
11/32	0.34375	8.7312	4	0.15748	0.4	10.16
23/64	0.359375	9.1281	5	0.19685	0.5	12.70
3/8	0.375	9.5250	6	0.23622	0.6	15.24
25/64	0.390625	9.9219	7	0.27559	0.7	17.78
13/32	0.40625	10.3187	8	0.31496	0.8	20.32
27/64	0.421875	10.7156	9	0.35433	0.9	22.86
7/16	0.4375	11.1125	10	0.39370	1	25.4
29/64	0.453125	11.5094	11	0.43307	2	50.8
15/32	0.46875	11.9062	12	0.47244	3	76.2
31/64	0.484375	12.3031	13	0.51181	4	101.6
1/2	0.5	12.7000	14	0.55118	5	127.0
33/64	0.515625	13.0969	15	0.59055	6	152.4
17/32	0.53125	13.4937	16	0.62992	7	177.8
35/64	0.546875	13.8906	17	0.66929	8	203.2
9/16	0.5625	14.2875	18	0.70866	9	228.6
37/64	0.578125	14.6844	19	0.74803	10	254.0
19/32	0.59375	15.0812	20	0.78740	11	279.4
39/64	0.609375	15.4781	21	0.82677	12	304.8
5/8	0.625	15.8750	22	0.86614	13	330.2
41/64	0.640625	16.2719	23	0.90551	14	355.6
21/32	0.65625	16.6687	24	0.94488	15	381.0
43/64	0.671875	17.0656	25	0.98425	16	406.4
11/16	0.6875	17.4625	26	1.02362	17	431.8
45/64	0.703125	17.8594	27	1.06299	18	457.2
23/32	0.71875	18.2562	28	1.10236	19	482.6
47/64	0.734375	18.6531	29	1.14173	20	508.0
3/4	0.75	19.0500	30	1.18110	21	533.4
49/64	0.765625	19.4469	31	1.22047	22	558.8
25/32	0.78125	19.8437	32	1.25984	23	584.2
51/64	0.796875	20.2406	33	1.29921	24	609.6
13/16	0.8125	20.6375	34	1.33858	25	635.0
53/64	0.828125	21.0344	35	1.37795	26	660.4
27/32	0.84375	21.4312	36	1.41732	27	685.8
55/64	0.859375	21.8281	37	1.4567	28	711.2
7/8	0.875	22.2250	38	1.4961	29	736.6
57/64	0.890625	22.6219	39	1.5354	30	762.0
29/32	0.90625	23.0187	40	1.5748	31	787.4
59/64	0.921875	23.4156	41	1.6142	32	812.8
15/16	0.9375	23.8125	42	1.6535	33	838.2
61/64	0.953125	24.2094	43	1.6929	34	863.6
31/32	0.96875	24.6062	44	1.7323	35	889.0
63/64	0.984375	25.0031	45	1.7717	36	914.4

1   Imperial gallon = 8 Imp pints = 1.16 US gallons = 277.42 cu in = 4.5459 litres

1   US gallon = 4 US quarts = 0.862 Imp gallon = 231 cu in = 3.785 litres

1   Litre = 0.2199 Imp gallon = 0.2642 US gallon = 61.0253 cu in = 1000 cc

Miles to Kilometres		Kilometres to Miles	
1	1.61	1	0.62
2	3.22	2	1.24
3	4.83	3	1.86
4	6.44	4	2.49
5	8.05	5	3.11
6	9.66	6	3.73
7	11.27	7	4.35
8	12.88	8	4.97
9	14.48	9	5.59
10	16.09	10	6.21
20	32.19	20	12.43
30	48.28	30	18.64
40	64.37	40	24.86
50	80.47	50	31.07
60	96.56	60	37.28
70	112.65	70	43.50
80	128.75	80	49.71
90	144.84	90	55.92
100	160.93	100	62.14

lb f ft to Kg f m		Kg f m to lb f ft		lb f/in^2 : Kg f/cm^2		Kg f/cm^2 : lb f/in^2	
1	0.138	1	7.233	1	0.07	1	14.22
2	0.276	2	14.466	2	0.14	2	28.50
3	0.414	3	21.699	3	0.21	3	42.67
4	0.553	4	28.932	4	0.28	4	56.89
5	0.691	5	36.165	5	0.35	5	71.12
6	0.829	6	43.398	6	0.42	6	85.34
7	0.967	7	50.631	7	0.49	7	99.56
8	1.106	8	57.864	8	0.56	8	113.79
9	1.244	9	65.097	9	0.63	9	128.00
10	1.382	10	72.330	10	0.70	10	142.23
20	2.765	20	144.660	20	1.41	20	284.47
30	4.147	30	216.990	30	2.11	30	426.70

Index

Printed by
Haynes Publishing Group
Sparkford Yeovil Somerset
England